FoxPro MAChete: Hacking FoxPro for Macintosh

Second Edition

by Lisa C. Slater

with Andy Griebel, J. Randolph Brown, and John R. "Doc" Livingston

Fox Pro MAChete: Hacking FoxPro for Macintosh Second Edition

by Lisa C. Slater
with J. Randolph Brown, Andy Griebel
& John R. Livingston

FoxPro MAChete: Hacking FoxPro for Macintosh, Second Edition

Library of Congress Catalog Number: 95-60411
ISBN: 1-56830-196-0

98 97 96 95 4 3 2 1

Interpretation of the printing code: the rightmost double-digit number is the year of the book's printing; the rightmost single-digit number is the number of the book's printing. For example, a printing code of 95-1 shows that the first printing of the book occurred in 1995.

Manufactured in the United States of America

CREDITS

Publisher
David Rogelberg

Managing Editor
Patrick Gibbons

Development Editors
Marta J. Partington
Don Eamon

Copy/Production Editors
Cathy Banguis
Tim Cox

Technical Editor
Robert Ameeti

Publishing Coordinator
Rosemary Lewis

Interior Designers
Fred Bower

Cover Designer
Karen Ruggles

Production
Gary Adair, Angela Calvert, Dan Caparo,
Brad Chinn, Kim Cofer, Jennifer Eberhardt,
David Garratt, Aleata Howard, Sean MacDonald
Joe Millay, Erika Millen, Beth Rago,
Erich J. Richter, Christine Tyner,
Karen Walsh, Robert Wolf

Indexers
Brad Herriman

Composed in
New Century Schoolbook

TO OUR READERS

Dear Friend,

Thank you on behalf of everyone at Hayden Books for choosing *FoxPro MAChete: Hacking FoxPro,* Second Edition to enable you to learn about the exciting world of FoxPro on the Macintosh. We think you'll enjoy the practical examples in this book and on the disk, while getting a true understanding of the power of FoxPro.

What you think of this book is important to our ability to better serve you in the future. If you have any comments, no matter how great or small, we'd appreciate you taking the time to send us e-mail or a note by snail mail. Of course, we'd love to hear your book ideas.

Sincerely yours,

David Rogelberg
Publisher, Hayden Books and Adobe Press

You can reach Hayden Books at the following:

Hayden Books
201 West 103rd Street
Indianapolis, IN 46290
(800) 428-5331 voice
(800) 448-3804 fax

Email addresses:

America OnLine:	Hayden Bks
AppleLink:	hayden.books
CompuServe:	76350,3014
Internet:	hayden@hayden.com

ABOUT THE AUTHORS

Lisa C. Slater

Lisa C. Slater is a FoxPro developer's consultant. She specializes in optimizing FoxPro techniques through customized training procedures and the review of applications under development by Xbase programmers.

Lisa has been a featured speaker at Fox Software and Microsoft's Fox Developer's Conferences and speaks widely at other FoxPro and database events. She is the writer and on-screen talent for Virtual Firmware's *FoxPro RAD* video training series. She has been editor of *FoxTalk*, Pinnacle Publishing's monthly journal for Fox professionals, a regular columnist in *DataBased Advisor,* and contributor to many other publications. With Steven E. Arnott, she has written Que's best-selling *Using FoxPro* series. She is also the author of the Report Writer volume of Pinnacle's *Pros Talk Fox Series One* and the Series Editor for *Pros Talk Fox Series Two*.

Lisa is CompuServe's Fox archivist and a Microsoft-designated Most Valuable Professional for her contributions to the FoxPro community. She holds the bug-hunting record for each of the FoxPro 2.0 and 2.5 beta cycles. You can reach her on CompuServe, using ID 71333,2565 on FoxForum or FoxGang, where she keeps a virtual whip hand over the mad antics of a large crew of Fox enthusiasts.

John Livingston

John R. "Doc" Livingston is principal of Database Online Computing Systems, where he develops business applications for Macintosh and Windows users. He is fluent in a number of computer languages and fourth generation development environments. He has studied advanced physics and chemistry, parachutes from airplanes, and completed Army Ranger training. Mr. Livingston received his B.S. from the United States Military Academy, his M.S. from the George Washington University, and his M.B.A. from the Stanford University Graduate School of Business. He can be reached on CompuServe at 71171,567.

Randy Brown

Randy is a consultant for Sierra Systems based in Northern California. He specializes in custom FoxPro development on Macintosh, Windows, and DOS platforms. Prior to founding Sierra Systems, Randy was engaged as a consultant in Ernst & Young's National Energy Practice based in San Francisco.

Last year, Randy completed his second book, *FoxPro 2.5 OLE and DDE,* a book for *Pros Talk Fox Series Two* by Pinnacle Publishing. His first publication, *FoxPro 2: A Developer's Guide* by M&T Books, continues to be one of the more popular selling titles. In addition to books, Randy has written numerous articles on a variety of FoxPro technical topics for major industry magazines and journals, including *Dr. Dobbs Journal* and *FoxTalk.*

Randy is an ongoing speaker with the FoxPro conference circuit, which includes the Microsoft FoxPro Devcom and the Minnesota FoxPro User's Conference. In his free time, Randy enjoys skiing, rafting, traveling, and eating Buffalo chicken wings. He can be reached electronically at the following addresses:

Internet: 71141.3014@compuserve.com

Compuserve: 71141,3014

America OnLine: Randy Brwn

Andy Griebel

Andy is president of Plaid Software Group, Inc., in Little Rock, Arkansas. He first became involved with computers while studying piano and saxophone in college. Having developed with FoxBASE+ for the Mac and FoxPro since they were released, he is currently teaching FoxPro for Windows and MS-DPS in a series of seminars across the country. Plaid Software's on-site training clients include Chevron, Glamour Shots, Universal Studios-based Anderson Video, the IRS, and the Pentagon.

Andy's book on the FoxPro Screen Builder is published by Pinnacle Publishing as part of *Pros Talk Fox Series Two*. He is the writer and producer of Plaid Software Group's *Video Training Series on FoxPro*, and is the on-camera talent for its all-new *FoxPro for Windows* series.

Andy can be reached on CompuServe at 71441,3452.

ACKNOWLEDGMENTS

More people than we can name helped us create this book. All four authors would like to acknowledge these special contributors:

Our tech editor, Robert Ameeti, who probably thinks we are lunatics by now.

The People On Our Side at Hayden Books.

The entire Microsoft FoxPro development and production team with special mention to the Beta folks—Susan Graham, Tony Pacheco, Lee Coward, and Ken Tittle—for working hard to provide us with a terrific product.

And the ghost of Fox Software, for starting it all.

Doc adds...

I would like to thank Lisa Slater for her encouragement and guidance during the preparation of my portions of this book. Thanks also to Jack Su and Jim Davis for their assistance with my chapter on the Library Construction Kit, and to Hayden Books for giving me the opportunity to participate. Finally, I would like to thank my other clients and friends, who graciously put up with me while I was working.

John Livingston

Palo Alto, California

Andy adds...

Thanks go out to Hunter Gray, Mimi San Pedro, Melinda Glasgow and Nancy Griebel for insight into the Ad biz. My office manager Becca Snider deserves a medal for being "continuity director" of my business life. A very special thanks goes to my daughter Greer, whose constant grins provide inspiration.

Of the Microsoft folks, additional thanks to Chris Cap, Bob Fortner, Susan Graham, Janet Walker and Marty for making it happen.

Andy Griebel

Randy adds...

I truly had a great time working on this book. Not too many authors will admit that they actually enjoy writing. In fact, many swear they will never do another book. Yet a year later, they put themselves through the same tortures again.

I must first acknowledge Lisa Slater (who?). She really gave 110 percent and is responsible for everything coming together on this fine effort. As a true Mac aficionado, I had my doubts about someone writing a Mac book whose roots were DOS-based. Now I think Lisa is a true Mac convert.

I would also like to thank a number of folks who provided some of the insight for my writing. Jim Simpkins (Microsoft) and Steven Black are both experts on International FoxPro, and their assistance on these matters rounded out the Localization chapter. Kudos to Joseph Schaller and Audrey Cole for showing me the light with QuicKeys and other Mac goodies. Also, many of the folks up north at Microsoft (including Susan Graham, Scott Cooper, Sherri and Walt Kennamer, and Meng-Khuan Phua) gave us help on many subject matters.

To my parents, I hope you two enjoy this book—it is the best so far. I hope you guys have room left on the coffee table for one more. And to my brother Terry, good luck with your WING-TIME venture—I want one of the first cases. If any one out there wants to try Terry's sauce, which is the best Buffalo Wing Sauce ever, feel free to contact me.

Finally, to Elaine for her great inspiration and patience. How about a teddy bear instead of the pig? Love ya.

Randy :)

Lisa adds...

Special thanks (and hugs) to Andy, Randy, and Doc (oh my!), for all their special gifts and their cooperation with a merciless schedule.

The FoxPro Mac Betazoids, especially John Van Aken and Peter Teeson, for merciless scrutiny and honorable criticism—both of the product and of my arguments—and Susan, Tony, Lee, and Ken at MSFT for being "real folks" about it. (Tony, would you like my LC II bronzed for your dashboard??)

The BobRed Company, my ultimate arbiter in all questions of taste.

Walt and Sherri Kennamer, who are true friends.

Bob Fortner, on whom it is now socially *de rigueur* to blame everything at MSFT because he takes it with such grace.

John Hosier, Ken Levy, Dave Lingwood, Keri Anderson Healy, Maurice Frank, Walter Nicholls, Matt Peirse and MicroMega (especially Alan Schwartz and Dale Kiefling for quick turnaround!), and PB&J at Cornerstone Software — all of whom provide tools in the service of rapid development.

Bill House, my OBJECTive friend and teacher.

Steve Arnott, for his faith in my ability to do this again.

Tom Rettig and George Goley, two people who serve as mentors with good humor and real affection.

Jordan Powell, Pat Adams, and Hank Fay, three people whose ears are probably permanently bent by now (besides I always wanted to mention Hank and Pat in the same breath <g>).

Sue Cunningham, Nancy Jacobsen, and Wayne Harless, for colorful advice.

nj(tpnts), with additional love, whether she wants it or not, for reminding me that the point of the Macintosh is true choice, having it your way, no matter what that way is.

Riley and Hallie and Tod, Stan and Jeanne, and Marcia and Larry, far away but always family.

Jonathan, Joshua, and Derek Slater, for traveling this difficult road with me as well as could be expected, with Kevin Jamieson, Merlin Love, Adam Rubinger, and Joshua Zygielbaum, all of whom saw some action along the way.

and Colin Nicholls, who inspires every step of the journey.

>*L*<

April 1994

CONTENTS

PART II PLAN FOR RAPID DEVELOPMENT: FOXPRO POWER TOOL DESIGN 127

Chapter 9: Provide Quick Results: Easy Rewards from the RQBE and the Report Writer 291

PART III SUPPORT THE APPLICATION SURFACE: FOXPRO CODE 353

Chapter 10: Assemble Application Modules: Multiple FoxPro Elements in a READ CYCLE 355

Chapter 11: Assure Comfort for Developers and Users: Cross-Platform Usability and Thoughtful Design 421

Chapter 18: Communicate with Other Mac Applications: Apple Events and AppleScript 703

Chapter 19: Enhance the Development Process and Polish Your Application: Third Party Tools and Extensions 739

FOREWORD

I owe Lisa Slater a goat.

One of the great pleasures of working first at Fox and now at Microsoft has been getting to know many of the people who make their living with FoxPro. I remember when I first met Lisa Slater on CompuServe in early 1990. In a few months, she progressed from being a beginner to one of the most knowledgeable FoxPro programmers in the world. I've never seen anything like it. She's one of the smartest people I have ever known. With her boundless energy, it makes for a formidable combination.

Lisa's first book was *Using FoxPro 2.0,* co-authored with Steve Arnott. Many of you who are reading this foreword probably picked up *FoxPro MAChete*, Second Edition, because you knew about *Using FoxPro 2.5,* one of the best of a large number of fine books about FoxPro. A lot of our customers learned how to use FoxPro by reading Steve and Lisa's book.

I have always hoped Lisa would continue to write about our products, so it is great news that she, Andy, Randy, and Doc have devoted their considerably combined talents to a book on FoxPro for Macintosh. I think *FoxPro MAChete*, Second Edition, should be required reading for FoxPro/Mac developers. Its key insight is that there are three distinct groups of people using FoxPro Macs:

- Experienced FoxPro users who do not use the Windows or MS-DOS versions
- Experienced FoxBASE+/Mac users moving up to FoxPro
- Newcomers to FoxPro

These groups face different challenges in learning about FoxPro/Mac and one of *FoxPro MAChete*'s strengths is the way it provides separate "getting started" sections for each group. This is valuable material, and it should help developers leverage what they already know to become productive with FoxPro quickly.

One final note. It is a special personal pleasure for me to write this foreword. Among many other accomplishments, Lisa introduced me to my bride, Sherri Bruhn Kennamer. Lisa assures me that a goat is the traditional fee for such matchmaker services. I have not yet paid up, but I do acknowledge how much I owe her.

Walter J. Kennamer

Redmond, Washington

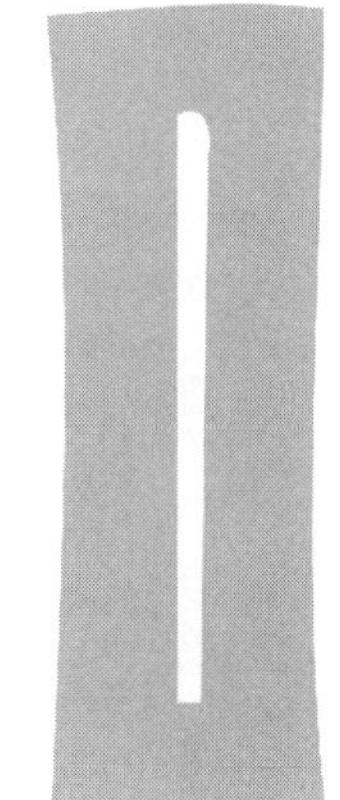

INTRODUCTION

Welcome to *FoxPro MAChete: Hacking FoxPro for Macintosh,* 2nd Edition. Get ready for an adventure.

FoxPro for Macintosh is a very special and exciting database development platform. I'm tempted to describe the product in Cecil B. DeMille terms: "*A sweeping epic ... five years in the making ... an all-star cast ...* "

Without Hollywood-style superlatives, there really isn't any way to describe the impact that FoxPro Mac is having on the Macintosh database market.

Record-Breaking Box Office Receipts

FoxPro Mac literally burst onto the software scene. In its initial appearance on the *MacWeek* Business Watch list (3/21/94), it placed fifth among all Macintosh products in the General Application category.

This distinction is even more significant when you consider that the list is calculated by *dollar volume*, and that the other products on the list were as much as five times the going price of FoxPro Mac. If you think in terms of *unit volume*, you can see how strong the sales actually were. Microsoft confirms that the company met FoxPro Mac's six-month sales projection in under two months.

At the same time, the product is complex and requires an investment of effort to learn. Adherents of other Mac DBMS software packages aren't easily convinced to switch, at least not quickly. Far from detracting from others' market share, FoxPro Mac is attracting a whole new audience to the Mac market. An early assessment, in the "Eddy Watch" of the March 1994 *MacUser* magazine, suggested that FoxPro Mac's "...robust cross-platform capabilities and speedy search language may help legitimize the Mac as a relational database platform."

The net effect of the product, then, is extremely positive: a broadening and deepening of the appeal and capabilities of the Macintosh environment. This effect fits perfectly with Apple's current strategy for the Macintosh.

The Mac is now over ten years old. For many people, the platform still has the reputation of a youthful rebel or upstart among personal computers. However, Apple knows that the Mac needs a corporate presence and corporate respect to survive. Apple is offering connectivity solutions, such as OpenDoc, and better hardware price-performance ratios in an effort to show the Mac as a true "team player" to the business community. The new Power Macs promise to bring Macintosh into an unprecedented level of compatibility with other operating systems.

FoxPro for Macintosh is a perfect application to showcase the Mac in this brave new world. How does FoxPro Mac perform this miracle?

Fast-Paced Action! Incredible Special Effects!

FoxPro allows developers to leverage their efforts across multiple platforms, writing code that works on DOS, Windows, Mac, and Unix machines. The resulting applications can handle databases of millions of records, in many cases, sorting and manipulating data at up to 40 times the speed of competing programs.

FoxPro's design tools allow many of the tasks of application development to be accomplished with minimal effort and maximum effect, creating screen, menu, and report definitions that are usable across multiple applications as well as cross-platform.

Where the design tools leave off, the FoxPro language comes in. This language, an Xbase dialect, is virtually limitless. What you can imagine doing with data, FoxPro has the syntax and depth to accomplish.

The Macintosh version of the product makes DOS and Windows FoxPro developers feel right at home. FoxPro Windows experts, in particular, find that their GUI design work transports well to FoxPro Mac.

Meanwhile, the Mac product includes Mac-specific support for AppleEvents, XCMDs, Macintosh-style long file names, and other features dear to Mac users' hearts.

All these features are built into the basic FoxPro Mac product, which also is by design fully multi-user. In addition, the Professional Edition includes everything that developers need in one box: the Standard product, a Distribution Kit for royalty-free distributable applications, a Library Construction Kit for calling the FoxPro API with C code, and a Connectivity Kit for creating front-end FoxPro applications for SQL Server-based databases.

Moreover, FoxPro has the muscle of Microsoft behind it. Although there are *few sure* things in the software world, Microsoft is not a vendor likely to disappear in the near future!

Bill Gates has stated that he views FoxPro as a developer's product "like C." You probably won't see FoxPro being touted as an easy "business solution" like Access, Microsoft's other database product on the Windows platform. FoxPro is undeniably difficult for end-users to master. However, FoxPro for Macintosh *is Microsoft's sole database offering on the Mac platform and has Microsoft's full support there.*

Recommended for Mature Audiences

You read me right in the last paragraph: FoxPro is not easy to learn, and FoxPro isn't for everybody. This book isn't for everybody either.

This book is for people who want to develop applications in FoxPro. We assume that you are a savvy computer user of *some* kind. You may be new to the Mac, new to FoxPro, or new to Xbase, but you're sophisticated and not afraid of a challenge. Part I of this book contains three Quick

Starts for people starting FoxPro from different backgrounds. These Quick Starts give each type of "new" reader the information that's needed to be prepared for work in FoxPro.

Parts II and III concentrate on rapid development strategy in FoxPro, beginning with use of the Power Tool system and continuing with the language constructs that support this system. Rather than attempting a complete overview of the vast feature set of FoxPro, these chapters provide a template development system and clear recommendations for efficient use of the product.

Part IV examines Macintosh-specific aspects of this product and its relationship to the Macintosh environment, including tools and features you can use to create polished, robust, and truly professional FoxPro Mac applications.

Each part of the book begins with a short introduction that tells you more of what to expect in its included chapters. Throughout the book, be prepared for surprises. In particular, if you're an expert FoxPro developer, you're going to learn things about FoxPro that you've never before seen in a book, applicable to FoxPro on *any* platform. If you're a Mac expert, you may learn a few things about working with System 7 that you've never considered.

The surprises don't end when you get to the source disk. Each author has contributed tools and examples that, in many cases, go far beyond the discussion these files receive in the book.

Behind the Scenes: The Making of FoxPro MAChete

Because FoxPro isn't really a film, there won't be a real "behind the scenes" documentary accompanying this book. (Instead, you get a source disk that's so packed with materials that I wondered up until the last minute how I was going to fit everything—compressed! —onto the high-density floppy. I'd hate to tell you how many "wonderful moments" ended up on the cutting room floor.)

Still, I want to take a moment to tell you why this book was a pleasure to write.

I love FoxPro, and I love talking about FoxPro. Watching this product take shape on the Mac platform and seeing my theories of application development prove their worth and flexibility in an entirely new environment was a joyful, validating experience for me personally.

Beyond that personal experience, however, came the real thrill of working with Randy Brown, Andy Griebel, and Doc Livingston, truly a "dream team" of FoxPro Mac authors. We all learned a great deal from each other.

I think we've achieved something I hoped for from the beginning, but wasn't sure was possible. You get to know us as four distinct personalities and voices, yet you still will hear a *consensus* on major issues and approaches. Our techniques dovetail nicely and work to extend one another's advice. The end result provides you with an integrated, workable developer's strategy that is open to adjustment for*your* personal needs and style.

You've Seen the Movie, Now Read the Book

If you're reading this introduction, you probably are already interested in FoxPro Mac, whether you own the product or are still considering it as a development platform. You don't need to see a promotional trailer. You're ready for the main attraction.

OK, I'll abandon the flashy movie metaphor now: FoxPro Mac is a big subject, and this book is already long enough, so I won't take up more of your attention with a lengthy introduction. If you're interested in FoxPro, you care about speed. You're probably ready to start.

So here's a wish of good luck, and *Happy Fox Trails* from Randy, Andy, Doc, and me. You'll find our CompuServe ID numbers in our listings in Appendix A. Stop by on FoxGang or FoxForum and let us know how you're doing! Popcorn and licorice whips are optional.

Lisa C. Slater

January 1995

PART I

MOVE UP TO FOXPRO FOR MACINTOSH: QUICK STARTS FOR DEVELOPERS

Right now, you may be an unwilling user of FoxPro for Macintosh.

Maybe you are an in-house database developer, expert in tailoring FoxPro for DOS and Windows to the needs of a large corporation. You were asked to support the desktop publishing group, who strangely insist that Macs are the only computers they'll accept. You know that FoxPro is up to the task, but you face the challenge of an unfamiliar operating system and conventions.

Or you may be an experienced FoxBASE+/Mac programmer. You want the latest and greatest features of the new FoxPro product. You need to stay competitive, whether you create custom programs or vertical market (commercial) applications. Along with the sexy FoxPro features comes a shock: radical changes in development procedures, and even in command syntax, from the FoxBASE you know and love.

Perhaps you use another Macintosh database management application such as 4th Dimension or Filemaker Pro. You can accomplish anything you want in your chosen environment, and you're apprehensive about switching to FoxPro's style and Xbase language. But you can't resist the lure of FoxPro's speed and power, plus the cross-platform advantage of the FoxPro product suite.

No matter which group of FoxPro for Macintosh users you're in, you share some needs and concerns with all other users of the product. You want to create portable, powerful applications—and you want these applications to take full advantage of FoxPro for Macintosh's unique capabilities.

You want a clear path through FoxPro's dense, often bewildering jungle of features—a path that takes you through the development process as rapidly and efficiently as possible.

Hacking this path through the FoxPro jungle is the aim of the rest of this book. First, however, you need to*outfit* for the journey according to your individual backgrounds and expectations.

Part I contains three separate Quick Starts for:

- Crossovers from DOS and Windows.
- Upgraders from FoxBASE+/Mac.
- New converts from non-Xbase DBMS products.

Once you have the basic survival skills you need to become comfortable and confident in FoxPro for Macintosh, you'll all take the journey together, starting in Part II.

With proper preparation, you will find this jungle an exciting, vivid, and rewarding place to live and work.

1

QUICK START FOR FOXPRO WINDOWS AND DOS DEVELOPERS

by
Lisa Slater

Moving to the Macintosh can be difficult for an experienced DOS or Windows developer. Suddenly, when you try to configure your environment, you're a rank beginner. There's no DOS prompt at which to enter commands to manipulate files. Even the behavior of icons on the screen confounds your Windows-based expectations.

FoxPro for Macintosh provides a wonderful bridge between the two environments because its behavior and use are astoundingly similar to the DOS and Windows FoxPro versions you know. This similarity is deliberate: Microsoft aims to make your use of FoxPro, and the FoxPro applications you write, uniform across platforms.

Even within FoxPro, however, you find that you occasionally need to adjust your use of the product to the needs of the Macintosh. This chapter is designed to give you the tools you need to feel at home in FoxPro for Macintosh.

The first section is devoted to your use of the Macintosh operating system and Desktop interface, using the FoxPro for Macintosh file set as an example. I'm not going to teach you all about the Desktop and its features; you can read dozens of Macintosh books to learn about the general capabilities of System 7, the Finder, and so on. Instead, this section is designed to give you a Macintosh tour with hints and shortcuts of particular interest to people working in FoxPro.

The second section addresses your second problem: how to adjust your use of FoxPro on the Macintosh platform. Of course you want your existing applications to run in the new environment, but you also want them to look and feel "Mac-like" to your users. If you follow this book's recommendations for rapid application development, you should be able to make the necessary changes in your generic code in one place and have them carry through all your work.

You'll find tricks to enhance cross-platform use—as well as warnings of potential cross-platform problems—throughout the book, along with power tips to use in the Mac's operating system. They'll look like this:

See Also

- "Locating and Referencing Files," Chapter 4
- "FoxPro's Use of File Extensions and Macintosh File Types," Appendix B
- PROCEDURE SaveSets, Source Disk: Library Folder: MAIN.PRG
- "Tools to Port Files between DOS and Mac Machines," Chapter 19

FOXPRO MAC HACK TIP

(This is an example of a cool trick to use on the Mac.) You can type a space to get to the top of a standard Macintosh GetFile dialog list, used by the FoxPro GETFILE() function. Add a space to the beginning of a file name if you want that file to appear at the top of the list. The tilde character (~) takes you, or a file name, to the bottom of the list.

CROSS-PLATFORM WARNING

(The same topic is also an example of something to watch for during cross-platform use of FoxPro.) File names with spaces in them, along with long Mac file names, cause problems for DOS. Use standard DOS file-naming conventions for any files you intend to share cross-platform.

With notes like these, every chapter of this book alerts you to issues of the Mac environment and cross-platform compatibility. This chapter gives you the information you need to get started with a minimum of false starts and frustration. For more information on any topic, follow the references that look like the notes in the margin beside this paragraph.

Introduction to the Macintosh Environment

This section introduces you to features of Macintosh System 7, its Finder, and Macintosh utilities that you use in your work as a FoxPro developer. Remember to consult the documentation supplied with your Macintosh, along with other third-party books, for more general information.

See Also

- "Additional Resources," Appendix A

Exploring the Macintosh Environment

If you haven't already installed a copy of FoxPro for Macintosh, now is the time to do it! Even if you have already installed it, reviewing the installation process is a good way to notice the special features of the Macintosh environment. You have to start by turning on the machine, of course. What happens when the Mac boots up?

Startup Procedures and the System Files

When you start up your Mac, you should see an image known as the "happy Mac" and hear a musical chord as the system boots. These two signals indicate that your System files were properly found and that your Mac is ready for work.

> **FOXPRO MAC HACK TIP**
>
> If you see a "sad Mac" or a disk icon that shows a question mark instead of the "happy Mac," you may have to boot from a floppy, just as you would if a DOS computer failed to find COMMAND.COM on your hard disk. Your System 7 disks come with a special Disk Tools Disk you can use to investigate your disk in an emergency. If you hear a different series of tones from the usual chord, your Mac probably has a hardware problem; see a service person immediately.

The Macintosh system is composed of a System file and a number of ancillary system components collectively known as "the System" and an application named Finder. The Finder creates your interface to the operating system, the Mac Desktop, menus, and file management procedures; most people think of it as an integral part of the System files.

• "AppleScript and Apple Events," Chapter 18

To run, FoxPro for Macintosh requires version 7 of the Macintosh operating system. At the time of this edition, the most recent release of the operating system is *System 7.5.*

Although you don't need System 7.5 to run FoxPro, you should upgrade your system files if you have System 7.0 or System 7.0.1 installed. The release of System 7.1 fixed a number of System 7 bugs and actually decreased the amount of memory taken by the system files. These changes affect your use of FoxPro. In addition, AppleScript, a feature you'll find particularly useful with FoxPro, was not included with the initial releases of System 7.

The Apple and Application Menus

To check your System Software, use the , or Apple menu icon, you see at the top left of your screen. If the Finder is the active application, the first option on the Apple menu is About This Macintosh. When you choose it, you see a dialog similar to figure 1.1.

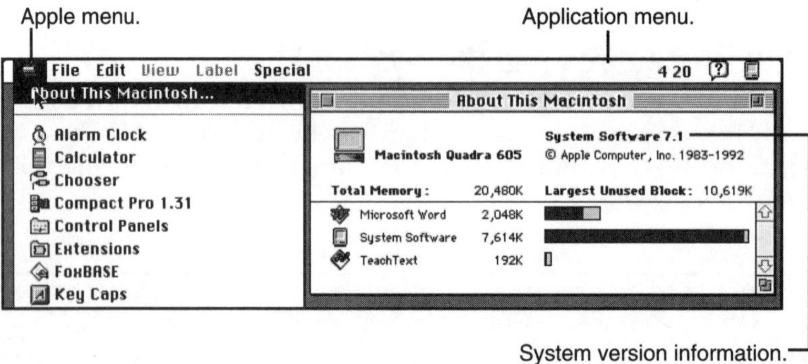

Figure 1.1 *The About This Macintosh dialog tells you which software is running, including your System version.*

If the Finder is not your active application, you may see a different About dialog on the Apple menu reflecting the current application. Like Microsoft Windows, System 7 is a *cooperative multitasking*, or task-switching environment. Although applications may run in the background, by time-slicing, one and only one application is always current—just as in FoxPro, one and only one window is "on top."

As in FoxPro and Windows, you can switch between Macintosh applications by clicking on their windows. When you click on the Desktop itself, or on an icon on the Desktop representing a file or collection of files, you make the Finder the current application.

Look to the right side of the menu bar. You see another symbol directly opposite the Apple Menu. Like the About dialog, this symbol reflects the currently active application. (As you see in figure 1.1, the symbol is an icon of the Macintosh when the Finder is active.) You can switch between the currently running applications by clicking on their names in the *Application Menu* under this symbol, just as you switch between applications in Windows' Task Manager or between FoxPro windows using the list on the FoxPro Window menu list. As you choose different applications from the Application Menu, the icon at the top of the menu changes and the appropriate application windows come forward.

System Extensions

When your Mac starts up, after you see the "happy Mac," you see a message welcoming you to Macintosh, just as you might see the sign-on screen while Microsoft Windows loads. You may also see a series of icons range across the bottom of your screen; these are system *extensions* and *control panels* used to extend the Mac operating system and the *Finder*.

System extensions and control panels are like TSRs (terminate-and-stay-resident applications) in DOS. Every Macintosh user collects his or her own personal set; it's almost impossible to imagine working on a Mac with no extensions or control panels. In fact, one extension, the Apple Shared Library Manager, is required to use the SET LIBRARY command in FoxPro on the Macintosh. As a cross-platform developer, you'll probably want to add at least one additional control panel to allow your Mac's floppy drive to recognize and mount DOS-formatted disks with a minimum of fuss.

Throughout this book, all four authors will describe extensions and control panels we find indispensable; a rapid application development plan requires that you use appropriate and available tools to streamline your work.

See Also

- "Third Party Tools and Extensions," Chapter 19
- Source Disk: Tools Folder

However, you should know that extensions remain loaded in memory just like DOS TSRs, and they have a similar potential for causing trouble. When multiple extensions conflict, you'll learn to remove extensions, or perhaps change the order in which they load, and reboot, until the conflict is resolved. There are even times when you should boot "clean," with no extensions, to forestall conflicts. Installing FoxPro for Macintosh is one of those times.

Make the Finder your current application, and use the Special menu option to Restart your Macintosh, holding the Shift key down. This time, when you see the "Welcome to Macintosh" message, it includes a second line, which reads "Extensions Off" (you can release the Shift key when you see this message).

> **FOXPRO MAC HACK TIP**
>
> You also saw an option to Shut Down on the Special menu. You should always shut down your Mac before turning off the power and educate your users to do this, too! Remember that the Finder is actually an application, like FoxPro—and remember the damage you can do to your files if you don't properly quit FoxPro before you flip the power switch. Think of Shut Down as quitting the Finder.

Disks and Files at Work on the Mac Desktop

With no extensions loaded, start the FoxPro installation process. Insert the first FoxPro installation disk, labeled Disk 1 - Setup. As your Mac recognizes the disk, its icon appears on the desktop with a label indicating its name.

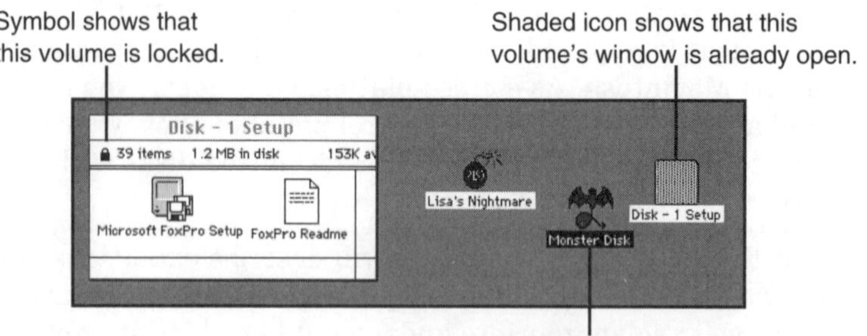

Figure 1.2 *Three mounted volumes, including the first FoxPro Installation floppy disk, show on the Desktop.*

Figure 1.2 shows a portion of my Mac Desktop, with icons for the first FoxPro installation disk and two other *mounted volumes* (Lisa's Nightmare and Monster Disk, my two hard disks). Volumes are disks or partitions of disks, and they are mounted if the system is currently aware of them. You'll notice immediately that my two disks have radically different icons, and that I've given them rather unusual names. Mac users typically personalize their Desktops in this manner; you probably will do it, too. Changing the icons on files or other Desktop elements doesn't affect your work—except in the sense that you can procrastinate for endless hours collecting, editing, and assigning the icons! However, the long names, which may include spaces and punctuation, have serious consequences for file-referencing in FoxPro. (Later in this chapter, I'll suggest a cross-platform strategy for handling file names.)

In this figure, you also see an open Finder window that shows some of the contents of the first FoxPro Setup disk. I didn't have to open this window myself, and you probably won't, either; each volume maintains a hidden *Desktop file*, something like the FoxPro FOXUSER file or Windows' .INI files, which stores Finder window positions and sizes for the different *folders* on that volume.

Folders are like DOS directories; they usually are hierarchical, or nested. The Setup disk has only one folder, which corresponds to the DOS root directory. When you mount the disk, the window that appears automatically shows you the portion of this folder that the person who planned the installation process decided you need to see.

Notice the little "lock" symbol under the title bar of the Setup disk's Finder window on the left. This disk was write-protected after recording the position and size of this window. No matter what changes you make to the window, your changes won't register in the Setup disk's Desktop file. The next time you use the disks, the window contents guide you through the beginning of the installation process again.

FOXPRO MAC HACK TIP

When you create distribution disks for FoxPro for Macintosh applications, you'll want to observe these same niceties. The Mac's well-deserved reputation for encouraging a high degree of confidence and a willingness to experiment, even among novice users, rests on hundreds of conventions like these, observed consistently by programmers. Some of these conventions are laid out in the Apple *Human Interface Guidelines*, but other conventions are a matter of unwritten consensus.

See Also

• "Additional Resources," Appendix A

> Regardless of the source, interface consistency is vital to the Macintosh community and to the success of Macintosh software. Your applications will gain acceptance in direct proportion to how well you assimilate and observe Macintosh interface conventions (such as the positioning of volumes on the desktop).

In figure 1.2, the icon for the floppy disk is shaded or dimmed, indicating that its window is already open. The icon for Monster Disk, to the floppy icon's left, has just been selected with a single mouse click, so it's highlighted. (Double-clicking on a volume's icon opens a Finder window showing its contents.) If you click directly on the volume's name, rather than its picture icon, wait a moment and the highlight changes color or the border of the text label changes. You can change the name of the volume when you see this change. As you add more elements to your Desktop, including icons for folders and single files, you'll use this method to alter their names constantly. The name is "selected on entry" (fully highlighted) at first, similar to many Windows dialog text boxes or the FoxPro @K GET format; if you type any character, the entire name disappears. Use a ← or → keypress, or click the mouse somewhere in the name, to avoid overwriting the name if you just want to edit. A ↓ press conveniently takes you to the end of the current name (if you experiment, you'll find that file names are limited to 31 characters).

See Also

• "FoxPro for Macintosh on the Network," Chapter 15

You *launch* (or execute) the FoxPro installation procedure by double-clicking on the icon labeled Microsoft FoxPro Setup in the Setup disk window. The installation procedure is very similar to installing other FoxPro products; you can choose a full, minimum, or custom setup, and there's a special option to install FoxPro locally if it's already installed on the network. If you have room on your disk and you don't have network access to the sample files already, do a full installation so you can explore them while you use this book. (You see the categories of installable files in figure 1.3.)

> **FOXPRO MAC HACK TIP**
>
> If you are installing the Professional version of FoxPro 2.6 or above, be sure to install the distributable library files for both standard and Power Macs, no matter which flavor of Mac you use. With the library files, you can create distributable applications for users of both types of machine.

You'll notice that you don't need to click on a button to continue the installation process after being prompted to insert a new disk. The Setup application also ejects a disk automatically when necessary. On the Macintosh, the system software controls the disk drive mechanism to accept and eject a disk. You may find this behavior unnerving at first, but don't worry. If the system fails to eject a disk properly, you can usually encourage it by performing a Restart. If all else fails, there's a small hole near the drive opening. Insert a paper-clip wire or similar tool in this hole to eject the disk mechanically.

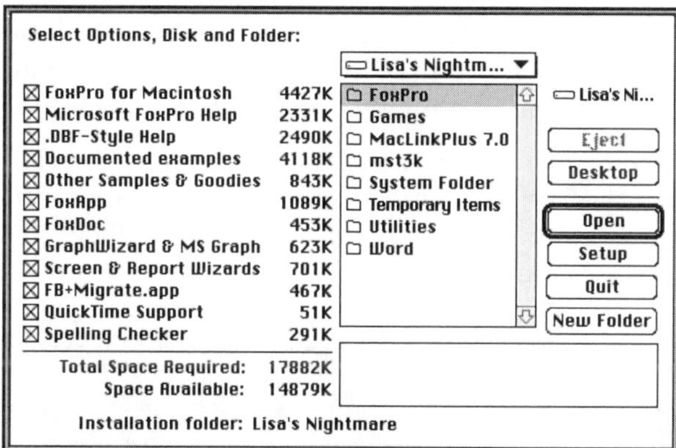

Figure 1.3 *The Custom Installation choices from FoxPro for Macintosh's Setup procedure.*

> **FOXPRO MAC HACK TIP**
>
> Before you complain that this reliance on software to eject a floppy disk is unnecessary, think about the number of times you've seen a "drive not ready" error under DOS. Because the Mac operating system is more drive- and volume-aware than DOS, these awkward errors don't occur on the Macintosh—and you don't need to code around them in your FoxPro applications.

Under the Special menu in the Finder, you also see an option to Eject a disk, with the shortcut ⌘-E. The ⌘, also known as the Command key, is different from the Control key, but you will find that FoxPro for Macintosh uses the two keys interchangeably. For example, you can press either

Ctrl-W or ⌘-W to close and save your work. If you issue an `ON KEY LABEL Ctrl-F10 WAIT WINDOW`, you get the WAIT WINDOW when you press either Ctrl-F10 or ⌘-F10. The equivalence of the Control and Command keys is critical to your ability to port FoxPro applications cross-platform. However, this behavior represents a departure from Macintosh interface standards; outside FoxPro for Macintosh, these modifier keys usually have different purposes. Don't expect Ctrl-E to Eject the disk in the Finder.

Insert a floppy disk, and try the ⌘-E shortcut. You see that the icon for the disk remains on your desktop. You haven't dismounted the floppy volume by ejecting it. While some good reasons exist to keep disks mounted at times (for example, during a multi-disk installation process), this behavior is usually irritating, because the Finder later may ask you for this disk at times you find highly inappropriate.

To dismount and eject a volume simultaneously, drag the volume to the Trash icon. Don't worry; this action doesn't erase the files, although the action of dragging other items (individual files and folders) to the Trash marks the items for deletion.

FOXPRO MAC HACK TIP

The dual-purpose nature of the Trash can is one of the few things that mars the consistency of the Mac Desktop interface. Even the most orthodox Apple Interface Guidelines proponents (people I like to call the "Mac Interface Cops" or "Jazz Police") agree this behavior is a mistake! You'll probably prefer, as I do, to use the Put Away option, which, oddly, is buried in the File menu instead of the Special menu's Eject. Select the disk and use the Put Away shortcut of ⌘-V.

You can perform this entire operation from your keyboard by tabbing through the items on your Desktop until the appropriate icon is selected. The Finder also has incremental seek like a FoxPro pop-up so that you can type the first letters of a disk's name until you select the right icon.

As part of the FoxPro installation process, Setup installs the Apple *Shared Library Manager,* a required extension, in your System files. FoxPro installation also adds FoxPro-specific library files to your Extensions folder.

Configuring FoxPro and Setting Up for Work

To continue exploring the Mac desktop, take a look at what you installed. (You can restart your Mac with your normal complement of extensions first, if you want to.)

Investigate the FoxPro Installed Files

If you don't see a Finder window listing the contents of the volume on which you installed FoxPro, double-click on the volume icon to open a window now. Find and double-click on your FoxPro folder to open a window of this folder's contents.

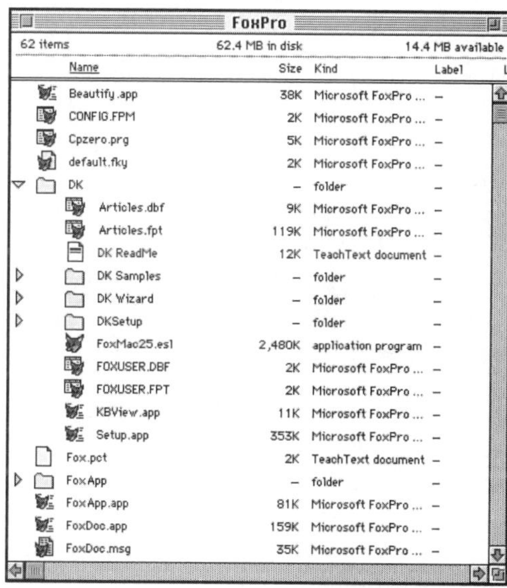

Figure 1.4 *The FoxPro folder in Name View, with the DK folder expanded.*

Using the Finder's View menu option, you can look at the contents of this window according to different systems of organization. Try the Name view to see files organized like a DOS directory listing or a Windows Program Manager listing. Notice the different kinds of files available, such as documents and executable applications, denoted by different Fox-associated icons as well as different file type descriptions. On the Macintosh, files that are not executable applications themselves are associated with a parent application (their *creator*), and each file also has a file *type* that tells you (and the application) how the application should respond if you double-click on the icon of this associated file.

CROSS-PLATFORM WARNING

As cross-platform developers, you should give your files conventional DOS file names and extensions. Your compiled applications, for example, should always be .APPs or .EXEs. Screen definition tables should always be .SCXs with associated .SCT memo files.

However, you must understand that FoxPro for Macintosh recognizes these files by their file types, not by their extensions. If you double-click on an .APP and FoxPro is not yet running, the Macintosh system looks at the .APP's creator attribute, which is FOXX for FoxPro for Macintosh, and launches FoxPro. Then the file's type of FAPP alerts FoxPro that you want to run the compiled application.

The same software that you use to get a Macintosh floppy drive to mount DOS volumes often has preference settings to allow you to set default associations for individual DOS file extensions. If you use this option, listing all the FoxPro file types for the translation or mounting utility, the tool automatically assigns the correct Macintosh creator and file type to each file that you transfer to the Macintosh. This procedure doesn't alter the files at all from DOS's point of view, but the automatic association makes your work in FoxPro for Macintosh much easier.

See Also

- "FoxPro's Use of File Extensions and Macintosh File Types," Appendix B

You see several READ ME files—labeled TeachText documents—within your FoxPro folder. Double-clicking on any of these files launches TeachText, a limited word processor installed as part of your Mac System files. (In System 7.5, *SimpleText* takes the place of *TeachText*. SimpleText opens the same files and has additional capabilities, such as speaking text if you have PlainTalk installed on your Mac.)

Make sure that you read these files carefully for additional information about the latest changes in FoxPro, including many corrections to the printed documentation and some information specific to the Macintosh version of FoxPro that you won't find anywhere in the manuals.

Use the ⌘ key with → and ← to expand or compress your view of a nested folder's contents; in figure 1.4, you see my FoxPro directory with the DK subfolder expanded. The DK folder is the location I chose for my FoxPro for Macintosh Distribution Kit files.

If you have the Professional version of the product, you can install the FoxPro for Macintosh Distribution Kit (known as the DK) using exactly the same procedure you used for the main files. (Remember, consistency is everything on the Mac.) The Distribution Kit asks you to select a location for the Kit's files. Be careful; neither the Setup dialog boxes nor the documentation explain this fact. Although you can install the DK into any folder you want, you must place one DK file, FOXMAC.LIB, in the home FoxPro folder for FoxPro to recognize the DK capabilities. The DK Setup doesn't take care of this vital detail for you.

Use this opportunity to practice moving a file on your Macintosh drive. (If you have not installed the DK, you can practice, using the steps below, with any other file of your choice.)

If you installed the DK, find the FOXMAC.LIB file by typing its name.

FOXPRO MAC HACK TIP

If you can't find a file, such as FOXMAC.LIB, use the Finder's File menu option to Find, as shown in figure 1.5 (shortcut ⌘-F10). This dialog box is indispensable in the graphical Macintosh environment. While you drag folders and their contents around to your heart's content just to rearrange your Desktop, you may inadvertently nest a group of folders inside another folder—and then you have no idea where they went.

As you search for a particular file when using Find and its companion Find Again (⌘-G), and watch various windows open to show you every MAIN.PRG you have on every mounted volume, you'll be glad the Finder lives up to its name.

Move FOXMAC.LIB to your FoxPro main folder by dragging it to the new location. (You can do this in any Finder View.) If you drag the folder to an open window of the FoxPro main folder's contents, just place the file within the confines of the window. You also can move the file by dragging it to the FoxPro main folder's icon, wherever that icon happens to be located. As you move the file to the folder icon, you see the folder icon darken. At that moment, if you drop the file, the Finder will place it inside the folder you chose.

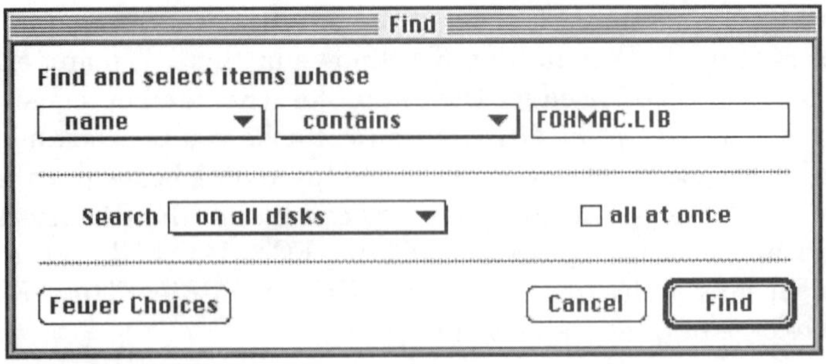

Find

Find and select items whose

name | contains | FOXMAC.LIB

Search on all disks | all at once

Fewer Choices | Cancel | Find

Figure 1.5 *The Finder's Find dialog, in expanded ("More Choices") view, helps you find the FOXMAC.LIB so you can move it to the main FoxPro directory.*

FOXPRO MAC HACK TIP

If you hold down the ⇧Shift and Option keys as you drag the file, you create a copy instead of moving the file. There's also an option to Duplicate a file on the Finder's Find menu (shortcut ⌘-D). However, it's more convenient to use this mouse shortcut when you want to copy a file to a new location. The Duplicate menu option copies the file in the same location as the original. To avoid duplicate file names in one folder, it assigns the new file the original file name plus the word "Copy" (or "Copy 2," "Copy 3," and so on, if you continue to Duplicate the same file). You need to edit the file name when you move the copy to its new folder. To avoid adding extra space characters to file names, you'll find it easiest to select the whole label with ⌘-A and retype from scratch.

This may be the first time you use the Option key. Although you notice that it has the word Alt on the keycap, this key is *not* an equivalent for the DOS keyboard's Alt key. I will discuss this FoxPro cross-platform issue later in the chapter.

After you move FOXMAC.LIB, explore the FoxPro files further. To customize your View of the files more thoroughly, use the Views control panel, one of the System files. For example, you may decide that you don't want to see the file type information if you're familiar with the various icons associated with documents for the applications you use.

Access the Views control panel by choosing the special System folder where your operating system resides on your boot disk. (The System

Folder that contains the running System files has a picture of the Macintosh on its icon. Mac people refer to this as the blessed copy of the operating system.) Within the System Folder you'll find the Control Panels folder. Double-click on this folder, and then double-click on the Views control panel item you find within it to launch the control panel and make your choices in the dialog you see in figure 1.6.

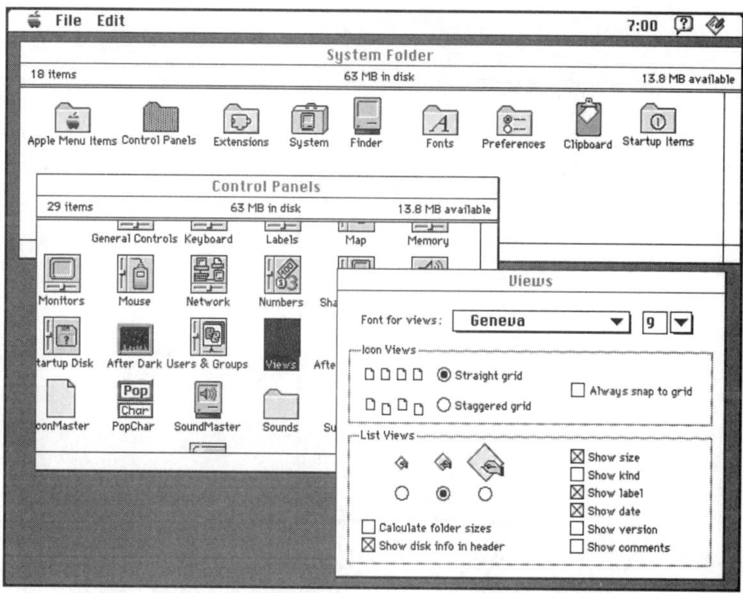

Figure 1.6 *The System Folder, its nested Control Panels Folder, and the Views Control Panel dialog.*

The changes you make in this dialog apply to all your Finder windows, while the decision you make about type of View from the Finder's View menu applies to one window at a time. The Finder saves the View type you set for individual windows, along with the size and position of open windows, in the Desktop file.

> **FOXPRO MAC HACK TIP**
>
> To speed window-opening, turn off the View option to Calculate folder size. You can always determine the size of a folder by selecting it and using the Get Info dialog that you will read about later in this chapter.

Besides the Finder, other applications save the custom settings you create for your work. Although each application can store this information in a different format, you'll find the *preferences* files for many applications, including FoxPro, in a Preferences folder nested in the System folder. If you look at the FoxPro Preferences file, as shown in figure 1.7, you see that it bears a striking resemblance to the definitions in a FoxPro for Windows .INI file.

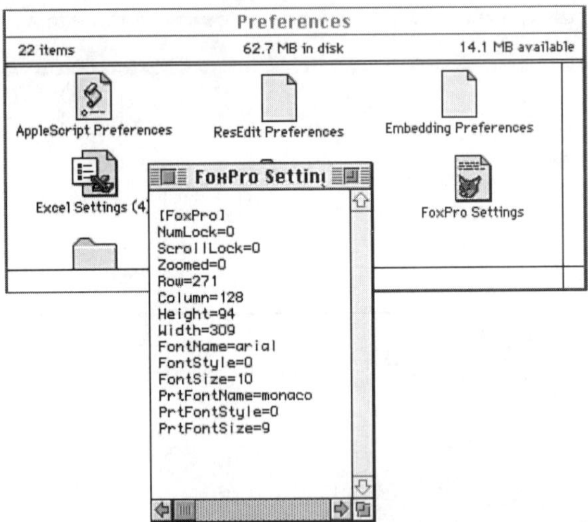

Figure 1.7 *The FoxPro Settings file, located in the System Folder's nested Preferences folder, along with preference files for many other applications.*

If you look in the Preferences folder, you may see a FoxPro for Macintosh 2.5 Preferences file even if you have never launched FoxPro. (Note that this file name differs slightly from the normal FoxPro Settings file.) This file is often left behind by the FoxPro for Macintosh Setup process. You can delete it. Drag the file to the Trash, and use the Special Finder menu option to Empty the Trash.

If you see a text editing window like the one in figure 1.7, you may have double-clicked on the FoxPro Settings file icon in the Preferences folder. The FoxPro Settings file is a document with the FOXX creator, and a TEXT file type; by double-clicking on it, you launched FoxPro with a MODIFY FILE command and opened the FoxPro Settings file in the FoxPro editor.

If you try to edit the FoxPro Settings file within FoxPro, your changes will not be effective because FoxPro overwrites this file when you quit. (You can, however, edit the file using another Text Editor, such as TeachText or SimpleText.) The entries, such as the attributes of the FoxPro Main Application window or the state of the NumLock key, are self-explanatory.

If you did launch FoxPro by double-clicking on the Settings file, use the File menu's Quit option to leave FoxPro now. Take a moment, before you Quit, to notice that you're using the same menu across the top of the screen formerly occupied by Finder options. It now shows the familiar Fox SYSMENU options, and the rightmost position (the Application menu) shows the familiar Fox head rather than the Finder's Mac icon.

Similarly, the Fox status bar appears across the bottom of the screen. Unlike the system menu and status bar in FoxPro for Windows, the FoxPro for Macintosh menu and status bar belong to the full *MACDESKTOP*. They are not confined to the space occupied by the FoxPro main application window and appear when FoxPro is the currently active application, just as the FoxPro windows come forward when FoxPro is active. I'll return to this important interface change later in the chapter.

Launching FoxPro

Along with its Settings file in the Preferences folder, FoxPro for Macintosh uses a CONFIG.FPM file much like the CONFIG.FPW and CONFIG.FP files of FoxPro for Windows and DOS. Unlike its DOS cousins, however, a CONFIG.FPM file *must* have the file name CONFIG.FPM for FoxPro to use and recognize it. There is no Macintosh equivalent for the FOXPROCFG, FOXPROWCFG, and FOXPROSWX environmental variables, or for the -C command line switch, which allows DOS and Windows to specify the name of a configuration file.

Similarly, you cannot pass FoxPro for Macintosh a command-line parameter with the name of a program to run. Instead, because you already launched FoxPro by using the FoxPro Settings file, you can double-click on a program or application file icon, launching FoxPro and the specified program at the same time. You also can double-click on a particular CONFIG.FPM, launching FoxPro with your choice of configuration. Your distributed applications can have CONFIG.FPM files bound to them; you may already follow this strategy for DOS- and Windows-compiled applications.

For most of your development work, you probably will use a default CONFIG.FPM file in FoxPro's home folder. But you don't want to dig through your folder structure to double-click on the CONFIG.FPM icon or on the nearby icon for the executable Microsoft FoxPro application icon in the home folder. Instead, System 7 provides the option of *aliases*, copies of icons, which you may place anywhere you like and which serve as pointers to the real location of the file or group of files they represent.

Returning to the main FoxPro folder, begin to type `Microsoft FoxPro` or scroll through the files until you find the icon for the main FoxPro executable file. Select it and then use the File menu option to Make Alias.

Figure 1.8 *Icons for a file (the FoxPro executable application) and its alias.*

In figure 1.8, you see the file and its alias in the Icon view, but you can create and use aliases no matter what view you use for your Finder windows. You always can tell an alias from the real file because its name label is written in italics. The Finder adds the word “Alias” to the label when you make the alias, but this addition isn’t required for aliases. The extra word is temporarily necessary because two items in one folder can’t have exactly the same name (just as two files in a DOS directory can’t have exactly the same name).

After you make the alias, you can move it to a more convenient position and double-click on it to start FoxPro whenever you like. (If you have a CONFIG.FPM in your home FoxPro directory, FoxPro will launch with the settings in this default CONFIG.FPM.) I like to keep one such alias directly on the Desktop, just as you might keep a dictionary ready-to-use on your physical desktop. Move the alias out of your FoxPro folder to a readily accessible location (you can change the alias name to remove the word “Alias” if you want, once it’s out of the FoxPro folder). You’ve begun to arrange your own Mac desktop in a manner that suits your working style.

Make as many aliases for FoxPro as you want. I keep an alias for my FoxPro application on my Apple menu along with the other tools I use daily. Placing an option on the Apple menu is simple, whether the item is an alias or a real file. Just move the item into the Apple Menu Item folder you find in the System folder. Similarly, if you want FoxPro to load when you start your Mac, move it or its alias into the Startup Items folder. You can see both of these folders in the System folder window in figure 1.6.

Launch Multiple Sessions of FoxPro

As you can see in figure 1.9, I have two FoxPro options on my Apple menu. Both are aliases, although aliases don't show as italicized on the menu. In fact, they are aliases for two separate copies of FoxPro! I arranged my system this way to allow me to run multiple sessions of FoxPro for testing purposes.

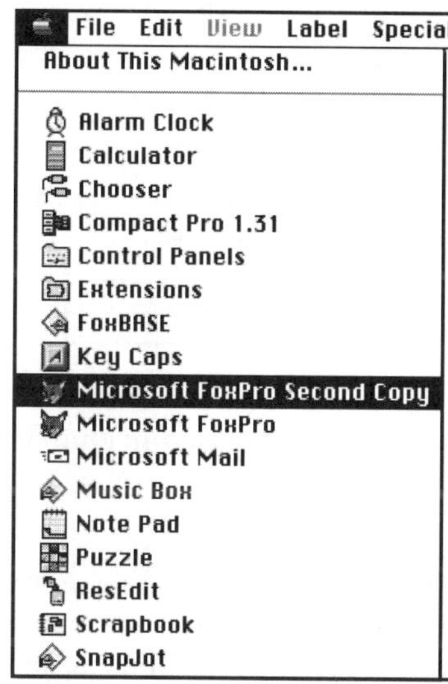

Figure 1.9 *A customized Apple menu shows multiple options for FoxPro.*

If you have sufficient disk space and memory for multiple FoxPro sessions, this method allows you to test your file- and record-locking code in FoxPro, even when a network is not available.

See Also

- "FoxPro for the Macintosh on the Network," Chapter 15

First, verify that File Sharing capabilities were installed with System 7 on your Mac by checking for a Sharing option on the Finder's File menu. If you don't see it, use the System 7 Installer to add these capabilities.

Next, launch the Sharing Setup control panel you find in the Control Panel folder to give your Mac a "network identity" and to turn on File Sharing using the dialog you see in figure 1.10. For now, don't worry about the "program linking" options at the bottom of the dialog.

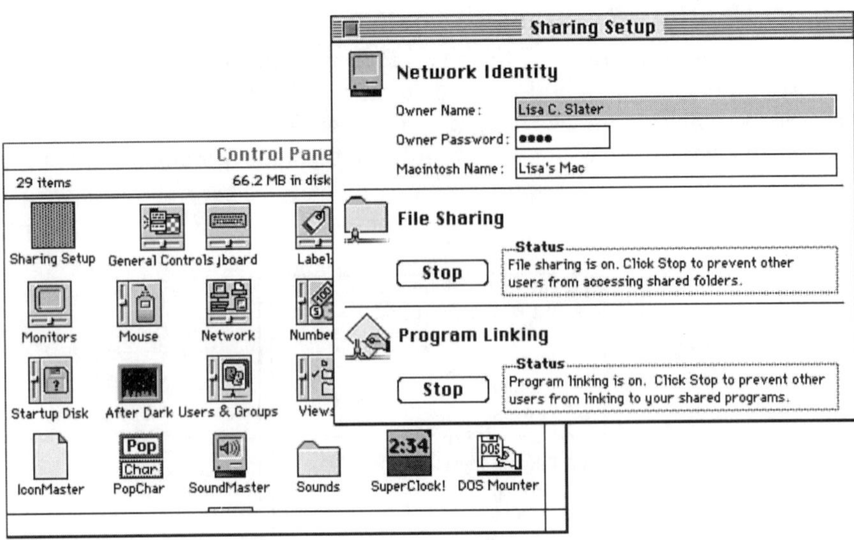

Figure 1.10 *The Sharing Setup control panel sets up File Sharing capabilities and can be used to enable multi-user emulation on a standalone Mac.*

Finally, turn on the native AppleTalk file sharing capabilities using the *Chooser*, a part of the Macintosh operating system that recognizes and selects network and printer drivers. The Chooser is an option on the Apple menu; select it and you see the dialog in figure 1.11. Use the option at the lower right corner of the dialog to enable AppleTalk and then restart your Macintosh. If you have two copies of the FoxPro application executable files and sufficient memory, you now can start two sessions of FoxPro and watch FoxPro's multi-user capabilities at work.

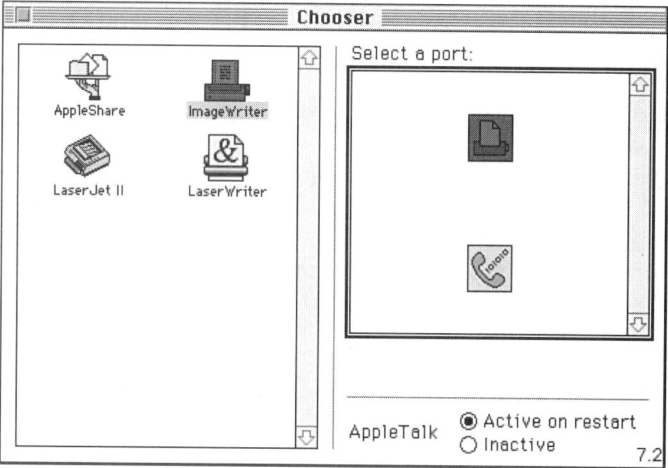

Figure 1.11 *Use the Chooser to turn on AppleTalk.*

FOXPRO MAC HACK TIP

If you can't enable File Sharing for any reason, don't worry. Although you may still have the capability to run two sessions of FoxPro, your data is in no danger, as it would be in a DOS or Windows multitasking environment.

As you probably know, a standalone Windows computer can run several sessions of FoxPro or other Xbase-table-reading applications, all of which "believe" they have EXCLUSIVE rights to the same FoxPro table—unless DOS SHARE is loaded on the computer! Without SHARE, each session can perform destructive commands usually restricted to EXCLUSIVE use or a file- or record-level lock—such as PACK—even though other sessions may have the same record or table in use.

Not so on the Macintosh. If you don't enable File Sharing, the worst risk you run with multiple sessions of FoxPro is an inability to test your own explicit locking code. Without file sharing, a session that opens a table receives true EXCLUSIVE rights to the table. All other sessions or applications attempting to open the table receive the message that the "file is in use by another," quite properly.

Tailoring Additional Macintosh Features for FoxPro Work

See Also

- Function Setup, Source Disk: Library/Template Code: MAIN.PRG
- "Setup Procedures," Chapter 5

I mentioned that the Chooser recognizes printer drivers available to your system, as well as network drivers. You can see the printer drivers available on my Macintosh in figure 1.11, and you may notice that one of them is a LaserJet driver. I use PowerPrint, from GDT Softworks, to connect my Mac printer port to the parallel port of my DOS printer. Along with the communicating cable, PowerPrint provides drivers that "speak TrueType" for most standard IBM printers, similar to the Microsoft Windows printer driver system.

Because the Chooser recognizes PowerPrint drivers like any other printer drivers installed on the Mac, the entire process is transparent to FoxPro.

> **CROSS-PLATFORM WARNING**
>
> PowerPrint is a great boon to the cross-platform environment, but it also serves as an illustration of a very important principle: *like FoxPro for Windows, FoxPro for Macintosh is dependent on the operating system for many services, including printing*. Like FoxPro for Windows, FoxPro for Macintosh does not "own the box" while it's running. Although as a DOS developer you may have specified every aspect of your application's environment, in Windows and on the Mac you give up some control, both to the operating system and to the user.
>
> In the case of printing, the user has the right to use the Chooser and specify another print device at any moment. The operating system takes care of interpreting the user's choice. In FoxPro, you can be aware of this choice and adjust your program to it, but you shouldn't override it with a programmatic choice of your own. As in Windows, this axiom proves most troublesome when FoxPro tries to print to a file. As you'll see in Chapter 15, however, the results are quite different on the Mac than you see in Windows.

See Also

- "Printing to File," Chapter 9

Besides the Chooser, there are other features of the Macintosh operating system and environment with specific consequences for FoxPro.

Memory Use

You've seen that you can start multiple sessions of FoxPro if you have sufficient memory. How much memory does FoxPro for Macintosh require? How do you configure memory on the Mac?

Select the icon for the Microsoft FoxPro application file and use the Finder's File menu option to Get Info. You'll see the dialog that appears in figure 1.12.

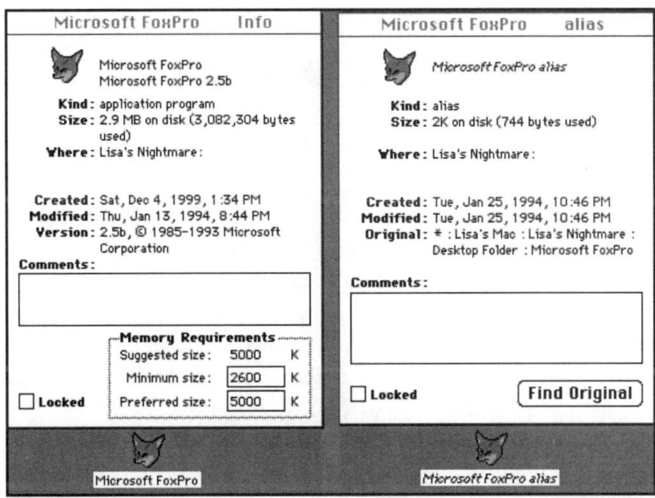

Figure 1.12 *The Get Info dialog for the FoxPro application file and for one of its aliases.*

At the bottom right, you'll see a Memory Requirements box; its first line holds the Suggested amount of memory for FoxPro as specified by Microsoft. The next two lines hold two memory settings that you can change—a *minimum* size, representing the amount of memory that must be available before FoxPro loads, and a *preferred size*, which is the amount of memory FoxPro will take from the available pool of memory if that much memory is available.

These settings are equivalent to the second and third arguments to the MEMLIMIT setting you use in CONFIG.FP and CONFIG.FPW files for FoxPro DOS and Windows. There is no equivalent setting to the MEMLIMIT first argument (percent of available memory FoxPro will take), but it isn't necessary. Edit the two available settings the same way you might experiment with MEMLIMIT—which means that you should be prepared for some unpleasant FoxPro session endings during your experiments!

In general, do not decrease the minimum memory size specified by Microsoft's default, which may change in different releases of FoxPro for Macintosh. Add memory to the preferred size setting if you have extra memory available. Remember that, like other versions of FoxPro, FoxPro for Macintosh can handle all the memory you give. The more memory you allow FoxPro for Macintosh, the more smoothly it performs. If you find that other applications complain that they don't have enough memory to load a document, change their preferred memory size and try again.

FOXPRO MAC HACK TIP

If you use the Get Info dialog for an alias rather than the original file, you can't adjust the memory settings. Instead, as you see in figure 1.12, you have an option to find the original file. When you change these settings, the changes affect *all* the aliases for this application, no matter where the aliases reside on your system or when you created them. Get Info boxes are tailored to different types of files. The Trash can's Get Info box lets you turn off the warning before the Finder executes the menu command to empty the Trash!

Earlier in the chapter, you saw the About This Macintosh dialog, which shows you the memory in use by each running application along with the version of the system software you are using. Take another look at this dialog now, comparing figure 1.1 to figure 1.13.

Notice the text indicating "Largest Unused Block" of memory under the System version information. (You can see it more clearly in figure 1.1.) As in Windows, Macintosh memory can become fragmented as you load and unload programs. The amount of memory you have available to load a program at any time is the "largest unused block," *not* the sum total of your memory minus the blocks of memory in use by other running programs.

In fact, the largest unused block can be much smaller than you might expect, no matter how much memory you have. You benefit by loading programs that require a great deal of memory *once*, and then avoiding unloading them, if, like FoxPro, you use these programs throughout your working day. You can easily follow this strategy if you add FoxPro to your Startup Items as described previously in the chapter.

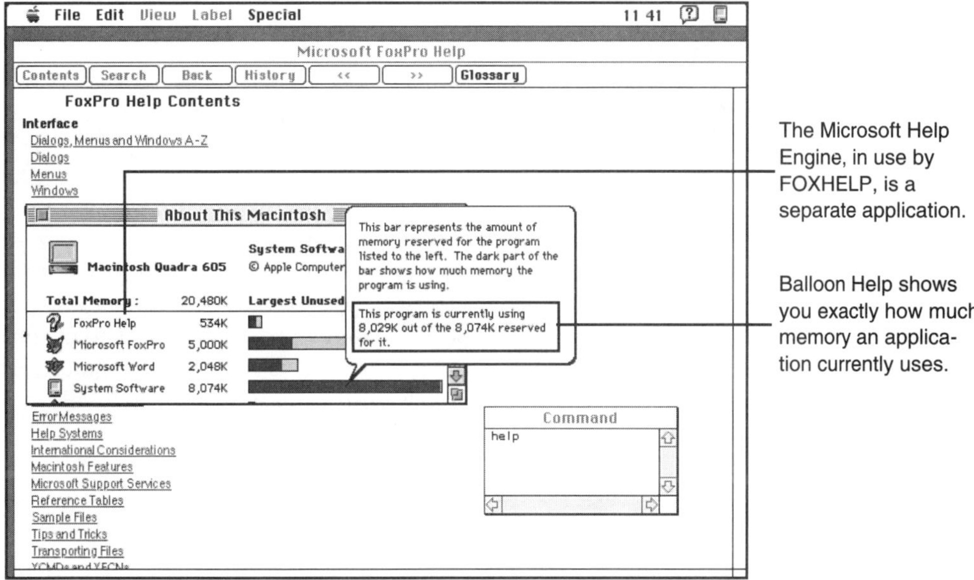

Figure 1.13 *Use the About This Macintosh dialog to monitor memory use.*

FOXPRO MAC HACK TIP

Use the Help Menu (to the left of the Application Menu on the menu bar with a Question-Mark icon) to turn on Balloon Help for a few moments. Most Mac users turn up their noses at Balloon Help, which provides short descriptions of interface objects as you move the mouse around on the Desktop. By almost universal consensus, Balloon Help is of limited utility, even for novice users. You'll certainly find Balloon Help annoying if you leave it on all the time, and it's not very well implemented in FoxPro for Macintosh's system objects.

However, as you see in figure 1.13, in the About This Macintosh dialog , Balloon Help has the intriguing capability to show you the *exact* amount of memory in use as you pass the mouse pointer over each application's memory bar.

> I'll show you some tricks you can do with Balloon Help in your own programs when you learn about FoxPro menus later in the book. You'll see that this underutilized Macintosh feature can add a very professional and helpful touch to your applications.

See Also

• "Cross-Platform Usability and Thoughtful Design," Chapter 11

While you experiment with FoxPro's minimum and preferred memory sizes, monitor the About This Macintosh dialog regularly. If you find that FoxPro's entry consistently shows the program to use almost all the memory you've allotted to it, perhaps you should increase the preferred size. If, on the other hand, you rarely see FoxPro's memory gauge reaching the midpoint of its allotted memory while you run your applications, you may safely decrease FoxPro's preferred size.

> **CROSS-PLATFORM WARNING**
>
> If your applications use the Windows-style help system (.HLP files), you can use this system on the Macintosh as well. Interactive FoxPro for Macintosh can take advantage of FOXHELP.HLP, too. But you should realize that the Microsoft Help Engine takes a considerable amount of memory—and it's a separate application from FoxPro.
>
> Be sure to leave sufficient memory for the Help engine when configuring your Macintosh and monitor the Help engine's separate use of memory in the About This Macintosh window. If necessary, use the Help engine's own Get Info box to change memory settings there. You'll find the Help Engine in a Microsoft Folder inside the Extensions folder nested in your System Folder.

Once you get a feel for the amount of memory FoxPro requires, you may decide that you just don't have enough memory! Of course, more RAM is always welcome. But the Macintosh has a *virtual memory* scheme, similar to Windows' swap files, which allows available hard disk space to take the place of memory. Virtual memory is slower than RAM, of course, just as swap files are slower than RAM in Windows, but it can allow the use of FoxPro on machines that would not support the application otherwise.

To manage memory, use the Memory control panel, shown in figure 1.14. Configure virtual memory the same way you approach Windows swap files, except there's no distinction between permanent and temporary virtual memory on the Mac. Turn off the option if you have sufficient RAM to support your work without using virtual memory.

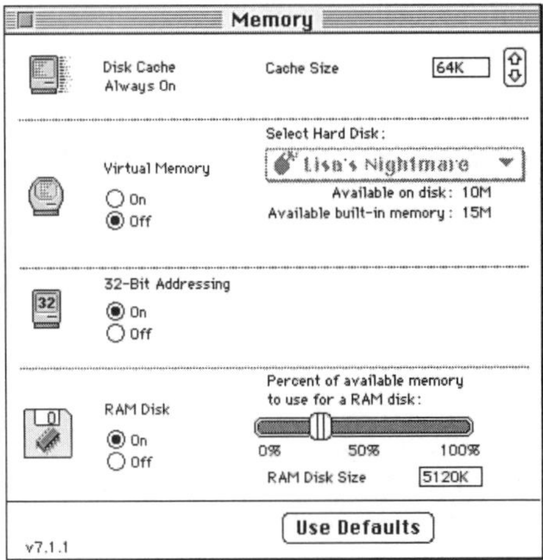

Figure 1.14 *Configure memory using the System's Memory control panel dialog.*

You'll see several other sets of memory options in this dialog. At the top, you can see a place to set the System's cache. Like FoxPro for DOS and Windows, FoxPro for Macintosh often performs far better using its internal caching without the interference of additional cache mechanisms. Although other programs may recommend much higher settings, you may notice far less disk thrashing if you set the cache in this dialog lower than its default value for your system.

Microsoft recommends a cache of 128k for FoxPro; in my experience, a cache limited to 64k is even better. This value also is the default value of SET BLOCKSIZE in FoxPro, the setting that governs the chunks in which memofields are written to the .FPT. My work often involves multiple memofields, so matching the BLOCKSIZE to the amount of information cached by the system may account for the performance gains I see with this setting. Your own mileage will vary.

You also can see a setting for 32-bit addressing. Since 32-bit addressing is necessary for the Mac to address the extra memory you know FoxPro loves to have, this one's a no-brainer; set it on if your machine supports it.

Depending on your version of the System files or your Mac model, the Memory control panel dialog may look different on your machine. For example, if you have an LC II, you won't see the RAM disk options. The lack of this option in the Memory dialog doesn't mean you can't use a RAM disk on the LC II, just that you can't use the built-in system RAM disk. Because many other RAM disks are more configurable and flexible, using an external utility is not an onerous requirement.

Be aware that different Macintosh RAM disks utilities exhibit different behaviors when you choose the Restart option. Some save your files until you Shut Down and physically turn off the computer; others don't save the RAM disk contents between Restarts; still others give you a choice.

I use a RAM disk to hold test files while I'm learning and creating new techniques in FoxPro. The RAM disk saves wear on my hard disk, and my repeated build-and-compile cycles proceed very quickly. A RAM disk also is a good place to put the temporary files *required* by FoxPro, notably PROGWORK, that are known to be a limited size. The other TMPFILES settings can create much larger temporary files, especially SORTWORK if you do complex SQL queries; never put them on the RAM disk.

However, you face the same performance issues with a RAM disk and FoxPro on the Macintosh as you do with DOS and Windows. The virtual disk takes memory that FoxPro could otherwise use. On the other hand, assigning temporary files to a RAM disk certainly is a good option if you would put these temporary files on a network drive. You have to balance the choices in your own environment.

On the Macintosh, people with FoxPro-class hardware may have huge amounts of RAM by DOS standards, especially if they customarily use high-end graphics and desktop publishing programs. In this situation, assigning a few megabytes of RAM to a virtual RAM disk makes good sense.

Monitor Settings

See Also

- Source Disk: Tools: RamDisk+
- "Configuration and Performance," Chapter 15

You'll find a Monitors control panel in the Control Panel folder. As you see in figure 1.15, this dialog enables you to set the number of grays or colors (known as *color depth*) if your system is capable of anything besides black and white. The Options button presents a second dialog with resolution choices if your video hardware can switch between resolutions.

FoxPro looks best if you choose 256 colors, but if you notice the screen refreshing slowly, change this Monitors setting to a 16-color display. However, FoxPro looks at the current color palette during startup, and it doesn't handle changes to the palette after startup very gracefully. Quit FoxPro and relaunch it if you have a need to use this control panel to change your color depth.

The Macintosh system has a curious distribution of color options among *three* control panels. The Monitors dialog controls the depth of color, or number of available shades; the Color control panel lets you select the editing text highlight and window border colors; and the General control panel controls the colors of the Desktop itself. Only the color depth is especially significant to FoxPro.

The Macintosh color system poses one of the knottiest problems of FoxPro cross-platform development. Its native notation for color references is different from both the FoxPro DOS character codes and the Windows RGB values. Also, FoxPro chooses its 256 colors from the available palette, regardless of how many colors you've set your Macintosh to display. You can expect some degree of imprecision in the 256 shades that appear in FoxPro regardless of how you attempt to assign color values. I'll cover this issue thoroughly later in the book because color-setting is a subject with which all FoxPro users must become acquainted.

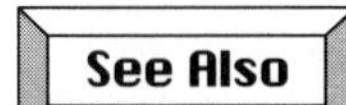

• "Color Use," Chapter 14

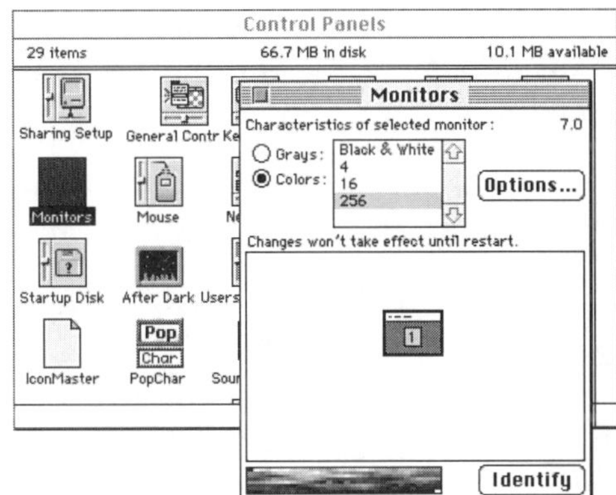

Figure 1.15 *Choose color depth and arrange multiple monitors in the Monitors Control Panels dialog.*

If you have multiple monitors connected to your Mac, the bottom half of the Monitors dialog shows more than one monitor. You can choose which monitor is your *primary* monitor: that is, which monitor FoxPro will recognize on startup and which one it uses to evaluate screen coordinates. You can arrange your monitors in relationship to each other, determining how FoxPro will evaluate the screen coordinates of the monitor that is not primary. The capability of the Mac to use more than one monitor has important consequences for FoxPro, as you'll see in the next section of this chapter.

Stationery Pads and Additional Features of the Get Info Dialog

If you use the Get Info dialog on a document, rather than an application, you see different options than the memory settings you saw in the dialog for the FoxPro executable file. Find a .PRG or other document file—even a .FKY with saved macros will do—and use the Get Info dialog now. In the bottom right, you see a check box for Stationery pad, and in the bottom left, you see a check box labeled Locked. The Locked setting makes a document READ-only. If you use the Stationery pad setting, the Finder creates a *copy* of the document when you try to edit or otherwise launch it, prompting you for a new name.

Stationery pads are a convenient way to create a template for a FoxPro program with your standard header and other information. Unfortunately, FoxPro doesn't recognize the Stationery pad setting internally; if you MODI COMM a .PRG you've previously identified as a Stationery pad, you can press ⌘-W and save the edited file. You need to double-click on the file from the Finder to get the benefit of a Stationery pad. In FoxPro, double-clicking on a .PRG executes the .PRG rather than issuing a MODI COMM for editing.

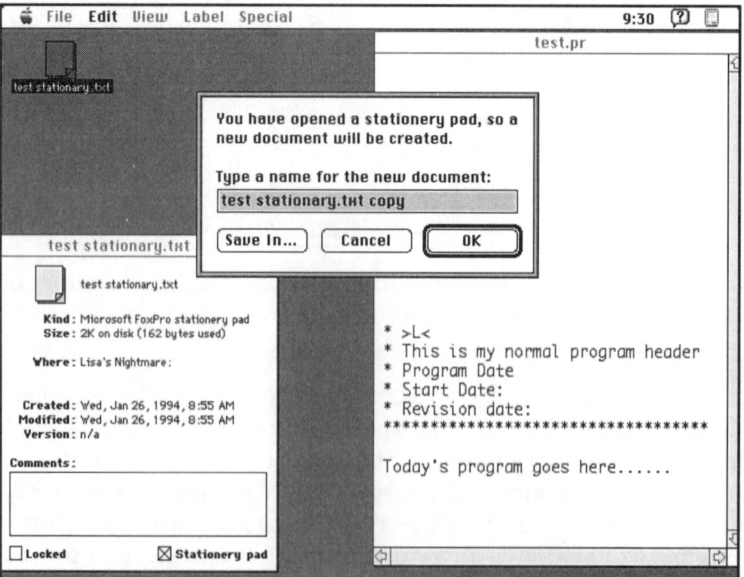

Figure 1.16 *Use Macintosh Stationery pads for template programs or standard text file headers.*

Instead, create your Stationery pad as a .TXT file, as you see in figure 1.16. When you double-click on it, the Finder asks you for a new name. Don't use a .PRG extension. You can edit and save the copy of your template, or many such copies, created by the Finder and then automatically open for editing by FoxPro. If you use a consistent extension for all the programs you create in this manner, you can use the FoxPro Filer later to rename them with a .PRG extension. You also can use Stationery pads for templates for any normal .TXT files in your application, of course.

Unfortunately, this trick won't work for template screens and reports because the Finder doesn't know enough about FoxPro to create a copy of the associated memo file when you opt to edit the stationery pad version of your .SCX or .FRX. However, on Macintosh, you can always keep a template screen or report handy on your Desktop, ready to be double-clicked for opening in a layout window. When you're finished editing, save the template as a screen or report with a new name in your current project's usual location.

Before you leave the Get Info dialog, notice the Created and Modified dates. The second date is the date that the file was most recently altered, identical to the date you'll receive if you use ADIR() to query the system about this file.

System Crashes

Yes, indeed it happens: you run out of memory, you program yourself into a corner, an extension misbehaves, and your system freezes. The crash isn't noticeably more amusing than it would be under DOS, and you probably have even *less* of an inkling of how to take care of it. I'd be remiss in my responsibilities to you if I didn't address this unpleasant subject.

To anticipate your first question, the DOS Ctrl-Alt-Del sequence has several near-analogies on the Mac. If an application stops responding, your first objective is to get back to the Finder, if possible, just as you'd try to get the Program Manager to take care of a problem you experience in Windows. Use the keypress ⌘-Option-Esc when your application freezes, and you'll see a dialog asking you whether you want to Force Quit or Cancel, as shown in figure 1.17.

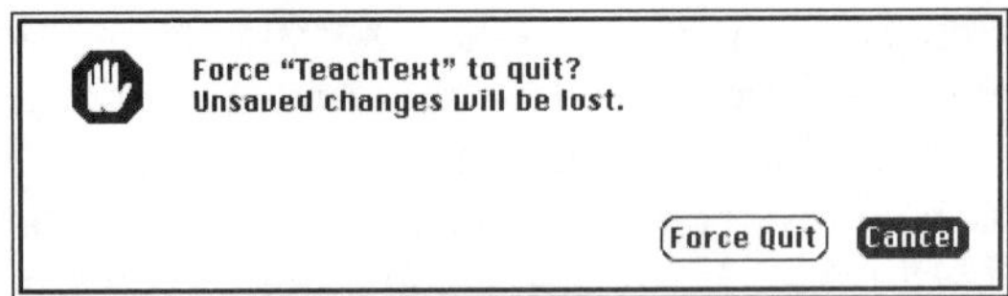

Figure 1.17 *The Force Quit dialog appears if you press* ⌘-Option-Esc.

This dialog is very polite and works nicely when nothing is wrong. For example, I was able to take the screen shot of figure 1.17, cancel the Force Quit, and return to work in TeachText with no difficulty. When you use it in a real crisis, however, you may see the dialog but be unable to pick either choice. You may have lost use of the mouse at that moment, which certainly limits your ability to press the buttons. The buttons may even be missing.

If you *can*, you should Force Quit from the errant application using this dialog, save all your other work, and then Restart as you would in a similar Windows situation.

If you can't use the dialog (or can't even summon the dialog), you can try the *programmer's switch* for either an interrupt or reset action.

When you press the interrupt button, you are suddenly in a small window with something suspiciously resembling a DOS prompt! (You'd probably be enjoying this, if you weren't about to lose the last three hours' work.) Type `G FINDER` and press the Return key. Be sure to hold down the Shift key for capital letters, even if they look like capital letters without the Shift. There is one space between the "G" and "F." After you press Return, if you're lucky, you will get back to the Finder and be able to perform a normal Restart. If it doesn't work, it's time for the Reset button.

Check your Macintosh documentation to find the location of these buttons for your model; not all Macintoshes have them. If you *don't* have the buttons, you can still use the *power key* (the left-facing button on your keyboard with a left-pointing arrow), pressed together with the ⌘ key for interrupt, and together with the Ctrl-⌘ keys for reset.

No matter which of these methods you use to recover from a crash, if there were any FoxPro tables open, they will probably be damaged, especially if they have associated memo fields. The tables may *open* without an error next time you USE them in FoxPro, but the memo fields may still be completely corrupt. Often the fields show a capital "M" in a BROWSE, indicating that the memos all have contents, but the fields still seem to be completely blank.

You can, of course, use the same memo-repair program available to you in DOS, if you move the affected .DBF and .FPT files to a DOS machine or if a Mac version of the repair program is available. But remember that you're especially vulnerable to crashes when you experiment in a new environment—so back up frequently!

After a crash, you may find a Temporary Items folder, either in the Trash or on your drive, containing the .TMP files that FoxPro and other applications were using at the time of the reset, as you see in figure 1.18. You can safely remove these files.

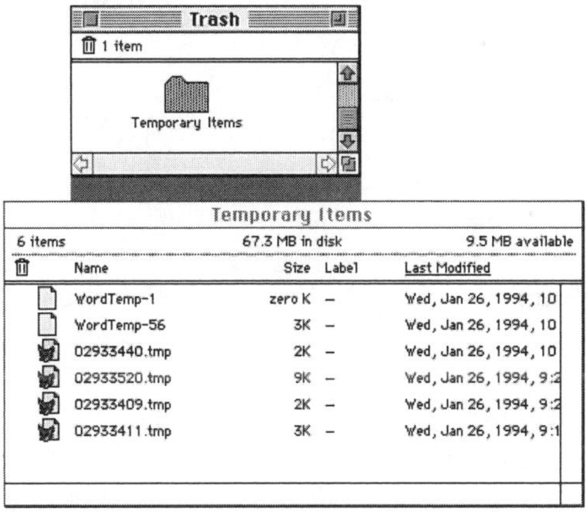

Figure 1.18 *A Temporary Items folder may be somewhere on your disk after a crash.*

FoxPro files probably are not the only files damaged in a crash. Along with documents from other running applications, the Desktop file that you learned about earlier in this chapter, used by the system to store Finder window attributes and file and icon associations, may be damaged as well.

If you find that documents don't seem to associate properly with their applications, or if your Finder windows are opening sluggishly, you may need to rebuild your Desktop file. Pressing Option-⌘ during startup, a Restart, or when you mount a volume, will bring up a dialog asking if you want to Rebuild the Desktop file. If multiple volumes mount at once, you get a dialog for each volume.

Sometimes rebuilding the Desktop isn't enough. The Mac retains some configuration information in parameter RAM (PRAM), and this information can become corrupted as well. You use the keypress Option-⌘-P-R while restarting your Mac to reset PRAM. You hear a second set of chimes during a slightly slower boot procedure to confirm the reset.

Although the system time and date are maintained by PRAM, they won't be reset when you follow this procedure. Use the Date & Time control panel to reset these items, if necessary.

FOXPRO MAC HACK TIP

Holding down those four keys while restarting is something of a feat, and every book I've read about the Mac complains about this key combination (it's new in System 7).

Before you object that you're not a contortionist, I found that I can reset PRAM by holding down the Option-⌘ keys while initiating the restart from the menu, just as I would to rebuild the Desktop file. After the restart procedure begins, I release the mouse with my right hand and press the P-R keys, continuing to press the Option-⌘ keys with my left hand. This process isn't difficult at all.

With all these cautionary notes grimly in mind, and with your newfound expertise in the Mac environment under your belt, proceed to the next section of this chapter. It's time to discuss how you *program* in FoxPro for Macintosh; specifically, how you adjust your FoxPro programming style to accommodate the Mac. At least you'll be able to minimize the crashes that occur because of FoxPro programming errors!

Adapting to FoxPro for Macintosh

In the last section, I gave you detailed instructions for performing tasks that (let's face it) Mac people think are elementary. You are a savvy computer user, but you were in unfamiliar territory. Now you enter the realm in which you are already proficient—FoxPro. I won't provide the same level of detail in these instructions, except in my descriptions of Mac-specific concepts.

Also, remember that the rest of this book continues the discussion of the task to which this section provides an introduction. Your fellow developers who do not come from a DOS and Windows background, for whom we wrote the other Quick Starts in Part I, are as interested in learning how to work in FoxPro for Macintosh as you are and need much the same information. This section is meant only to give you the information you need to change your existing code—and, more importantly, your existing coding habits—so it won't crash and burn on the Mac.

Volume and File Name Setting

You already noticed that my volumes and drives have long names, including spaces and punctuation, illegal in DOS names. File names on the Macintosh can be up to 31 characters, and they often contain these illegal-to-DOS characters, too. The elements of a path (volume, folder, and file names) are all separated by colons, unlike the DOS convention of a colon following the drive letter and backslashes for the rest of the path.

How does FoxPro for Macintosh cope?

Volume Name Translation

FoxPro understands Mac file and path notation, but it also handles the DOS-style notation in programs you've already written and projects you've already built. If you name your Mac folders with the same path structure you use in DOS and Windows development, you can reference them by using either the colons common to Mac notation or DOS-style backslashes. You even can use a mixture of the two, if you type carefully.

No matter how *you* type the notation, FoxPro functions such as GETFILE() and ADIR() return standard DOS notation (colon after volume name, followed by backslashes for other segments of the path). This consistent behavior is crucial when you parse the return values by using FoxPro's string functions.

However, standard notation doesn't necessarily make a legal DOS path, especially in the case of verbose Mac volume names. To be able to share projects and the PJX file's file name references between environments, you can assign temporary drive letters to your Macintosh volumes or individual folders within the volumes by using the new SET VOLUME command. The syntax looks like this:

```
SET VOLUME C TO "Lisa's Nightmare:"
```

Notice the quotation marks, necessary because of the space and punctuation in my volume name. Now I can issue commands such as these:

```
MODIFY PROJECT C:\APPS\TEST\NewProj
SET DEFA TO C:\APPS\TEST
* the following line edits a READ.ME file
* in the Lisa's Nightmare:Apps:TEST folder
MODI FILE Read.ME
```

> **CROSS-PLATFORM WARNING**
>
> You can think of SET VOLUME as performing the same function as the DOS SUBST command you may have used on PCs. Be careful; SET VOLUME appears to work in a limited fashion in FoxPro for Windows (not DOS), but it works the way DOS ASSIGN does in FoxPro Windows, not SUBST!

After VOLUME is SET, any project file you open or environment you save in a screen or report stores DOS-style drive references such as C:\ instead of the Macintosh volume names. FoxPro DOS and Windows understand the references without difficulty. Figure 1.19 shows the file references in one of the sample projects that ships with FoxPro for Macintosh (LASER.PJX).

Even if you don't expect to take a project cross-platform, you may prefer to SET VOLUME for convenience. It's a lot easier to type `MODI COMM D:\test\main` than `MODI COMM "Monster Disk:\test\main".` — again, notice that I need to use quotation marks, or other delimiters, if some element of my path or file name contains a character illegal in DOS (in this case, the volume has a space character).

At first I thought volumes were so convenient that I SET VOLUME <letters> TO various individual folders all over my disk to save typing. I changed my volume settings often during my FoxPro work sessions. I found that this tactic is more trouble than it's worth because many utility programs, along with your FoxPro projects, depend on saving and remembering a path. When you re-SET VOLUME, the path these programs saved previously, and in which they expect to find their files, may no longer exist. For example, the Run menu items get terminally confused if you SET VOLUME in the CONFIG.FPM and then remove the VOLUME designations later.

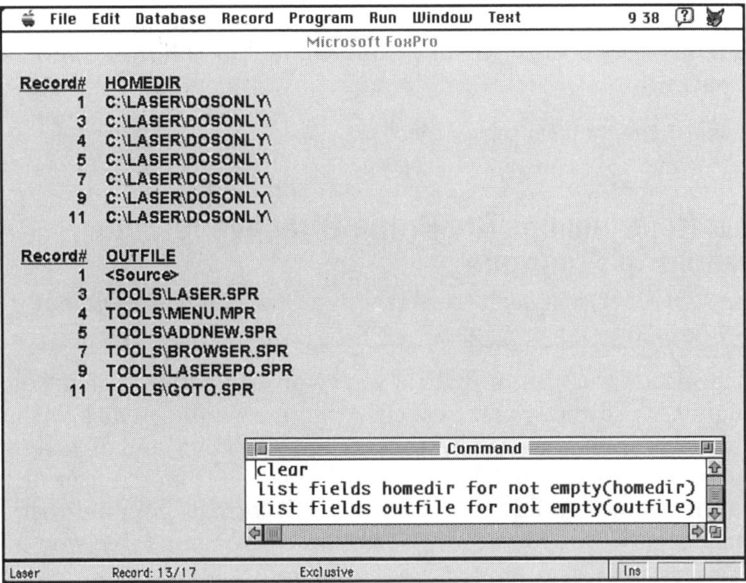

Figure 1.19 *DOS-style references are stored in a FoxPro PJX file used in FoxPro Mac.*

For my development work, therefore, I set up volume assignments in the CONFIG.FPM file and I don't change them thereafter. The relevant lines of the CONFIG.FPM look like this:

```
volume c = "Lisa's Nightmare:"
volume d = "Monster Disk:"
volume e = "Ram disk:"
```

Notice the delimiting quotation marks, again, required when you have spaces or other illegal characters in your Mac names.

To refer to the root of your current volume, you can use a single space (`SET VOLUME C TO \` , or `VOLUME C = \` in the CONFIG.FPM). If you move your programs to a differently named volume, this notation is conveniently portable.

The items on your Desktop reside in a "Desktop Folder" from FoxPro's point of view. If, like me, you work with a messy Desktop covered with your current work-in-progress, you want to refer to files on the Desktop easily. You can SET another VOLUME assignment to the Desktop like this:

```
SET VOLUME F TO "Lisa's Nightmare:\Desktop Folder"
```

Because volume assignments are cumulative, if I've already SET VOLUME C to my disk, I can also express the new volume assignment as follows:

```
SET VOLUME F TO "C:\Desktop Folder"
```

Indirect Referencing: The Prime Directive for File References in Programs

SETting VOLUME is a boon to interactive development work, but it's inappropriate for your programs.

In your previous work with FoxPro, you've probably already learned that you should *never* directly and explicitly reference a file on disk with a fully qualified path. A user is entitled to have any directory and disk structure that he or she wants. You collect path information from the user or the current environment, and then you use this information in indirect references to any files you need. For example, to open a table, you might `USE (m.datapath+"mydata.dbf")`.

In FoxPro for Macintosh, this rule becomes far more stringent than before. Mac users of FoxPro programs should not be denied the privileges to which they are accustomed in their environment. That means that they have the right to volume and path names that are illegal by DOS standards.

Your programs can, and should, create file and folder names that are readable in both environments when possible; you'll see that the source code for this book follows this principle. But when you *distribute* an application, the folders and volumes in which users keep both programs and data may be named almost anything.

You may also already know that the indirect referencing syntax that I used in my USE example, with a name expression enclosed in parentheses, is more efficient for FoxPro file-referencing than macro-expanded expressions such as `USE &filename`. If so, you probably already are in the habit of using the indirect referencing form.

If you're not using indirect referencing, or if you're using it inconsistently along with macro-expansion, now is the time to switch! Macro-expansion can fail if there is a space or a character used by FoxPro as a delimiter somewhere along the file's path.

Indirect referencing sometimes can be necessary *inside* a macro expression that will be executed as code at runtime, perhaps in a dynamically created SQL SELECT statement. For example, to save and restore the existing environment, my old DOS and Windows code performed operations like this:

```
* in setup:
Savesets(2,2) = "SET HELP TO "+SET(HELP,1)
* in cleanup:
&Savesets(xx,2)
```

You see immediately that this code won't work on the Macintosh because the expression the array element holds might be a line like this:

```
SET HELP TO Lisa's Nightmare:FoxPro For Macintosh:FOXHELP.HLP
```

Without delimiters, such a file name causes an error in the SET HELP command when the line is executed as a macro. I next tried code like this:

```
Savesets(2,2) = "SET HELP TO ["+Savesets(2,2)+"]"
```

I hoped that the delimiters would solve my problems in the macro. However, adding delimiters isn't safe—all the possible delimiters are legal characters in Mac file names, also. Just because *my* path happened to contain a single quotation mark doesn't mean that my user's path doesn't contain brackets (the character I chose for delimiters) instead, or both.

The solution—create an indirect reference to be included in the macro expression when it executes, like this:

```
Savesets(2,1) = "SET HELP "+ SET("HELP")
Savesets(2,3) = SET("HELP",1)
* have to check for EMPTY() because
* SET HELP TO <nothing> causes
* a "file does not exist" error in
* a distributed application in FoxPro Mac
IF NOT EMPTY(Savesets(2,3))
 Savesets(2,2) = "SET HELP TO (Savesets(2,3))"
ENDIF

* the matching cleanup code runs through
* the Savesets array rows,
* executing the first two elements, like this:
FOR xx = 1 TO ALEN(Savesets,1)
 IF NOT EMPTY(Savesets(xx,1))
        &Savesets(xx,1)
 ENDIF
 IF NOT EMPTY(Savesets(xx,2))
        &Savesets(xx,2)
```

```
    ENDIF
    * column # 3 is used in indirect refs in
    * columns # 1 and 2
    * it's never executed directly
ENDFOR
```

Don't worry too much about where this code fits into a systematic approach to FoxPro development; I will discuss it thoroughly in Part II. For now, it just represents a convenient illustration of the fact that you *must* indirectly reference path and file names on the Mac, no matter what the circumstance.

See Also

- "The Template Main Program," Chapter 5
- PROC SaveSets, Source Disk: Library/ Template Code: MAIN.PRG

Be sure to follow the rule of indirect referencing no matter where or how you reference file and path names. For one additional example, suppose that you want to make sure a particular folder or directory is on the current FoxPro PATH.

First, collect your folder name into a variable by using GETDIR() or retrieving it from a system file in your application that stores this information. Then check, as you always should, to see if the folder is already on the path; `ATC(my_folder,SET("PATH",1)) = 0` determines that you need to adjust the PATH.

Finally SET PATH to an indirect reference, as follows:

```
SET PATH TO (SET("PATH",1)+","+my_folder)
```

Avoiding any explicit or direct file references, you ensure that this code will work on all FoxPro platforms, no matter what names the user gives various elements of the path.

Reverse Name Translation

I'm sure that you can see why you must be very careful of the order in which you placed any saving, changing, and restoring of VOLUME names with respect to the saving and restoring of any file and path names. Whenever possible, ruthlessly remove any VOLUME-setting shortcuts from programs that you distribute to other users.

Sometimes, leaving the VOLUME-setting at home and using indirect referencing consistently isn't sufficient for success, however. Your programs may run in environments where other developers have SET VOLUME. Even if you are sure no VOLUMEs have been SET by others, so that a GETFILE() returns "Lisa's Nightmare:\TEST.PRG" instead of "C:\TEST.PRG," for some operations, you need the proper Mac *notation* for the file name.

For example, passing the file name to another Macintosh program, using AppleScript, requires the Mac file name. You'd hardly expect Excel for Macintosh to know what VOLUME you SET in FoxPro, or even the DOS-style notation FoxPro functions use for cross-platform compatibility!

Even closer to home, the FOXTOOLS.MLB (API library file) supplied with FoxPro for Macintosh manipulates Macintosh files and folders in a variety of useful ways. Its functions require the true Macintosh names of the files you want to affect.

FoxPro for Macintosh provides the SYS(2027) function to handle this need. When you pass it a file name, it returns the Mac notation for that file name. It doesn't matter whether you've used a VOLUME setting or not, and you can use wildcards if you like. For example, if I have SET VOLUME F to my Desktop Folder, as I suggested earlier, I can do the following reverse translation:

See Also

- "AppleScript and Apple Events," Chapter 16

```
* ? SYS(2027,"F:\*.*")
* resulting string is:
LISA'S NIGHTMARE:DESKTOP FOLDER:*.*
```

Notice that, along with using the correct volume name, SYS(2027) changes the delimiters between different path segments to the correct Macintosh colons.

CROSS-PLATFORM WARNING

Before version 2.6, FoxPro for DOS and Windows didn't reject SYS(2027) with an error, but the function returned a null string if you used it in those environments. When you need to use SYS(2027), therefore, you need to *bracket* the function so that it is only called on the Mac platform, like this:

```
m.filename = GETFILE()
IF _MAC
        m.filename = SYS(2027,m.filename)
ENDIF
* now go on and do something with the filename
* in all environments.
```

In FoxPro for DOS and Windows 2.6, SYS(2027) is smarter. The function simply returns the argument that you passed it, which is a perfectly good DOS or Windows filename. If you haven't yet upgraded your copy of FoxPro DOS or Windows, this is one of many subtle changes that affect cross-platform development.

See Also

• "FoxPro for Macintosh 2.6 and Beyond," Appendix E

There may be times when you must remove *all* volume settings from the environment temporarily, rather than reverse-translating specific file and path names. I write programs destined to be called as developers' tools in interactive FoxPro. Such tools often require special precautions against conditions developer-users may have introduced into their working environment, including VOLUME assignments.

APPSETUP, which I wrote for Part II of this book, is one such tool: a utility to help developers prepare file-maintenance code. I decided that APPSETUP should make use of .VUE files, if the developer had prepared them, to initialize the file relationships that APPSETUP would replicate as generated program code.

Unfortunately, I discovered that FoxPro for Macintosh .VUE files were often confused by VOLUME assignments, even if the VOLUME settings remained consistent between the time the developer CREATEd VIEW and the time my program SET VIEW to the .VUE file.

I SET LIBRARY TO FOXTOOLS so that I can use its FXGVolume() function to determine existing VOLUME assignments. The following code strips VOLUME settings out of the environment:

```
IF _MAC
        * m.volumes initialized in APPSETUP's
        * top-level program so it's available
        * to all the subroutines
        m.volumes = FxGVolume()
        * turn off volume-setting
        IF NOT EMPTY(m.volumes)
         FOR m.xx = 1 TO ;
             OCCURS(SPACE(5),m.volumes)
                 m.yy = AT(SPACE(5),;
             m.volumes,m.xx)-2
                 SET VOLUME ;
             (SUBSTR(m.volumes,yy,1)) TO
         ENDFOR
        ENDIF
ENDIF
```

At APPSETUP's conclusion, I replace the previous VOLUME settings like this:

```
PRIVATE m.xx, m.yy, m.zz
IF _MAC AND NOT EMPTY(m.volumes)
        FOR m.xx = 1 TO ;
          OCCURS(SPACE(5),m.volumes) -1
```

```
          m.yy = AT(SPACE(5),m.volumes,m.xx)-2
          m.zz = AT(SPACE(5),m.volumes,m.xx+1)-7
          SET VOLUME ;
                  (SUBSTR(m.volumes,yy,1)) TO ;
                  (SUBSTR(m.volumes,yy+7,zz-yy-3))
        ENDFOR
        m.yy = RAT(SPACE(5),m.volumes)-2
        m.zz = RAT(CHR(10), m.volumes)
        SET VOLUME ;
                (SUBSTR(m.volumes,yy,1)) TO ;
                (ALLTRIM(SUBSTR(m.volumes,;
                       yy+7,zz-yy-7)))
ENDIF
```

You won't have to take such precautions routinely, but in a special case like APPSETUP you will be glad that FXGVolume() is available.

FoxPro's MACDESKTOP

Beyond the issue of file-referencing, the most obvious differences among the different FoxPro products are the appearance and attributes of the main application window.

Contrasting FoxPro Main Application Windows

In FoxPro for DOS, the main application window is literally the screen, the entire surface of the display. Even if you run FoxPro for DOS in a Microsoft Windows window, or session, FoxPro's main application window is the entire area allocated to its session. When you refer to this surface, you use the name SCREEN (ACTIVATE SCREEN, for example).

In FoxPro for Windows, the FoxPro main application workspace is not always the full display area of your monitor. Instead, it is a *special window named* SCREEN, which you can size and alter whenever you want. You use the commands ZOOM WINDOW SCREEN, MODIFY WINDOW SCREEN to alter this window, just as you would use the ZOOM WINDOW and MODIFY WINDOW with other windows that you DEFINEd. The special SCREEN window shares display territory with other Microsoft Windows applications floating in the Microsoft Windows Desktop.

By default, all the windows that belong to FoxPro for Windows—the Command window, system windows such as BROWSEs, and windows you DEFINE—exist within the confines of the FoxPro main application workspace, the window with the name SCREEN. If you want a FoxPro for Windows window to break free of this boundary, you can DEFINE that WINDOW with the special IN DESKTOP clause. For example, you may want to make sure that a dialog is always centered on the monitor, even if the user moves your FoxPro application to one corner of the monitor display area.

The Mac default is just the opposite: all windows *float free in the full Desktop area*, which FoxPro for Macintosh calls MACDESKTOP. When you activate the main FoxPro window by clicking on it, you find that your Command window, the programs you were editing, and any other FoxPro windows on the screen may disappear behind the main window. In the default state of FoxPro for Macintosh, these windows have no connection with each other.

Using SET MACDESKTOP

FoxPro for Macintosh terms this default state SET MACDESKTOP ON. If you DEFINE a WINDOW with SET MACDESKTOP ON, you find that the function WPARENT(<window name>) returns the string "MACDESKTOP".

If you SET MACDESKTOP OFF, you see windows behave as they do in FoxPro for Windows; they are now *clipped* to the main application window, child windows defined relative to it. If you DEFINE another WINDOW now, WPARENT(<window name>) returns the null string, which denotes the main application window, SCREEN, instead.

No matter what the current SETting of MACDESKTOP, in FoxPro for Macintosh you can use the DEFINE WINDOW clauses IN SCREEN or IN MACDESKTOP to specify a particular window's parent.

If this isn't confusing enough, in all three environments the Screen Builder talks about the Desktop window when it really means the "main application window," with the window name SCREEN—*not* the Windows Desktop or the Mac Desktop.

In the previous paragraphs, I specified window behavior relative to SCREEN or the larger Desktop by stipulating the parent surface in which the WINDOW was DEFINEd. Like human children, windows only get natural parents once: at the time they are DEFINEd. However, also like human children, windows can have adoptive parents: you can use the ACTIVATE WINDOW command with the IN clause to force a window to appear wherever you want.

Because the Command window is DEFINEd only once at startup, it can never have the main application window as its parent unless you put the line MACDESKTOP = OFF in your CONFIG.FPM. However, you can ACTIVATE WINDOW Command IN SCREEN at any time. In figure 1.20, the Command window is floating free in the Macintosh Desktop. I've issued a MODI COMM MAIN.PRG with no IN clause, so that with MACDESKTOP left at the default state of ON, MAIN.PRG floats free of the main application window as well. Meanwhile, I have forced the View window to be clipped to the main application window using the command ACTIVATE WINDOW View IN SCREEN.

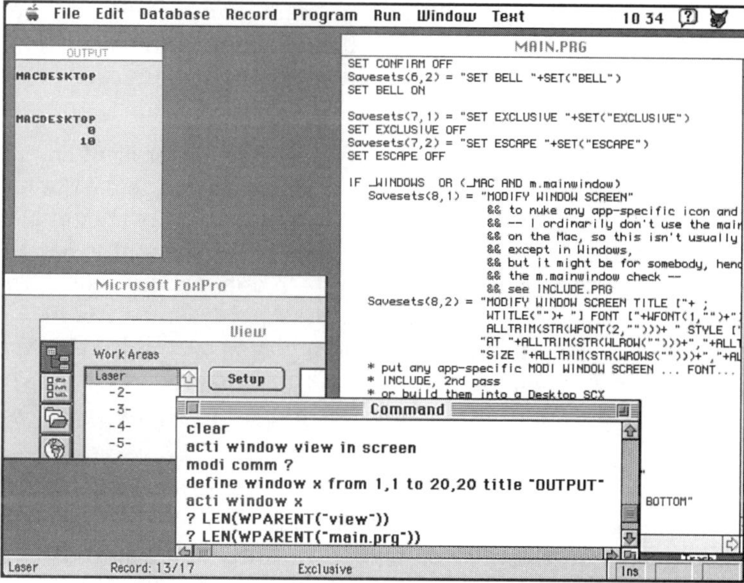

Figure 1.20 *The View window is inside the FoxPro main application window (SCREEN), while the Command window, a small output window, and the MAIN.PRG float free IN MACDESKTOP.*

What does all this mean to you as a cross-platform developer? The easiest strategy for your current code, if you want to port without reference to Macintosh interface considerations and without modification, is to put the line MACDESKTOP = OFF in your CONFIG.FPM so that FoxPro for Macintosh windows behave exactly like FoxPro for Windows.

The easiest strategy is not the best strategy. Leave SET MACDESKTOP at its default ON value in FoxPro for Macintosh. The Microsoft Windows interface relies on a relationship between main application windows for each running program and their multiple child, or document, windows. This interface doesn't work particularly well for FoxPro applications even in Microsoft Windows, and it looks completely out of place on the Macintosh.

Look at the other Macintosh applications available. Whether they are editable documents or modal dialogs, windows float free on the Macintosh desktop in every application.

A Macintosh application does not signal its presence by presenting a window to enclose its various activities. You already saw that the currently active application has control of the menu bar at the top of the screen and the icon for the Application menu. When a Macintosh application is active but idle, the menu is all that you see. A window means work is going on.

Your applications should behave this way, too. If the user is sitting in a GETless Foundation READ, in which the application waits for the user to choose a new task from the menu, the only FoxPro display should be your customized version of SYSMENU, and, if you use it, the status bar across the bottom of the screen. Like other Macintosh applications, your program can have an About dialog box attached to the Apple menu. (The new command SET APLABOUT gives you the ability to customize the Apple menu with your own dialog instead of FoxPro's.) No other splash screen, logo, or background is appropriate, and certainly not one that you force the user to see at all times.

In FoxPro for Macintosh, you probably will find that the main application window is a nuisance, even when you work interactively. Unless you make it very small, you'll tend to click on it inadvertently and lose your Command window and other work tools behind it.

Close the main application window completely by using its close box or the command HIDE WINDOW SCREEN. If you need to display output at any time, use a WAIT WINDOW or DEFINE an output WINDOW explicitly, as I've done in figure 1.20. (If you want to bring the SCREEN window back for any reason, and without obscuring other FoxPro windows, use the command SHOW WINDOW SCREEN BOTTOM.)

After you work this way for a while, you will find that FoxPro for Macintosh seems much more like other Mac applications than it does if you SET MACDESKTOP OFF and work within the confines of the SCREEN window. Design *your* FoxPro applications to work the same way so that your Mac users feel comfortable using them, too.

The template application code you use to build an application in this book automatically rids the display of the main application window if the code determines that the current platform is _MAC. I provided an application-specific switch to allow you to retain the main application window if you like. In some applications, which I call *switchboard apps*, a dialog is continually present at the foundation READ level with options from which the user selects further activities. Such a dialog, as contrasted with the usual GETless foundation READ wait state, presents a reasonable opportunity for the main application window to make itself useful.

However, later in the book, you will see that even this limited use of the main application window is fraught with difficulty. The special SCREEN window and its handling by GENSCRN have a few bugs you won't encounter if you DEFINE a regular WINDOW for your switchboard instead. I currently use DEFINEd WINDOWs even for switchboard apps.

Don't rely on the main application window or the Windows-compatibility crutch of SET MACDESKTOP OFF for one program longer than necessary. Once you get used to SETting MACDESKTOP ON, you'll find that this change from Windows doesn't make your job of porting applications any harder. After all, even within the Windows environment the available display space and resolution may vary from one user to the next. Think of the MACDESKTOP as a similar condition your programs must evaluate.

Evaluating MACDESKTOP Metrics

When MACDESKTOP is ON, you can use the SROWS() and SCOLS() functions to evaluate the screen area within which your windows may move. Although these functions are expressing the Fox rows and columns available on the entire screen, the rows and columns are expressed *relative to the current font of the main application window* because the MACDESKTOP area has no FoxPro-assigned font of its own. WFONT() using a second argument of "" gives you the font information you need for the main application window. Be careful not to use the WFONT() function without the second argument, or you'll get font information for the current output window instead.

When MACDESKTOP is OFF, SROWS( ) and SCOLS( ) tell you about the rows and columns of the main application window instead. You still can use SYSMETRIC(1) and SYSMETRIC(2) functions to get the dimensions of the full MACDESKTOP. Because SYSMETRIC() returns values in pixels, you must translate its results to rows and columns to evaluate the position and size of any MACDESKTOP windows you wish to affect. Again, you convert the values to rows and columns by using the font metrics of the current font for the main application window, even though you want information about the screen because MACDESKTOP doesn't have a font.

Using the WLROW() and WLCOL() functions works similarly. These functions tell you about the positions of a window with respect to its parent, using the parent font as a reference, so you just follow the same rule (MACDESKTOP font is the main application font) to understand the values they return.

On the other hand, the MROW() and MCOL() present a problem with MACDESKTOP ON. You have no way to tell these functions that MACDESKTOP is the space with reference to which MROW() and MCOL() return a result. They default to the active output window (WOUTPUT())—and the Mac DESKTOP never holds FoxPro output. If you use the null string as an argument instead, this designation refers to the main application window whether MACDESKTOP is ON or OFF.

If you need to evaluate the mouse position, make the main application "shadow" the desktop with the following commands:

```
ZOOM WINDOW SCREEN MAX
HIDE WINDOW SCREEN
```

Now you can use the MROW("") and MCOL("") functions with the null string denoting a request for information about the main application window—but these values will be equivalent to information about the Desktop.

Multiple Monitors

See Also

- "Window and Font Handling in MACDESKTOP," Chapter 12

I realize the discussion in the last section sounds a little forbidding and that I'm not providing examples here. You'll return to this topic later in the book.

Meanwhile, it's important not to get too caught up in the formulae for positioning windows on the Desktop in Macintosh. Remember that the user should be able to position these windows at will.

There's yet another reason not to port code that positions windows unmodified from DOS and Windows: remember that, earlier in the chapter, you looked at the Monitors control panel? Refer to figure 1.15 and the accompanying discussion again. A Macintosh may have multiple monitors attached to it. Users can position the monitors in any relative positions they choose. FoxPro is aware only of the primary monitor when it provides coordinates. However, *FoxPro windows can move freely within ALL the screen real estate provided by the multiple monitors.*

How does this work in practice, and why does it present a problem?

Suppose that you use the DOS and Windows trick of positioning a window at negative screen coordinates to hide it from the user's view. On the Macintosh, if the user has positioned a second monitor to the left of the primary monitor or above the primary monitor in the Monitors control panel, these negative coordinates may be visible on the second monitor!

Code that performs this trick *must* be changed to be safe on the Macintosh. Instead of MOVE WINDOW TO negative coordinates, use the HIDE WINDOW command to "disappear" your windows. You may need to ACTIVATE another WINDOW first because the active output window won't HIDE, and you should SHOW GETS WINDOW <window name> DISABLE for this window too, so the window doesn't come forward as part of a READ CYCLE when one of its GETs receives the focus.

Some people save FoxPro window positions in a custom-designed preferences table so that each user can see windows in the preferred arrangement when starting up a task. At first thought, this technique seems very Mac-like indeed. However, a user may change the designation of the primary monitor between sessions of a FoxPro application. If the monitors are different sizes or resolutions, the saved coordinates may be inappropriate to the real estate available on the primary monitor from one session to the next.

Code like this should be abandoned in FoxPro for Macintosh, unless you decide to save SYSMETRIC() information and restore window positions based on relative positions and ratios rather than on the absolute coordinates you saved.

You may find that multiple monitors create problems even in interactive FoxPro. Recall that the FoxPro Settings file in the Preferences folder, described earlier in the chapter, saves a position for the main application window. If you change your primary monitor to one with a smaller view area or lower resolution, or if you turn off one monitor occasionally, you may not be able to find the application main window *or* the Command window when you start up.

If you can't see the Command window, this doesn't mean you can't type commands. Type `MOVE WINDOW Command TO 2,2` (carefully!) to find the Command window again. If this doesn't work, you may have a Command window clipped to the main application window. Type (still carefully!) ACTI WIND Command IN MACDESKTOP, and you should be able to see your Command window again.

Portable, and Not-So-Portable, Fonts, Graphics, and Screens

With all the differences between Mac and DOS displays (aspect ratios, pixel shapes, resolutions, and so on), I confess I'm amazed that the FoxPro Transporter manages to convert my more bizarre screen designs at all!

Although the Transporter does a reasonable job of converting a Windows screen to an equivalent Mac layout, it makes a few unfortunate choices in the process. Because both FoxPro for Windows and FoxPro for Macintosh use TrueType fonts, the Transporter tries to use identically named fonts in its conversion process. However, identically named TrueType fonts don't necessarily have the same font metrics (character width and height) on the two platforms, so, very often, this approach doesn't provide a screen with the same object positioning and sizing that you expect.

See Also

- Source Disk: Cosmic Converter
- "Window and Font Handling in MACDESKTOP," Chapter 12

Randy Brown has written a wonderful utility, shown in figure 1.21, to aid GUI-platform transporting that takes a different approach to assigning fonts for imported objects: Randy checks the font metrics for objects' fonts and looks for a near match between these fonts and the Mac fonts available. You'll find the Cosmic Converter on your source disk, and Randy discusses the rationale behind this approach later in the book.

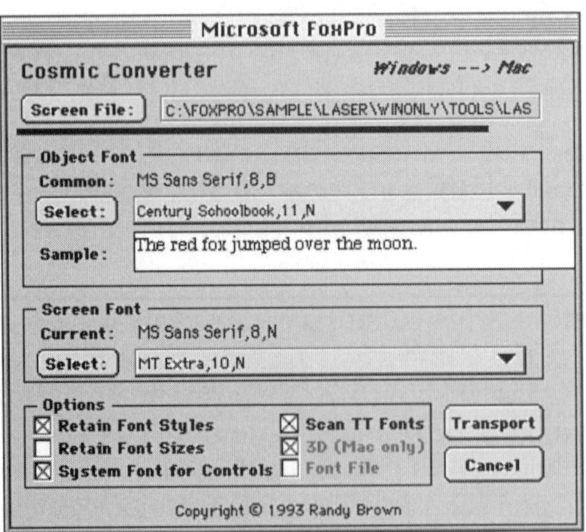

Figure 1.21 *Randy Brown's Cosmic Converter.*

CROSS-PLATFORM WARNING

Although Microsoft delivers FoxPro for Macintosh with some TrueType fonts, you aren't licensed to redistribute these fonts to your user by the terms of the Distribution Kit—another reason to use Randy's approach to font translation instead of straight conversion between like-named TrueType fonts.

You can distribute FoxFont and FoxPrint fonts that come with FoxPro for Macintosh, but you should be aware that FoxPrint for Macintosh doesn't include the DOS line-drawing characters as perfectly as does FoxPrint for Windows. Also, if you deliver your distributable application using the DK's Setup Wizard to prepare installation disks, the Setup procedure won't put these font files where the Macintosh system needs to see them (inside the Font folder in the System folder). You have to move the fonts yourself or instruct your users to do so.

FoxPro for Macintosh will use the .BMP graphics you designate for your FoxPro for Windows screens without difficulty, performing an internal, on-the-fly conversion to coax the Macintosh to display this foreign format. If you use the PICT format native to Macintosh, the graphics may display slightly faster because they don't require the conversion. Many file-translation utilities exist, and you can probably prepare PICT copies of your .BMPs without trouble.

When you take your Macintosh screens back to Windows, however, if they use PICTs, you must create .BMP copies of these graphics (FoxPro for Windows can't read PICTs). FoxPro for Macintosh ships with a utility named PICT TO BMP to perform this conversion, although it only works for small graphics.

As you see in figure 1.22, PICT TO BMP also creates default file names for its conversions that may not be legal DOS file names. You have to change these names before bringing your BMPs to FoxPro for Windows.

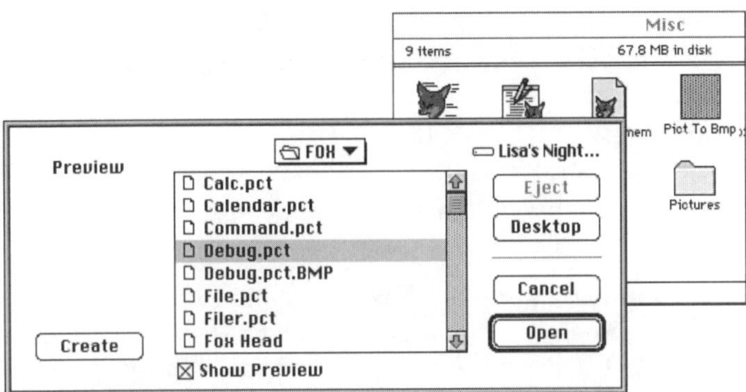

Figure 1.22 *PICT TO BMP converts the common Macintosh graphics format to bitmaps FoxPro for Windows can use.*

CROSS-PLATFORM WARNING

The Transporter doesn't handle Macintosh screens with PICT-format graphics in them very well. When FoxPro for Macintosh was first released, if you chose to Transport a Macintosh screen in FoxPro for Windows, the Transporter didn't recognize a problem with the graphics file format. When you tried to edit the screen, FoxPro for Windows couldn't open the layout (because of the PICT). You had to USE the .SCX table and manually change the PICT filenames to names of .BMP files.

This behavior changed in later releases of the Transporter, although it still isn't perfect. It prompts you for the name of the appropriate file using the PICT file name (complete with .PCT extension, if you used one), but suggests a filemask of *.BMP for the file to locate! I'm happy to trade the crash for slightly confusing behavior, and I'm sure that the Transporter will continue to improve. *Always check with Microsoft to get the latest version of the Transporter and GENSCRN and GENMENU,* the two generating programs in FoxPro. It doesn't matter which platform is officially associated with the latest version; TRANSPRT.PRG, GENSCRN.PRG, and GENMENU.PRG are cross-platform programs. They also are extremely complex programs, and Microsoft Fox Team (MSFT) upgrades them with bug fixes along with enhancements to support new releases.

A final problem with screens and screen behavior, for seasoned FoxPro developers, is a difference in the way GET controls behave in a Macintosh dialog. Macintosh control objects never get the focus in a dialog, because you can't move to them with the keyboard. If you have code that depends on setting _CUROBJ to the object number of a button and KEYBOARDing "{ENTER}" or "{SPACEBAR}" to run the button's VALID code, this code will fail on the Mac.

You have two choices: either alter your code to run the button VALID procedure directly (instead of setting _CUROBJ and KEYBOARDing), or SET KEYCOMP to either DOS or WINDOWS, which will model the behavior of GET controls on the environments with which you're familiar.

As usual, taking the easy way out, SETting KEYCOMP to DOS or WINDOWS to gain instant compatibility, is not necessarily the best choice in the long run. It will alter other FoxPro for Macintosh behavior at the same time, as I describe in the next section, and it may also confound the expectations of your Mac users. However, depending on the kinds of data entry and dialogs your applications require, even your Mac-only users may enjoy being able to tab between GET controls.

The best choice is probably giving your *users* a Preferences menu option to change the SETting of KEYCOMP themselves so they can experiment and see which way they prefer to work. Grace and flexibility on the part of your program comes at a price; naturally, your code needs to be altered so it works no matter what the user chooses.

You often have to support ease of use with hard work on the programming end. You may already have chosen this strategy in your FoxPro work on the DOS or Windows platform. It's amazing how many times you reach this conclusion on the Mac, isn't it?

Mac developers have a saying: "Easy is hard." Now you know why.

Keyboard Differences

The SETting of KEYBOARD influences dialogs and menu hot key behavior as well as the GET focus. The SET KEYCOMP TO MAC default behavior doesn't highlight or underscore hot keys on SYSMENU or in GET control labels. You still can navigate to the SYSMENU options by pressing F10 to activate the menu and then using arrow keys. However, in a SET KEYCOMP TO MAC READ, GET controls such as push buttons are accessible only with the mouse.

You should be aware that not all Macintosh keyboards are the same. Although this is true of DOS keyboards as well, the differences are more profound here; some Mac keyboards have no function keys at all.

Because some keyboards have no function keys, the ⌘ key can be pressed with the numeric keys as an alternative. For example, to get to the Command window, you can either use the standard Ctrl-F2 or ⌘-F2 if your keyboard has function keys, or Ctrl-⌘-F2. (In my tests, this method works on both sets of numeric keys, and it doesn't matter whether Num Lock is on or off.)

Users can press ⌘-O to access the System Menu, just like F10, or, if your code issues an ON KEY LABEL F10 assignment, users can press ⌘-O to achieve the same effect. Be sure to make this clear in documentation for your programs. You can use the FoxPro FKMAX() function to determine the number of function keys, and you also can use the FOXTOOLS FxKeyBoard() function to determine the Mac keyboard type in greater detail. You even may want to change the menu shortcuts that refer to function keys dynamically, depending on the keyboard you find.

I mentioned earlier that you can use the Ctrl and ⌘ keys interchangeably in FoxPro for Macintosh. Refer to this keypress using the CTRL key label, as you have done previously, so your code will remain portable back to Windows and DOS. (The CTRL key label appears as ⌘ in your FoxPro for Macintosh menus.) If your Windows and DOS programs include menu shortcuts, ON KEY LABEL assignments, or macros that use the ALT label, these assignments are mapped to a keypress of Ctrl-Option.

To hide all windows in front of the current output window in FoxPro for Windows or DOS, you press Shift-Ctrl-Alt; in FoxPro for Macintosh, you press Shift-Ctrl-Option-⌘.

You may wonder why ALT wasn't mapped to a simple Option keypress in FoxPro, especially since the Option key shows the word "alt" on your keyboard. The Option key plus a second keypress is reserved to type special characters on the Macintosh, much as you can press the Alt key on your DOS keyboard and numeric values to type extended ASCII characters.

Typing special characters with the Option key doesn't work the same way Alt does in DOS, however. In figure 1.23, you see Key Caps, a System extension that lets you see the characters your keyboard can produce. You hold down Shift keys and the pictures on the key caps change.

Although Key Caps shows Chicago font at the moment, you can pick any available font from the Key Caps menu and check the characters it produces with various Shift keys or combinations of Shift keys. You probably want to check FoxPrint, for example. You can put example characters in the text box by clicking on the keys. Then copy and paste the symbols into your FoxPro for Macintosh file.

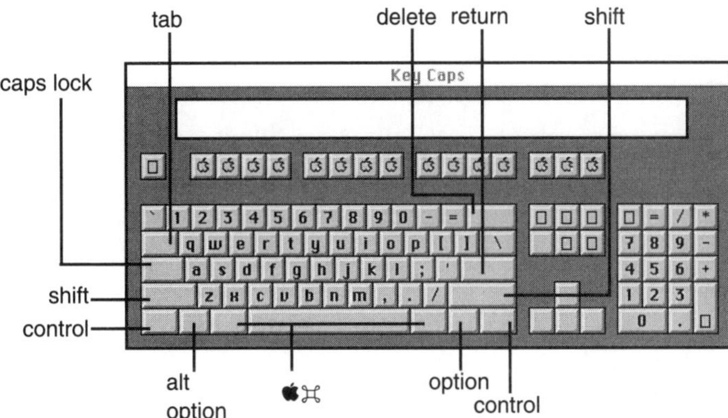

Figure 1.23 *Use Key Caps to see what characters result from different keypresses or shifted keypresses in different fonts.*

When you need the ASCII value of a keypress, Key Caps doesn't help, and FoxPro for Macintosh doesn't have the ASCII chart you find in FoxPro for DOS. A freeware control panel named PopChar comes to your rescue. You can see the way it displays the ASCII value of a character in the upper-left corner of its window, in figure 1.24, and you will find this utility on your source disk.

Figure 1.24 *The PopChar utility provides a different method of looking at character values.*

In case you miss your DOS capability to type the Alt key followed by the digits representing an extended ASCII character, I created the following procedure for your use:

```
* X_ASCII.RG
* by Lisa C. Slater
* for FoxPro MAChete, published by Hayden Books
```

```
* assign this program to an ON KEY LABEL,
* such as ON KEY LABEL F9 DO X_ASCII
* To type extended ASCII values, press the
* ON KEY LABEL assignment followed by
* the numeric digits
* representing the character you want.

PUSH KEY CLEAR
PRIVATE m.results, m.xx, m.invalue, m.tempvalue
m.results = ""
m.tempvalue = ""
FOR m.xx = 1 TO 3
        * collect up to three keypresses
        m.invalue = INKEY(0)
        IF NOT ISDIGIT(CHR(m.invalue))
         * user is finished typing digits
         m.results = CHR(m.invalue)
         EXIT
        ENDIF
        * if you got a digit,
        * concatenate with digits
        * already pressed
        m.tempvalue = m.tempvalue + CHR(m.invalue)
 ENDFOR
IF NOT EMPTY(m.tempvalue)
        IF TYPE("CHR(EVAL(m.tempvalue))") # "C"
         * illegal code, outside range
         * of extended ASCII set
         m.tempvalue = ""
         ?? CHR(7)
        ENDIF
        m.results = CHR(VAL(m.tempvalue))+m.results
ENDIF
KEYBOARD m.results
POP KEY
RETURN
```

Just issue the statement ON KEY LABEL <some function key> DO X_ASCII. Then you can press the function key whenever you would press Alt on your DOS keyboard (don't hold it down), followed by the digits of the character as you know them from the ASCII set, remembering that your current font will influence the results you get, of course. X_ASCII is smart enough to recognize two-digit codes (without a leading zero) if you type a third non-numeric character. You can even use this ON KEY LABEL to type graphics characters into text labels in the Report and Screen Layout windows!

I wrote X_ASCII.PRG as something of a tour-de-force to prove you can do this trick on the Mac because I couldn't find a utility that exactly mimicked this DOS feature. Most Mac people would never miss it. They are more used to selecting a special character with the mouse, as you do in PopChar or Key Caps. But, hey—you're a Mac person now, too! You have as much right to choose the way you *enjoy* working on the Macintosh as everybody else. That's what makes writing applications and working in the Macintosh environment so challenging—and enjoyable.

Chapter Wrap Up

I think that's quite enough for now, don't you? Take some time to let this information sink in and try not to be overwhelmed. As you'll see when you roll up your sleeves to work in FoxPro for Macintosh, even with all these caveats, the similarities between this product and the DOS and Windows incarnations far outweigh the differences.

See Also

- Source Disk: Tools: PopChar
- Source Disk: Miscellaneous Code Examples: X_ASCII.PRG

If you come away from this chapter with one general impression, it should be this: don't work too hard to mimic your DOS or Windows environment. Where FoxPro differs across platforms, you will find the work to *adapt* to Macintosh in ways much more rewarding than the work to force Macintosh ways into a DOS mold.

Although all four authors will continue to add tips and warnings from our cross-platform experience, Parts II and III of this book are really about using the FoxPro you already know and love better than you've used it before—on *any* platform. Then, in Part IV, you learn about the Mac-specific features of FoxPro for Macintosh that distinguish this version of the product from earlier versions and make it especially fun to use.

2

QUICK START FOR FOXBASE+/MAC DEVELOPERS

by
Andy Griebel

The last significant upgrade of FoxBASE+/Mac preceded FoxPro for Macintosh by about five years, which is a long time. In computer years, this is an exceedingly long time.

Things change. Products get more robust. Bigger, faster hardware becomes more prevalent. The envelope gets pushed all along the way.

FoxBASE+/Mac was something of a "stepchild" product for many years. On one hand, it still was the best thing out there. On the other hand, if it were a car you would see the paint starting to peel, the transmission slipping, and the upholstery fading. In short, it's time to get a new one.

Finally, FoxPro for Macintosh shipped, one year after its Windows and DOS sister products were out the door. We get our glitz and glory, but at a price.

Making the Change to FoxPro

I was developing on the Lisa and Macintosh in Omnis 3+ and using Clipper on DOS machines when FoxBASE+/Mac became available. I quickly transitioned all new Mac work to FoxBASE+/Mac, so I had a lot of code in the Mac product before FoxPro version 1 for DOS shipped. After porting our Mac apps into FoxPro, I changed a lot of code to make it work.

Overall, though, for a DOS program FoxPro Version 1 was more "Mac-like" than anything else I had used at the time. I was hooked. Fox told everybody they would be upgrading the Macintosh to the same FoxPro level.

Then came FoxPro 2.0, about a year and a half later. Wow! Everything I had in FoxPro 1.0 still ran, but it wasn't "2.0-like." I rewrote a lot of apps. Fox told everybody they would be upgrading the Macintosh to the same FoxPro 2.0 level.

I told all my clients it wouldn't be wise to spend a great deal of money in FoxBASE+/Mac code development. I knew from experience that going from FoxPro 1.0 to 2.0 basically required a rewrite, and besides, FoxPro for Macintosh was going to be out *Real Soon Now*.

So my Mac development idled—I just patched things here and there, adding reports and new data items only if absolutely required. Not a happy situation, but prudent, all things considered. Some of my Mac clients reluctantly fell to the "other side" and asked about having their apps ported to FoxPro for Windows. Of course, they expected the transition from Macintosh to Windows to be largely a rewrite.

Finally—and happily—we've got it: FoxPro for Macintosh, and only four years later. Lots of things have changed since FoxBASE+/Mac, but practically all for the better!

Keeping Compatibility with FoxBASE+/Mac

The developers at Fox have a sort of unwritten credo: *thou shalt not break existing code*. No new version should introduce code that creates problems for existing code, and all old commands should be supported. This is why some commands, such as SET FORMAT, are supported even though practically no professional developer ever uses them. This credo, however, presented some major problems for the FoxBASE+/Mac crew.

FoxBASE+/Mac's status as a commercial product was an accident to begin with. The Fox people started working in the current version of Windows way back then, but found the development environment too unstable. On the other hand, the Mac operating system was pretty secure and offered an event-driven windowed environment in which to work. Fox decided it would be more prudent to "practice" writing a windowed style database management program by using the Macintosh until Windows matured. And, as a bonus, they got to sell to Mac developers like you and me!

It was the first time they got their feet wet with a real GUI. They learned a lot. They also made more than a few mistakes. By the time they got started on FoxPro for Windows, they had a better handle on how they wanted to deal with the finer points of a GUI database product.

Along the way, some radical changes took place. The biggest change occurred when FoxPro 2.0 was released. FoxPro 1.0 programs would work without a great deal of change in 2.0, but this didn't mean they were 2.0 programs. Most 2.0 developers started from scratch, trashing almost everything except perhaps some behind-the-scenes validation code and their data structures and designs.

FoxPro 2.5's Goals

From observations, conversations, and Power Point Presentations out the wazoo, I think I can give you an idea of what Microsoft Fox had in mind with the 2.5 series.

The mission of the MS-Fox development team was to:

- Take over the Windows database market.
- Make the new stuff in Windows run in DOS.
- Make it run in Macintosh.
- Have as close to "seamless" cross platform capabilities as imaginable.
- Continue to propel all three platforms into the future, picking up Unix along the way...
- ... and oh yeah, have the same executable image (compiled PRG) run in all four platforms—without modification.

This last item is a pretty good trick. There are some problems with meeting all of these goals. Some problems are obvious, some are artificial, and some are extremely subtle.

The Fox (now Microsoft Fox) developers got together, looked at all the goals, and made a tough decision. They decided to abandon a great deal of the approach they took in the original FoxBASE+/Mac product. Understand that this is not the light-hearted, "wake-up-Saturday-morning-with-a-smile" kind of decision. A great deal of money and time was invested in the way that FoxBASE+/Mac developers work, but they couldn't do some things, given the current FoxBASE+/Mac approach and their FoxPro 2.5 goals.

In so doing, the developers created another problem. They broke their own prime directive, "Thou shalt not break existing code." They dropped many of the features that made FoxBASE+/Mac work. They knew this change wouldn't sit well with FoxBASE+/Mac, so they struggled for another solution.

Enter the Migration Kit

FoxPro for Macintosh has a Migration Kit, which Microsoft Fox designed to answer this need (see figure 2.1).

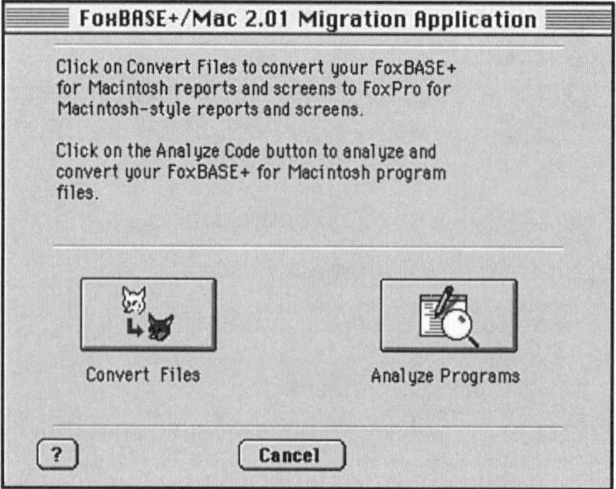

Figure 2.1 *The FoxBASE+ / Mac-to-FoxPro for Macintosh Migration Application's opening dialog.*

When I started working on this chapter, I had a pretty dim opinion of the Migration Kit (MK). The file conversion half of the MK just updates older screen and report files to current versions the FoxPro power tools can use. That works great for most cases—no muss, no fuss.

And then there's the Code Analyzer. The Code Analyzer is supposed to work its way through all of your old programs, making notes of syntax and other things that are out of date, correcting or offering suggestions. Look, I've got friends at MS-Fox. I wanted this to work in a useful fashion. I kept slugging through it, hoping to find some good things to say about it.

Folks, it just isn't there.

I've gone through this story to explain why it exists so that you understand *whose* problem it cures. This gets Fox off the "breaking code" hook, but it doesn't really do much to help you. If you're interested in running yesterday's programs without modification or upgrading to current levels of performance, OKAY. This is about all you can count on.

You'll have to evaluate the Migration Kit on your own, but the following sections show some of the things where I find fault and have to say "oi!".

Speed

Is this thing slow or what? If you ask the MK to update what I would consider to be one of my more moderate apps from the old days, it goes away for a long, long time. This occurs on one of the fastest microcomputers available today!

Results

Most of the time, the MK works, converting old-style code to new FPM code properly. However, at many points it just says the equivalent of "This doesn't work any more, you need to fix it yourself...." How effective is this? Not very, if you still have to rewrite your app!

Bugs

At the time of this writing, the FXALERT conversion function the MK supplies causes your FoxPro session to die if you call it 19 times in a row. Sorry, I missed it in the beta, but be aware! Microsoft is now aware of the problem, and I'm sure it will be fixed—probably before you see this text on your bookshelf. Just in case, make sure that you have the latest version of FoxPro Mac!

FOXPRO MAC HACK TIP

Always bug your vendor—any vendor—for a current release! Sometimes products sit on the distribution warehouse shelves for a long time. I always make it a point to check on CompuServe for the latest version number of a product before I beat my head against a wall rediscovering a bug that was already fixed.

Waste

Some of the Migration Kit's internal shortcuts translate to extra work. Most critically, it duplicates a few pieces of code all over the place, which is something Lisa, Randy, Doc, and any other reputable programmer—on any platform—would tell you is "the big no-no."

The FXALERT routine I referred to on the previous page, along with the Pixel Conversion functions, window definition functions, and any other facility of the Migration Kit, gets pasted into every PRG that the MK converts! Not only is this a waste of disk space, but you also get to fix a UDF dozens of times if you need to modify it. It would have been *much more, tremendously much more* efficient from a long-term standpoint to leave the functions "loose" as individual .PRGs or bound into a single SET PROCEDURE file.

The bottom line: The Code Analyzer gives you—at best—a stop gap conversion to FoxPro for Macintosh.

In the rest of the chapter I describe the things that are different in FoxPro Mac from FoxBase+/Mac. I think you'll come to see why I feel so strongly about approaching FoxPro Mac as a rewrite of your existing FoxBASE+/Mac applications.

What's Really Different in FoxPro?

Understand that in this section I'm not discussing taking advantage of new features. Just to *run*, to execute old FoxBASE+/Mac programs, there are more than a few things that must be recoded, either by you or the Migration Kit.

I will give you a list of the "big problem" code changes, but the really important change you make is more than syntax: it is a way of writing applications.

Screens

In FoxBASE+/Mac, you used the screen design tool once to generate a screen, and then copied and pasted the generated code into a PRG. Thereafter, you did all manipulations of the screen by hand in the code, manipulating Pixels, Fonts, and Styles—something very hard to do.

In FoxPro (on any platform), I recommend that you never touch the screen code directly. Instead, stay in the design tool (Screen Builder) to make changes.

Menus

No Menu Builder existed in FoxBASE+/Mac. Many developers created all our menus in arrays. At least for me, this technique tended to be a bit flaky on some systems. You also had to pay close attention to declaration of arrays and so on with multiple menu systems.

In FoxPro, the Menu Builder supplies a simple "point, click, and type" sort of arrangement for creating menus.

Reports

Although I gave up on this after my client said, "Oh, this is Helvetica—it should be in Palatino!", a lot of Mac developers hand-code reports. I would suggest strongly that you avoid this approach in FoxPro. I groaned when the client followed up his previous comment with "Just use your mouse!"—not realizing that simple font change was going to translate into hours of recoding for me, recalculating pixel locations, page lengths, and so on.

The Report Writer in FoxPro Mac looks a lot like the one in FoxBASE+/Mac. In fact, you'll probably feel most at home there. To take real advantage of FoxPro (and have a truly upwardly compatible, cross-platform solution), you need to get all of those hand-coded reports into the Report Writer.

Let's see: Screens, Menus, and Reports. The first two are radically different, and the last is different if you haven't used the Report Writer. Hmmm. Sound like time to rewrite? It should.

Differences on the Code Level: Screen Coordinates

There are a few things that are radically different on the coding level. Microsoft Fox changed the way the screen coordinate system works. You'll have to get used to it because it isn't going to change back any time soon.

In FoxBASE+/Mac, you addressed pixel locations on the screen directly with syntax that looked like this:

```
@20,20 SAY "Here I Am!"
*or
@PIXELS 237,127 SAY "Here I Am!"
```

In the first line of code in this example, the code is listed in typical "DOS-style" 80 × 25 grid format. In the second, I added the keyword PIXELS to identify the exact Pixel location where I wanted the item to appear.

Very few FoxBASE+/Mac programmers wrote applications that looked like DOS apps. That's sort of against our creed, right? That means practically every FoxBASE+/Mac program in existence uses the second form of code, with the keyword PIXELS.

One of the Microsoft Fox goals listed previously is *make the same program run on any of the platforms*. That presents a problem for PIXELS type code. Do you see that if you ran @245,123 PIXELS on a machine that can do only 80 × 25 grids (i.e., a DOS-box) you have to convert on the fly? 245 by 123 pixels on a Mac screen would translate into something like, oh, 10 rows by 15 columns in DOS-land.

When Microsoft opted for row and column coordinates in FoxPro, I don't think they had the Mac in mind. Many Mac owners couldn't care less about owning a DOS machine or running code that works on a DOS machine. However, by definition, every Windows user owns a DOS machine. Giving these users a coordinate system they could use in both DOS and Windows proved to be a thorny skull-scratcher of a problem for the developers.

Finally, they arrived at a novel solution to a complex problem. They decided to allow decimal places in @row,col code.

The new code looks like the following:

```
@10.456,13.272 SAY "Here I am!"
```

If you're running on a platform that supports pixels (Windows and Macintosh), the decimals are significant. If you're running on one that does not (DOS), FoxPro ignores the decimal place. You've just become acquainted with the *foxel*, Microsoft's term for this particular concept. Randy will tell you more about this concept in Chapter 12.

I know you are about to say, "But how do I define a specific pixel? What is this decimal point stuff supposed to mean?"

Bear in mind that the first time I saw FoxPro for Windows I was in the same boat that you are in relation to the GUI environment. I couldn't figure out why they would do such a thing—I need to be able to identify a pixel point exactly, right?

Don't panic. You still can.

The foxel is a pixel coordinate locator in a GUI environment, and it happily becomes a row-and-column grid locator in a character-based system. To fully understand how it works, try it out in the Command window. Type the following:

```
ACTIVATE WINDOW SCREEN
```

This will establish the FoxPro for Macintosh desktop window as the current output window. If you don't see the window, select it from the Window menu list even though it's already checked. If the desktop window is off-screen somewhere, reselecting it will bring it to visible coordinates.

Now enter the command:

```
MODIFY WINDOW SCREEN FONT "Helvetica",12 STYLE "B"
```

This command forces the current output window you see right now into Helvetica, 12 point, bold.

Now issue this command:

```
@3,3 SAY "This is a piece of text at row 3 column 3"
```

Your result should look something like figure 2.2.

In the Command window, issue the following:

```
MODIFY WINDOW SCREEN FONT "Helvetica",55 STYLE "B"
@3,3 SAY "this is a piece of text at row 3 column 3"
```

Take a look now! The text item appears further to the right and down. Now try going the other way.

```
MODIFY WINDOW SCREEN FONT "Helvetica",3 STYLE "B"
@3,3 SAY "this is a piece of text at row 3 column 3"
```

You see a screen something like figure 2.3, and your first instinct is to say, "Argh!" I know I did. But relax, there is something reasonable and predictable going on here.

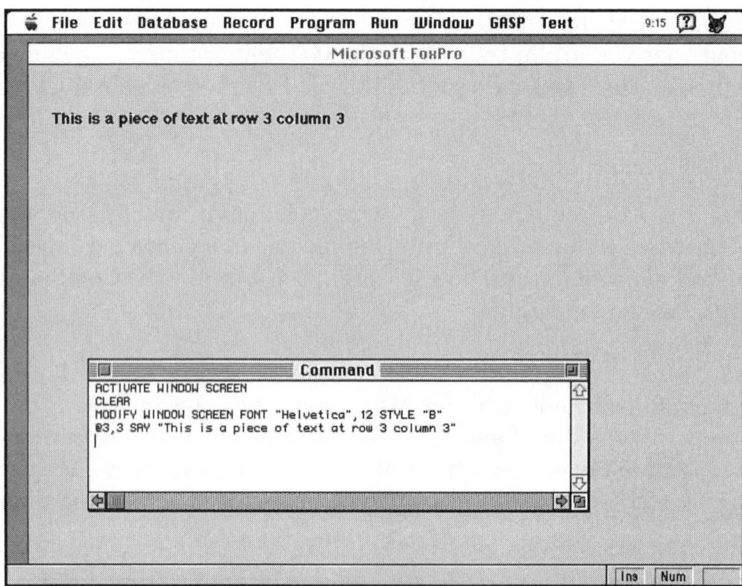

Figure 2.2 *Testing pixel-addressing with foxel coordinates interactively.*

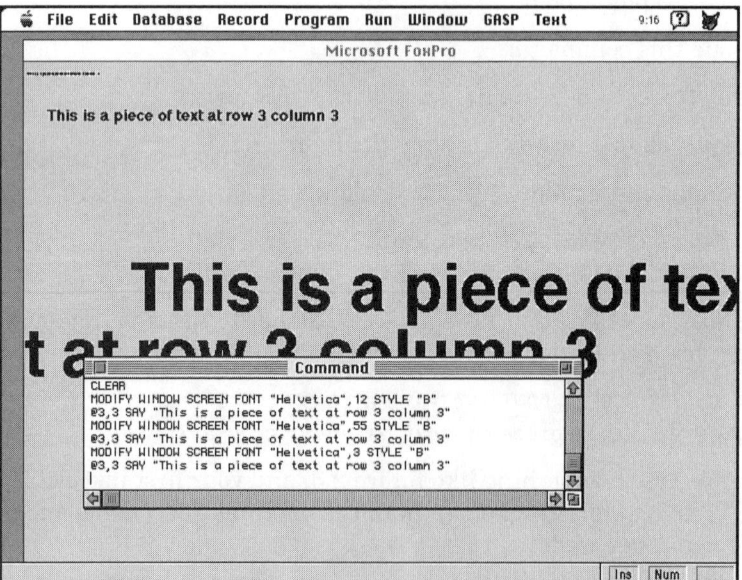

Figure 2.3 *Address the same foxel coordinates using a different font, and you get different results.*

In DOS land, the screen font can't be changed, so the 3,3 type coordinates will always be a constant. However, as demonstrated in this GUI environment, *the row and column coordinates are relative to the current output window's font, point size, and style.* This rule seems nerve-wracking at first. Why couldn't they just let us use pixels? How will I ever hard code a pixel location on the screen?

First, for most purposes you won't have to deal with it. I'm going to recommend, *LOUDLY*, that you do all screen design within the Screen Builder. If you do this, you don't have to know a *thing* about how the foxel works. It works exactly the same way in FoxPro for Windows, and I dare say that only a handful of FoxPro Win developers have a clue as to what a foxel is. This is OK. FoxPro Win developers don't particularly need to know, and after you make the transition to FoxPro Mac, you probably won't either.

How Foxels Work

I promised you a reasonable explanation. There are many valid reasons that caused Fox to implement the foxel concept as opposed to the PIXEL clause from FoxBASE+/Mac, and I hope that you keep an open mind about it. Remember that cross-platform technology is one of the things that makes FoxPro Mac such a powerful tool.

FoxPro has a new FONTMETRIC() function with an extensive list of arguments and return values. Of these, the ones that primarily concern you here are FONTMETRIC(1) and FONTMETRIC(6).

FontMetric(1) returns the average character height of a particular font, size, and style in pixels. FontMetric(6) returns the average width of the same. Convert foxels to pixels by performing this calculation:

```
Vertical Pixels = <row coordinate> X <FontMetric(1) of current window
font>
Horizontal Pixels = <col coordinate> X <FontMetric(6) of current window
font>
```

> **CROSS-PLATFORM WARNING**
>
> The calculation for vertical pixels in FoxPro Windows differs slightly (wouldn't you know it): you have to add FontMetric(5), which returns extra leading, to FontMetric(1), the height of the font at this point size, before you can multiply by the row coordinate. If you write code to perform these calculations, *bracket* the code by platform.

See Also

• "Bracketing Code for Cross-Platform Applications," Chapter 11

When you say `MODIFY WINDOW SCREEN FONT ...` you change the current window font. If you design a screen in the Screen Builder, or even execute a window command that the Migration Kit created, you are then using this window's font.

> **FOXPRO MAC HACK TIP**
>
> This terminology of "windows" as opposed to "screens" is sometimes confusing. I usually say "screen" to mean a "data entry screen" or dialog. The only time I say SCREEN as a FoxPro keyword is when I use it to refer to the main FoxPro "background" screen.

Here, in FoxPro code style, is a sample conversion from Foxels to Pixels:

```
*current screen font is "Helvetica",12 STYLE 'B'
@4,7 Say "Here I am!"
m.vertfactor = FONTMETRIC(1,'Helvetica',12,'B')
m.horizfactor = FONTMETRIC(6,'Helvetica',12,'B')

m.vertpix = 4 * m.vertfactor
*this equals 52
m.horizpix = 7 * m.horizfactor
*this equals 49
*EquivalentFoxBASE+/Mac code would be...
@ PIXELS 52,49 SAY "Here I am!"
```

If you want to go back the other way, simply divide the pixels instead, as shown in the following code:

```
*convert Pixels to Foxels
*current screen font is "Helvetica",12 STYLE 'B'
m.vertpix = 234
m.horizpix = 114
m.vertfactor = FONTMETRIC(1,'Helvetica',12,'B')
m.horizfactor = FONTMETRIC(6,'Helvetica',12,'B')
m.foxvertical = m.vertpix / m.vertfactor
m.foxhorizontal = m.vertpix / m.horizfactor
```

Given these facts, you can write a routine that changes your old FoxBASE+/Mac @..PIXELS type code into FoxPro Mac code. If you are really slick, the routine might look something like this:

```
*: Function: _pix2fox
*:
*: Added by FB+MIGRATE.APP
*:
*: Converts pixel coordinates to foxels
*:
*: PARAMETERS:
*: nPixel     N  a pixel value
*: cDimension C  "H" = horizontal (col) conversion
*: "V" = vertical (row) conversion
*: cFont       C   Font
*: nFontSize   N   Font size
*: cFontStyl   C   Font style
*:
*: RETURNS: foxel value (numeric)
*:
*:***************************
FUNCTION _pix2fox
PARAMETER m.nPixel,m.cDimension,;
          m.cFont,m.nFontSize,m.cFontStyl
IF PARAMETERS() < 3
  RETURN ;
  m.nPixel/;

FONTMETRIC(IIF(UPPER(m.cDimension) = "H",6,1))
ELSE
 RETURN ;
 m.nPixel/;
 FONTMETRIC(IIF(UPPER(m.cDimension) = ;
 "H",6,1),m.cFont,m.nFontSize,m.cFontStyl)
ENDIF
```

This is the conversion function the Migration Kit automatically sticks into your code when you Migrate to FoxPro Mac. Notice the parameter for "H" or "V," which is how the function determines if you're looking for a horizontal or vertical position. This is how the Migration Kit converts old-style code.

The Problems with Pixel-to-Foxel Conversion

Let's say the MK makes the transition for you to modern style code by using the PIX2FOX function. Are you any further along? Nope. Now you have to decide whether you want to hand code screens in foxels or pixels.

If you decide to stick with pixels, you have to include the conversion function on every line of screen code you draw, which is a total pain.

Next on the Code Change Hit List: SCREEN/ Window Definitions

In FoxBASE+/Mac, you had a total of nine "Screens" available that you could define, size, locate, and activate. As you know, to bring one up you would issue this command in your code:

```
SCREEN 2 TOP
```

Other attributes define the size, type, and location.

FoxPro Version 1, and now FoxPro Mac, use another scheme. In this scenario, you DEFINE WINDOW <window name> with attributes, and then ACTIVATE WINDOW <window name>. An example of the FoxPro Mac style is shown in the following code:

```
DEFINE WINDOW raoul FROM 3,3 TO 20,20
ACTIVATE WINDOW raoul
@1,1 SAY "Hello there!"
```

You see the results in figure 2.4. This syntax has some distinct advantages. Most importantly, you have a much greater maximum number of windows available, with the actual upper limit relative to the amount of RAM you have. Second, the windows can take on "realistic" names—that is, you can name a window GL_DATA or INVOICES. This allows for code that is a little more readable than SCREEN 3 TOP.

The biggest reason to use the new method is that, just as they ignore foxels, many FoxPro developers are clueless about the code that defines windows. Again, this is because the Screen Builder emits all the code for you.

So with this in mind, you would expect the Migration Kit to do a bang-up job converting all of your SCREEN definitions in Mac to something the new Screen Builder could use, right? I'm afraid this isn't the case. Once again, you get a cookie-cutter function that barely provides a gateway into the new FoxPro Mac world.

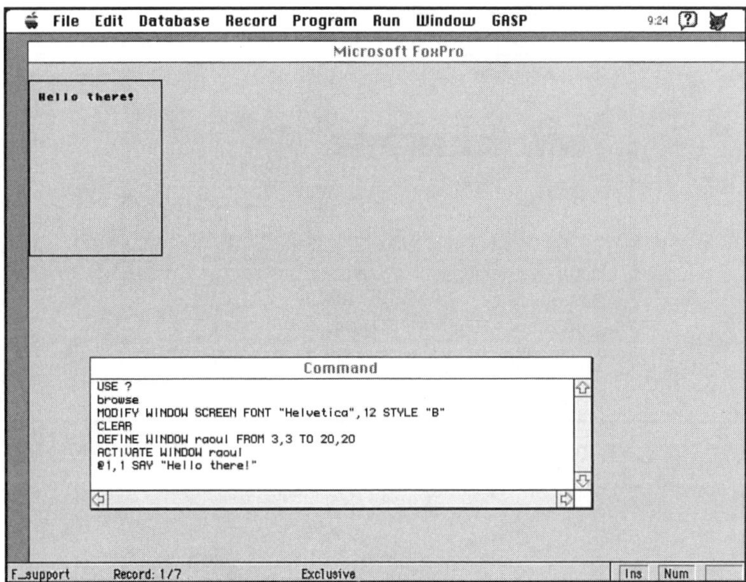

Figure 2.4 *The new DEFINE WINDOW syntax can be issued in the Command window as well as in programs.*

There's More

I could spend the rest of the chapter talking about what the Migration Kit doesn't do, which really wouldn't help you. Instead, let me show you in Microsoft's own words what doesn't work. In the same folder where you find the Migration Kit, look at the table F_SYNTAX.DBF (see figures 2.5 and 2.6).

This table is the part of the Migration Kit that contains the "issue" and "rules" messages that you see when you run the MK. Just browse through the "Rules" memo field. You soon will find yourself stumbling over and over onto the sentence, "There is no equivalent in FoxPro Mac." Read the rules and issues, and consider whether the "no equivalent" items concern you; if you used Screens, Menus, and a host of other required FoxBASE+/Mac elements, they probably will.

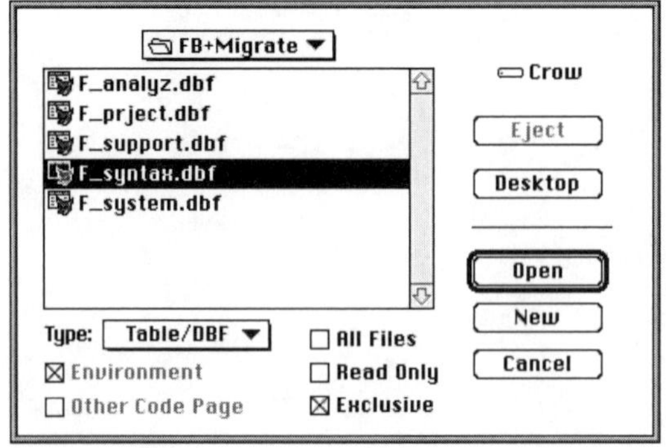

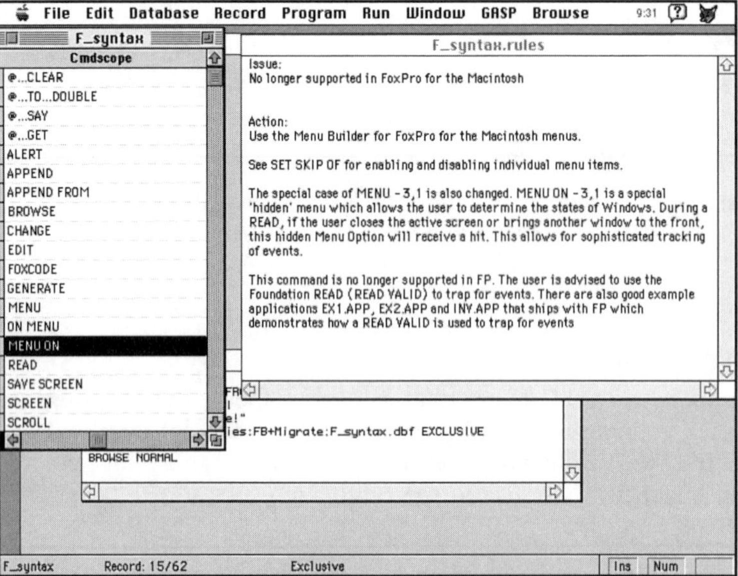

Figures 2.5 and 2.6 *The Migration Kit source code includes a useful table of syntax problems.*

Don't take it too hard. Instead, look at this situation as an opportunity to rewrite that dusty old app — starting from scratch with only the data and structures from the previous life. You might get a leg up if you used the Report Writer and Screen Builder religiously in FoxBASE+/Mac. The MK conversion of those files to modern FRX and SCX files is pretty smooth. You will probably end up doing a lot of tweaking when you try to hook the new screens into your FoxPro-style versions of the old programs.

Hello, FoxPro Mac!

Assuming that you made the decision to rewrite the existing app, you can enjoy some of the process. This section discusses some FoxPro features you won't want to miss.

What is really new and different in FoxPro/Mac? How important are the new enhancements in your day-to-day application development life? I identified the things that you will find are the biggest advantages of the product:

- Performance
- Maintenance with the Power Tools
- SQL

Performance, Indexes, and Rushmore

The database world changed dramatically with the introduction of FoxPro 2.0. Utilizing a new technology named Rushmore, ordinary DOS machines, roughly the equivalent of SE-30s, now could give truly amazing results. Suddenly, these PCs could tell you the answer to *"How many people own blue cars, have license plates that start with WX, and have brown hair?"* With this kind of information in a FoxPro table — even one containing around 3 million records—you could get the answer in about 3 seconds or less.

Optimization of FoxPro queries relies on a few rules. First, anything on the left-hand side of a conditional operator has to be "tagged," that is to say, indexed. This index must match *exactly* the expression on the left of the relational operator. Substring searches, such as searching for the letters "came to my party" in a memo field, are not generally maintained as TAGged expressions, and therefore cannot be optimized.

Second, all commands that take the FOR operator, SET FILTER, and SQL — SELECT's WHERE are potentially optimizable.

Third, if only it were just that simple! You will find that the right way to locate data in FoxPro is dependent upon what you look for. Always remember that SEEK is the fastest way to get anywhere in a FoxPro table. Of course, you can't select multiple items with a SEEK unless you have an index built on all of the items. Multiple, complicated indexes bring with them the downside of devouring both disk space and overhead in processing.

Don't believe anybody when it comes to performance. Often, the best way to get the desired data from a table is a function of *what* you look for. Give it your best shot with the way that you *think* is fastest, and then test different approaches. Use the FoxPro SECONDS() function (which has a resolution of 1000ths of a second) as a stop watch. See what works best for your situation.

You will discover that sometimes the FOR Rushmore Optimization may not be as fast as a traditional SEEK/WHILE type of construction. On the other hand, writing `BROWSE FOR <exp1> AND <exp2> AND <exp3>` is simple, direct, and unlikely to break, nor does it require an index built on <exp1>+<exp2>+<exp3>. If you test this command on the data with realistic loading levels (anticipated size of the data set plus gobs more than that) and you find it delivers acceptable results, use it. If it doesn't, investigate another method.

You learn more about using different methods to query your data and display the results of queries in Chapter 9.

The Old Way

In FoxBASE+/Mac, the standard practice was to create multiple index files that you had to maintain separately. A prime location for a bug to creep into your program was forgetting to USE the data file with all of the indexes it needed. The program would either bomb because an index wasn't available, or when the program next used the index, it would be out of date. You needed careful attention to track index files.

In FoxPro Mac you use *Structural indexes*, or CDX files. To create a structural index, you modify your old-style code only slightly.

Here is an example of the FoxBASE+/Mac way:

```
USE a_table
INDEX ON lastname TO lastname.idx
INDEX ON address TO address.idx
INDEX ON city TO city.idx
...and so on
Using the table in another module would look like this:

USE a_table INDEX lastname,address,city
```

If you forgot to include CITY in the index portion of this statement, it didn't get updated. Worse, if you had a Vendors table that held a city field and you overwrote one IDX with another, things really got weird. Code like this was a good way to break your programs.

In FoxPro Mac, do this instead:

```
USE a_table
INDEX ON lastname TAG lastname
INDEX ON address TAG address
INDEX ON city TAG city
```

This code creates a CDX file with the same name as the table. Now, any time you issue the command USE a_table, the indexes open up automatically. All changes made to records in the table update all of the CDX tags.

The default order when using CDX type index is *natural*, or no order. To establish a tag as the current order, perhaps to perform a SEEK, use the SET ORDER TO command. The following example shows this:

```
USE a_table
SET ORDER TO city
SEEK "Dallas"
```

Locating Result Sets of Records

Another standard FoxBASE+/Mac practice was to isolate specific data with code like the following example:

```
USE sales
INDEX ON inv_date FOR salesid = 23 TO temp.idx
BROWSEDELETE FILE temp.idx
```

In FoxBASE+/Mac this method is usually the most efficient way for preparing data for a report or browse. Particularly on a network and depending on the size of your tables, however, this code can take a long, long time to execute.

In FoxPro this requirement can be handled by using a CDX TAG. In the preceding example, if the "salesid" field is TAGged into the CDX, you can issue this command instead:

```
BROWSE FOR salesid = 23
```

You should see nearly instant results, even on large numbers of records.

You can combine multiple logical expressions, and FoxPro's Rushmore optimization still kicks in provided that you followed rules 1 and 2. In the following lines, you see some examples of optimizable expressions based on the TAGs created in this code as well:

```
USE company
INDEX ON address TAG address
INDEX ON compname TAG compname
INDEX ON city TAG city
INDEX ON state TAG state
BROWSE FOR compname = "Exxolot"

REPLACE balance WITH balance * 1.3 ;
    FOR compname = "Bill's Garage";
    AND city = "Austin"
REPORT FORM myreport.frx FOR state = 'VA'
```

Based on the above code, here is an example of a NON-optimized expression:

```
BROWSE FOR UPPER(compname) = "EXXOLOT"
```

Subtle difference, isn't it? The UPPER() function doesn't match EXACTLY the expression the TAG was built on. However, most developers make search screens case-insensitive so the users don't have to match case exactly. The difference between an optimized expression and a non-optimized one is significant to staggering, depending on the number of records in your database tables.

For example, I can routinely demonstrate selecting 23 records out of 1 million in under 2 seconds if the expression I'm looking for is TAGged. Yet, if I asked a non-optimized question of a 20,000 record table, I expect the results to come back in 45 seconds or longer. With a million record table, the time might run from several minutes to an hour!

If you want to do an UPPER() conversion in your selection statements, just build the TAG on the expression instead! Or use both the normal *and* the UPPER() TAGs. FoxPro looks for the expression, not the TAG name, when performing a query. Here is an example:

```
INDEX ON UPPER(compname) TAG compname
```

At this point, I can issue the previously non-optimized expression and Rushmore kicks in. Make sure that you pay attention to this detail. I've walked in on consulting jobs and changed tasks from taking several minutes to less than one second by building the TAGs (and/or queries) properly. It really can make you an office hero, and it is frighteningly easy to master.

> **FOXPRO MAC HACK TIP**
>
> How can you tell what your TAGs are? FoxPro gives several methods. Interactively, USE the_table, then type DISPLAY STATUS, or use the View window's Setup panel to look at a table's associated tags and indexes. The KEY column in the Status listing or the Index Expression listing in the View panel is the item that must match exactly to what is on the left-hand side of the relational operator to optimize a condition.

So, I'll TAG Everything!

TAGging everything may be your first inclination, but this isn't necessarily a great idea. First, everything you TAG takes a portion of disk space. It isn't uncommon for CDX files to be almost as large as the tables (DBFs) from which they are drawn. When you add, edit, or delete a record, each TAG must be updated.

You have to evaluate for yourself and for your situation. If your data is more static in nature, you probably will lean toward having many TAGs. If, however, the data is very dynamic—say, a head-down data entry system—you will lean toward having fewer TAGs. I usually advise folks to TAG more rather than less and then back off if they experience performance problems.

Use the Screen Builder

DO NOT copy and paste code generated from the Screen Builder into PRGs and attempt to modify it by hand. This is a particularly nasty habit and it does a world of harm to you in the long run. The following are reasons to give up hand-coding a screen:

- Foxels are hard to visualize (and really, pixels aren't much better)
- Increases the chances of a mistake (what I call "code-exposure")

- You have to learn a bunch of syntax (yuck!)
- It takes a long time to redesign screens
- It is absolutely not necessary

Your first inclination (everybody's!) may be to continue working along as you used to. You probably have a set of code that handles the basic tasks (such as add, edit, delete), and you can paste a new screen into it. At Plaid Software, we used to call our basic code "the frame," and we made a new copy of it each time we started a new FoxBASE+/Mac program.

Give yourself some time, but do yourself a favor and forget the FoxBASE+/Mac way of doing things. Parts II and III of this book show you how to make the Power Tools work together with one set of your framing code for a different style of work and a much easier way to maintain this code.

SQL

SQL, or Structured Query Language, adds a wonderful dimension to application development with FoxPro. This is an area you'll want to get familiar with right away.

A big advantage in dealing with SQL is that it maintains its own set of Parent and Child relationships irrelevant to the current settings of SET RELATION TO, orders, and other xBase conventions.

Occasionally—particularly when you stumble into one of those frequent real-life situations called the "Many to Many" relationship, for which Xbase syntax has no natural representation—you have to flip-flop between who is the Parent and who is the Child. Further examples in this book demonstrate a typical Many to Many relationship —that is, between ad agency employees and the agency's jobs. One or many employees may be involved with one or many jobs. If you want to know all of the jobs to which an account executive is assigned or on which an employee logged time, you make the Account Executive table the Parent, and the Job table the child. If instead you want to see which Account Executives are involved with a particular Job, you make the Job the Parent and the Account Executive the Child.

This scenario is evident in all kinds of real-life situations—Students and Classes, Workers and Teams, Lobbyists and Industries, Cases and Evidence, and so on.

These scenarios become particularly cumbersome for data entry operations. You want to allow the user to hit a button and see the "other half" of whatever side they're currently working on. In FoxBASE+/Mac, this would mean a bunch of SET RELATION TO statements, and it gives you yet another great place to bomb your programs. Xbase relationships can't be cyclical, by definition.

With a SQL SELECT, you can hook up ONE line of code that gives you the desired effect and not have ANY impact on your data entry operations.

Lisa discusses SQL in Chapter 9. Read that section: it will change your life for the better. You also will see a different way to achieve the same effect in FoxPro, the USE AGAIN command, demonstrated in Chapter 6.

Miscellaneous New Features and Concepts

If the changes I've mentioned above were the only broad differences between FoxBASE and FoxPro, your life may be easier at first—but the FoxPro world would be a poorer place. This section includes other changes that you have to get used to as part of your initial move to FoxPro.

Tables versus Databases

Wayne Ratliff, the creator of dBase, came up with the extension DBF to indicate "DataBase File" well over a decade ago. He has since apologized to everyone.

The files FoxBASE+/Mac developers commonly refer to as DataBases really are Tables. The collection of all the Tables, along with the application that allows you to retrieve, add, and change data in the tables, is referred to as a Database.

In a world moving toward greater connectivity between different types of data management systems and platforms, it pays to get the terminology straight. Tables are the individual files—like Customers, Vendors, Invoices, and Products. Each Table is composed of Rows (Records to you and me) and columns (fields). Think of what a BROWSE window shows and it makes more sense.

Line Continuation Character

Commands now can be broken across multiple lines—both in code and the command window—by using the semicolon. Semicolons help make your code more legible, as in the following example:

```
REPLACE;

 lastname WITH "Simms",;
 firstname WITH "Davis",;
 address WITH "1400 West Place",;
 state WITH "CA"
```

READ CYCLE

FoxBASE+/Mac data entry READs usually were encapsulated within a DO/WHILE loop. This loop is no longer required for FoxPro. Instead, you add the CYCLE option for a similar effect.

Here is an example of the old-style code:

```
m.exit = .F.
DO WHILE NOT m.exit
       DO gets
       READ
ENDDO
*somewhere another control would turn
* m.exit to TRUE and end the loop.
```

This code can be replaced with the following:

```
DO gets
READ CYCLE
```

CYCLE has the effect of allowing the user to tab from the last field back to the first, which would usually just drop out of the READ. GENSCRN, the screen generator program that emits code from the definitions you create in the Screen Builder. It generates the READ CYCLE clause by default, so the two lines above are reduced to the single line DO the.SPR (SPR is the extension for the generated screen program).

SHOW GET/SHOW GETS/ENABLED/DISABLED

You use the SHOW GET and SHOW GETS commands often. SHOW GETS refreshes all current GETS involved with the READ session. SHOW GET <get_fld> refreshes an individual element. Adding the DISABLE and ENABLE clause dims or makes available fields for editing.

It is much more preferable from a user's and designer's standpoint to prevent users from being in a field they're not supposed to be in by having the field appear dim and unavailable. The only other solution is to wait until they're in the field and tell them, "Hey, you're not supposed to be here!" The second method is the hallmark of an amateurish application in FoxPro. You will see the enabling and disabling of objects play a central role in the design of screens throughout Chapters 8 and 10. In Chapter 11, Lisa summarizes this style of validation, designed to have WHEN and VALID clauses on a GET RETURN .T. almost universally. This *permissive* validation style is especially appropriate to Macintosh applications.

Here are some examples:

```
*in the VALID (lost focus) CLAUSE
* of an ITEM field on an invoice
IF EMPTY(item)
   SHOW GET quantity DISABLED
ELSE
*they have an item selected...
  SHOW GET quantity ENABLED
ENDIF

*or for toggling an entire
*screen on and off...
*
IF m.in_edit_mode
  SHOW GETS ENABLED
ELSE
  SHOW GETS DISABLED
  SHOW GET m.control_bar ENABLED
*Note that if you show GETS disabled,
*the READ will terminate
*It is for that reason that you usually
*follow it with a SHOW GET.. ENABLED
*to turn your control (buttons or whatever)
*object back on
ENDIF
```

_CUROBJ

This little guy is a happy member of the club called System Memory Variables. You can see these variables by typing DISPLAY MEMORY right after you start up FoxPro. Although they report values that FoxPro has assigned to them by default, you also can assign new values to the system variables.

For example, if you wanted the user's cursor to move immediately to the first object after adding a blank record, the code would look like this:

```
APPEND BLANK
_CUROBJ = 1
*last line forces the cursor to
*jump to the first object
```

OBJNUM()

This function is a companion to the _CUROBJ function. You can supply a GET field expression in the OBJNUM() as a parameter, and it reports the number of that object. OBJNUM() is handy to move the cursor to some particular field. For example:

```
*in the valid clause of a field called Vehicle
IF vehicle = 'MOTORCYCLE'
  SHOW GET helmet ENABLED
  _CUROBJ = OBJNUM(helmet)
ELSE
 SHOW GET helmet DISABLED
ENDIF
```

> **FOXPRO MAC HACK TIP**
>
> Refer to Appendix E for OBJVAR(), a new function in 2.6 that is a superior variant of FoxBASE's SYS(18) or FoxPro's VARREAD().

WAIT WINDOW

This handy little gizmo displays any character expression that you supply. I use it all the time in applications and during the development cycle. If you use the CHR() function with a parameter value of 13, you can insert line feeds for multi-line wait windows. Here is an example:

```
WAIT WINDOW ;
"This is the "+CHR(13)+;
"multi-line"+CHR(13)+'message!'
```

.NOT.DOT.

FoxBASE+/Mac requires that logical expressions such as AND, NOT, and OR be surrounded with periods. This is not required in FoxPro. If your fingers just do it automatically, don't fret about it, the old style still works. However, most of us quickly gave up typing the extra characters.

.T. and .F. still require the dots around them.

Alias and Field References

First, let me say that if you're still referring to tables (DBFs) by their workarea name (A, B, 3, 4), stop. This mode of thinking makes it harder to tell what's going on when reading your code. The following example shows a proper code sequence for opening a table into a workarea for general purpose:

```
*select 0 picks the lowest available work area
SELECT 0
*open the table
USE company

*and repeat the sequence for each new table
SELECT 0
USE job
```

With this method, you have no idea exactly which workarea a particular DBF is going to be opened into. Nor do you care! You don't write code that looks like this:

```
SELECT A
BROWSE
SELECT B
BROWSE
*the above example assumes that the 1st and 2nd work areas were used...
*SELECT 0 actually picks its own work area
```

Instead, write code like the following, which is much more legible to anyone:

```
SELECT company
BROWSE
SELECT job
BROWSE
```

If you wanted to see the address field (column) from the company table—and it was opened into the A (first) workarea—any of the following code would execute properly:

```
? A->Address
? Company->Address
? Company.Address
```

Most of us prefer the "dot" method because you only have to type one character, and this character doesn't even require the shift key! Second, have you ever been tongue-tied trying to say, "Company dash greater than sign address" on the phone? It may seem like a silly reason to change, but "company dot address" is one heck of a lot easier to say aloud.

You have a third reason to use the dot instead of ->: this style is consistent with the return values you get from FoxPro functions and other internal references to aliased fields (including memory variables, as you will see in the following section). Look back, for example, at figure 2.6. Whether I opened the memo window on the right using a MODIFY MEMO command or by double-clicking on the Rules memo placeholder in the BROWSE on the left, FoxPro uses the name `F_syntax.rules` as the memo window's default title. If I use the various window functions (such as WTITLE()) to refer to this window, it's important to be aware of the difference. For example, WVISIBLE("F_syntax.rules") returns .T., while WVISIBLE("F_syntax->rules") returns .F.

The "M Dot"

For some reason, FoxBASE+/Mac developers—myself included—greatly missed the "M." reference for memory variables. I suspect that a lot of you readers already know this, but for the benefit of those who don't, I'll explain how it works.

In both FoxBASE+/Mac and FoxPro Mac, you can create a memory variable by using the equal sign. An example is given in the following lines of code:

```
myvar = 2445
? myvar
```

I see a lot of old code with all memory variables prefaced by the letter M. Examples would be:

```
mAvalue = 24
mSomeData = 56
mROI = 1.56
mName = "Andy"
```

The idea was to arrive at a naming convention that prevented a conflict from arising between memory variables and field names. In case you didn't know this, try the following example:

```
CLOSE ALL
address = "This is some test data"
? address
USE company
? address
* address is the name of a field in the
* company table
USE
? address
```

If Fox sees a duplicate of a memory variable in a table as a field name, it defaults to using the table value. You can see how this default might produce undesired effects!

The "m" as a leading character is OK, but it doesn't prevent you from having the same problems if you create a field name with a leading "m"!

A simple cure exists for this problem. Execute the previous example, but this time add an "M." before the address.

```
CLOSE ALL
address = "This is some test data"
? address
USE company
? address
? m.address
USE
? address
? m.address
```

I always refer to memory variables with a leading "m.", as does Lisa, except when she references a passed parameter or expands a macro-expression. Other developers have different styles for handling these conflicts.

SET RESOURCE

When you read Randy's Chapter 16 on XCMDs and XFCNs in FoxPro, you can see why the SET RESOURCE command has a different meaning to FoxPro than it did in FoxBASE. (Lisa tells you about the new FoxPro-style resource file in Chapter 14.)

To access external commands and functions, you can use SET XCMDFILE instead—but to include pictures in dialogs, you can no longer store them in a resource fork. Pictures have to be separate files on disk. Don't worry, though. In the applications you distribute, FoxPro combines them in a single .APP file along with the rest of the program files the applications need. For cross-platform reasons, however, all elements of the application are treated as data. The .APP has no resource fork.

Menus

Menus are handled far differently in FoxPro than in FoxBASE. First, play with the Menu Builder and get a feel for just how easy it is to lay out a menu. Make a Quick Menu and notice all the system-defined menu bars. FoxPro turns these on and off as it deems appropriate during your application. Some of them have no business being in the production version of your finished application (Trace and Debug come to mind); but others, such as Edit's Copy and Paste capabilities, offer extensions to the functionality of an application.

Being Mac people, you won't appreciate the fact that you get the "desk accessories"—that is the Calculator, Puzzle, and Calendar—free of charge by simply including them in your application's menu. If you're a Windows or DOS person, this is a big deal. (Often, I just shake my head and wonder why Mac is still the underdog here... but if you read Chapter 7, you'll see that you can remove these items easily from the menu on a platform-basis, if you want.)

When you execute a menu (DO mymenu.mpr, the generated code product of the Menu Builder and GENMENU, the generator program) it replaces the System menu bar in FoxPro with your menu. No program is running (other than FoxPro, that is) after the MPR completes its execution. You're back in interactive mode, although your system menu is customized. That menu is established, and it will remain until you type something like:

```
SET SYSMENU TO DEFAULT
```

In FoxBASE+/Mac you loaded menu options in arrays. To change a menu or its status (dimmed or available), you reloaded the array. In FoxPro the SKIP FOR option is available for each menu pad and bar. When the expression evaluates to TRUE, the option is dimmed. Evaluation takes place whenever a "hit" occurs on the menu.

You can use this clause for a variety of purposes. For example, it is possible in a multi-user system to dim menu options dynamically, based on user-privilege levels.

The Project Manager

You will want to start using the Project Manager early on. The Project Manager combines all the elements of your application into a single executable image — either as an APP or EXE. This file is more efficient at execution time, and has the side benefit of allowing you a more organized view of everything going on in the app during development.

You establish the Main file (outermost level) of your application, and then press the Build button. The Project Manager analyzes the requirements of your application by investigating the references to other files in your Main file.

File Name Extensions

When FoxPro sees "DO myscreen.SPR," the SPR extension indicates to the Project Manager, "Ah-ha! A 'myscreen.SCX' must be around here somewhere" and goes looking. If it can't find it, it asks you to locate it. For this reason, if you don't have a specific reason not to, adhere to the defaults for generated code from screens and menus. Otherwise, you'll have to manually link up the two in the Project Manager.

A Strategy for Converting

I will assume that I made a believer of you, and you want to rewrite your applications in FoxPro the proper way. But let's face it, if you have a robust application, this might be a fairly lengthy task.

Make sure that everybody on the network is running a Mac capable of handling FoxPro Mac. This means about 8 megs of RAM minimum. Realistically, I wouldn't want to have my clients expect great results on anything less than an '040. If you've got 60 percent '020-based computers on the LAN, make sure that everybody knows this new great product you're writing won't run on many weaker machines.

You can straddle the fence, running both FoxPro Mac and FoxBASE+/Mac simultaneously on the network. The data and older style index files are visible to both systems. However, you now have about twice as much work to do, and for this reason, I recommend trying to stay away from it.

How can you take advantage of FoxPro Mac immediately in existing applications? First of all, you'll have to update the "drop dead, no-way" code issues that the Migration Kit can't handle for you. This is not a trivial matter, and unfortunately, I don't have an easy trick to help you out here.

After you get the application running in FoxPro, here are some areas where you can improve performance immediately without having to worry too much about breaking code.

Look through your code for any of the following and change to the more modern style. Note that the Migration Kit isn't going to be concerned with this—both styles of code execute, it's just that the old method is much slower.

> **FOXPRO MAC HACK TIP**
>
> Remember when I said to keep in mind whose problem the Migration Kit really solves? Microsoft's failure to build advice about performance issues into the MK is a good example of what I meant.

INDEX ON <expression> FOR <condition> TO <name of a temp file>

Building temporary indexes takes a relatively long time. Usually the above line of code will be followed by something like a BROWSE or REPORT FORM, and in most cases you'll find that you could just comment out the line and add the FOR condition to the command itself.

Remember to SET ORDER TO <expression> so that your data still appears in that sort order. You still need a tag built on <expression>; you just don't have to build additional indexes for every new <condition>.

INDEX ON <expression> TO <name>

To get rid of old-style IDX files, simply change the word "TO" to "TAG" and you're done! Delete the IDXs—you won't need them anymore. Remember to comment out any code that says SET INDEX TO because you'll be using CDXs automatically now.

CROSS-PLATFORM WARNING

If you're supporting other platforms (i.e., FoxBASE+/Mac) that don't support CDXs, you can't do this.

DO WHILE /ENDDO

Replace these statements with SCAN/ENDSCAN. Comment out the SKIP line (SCAN implies a skip), and you won't need to worry about the EOF() because it automatically stops at the end of file. If you SELECT tables within the loop and re-SELECT the table through which you're moving before the ENDDO, you can comment out the re-SELECT too. ENDSCAN automatically re-SELECTs the SCANned table!

This one change may provide the most performance gain for the least amount of your effort.

INDEX ON <expression>+<expression>+ <expression> TO ...

Concatenated indexes were a common way of identifying multiple elements quickly in FoxBASE+/Mac. I would (and have) done this with something like "lastname+firstname+state" to locate a record via seek.

This is hardly ever necessary anymore. Instead, investigate using SQL by playing with the RQBE. You'll discover that SQL can combine TAGs built on individual fields in a very flexible fashion. Here is an example:

```
SELECT *;
  FROM company;
  WHERE state = 'TX';
     AND lastname = 'F';
   ORDER BY lastname,firstname,state
```

Caution: You'll love the results so much that you'll decide to rewrite the entire application—tonight!

Cross Platform Planning

It is a fact that only a few shops are totally Macintosh. In fact, Apple's new Power Mac ads are touting *"Mac because you want to—DOS because you have to."* For this reason, you need to keep some basic cross-platform concepts floating around.

From DOS's point of view, the Mac can have long file names, as you know. DOS—brain dead as it might seem — can only have eight character file names, plus a three character suffix (extension) following a period or full-stop character. Mac-style file names can also contain special characters DOS thinks are illegal, and they often contain spaces that throw normal DOS application programs for a loop.

If you think there's a chance that you might be porting your Macintosh application to Windows, DOS, or Unix, make your file names DOS-compatible. This can be tougher than you might imagine. For example, Alias names can have 10 characters. File names in DOS can have only 8. More than once I've written code in DOS that said something like USE CUSTOMERS. In DOS, that has an alias of CUSTOMERS, but the file name has only eight characters, that is CUSTOMER.DBF (no "s")! What happens is the code works great on the DOS box, but then the Mac starts looking for a CUSTOMERS.DBF (with the "S"). There are countless variations on this theme, back and forth. Keep an eye out for it.

CROSS-PLATFORM WARNING

Oh, guess what? Windows/NT and the not-yet-shipping Windows 95—Microsoft's newest Windows operating system—support long file names, although they provide long file names using completely different methods! Users of FoxPro Unix, moreover, encounter an entirely new set of file-naming requirements, including case-sensitivity in file names and a different understanding of "drive" or "volume." So things will get better, and things will get worse.

Whether or not you think you are going to develop cross-platform, be aware that FoxPro for Macintosh functions return file name and path information using DOS-style notation. This means drive and volume names are separated from path information with a colon and backslash, and the rest of the path elements (folders on the Mac, directories in DOS) are separated by backslashes.

You can use the SYS(2027) function to find out what a file's "real Mac name" is, especially if you need this information to pass to other Macintosh programs that don't understand DOS notation.

FoxPro's own functions understand either style of notation when you pass them information. However, they're still DOS-headed to a degree; use delimiters (quotation marks or square brackets) around any file and/or path information that might include spaces or other "DOS-illegal" characters. Lisa has additional information on file name translation and indirect file referencing, a good habit that solves many of these problems, in Chapter 1.

Chapter Wrap Up

You'll love FoxPro Mac once you finally get your new stuff into it. The size of your application determines whether it is even advisable to spend the time running it through the Code Analyzer portion of the Migration Kit. I can tell you that it wasn't worthwhile for any of my applications.

If you can't migrate totally due to time constraints, get started with some of the most important features listed in this chapter, especially Rushmore optimization. All it takes is going through the code and changing your indexing style.

See Also

- "In direct Referencing: The Prime Directive for File References in Programs," Chapter 1
- "Reverse Name Translation," Chapter 1

3

QUICK START FOR NON-FOXFOLKS

by
Andy Griebel

Microsoft got to you. Because of the low price, the promise of unbelievable performance, the cross-platform technology, or whatever other motivations, you purchased FoxPro for Macintosh. Perhaps you have never used a database before. Perhaps you've used a less complex product, like FileMaker Pro.

You cleared off disk space, installed FoxPro for Macintosh, and said, "Now what?" Soon you knew that this wasn't FileMaker Pro—this was hard. At that point, you decided you needed more help, and you bought this book.

The purpose of this chapter is to provide you with some basic direction into the Fox way of doing things. I'll discuss terminology and concepts of FoxPro for Macintosh, isolating differences between it and other products.

Defining FoxPro for Macintosh

FoxPro is a *relational database management system*. Right away, that contrasts it to currently shipping versions of FileMaker and other similar products. FoxPro can be (and is intended to be) used on at least three levels. First, a user can use it interactively, not unlike the way you may approach using a spreadsheet program. Second, it may be used as an application development platform—that is to say, as a "real" programming language. The end result of application development yields the third level, on which a data entry person is running a FoxPro Application you created—totally unaware of the fact they are even using FoxPro.

It is the second use of FoxPro that requires the most expertise—and to which a great deal of this book is devoted.

Flat-File Versus Relational Databases

What is a relational database? Why is it important to you?

A couple of the easiest reasons to consider using a relational database product like FoxPro are to:

- Make data more accessible by logically grouping data elements
- Avoid duplicating data

There are many other reasons and scenarios where relational databases prove to be greatly beneficial, but the motivation for using a relational database usually boils down to some variation of the items in the preceding list.

To contrast FoxPro with non-relational database technology, let me design this scenario in FileMaker Pro.

> **FOXPRO MAC HACK TIP**
>
> I don't want you to think I'm picking on FileMaker Pro. In fact, there are a great many things I like about the package. FMP is popular on the Mac and is currently a non-relational product. These facts make FMP a good common-ground example to which I can contrast FoxPro and in comparison with which I can explain some FoxPro concepts.

You want to create a simple customer and invoice system. The example that ships with FileMaker Pro has fields for each invoice called Company Name, Company Address, etc., as well as "repeating" fields for each line item of the invoice. You type an account number in the appropriate field, and FMP fills in the blanks for the customer address and the like. The lookup information is drawn from the contact file.

What's wrong with that? The example looks fine, even pretty (see figure 3.1).

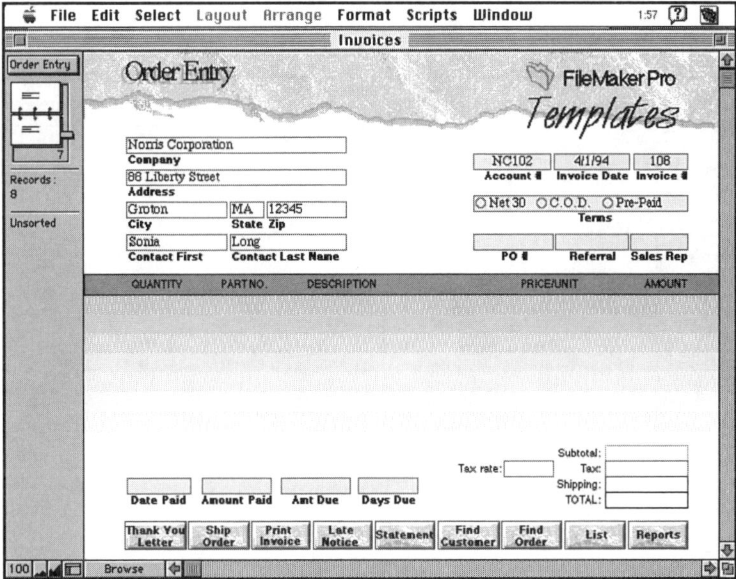

Figure 3.1 *The FileMaker Pro Invoice template.*

The problems creep in when you change data. In the FileMaker Pro example, the customer address is stored in each and every invoice.

Why is this a big deal? If the customer gets 23 invoices, and then calls to say "You've got our address wrong on all of these" or "I've moved," you'll need to edit all 23 invoices, as you see in figure 3.2. This storage method is wasteful. The customer is a single entity, right? Why should you be tracking around 23 different copies of his address?

The problems magnify significantly as you increase the number of invoices each customer has. Next comes the problem of finding all the invoices that belong to a single customer. Although you can use the Account Number to bind invoices to a single customer, in the FileMaker Pro example this important information is optionally keyed in.

Do you see how difficult it would be to identify like invoices if you had to consider all of the company names in the previous screen shot as one? For example, Norris Corp. is the same as Norris Corporation, Norris Brothers Corp., etc. Locating a particular customer rapidly becomes a total zoo (not a jungle, just a zoo...).

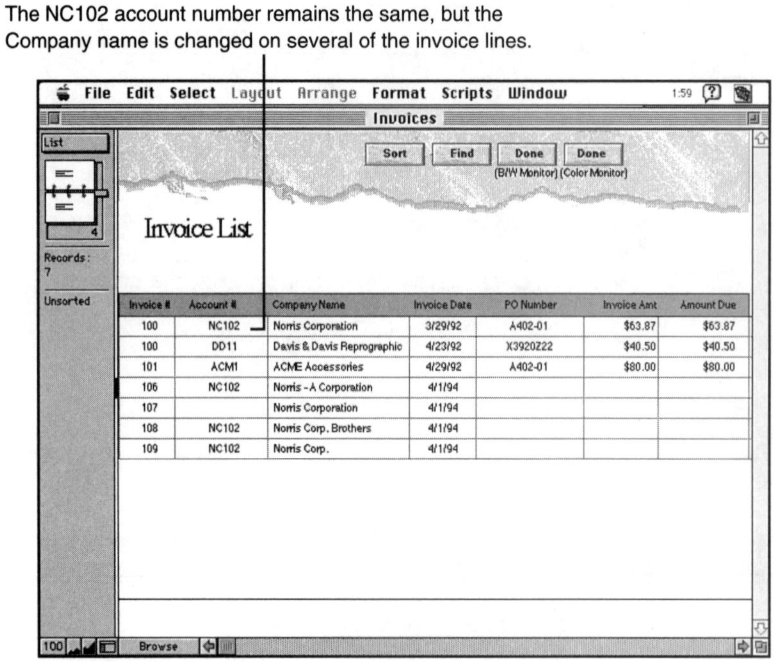
The NC102 account number remains the same, but the
Company name is changed on several of the invoice lines.
File Edit Select Layout Arrange Format Scripts Window
Invoices
List
Sort
Find
Done
Done
(B/W Monitor) (Color Monitor)
Invoice List
Records:
7
Unsorted
Invoice # Account # Company Name Invoice Date PO Number Invoice Amt Amount Due
100 NC102 Norris Corporation 3/29/92 A402-01 $63.87 $63.87
100 DD11 Davis & Davis Reprographic 4/23/92 X3920Z22 $40.50 $40.50
101 ACM1 ACME Accessories 4/29/92 A402-01 $80.00 $80.00
106 NC102 Norris - A Corporation 4/1/94
107 Norris Corporation 4/1/94
108 NC102 Norris Corp. Brothers 4/1/94
109 NC102 Norris Corp. 4/1/94
Browse

Figure 3.2 *A List view of the FileMaker Pro invoice system.*

With FileMaker Pro and other products like it, you don't really have a choice. You have to repeat data over and over and over in each record because these products are *flat-file* database management systems. By nature, they are easier to use—and less useful in the long run. A flat-file is no different from a Rolodex on your desk.

To keep track of customers and invoices "correctly," you need a relational database.

Enter Relational Databases

A relational database developer looks at the scenario of customers and invoices and thinks, "Hmmm. One customer can have one invoice. Or, one customer can have several invoices. In fact, because the sales department picked up the new division last year, we have some customers that have thousands of invoices."

If you handle this situation with flat-file technology, each invoice will contain the address *and* sales information (what they bought, how much it costs, etc.). If indeed you have thousands of invoices per customer, this might translate to real dollars—in required disk space—very quickly.

The proper way to solve this with FoxPro is to create two files: one for customers, and one for invoices. Verbalizing the scenario again, the relational developer says: "One customer, one invoice, or One Customer a bunch of Invoices... One customer To Many invoices — ah ha! A One To Many Relationship!"

In this scenario, the Customer becomes the Parent table, and the Invoice becomes the Child table.

This process of data analysis, determining which data is the Parent and which belongs to the Child and other ancillary issues, is called *normalization*.

We've developed this scenario sort of backwards, starting from the invoice side. Let me show you another example of the same thing. This is usually where I find developers "doing it wrong," and it is a subtle way to creep into problems.

Let's say that you have a literal Parent and Child relationship: a day care center. You started using FileMaker Pro or some other flat-file data manager. You quite naturally make a file called Parents, which has fields for the parents' address, city, state, and so forth. In addition, being the hip, savvy flatfile developer you are, you include multiple fields for children, with fields named Child1, Child2, and Child3.

There's some kind of natural law about putting numbers in field names. As soon as you create Child1, Child2 and Child3, you can almost always count on adding fields for Child4, Child5, Child6 and so on. Trust me, it usually happens. Of course this means that for those parents that have only one child, you're tracking around unused space for Child2 through Child6.

The other downside is searching for a specific child. If you happen to know the name of the child ("We found him in the park wandering around...") and you want to know who his parents are, you can't just search the Child1 field. You need to look at all the Child fields individually, as "Ronnie" might easily be the fifth offspring of Mr. Jones. The "Argh" factor goes way up as you add more children per parent and increase the total number of records.

When you are ready to print a report, you also have to deal with these multiple fields. In reporting, the "Argh" factor increases immediately.

FOXPRO MAC HACK TIP

Just to underline the difference in power you have available to you in FoxPro, think about this:

FoxPro Mac is *quite* capable of tracking a city with a population of two or three million people. Assume that you had the data—which is largely available—contained on a system running FoxPro Mac. You could find all parents who have children with blue eyes, greater than four years old but less than seven, named "Ronnie" in less than 20 seconds.

That's a fairly conservative guess; your actual time would probably be much, much less. If nothing matched, let's say you looked at the kid's eyes again and decided somebody might have considered them to be "hazel." You could issue the modified query again and have the response back even faster than before.

The goal of a relational database is to store data only once, in one location. This eliminates confusion ("Hmmm, I wonder if the Norris Brothers Corporation at 2727 Beamon Street is exactly the same as the Norris Corporation at 2727 Beaumont Street and they just typed it in wrong?") and, more importantly, allows you to edit the change in a single spot.

Lisa describes a complex, real-life data scenario in Chapter 6 and helps guide you through the process of establishing Parent and Child relationships. After you make the jump to related files, you'll be greatly rewarded with efficient, reliable data storage.

The basic technique depends on a *unique identifier* being assigned to each parent record. Any child records that are associated with a parent are "stamped" with the same unique identifier.

A How-To Guide for FoxPro Mac

Now that you're convinced you have a reason to use FoxPro Mac, you need to figure out where to start.

This section describes a few commands and concepts I refer to as the "hot hit list." You need to know these commands — or use a template that already has them—to write applications in FoxPro Mac.

You can execute practically all of these commands from the pulldown menu system and subsequent dialog sin interactive FoxPro for Macintosh. However, since you're going to be a developer now, you probably should become accustomed to entering them from the Command window.

I've given you the "lite" version of each command—streamlined here to give you a leg up on developing applications quickly. Keep in mind that practically every command has additional functionality in the form of additional keywords and clauses. Be sure to look in the Help file if one of these commands falls a little short of what you need it to do.

SET DEFAULT TO

```
SET DEFAULT TO [My hard disk:folder:other folder:]
```

Use the SET DEFAULT TO command to change your current working folder.

CLEAR

Without an argument, CLEAR erases the screen or the current output window and releases all pending GET statements.

In practice, you will find yourself assigning a keyboard macro with the commands:

```
CLEAR ALL
CLOSE ALL
CLEAR
```

to reset your environment as you begin developing with FoxPro. This is essentially the "wipe all this junk out and let me start over" sequence.

CREATE [<table name>]

```
CREATE myfile
```

Use this command to create a new table. A path and extension, such as `F:\PUBLIC\MYDIR\MYFILE.DBF` may be added to the command.

CREATE <table name> displays the structure dialog dn <file> into the current work area. It also closes any file that may have been opened in that work area previously. Attempting to create a new structure with an existing name causes FoxPro to issue overwrite warnings (see SET SAFETY).

QUIT

The QUIT command closes down FoxPro, shutting down all databases and open files automatically.

USE [<table name>]

```
USE myfile.dbf
```

This command opens a database table for use. You can add a path to the table name, such as `[PUBLIC:MYDIR:MYFILE.DBF]`.

USE <file> opens <file> into the current work area and closes any table that previously might have been opened. Entering USE without a file name closes any file that was previously open in that work area.

MODIFY STRUCTURE

```
MODIFY STRUCTURE
```

This command redisplays the table structure dialog for the current work area. If no table is in use in the current work area, FoxPro prompts for a .DBF to open.

APPEND [BLANK]

The APPEND command adds a record to the end of the table. The only time you use APPEND without the BLANK keyword is if you are working interactively from the Command window and want to add several records. Entering APPEND without the BLANK clause is exactly the same as responding "Yes" to the `Input Data Records Now?` prompt you get after you create a new structure. It is fairly uncommon to use APPEND without BLANK in programming.

There are also more efficient methods of adding data to tables. Doc and Lisa demonstrate the INSERT INTO command later in the book.

REPLACE [scope] <field1> WITH <expr1>, <field2> WITH <expr2> ...

```
REPLACE name WITH "Michael Burton",;
        city WITH "Tulsa",;
        state WITH 'OK'
REPLACE ALL totdue WITH balance - amtpaid
```

REPLACE updates database information by transferring information on the right side of the WITH clause into the field name on the left side. You can update multiple fields with a single REPLACE command, each field having its respective WITH statement in a comma-delimited list. In the REPLACE examples above, you see the semi-colon " ; " used to continue a statement across lines for clarity. The optional ALL statement causes the REPLACE to take effect across the entire database, as opposed to only the current record, REPLACE's default scope.

You can also use scopes such as NEXT 10 or REST on the REPLACE command. You can apply a FOR condition to limit the scope of a global REPLACE. For example:

```
REPLACE wordstate WITH "Arkansas" ;
        FOR state = 'AR'
```

? <expr>

```
? 23 + 14
* displays the number 37 in the
* current output device
```

The ? and ?? commands evaluate expressions and display the results. They have a horizontal positioning attribute (the AT clause) but no vertical positioning attribute. The ? command displays its results on successive lines, preceded by a carriage return and line feed, and the ?? command displays its results at the current position of the current line of the current output device. You often use these commands while working and debugging, or when you SET PRINT TO a file for character-based report or log of current program activity.

Math, Memory Variables, and Fields

FoxPro supports standard mathematics operators for most operations. They are:

+	Addition
-	Subtraction
*	Multiplication
/	Division
%	Modulus
^	Exponent

Values may be stored in fields or *memory variables*. Memory variables are temporary storage areas that live a maximum time period exactly equal to your current FoxPro session (they may be removed during a session if you so choose). You can use the = sign to transfer information into a memory variable. For example, the following equation places the value "FRED" into the memory variable tempname.

```
tempname = "FRED"
```

If you were to now type ? tempname, "FRED" would be displayed on the FoxPro output screen.

The = sign and STORE perform virtually identical functions with memory variables. The above equation could also be expressed like this:

```
STORE "FRED" to tempname
```

The STORE statement is useful in assigning a value to multiple variables simultaneously. The following statement assigns the value of 0 (zero) to four memory variables.

```
STORE 0 TO m.val1,m.val2,m.val3,m.val4
```

If you used the = sign, you would be forced to enter the following:

```
m.val1 = 0
m.val2 = 0
```

```
m.val3 = 0
m.val4 = 0
```

The = sign and STORE may not be used with fields to assign values; instead you'll probably use REPLACE or GATHER. The REPLACE command is the only direct method of altering a field value.

FoxPro (or Xbase in general) is not a strongly typed language. This means variables can be declared or created on-the-fly, or they can change data types suddenly. The following code won't produce any errors at compile or execution time.

```
m.charname = 'Flo'
m.charname = 123.498
m.charname = 'Bubba'
```

Follow these two basic memory variable rules to be on the road to better FoxPro programming:

- Refer to memory variables with an "m."
- Make sure that you use a consistent method of defining variables.

@ <row,column> GET/ SAY

```
@20, 15 SAY "Here is a sentence "
@10, 10 GET a_field
```

This syntax performs input and output at the specified row and column.

@GET/SAY is the heart of FoxPro interactive programming. You typically use the FoxPro Screen Builder to construct @GET/SAY code. You may, however, create your own screens by hand with this code. The best way to get a feel for @GET/SAY is to create some screens with the Screen Builder, Generate the code, and take a look at the completed code. @...GET's are made available for input when a READ statement is encountered. For example, you could enter this from the Command window:

```
m.value = 0
* create memvar with value zero
@2,1 GET m.value
READ
```

At this point a GET input box, showing the initial value of 0 and accepting values of numeric type, will become "live" onscreen for editing and remain so until the user presses a terminating key, such as Return, to leave the box. After the READ ends, m.value will contain whatever the user typed. If an actual field name had been used instead of a memory variable, the database record would be updated (without you having to use a REPLACE command) automatically.

ALIAS names and ALIAS() Work Area Names

By default, FoxPro always opens a table with an ALIAS name exactly the same as the file name. For example, typing the command `USE myfile` opens the file MYFILE with the alias name MYFILE. You may refer to a specific table by its ALIAS name. If you have two or more tables open with identical field names in each, it becomes important to identify specifically which table contains the field you are currently interested in. For example, if the tables OWNERS and PETS are both open and the field COMMENT was in both tables, you would address each like this:

```
@1,1     SAY pets.comment
@10,20   SAY owners.comment
```

It is generally a good idea to include ALIAS names in your coding efforts. Later on, the code is not only easier to read, but less likely to be subject to bugs.

ALIAS() is a built-in FoxPro function that returns the ALIAS name of the currently selected work area. For example, if the OWNERS table were open in the currently selected work area, the memory variable m.alias would be set equal to "OWNERS."

```
m.alias = ALIAS()
```

SELECT [area]

```
SELECT 1          && first area
USE myfile
SELECT 2          && second area
USE myfile2
```

SELECT [area] is used in multi-table programs to switch among different tables. You usually SELECT a table by its alias, which is the same as the file name by default. For example, after the above example had been executed you could enter the following code:

```
SELECT myfile     && select area one
SELECT myfile2    && select area two
```

This syntax allows the programmer to refer to areas with "real" names, rather than having to mentally keep track of what database is in what work area. Typically, a FoxPro programmer has no need to know in what area a table is open.

SELECT()

```
m.sele = SELECT()
```

SELECT() returns the currently selected area. You generally use it before SELECTing a table (using its alias), which may change the currently selected area. Later, after the procedure involving the specified table finishes, you issue the following:

```
SELECT (m.sele)
```

Now you've restored the work area you were in before the switch.

SELECT 0

```
SELECT 0
USE a_file
```

This syntax selects the lowest unused work area. This syntax is the typical way to open a table in FoxPro. You don't have to be aware of the actual work area number in which the table is open. From this point forward you refer to the table by its ALIAS name. This syntax works well when you need to work with the table you're opening immediately. If you just want to open the table in some work area without SELECTing it, for later use, use this alternative:

```
USE a_file IN 0.
```

SQL SELECT

```
SELECT *;
   FROM owners ;
   INTO CURSOR curbrow
```

The Structured Query Language SELECT command selects a result set of records or information drawn from records into a target format of your choice. You learn about this SELECT in Chapter 9. I mention it here to emphasize that although the word SELECT appears in this command as well as those commands referencing work areas, they have no connection.

INDEX ON

```
* This creates an IDX file
INDEX ON lastname TO lastname
* This creates a tag in the structural CDX
INDEX ON lastname TAG lastname
* This creates a tag in a non-structural CDX
INDEX ON lastname TAG lastname OF cdxfile
```

INDEX ON creates information outside the .DBF table that FoxPro uses to order the information in the table. The example above creates an "old-style" IDX file that contains information about just one order. FoxPro's "new-style" CDX (compound) index system is far superior to using IDXs for most purposes because CDXs are much easier to keep track of. The CDX file may be saved as any legal DOS file name, but will be opened automatically (as a *structural* CDX) only if it is the same name as its table. If you are using IDX files, be sure to include the keyword COMPACT (`Index on ... TO ... COMPACT`). The COMPACT keyword ensures maximum performance. CDX files are COMPACT by nature; you don't need the keyword.

SET ORDER TO TAG <tag name>

```
SET ORDER TO TAG state
```

This command orders the data in the table by one of the index expressions you've made available with the INDEX ON command. A table must be arranged in index order by the value you wish to locate if you are using the SEEK command or displaying ordered data. Other indexes remain open and are updated automatically regardless of the current order. The index to which you refer in the SET ORDER TO command must already be open—it is open automatically if you are using structural CDX indexes.

SEEK <value>

```
SEEK 1039
```

SEEK searches for a record by its index value in the current order. The example above would look for customer number 1039 in a table ordered by customer numbers.

FOUND()

```
* after a SEEK
IF FOUND()
    *...do some processing
ELSE
    *tell them you couldn't find it...
ENDIF
```

You use FOUND() following a SEEK to check the results. The SEEK() function can be used as a combination of the two, like this:

```
IF SEEK(1039)              && .T. implies it was FOUND()
*...do some processing
ELSE
*  couldn't find it...
ENDIF
```

DELETE [scope]

```
DELETE
*or
DELETE FOR STATE = "VT"
*or
DELETE ALL
```

In FoxPro, records are not automatically removed from the table when you issue the DELETE command. Rather, deletion flags, or marks the records for later removal using the command PACK. You can restore a deleted record to normal status by issuing the command RECALL. After a PACK, the record is truly gone and no longer RECALLable.

The default scope of DELETE is the current record (NEXT 1), but it can take any scope. DELETE ALL is similar to ZAP (later in this section), but you can still RECALL ALL or RECALL specific records by scope.

SET DELETED ON

Normally, the user expects deleted records to disappear. Because the FoxPro DELETE command doesn't remove records from the table, you use the SET DELETED ON command to have FoxPro ignore deleted records during normal operations. SET DELETED OFF makes these records visible again.

DELETED()

```
IF DELETED()
    *ask if the user wants to
    * recall the record...
ENDIF
```

The DELETED() function RETURNs .T. if the current record is deleted.

SKIP [n]

```
SKIP        && moves to next record
SKIP - 1    && moves to previous record
```

SKIP moves the record pointer in a table a number of records relative to the current position. The expression [n] may be any value, but it is most often nothing or negative. In this form, you often attach it to a "next and previous" pair of buttons or menu controls that are designed to allow the user to step through records.

GOTO [n]

```
GOTO 3
```

The GOTO command moves the record pointer to the record number you specify. The example above makes the third record *in the table's natural or physical order* the current record.

RECNO()

```
mrec = RECNO()
```

RECNO() tells you the record's position in the table's natural or physical order (the order the table has if you SET ORDER TO 0, or no index expression at all). You often use RECNO() as a placeholder while you're SEEKing another record. The following code sequence looks for a new record with the name "BILLY" as the value of its index expression. After an unsuccessful SEEK, the record pointer is positioned at EOF() (the *end of file*), so you want to go back to the record you were on originally.

```
m.rec = RECNO()
IF SEEK('BILLY')
      * code that does something with the new record...
ELSE
      GOTO m.rec     && back where we started
ENDIF
```

ORDER()

```
m.order = ORDER()
SET ORDER TO another
*processing in the new order
SET ORDER TO (m.order) && back to what we were...
```

In FoxPro, it is a good idea to design your software modules so that they "clean up after themselves." In the above example, you really don't care what the order was going into the sequence, as long as you know you return it to what it used to be when you're through with the present action.

EOF()

Check EOF() (end of file) to see if a filter condition has no matching records or a SEEK has failed; EOF() is the same as NOT FOUND() for a SEEK. Xbase loops to process records used to use the command `DO WHILE NOT EOF()... ENDDO`, accompanied by a SKIP within the loop, but this construct is commonly replaced by a `SCAN... ENDSCAN` in FoxPro.

Also check EOF() after a SKIP to make sure you haven't gone past the existing records in the table. Check BOF() (beginning of file) after a SKIP -1. If you filter a table's records with SET FILTER and then issue the GO BOTTOM command (described below), or if the table is empty, BOF() and EOF() are both .T.

GO TOP / GO BOTTOM

These commands move the record pointer to the top and bottom of the table, respectively, according to its currently indexed order.

BROWSE [FIELDS] [NORMAL][LAST] [NOMODIFY][NODELETE][NOAPPEND][FOR]

```
BROWSE NORMAL NOMODIFY NODELETE;
    NOAPPEND FOR state = 'TX'
```

This command displays records in a BROWSE window, a format similar to a spreadsheet, in which the records show as rows and the fields show as columns. The above example would display all states that equal “TX” in the currently selected table. The FOR clause is optional and may contain more complex expressions. NORMAL ensures that the browse window will take on system window attributes, and NOMODIFY prevents the user from altering information. Typically, a browse option like this is used to present a list of possible matches to a search condition.

The BROWSE command is one of the most powerful in FoxPro and has a great many more keyword options available. Using the FIELDS keyword allows you to specify a list of fields, which might include fields from related tables or calculated expressions.

The FOR clause

```
COUNT FOR state = "TX" TO m.val
```

The FOR clause is a potentially (usually) optimizable method of focusing in on a particular set of information within your table(s). It limits the scope of a command’s action. The above example counts all records matching the condition and stores the result in m.val.

SUM [field] FOR [expL] TO <memvar> CALCULATE <expression list> TO <memvar list>

```
SUM paidamt FOR state = "TX" TO m.sum
```

The SUM command totals the contents of a field using any scope you give it, referencing any filtering conditions you set. If you don’t use a scope, SUM defaults to ALL records.

Often, you have to do several sums or other operations on the same scope of records. In that case, avoid doing several passes through the table by using the CALCULATE command to do the operations at the same time, like this:

```
CALCULATE ;
    SUM(paidamt) , AVG(balance), MAX(invtotal) ;
    FOR <conditions> ;
    TO m.sum_paid, m.avg_bal, m.max_inv
```

PACK

PACK physically removes records marked for deletion in a database file. There is no way to retrieve deleted records after the PACK is finished.

ZAP

ZAP deletes all records in the current work area. ZAP is functionally equivalent to DELETE ALL followed by PACK, but it is much faster. Records deleted by ZAP are not RECALLable. They are immediately gone forever. Be sensitive to the setting of SET SAFETY (see below) when using ZAP.

SET commands and the SET() function

Use SET commands to tailor the FoxPro environment. The following are some typical settings that I use during the development phase. You can turn them on and off through a program to achieve a particular effect.

```
SET BELL OFF
```

This disables the beep as each GET field is completed. It's very annoying otherwise.

Even though the automatic bell is turned off, you can still ring the BELL by issuing the following code:

```
?? CHR(7)
```

BELL can be SET TO a frequency and duration as well as OFF and ON. In FoxPro for Macintosh, instead of a frequency, you can supply the name of one of the standard system sounds, as shown in this example. Although you still supply a number as the second parameter of the command, it has no effect on the sound.

```
SET BELL TO "Quack",3
```

```
SET CONFIRM OFF
```

If CONFIRM is on, the user must press ENTER to exit each GET field, even if the number of characters typed match the number expected, i.e. 72201 in a zip code field.

```
SET SAFETY OFF
```

The setting of SAFETY controls the "overwrite" checks FoxPro gives you during various operations. During development, as well as when your application runs, you may want to remove those annoying alert dialogs which look like error messages. If your programs are handling overwrite confirmation, you don't need FoxPro to ask for you again. SETting SAFETY OFF does mean, however, that you are working without a net, so be careful!

```
SET TALK OFF
```

TALK is one of those settings you will use both ways. Having TALK on means the result of every command you execute will be echoed to the current output window, which will slow performance and clutter up the screen. In almost all cases your programs should SET TALK OFF. You may, however, use SET TALK ON to watch results as you are debugging.

You can retrieve many of the environmental SETtings by using the View window interactively. To see them all, issue the command DISPLAY STATUS. In a program, find the ON or OFF value of a SETting by using the return value of `SET("the setting")`. With a second argument of 1, the SET() function gives you settings that are more diverse than ON or OFF, for example the name of a file TO which HELP is SET:

```
? SET("HELP")
* displays ON or OFF
? SET("HELP",1)
* displays the name of the current help file
```

SET FILTER TO <expL>

```
SET FILTER TO state = 'TX'
```

This command limits the scope of records to those that match the condition. Subsequent commands, such as BROWSE, will respect that condition. When you issue the SET FILTER command, you need to *activate* the filter by moving the record pointer, in case the current record is not part of the filtered set, before the filter is respected by your next command. BROWSE is an exception to this rule; it activates the filter automatically.

TRIM(<expC>) and variants

```
? TRIM(contact.lastname)+', '+ ;
            TRIM(contact.firstname)
```

Because FoxPro has fixed-length fields, character data is always padded out to the right with spaces up to the structure definition of field width. To produce the result "Jones, Barney," you have to remove the trailing spaces using the TRIM() function or the identical RTRIM(). If you only want to remove leading spaces, use LTRIM(). ALLTRIM() is the version you'll find you need most often; it removes both leading and trailing spaces.

Nothing Is for Free

If you're coming from a program like FileMaker Pro, it will seem like you have to write code for everything! The method for application development that we outline in this book helps to minimize the work; however, you'll discover there's a lot of work to be done.

So why should you fool with FoxPro? *Simply because it is the only Macintosh database that can deliver results very quickly from large record sets.*

Beyond that reason, however, once you get used to writing FoxPro code, you'll find that you can duplicate the features of any other database management program with a little effort.

One of the basic functions I like in FileMaker is the Query by Form mode. You lay out your screen design, and then choose the Find option. Suddenly, your data entry screen becomes a Query screen.

I wanted to re-create this capability in FoxPro, so I wrote the example SEARCH.PRG that you find on the source disk. I'm not going to try to describe all the functions and concepts it uses in this Quick Start chapter; rather I'm going to show you how you use it.

See Also

- Source Disk: Miscellaneous Code Samples: SEARCH.PRG

To use the search function I've provided for you with any table, follow these steps:

1. USE the_table.
2. MODIFY SCREEN <name>, where <name> is what you'll be calling it when you search. Call it something like "CompFind".

3. Go to Quick Screen on the Screen menu.
4. Click on Memory Variables (see figure 3.3).

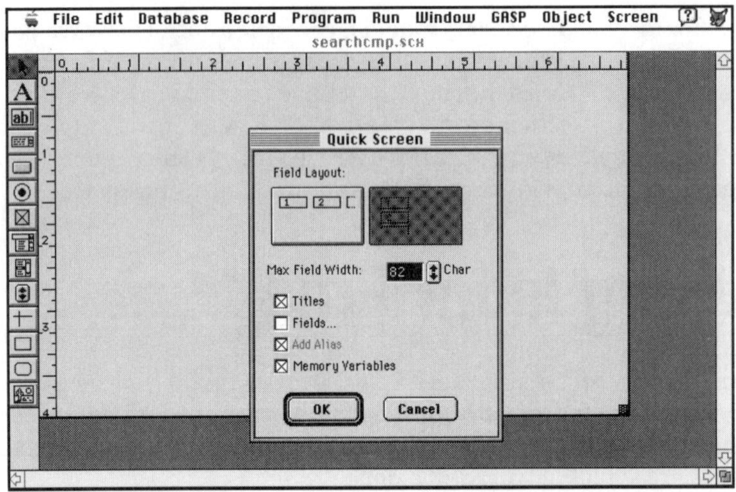

Figure 3.3. *Create a Quick Screen to test the Search function.*

5. Then press OK. I'm using the Company DBF that's part of the sample data set on the source disk so that my screen looks like figure 3.4.
6. Now delete any fields that you don't want to be part of the query.
7. Add a push button with a prompt that says *Search* or *Locate*. Name the memory variable `m.sbutton` or whatever you wish. In the Valid Clause of this button add the following single line of code:

   =search("key")

8. In this line, replace "key" with the name of the unique identifier field in your table (it's really Key for COMPANY.DBF). Note that this key field MUST have a tag built on it for the search program to work. If your unique identifier or key field in another table was "Acct_num," then use the following instead:

```
=search("acct_num")
```

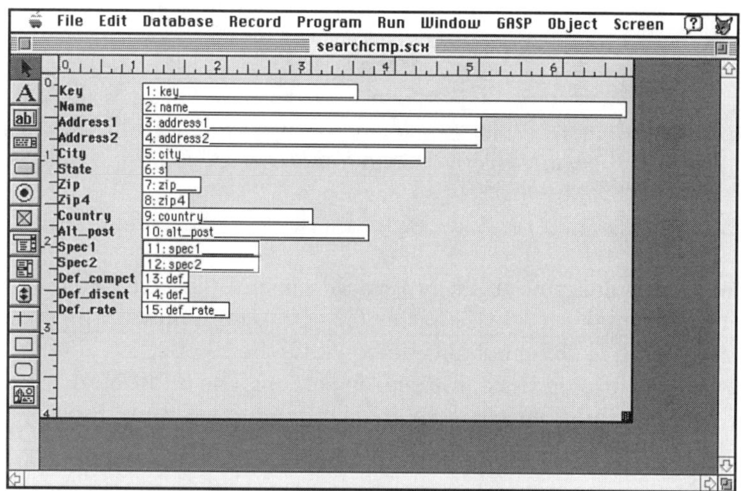

Figure 3.4 *The Company table Quick Screen.*

9. Go to the Screen Layout and add this line of code in the screen setup code:

```
SCATTER MEMO MEMVAR BLANK
```

10. Use the Program menu's Generate option to Generate this screen with the default name of COMPFIND.SPR (or whatever you called your screen, plus an .SPR extension). If you prefer, modify the layout further before you Generate. Make sure that FoxPro knows where to find SEARCH.prg; if nothing else, copy it into the same folder in which the freshly generated SPR is located. Now you can execute the new "compfind" screen by typing:

```
DO compfind.spr
```

11. Type as much or as little into as many or few of the fields as you like. You'll find the system tells you how many matches there were. If there was more than a single match, a browse window displaying all matches is presented.

12. From a data entry screen, you would probably attach this routine to a button on the control panel and add the code SHOW GETS to update your current data. An example would be:

```
DO compfind.spr
SHOW GETS
```

> **FOXPRO MAC HACK TIP**
>
> The SEARCH.prg looks for tags on the UPPER() versions of character expressions to provide case-insensitive search capabilities. If you do a query and results aren't snappy, make sure you have tags built properly on the table you chose.

The above steps describe the way I would normally use this function in an application. To make it a little easier for you to get started, the screen on the source disk has some extra code beneath the SEARCH() line that displays the results on the same search screen. The additional "Clear Search" button wipes out the screen for immediate re-searching.

You can copy and paste these buttons into a quick screen of your own design. Remember to make your fields onscreen Memory Variables or it won't work. Later, if you want the screen to automatically go away after you press Search, check the Terminate Read option on the Search button.

Chapter Wrap Up

Looking at all the effort you have to go through to create something FileMaker Pro does with a button, you might wonder why you would want to change. The answer is simple, really. Run up some data to 200,000 records in both products, and issue a query against a single table for something like *All sales greater than $20,000 and invoice date between January 1, 1994 and January 15, 1994*. This query represents a very common business need.

I don't want to provide any official-sounding benchmarks, but it won't take a stopwatch for you to measure the difference. FoxPro will give you those answers back in a couple of seconds or less. FileMaker Pro will return that result in minutes—several of 'em.

Spend the extra time it takes to get familiar with FoxPro and relational database management systems.

PART II

PLAN FOR RAPID DEVELOPMENT: FOXPRO POWER TOOL DESIGN

In Part I, you received information about the aspects of FoxPro that were necessarily new and possibly uncomfortable. Now, in Part II, you delve into a subject you may know well—the design of a database application. You have a single objective—to discover an efficient and practical way to do this job in FoxPro for Macintosh.

FoxPro often has many commands and functions that you can use to accomplish any specific task. The FoxPro development environment sometimes offers competing dialogs and tools that offer different routes to the same end. Even experienced FoxPro developers often try several approaches before settling on an optimal combination of features and syntax.

Experimenting with FoxPro capabilities is definitely not a waste of effort. But when you're trying to deliver an application, you don't always have the luxury of R&D time.

The four authors of this book present you with the *conclusions* of our own R&D, so that you can develop applications rapidly in FoxPro. We acknowledge, up-front, that our ways are not the only ways to work in FoxPro, but we won't get sidetracked in describing the FoxPro approaches we investigated and discarded.

We're breaking the job of implementing an application into discrete tasks and presenting the FoxPro tools responsible for managing each task. Where FoxPro falls short of an ideal rapid application development environment, we suggest—and provide—additional tools.

Chapter 4 is a quick overview of a rapid application development path using the various sample applications that ship with FoxPro for Macintosh to point out the path's components. You are introduced to the template code that we provide to coordinate these components.

In Chapter 5, you'll investigate the template code so that you can adjust it for your own style of work and establish it as a solid foundation for your applications. Beginning in Chapter 6, Part II applies this foundation and our design principles to a real-life business model: a job-tracking application for an advertising agency.

Let's get started!

MEET THE FOXPRO POWER SYSTEM

by Lisa Slater

The requirements of a database management application don't vary much from application to application. They don't even change from platform to platform or language to language. When people ask you to write a program to manage data, they are interested in one or more of the following tasks:

- Acquiring information of material interest to them, through direct methods (data entry) and indirect means (data import)
- Organizing information so they can assimilate and use it easily
- Processing information so they get answers they need in formats they can understand, and which they can communicate to other people
- Storing information so they can use it again

In Xbase you accomplish the last task, storing information, by using a .DBF or table format. You may interpret data stored in other formats, but the .DBF is still the basic structure that Xbase uses to do its own work.

The .DBF structure mandates the way Xbase handles all the other data management tasks; "acquiring information" means getting data into tables, "organizing information" means ordering and relating tables, and "processing information" means querying tables and displaying the result.

Because the table structure doesn't change from one application to another, the Xbase methods your FoxPro applications use to handle all these table management tasks don't change from one application to another. You don't have to return to first principles every time you sit down to start a new application.

You shouldn't have to write the same program over and over again, either. Instead, you can isolate the common tasks that every program must accomplish, decide how the .DBF structure accommodates each task, and identify the methods that you use to manage the task. You can write a module or limited procedure that handles each task, literally codifying your standard methods and thoroughly debugging each one. You build these modules into every application.

With all this work done before you even start developing a specific application, you are left with a lot of free time, right? Not really. The *surface* of the application varies enormously from one application to the next. This surface includes the methods you use for presenting data, the opportunities you provide the user to manipulate data, and the integration of computerized data with the user's life or business.

I deliberately say the "surface" of an application varies rather than using the word "interface." The application's interface consists of such elements as window attributes, editing keystrokes, the behavior of control objects, even the style of language you use in dialogs. Esecially on the Macintosh, as you know, the application interface should be standard and consistent. You should work out an application interface that makes sense to you and that conforms to what your users expect from their use of other applications. You maintain that interface throughout your work, just as you write file management code and reuse it repeatedly.

By contrast, you *custom-tailor the surface of the application* for an individual user and the needs of the task at hand by closely following the way the user handles the application's data when he or she steps away from the computer. Here are just a few of the criteria you can use to evaluate your progress in tailoring the application surface appropriately:

- The data should change intelligently (without user intervention) in response to conditions and business rules that reflect the user's own decision-making process.
- The vocabulary the user employs to speak about his or her tasks should dominate the program's communications about the data.

- The physical layout of data onscreen and in reports should accurately match the user's manual forms and vision of his or her information.
- The tasks of the application should follow each other in the same sequence that the user would choose if he or she were doing them manually, completely uninfluenced by the needs of the program.

You should spend a lot of time and hard work *listening* to users and then properly design a system to meet those requirements based on what these users teach you.

The good news is that you have the time and attention to pursue these goals when you don't waste energy re-creating standard file-management techniques for every application. The even better news is that FoxPro provides tools designed to pursue these goals, and FoxPro smoothly integrates the results of your tailored design work with your standard modules.

In this chapter, you take a quick look at the FoxPro tools that speed your design process and investigate a standard framework on which you can support the results of your design.

Discover the Sequence of a Rapid Development System

The secret to rapid development, as you've probably already concluded, is to appropriately divide the work of an application into generic and application-specific elements so that you spend time on the right parts of your job.

You provide the generic elements from libraries that you collect. Some elements are the standard modules that you write yourself, and others are tools that you integrate or adapt from the work of other developers.

Then you quickly "sketch" the application-specific elements as you learn about them from your users. Using FoxPro's graphical design tools, you provide a layout of the finished application.

The tools' underlying code generators create a quick, visually-correct prototype that you can use to corroborate your design strategy with users.

When you're sure you've understood users' needs correctly, you attach programs to process the special needs of this application's data to your generic file management code.

Tour a FoxPro Project

The FoxPro Project Manager is the tool that keeps track of an application's various elements throughout the process I've just described. To get a feel for the elements of a FoxPro application and the Project Manager's role in controlling them, look at some of the sample projects that you installed along with the base product.

To pick a project file, use the File menu's Open dialog (shortcut ⌘-O), or type `MODIFY PROJECT ?` in the Command window, followed by (Return), to execute the command. If you used the menu option or its shortcut, choose files of Type Project from the pop-up menu at the bottom of the dialog, as shown in figure 4.1.

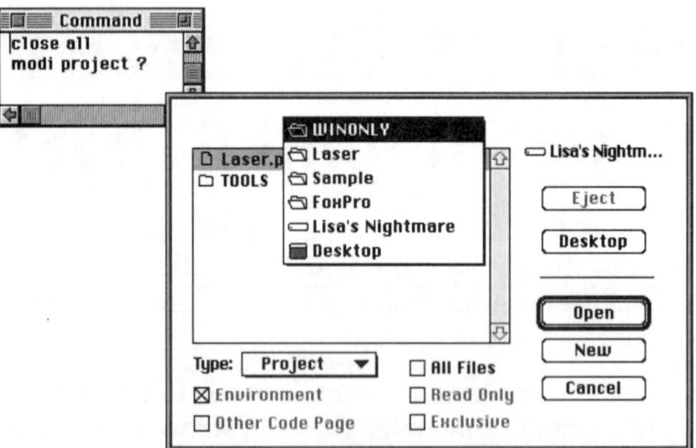

Figure 4.1 *Pick the WINONLY version of the Laser project from the sample files.*

I'm using the WINONLY folder's version of the LASER.PJX project file to give you a quick tour of project features. (You can see its full path in figure 4.1.) You can investigate any of the sample projects to follow along.

Assigning a Project Home Folder

When you select a project, you probably will see the alert dialog shown in figure 4.2. A project file keeps track of the application's components using file names, relative to the project's *home folder*, the location of the project file. Because the developer who worked on this project has a different volume and folder structure from the one on your disk, the Project Manager has to adjust its file references.

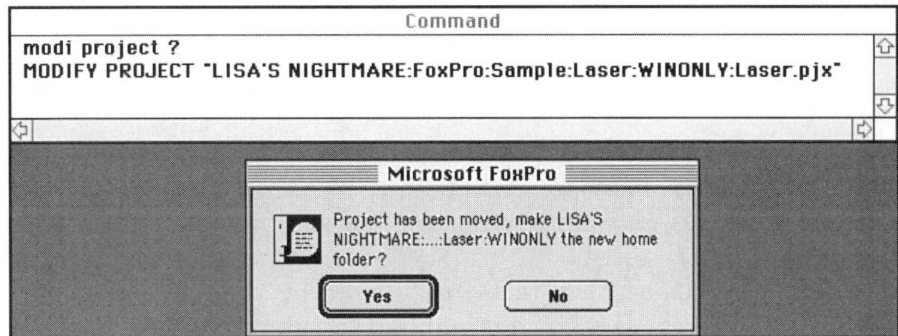

Figure 4.2 *When you move a project, the Project Manager adjusts the project's Home Folder.*

Most people keep different elements of projects (screens, menus, and so on) in separate folders. However, if these locations remain in the same relative path to the main folder (for example, if they remain in folders with the same names nested within the project folder), the Project Manager can resolve references without difficulty.

You may work on projects with different people who have different volume names or different folder structures. You can use the SET VOLUME command to create a uniform home folder reference for everyone, even if you work on different FoxPro platforms.

FOXPRO MAC HACK TIP

Ordinarily, you should keep VOLUME settings stable during a single FoxPro session to avoid confusing any developers' tools that rely on path information, as well as the system variables holding the locations of _GENSCRN and other FoxPro components.

See Also

- "Volume Name Translation," Chapter 1

> However, if you get the yen to *change* the name of a volume or folder while FoxPro is loaded—as Mac developers are wont to do—change SET VOLUME to match FoxPro's new path. FoxPro then finds all of its components correctly.
>
> For example, if I have the setting VOLUME C = `"Lisa's Nightmare:"` in my CONFIG.FPM, _GENSCRN might hold the value "C:\FOXPRO\GENSCRN.FXP". I click on the label for this volume's icon and change it to read "Boring Internal Drive Name". The next time I try to work with screen files, I get the error message that FoxPro can't find GENSCRN. I set volume C to `"Boring Internal Drive Name:"`, and I'm in business.

Choose to adjust the home folder, and you see the Project Manager main dialog, as shown in figure 4.3. This dialog is a container for the application's components. Use the scroll bar on the file list to scroll down until you see the item marked with a bullet. In the WINONLY:LASER project, this file is the Laser Screen Set; the marked item may be a different type of program in the project you have opened. However, every product has *one* file marked in this manner to indicate the project's *main* program.

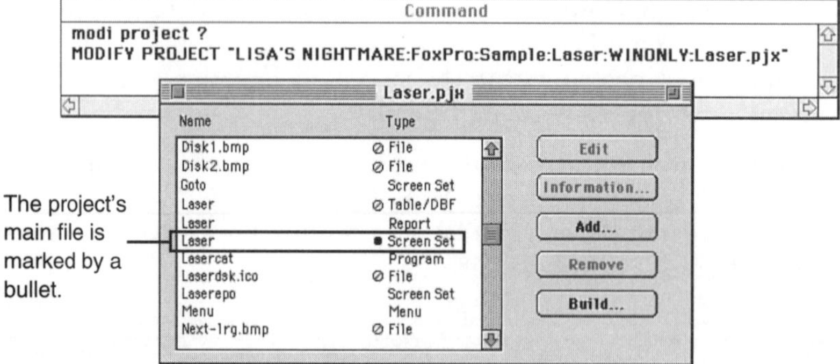

Figure 4.3 *The main Project Manager dialog shows the Laser project's main file (a screen set) and additional application components.*

The Project Manager builds the list of project resources—menu and screen definitions, queries, reports, utility programs, graphics, and other resources—by reading the program you designate as the main file. As the Project Manager discovers references to other programs and application elements, it adds items to the project list. It reads the new files to find more references to still other application elements.

If it can't find a file required by one of your programs, the Project Manager asks you to resolve the reference by locating the file in another folder. When you provide one reference to another folder, the Project Manager will know enough to check that folder for additional unresolved references as it continues its search.

Editing the Project Components and Building the Application

After you have a list of application elements in a project, you can use the Project Manager container to call FoxPro's various tools to edit these files. Try double-clicking different items on the list or highlighting them and pressing the Edit button. If the item is a Program, the FoxPro Editor will open; if it is a Menu, you'll get the Menu Builder; if it is a Table/DBF, the Project Manager USEs the table and opens a BROWSE window.

If you pick an item that requires changes when it moves among platforms, a Screen, or a Report, the appropriate editing tool (the Screen Builder or Report Writer) checks to see if this is the first time the file was edited on this platform. It also checks the item's definitions for *timestamps*, showing that this file was edited on another platform more recently than its editing sessions on this platform. If the editing tool discovers either of these conditions, it calls a program known as the Transporter to ask you to decide on cross-platform adjustments before opening the file for editing.

CROSS-PLATFORM WARNING

FoxPro DOS developers may wonder why I talk about screen and report definitions without mentioning labels. In FoxPro for Macintosh and FoxPro for Windows, there is no separate Label Designer tool; the Report Writer has label capabilities built in.

You still can use the commands CREATE and MODIFY LABEL, and subtle differences exist between the default layout if you choose to create a new label rather than a report. However, .FRX and .LBX tables, the definition files for reports and labels, have identical structures. There is only one layout tool to edit both formats, and the LABEL FORM and REPORT FORM commands call the same output engine.

Figure 4.4 shows the Laser project with several types of files open in editing windows. The Transporter dialog is ready to import a report file from its FoxPro for Windows version. (You see a slightly different dialog if the report has been edited under Windows but already includes a Macintosh definition.)

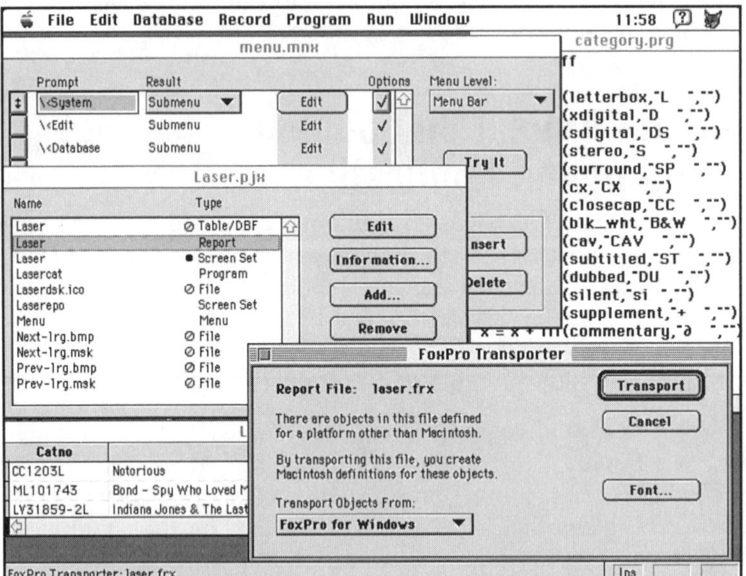

Figure 4.4 *The Project Manager provides access to FoxPro's editing facilities for different file types. The Transporter intervenes if you select a report or screen created or edited on another FoxPro platform.*

Press the Build button in the Project Manager dialog, and you'll see the modal dialog in figure 4.5. This dialog doesn't look like much, but one of the commands it invokes, BUILD APPLICATION, is the nerve center of FoxPro development. Select the Build Application button, as shown in the figure, and then press OK. After asking for a destination for its resulting .APP file (see figure 4.6), the Project Manager proceeds to generate programs from the project's menu and screen definition tables, compile both the generated and standard programs on the list, and meld the compiled versions together with all the other components specified in the project list into a single, runnable .APP file.

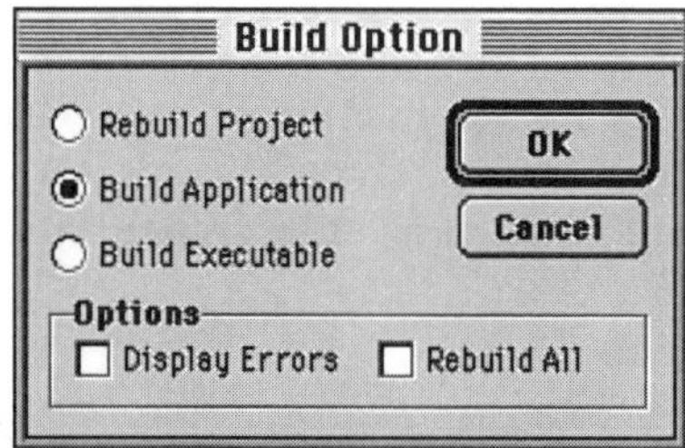

Figure 4.5 *The Project Manager's Build Option dialog.*

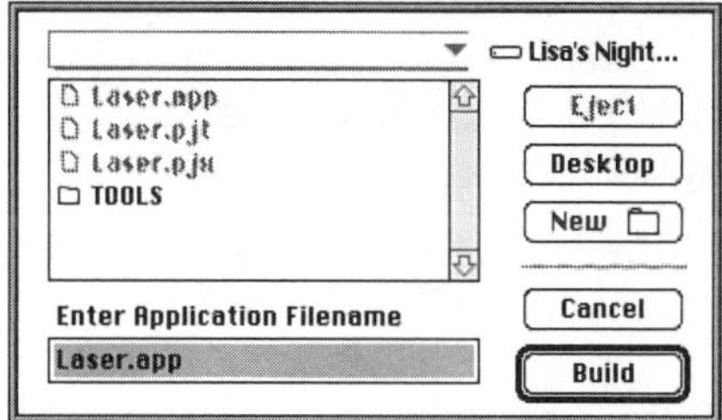

Figure 4.6 *The Project Manager's result is a compiled .APP (application) file.*

You probably noticed the check box to select Rebuild All from the Project Manager's Build options. Although you didn't use it, you still see all the generated elements of the project (screens and menus) re-created during the Build Application process. The Project Manager does a Build All whenever you move the project to a new home folder or directory, one reason to use a consistent SET VOLUME convention with your co-workers.

Handling Cross-Platform Project Elements

Although the various screens and menus are regenerated during a Build All, they don't receive new Macintosh definitions automatically when they are regenerated. No item in the project is Transported *until you choose that item for a direct edit.*

See Also

- "Adapting to FoxPro for Macintosh," Chapter 1
- "Cross Platform Usability and Thoughtful Design," Chapter 11

FOXPRO MAC HACK TIP

Project elements that remain untransported (or *unmodified*, as the documentation terms it) will run successfully in the Macintosh environment if they don't use DOS- or Windows-specific capabilities. (For example, the RUN command, which shells to DOS, generates a `feature not available` error in FoxPro for Macintosh.)

You can move an entire compiled .APP file from FoxPro for Windows or DOS and run it immediately in FoxPro for Macintosh. The Mac product tries to map fonts and positions from the Windows platform and creates equivalent objects for DOS GET controls using a special DOS-style FoxFont. The Mac product even calls the DOS Report Writer engine to run REPORT FORM commands on DOS-only .FRX tables.

The ability to use project elements without Transport is a boon to developers of large projects. You can attend to the screens and reports in your project individually, gradually, while the full application still runs. However, in most cases you want to Transport each element as soon as possible for Mac-like appearance and behavior. Figure 4.7 shows you an unmodified LASER.APP from the DOSONLY folder, running in FoxPro for Macintosh. If you investigate the LASER.APP from the WINONLY folder, it will *look* much better, but there will still be a few features of the .APP that won't function properly in the Mac environment.

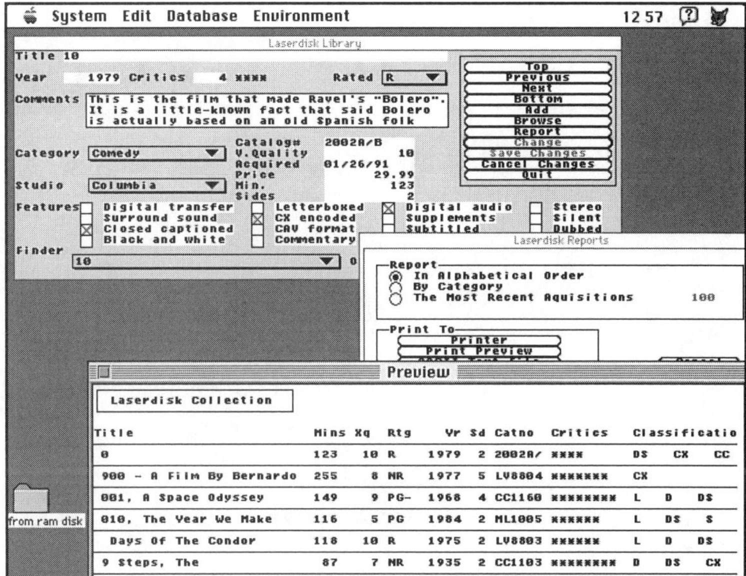

Figure 4.7 *An unmodified DOS .APP running in FoxPro for Macintosh.*

Using a Generic Dialog

Using either the Program menu's Do option (shortcut Option-D) or the Run menu's Application dialog, execute any LASER.APP file. Figure 4.8 shows the WINONLY LASER.APP running with its Project dialog still showing onscreen. I've pressed the Browse button on the Laser screen, bringing up the generic Browser modal dialog designed to set filter conditions on open tables in a database.

Experiment with this dialog and its counterparts in the other sample FoxPro for Macintosh applications. You find BROWSER.SCX objects in the ORGANIZE and FNDATION screen folders, as well as each of the LASER project file groups.

When you're satisfied that you understand the purpose of this screen, edit BROWSER in any of the sample projects. Double-click on Browser in the main project dialog and then choose to Edit the Browser screen in the Edit Screen Set dialog that appears next.

Figure 4.8 *The Windows version of LASER.APP, showing the generic Browser dialog.*

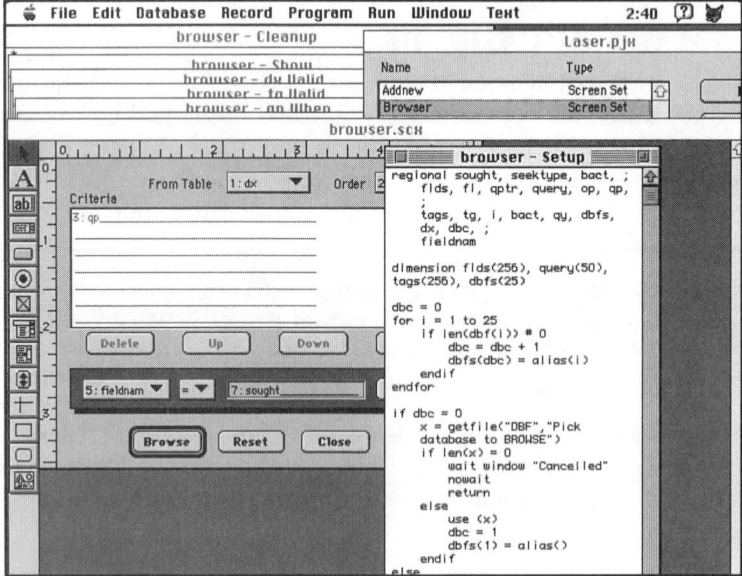

Figure 4.9 *Examine the BROWSER.SCX Setup code.*

You can look at BROWSER's code by choosing the Screen menu's Show All Snippet's option (shortcut Option+N). Choose the Setup snippet window from the cascading editing windows that open (use the Window menu list to find the Setup snippet). Depending on which BROWSER you open, the screen layout may look a little different from figure 4.9, but in each Setup window you'll find code that looks like this:

```
* code extracted from Setup snippet,
* BROWSER.SCX, FPMac sample files
dimension flds(256), query(50), ;
tags(256), dbfs(25)

dbc = 0
for i = 1 to 25
    if len(dbf(i)) # 0
       dbc = dbc + 1
       dbfs(dbc) = alias(i)
    endif
endfor
```

This code doesn't reference any tables directly. Instead, it checks the environment for open tables, saving their aliases into an array for later use. The dialog's designer wrote the code generically to support whatever tables it found in its environment into which a developer incorporated the BROWSER feature.

This code is also incorrect. The designer wrote BROWSER before FoxPro 2.5. You can tell by looking at the line `for i = 1 to 25`, which indicates that BROWSER looks at the contents of only 25 work areas out of the 225 available to FoxPro for Macintosh. FoxPro for DOS Standard edition has only 25 work areas, even in versions 2.5 and above, but code like this should be adjusted to accommodate *all* available environments, not just the lowest common denominator. Even when an application has fewer than 25 work areas in use, they are often not the lowest 25 in FoxPro for Windows, FoxPro for DOS Extended, and FoxPro for Macintosh. FoxPro developers have learned to open tables without regard for the number of the work area. They refer to tables by alias instead of number at all times because they know that SQL SELECT commands may commandeer work areas indiscriminately when they run queries.

In other respects, BROWSER is an admirable example of a generic dialog: independent of its environment and serving many different databases. In fact, I like it so much that I adapted it to provide filtering conditions for other purposes, rather than always resulting in a BROWSE, as you'll see in the next section. You can often incorporate such a dialog into your own applications without understanding all of its supporting code. As this example also shows, however, writing generic code means taking more considerations into account than writing a simple application-specific dialog over whose environment you have complete control. When possible, you *shouldn't* trust the code without checking it against your environment and standards.

The sample projects' *use* of BROWSER doesn't teach you much about managing FoxPro projects for rapid development. Each project maintains its own copy of BROWSER, and each BROWSER is subtly different. If I correct the work areas error in the ORGANIZE copy, the LASER copies are still wrong.

To see the way to incorporate generic elements such as BROWSER into your development projects for efficient use, you need to leave the sample files installed with FoxPro and look at the sample files for this book.

Growing a FoxPro Project from Seed

If you haven't installed the sample files for this book yet, now is the time. Copy the source disk files to a new folder on your hard disk and expand the self-extracting archive you find included there.

Now create a new folder. It doesn't matter where you put it on your disk in relation to the Source Code folder, or whatever you call it; you won't use this new folder again after this chapter.

To get into the Files Selection panel, use the View Window option you find on the Window menu and click the third button on its left border. Use the Working Folder button to set your FoxPro *default* folder to the folder that you just created. Alternatively, execute the command `SET DEFAULT TO (GETDIR())` in the Command window. (You can see both methods in figure 4.10.)

Now you can create a new project with this folder serving as the project home folder. Choose the File menu's New option to start a new project, bringing up an Untitled (empty) project list. Click on the Add button, and the Project Manager asks you for the name of the file you want to add. If the pop-up menu at the bottom of the dialog doesn't already suggest files of Program type, change it to read Program. Then navigate to the folder in which you stored the source code for this book. You should find a nested folder labeled Library/Template Code. Within this folder you'll find a MAIN.PRG (see figure 4.11). Double-click on the file name, and you'll return to the Project Manager with the Main program added and marked with the bullet indicating that this file is the top-level program for this project.

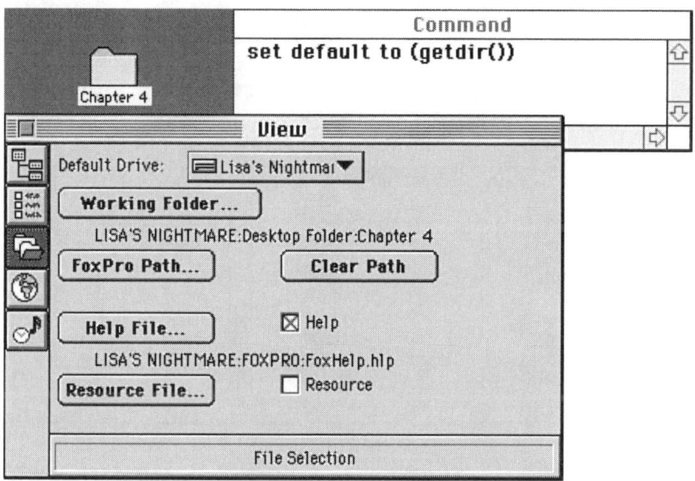

Figure 4.10 *Set your default, or working, folder to your project's home folder.*

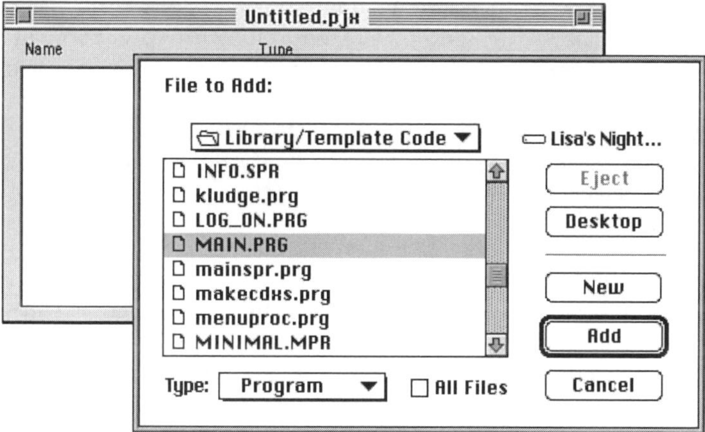

Figure 4.11 *Start building your project with a MAIN.PRG from the library code provided with the book source code files.*

That's it. Now use the Build dialog to Build Application, providing the project with any name you like for your new project and .APP file, and watch what happens. You should see the Project Manager pull a variety of programs automatically into the project (and the resulting .APP file) as shown in figure 4.12.

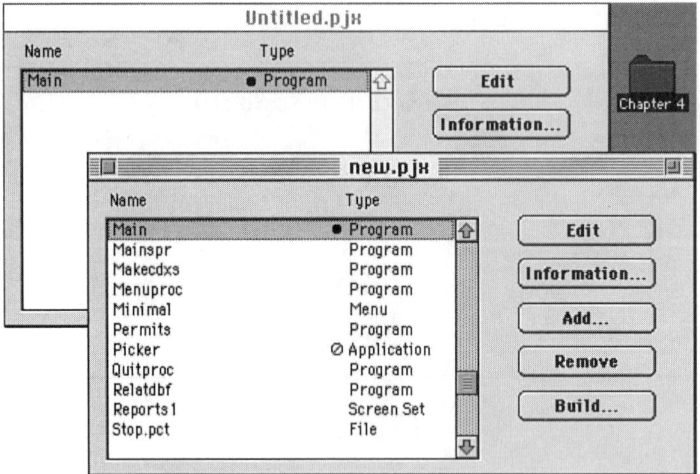

Figure 4.12 *The seeded application, before and after a Project Manager Build procedure.*

Your project has been seeded with generic objects and procedures, but none of these files exist in the new folder that holds your .PJX file. They are all template files which can be shared among *all* your applications. The Project Manager knew they were necessary for the project because they are referenced by MAIN.PRG, and it could find them because all the files were in the same location as MAIN.PRG. (If you keep your template code in a separate folder for separate kinds of files, you need to Locate each separate location once for the Project Manager the first time you Build.)

You will investigate MAIN.PRG in the next chapter to see how it organizes the application's tasks. For now, you only need to know that this program represents the code that *never changes* in any of my projects. The Library/Template Code folder also has separate programs that provide defaults for procedures that *usually* are the same. Because they're not built into MAIN.PRG, I can override these procedures with application-specific versions when necessary using the project's home folder or another location of my choice.

> **FOXPRO MAC HACK TIP**
>
> You can use the Macintosh Labels feature to color-code generic project elements and clearly distinguish the application-specific objects belonging to different projects. Although the Label colors won't show up in the FoxPro dialogs, the colors will prevent you from confusing default procedures with application-specific override versions with the same names. You'll also be able to recognize your template objects at a glance when you're backing up or double-clicking on objects to edit them directly from the Finder.

In a moment, you will see that generic procedures can handle quite a number of prosaic tasks without you giving them any more thought than you took to build this application. First, however, there's one bit of editing you may want to do to personalize this application.

Double-click on the Include Program you see in the new project's file list. This program ordinarily exists in your project's home folder because it is specifically designed to add the *non-generic* aspects of each individual application to your generic code. Using the Edit Find menu option (shortcut Option-F) to look for **LCS**, find the lines that store the developer- and application-specific strings. You can see them in figure 4.13.

Replace the m.developer variable's value with your own name, the m.dev_id with any three-letter code you like, and the m.app_title value with the name that you want to give this application.

Now re-Build the Application. Use the Build dialog from the Project Manager again or (as I prefer) type `BUILD APP <application name> FROM <project name>` in the Command window. Either way you initiate the Build process, you should find that it goes very quickly this time because the Project Manager checks the references for all the files except INCLUDE.PRG and finds that you haven't edited any of them. Nothing else has to be regenerated or recompiled.

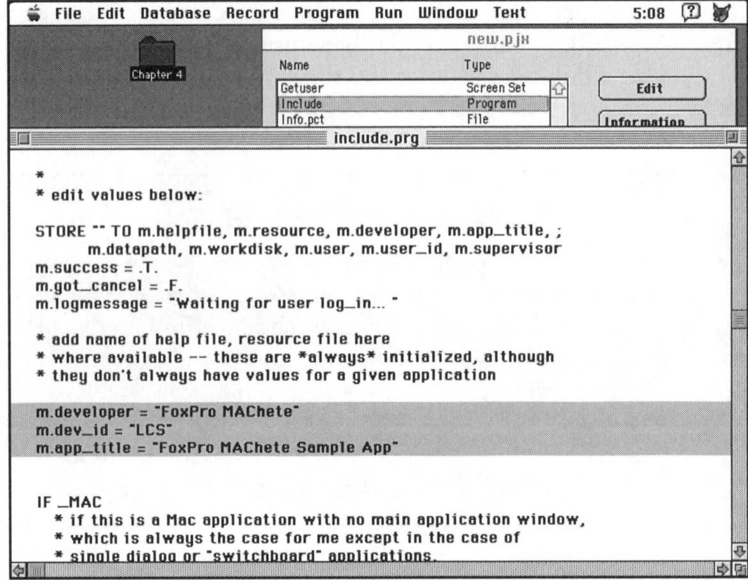

File Edit Database Record Program Run Window Text 5:08
new.pjx
Chapter 4
Name Type
Getuser Screen Set
Include Program
Info.pct File
Edit
Information
include.prg
*
* edit values below:
STORE "" TO m.helpfile, m.resource, m.developer, m.app_title, ;
m.datapath, m.workdisk, m.user, m.user_id, m.supervisor
m.success = .T.
m.got_cancel = .F.
m.logmessage = "Waiting for user log_in... "
* add name of help file, resource file here
* where available -- these are *always* initialized, although
* they don't always have values for a given application
m.developer = "FoxPro MAChete"
m.dev_id = "LCS"
m.app_title = "FoxPro MAChete Sample App"
IF _MAC
* if this is a Mac application with no main application window,
* which is always the case for me except in the case of
* single dialog or "switchboard" applications.

Figure 4.13 *Edit the application-specific INCLUDE.PRG quickly for your first change to the seeded project.*

Execute the application using Program Do, the Run menu option to start an Application, or the DO <app name> command in the Command window. You'll first see a request for a data folder, as shown in figure 4.14. This requirement doesn't mean very much right now because this application has no data; you can just select any folder. I'll show you how to avoid this dialog when you have a real application with no data, as happens occasionally. However, ordinarily this dialog occurs because the application is looking for data and will provide the user with an opportunity to create it in a new location if necessary.

Next, you see a log-on screen, as shown in figure 4.15. Type your name here if you edited INCLUDE.PRG to store it as the m.developer value. Type `FoxPro MAChete` if you didn't edit INCLUDE.PRG. (The dialog is case-sensitive.) The developer is automatically a registered user of this system.

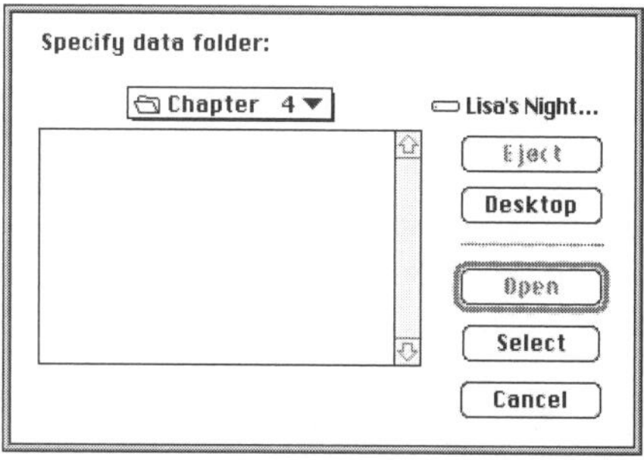

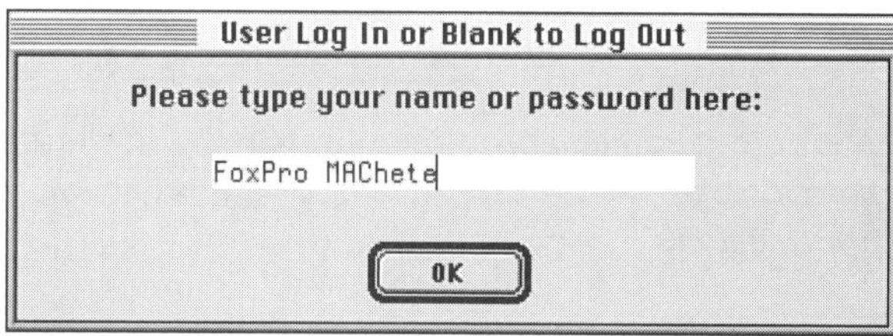

Figures 4.14 and 4.15 *The Template application's opening dialogs.*

You'll see a confirming WAIT WINDOW in the corner of the screen, and then the application menu waits for further instructions.

CROSS-PLATFORM WARNING

This WAIT WINDOW is a WAIT WINDOW NOWAIT, so the confirming message doesn't stick around if you move the mouse at all. In DOS or Windows, I prefer to leave the WAIT WINDOW up. However, on the Macintosh, clicking the mouse anywhere on the desktop brings the Finder forward instead of clearing the WAIT WINDOW. Because there is no main application window to click on, you have to click *directly on the WAIT WINDOW* to clear it and stay in FoxPro. I found this behavior too confusing to retain.

You will have plenty of time to investigate the generic options of this sample application later in the book, but right now you might want to verify that your custom INCLUDE.PRG has in fact supplanted my default copyright information on both the Apple menu's About prompt and the attached About dialog as well as on the Macintosh Help menu, as shown in figure 4.16. (The Help option is dimmed because you didn't supply a help file name in INCLUDE.PRG.)

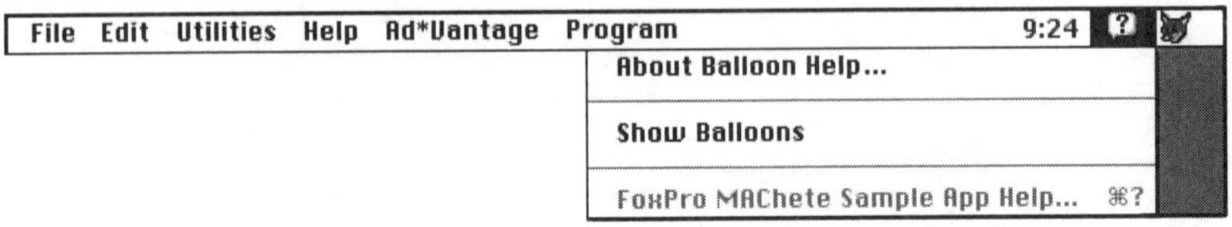

File Edit Utilities Help Ad*Vantage Program 9:24

About Balloon Help...

Show Balloons

FoxPro MAChete Sample App Help... ⌘?

Figure 4.16 *A single replacement of the application title name personalizes various aspects of this FoxPro for Macintosh application.*

Chapter Wrap Up

You can quit the template program at any time by Logging off (under the File menu), by blanking the default entry and then choosing the File menu's Quit option. But first, if you want to see my version of BROWSER while you're touring the seeded application, it serves as the Filter Conditions dialog under the Report Picker screen on the Utilities menu, as shown in figure 4.17. You can check the changes I made to BROWSER by editing the screen through your own project. Use the Screen menu option to Open All Snippets again and use the editor to search for comments beginning with the symbols *&* to find my changes. You'll probably be surprised that there are so few changes necessary.

The Report Picker dialog itself is usable but primitive. It employs a standard GETFILE() dialog to find available report and label forms, which means that it may not produce appropriate results for you if you pick a report from the Microsoft-supplied sample files that depend on a User-Defined Function currently unavailable. The dialog has error-checking built in, but it can't take care of every eventuality, *especially* since the Report Preview option is really a separate application from FoxPro for Macintosh. You can't prevent *every* failure, especially when you create generic objects meant for a multitasking environment. You can concentrate on making the failures as few, and as graceful, as possible.

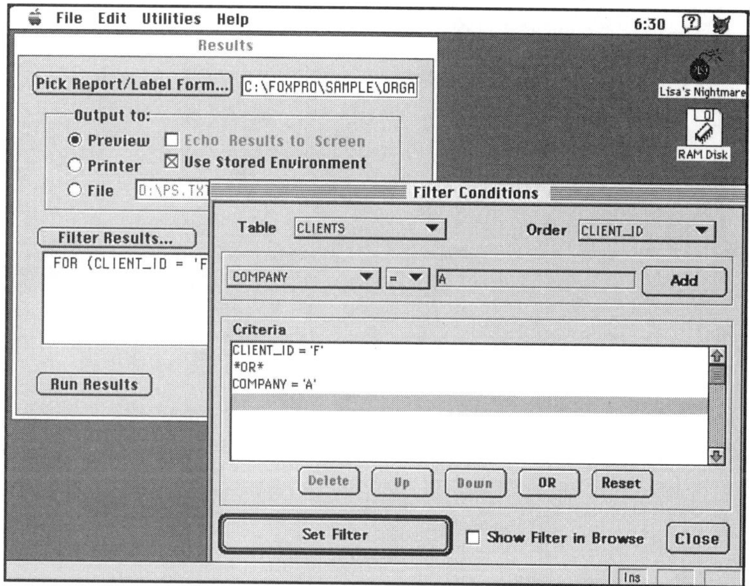

Figure 4.17 *BROWSER, in disguise, providing Filter Conditions for a Report Picker dialog in the seeded application.*

Later in the book you will see how to make such a dialog *data driven* and provide finer control over both the output formats the user can choose and the filtering mechanisms at the user's disposal.

However, with the nested Filter Conditions dialog, the Report Picker provides quick rewards for users during the early, prototyping stage of rapid development. With some simple reports, and with their first sample data entry screens, users have a chance to see if they can retrieve the results from their data that they really need. Even when they don't like what they see, having a model to react *against* makes it easier for people to communicate their needs to you.

With users' feedback, and with the framework of solid generic code that provides most of your project, you can add custom elements to meet the objectives of the application.

5

DESIGN AN APPLICATION FROM THE TOP DOWN: THE TEMPLATE PROGRAM STRATEGY

by
Lisa Slater

The FoxPro project file is a container into which you pour your development files. You press a Build button, and the Project Manager whirls your application ingredients into a new, compiled form: an .APP file or (with the Distribution Kit) an .EXE.

In Chapter 4 you saw how these files can include graphical layout descriptions. The Project Manager calls programs to read the description tables and generate program code so that it can compile the code into .APP form. For example, the Project Manager processes Screen description tables (.SCXs), grouped together as *screen sets*, by calling the program whose name is stored in the system variable _GENSCRN (GENSCRN.FXP in FoxPro's home folder, by default) to generate screen code (normal programs with the extension .SPR, by default).

Your ability to describe screens, reports, and menus in graphical layouts, rather than having to write code by hand, is critical to a rapid development process. In fact, FoxPro's few weaknesses as a rapid development tool correspond to the functions for which the Project Manager does *not* coordinate graphical design tools with supporting code generators.

In Chapter 6, you'll investigate the area of database management least controlled by the Project Manager and the existing design tools: table maintenance code. I provide some alternative tools to bring this area of application design under control. In the balance of Part II, you'll use the native FoxPro design tools to create most application elements quickly and visually.

However, your first experiences with the Project Manager in Chapter 4 also showed you that the application-building process is dependent on some program code, which is in a file designated as the project's Main program. The Project Manager reads this code to find references to other application elements and to pull your application together. (In the LASER project, the main file is a generated screen program, but somebody had to write supporting lines of code in the LASER.SCX screen definition file for the Project Manager to work.)

You still have to write programs. Rapid application development in FoxPro is not code-free; in fact, the supporting code for my template application is quite extensive and fully cross-platform. The better you understand this framework, and the more you work to adapt it to your own style and needs, the less code you'll write for each individual application you build on the framework.

For this reason, I present the key template code in this chapter *before* you begin to use the design tools.

See Also

- "Quick Start for FoxBASE+/Mac Professionalism," Chapter 2
- "Quick Start for Non-Xbase Database Designers," Chapter 3

If you're just beginning in FoxPro, you will want to look up unfamiliar commands, functions, and keywords in the Language Reference volume of your FoxPro documentation as you follow along, or simply ignore any syntax you have never seen before. Understanding the basic layout of these programs is more important than understanding every line of code.

Even if you are an experienced FoxPro developer, you may encounter commands and functions in FoxPro for Macintosh that don't work as you expect. Your first reaction should be to check the Language Reference to see if there is some specific Macintosh exception for this FoxPro syntax. Check the online helpfile because it is often more up-to-date than the printed manuals.

> **CROSS-PLATFORM WARNING**
>
> Be sure to check the READ.ME files included with FoxPro for even later changes. FoxPro for Macintosh had a very short beta period, and the READ.ME files make a number of important corrections to the manual and the helpfile. For example, ON KEY LABEL RIGHTMOUSE is a feature listed in both the manual and helpfile, but it doesn't really exist in FoxPro Mac. Microsoft decided not to try to imitate this DOS capability during the beta, but forgot to change the documentation. You'll also find that the READ.ME files pay special attention to problems and features that occur only in the Macintosh product. As you can see in figure 5.1, the FoxPro READ.ME file in FoxPro's home folder lists the other READ.ME files that you install with the product.
>
> If you check all available documentation, and still can't resolve the difficulty, log on to CompuServe's FoxForum or call Tech Support. You may have found a genuine bug.

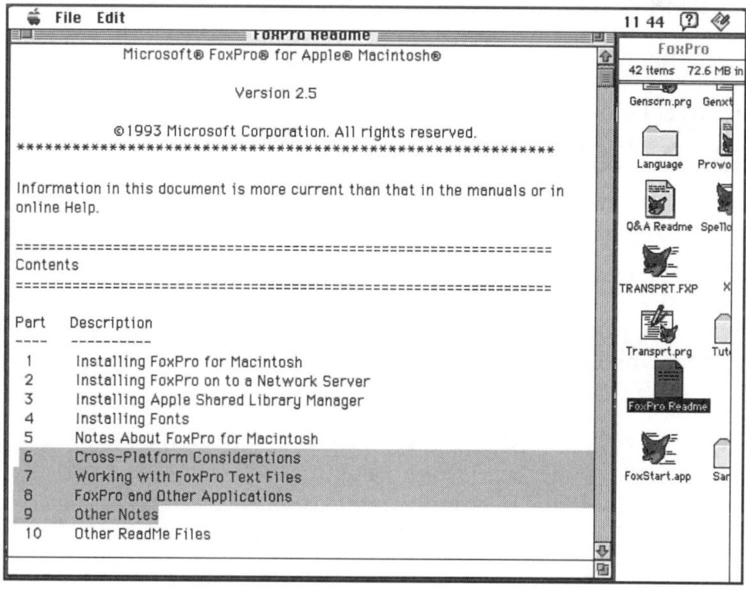

Figure 5.1 *FoxPro's home folder contains a main READ.ME file with vital information, including references to other READ.ME files.*

If you prefer not to examine code at this stage in your FoxPro development, you still should read the first major section of this chapter to understand the template structure. Then skip ahead, read about the tools, and come back to this chapter when you're ready.

The MAIN.PRG/INCLUDE.PRG Scheme for Rapid Development

In Chapter 4, you learned that the secret to rapid development in FoxPro is dividing your work into generic and application-specific elements. When you built your first application from the template code, you saw two programs at work: MAIN.PRG and INCLUDE.PRG.

In my template system, MAIN.PRG represents the generic programs, and INCLUDE.PRG represents the application-specific elements.

Distinguish between Types of Generic Procedures

Of course, you saw the Project Manager add a lot more files into the project container as it examined the file references in MAIN.PRG. In your sample, these programs all came from the Library/Template Code folder. These programs provide default behavior that you may want to change for a particular application. Your application directories override the default behavior for any special application needs by holding programs with the same name as the Library/Template folder's files.

How do you divide procedures into those held by MAIN.PRG and those included as separate Library/Template Code files? Here's my basic rule-of-thumb: every internal file management need, everything transparent to the user, should inspire you to write a MAIN.PRG procedure. Work out the best way to handle the requirement and use this best method all the time.

If I discover an improvement I can make in any generic method, I change the method in MAIN.PRG, secure in the knowledge that the change will carry through to *all* my applications when I next compile them. For example, the version of MAIN.PRG on your source disk includes Randy

Brown's cascading delete function. My code to accomplish the same task was completely different, but I like Randy's better, so I've made this global change.

By contrast, external Library/Template procedures should handle application requirements the user notices, or the results of which the user is aware. This division means that I can easily adjust external procedures to match any users' requests for a custom application surface by incorporating a local-directory override version into a specific project.

For example, as you saw during your quick tour in Chapter 4, my template code calls a "log-on" procedure to register users on a system. This procedure involves several surface elements, including a dialog into which the user types his or her name and an internal separation of users into classes. You may not have been aware of the second element. The classes exist to allow some users to log on after an interrupted or abnormally terminated (*abended*) previous session, while others have to check with an application supervisor. You *did* notice that you had to type your name to log on. Perhaps you would prefer a masked password in that dialog, or perhaps some users need a log-on procedure that looks entirely different.

Override or Alter Generic Procedures at the Proper Level

If you thoroughly dislike my LOG_ON.PRG procedure, change the Library/Template Code folder version to suit your defaults. For example, Andy Griebel's first comment to me about data entry, when we began to discuss the business rules for this book's model application, was that nobody on earth wants to bother with case sensitivity. Andy notes that "the relative benefit (hard passwords) is hardly worth the training time you have to pass on to the users." I disagree, where security is concerned, although his argument makes good Mac interface sense. But if Andy wants to extend his preference to password entry, he can easily make this change to his Library/Template version copy of LOG_ON.PRG.

However, even when you are satisfied with the edited default LOG_ON.PRG, you may have a *specific* application that calls for a completely different log-on process. For instance, I wrote a baseball card inventory system for children. In this application, I present the registered users in a scrollable list at log-on, so the child using the program can choose to see his or her own card records. You can build a LOG_ON.PRG in your application's directory to override the normal default procedure in a case like this, or to make much less extreme changes.

Some of the external programs are simple placeholders, providing you with an opportunity to accommodate common application needs without forcing them on every application. For example, once a user logs on to the system successfully, you may want to custom-tailor the application for that user, but you may not use this capability all the time. LOG_ON calls an external program named PERMITS.PRG, in which you place the necessary code. My default PERMITS.PRG in the Library/Template Code Folder, however, does a simple RETURN, with no instructions at all.

In some applications, I re-issue the application menu in PERMITS.PRG and RELEASE menu BARs and PADs that a particular user shouldn't see. You might want to save user preferences, such as SETting of KEYCOMP or sounds or colors, and restore these preferences in PERMITS.PRG. The moment of log-on, which is the moment when your application becomes aware of a change in the individual interacting with it, is a natural place to make these adjustments.

See Also

- "Thoughtful Design," Chapter 11
- "Color Handling," Chapter 14

You could choose standard default instructions for this program if you want—or, like me, you may prefer to create local PERMITS.PRGs on an occasional, application-specific basis. Either way, PERMITS.PRG remains a separate procedure from MAIN.PRG so that you can tailor it to depart from your defaults when necessary.

Conveniently, the screens and menu code for an application (.SPRs and .MPRs) *always* reside separately on disk from the MAIN.PRG, because these files are generated from system tables (.SCXs and .MNXs) rather than handwritten. These application components make obvious contributions to the application surface, and thus they may require frequent tinkering. Because generated programs always exist separately, I can override even the most generic alert dialog with a local version if a user requests a custom appearance.

In some cases, I further isolate the generated code inside a *framing program*. Rather than directly issuing a call to `DO APP.MPR` in MAIN.PRG, for example, I may `DO APPMPR`, a normal .PRG. The default APPMPR.PRG in the Library/Template Code does the simple call to APP.MPR. However, a local version of APPMPR.PRG may call a file with another name or surround the call to APP.MPR with reams of additional conditions. The local APPMPR.PRG may even RETURN after doing nothing—some applications don't have menu pads at all.

Take Charge of the Template Code

I explain my system of distinguishing program elements at some length here, but not because I think it is perfect. I want you to feel *knowledgeable and in command* of this system, because inevitably you will disagree on the best way to make some of these decisions. You will even find instances in which your organization of these procedures doesn't perfectly match my description of the principles of the system.

Go ahead: change the code! Because you make your decisions in one place, the one set of template procedures, and watch the results ripple through all the projects you develop, changes are relatively painless and immediately satisfying.

Customize with INCLUDE.PRG

There are some aspects of an application's work, notably setup and cleanup procedures, which you have to do for each application. Although you do these procedures for each application, you also know these particular aspects *must be* different for each application. For example, each application has a name.

There are other aspects of an application's environment that you want to make sure to *reconsider* for each application, rather than blissfully relying on default behavior in most cases. For example, you may want to evaluate the conditions under which a particular application should refuse to load.

These are the aspects of an application I isolate in INCLUDE.PRG. When I begin development of a new application, I generate an application-specific INCLUDE.PRG (you see how to create the program in Chapter 6). INCLUDE.PRG is the first program I edit for each new application, and it's the one in which many decisions affecting the whole application are made.

I incorporate calls to INCLUDE.PRG at strategic points of MAIN.PRG, as you see in detail in the next section. The first call occurs at the very beginning of the application, the moment my generic environment-setting is in place. The last call occurs as part of generic environment-restoration. INCLUDE.PRG takes one parameter to indicate to the program which call is in progress.

Astute FoxPro developers recognize this set of calls from the organization of a generated .SPR file: I provide opportunities (or *hooks*) into your code at approximately the same points as GENSCRN inserts #SECTION 1 and #SECTION 2 of the Setup snippet and the Cleanup snippet.

For my needs, these three hooks in MAIN.PRG are sufficient, *but you can create additional hooks at any point in MAIN.PRG requiring customizing for each application*. Just add a DO INCLUDE WITH <section number> line in MAIN.PRG wherever you need an additional hook to hang your customization code.

Don't add these hooks, however, without serious thought. Although the added flexibility is helpful, remember that the aim of a rapid development technique is to *limit* the code that you write for each application. Each call to INCLUDE.PRG is a point at which you have found application-specific code unavoidable. Consider alternatives, with this principle to guide you, before you give INCLUDE.PRG additional responsibilities.

In the next section, you become familiar with the code and structure of MAIN.PRG and INCLUDE.PRG so that you can begin to adjust them.

The Generic MAIN.PRG Components

The basic tasks of MAIN.PRG look like this:

- Perform setup procedures, including saving the environment and initializing variables
- Customize the menu and options for the program
- Enter a wait state, in which the program looks for, accepts, and processes user instructions
- Perform cleanup procedures when the user instructs the program to end

This structure is familiar to those of you who have worked in FoxPro before. You should be aware that not only the main program of the application but also subsidiary programs that launch application tasks all follow the same basic pattern.

Rapid development strategy requires MAIN.PRG to perform each of these tasks as flexibly as possible. In this section, I'll show you the special features of *this* MAIN.PRG so that you can extend it as necessary. If you want to follow along in the source code, you will find most of this section written directly into MAIN.PRG as comments, as you can see in figure 5.2.

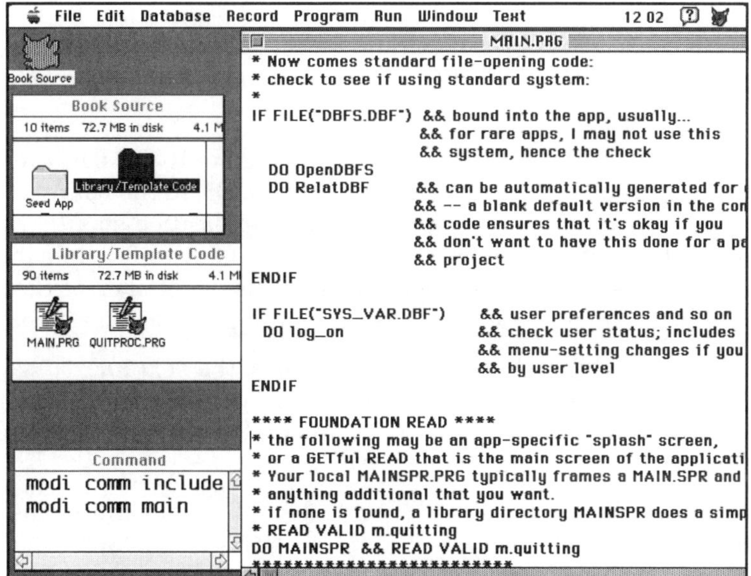

Figure 5.2 *MAIN.PRG in the Library / Template Code Folder on your Source Disk is replete with comments on the structure and design of this important program.*

See Also

- Source Disk: Library/ Template Code Folder: MAIN.PRG

Setup Procedures

MAIN.PRG's Setup procedures are the most extensive part of the program, with calls to numerous subprocedures.

Because a PARAMETERS statement must be the first line in any program if you want to pass parameters, naturally MAIN.PRG has a PARAMETERS statement as the first line. Ordinarily, I don't pass parameters to my APPs unless they are designed to function as subordinate tools to other applications. Recall that you can double-click on an .APP file in the Finder, but there's no way to pass values to the .APP when you use this method to launch the program.

However, MAIN.PRG functions on all FoxPro platforms and also serves well as the organizing program for subsidiary tool .APPs, so it must be flexible. MAIN.PRG's PARAMETERS line has one parameter (`passed_to_main`). If you have multiple parameters for a particular .APP, you can pass a delimited string with several values, or you can pass an array by reference.

The parameter becomes a global variable for the application. Because the contents of this parameter is inevitably specific to applications, you edit the application's INCLUDE.PRG to parse, evaluate, and apply the contents of this variable.

Following the PARAMETERS line is the first call to INCLUDE.PRG. I suggest uses for this early appearance of INCLUDE in the next section, but it should *always* include initializing some application-specific values required by the rest of setup procedures (you will see an example in a moment). Because this call precedes any establishment of error checking and other environmental precautions by your application, use it sparingly.

When the initial INCLUDE.PRG call concludes, the next line, `DO SaveSets`, saves all factors of the current environment to an array. As each factor is safely stored in an array element, SaveSets replaces its SETting with the default states for my applications.

Look over this procedure thoroughly and add additional array elements for FoxPro SETtings your programs depend on. Adjust the DIMENSION statement at the beginning of the procedure to handle additional settings you require.

The SaveSets array has three columns. The first two columns store FoxPro commands as a string, which are executed during Cleanup using macro-expansion. The third column stores file names these commands include as indirect references.

See Also

- PROCEDURE Save Sets, Source Disk:Library/ Template Code Folder: MAIN.PRG

Some settings are straightforward, like this:

```
Savesets(5,1) = "SET EXACT "+SET("EXACT")
SET EXACT OFF
Savesets(5,2) = "SET DELETED "+SET("DELETED")
SET DELETED OFF
```

Other aspects of the environment take more work and more platform-specific consideration to save properly:

```
Savesets(3,3) = SET("RESOURCE",1)
* Check for EMPTY() because if
* RESO = OFF in the CONFIG.FPM
* file the named resource file
* (default of FOXUSER)
* may not exist.
* also check for nonexistent
* resource file name
* because it's possible for
```

```
* somebody to do this:
* RESOURCE = OFF
* RESOURCE = Filename that doesn't exist
* in the CONFIG.FP? file...
* ... the resource file won't
* get created, but
* *will* be held in SET("RESOURCE",1)
* in some circumstances —
* also if it was never
* ON, it could have been erased
* by the user during
* the run of the app <sigh>...

IF NOT EMPTY(Savesets(3,3)) AND ;
       FILE(Savesets(3,3))
   IF _MAC
      Savesets(3,3) = ;
      SYS(2027,Savesets(3,3))
   ENDIF
   Savesets(3,1) = ;
      "SET RESOURCE TO (Savesets(3,3))"
ENDIF
* Always SET RESO TO a
* filename *before* SETting
* it ON or OFF, because the act of
* SETting RESO TO a filename
* automatically SETs RESO ON.
Savesets(3,2) = "SET RESOURCE "+ ;

         SET("RESOURCE")
IF EMPTY(m.resource)
   SET RESOURCE OFF
ELSE
   SET RESOURCE TO (m.resource)
ENDIF
```

The `m.resource` variable in the excerpt from SaveSets above is established by INCLUDE.PRG. The default INCLUDE.PRG initializes the m.resource variable. According to your needs, you can add code to INCLUDE to assign a standard file name to this variable after checking for the existence of the file, generate user-specific resource files on a network, or leave the variable empty if this application does not require a resource file. SaveSets takes care of the rest.

You also see a call to SYS(2027) in this code. I save the Macintosh style file name, rather than any VOLUME version of the file name that FoxPro may be using, in case I call a library procedure written by someone else who carelessly changes the VOLUME SETtings and does not restore them. I know the Macintosh style file name will work to restore the old resource file in spite of any problems like this. Refer to Chapter 1 for a discussion of FoxPro's SYS(2027) and for a full explanation of the rationale for indirect file referencing, if you don't use this style of file referencing consistently in your code already.

See Also

- "Indirect Referencing," Chapter 1
- "Volume Name Translation," Chapter 1
- "Reverse Name Translation," Chapter 1

CROSS-PLATFORM WARNING

Pay particular attention to the many instances of *bracketed* code in PROCEDURE SaveSets. In FoxPro, the term bracketed code refers to code that should only execute on specified platforms. The "brackets" are IF/ENDIF or CASE constructs that restrict the execution of the code by using FoxPro's system variables _MAC, _WINDOWS, _DOS, and _UNIX to evaluate the current platform at runtime.

Because environment-setting requires more bracketed code than almost any other part of your application (with the possible exception of addressing the printer), the bracketed code in SaveSets gives you a good introduction to areas of cross-platform conflict.

When you examine the code directly, specifically at the _MAC platform in SaveSets, you also get an introduction to some of FoxPro for Macintosh's Mac-specific enhancements. For example, the following section of SaveSets executes only on the Mac:

```
IF _MAC
   Savesets(13,1) = "SET APLABOUT "+;
                    SET("APLABOUT")
   Savesets(13,2) = [SET APLABOUT PROMPT "]+;
                    SET("APLABOUT",1)+["]
   SET APLABOUT ENABLED
   SET APLABOUT PROMPT ;
                   "About "+IIF(EMPTY(m.app_title), ;
                   "this application... ",;
                    m.app_title+"...")
   Savesets(14,1) = "SET MACHELP "+SET("MACHELP")
   Savesets(14,2) = [SET MACHELP PROMPT "]+;
                    SET("MACHELP",1)+["]
```

```
SET MACHELP ENABLED
SET MACHELP PROMPT ;
                 IIF(EMPTY(m.app_title), ;
                 "Application Help...",;
                 m.app_title+" Help... ")
Savesets(15,1) = "ON APLABOUT "+ON("APLABOUT")
Savesets(15,2) = "ON MACHELP "+ON("MACHELP")

* if no APPABOUT proc is found locally,
* a simple library procedure
* will do a WAIT WINDOW
ON APLABOUT DO appabout

IF EMPTY(m.helpfile)
   ON MACHELP WAIT WINDOW m.app_title+;
      " Help goes here!" NOWAIT
ELSE
   ON MACHELP DO helpproc
ENDIF

* only on the Mac do I load FOXTOOLS up-top
* I don't always need it otherwise, but
* for the Mac product INSTALL.DBF has to
* have it available to change file & creator
* type if necessary to install files on disk.
* I also use FxAlert() whenever possible
* instead of SPRs.
Savesets(16,1) = SetLib("FoxTools")
DO CASE
CASE EMPTY(Savesets(16,1))
   * However, I won't crash out
   * of the whole project
   * at this point —
   * if INSTALL.DBF can't use
   * the library it won't do the
   * file type setting
   * — but it's not crucial enough
   * to bail out
CASE Savesets(16,1) = "loaded !"
  * library was in the environment already
  Savesets(16,1) = .F.
  * don't execute anything here on the restore
```

```
 OTHERWISE
     * set up the environment restore:
     Savesets(16,1) = ;
               [RELEASE LIBRARY ("FoxTools")]
 ENDCASE
ENDIF
```

This code shows you the syntax for the new SET APLABOUT and SET MACHELP commands. You also see a Mac-specific command to SET LIBRARY TO FOXTOOLS. On the Macintosh, a FOXTOOLS capability is integral to my installation procedures, as you'll see later in this section. I use it throughout my applications, so I load this library routinely.

If FOXTOOLS can't load, however, I show a warning message rather than ending the application at this point. Because not every session of the application must run through the required installation procedure, I prefer to reserve that judgment call to any procedure that relies on FOXTOOLS or other library. In many cases, the procedure can offer an alternative rather than shutting down.

The actual library loading, and the warning message if the library cannot load, occurs in another MAIN.PRG procedure, FUNCTION SetLib. This important generic function defaults to FPATH in FoxPro for DOS and FOXTOOLS in FoxPro for Windows and Macintosh but loads any library you need. SetLib uses the SET LIBRARY ADDITIVE syntax to leave other libraries undisturbed.

See Also

- FUNCTION SetLib, Source Disk:Library/ Template Code Folder: MAIN.PRG
- "Specific Areas of Cross-Platform Incompatibility," Chapter 11

CROSS-PLATFORM

SetLib is a function that begged to be written as part of template code. Not only is loading libraries a system function whose method should never need adjustment, but it is also a function that has many cross-platform nuances you don't want to bother thinking about every time you load a library.

On the DOS and Windows platforms, the library must be located, and you must store a string showing its location, with full path, so that you can RELEASE the LIBRARY later. On the Mac, the library is always in the Extensions folder. However, on the Mac there's an additional headache: if the Apple Shared Library Manager Extension isn't properly installed, you can't load your library.

If SetLib finds that the requested library is already in the environment, it RETURNs the string "loaded !" as a signal to the calling program not to try to RELEASE this library later.

After the environment is saved and set, normal setup procedures continue in MAIN.PRG with the following code:

```
SET DEFAULT TO SUBSTR(SYS(16),1,;
                      RAT("\", SYS(16)))

* Now do rest of common-code setup:
IF NOT Setup()

   SET COLOR OF SCHEME 5 TO SCHEME 7
   WAIT WINDOW ;
         "Application can't start successfully"+ ;
         IIF(TYPE("m.developer") # "C","!", ;
         " — call "+m.developer+"!")
   SET COLOR OF SCHEME 5 TO
   DO Setsets
   DO Cleanup
   RETURN
ENDIF
```

The first line above SETs DEFAULT to the APP file's own directory, where many other control files crucial to the application reside. (These are not data files, which the user may place anywhere on the system.) The evaluation of SYS(16) to provide the location of the .APP file *must* occur in the main program; otherwise, I'd put it in SaveSets, where I have already saved the old DEFAULT for later restoration.

The Setup function then proceeds with global setup duties. You can place anything in Setup you want, including PUBLIC declaration of variables that all your applications need. Notice that Setup returns a value to indicate success or failure. MAIN.PRG provides a normal cleanup path when failure occurs.

CROSS-PLATFORM WARNING

The SET COLOR OF SCHEME code here doesn't accomplish anything in FoxPro for Macintosh; WAIT WINDOWs are only affected by the FoxPro color system in FoxPro for DOS. However, this code won't produce an error and is a perfect example of code you don't have to *bother* to bracket.

See Also

- FUNCTION SetLib, Source Disk:Library/ Template Code Folder: MAIN.PRG

The global Setup function is short enough and important enough to cite in full here:

```
FUNCTION Setup
PRIVATE m.success, m.havelib
m.success = .T.

* all your global variables can go here, except
* app-specific stuff (see call to INCLUDE):
PUBLIC m.quitting
m.quitting = .F.

PUSH MENU _MSYSMENU
SET SYSMENU OFF
HIDE MENU _MSYSMENU
PUSH KEY CLEAR

* get pieces that must exist on disk
* out of the app if necessary...

IF FILE("INSTALL.DBF")
   USE Install && DBF included in .APP
   m.havelib = "FOXTOOLS" $ ;
                UPPER(SET("LIBRARY",1))
   SCAN
     IF NOT FILE(ALLTRIM(Name))
      WAIT WINDOW NOWAIT ;
         "Installing "+ALLTRIM(Name)+"... "
       COPY MEMO Contents TO (ALLTRIM(Name))
       IF _MAC AND m.havelib
          = FxSetType(SYS(2027,ALLTRIM(Name)),;
                       Filetype,Creator)
       ENDIF
     ENDIF
  ENDSCAN
  WAIT CLEAR
  USE
ENDIF

* initialization of any globals that
* are app-specific, along with
* addition of app-specific conditions
```

```
* or flags, is done in INCLUDE, which
* you keep in the application directory,
* not with your library files...

DO Include WITH 2

IF NOT EMPTY(m.helpfile)
   SET HELP ON
   SET HELP TO (m.helpfile)
ELSE
   SET HELP OFF
ENDIF

IF m.success AND (_DOS OR _WINDOWS)
   m.success = MultiUse()
   * this is necessary because otherwise they
   * can start multiple sessions without hindrance
   * from the operating system —
   * they *have* to be thrown out, if so, it's
   * not safe
ENDIF

RETURN m.success
```

The Setup function checks for pieces of the application using an INSTALL.DBF that stores file names in a character field and the contents of the files in a memo field. If any required file is not available, Setup can copy the file out from the memo file on disk.

> **CROSS-PLATFORM WARNING**
>
> This code requires some special attention on the Macintosh. Don't try to use INSTALL.DBF with files that include resource forks, such as XCMD resource files or executables. Even when you can coax such files into the memo field (you can't do it with executable applications), their resource fork is lost.
>
> The file type and creator is also not properly restored when you COPY the file back out onto disk. You can see that Setup() uses a FOXTOOLS function, FxSetType(), to remedy this problem. If FOXTOOLS isn't available, this step is omitted, but your FoxPro

application will still be able to use the files properly (the user just won't be able to see the correct icon or double-click on the file to launch it normally).

Even with its platform limitations, this method provides a convenient way to distribute applications with many types of files that *must* appear on disk, rather than being built into the .APP. The Microsoft Engine-style Helpfile (.HLP) is one such file. Because it must exist on disk, you notice I SET HELP TO <the helpfile> in Setup(), rather than Savesets(), because I'm not sure the file is available until after the SCAN of INSTALL.DBF.

FOXPRO MAC HACK TIP

You may not have the Distribution Kit, but you may still need to distribute applications to other FoxPro users in your organization. With INSTALL.DBF, you don't need to use the Setup Wizard supplied by the Distribution Kit to install your application's files. The user doesn't even have to know the file-copying takes place, and there are no floppies to swap. Even if a crucial file gets erased after the initial application installation, Setup() performs its quick check each time the application is launched and remedies the problem without user intervention.

All you need to do is build the correct INSTALL.DBF into your Project containing the appropriate application files, their names, file types, and creators. These files may be .DBFs "seeded" with data, report forms you want the user to have a chance to edit, and more.

After doing global setup procedures, Setup() makes the second call to INCLUDE.PRG to see if you have any application-specific tasks to add. Finally, it SETs HELP to a helpfile if the application has one, now that you can be sure a copy of the file exists on disk.

The final Setup() check deserves special comment. In DOS and Windows it's possible to start multiple sessions of FoxPro and be unprotected by FoxPro's automatic file and record locking. This check stops the application from proceeding if the MultiUse() function determines this situation is a possibility on the user's machine. As I explained in Chapter 1, this horrific behavior doesn't occur on the Macintosh.

If you don't enable filesharing on the Macintosh, FoxPro opens all tables EXCLUSIVEly so that there's no chance you could PACK in one session of FoxPro while the tables are in USE in a second session.

See Also

- FUNCTION MultiUse, Source Disk:Library/ Template Code: MAIN.PRG
- "Launch Multiple Sessions of FoxPro," Chapter 1

However, this presents your applications with an additional problem on the Macintosh: multiple sessions won't be able to get the files they need because of the true-EXCLUSIVE use without filesharing. This isn't dangerous, and you certainly don't need to send users out of your application simply because they've loaded without enabling file sharing in their first session. The application can function quite successfully in EXCLUSIVE mode.

However, if they start a *second session* or a second FoxPro application that accesses the same tables without enabling file sharing, they certainly will make an application crash resoundingly.

The only answer is to do a check the first time you open a table that isn't bound into the application or otherwise marked READ-only. If you get an error, you know they've started a second session on an unprepared Macintosh. You can send them out of the application at that point by using a dialog like the one in figure 5.3. (The dialog will be proceeded by my standard error-handler message indicating a locking problem on the error, and they'll receive a message after the dialog indicating that they should call the developer for help if necessary.)

Figure 5.3 *Send users out of the application if they try to start a second session of FoxPro without enabling file sharing.*

I can't tell you exactly when to make this check. I do it in OpenSys(), the function that opens my SYS_VAR.DBF, but you may not use this table in your application. Perform the check whenever you open a table in read-write mode for the first time.

This check concludes the global setup for the application.

Menu Handlers

Next, MAIN.PRG proceeds to set the menu for this application. For maximum flexibility, I've broken the menu into several parts. The first menu component, MINIMAL.MPR, contains the two pads (File and Edit) that every Mac menu must have, with standard elements. This menu replaces the previous version of SYSMENU. The second component appends a Utilities pad that, like log-on procedures, is usually standard but may be overridden for a particular application.

See Also

- Source Disk:Library/ Template Coder Folder: APPMPR.{RG

The third menu component is an Application-specific pad for the tasks global to this application. (Each application task may add another pad, just as the Project Manager and other FoxPro tools do, for its own use.) Because this third component is different for every application, I choose to have it "framed" by an APPMPR.PRG. Besides calling an .MPR generated menu program to add the Application-specific menu options, this program has a chance to RELEASE options from the File, Edit, and Utilities pads that are inappropriate to this application or this platform. The default APPMPR.PRG in your Library/Template Code folder provides examples of these RELEASE calls, as comments, for all the File and Edit menu bars.

See Also

- Source Disk:Library/ Template Code Folder: DEBUG.MNX

The last menu component provides a Debugging tool menu conditionally, as follows:

```
F TYPE("_DEBUG") = "L" AND _DEBUG
  * append your personal debugging tools
  * pad here...
  DO Debug.MPR
ENDIF
```

> **FOXPRO MAC HACK TIP**
>
> You can provide any condition you prefer to the IF evaluation in this code to permit your debugging menu to appear only when you need it. Some developers use a check for a file with an unusual name, which they create on disk whenever they want to run tests.

The next Setup task is file opening and setting file relationships. MAIN.PRG checks to see if its default system, which uses a DBFS.DBF control file, is in place before opening tables. You examine this system thoroughly in the next chapter. You can override this system very simply by adding file opening procedures to INCLUDE and omitting the

DBFS.DBF table for any application. You normally INCLUDE the DBFS.DBF table in the Project, however, as simply another invisible, read-only component of the .APP file.

Finally, MAIN.PRG performs its first log-on procedure, if INCLUDE has performed some key steps to make log-on a feature of this application, as you'll see in the next section. The application is ready to enter its wait state, either waiting for a new user log-on (if none occurred) or waiting for the user to make a menu choice.

The Application Wait State: Foundation READ

In FoxPro, this wait state is usually implemented as a *Foundation READ*. This READ statement is often *GETless*: it doesn't present the user with anything to do. It doesn't have to be GETless, however. Several of the developer tool utilities supplied with this book have foundation READs that present the user with a series of choices as GET controls. I call this type of application a *switchboard* app because the GET controls on the main window provide the connections to all the tasks "underneath."

MAIN.PRG implements the foundation wait state as a call to a procedure named MAINSPR.PRG. The Library/Template Code default version of MAINSPR.PRG provides the simple GETless foundation READ that many people use for every application:

```
* default MAINSPR.PRG
IF _WINDOWS
    DEFINE WINDOW xout ;
      FROM -3,-3 TO -2,-2 NONE
    ACTI WINDOW xout
ENDIF

READ VALID m.quitting

IF _WINDOWS
    RELEASE WINDOW xout
ENDIF
```

See Also

- Source Disk:Library/ Template Code Folder: MAINSPR.PRG

The WINDOW xout code is necessary in Windows to avoid problems with a GETless foundation READ in the main application window. The most obvious problem is that the READ window cannot be resized, and many people want to resize the main application window. My WINDOW xout is a workaround to provide the capability. You can refer to the expanded comments in MAINSPR.PRG on disk if you're curious about the other reasons for this trick in Windows.

Problems traceable to use of the main application window, thankfully, need not afflict us on the Macintosh. If you are using the main application window in your application, you have presumably put GETs in it to make it a switchboard app. If you have GETs in FoxPro, you know what size their window should be: the size that you designed for this series of GETs. If you don't have switchboard GETs at the foundation READ level, you shouldn't be using the main application window at all.

See Also

- "Contrasting Main Application Windows," Chapter 1
- "Using SET MACDESKTOP," Chapter 1

As always, you provide a local MAINSPR if your application requires a different approach from the simple default foundation READ—or change the default version, if you customarily use another approach, such as the READ VALID Handler() you find in the FoxPro for Macintosh sample FNDATION folder's EX1 and EX2 projects.

Restoration

Cleanup in MAIN.PRG is much less elaborate than Setup. There is, of course, a call to your local INCLUDE.PRG in case you want to add to Cleanup's generic procedures. The Setsets procedure handles restoration of all the environment factors you saved to the SaveSets() array as follows:

See Also

- PROCEDURE SetSets, Source Disk:Library/ Template Code Folder: MAIN.PRG

```
PROCEDURE SetSets
PRIVATE xx
FOR xx = 1 TO ALEN(Savesets,1)
   IF NOT EMPTY(Savesets(xx,1))
      &Savesets(xx,1)
   ENDIF
   IF NOT EMPTY(Savesets(xx,2))
      &Savesets(xx,2)
   ENDIF
ENDFOR
RELEASE Savesets
RETURN
```

As you can see, no matter how much you change the SaveSets procedure, you won't have to adjust the SetSets code as long as you store executable statements into the first two columns of the SaveSets array.

I have glossed over some aspects of the MAIN.PRG code and completely omitted other features you'll discover later in the book, such as its extensive error handler. Still, you probably see that having this much of your application handled generically saves a tremendous amount of work for each new project.

In the next section, you'll see the code elements you should be sure to edit in each application-specific INCLUDE.PRG. You'll be glad to see that they are very limited compared to the amount of support work done by MAIN.PRG without your intervention.

The Application-Specific INCLUDE.PRG Elements

INCLUDE.PRG takes a single numeric parameter, which serves to tell the program which part of MAIN.PRG is placing the call to it. INCLUDE processes a single CASE for each call. (You could provide separate INCLUDE programs and dispense with the parameter, but that would defeat the purpose of keeping all application-specific code in one place.)

As you have seen, MAIN.PRG calls INCLUDE.PRG at three points by default: at the very top of the program; after generic Setup routines have run; and during cleanup. You can add other calls to INCLUDE at any other point of MAIN; just give each a unique numeric argument to pass. (As all my programs do, INCLUDE makes sure it has received an appropriate numeric parameter and assigns a dummy value, processed by none of the CASEs, if you mistakenly call it without a numeric argument.)

The first call to INCLUDE is a place for you to accomplish two tasks:

- Evaluate the environment to make sure there is no reason the program should refuse to run at all
- Initialize application-specific values required by the rest of the application

INCLUDE accomplishes the first task with the following code:

```
* CASE m.section = 1

   m.disallowed = ""

   IF TYPE("m.disallowed") = "C" AND ;
      NOT EMPTY(m.disallowed) AND ;
      EVAL(m.disallowed)
      SET COLOR OF SCHEME 5 TO SCHEME 7
```

```
    WAIT WINDOW ;
       "Sorry — your configuration or "+;
       "version of FoxPro"+CHR(13)+;
       "doesn't support this application!"+;
       CHR(13)+CHR(13)+;
       "Disallowed: "+m.disallowed
  SET COLOR OF SCHEME 5 TO
  CANCEL
ENDIF
```

See Also

- INCLUDE PRG, first call, default version, Source Disk: Library/ Template Code Folder

This default version of INCLUDE.PRG provides an empty definition for the variable m.disallowed, ready for you to add the necessary conditions for this application. For example, if your application requires more than 25 work areas, you might use this condition:

```
m.disallowed = ;
     "(_DOS AND NOT '(X)' $ UPPER(VERSION(1)) )"
```

If your application runs only on the Macintosh, you could add:

```
m.disallowed = ;
     "NOT _MAC"
```

If your application's screens won't fit on a Mac Classic monitor, you might not restrict its platform. You could restrict its display like this:

```
     m.disallowed = ;
        "_MAC AND SYSMETRIC(1) < 640"
```

I isolate the `m.disallowed` variable from the IF construct that evaluates it to make sure it is easy to edit and easy to see. I use the TYPE() and EVAL() checks in the IF construct to ensure that the program runs properly even if you never touch this variable. However, if you become accustomed to editing your INCLUDE.PRG for each application, you may just make the initial IF condition an IF .F. and then edit this condition to hold application-specific checks as necessary.

Similarly, you may want to tailor the WAIT WINDOW I use in the cancellation phase, if the program should not run, to an alert that fits your style better or at least a more attractive message.

Don't make this alert procedure *too* complex, however; remember that, at this point of the program, you don't have your usual resources. Error checking is not in place, you haven't loaded libraries yet, and no variables are initialized. This is an *emergency* procedure, and a WAIT WINDOW, which uses only native FoxPro resources, is an appropriate tool to use. When you CANCEL, you don't want any cleanup to worry about.

Following this initial emergency check, the first call to INCLUDE declares application global variables PUBLIC and assigns values, such as the application title and developer's name you edited in the last chapter. I provide one special variable, m.mainwindow, used only for the Mac. This is the switch you can set to .T. if you want the main application window to remain available during the application.

Because a PUBLIC variable is automatically .F., if you never touch this variable my template code will hide the main application window and restore its original characteristics at the conclusion of your program. This capability is built into the SaveSets procedure you have already investigated in MAIN.PRG. You may want to use the relevant SaveSets code to understand window-handling syntax as it applies to the special FoxPro SCREEN window:

```
IF _WINDOWS OR _MAC AND m.mainwindow
   Savesets(8,1) = "MODIFY WINDOW SCREEN"
     * to nuke any app-specific icon and wallpaper
     * — I ordinarily don't use the main app window
     *  on the Mac, so this isn't usually a problem
     * except in Windows,
     * but it might be for somebody, hence
     * the m.mainwindow check —
     * see INCLUDE.PRG
ENDIF
IF _WINDOWS OR _MAC
   Savesets(8,2) = ;
          "MODIFY WINDOW SCREEN TITLE ["+ ;
           WTITLE("")+ "] FONT ["+WFONT(1,"")+"], "+ ;
           ALLTRIM(STR(WFONT(2,"")))+ ;
          " STYLE ["+WFONT(3,"")+"] " + ;
          "AT "+ALLTRIM(STR(WLROW("")))+;
          ","+ALLTRIM(STR(WLCOL(""))) + ;
          " SIZE "+ALLTRIM(STR(WROWS("")))+ ;
          ","+ALLTRIM(STR(WCOLS("")))
   * put any app-specific MODI WINDOW
   * SCREEN ... FONT... SIZE... ICON.. etc in
   * INCLUDE, 2nd pass
   * or build them into a Desktop SCX
ENDIF
```

```
IF _MAC
   DO CASE
   CASE NOT WVISIBLE("")  ;
             AND m.mainwindow
        Savesets(9,1) = "HIDE WINDOW SCREEN"
   CASE WVISIBLE("")  ;
          AND NOT m.mainwindow
       Savesets(9,1) = ;
            "SHOW WINDOW SCREEN BOTTOM"
       HIDE WINDOW SCREEN
OTHERWISE
      * we already have what we need — either
      * mainwindow visibility or not!
ENDCASE
IF  SET("MACDESKTOP") = "OFF"
    Savesets(9,2) = "SET MACDESKTOP OFF"
    SET MACDESKTOP ON
  ENDIF
ELSE
  IF NOT ( EMPTY(Savesets(9,1)) OR ;
          Savesets(9,1) = ;
              "SHOW WINDOW SCREEN BOTTOM")
     ACTI SCREEN
     * must be done to make sure
     * nothing but SCREEN is WOUTPUT()
     * before the HIDE WINDOWS below
  ENDIF
ENDIF

HIDE WINDOWS ALL
* HIDE WINDOWS ALL doesn't do
* anything about the SCREEN
* window, even on the Mac,
* so this is a safe position
* to put this code
```

The second call to INCLUDE.PRG occurs after MAIN.PRG has properly set up its own environment so that you can add any application-specific Setup here secure in the knowledge that your error handler is initialized.

The only line of code in this default version of INCLUDE's second CASE is a call to DO OpenSys. OpenSys is a procedure in MAIN.PRG that uses a control file to assign system parameters to an application. You saw it at work when you generated an application in the last chapter. OpenSys didn't find the file it needed, SYS_VAR.DBF, so it created this file, installed the developer's name as a registered user, and asked you for some initial information (a data path for the application). If you don't want log-on procedures or registered users for an application, you omit the DO OpenSys call in the local INCLUDE.PRG, SYS_VAR.DBF is never created, and Log_On doesn't do its usual work.

I use SYS_VAR.DBF to store registered users' names, the current data path, and additional information in memo fields, like a custom resource file. Later in the book, you see examples of extending SYS_VAR.DBF to include other information of any type an application demands.

You can adapt this approach; you can remove the call altogether if you don't like SYS_VAR.DBF handling these tasks, or you can comment out the DO OpenSys line in INCLUDE.PRG for those applications that don't need it.

If you read the notes in this section of INCLUDE.PRG, you'll notice that I suggest placing a deliberate error at this point in your program. If you want to watch my template code's error handler at work and use the Utilities menu options that give users access to the error logs, remove the asterisk from the line `* error test here`, recompile your seeded application, and run the program. (You may also want to set `_DEBUG = .T.` before executing the application to see the Debug menu appear.)

My error handler saves many different types of information in its memo fields. If one error cascades to create many others, even if they're all trivial after the first, the log may accumulate until it runs out of disk space. Don't worry; it will eventually stop, and you can safely delete the error log file afterwards if you like.

I often force disk space to run out by running applications on a RAM disk to check this important species of error. If the error handler fails because the disk space runs out while it is in the middle of writing information, you may find that FoxPro reports that the file is corrupted when you try USE it as a table later. You can still open its memo file: by using the command MODI COMM ERRORLOG.FPT, go to the bottom of the file and salvage very valuable information.

Whatever you do, don't get frustrated and turn off your Mac! If you find that my error handler takes its job too seriously, creating many spurious log entries after the first critical error in a series, you can make sure that the application terminates after it's been through the logging process once. Simply edit PROCEDURE APPERROR, in MAIN.PRG, to CANCEL for any conditions you choose.

FOXPRO MAC HACK TIP

No error handler is perfect, and there are always situations from which even a well-designed ON ERROR program cannot recover. Although I created this opportunity for a "safe" error in INCLUDE.PRG, you may sometimes have an unrecoverable error. There are some errors that cannot be managed inside FoxPro. For example, if you properly SET a DEFAULT directory, but your users rename the folder while your application is running, the error handler (APPERROR) may give up in disgust.

While you're working on adjusting the template code for your own needs, the error handler may fail completely at some point and send you back to interactive FoxPro.

The first thing you notice is that you can't seem to quit FoxPro. FoxPro is still looking for APPERROR to handle the problem, but it can't find APPERROR any longer. *Don't panic and switch off your Mac!*

FoxPro can't find my ON SHUTDOWN program if normal Cleanup procedures didn't get a chance to clear it out. Simply type `ON SHUTDOWN <nothing>` in the Command window and you should be able to `QUIT` without difficulty. If you want to stay in FoxPro, type `ON ERROR <nothing>` to remove the error handler, too.

This isn't really a problem with my procedures; ON SHUTDOWN is notorious for stymieing people after a crash. Being aware of annoyances like these so that you can overcome them with aplomb is important to your continued freedom to experiment in FoxPro.

INCLUDE.PRG's third CASE handles the Cleanup call to application-specific tasks. In the default version of INCLUDE, this CASE consists simply of a RELEASE statement copied directly from the PUBLIC statement in the first CASE. If you handle all PUBLIC declarations in this one place, you can be sure to mirror them in the RELEASE in the same program.

Chapter Wrap Up

You've now looked at the procedures at the heart of my template system, although there are lots of ancillary capabilities and components you'll investigate in later chapters. You may be wondering why I started this chapter by extolling the virtues of the Project Manager as a central part of FoxPro's application-building process when you spent the whole chapter investigating two .PRGs. You may have opened these programs without going near a project file.

Here's my answer: you've really been working *within the Project Manager's build capabilities*, and relying on them all the time, even though you never saw the Project Manager's container window.

To work within a FoxPro project means to work within the framework of the compiled program format (the .APP and .EXE) that the Project Manager and its BUILD command create from your programs, not necessarily to use the Project Manager dialogs.

My MAIN.PRG and INCLUDE.PRG would be useless if I couldn't depend on the BUILD command reading their references and pulling all the pieces of the application together in an .APP. I also could never design a system like this without the APP file's consistent *calling chain* so that I have confidence in which version of a procedure (local or global, override or default) the .APP calls.

As you go on to read the next chapters and work in FoxPro for Macintosh, you may find yourself developing the same reliance on the Project Manager. Whether you approach it as a set of dialogs and a tool or in the "invisible" form of the BUILD command is immaterial to the very real help it gives you.

CREATE APP-SPECIFIC STRUCTURES: TOOLS TO DESCRIBE AND TEST DATA

by Lisa Slater

In Chapter 5, you saw a lot of code designed to handle generic tasks. In this chapter, I'll add a few more crucial file-handling routines to your arsenal. You should understand these procedures so that you feel comfortable adapting them to your working style.

After you understand MAIN.PRG and INCLUDE.PRG, which control the design of the template application, relax and forget about it.

The code isn't your goal. Your objective is to solve a business problem. *My* objective, in providing the template structure and procedures, is to get the code out of your way. With standard tasks handled for you, you can concentrate on the design of the application features that solve your business problems.

Your first job, on the agenda for this chapter, is to describe the information the business needs in FoxPro terms and with FoxPro data structures. In the next few chapters, you'll design ways of *presenting* those structures to the user.

To concentrate on design, and not code, you need suitable tools. You have already had a brief glimpse of the FoxPro design tools in Chapter 4. The Menu Builder, Screen Builder, and Report Writer handle the design of the application *surface*. The Project Manager coordinates these pieces, welding them into an application.

That's the surface. I don't know how to break this news to you gently: FoxPro has no equivalent native tool to design the underlying data structures of an application.

It's not entirely a lost cause. You can design the data in FoxPro interactively and visualize the results of your work, much as you plan a screen layout in the Screen Builder. However, FoxPro has no facility for *incorporating* your design work into an application; the Project Manager doesn't know how to coordinate your results.

As soon as you identify this limitation, however, you begin to see it as a standard problem. Any problem you face in every application deserves a comprehensive solution, a method and tool you can add to FoxPro's native set.

This is a standard principle of rapid development: if you find yourself doing something repeatedly, figure out the elements of the task and devise a better way to handle them.

You have two alternatives: design the tool in FoxPro, or find an external tool that already solves the problem. The first approach offers you ease of integration and customization. The second strategy allows you to take advantage of the tool designer's expertise, as well as features unavailable within FoxPro, but may be difficult to coordinate with your FoxPro Project.

In this chapter, you'll begin the process of solving a real-life business problem: tracking work flow and money for an advertising agency. As you confront the application's data requirements, I'll present both these alternatives.

Learn about the Data

You can't use any tools (no matter how good they are) to design an application until you figure out what the application is supposed to do. Your first job as a designer is to listen, intently and at length, to your users.

With what users say, and from the current system they demonstrate, you piece together a narrative of their work habits and needs.

If the system is large, with many different users, you'll hear many different stories. Your narrative may be hazy or convoluted and incomplete in spots, rather like a Robert Altman script. This can't be helped! Don't ignore complexity at the beginning. Simply gather *all* the details you can without attempting to reconcile them. If you initially omit requirements because you're anxious to provide comprehensive solutions, you usually have more trouble adding the overlooked requirements later.

Effective Communication at the Design Stage

Whenever possible, designate one contact person among the user group as a conduit for everybody's wish lists and work descriptions. This strategy has several important results:

- The contact person becomes well versed in describing design requirements, and the two of you learn to communicate with each other. This is easier than becoming acquainted with the nuances of each user's language and thoughts.
- The users have to confront some competing specifications *before* you hear about them. Sometimes the requirements are incommensurable. For example, the personnel department wants all data encrypted while top management expects easy, interactive use of the data from a variety of outside sources. At other times, the competing needs of different parts of the organization cannot be handled within the current scope and budget of the project. There's no reason for you to handle all such problems when users can identify them and work out some compromises on their own.
- The users often develop creative extensions and enhancements of their original application goals. Sometimes an organization has no productive internal mechanisms for brainstorming and capturing useful ideas until *you* provide an external requirement.

Of course the contact person must be fair-minded and intelligent, and the organization must be psychologically healthy for a cooperative design process to be successful. There are always individuals who want to sabotage a project within a group. If you can identify the source of their fears and address their concerns early in the process, however, the original skeptics can become your application's adept and enthusiastic evangelists.

You won't always succeed in this effort, but it's always worth trying. Remember that the information you process is your users' area of expertise. The more creatively they work to help you design, test, and implement the application, the more exciting and rewarding your results will be.

AD*Vantage FoxPro: The Story Opens

The specifications for this book's model application (working title: AD*Vantage) were "translated" from the client's requirements to me by Andy Griebel.

Because Andy is an expert applications developer, his narrative gives you a much clearer perspective on the application than you often get in interviews with prospective users. If you find one contact person who enjoys thinking about information in an organized fashion, however, your job is much easier. Whether they know anything about computers or databases is unimportant.

Even a narrative from a contact person who's also a developer does not prevent application requirements from being confusing! Below, I excerpt from Andy's vivid description of the agency's work. You see that it is in the form of a story:

> The agency interacts with outside people. People, particularly in the ad biz, change jobs all the time. Also, it isn't uncommon for a person that used to be a customer to become a vendor and vice-versa.
>
> On the agency side, we keep track of:
>
> Jobs (usually assigned a "job number" regardless of agency)
> People, sub-categorized as:
> Bosses (they don't work <grin>)
> AE's (account executives, essentially "waiters")
> the "chefs"
> creative copy
> creative artists
> the "cooks"
> Production
> Audio/Video
> Print
> typesetters/graphic video artists

> A job has an "inventory." The inventory stores everything that goes on during a job. A line-item in the inventory might be any one of the following:
>
> Time Entry: (hours by person)
> Purchase Order: (say, for printing or other "real" costs)
> Insertion Order: (magazine ads)
> Broadcast: (TV/radio)
> Something else I can't remember right now.<frown>
>
> Purchase orders are like a normal sales invoice. Dollars X for Items Y. The only problem is sometimes you create a PO without an assigned value. You might "estimate" that printing labels that say "I love California" to be placed on fourteen thousand stuffed bears will run $xxx, only to change that to a "real" value after the folks have completed assembly of said unit. You estimated to give the AE an idea (often they are clueless) what they had "ordered" was gonna cost the client. For the sixty days during the process you carried the estimated profit/loss, but that became a "real" profit/loss when the estimate became an invoice. Make sense?

At this point in Andy's narrative, I was entertained, but somewhat overwhelmed. I was tempted to answer "No!" to his question in the last sentence.

Remember to reserve judgment. Gather information, don't rush to provide a solution at this stage.

Both my amusement and my confusion deepened, as he continued:

> Insertion orders are similar, but include discount schedules for multiple insertions, frequency, size, number, colors, and contacts at the pub. It would be handy to keep track of how many times a given publication had let you "push" a deadline.
>
> The category of insertion orders also covers billboards, called Outdoor by the industry. Actually, they're not *exactly* the same thing, but most folks use the same "form" to record the data on paper.
>
> For broadcasts, store the name of the piece, frequency, duration, station, and rates. Broadcast has to carry special requirements. For example, you wouldn't want to schedule spots for the local nuclear power agency during "The Simpsons." The powers-that-be would not be amused (but, man, I would be!).
>
> I *know* I'm missing something...

> Ad agencies are notorious for billing arbitrarily. They sometimes "eat" the extra time given to a job (it was harder than we thought) or money (they printed a word wrong and our copy editors missed it). The industry standard billing terms are "net" and "gross" for the internal costs versus what they bill the clients, with the difference (profit) usually standardized at a percentage. As well as "eating" the over-runs, they sometimes inflate the charges.

Having described the information the agency uses, Andy told me what the agency needs to know:

> At any given time, you want to know the following:
>
> How much money has client X spent with us?
> How much do they owe us?
> When will their job be delivered?
>
> If something goes wrong:
>
> Who is involved? (AE's, production)
> Why is it delayed (whose fault?)
> What is the revised delivery date?
> Are additional costs associated?
> Who pays for cost over-runs (agency or client)?
>
> Here are the kinds of things that can go wrong:
>
> AE's might forget to show a sample for approval, or forget to get the client to sign-off on the sample, or forget to place the insertion order for a newspaper/mag until after the deadline, or forget to remember that lead-time for job "x" is six weeks and they want it tomorrow.
>
> Creative people might blow off working on "X-RAYS and Your Prostate" brochures because they find it distasteful.
>
> Production people might forget to call the printer and say "the blue-line is fine, print it..." or be available to approve the colors of Company Z's annual report as they come off the press.

What the agency people want to know has implications for application output:

> At any agency, there is a constant *finger-pointing*. This is where ad-agency programs have to differ from normal accounting systems. A bill is rarely sent "as-is." If you buy 124 widgets at $24.95 each in a hardware store, you pay the extended cost. *Every* bill in an agency, on the other hand, is examined with an eye that usually says "The client won't stand for this! Uh, take off the $134 charge for "courier service," and throw away the AE's time (15 hours at $98/hour)...."

> On the other hand, it's important for them to keep track of real costs, whether they've been billed or not, to justify internal expenses. "My department billed ?XXXXX last year, eating $0 dollars in errors...."
>
> Jobs need to be totaled by Client, AE, and Department.
>
> At any time, we might put together a "total-cost" for client, but involve elements that we don't know how much will cost. There are countless variations on this theme, but mostly it means that we never use "real" numbers practically anywhere. Reports they need are based on both the real and adjusted figures:
>
> How much did each employee bill?
> How much did we charge per billed employee? (profit)
> How much was biz per client?
> How much was biz per job?
> How much $ per department?
> How much did we eat (disallowed costs)?
> What's wrong with job X?
> What jobs are employee X involved with?
> What employees are involved with job X?

Well! Microsoft marketing people are fond of using the slogan *"Challenge Me!!"* when they talk about FoxPro. If you don't find Andy's description of real-life requirements a little more *challenging* than the LASER application that ships with FoxPro, I'll eat my Rules of Data Normalization wall poster.

Luckily, AD*Vantage is up to the challenge—when you put the task in terms that FoxPro understands.

Describe the Data in FoxPro Terms

If you haven't a clue about the basic database concepts of entities, attributes, and keys, or the way these concepts are expressed in FoxPro tables, fields, indexes, and relations, you need to review FoxPro documentation or another book before reading this section. You should also review Chapter 3, "Quick Start for non-FoxFolks", if you're new to the FoxPro database management vocabulary.

I'm going to tell you how I translated Andy's specs into FoxPro structures, but I expect you to know how those structures work.

Identify the Prime Suspects

See Also

- "Quick Start for Non-Xbase Database Designers," Chapter 3

I feel like a detective in the dénouement of a murder mystery about to disclose the secret of the solution to the crime. Some fictional detectives accomplish brilliant feats of observation and deduction unattainable by their admiring listeners. Others make progress through a series of very ordinary accomplishments which gradually amount to a solution.

Don't worry, I'm the second kind of detective, and arranging data into normalized structures is the second kind of activity. *You can do it.*

You start with a small piece: examine it closely, make sure you understand it thoroughly, and then relate it to the next piece. Eventually, you'll get a clear picture of the whole database.

To begin, I determined that the concept of a Job and a Job's Inventory was central to the work the agency did. Along with Inventory, a Job also had zero-to-many Change Orders, representing an audit trail of adjustments to the original job specifications. The Change Orders would not necessarily have any connection to individual Inventory items.

Figure 6.1 shows you the FoxPro View window and its subsidiary 1-To-Many relationship dialog box. If you're new to FoxPro, you can use these tools to learn FoxPro syntax (in this case, SET SKIP); the choices you make are echoed as FoxPro code in the Command window.

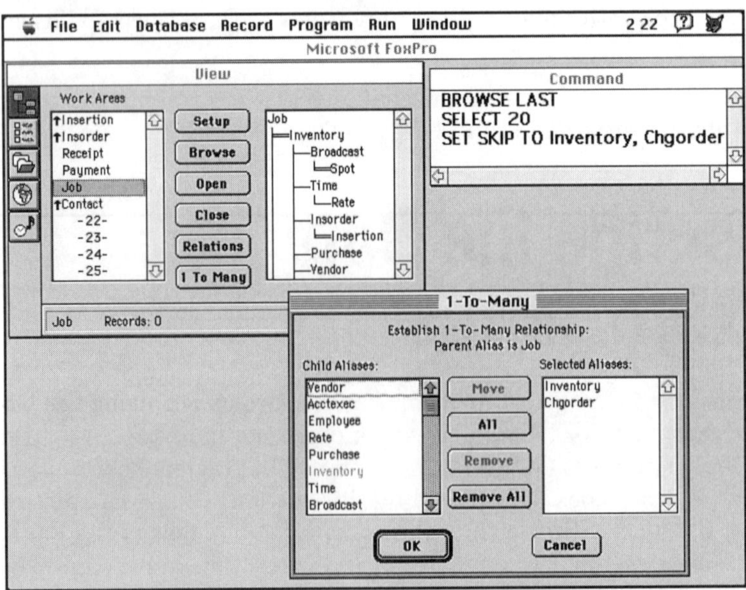

Figure 6.1 *The View window provides a graphical view of data and processes your requests as FoxPro code in the Command window.*

FOXPRO MAC HACK TIP

Along with the good it does, the View window teaches some bad code habits. In figure 6.1, you can see the View-window-created code `SELECT 20`, which makes the Job table the current work area before the SET SKIP commands on Job's child tables can be issued. *Never use workarea numbers to refer to your tables.* You shouldn't care what workareas FoxPro uses to open your tables, especially because FoxPro's SQL SELECT command opens tables in any workarea available. When you open a table, use the commands `SELECT 0` followed by `USE <tablename> ALIAS <aliasname>`, or `USE <tablename> IN 0 ALIAS <aliasname>`. Then you can refer to the table using its alias without ever knowing its workarea number. This code is easier for other programmers to understand and is more portable and more safe than explicit workarea references.

The Job had to be linked to one responsible account executive inside the agency and one client outside the agency. Each Job would also have a link to one or many vendors, one for each line item of its Inventory. The vendor for a broadcast order or printing purchase is obvious. But even a time charge for an agency employee has a vendor: the department inside the agency which bills the hours and the salaries that have to be justified.

Link to the Outside: The Address Book

Andy's first statement about people changing jobs and relationships to the agency was highly significant. I decided that this application didn't really have Vendors and Clients, it had an Address Book. I named the address table Company, rather than Address, to underscore the fact that the significant entity is the business, not the location. The agency may send bills to a specific Company, or receive payments from it, or both. Agency personnel simply wanted to reach for their Address Book and add information while they worked.

In FoxPro, it's easy to view a single table in two guises using the USE AGAIN syntax. Each guise of the table has a unique ALIAS, with which you refer to the table within the application. In this case, I `USE Company AGAIN` in two different workareas, `ALIAS Vendor` and `ALIAS Client`. You see the results in figure 6.2. Notice that the tables can maintain different orders. This capability is useful for reporting, but it also permits relationships based on different key values for each alias.

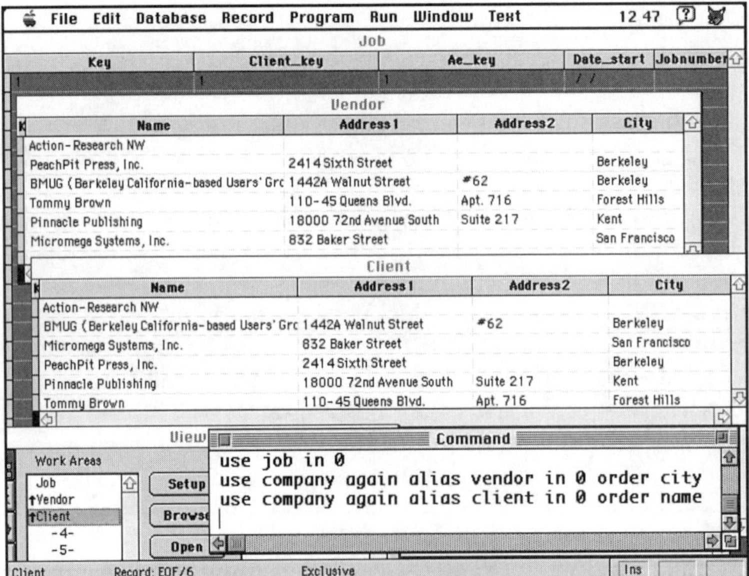

Figure 6.2 *A single Address table provides views of Clients and Vendors.*

An agency or other business may have many relationships with outside entities besides Clients and Vendors, such as government regulatory agencies, but address information is always the same and shouldn't be split up into separate tables. You can always filter out companies that have never received an industry purchase order, if you want to print a Vendor Address book.

Similarly, a Job has one and only one Account Executive, and it also has an employee responsible for each Inventory line. However, Account Executives are employees, too. Instead of an account executive table, I `USE Employee AGAIN ALIAS AcctExec`. Then I use the Department table with two aliases, (DEPT and AE_DEPT). Now each Account Executive is properly identified by his or her department, but each line item is the responsibility of a particular department, according to the employee information in the Inventory record.

A Company may have zero, one, or many contacts associated with it, so I created a child table of Company, named Contact, and a Number grandchild table to hold all methods of reaching a Contact (e-mail, voice-mail, fax, home, and so on). These contacts are associated with the Company whether the Company is currently viewed as Vendor or Client. Figure 6.3

shows the Setup dialog box of the View window and the Company-Contact-Number relationships as I work on the Number table structure and index keys. Notice that the order is set to Cont_key, the unique ID value of the Number table's parent Contact.

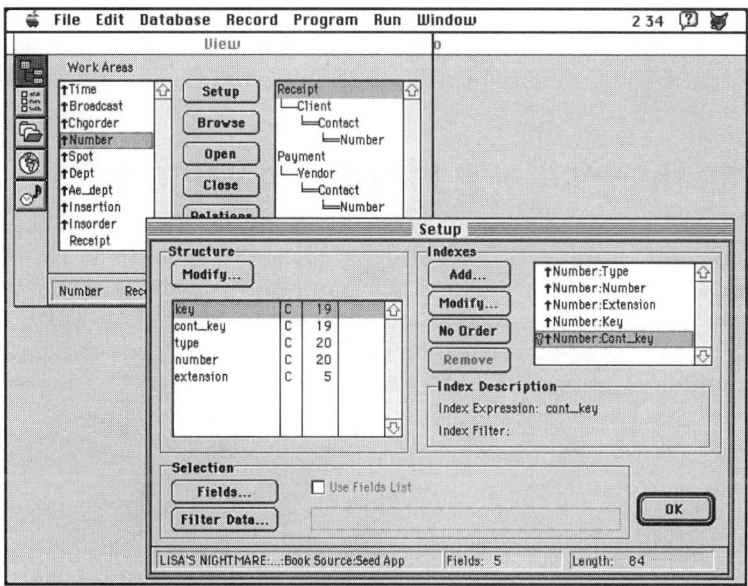

Figure 6.3 *The View window provides a way to edit table structures as well as relationships.*

The association of a Job to a contact is not as critical as the Job's Company link. The agency's bills or purchase orders don't follow the individual when he or she changes employers. I omitted a field in the Job table to link a Contact directly with the Job, reasoning that the agency might decide to link this information on an Inventory-item basis, rather than for the whole Job at once.

Specifying a contact for each detail line shouldn't cause extra data entry work. To minimize the drudgery, the agency might specify that the Contact for an Inventory record be repeated within a Job until the user enters a new value. The contact information is a *lookup* (it's chosen from available values in the Contact table, not entered directly), so even a new value doesn't take much work.

In later chapters, you'll see that such data entry aids are no difficult trick, but you should still be sure of the user's intentions and needs before creating a solution. (This is *not* the same as oversimplifying or omitting real requirements, which I cautioned you against earlier in this chapter.) There was no basis on which I could make an arbitrary or unilateral decision about which relationship (Job to Contact or Inventory to Contact) would best serve the agency. At this stage, I concentrated on the aspects of data that I knew were required to link the data into meaningful form.

Link to the Inside: A Flexible Inventory

The other side of the application was a little trickier to envision in physical terms than an Address Book: A Job clearly had a one-to-many relationship with Inventory items, but what information was stored in an Inventory record? Andy's description of different detail lines (Time, Purchase, Broadcast, and Insertion Orders) did not indicate much common ground among them. What's more, I was troubled by the inference that there could be many more kinds of Inventory lines we hadn't encountered yet.

How could I design an Inventory table to encompass them all?

I couldn't. And, in fact, there isn't any need to do it. The Inventory record is the *header record* for many different types of information, each going into its own table. Each Inventory record has a one-to-one relationship with one record in one of those child tables. Some of the child tables have additional one-to-many relationships; for example, a Broadcast record may be an order for many Spots.

The Inventory record simply receives the common *results* of each child record's variable contents: the actual and estimated cost figures, the dates and times, and the employee responsible for this activity.

After I removed the variable contents from Inventory, I could easily encompass as many different types of Inventory items as might eventually appear, by adding additional child table and data entry screens. Later in the book you see that the calling procedures won't even know anything has changed if you add additional Inventory child tables. You could put the application into production use and make this change months later with no problem.

As I began to understand the agency work flow, and as the structures fell into place, so did a physical world metaphor for the Job to match the Address Book metaphor for the Company. My screen would show the

Job-global information as it might be written on a manila file folder: the Job title on a tab, its dates, and perhaps some free-form notes. "Within" the Job Folder each "Inventory page" might look completely different from the next, depending on the type of Inventory, just as the original paper work orders did. These metaphors would make the application's main tasks comfortable and familiar for its users.

With these two images in mind, I felt the main hurdles of the structural design process were over. Simple queries in FoxPro's RQBE (Relational Query By Example dialog) convinced me that I could, indeed, answer the questions that Andy specified as application output and results.

For example, in figure 6.4 you see the RQBE-generated SQL SELECT statement to process the following English-language query: *Show me all overdue job numbers with the names of the clients to whom I'm going to have to apologize plus the names of the employees responsible for the overdue items, under whose tails I'm going to have to light a fire.*

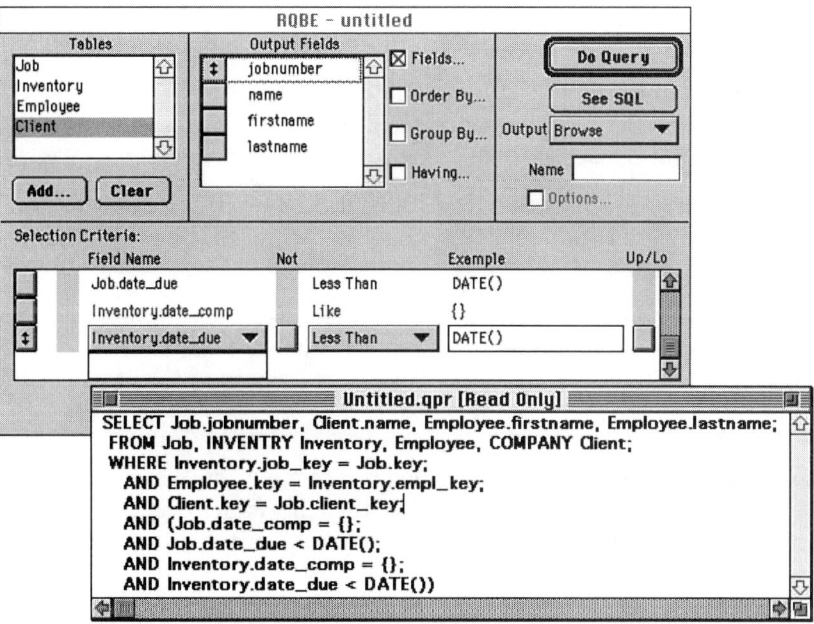

Figure 6.4 *Check the results of your table design work in the RQBE. Can you get the results you want?*

You don't have to know SQL SELECT syntax to write this query; the RQBE does almost all the work for you. If you have your tables open when you work on the tables, the RQBE makes very intelligent guesses. When I specified the Company table for the query in the figure, I was especially impressed to see that the RQBE knew enough to use the Company opened under its current Client alias, rather than re-opening it under its own name.

The RQBE won't actually write apologies or light fires for agency executives. There are limits, even in a FoxPro executive information system (the executive still has to take action on the results of the query). However, if your tables are properly designed, manipulation of their information is almost limitless.

Visualize the Data in FoxPro

The figures in the last section show you some of the work I did in FoxPro to arrive at my conclusions, in FoxPro's View window and its subsidiary dialog boxes along with the RQBE and FoxPro's Command window.

See Also

- Source Disk: Seed App (startup) Folder

If you want to investigate the full structures of the AD*Vantage application, you'll find a Seed App (startup) folder on your source disk with the FoxPro AD*Vantage set of tables.

Make a duplicate of this folder and SET DEFAULT TO the new folder. You'll see the View window's Files panel method of SETting the DEFAULT in figure 6.5.

Be sure that the current folder is properly set; use the command `WAIT WINDOW CURDIR()` in the Command window to check. Then execute this command:

```
SET VIEW TO APP
```

Alternatively, use the File Open dialog box to open the View file APP.VUE that you find in the default folder. Checking the View window after opening the View file, you should see the full set of tables and relationships for AD*Vantage set up for you.

View files store relative paths from the current folder to the open tables (although it doesn't matter what the current folder's name is), so they only work as long as the tables and the .VUE file remain in the same locations, relative to one another. In APP.VUE's case, it only works if you have properly SET the DEFAULT folder to the folder in which APP.VUE resides, and nested in which you find the DBFS folder. This fixed-folder relationship makes View files unsuitable for application work. They are still very handy while you design the tables and relationships.

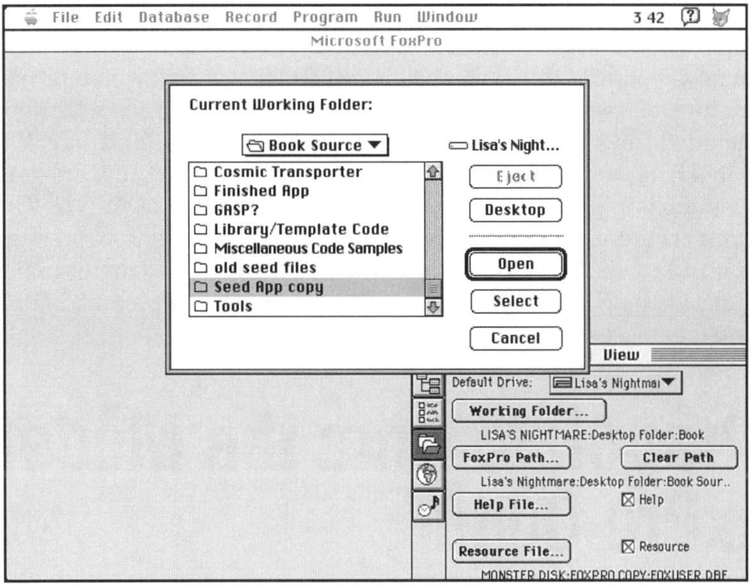

Figure 6.5 *SET DEFAULT TO the Seed App Copy folder before you try the .VUE file.*

> ## CROSS-PLATFORM WARNING
>
> You create and edit View files by changing the currently open tables, their tags or relationship, or other factors in your environment, followed by the File menu's Save As command or the command `CREATE VIEW`. However, in my experience, View files written in FoxPro Mac are easily confused, possibly because of some internal confusion about VOLUME-settings. The APP.VUE file on your source disk was saved in FoxPro for Windows; FoxPro Mac also doesn't seem to like FoxPro for DOS .VUE files. Because you need the APP.VUE file for work in the rest of the chapter, don't overwrite it with a Mac version, just in case!

The file structure of the .VUE is difficult to read, which is another reason why View files are not suitable for inclusion in applications. In fact, the Project Manager knows nothing about them. Your interactive visualization of the data doesn't help you manage the data within your application.

In an ideal FoxPro, a .VUE would be a normal FoxPro table, like an .SCX or .MNX (screen and menu definition files). You'd create the View file as you do now, opening tables in the graphical View window and other FoxPro interactive dialog boxes or by executing commands interactively. If you included the View file in your Project or issued the SET VIEW command in a program included in an application, the Project Manager would call a generating program similar to GENSCRN or GENMENU. The generator would read the View file you created in the graphical View window and its dialog boxes. It would then generate file maintenance code, just as the Project Manager currently causes .SPRs and .MPRs to be generated as necessary.

Extrapolate from the Model to FoxPro Code

Enter APPSETUP, the developer's tool I wrote to generate file-handling code.

APPSETUP: A Data Description Tool

You'll find the APPSETUP project file in its own folder on the source disk, along with full source for this tool. Before running the APPSetup application, you need to SET DEFAULT TO this folder and issue the command BUILD APP APPSETUP FROM APPSETUP, as described in the disk's readme.1st file and as you've already done in Chapter 4. (We omitted this compiled file from the source disk to save space.) Then you can execute APPSetup.APP from the Run or Program menus as you executed LASER.APP and your test application in Chapter 4.

See Also

- Source Disk: APPSetup: APPSETUP.APP

APPSETUP makes use of a .VUE file if you've prepared one, so you should know that it SETs DEFAULT to the folder you designate as your application's home folder. It also expects to find the data for the development copy of your application to exist in a folder named DBFS under the home folder. Of course, this restriction doesn't affect the distributed version of your app because the template code indirectly references all table names with the data path they specify. However, if you create View files to use with APPSETUP, you can arrange your files and SET your DEFAULT according to this system before saving the .VUE.

You can start APPSETUP using any default. The tool's first visible action is a dialog box requesting your application's home folder. If you choose one, APPSETUP checks for the files that it needs and the development folders that it expects to find nested there. If you don't, APPSETUP tells you what it wants (using the alert you see in figure 6.6) and waits at its main dialog box for you to choose a folder.

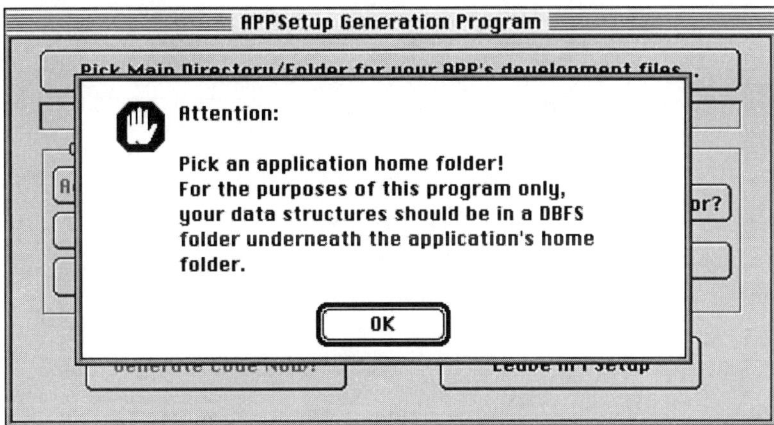

Figure 6.6 *APPSETUP requires a home folder name and a DBFS folder within it.*

Choose your Seed App Copy folder, either initially or using the appropriate button in the main APPSETUP dialog. Take a moment to read the help screen (shown in figure 6.7) using another button in the dialog box. It will familiarize you with the programs and folders APPSETUP creates and how you can use them.

Besides the DBFS folder and at least one table in it, APPSETUP requires a table named DBFS.DBF in your application home folder. It creates this table if you don't already have it to identify the tables in use by your system and their aliases. (When you set your home folder to the Seed App Copy folder, which has this file prepared for you, you should see a message as APPSETUP opens all the tables it finds listed in DBFS.) Use the button with the prompt "Adjust DBFs.DBFS," and the dialog changes to the BROWSE you see in figure 6.8 so that you can change aliases or add tables as necessary.

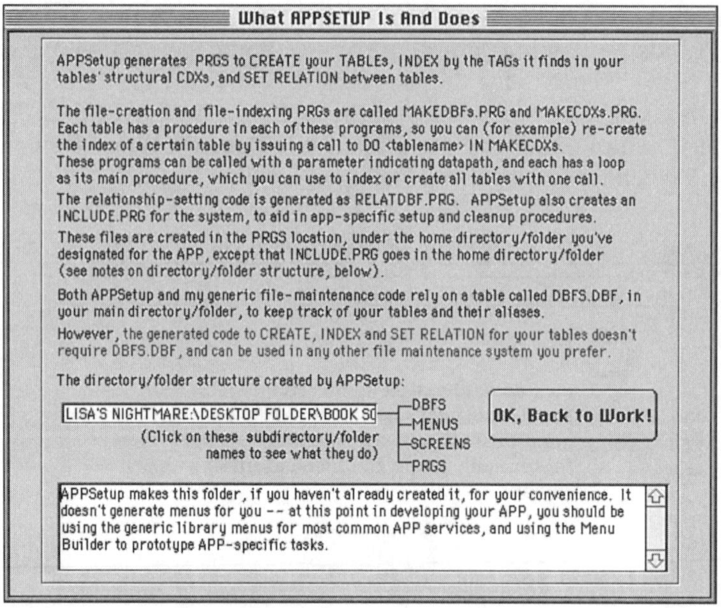

What APPSETUP Is And Does

APPSetup generates PRGS to CREATE your TABLEs, INDEX by the TAGs it finds in your tables' structural CDXs, and SET RELATION between tables.

The file-creation and file-indexing PRGs are called MAKEDBFs.PRG and MAKECDXs.PRG. Each table has a procedure in each of these programs, so you can (for example) re-create the index of a certain table by issuing a call to DO <tablename> IN MAKECDXs. These programs can be called with a parameter indicating datapath, and each has a loop as its main procedure, which you can use to index or create all tables with one call.

The relationship-setting code is generated as RELATDBF.PRG. APPSetup also creates an INCLUDE.PRG for the system, to aid in app-specific setup and cleanup procedures.

These files are created in the PRGS location, under the home directory/folder you've designated for the APP, except that INCLUDE.PRG goes in the home directory/folder (see notes on directory/folder structure, below).

Both APPSetup and my generic file-maintenance code rely on a table called DBFS.DBF, in your main directory/folder, to keep track of your tables and their aliases.

However, the generated code to CREATE, INDEX and SET RELATION for your tables doesn't require DBFS.DBF, and can be used in any other file maintenance system you prefer.

The directory/folder structure created by APPSetup:

LISA'S NIGHTMARE:\DESKTOP FOLDER\BOOK S(

(Click on these subdirectory/folder names to see what they do)

DBFS
MENUS
SCREENS
PRGS

OK, Back to Work!

APPSetup makes this folder, if you haven't already created it, for your convenience. It doesn't generate menus for you -- at this point in developing your APP, you should be using the generic library menus for most common APP services, and using the Menu Builder to prototype APP-specific tasks.

Figure 6.7 *APPSETUP's help screen.*

FOXPRO MAC HACK TIP

The BROWSE in APPSETUP is a simple data entry method with just enough data validation to make sure that you can't enter an invalid alias name. In normal applications, I reserve BROWSEs for READ-only lists of records, a selection which brings up an editing screen. However, APPSETUP is a tool for developers and a BROWSE is acceptable for data entry in this context.

Using the BROWSE rather than a fully developed data entry dialog for table and alias names in APPSETUP illustrates an important rapid development principle: *Don't overcode*. When FoxPro has a native capability to take care of your needs, use it. However, in the shipping version of FoxPro Mac, the BROWSE command has a few quirks. Make sure that your main application window is on-screen and more than a few rows and columns in size before starting APPSETUP or the BROWSE may not appear. This is a FoxPro bug for which I've made provision in the application-building template code you'll use later in the book.

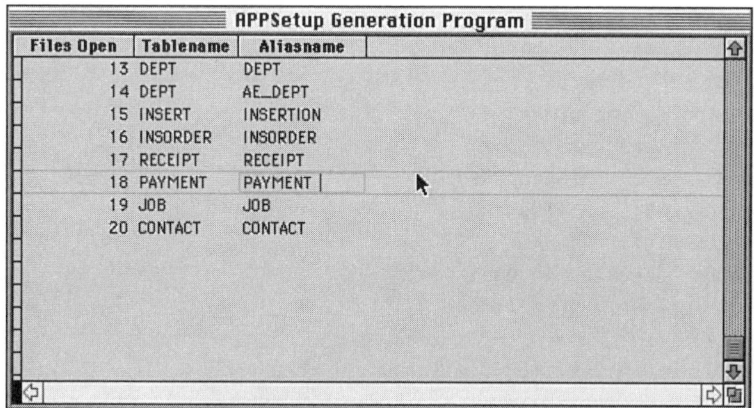

APPSetup Generation Program

Files Open	Tablename	Aliasname
13	DEPT	DEPT
14	DEPT	AE_DEPT
15	INSERT	INSERTION
16	INSORDER	INSORDER
17	RECEIPT	RECEIPT
18	PAYMENT	PAYMENT
19	JOB	JOB
20	CONTACT	CONTACT

Figure 6.8 *DBFs.DBF stores table and alias names for APPSETUP and also for the template code's file-handling procedures.*

My template code uses DBFs.DBF to identify these tables in file-handling procedures, as well. For example, the procedure to open tables for the application reads as follows:

```
PROCEDURE OpenDBFS
PRIVATE m.errorprog, m.oldbell
IF NOT USED("Dbfs")
   USE Dbfs AGAIN ALIAS Dbfs IN 0
* You bind the table into app
ENDIF
SELECT Dbfs
m.oldbell = SET("BELL")
SET BELL OFFWAIT WINDOW NOWAIT "Opening data files... "
SCAN
DO Open_one ;
         WITH ALLTRIM(Dbfs.tablename), ;
         ALLTRIM(Dbfs.aliasname)
ENDSCAN
* PROCEDURE Open_One
* is built to handle any tables
* that can't be opened, whether
* they are corrupt, have missing
* or corrupted memo files or
* structural indexes, or whether
* they are simply missing from
* the file.
```

```
* Now do a second pass —
* some files may have been
* created on the first pass, and
* depending on the order
* of the failures you don't
* know for sure what happened
* with any USE... AGAINs and
* relationships.
* The error checking in Open_one
* is not necessary this time.
SCAN
   IF NOT USED(ALLTRIM(DBFS.aliasname))
       USE (m.datapath+ ;
            ALLTRIM(DBFS.tablename)) ;
           AGAIN ALIAS ;
           (ALLTRIM(Dbfs.aliasname)) IN 0
   ENDIF
ENDSCAN

SET BELL &oldbell
WAIT CLEAR
RETURN
```

See Also

- PROCEDURE OpenDBF's, Source Disk:Library/ Template Code:MAIN.PRG
- PROCEDURE Open_One, Source Disk:Library/ Template Code:MAIN.PRG

Besides the tablename and aliasname fields, AD*Vantage's copy of DBFs.DBF uses an additional field in DBFs.DBF, Subform, to identify the Inventory child files and their one-to-many subfiles.

You can add additional fields to DBFs.DBF in your own tables; APPSETUP won't mind. In fact, in subsequent chapters, you'll see that the AD*Vantage version of DBFs.DBF uses fields not required by APPSetup to handle file relationships in multi-table screen sets. The DBFs table thus becomes the beginning of the *data description* table we wish the native View file could be. I won't go so far as to call it the data *dictionary* that FoxPro developers would like to have, but you could extend the concept in many directions.

APPSETUP's generated code, however, is independent of my system and doesn't require DBFs.DBF, as you'll see when you create it in a moment.

As a shortcut to setting up the application's data and relationships, use the button to select a View file and choose the same APP.VUE file that you used interactively before. Use the button to access the View window so that you can verify the tables and watch as APPSETUP works. Then press the button to Generate code.

APPSETUP lets you know which tables it finds as it works. If you have the View window open, you can see all available workareas being checked. When the generation process completes, press the button to View Generated Code. Your screen looks something like figure 6.9.

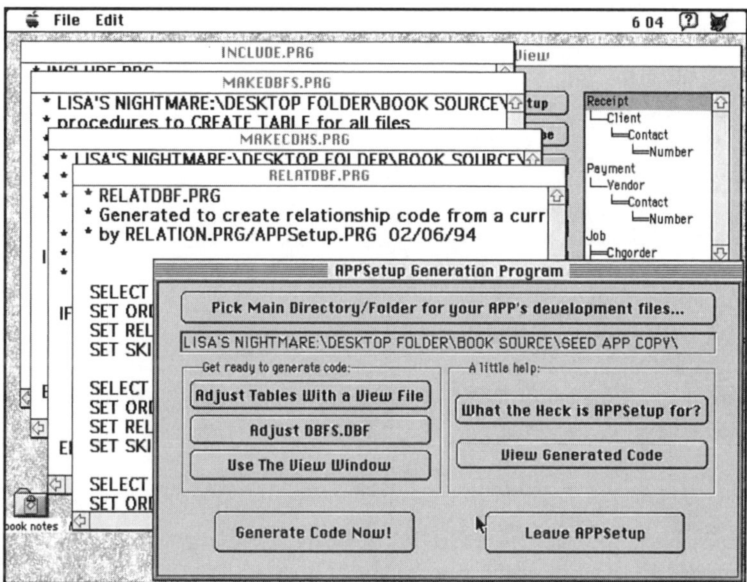

Figure 6.9 *APPSETUP shows you the code that it generated.*

APPSETUP's Generated Results

Editing the RELATDBF.PRG, you find code that looks like this:

```
SELECT VENDOR
SET ORDER TO COMP_KEY IN CONTACT
SET RELATION TO VENDOR.KEY INTO CONTACT ADDITIVE
SET SKIP TO Contact
```

```
SELECT CLIENT
SET ORDER TO COMP_KEY IN CONTACT
SET RELATION TO CLIENT.KEY INTO CONTACT ADDITIVE
SET SKIP TO Contact
```

These are the relationships "hidden" in the View file, made available as a .PRG for your project.

The generated MAKEDBFs.PRG starts with a loop that you can use to create all tables at once, by executing the command `DO MAKEDBFs.PRG [WITH datapath memvar]`:

```
IF FILE("DBFS.DBF")
SELECT tablename DISTINCT ;
  FROM DBFS INTO ARRAY dbfsarray
* DISTINCT because of USE AGAIN files
PRIVATE dbfsarray, m.xx
FOR m.xx = 1 TO ALEN(dbfsarray)
    DO (ALLTRIM(dbfsarray(m.xx))) WITH m.datapath
ENDFOR
ELSE
  WAIT WINDOW NOWAIT      ;
      "Your app-specific TABLE-CREATEing program "+ ;
      "ordinarily goes here... "
ENDIF
RETURN
```

Following the loop, you see a PROCEDURE for every table in the application's DBFs list, each one in the following form:

```
PROCEDURE RATE
PARAMETERS dpath
IF TYPE("dpath") # "C"
   dpath = ""
ENDIF
PRIVATE m.safety
m.safety = SET("SAFETY")
SET SAFETY ON* prevent overwrites
* LISA'S NIGHTMARE:\BOOK SOURCE\SEED APP COPY\DBFS\RATE.DBF - 02/06/94
PRIVATE sqlarray
DIMENSION sqlarray(3,4)
   sqlarray(1,1) = "key
   sqlarray(1,2) = "C"
   sqlarray(1,3) = 19
   sqlarray(1,4) = 0
```

```
   sqlarray(2,1) = "descr
   sqlarray(2,2) ="C"
   sqlarray(2,3) = 40
   sqlarray(2,4) = 0
   sqlarray(3,1) = "hourly
   sqlarray(3,2) = "N"
   sqlarray(3,3) = 6
   sqlarray(3,4) = 2
CREATE TABLE (dpath + "rate.dbf")    FROM ARRAY  sqlarray
SET SAFETY &safety
RETURN
```

You can create a single table using the command `DO <tablename> IN MAKEDBFs [WITH datapath memvar]`. (This is how PROCEDURE Open_one in my template code creates the table after an error during file-opening procedures.)

MAKECDXs is similar to MAKEDBFs, with the same loop at the top, and you can call it in the same ways. Its individual procedures for each table look like this:

```
PROCEDURE DEPT
PARAMETERS dpath
IF TYPE("dpath") # "C"
   dpath = ""
ENDIF
PRIVATE m.safety
m.safety = SET("SAFETY")
SET SAFETY OFF
* Structural cdx: LISA'S NIGHTMARE:\BOOK SOURCE\SEED APP
ÂCOPY\DBFS\DEPT.CDX
IF USED("DEPT")
   SELECT DEPT
ELSE
   SELECT 0
ENDIF
USE (dpath + "DEPT.DBF") ;
      AGAIN ALIAS DEPT EXCLUSIVE
DELETE TAG ALL
INDEX ON upper(descr) TAG descr
INDEX ON key TAG key
INDEX ON topemp_key TAG topemp_key
SET SAFETY &safety
RETURN
```

APPSETUP doesn't have the intelligence to decide which index tags a table needs or what relationships an application needs. It simply looks at the open tables in their existing relationships and the current tags in their structural index files to generate RELATDBF.PRG, MAKEDBFs.PRG, and MAKECDXs.PRG. In addition, it creates a copy of INCLUDE.PRG for this application's use in the home folder.

If you start development of a new project using APPSETUP, you can edit INCLUDE.PRG at this point with a new m.app_title for the new project and other customization. For awhile, you can continue to make structural changes in the app (for example, adding the new linking field to relate either Job or Inventory to Contact). You can access the View window and its Setup dialog box directly from APPSETUP to edit the file structure and regenerate whenever you like.

INCLUDE.PRG is designed for you to customize it for each new application so APPSETUP won't overwrite your edited version when you regenerate.

However, don't edit the generated file-maintenance code in the other .PRGs directly. Think of these programs as an interim processing step in the Build process like .SPRs generated from .SCXs. (In fact, in Chapter 11, I'll suggest a way that you can force the Project Manager to run APPSETUP or other additional processes for you when you Build.)

APPSETUP as a FoxPro Program

APPSETUP uses my Library/Template code and MAIN.PRG just as AD*Vantage does, with very different results, based on a different INCLUDE.PRG and a radically different MAINSPR.PRG. APPSETUP is the species of application I termed a "switchboard app" in Chapter 5. Instead of a GETless Foundation READ in which the application waits to accept the user's menu choices, MAINSPR.PRG holds almost all the code for APPSETUP, surrounding a call to the main APPSETUP dialog box in which all action of this application takes place.

The APPSETUP folder contains full source for the tool—or at least all the APPSETUP-specific source it doesn't "borrow" from the Library/Template code folder. You'll find this project an instructive example of just how far you can stretch my template.

You should also examine the generating code in MAINSPR.PRG to learn about the SET TEXTMERGE command. When you identify other FoxPro toolkit omissions, you can easily design programs similar to APPSETUP to generate the additional code you need.

FOXPRO MAC HACK TIP

APPSETUP's generating code is an evolved version of utilities written by Maurice Frank, an excellent FoxPro developer in Atlanta, Georgia. It demonstrates yet another important rapid development principle: *never reinvent the wheel*. If there's no FoxPro feature to take care of your needs, see if anybody else has already addressed that need and is willing to share. Thank you, Maurice!

See Also

- PROCEDURES GdMain, GdSqlct, and GdCDXTag, Source Disk:APPSetup: PRGS:MAINSPR.PRG

Model the Data in a CASE Tool

I've stated that the FoxPro View window is a graphical design tool for table structures. It actually has only limited capability to display structures graphically, and limited capability to describe the behavior of each structure.

In a large system, multiple programmers try to decipher the kind of narrative that you read at the beginning of this chapter and work out solutions. You need better images with which to communicate your thoughts about the application and a better storage device to hold the business rules and data entities you discover. A CASE (Computer Aided Software Engineering) tool provides *entity relationship diagrams* and a repository underneath to store this information.

You also need to capture and display the flow of data between application tasks. In the next two chapters, you'll see this flow of data and the variety of application tasks prototyped in the Menu Builder and Screen Builder. However, in a large system, a CASE tool's *data flow diagrams* or some other design method (even if it's a sketchpad and paper) help you translate the users' current work flow into separate activities and to visualize those activities' dependencies on each other.

Figure 6.10 shows the data entities for AD*Vantage being described in AUT2, Model Systems Consultants, Inc.'s CASE tool for Macintosh.

See Also

- "Additional Resources," Appendix A

You can see that the diagram allows a long English description of the Company table's attributes (fields), along with its type and length. Most CASE tools have room for additional notes in which you can specify the business rules, or validation requirements, for individual attributes, along with the details of the required relationships among tables. For example, you may want to specify that every Company has at least one Contact (a one-to-many relationship) while a Contact record does not necessarily have attached Numbers (a zero-to-many relationship).

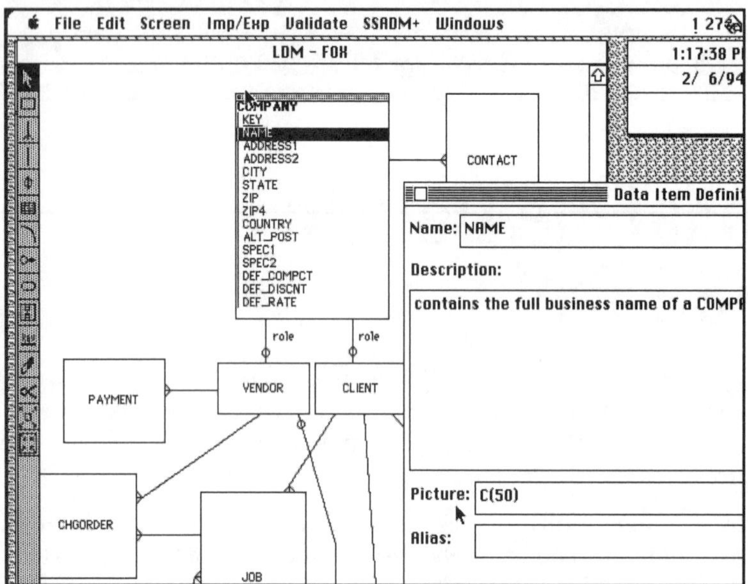

Figure 6.10 *Entities and relationships diagrammed in AUT2.*

Extrapolate from the CASE Model to FoxPro Code

Large systems deserve more painstaking description than APPSETUP or the View window can get them. However, to import this level of detail into

FoxPro form requires an extra step (the import itself) and additional planning (you devise programs to use the detailed information FoxPro doesn't handle automatically).

The following short procedure brings a tab-delimited text file, output by AUT2's repository into a FoxPro table. Notice that all data in the file is treated as character strings by the low-level file function, FGETS(), that reads the file. You can translate the data into appropriate types as you go along.

See Also

- Source Disk: Miscellaneous Code Samples: AUT2.PRG
- Source Disk: Miscellaneous Code Samples: ENTITY DEFS.TXT

```
* AUT2.PRG

PRIVATE m.handle, m.thisline, m.front, m.back,;
        m.min_no, m.av_no, m.max_no, m.workav, ;
        m.tablename, m.descr, m.oldselect,;
        m.fullpathname

* define a constant to represent
* the tab character for convenience
#DEFINE tab CHR(9)

* create a temporary table
* for this limited example;
* in the real application,
* save this information
* in a DBF on disk for use in
* diskspace estimates and checks

m.fullpathname = "Entity Defs.TXT"
IF NOT FILE(m.fullpathname)
    * find it!
    m.fullpathname = GETFILE(m.fullpathname, ;
                     "Find '"+m.fullpathname+;
                     "' file")
ENDIF

m.handle = FOPEN(m.fullpathname)
IF m.handle = -1
   * error check!
   WAIT WINDOW "Couldn't open Entity Defs file!"
   RETURN
ENDIF
```

```
m.oldselect = SELECT()

CREATE CURSOR Limits (tablename c(8),;
                      descr m,       ;
                      min_no n(10),  ;
                      av_no n(10),   ;
                      max_no n(10),  ;
                      workav n(10))

DO WHILE NOT FEOF(m.handle)
   * pick up the file a line at a time
   m.thisline = FGETS(m.handle)

   m.back = AT(tab, m.thisline,1)
   IF m.back = 0
      * this table's line isn't filled out
      LOOP
   ENDIF

   m.tablename = LEFT(m.thisline,m.back-1)

   m.front = m.back + 1
   m.back = AT(tab,m.thisline,3)
   m.descr = SUBSTR(m.thisline,;
                    m.front, m.back-m.front)
   * remove @ symbols, used internally by
   * AUT2, from the description field:
   m.descr = STRTRAN(m.descr,"@","")

   m.front = m.back + 1
   m.back =AT(tab,m.thisline,4)
   m.min_no = CheckType(SUBSTR(m.thisline,;
                        m.front, m.back-m.front))
```

```
   m.front = m.back + 1
   m.back = AT(tab, m.thisline,5)
   m.av_no = CheckType(SUBSTR(m.thisline,;
                    m.front, m.back-m.front))

   m.front = m.back + 1
   m.back = AT(tab, m.thisline, 6)
   m.max_no = CheckType(SUBSTR(m.thisline,;
                     m.front, m.back-m.front))

   m.front = m.back+1
   m.workav = CheckType(SUBSTR(m.thisline,;
                            m.front))
   INSERT INTO Limits FROM MEMVAR
ENDDO

* close the file:
=FCLOSE(m.handle)

MODI COMM (m.fullpathname
                ) NOWAIT
BROWSE TITLE "Your Results... "

* get rid of temporary table
* for this example
USE IN Limits
SELECT (m.oldselect)
 RETURN
FUNCTION checktype
PARAMETER the_value
RETURN IIF(TYPE(the_value) = "N",;
VAL(the_value),0)
```

Figure 6.11 shows you the results that you'll get when you run this demonstration program.

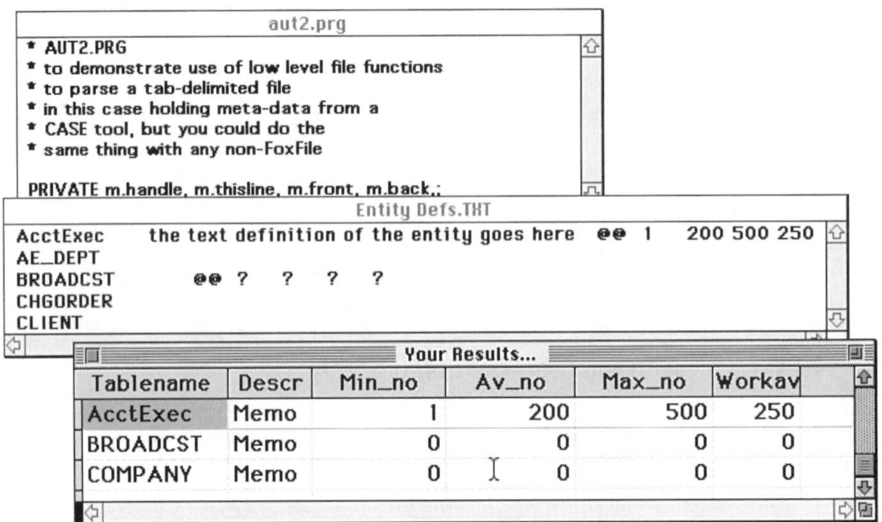

Figure 6.11 *FoxPro's low-level file functions bring CASE meta-data into a FoxPro table.*

The AUT2 text file in this example holds entity (table) names, a long English description of each table, and numbers indicating minimum, average, maximum, and working average quantities of records for the table. Although I import the values into a temporary cursor in this demonstration program, you could create DBFs.DBF fields to store the values for each table. The numeric values would provide information for disk space estimates, and the long table description would appear in help messages or menu prompts.

You might never use a CASE tool to create data-describing-data. However, you need to understand these import techniques to bring *normal* data from other database management programs along with meta-data. FoxPro allows a direct APPEND FROM the ubiquitous tab-delimited format, but you can use the low-level file function and string-handling techniques shown here on almost any format.

Conversion of data, investigating the formats in which data is organized and used in users' existing systems, is a critical part of the data structure design process you investigate in this chapter.

FOXPRO MAC HACK TIP

Besides handling file import requirements, low-level file functions can avoid the line feeds that FoxPro adds to text files before you *export* data. The line feeds are required for cross-platform compatibility with FoxPro DOS and Windows, but they are not expected by other Macintosh programs.

You can use a FOXTOOLS function, FxStripLF(), to strip the line feeds from a file you create in FoxPro by some other method. Often, however, it's more convenient to create the file using the low-level file function FWRITE() to write the data without the line feeds and without the need for any conversion process.

CROSS-PLATFORM WARNING

Similarly, FoxPro exports to a DELIMITED WITH TAB flat file using the tab character as a *field separator* and with double quotation marks as the true field delimiter. This technique is necessary because the tab character is a legal character in FoxPro character and memo fields. Most Mac programs' import facilities for tab-delimited files don't expect the quotation marks. You can use the low-level file functions to write an export file that matches the other Mac program's needs exactly.

Chapter Wrap Up

When you have the structures and relationships correct, the rest of your application just flows. When you have them wrong, you'll also know because every FoxPro task, even the design of a simple report, becomes difficult.

For example, while prototyping AD*Vantage's data entry processes, I couldn't get the Inventory child files to show the appropriate records. I searched through my code for hours to no avail. I finally realized that I'd set a double relationship between the Inventory file and the subfiles. Each Inventory record carried the unique key of its subfile-twin and the subfiles also carried the Inventory key. I was SEEKing and relying on one key in one place in my code and the other key elsewhere. Removing the redundant information solved the problem immediately.

Trust the symmetry and ease of use you get when structures are correct. Also, learn to see the patterns in relationships. A lookup file ordinarily has its order set to its own unique key. The controlling file in relationship with the lookup SETs RELATION to the lookup file's key value. By contrast, the child records in a one-to-many relationship have their order set to their parent's key value. The controlling parent SETs RELATION to its own key value. If you don't see these patterns in your own application, something is probably wrong.

You've added to the FoxPro tool kit and accomplished one of the most difficult aspects of application design. In the next chapters, you'll go on to design the application surface, an area in which FoxPro and its native tool set really shine. Get ready to be creative!

7

PROTOTYPE APP-SPECIFIC TASKS: THE MENU BUILDER AND DATA FLOW

by
Lisa Slater

In Chapter 6, you constructed data structures and relationships suitable to a business's data management objectives, by listening to the stories of the application's users. As you learn about your users' jobs and daily routines, you have a second, critical goal—identification of the application processes that maintain and use the information in those data structures.

Although some of these processes may run automatically (for example, at the end of a month), most of an application's action occurs when the user chooses to initiate it. In FoxPro, users initiate major tasks by choosing a menu option from the system menu known as SYSMENU.

Accordingly, FoxPro programmers create an outline of an application's tasks in relation to each other by building the system menu structure for the application. The syntax for creating each SYSMENU element is baroque, but you don't have to learn the actual menu-defining commands. Instead, use the FoxPro Menu Builder to sketch the menu options and save them in a menu description table (an .MNX). The menu generation program (GENMENU) reads the .MNX and creates the appropriate code in an .MPR file.

The Project Manager coordinates this process by causing GENMENU to regenerate .MPRs every time you rebuild your application after using the Menu Builder to make a change to one or more of your .MNXs. The Project Manager's Build process then recompiles the newly generated .MPR and binds the resulting compiled version of the file into the .APP file that you use to execute the entire application.

As you'll see in the next chapter, you complete your prototype by using the Screen Builder to create simple programs that you attach to the menu options. You show the resulting working .APP to your users, make adjustments in menu and screen layouts based on their reactions, and rebuild. When your programming team and your users agree that the data set and tasks have been properly identified, the design phase ends. You proceed to flesh out the prototyped menu options and screens with supporting code.

The more complete the prototype, and the less you leave to your user's imagination, the more satisfying this design process will be for everyone and the faster you can reach a consensus. However, you don't have to write a lot of code in menus or screens to provide a fairly elaborate prototype if you properly distinguish between generic processes and application-specific processes. Just as your MAIN.PRG, which doesn't change between applications, performs many standard application tasks, your library or template menu options and screen dialogs supply your application with broad areas of functionality. Only the application-specific menu options and screens, analogous to INCLUDE.PRG, require prototyping.

People usually spend much more time learning to use the Screen Builder than the Menu Builder because the Menu Builder gives satisfying results very quickly. Don't be fooled into thinking that the benefits of this tool end with freedom from DEFINE MENU syntax. The Menu Builder is so easy to use that many developers overlook some of its deeper virtues, both as a prototyping tool and as a management device for dynamic event management in the finished application.

As always, read your FoxPro manuals for basic information on using the Menu Builder. This chapter concentrates on ways to *extend* the Menu Builder to promote rapid development. Following the same procedures you used to learn about the template code, you can first investigate the template menu elements. You can familiarize yourself with the options they provide and how you can adjust them for your programming style, or for the needs of a particular application. Then you can add application-specific menu elements to the menu.

Planning the Generic Menu Skeleton and Style

MAIN.PRG's menu-defining code breaks the menu into several parts. Each .MNX file generates a separate .MPR element for the system. I use the separate .MPRs to distinguish not only between generic and app-specific menu sections but also between different types of generic menu sections requiring different treatment:

- The first menu section, represented by MINIMAL.MNX in the template code, includes pads that every application must have. Later in this system, you'll see how its standard elements can adjust for each application, but the pads exist in every case and form a basis for the rest of SYSMENU.
- The second menu section, represented by UTILITY.MNX in the template code, includes pads and options that exist in most applications. You can omit them entirely, or give them completely local behavior for certain classes of applications, using a different method than you use to adjust MINIMAL.MNX.
- The third generic menu section, represented by DEBUG.MNX, includes options you want to appear conditionally for testing purposes.

You may find that a different system of classification works for you, or you may be happy with mine. Either way, you can easily accumulate a menu system out of your chosen components by using the Menu Builder's ability to *append* menu pads to SYSMENU. This method is in stark contrast to the default behavior of an .MPR file, which ordinarily *replaces*, or substitutes, its menu definition for the entire existing system menu. You make this crucial non-default choice in the Menu Builder's General Options dialog that you see in figure 7.1. Later in the chapter, you can use the same method to append application-specific pads into a complete, tailored SYSMENU.

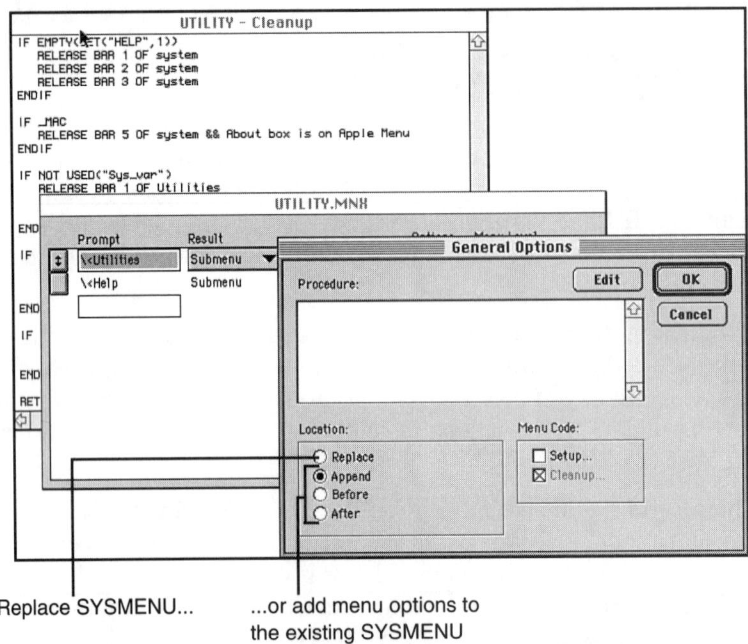

Figure 7.1. *After your general MINIMAL.MNX version of SYSMENU replaces the previous version, you can append additional menu items, such as UTILITY.MNX's Help and Utilities pads, using the Menu Builder's General Options dialog.*

The Minimal Menu Base Design

Conveniently, applications in both Microsoft Windows and the Macintosh operating system commonly have the same two standard menu pads to the left: File and Edit. Therefore, these two pads form the basis of the menu system that I provide for every application.

Macintosh adds the Apple menu to the far left and the Help and Application menus to the far right. You never DEFINE these pads directly. These native Macintosh features remain available during FoxPro programs, even if you SET SYSMENU OFF.

> **CROSS-CROSS PLATFORM WARNING**
>
> In the current version of FoxPro for Macintosh, even normal FoxPro pads remain available during FoxPro programs with SET SYSMENU OFF! Both the online help file and the documentation indicate that SET SYSMENU OFF should work in FoxPro for Macintosh just as it does in FoxPro for Windows and DOS, so this behavior may be a bug. You can test for it in your version of FoxPro Mac with the following code:
>
> ```
> HIDE WINDOWS ALL
> SET SYSMENU TO _msm_file
> SHOW MENU _msysmenu
> DEFINE PAD x OF _msysmenu PROMPT "Trial"
> ON SELECTION PAD x OF _msysmenu WAIT WINDOW
>      SET SYSMENU OFF
> BROWSE
> READ CYCLE VALID LASTKEY() = 27
> SHOW WINDOWS ALL
> SET SYSMENU TO DEFAULT
> ```
>
> If FoxPro Mac's behavior hasn't changed, you'll be able to Close the BROWSE using the File menu option and see the WAIT WINDOW if you click the Trial pad. (After testing, press Esc to clear the READ and end the test program.)
>
> If this behavior changes in later versions of FoxPro Mac (so you can't access the FoxPro pads with SET SYSMENU OFF), however, the native Macintosh Apple, Help, and Application options will almost certainly remain available at all times.

Examining your other Macintosh applications, you can see that there are standard File and Edit pop-up menu options. To provide the normal Edit menu options to your FoxPro application, you can use internal system capabilities, referred to in the menu system as *system bar numbers*. As you see in figure 7.2, I've kept my MINIMAL.MNX Edit menu options substantially the same as the default Quick Menu that you create in the Menu Builder. I've added the Macros dialog, usually found on the Program pop-up menu, because a macro recorder is an editing convenience appropriate to most applications.

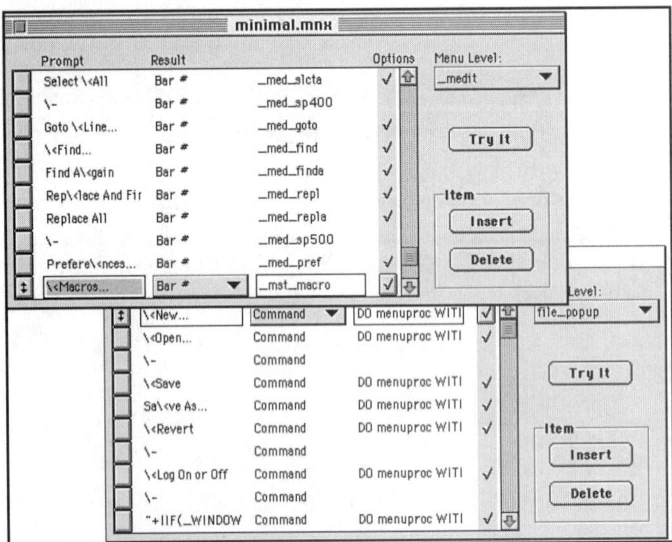

Figure 7.2. *Two copies of the MINIMAL.MNX show you its standard Edit pop-up options contrasted with its customized File pop-up options as you edit both in the Menu Builder.*

You see that the Macros dialog bar number has an _mst_ prefix, unlike the other Edit options' _med_ prefix. This difference reflects the dialog's origin on the System pop-up menu in FoxPro for DOS, although it was moved to the Program pop-up menu in FoxPro for Windows and Macintosh.

Microsoft's ambivalence about the placement of this option should make you think further about your own optimal placement of this and other menu items. You should follow standards where users already have developed expectations from other applications. Also, think long and hard about developing useful standards of your own where no external standard exists.

FOXPRO MAC HACK TIP

The native _mst_macro bar capabilities are not available in the runtime (Distribution Kit) edition of FoxPro. Instead, you can provide macro recording capabilities with the SET MACKEY option by default Shift-F10 or Shift-Option-⌘ on Macintosh keyboards that don't have function keys.

To provide menu access to macro recording in a distributed application, simply give your Macros option the Command result of `KEYBOARD "{SHIFT-F10}"` (or whichever MACKEY you've SET), rather than the Bar result of _mst_macro. Then you can add the capability to save, clear, and restore sets of macros to your distributed application using custom dialog options. You can model your custom macros dialog on the system Macros dialog if you like, but a simpler approach will probably be more suitable.

You can see the difference between the native _mst_macro dialog and the SET MACKEY dialog in figure 7.3. Although I've chosen to use the native behavior for my standard MINIMAL.MNX, you could easily decide the SET MACKEY dialog is more appropriate to *all* applications, even when you distribute them using the full development version of FoxPro.

Extend careful attention to the design of *each* generic menu element. You'll be repaid many times over in development time as you incorporate these elements in your applications.

CROSS-PLATFORM WARNING

FoxPro for DOS' System pad, on the left, was replaced by a Help pad on the right in FoxPro for Windows. On the Macintosh, the options on the System/Help pad are omitted from the default SYSMENU list in favor of native Macintosh capabilities. You can use FoxPro code to summon some of these features (for example, you can `ACTIVATE WINDOW Calculator` or include the native bar _mst_calcu on a FoxPro for Macintosh menu) and not others (`ACTIVATE WINDOW Special` or the native bar _mst_specl gives you a "feature not available error" instead of the Special Characters chart). The System About option and Help option have special positions in the native Macintosh Apple and Help menus, although you can move them to standard FoxPro menu positions if you like.

The System pad was Fox Software's attempt to reproduce the Apple menu features in DOS when they created FoxPro 1.0, using FoxBASE+/Mac as a model. This pad doesn't represent any sort of interface standard in the DOS world, as the File and Edit pads do in Windows and on the Macintosh. You don't need to imitate it on the Mac, and you don't even have to include it in your FoxPro for DOS menus. In the section on the Utility menu, below, you'll see my recommendation for providing the System pop-up's features cross-platform, but at this point there is no stable interface model to follow for these options.

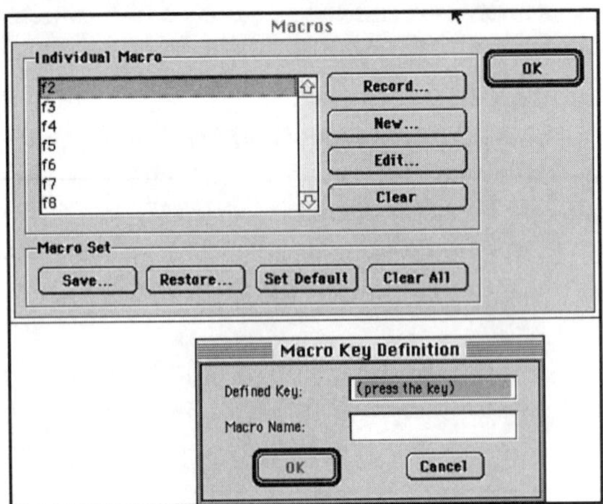

Figure 7.3 *Contrast the native _mst_macro Macros dialog (top) with the simple SET MACKEY dialog (bottom) running in a second copy of FoxPro. A combination of the SET MACKEY dialog plus a custom version of the save, clear, and restore capabilities of _mst_macro is a good choice for distributed applications.*

Compared to their use of Edit pop-up menu options, Macintosh applications are much less consistent in their use of the various File options. Although the names of these options don't vary from application to application, you may be at a loss to know what each of these options actually does until you try it.

Microsoft Windows applications provide even less consistency in their use of the File menu pad than Macintosh programs. If you develop a consistent approach to File menu handling and impose it on *both* environments, you can make a real contribution to the development of a usable interface standard.

In addition, unlike the Edit options, most of the native system bar numbers on the File menu are inappropriate to running programs. In figure 7.2, you see that I've replaced these bar numbers with a Command result in each case: `DO Menuproc WITH <character string>`. The character string parameter sends the Menuproc procedure a message indicating what action the menu procedure should take. (This message is usually the same as the File menu option prompt, for clarity.)

Using a standard Command result in the MINIMAL.MNX doesn't mean that every application has to perform the same action for a menu option. In Chapter 5, you saw that each application creates a foundation wait state by making a call to a program named MAINSPR.PRG, but that each application can have a different type of foundation wait state by having a *different* MAINSPR.PRG. My template code includes a default copy of MAINSPR.PRG, which performs a simple `READ VALID m.quitting`, but any application can have a *local* MAINSPR overriding this standard version. For example, a local MAINSPR.PRG can call a logo or "splash" screen before waiting at a GETless READ. Instead, in the case of a "switchboard" application like APPSetup, the MAINSPR.PRG can initiate a GETful dialog READ, in which the application remains until quitting. (I'll return to the important principle of the foundation wait state later in this chapter.)

See Also

- Source Disk: Library/ Template Code Folder: MENUPROC.PRG
- Source Disk: Library/ Template Code Folder: LOG_ON.PRG
- Source Disk: Library/ Template Code Folder: QUITPROC.PRG

Similarly, my template code contains a bare-bones copy of MENUPROC.PRG, as follows:

```
* default MENUPROC.PRG
PARAMETER whatcall
DO CASE
* CASE whatcall = "New"
* CASE whatcall = "Open"
* CASE whatcall == "Save"
* CASE whatcall = "Save As"
* CASE whatcall = "Revert"
CASE whatcall = "Log"
   DO log_on
CASE whatcall = "Quit"
   DO quitproc
```

```
OTHERWISE
   WAIT WINDOW NOWAIT ;
      "Feature not implemented!"
ENDCASE
```

You can see that the default MENUPROC.PRG doesn't do much work because I *expect* this procedure to be overridden by local versions on a regular basis. Each local version of MENUPROC.PRG interprets the same message parameters to mean a different action appropriate to the application. The default MENUPROC.PRG serves as a "placeholder," while you're prototyping an application, until you decide what the behavior of each of the File menu options should be.

Later in this chapter, you will learn how to remove the File options that are inappropriate to a specific application completely, but MENUPROC's inclusion of an OTHERWISE case with a simple WAIT WINDOW message is a backup method of handling any bars that you haven't implemented and forgot to remove.

The default MENUPROC.PRG has only two implemented CASEs: two standard template procedures for the "Log" and "Quit" messages. Just as you can override MENUPROC itself, you can override the default LOG_ON.PRG and QUITPROC.PRG by local versions whenever necessary (that's why they're not included in MAIN.PRG itself). I place these CASEs in the default MENUPROC.PRG because you will probably adapt these two procedures to your own system and then use them unchanged for most applications.

What kinds of work should the other options on the File menu do? Use a simple rule: if the standard File menu prompt has an obvious meaning in the application's context, you'd be foolish to place this same action on another pop-up menu with the same or a similar prompt. For example, Save can confirm the current data entry editing session underway, and Revert can cancel the same edit.

In many cases, this menu option is a second method to perform an action for which you already provide a button on the screen. Although giving users a choice of methods to perform the same action may seem redundant or confusing, this choice gives users a chance to work in whatever manner they feel comfortable. Using menu options and buttons for the same actions also gives your programs a convenient method to assign menu key shortcuts for these actions.

Of course, you don't write two separate procedures for the same action. Both a menu option's Command result and a button's VALID clause perform the action using exactly the same code. During the prototyping stage, this procedure can be another simple placeholder, such as:

```
PROCEDURE DO_Save
WAIT WINDOW ;
   "You chose to save your work!"
RETURN
```

Now your application-specific version of MENUPROC.PRG looks like this:

```
PARAMETER whatcall
DO CASE
* CASE whatcall = "New"
* CASE whatcall = "Open"
CASE whatcall == "Save"
   DO Do_save
* CASE whatcall = "Save As"
* CASE whatcall = "Revert"
CASE whatcall = "Log"
   DO log_on
CASE whatcall = "Quit"
   DO quitproc
OTHERWISE
   WAIT WINDOW NOWAIT ;
       "Feature not implemented!"
ENDCASE
```

Your Save button's VALID clause contains a call to the same code, either by including the line `DO Do_Save` in the VALID procedure snippet or by using the procedure's name as the VALID expression: `Do_Save()`.

If you find that you always want a Save prompt on your File menu and you can standardize its behavior for most applications, you may make this change to your template version of MENUPROC.PRG. I prefer to leave the template version severely empty. I find that looking closely at the individual File menu choices for each new application, as part of the process of creating each application's local MENUPROC.PRG, forces me to make application-appropriate use of each option.

Menu Items as Polymorphous Objects

Take a quick look at the File menu procedure for my Color Tutor application, which you'll use in Chapter 15 to explore the FoxPro for Macintosh Color system. (This local copy is a procedure inside the COLORS.PJX's local MAINSPR.PRG. COLORS.APP is another "switchboard" application similar to APPSetup. Because its highly complex local code affects just one dialog, in which the application remains from start to finish, I've placed all the code within COLORS.APP's unusual MAINSPR.PRG for editing convenience.) This version of the Menuproc CASEs contains very idiosyncratic interpretations of the standard File menu options, only some of which are also available as buttons in the application dialog. Yet all these options make sense in the context of the Color Tutor application:

```
PROCEDURE Menuproc
PARAMETER whatcall
DO CASE
CASE whatcall = "New"
   m.whichset = "_New Color Resource_"
   SHOW GET m.whichset
   SEEK m.whichset
CASE whatcall == "Save"
   DO SaveColorSet
CASE whatcall = "Revert"
   IF m.whichset = "_New Color Resource_"
      WAIT WINDOW NOWAIT ;
          "Reverting to default colors..."
      SET COLOR SET TO
      DO SetArray
      DO SetRGBs
      DO Example
   ELSE
      DO SetColorSet
   ENDIF
CASE whatcall = "Quit"
   DO quitproc
OTHERWISE
  * should never get here because any unused
  * MINIMAL.MPR options should be RELEASEd
  * local APPMPR.PRG
  WAIT WINDOW NOWAIT ;
      "Feature not implemented yet!"
ENDCASE
```

The Color Tutor's local Menuproc should give you a clear idea of the latitude you have in interpreting the File menu options, depending on the scope and nature of each individual application.

See Also

- "Set Up Your Application for Efficient Help Systems," Chapter 14

Because each File menu option presents a standard prompt but may act differently in each application, you have a special responsibility to make sure the user knows what to expect from each choice. You may want to use variables to provide the MESSAGE clause for each bar, which you adjust for each application depending on the use you make of each bar. In FoxPro for Macintosh, you can provide a more verbose message by using Balloon Help, which the user can turn on for initial exploration of the application and remove later.

If you are familiar with the terminology of *object-oriented programming* (OOP), you may recognize this ability of a single menu option to perform differently according to different circumstances as a FoxPro implementation of *polymorphism*.

When a programming element is polymorphic, the programmer has defined some basic behavior for the object without regard for the exact target of its actions. In this case, the programming elements are the bars on the File menu. They always appear in the same position and they have the same Command results. The programmer does not need to redefine these attributes for each *instance* of the File menu (each application in which s/he uses the File menu). However, each instance of the File menu adapts to its current environment. The object is defined once, but acts in many different ways.

If you look at the prompt for the final option on the File menu (shown at the bottom of figure 7.2), you see a simple trick I use to evaluate the current platform and define a menu prompt appropriately. Instead of using a literal Quit prompt, as appropriate for DOS and the Macintosh, or the Exit prompt appropriate to Windows, I've typed the following expression into the text box holding this menu prompt:

```
"+IIF(_WINDOWS,"E\<xit","\<Quit")+"
```

When GENMENU generates the code for this menu bar, it will surround the expression with another pair of quotation marks because it expects a literal string. The resulting generated code in the .MPR looks like this:

```
""+IIF(_WINDOWS,"E\<xit","\<Quit")+""
```

FoxPro evaluates this expression at runtime, when the menu code executes, and properly shows a Quit prompt in FoxPro for DOS and Macintosh but an Exit prompt in FoxPro for Windows.

In the next sections, you'll see how you can continue refining the behavior of the File pop-up menu and the rest of the system menu's generic components to fit the current application and the current platform. As you continue to work through the rest of this book, you will see that the FoxPro design tools provide an opportunity to create *reusable* and *extensible* application components, keys to an OOP strategy.

FoxPro's implementation of these concepts is not exactly standard because FoxPro itself is not an object-oriented language, but your awareness of these concepts is critical to a rapid development path in any language. For this reason, I'll continue to point out your FoxPro opportunities to implement OOP concepts as they arise.

Adaptable Utility Menu Options

After MAIN.PRG calls MINIMAL.MPR to design the required menu base for every application, it calls UTILMPR.PRG, a *framing program* for the Utility menu definition. The default version of UTILMPR.PRG executes a simple `DO UTILITY.MPR` and RETURNs to MAIN.PRG. However, the use of the framing routine gives you a chance to substitute a completely different set of utility options from your normal tool set for a particular application, simply by executing a different .MPR in a local version of UTILMPR.PRG.

If you don't need any utilities at all, a local UTILMPR.PRG can even avoid any appearance of utility options on your menu by omitting *any* call to an .MPR. COLORS.APP takes this approach with a UTILMPR.PRG that contains a simple RETURN with no other statements.

In spite of occasional odd requirements, you'll develop your own group of standard UTILITY.MNX options that serve you well for most applications. Two pads comprise my Utility group: a Utilities pad and pop-up for generic data-management dialogs, and a Help pad and pop-up for desk accessories and other non-data management application features, most of which came from the FoxPro for DOS System pop-up originally. In figure 7.4, the Utilities pop-up options are showing in what appears to be the Menu Bar but is actually the mockup of the Menu Bar created by the Menu Builder's Try It feature. Meanwhile, the Help pop-up options appear in the Menu Builder's main layout window.

You have already been introduced to the Utility menu options when you built an application from the template code elements in Chapter 4. You may be surprised to see that there are additional options on both the Utilities pop-up and Help pop-up that didn't appear on your generated application menu. As a well-behaved, polymorphous object, the Utility menu checked its surroundings when you executed it, and only showed you the options appropriate to its current environment.

Because the UTILMPR.PRG is a single line of code executing UTILITY.MPR, when and where does the menu perform these checks? An .MNX file contains two snippets into which you can place code (Setup and Cleanup). This code runs directly before and directly after the generated .MPR's definition of menu pads and bars. UTILITY.MNX's Cleanup snippet contains code that examines the current environment and then RELEASEs any menu options that are inappropriate.

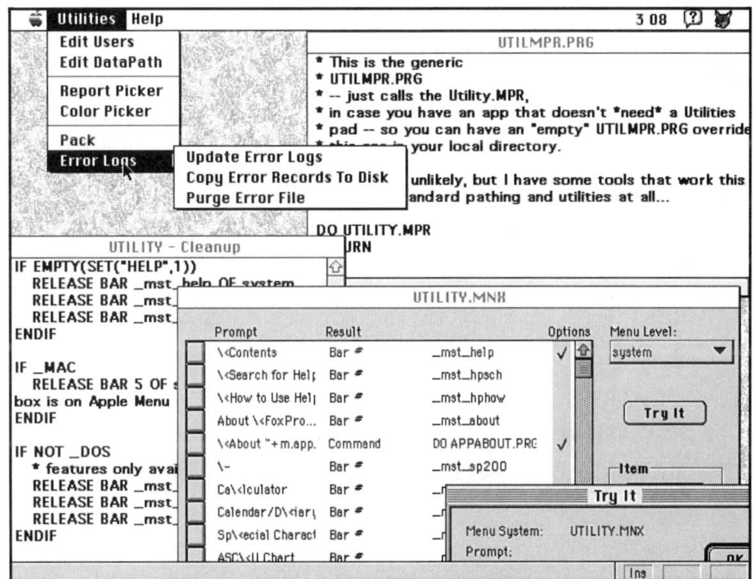

Figure 7.4 *Both the template UTILITY.MNX's Utilities options (in the Menu Builder's Try It feature) and Help options (in the main Menu Builder layout window) are visible, along with the menu's framing program (UTILMPR.PRG) and cleanup code.*

You get access to the Setup and Cleanup snippets of a menu using the same General Options dialog that you use to specify Append, rather than Replace, for this menu's association with the existing SYSMENU (see figure 7.1). UTILITY.MNX's Cleanup contains the following code:

```
IF EMPTY(SET("HELP",1))
   RELEASE BAR _mst_help OF system
   RELEASE BAR _mst_hpsch OF system
   RELEASE BAR _mst_hphow OF system
ENDIF
IF _MAC
   RELEASE BAR 5 OF system
   * About box is on Apple Menu
ENDIF

IF NOT _DOS
   * features only available under DOS
   RELEASE BAR _mst_specl OF system
   RELEASE BAR _mst_ascii OF system
   RELEASE BAR _mst_captr OF system
ENDIF

IF NOT USED("Sys_var")
   RELEASE BAR 1 OF Utilities
   RELEASE BAR 2 OF Utilities
   RELEASE BAR 3 OF Utilities
ENDIF

IF NOT FILE("COLORRSC.DBF")
   * bound into the app if you provide this
   * capability
   RELEASE BAR 5 OF Utilities
ENDIF

IF NOT FILE("DBFS.DBF")
   * this is usually bound into the app
   RELEASE BAR 7 OF Utilities
ENDIF

RETURN
```

As you can see, this code examines and responds to a variety of disparate conditions. First, it checks for a name of a help file that is available; if none exists, it removes the options on Help pop-up that access the help file.

See Also

- Cleanup Snippet, Source Disk:Library/ Template Code Folder: UTILITY.MNX

> **FOXPRO MAC HACK TIP**
>
> You could change this check to SET("HELP") = "OFF," checking the state of the help system rather than the availability of a file. However, an application might SET HELP OFF occasionally to allow help file editing. My template code allows an application to SET HELP OFF without disturbing the name of the help file previously SET if the application doesn't have a replacement file of its own. If HELP is SET OFF, but SET("HELP",1) shows that a help file *is* registered, these native menu items will automatically appear dimmed.

Next, the menu cleanup code checks for the Mac platform on which the "About this Application" option is removed from the Help pop-up because this option moves to the Apple menu (using SET APLABOUT) in FoxPro for Macintosh.

> **FOXPRO MAC HACK TIP**
>
> Look carefully at the prompt for this option, which appears in figure 7.4. I use the same trick that I used in the Quit/Exit prompt on the File pop-up to provide a variable prompt for this option, incorporating the application's name. Because this variable prompt uses m.app_title, an external component ordinarily supplied by INCLUDE.PRG, I *encapsulate* "knowledge" about this variable in UTILITY.MNX's Setup snippet, in case UTILITY.MNX is somehow used outside my template-application system. A well-behaved object is always protected from changes in its environment by checks of this nature:

```
IF TYPE("m.app_title") # "C"
   PRIVATE m.app_title
   m.app_title = "This Application"
ENDIF
```

The syntax for RELEASE BAR or PAD mirrors DEFINE BAR and PAD syntax from which you are usually insulated by GENMENU. I use the variables that represent native bar numbers to RELEASE native options like the desk accessories and help options, such as _mst_help, but I use an explicit bar number, based on position in the pop-up, to RELEASE my home-grown "About this Application" menu option with its Command result.

The next IF construct removes the desk accessories (Special Character Chart, ASCII Chart, and Capture feature) unique to FoxPro for DOS when the application is not running on the DOS platform.

Next, it checks for the presence of SYS_VAR.DBF, a system table I use to provide user registration capabilities. If this application doesn't use SYS_VAR.DBF, I have removed the call to Open_Sys from its INCLUDE.PRG, described in Chapter 5. Then I remove the menu options that require SYS_VAR.DBF (user name editing and data path location) and a third bar that serves as a delimiting line between this and the other Utilities options if SYS_VAR isn't present.

The Utility Cleanup code then checks for the presence of another table, COLORRSC.DBF, required by my application Color Picker. When I want this feature to be available in an application, I use the Project Manager's explicit Include feature to bind COLORRSC.DBF into the .APP file. The presence or absence of COLORRSC.DBF in the .APP is detected by the FILE() test, and determines the Color Picker's appearance on or removal from the Utilities list.

Similarly, if this application doesn't use my file maintenance system, which relies on a DBFS.DBF table to recognize all the data tables used by this application, I remove the final bar on the Utilities menu, a PACKing utility, because this procedure relies on DBFS.DBF.

Once again, a single menu object exhibits polymorphous traits in accordance with its surroundings. In OOP terms, you *subclass* your applications as including the Color Picker feature or omitting it, by the simple act of Including the required COLORRSC table in the Project Manager's list. You have also subclassed your application using my system of user log-on and registration as well as file maintenance by the availability of two other tables. Your FoxPro project and its resulting application display the OOP capability of *multiple inheritance*; they're deriving their features from several different classes of applications.

You can add more Utilities options over time, as you develop or encounter generic utilities that can benefit your applications. (I'll suggest some additional tools for this pop-up menu later in the book.) The fact that all of your projects build their menus using just one template version of UTILITY.MNX means they all have access to the improvements as soon as you rebuild their .APPs.

As you incorporate these new features, you adapt the Cleanup code in UTILITY.MNX to implement or remove them intelligently according to the special needs of their runtime environment. Because the Cleanup code is bound into the menu definition file (*encapsulated*, in OOP terms), you ensure that each Build of an application that has access to new UTILITY.MNX features also has access to the rules governing their use.

Different Strategies for Dynamic Menu Behavior

You can encapsulate the UTILITY.MNX rules in the menu definition because the rules *remain the same for every application,* even though the results of evaluating the rules change.

By contrast, the rules governing the appearance and behavior of File pop-up menu options are intimately connected with the nature of the individual application, as you saw in COLORS.APP. You can't encapsulate these rules in the template MINIMAL.MNX without destroying the generalized behavior of the menu definition file.

You might create a menu framing program, similar to UTILMPR.PRG, which you'd edit for each application, to handle the removal of File pop-up menu options for MINIMAL.MNX. I choose not to create this program for several reasons:

- I never need to consider the possibility of complete removal or replacement of MINIMAL.MPR's two pads, as I do for UTILITY.MPR's pads. UTILMPR.PRG, as you recall, allows me to omit the call to UTILITY.MPR altogether.
- A framing program for MINIMAL.MPR would require editing for *every application,* not just an occasional override of the default version, which is work that I avoid if necessary.
- I already have an application-specific menu evaluation program: APPMPR.PRG, which governs the application-specific pads that I add to my template menu options.

Because *APPMPR.PRG* already exists and must be edited for each application, I prefer to add the application-specific rules for MINIMAL.MNX options to this program.

The template version of APPMPR.PRG contains the code you need to release *everything* from the File and Edit pop-ups of MINIMAL.MNX, included mostly as comments. This program also has certain default behavior built in to handle cross platform differences and to check for my SYS_VAR.DBF user registration system:

```
* default APPMPR.PRG
IF _DOS
  * release OLE options
  RELEASE BAR _med_pstlk OF _medit
  RELEASE BAR _med_insob OF _medit
  RELEASE BAR _med_obj OF _medit
  RELEASE BAR _med_link OF _medit
  RELEASE BAR _med_cvtst OF _medit
  RELEASE BAR _med_sp300 OF _medit
ENDIF

IF NOT FILE("sys_var.dbf")
  * not using log on system...
  RELEASE BAR 8 OF file_popup
  RELEASE BAR 9 OF file_popup
ENDIF

* DO your app-specific appended pad here

RETURN

* The File menu pad of MINIMAL.MPR:
* RELEASE BAR 1  OF file_popup && New
* RELEASE BAR 2  OF file_popup && Open
* RELEASE BAR 3  OF file_popup && --
* RELEASE BAR 4  OF file_popup && Save
* RELEASE BAR 5  OF file_popup && Save As
* RELEASE BAR 6  OF file_popup && Revert
* RELEASE BAR 7  OF file_popup && --
* RELEASE BAR 8  OF file_popup && Log On/Off
* RELEASE BAR 9  OF file_popup && --
* RELEASE BAR 10 OF file_popup && Quit
```

```
* The Edit pad of MINIMAL.MPR:
* RELEASE BAR _med_undo OF _medit
* RELEASE BAR _med_redo OF _medit
* RELEASE BAR _med_sp100 OF _medit
* RELEASE BAR _med_cut OF _medit
* RELEASE BAR _med_copy OF _medit
* RELEASE BAR _med_paste OF _medit
* RELEASE BAR _med_pstlk OF _medit
* RELEASE BAR _med_clear OF _medit
* RELEASE BAR _med_sp200 OF _medit
* RELEASE BAR _med_insob OF _medit
* RELEASE BAR _med_obj OF _medit
* RELEASE BAR _med_link OF _medit
* RELEASE BAR _med_cvtst OF _medit
* RELEASE BAR _med_sp300 OF _medit
* RELEASE BAR _med_slcta OF _medit
* RELEASE BAR _med_sp400 OF _medit
* RELEASE BAR _med_goto OF _medit
* RELEASE BAR _med_find OF _medit
* RELEASE BAR _med_finda OF _medit
* RELEASE BAR _med_repl OF _medit
* RELEASE BAR _med_repla OF _medit
* RELEASE BAR _med_sp500 OF _medit
* RELEASE BAR _med_pref OF _medit
* RELEASE BAR _mst_macro OF _medit
```

Your local copy of APPMPR.MPR appends an application-specific pad or pads to the menu using a call to another .MPR file, right before the RETURN, as indicated in the comments in the code above. The additional commented-out lines after the RETURN are designed to be moved before the RETURN line without the comment mark for any File and Edit options that are not appropriate to your current application.

See Also

- Source Disk: Library/ Template Code Folder: default APPMPR.PRG

The Utility menu encapsulates RELEASE strategy within its menu definition, and the Minimal menu delegates RELEASE strategy to the individual application. The third generic menu element, DEBUG.MNX, follows a third strategy entirely: I hardcode a check for debugging conditions into MAIN.PRG itself, and only `DO DEBUG.MPR` if those conditions exist.

Why the difference? The Debug or Program pad does not always appear, unlike the File and Edit pads. When it does appear, its contents don't vary, so you don't have to allow for the release or instantiation of individual Debug options, as you do for the options on the Utilities and Help pop-ups. Instead, its appearance is governed by an external condition (whether or not you're in testing mode). You can set this condition according to any system of your choice, consistently across all your application development work. *Anything you can do the same way for every application can safely be placed in MAIN.PRG, where you never have to repeat it or worry about including it.*

Figure 7.5 shows you the options on my Debug menu and the call to DEBUG.MPR in MAIN.PRG. Both your evaluating conditions and your Debug menu options could be entirely different.

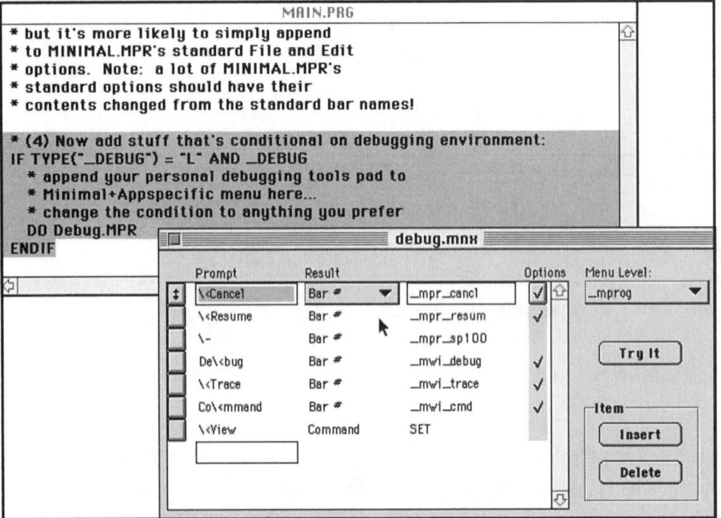

Figure 7.5 *The Debug menu appears in your applications according to any conditions you decide to evaluate in MAIN.PRG and can contain any personal tools you use while developing an application.*

Intelligent Menu Changes During an Application Session

So far, you've seen the tremendous flexibility that FoxPro menu syntax allows for menu definition according to the needs of the current platform, the specific application, or the mode of operation (production or debugging). However, FoxPro menus can also change their behavior to dynamically reflect the changing conditions and events that occur *during a single session of a single application*. In this section, you'll learn how to create these dynamic changes, using capabilities that make SYSMENU an integral part of the event-handling techniques in FoxPro.

Within a single application session, you can RELEASE a FoxPro menu item entirely so that the user can't see it, or you can *disable* the menu item so that the user can see the option, but choosing it produces no results.

RELEASE and REDEFINE Menu Options

The first method is appropriate when your application supports different classes of users. Each time a new user logs onto the system, you can re-issue any .MPRs, which contain items not all users should see, and then RELEASE any items that the current user shouldn't have. My LOG_ON.PRG contains a `DO PERMITS` call, after a new user has been recognized, to support dynamic menu configuration on a user level.

The default template PERMITS.PRG is a "placeholder," with a simple RETURN, but local PERMITS.PRGs can be quite elaborate. You may wish to extend SYS_VAR.DBF with information about each user's permitted options, or to maintain a user "class" system and a separate system table that indicates which options are appropriate to which class of users.

Enable and Disable Menu Options with SET SKIP TO and SKIP FOR

Dynamic enabling and disabling of menu options, by contrast to RELEASE, can occur constantly throughout the application session. If you use FoxPro's native bar numbers, the associated menu options may enable and disable themselves without any instructions from you. For example, two of the three Help options on my UTILITY.MNX's Help pad work only with Microsoft Help engine-style help files (.HLPs). If you use the .DBF-style help system, these options automatically dim; if you switch to the .HLP-style help file mid-session, they automatically re-enable.

Your own menu options should emulate this behavior, becoming available only when their results are applicable to the current state of the application. The SYSMENU syntax includes two methods of enabling and disabling menu options:

- The SKIP FOR <logical expression> clause on DEFINEd BARs and PADs, which you access using the Options check box for menu elements in the Menu Builder.
- The SET SKIP OF BAR <number> OF <pop-up name> |PAD <name> OF _MSYSMENU|POPUP <name> OF _MSYSMENU <logical expression> command.

Both these methods can be used with the native pads, pop-ups, and bar names along with menu options you define yourself.

FoxPro evaluates the SKIP FOR clause dynamically, whenever the user accesses the menu. For example, my Error Log management pop-up (a submenu on the Utilities pop-up, as you see in figure 7.4) uses the SKIP FOR expression `SKIP FOR NOT FILE("errorlog.dbf")`. If no error log file exists, these options are unavailable. If an error occurs during an application session, my error-handling program creates ERRORLOG.DBF and adds an entry. The Error Log management options become available immediately.

FOXPRO MAC HACK TIP

The SKIP FOR clauses are actually evaluated more often than the user chooses to access the menu. Microsoft Fox staff generally say that the evaluation occurs whenever FoxPro encounters a “null event,” which I think of as a programmer’s way of saying “whenever FoxPro has a spare moment.” However, FoxPro’s internal behavior has changed from version to version on this point. Clearly, FoxPro’s developers want to have the benefit of constant SKIP FOR evaluation without a performance penalty for this check, and they’ve experimented with different methods of achieving this goal. If you find that SKIP FORs are not evaluated at a point during your program when you’ve changed a particular condition, you can often use a `SHOW MENU _MSYSMENU` command to force evaluation.

You may also find that options on a pop-up menu under a menu pad disabled with a SKIP FOR don’t always dim appropriately on the menu, even though you can tell they’re disabled because they don’t work when you choose them. This problem is not an issue of timing; it’s probably a bug that future versions of FoxPro Mac will correct.

SET SKIP OF <menu element> TO <logical expression> commands, by contrast, are commands that you execute explicitly. Their logical expressions are always evaluated once, and you always know exactly when they're evaluated (at the time you execute the command). For example, if I issue the command SET SKIP OF BAR 5 of system EMPTY(m.user), this bar is disabled if no user is logged on at the moment I issue the command. If a user subsequently logs on, the condition of the bar does not automatically change unless I reissue the SET SKIP command.

Because the SKIP FOR clause on menu element definitions is evaluated repeatedly, if you use both a SKIP FOR clause and a SET SKIP OF command to affect the same menu element, the SKIP FOR clause will always take precedence.

Since the SKIP FOR clause is obviously more powerful, under what conditions should you enable and disable menu elements using SET SKIP OF commands instead? Multiple SKIP FOR conditions require FoxPro to do some work to reevaluate conditions, and can slow down a program. If you have a condition that rarely changes, or that only changes at times when your program can intercede with an explicit command, you may be better off removing the constant reevaluation of the enabling condition from the SKIP FOR clause and adding the explicit SET SKIP OF command instead.

Suppose that you decide that AD*Vantage shouldn't allow any Job or Inventory editing until the user has defined at least one Client/Vendor record and at least one Employee. You could add a SKIP FOR RECCOUNT("Company") = 0 OR RECCOUNT("Employee") = 0 to the Jobs menu option, but this causes a great deal of evaluation, throughout the life of the program for a condition that rarely occurs. Instead, you can check these conditions during Company or Employee editing and issue the appropriate SET SKIP OF command when the first record is added or the last one is deleted.

The explicit check also gives you the opportunity to issue a WAIT WINDOW or other instructions to the user, explaining why this option is suddenly disabled or enabled at the same time that you issue the SET SKIP OF command. By contrast, the SKIP FOR clause when it represents an unusual condition may produce results that the user finds puzzling.

Where a menu option provides access to a task already handled by a dialog button, you have another perfect reason to use SET SKIP OF. Because your code already issues explict SHOW GET <button get> DISABLE | ENABLE instructions whenever the relevant condition changes, you might as well add an explicit SET SKIP OF command for the analogous menu option.

Use a SKIP FOR clause, not SET SKIP OF, for conditions that change rapidly throughout an application, in response to many different events, and which therefore deserve dynamic reevaluation by FoxPro rather than constant attention in your code.

For example, many of my utility options are designed to be available only when the user is not engaged in any other application activity. To limit access to the Report Picker, the Color Picker or other such utility options, I use a `SKIP FOR RDLEVEL( ) > 1` clause on the Utilities pad. Now this pad only allows access to its options when the application is waiting in its foundation READ state. If you tried to issue equivalent SET SKIP OF commands, you'd have to maintain lists of all the menu options deserving this treatment. You'd issue SET SKIP OF commands for each of them every time you initiated a nested (second level) READ during the run of the application—creating a guaranteed maintenance nightmare, unless you never change a single option in your menus.

Exploring Menu-Based Event-Handling

I mention the RDLEVEL() check because it's extremely significant to FoxPro event-handling during an application. You can divide program activities that occur over a period of time into two main groups: those that require user interaction, such as data entry, and those that do not, such as outputting a report, importing data from a foreign file source, or performing a query. In an activity that doesn't require user interaction, program statements execute consecutively, without pausing until the activity finishes. If a program activity requires any user interaction, the program pauses in a wait state, receptive to choices the user makes.

In FoxPro, the program can pause for user interaction in many different ways. Even a WAIT WINDOW is a wait state, with the program paused until the user presses a key to continue. However, most FoxPro-user interactions occur through the wait state known as the READ, which activates GET objects (text boxes and controls) into which FoxPro collects the user's choices.

In Chapter 5, you saw that FoxPro programs have a base, or *foundation*, wait state in which the program waits to receive the user's choice among its various activities. Although this wait state may be a "switchboard" dialog like APPSetup's, with button choices from which the user chooses tasks, it's typically a *GETless READ*, which holds the user in the application until the end of the program. During this foundation READ, the user chooses program activities by picking different menu options.

If these menu options require further user interaction, the programs they run contain additional READs, referred to as *nested* READs within the foundation READ. *Because FoxPro has a limit of five nested READ levels, you cannot choose additional menu choices indiscriminately while other tasks are in progress.*

Choosing one menu choice after another will quickly escalate the nested READs beyond the five levels FoxPro allows.

FoxPro programmers know that there is a Microsoft-recommended technique for getting around the READ level limitation, which you can see demonstrated in the EX1 and EX2 applications in the FoxPro sample files. It works by CLEARing current READs in progress when the user makes any new activity choice, but leaving these READs' windows on the screen.

When the user opts to return to any activity by selecting its window on the screen, EX1 and EX2 CLEAR the current task's READ and reissue the READ appropriate to the new top window with all its attendant code, so the user doesn't know this READ ever ended. This technique carries a speed penalty and has other inherent limitations when you try to add multiple FoxPro system windows, such as BROWSEs and desk accessories, to the screen.

If you follow the suggestions in this book, you may never need to use the EX1/EX2 system. You'll see that FoxPro allows plenty of real activity in carefully-managed READs without pretending that multiple READs are active. The READ level limit is actually a programmer's hangup. Users don't know or care how many nested READs are in progress; they are satisfied because FoxPro allows them to do all the tasks they need to do at one time, without interruption.

See Also

- FoxPro Samples files: GOODIES: FNDATION Folder:EX1.PJX and EX2.PJX
- "Modality and Event-Driven Programming," Chapter 12
- "Additional Resources," Appendix A

FOXPRO MAC HACK TIP

If you decide to follow the EX1/EX2 method, be sure to investigate its extensions in *The FoxPro Codebook*, written by Yair Alan Griver and additional members of the Flash Creative Management team. *Codebook* implements OOP principles, as implemented by Bill House of Flash, to make the EX1/EX2 method more workable. You'll find that you'll be able to incorporate *FoxPro MAChete's* template code and the other techniques you learn throughout this book into whatever flavor of FoxPro event-handling you choose.

Most of the generic system utilities I provide in the template code represent *modal READs*, designed to prohibit further choices until the user finishes with this activity. You encounter modal dialogs throughout the Macintosh environment because there are many actions a user *must* complete before continuing with further work. The user doesn't perceive this limitation as onerous in any way.

However, application-specific, data-entry activities may be combined with additional activities for maximum efficiency and a reasonable approximation of the way the user behaves in real life. For example, in AD*Vantage, the user may begin entering new job information and then realize that s/he has to create a new customer record for this job. Just as s/he might open an address book and add a new entry, pushing aside the job order sheet for a moment, the user expects to enter a new customer record without abandoning work done on the job record.

Even in real life, the user doesn't actually make the address book entry at the same instant as s/he completes the job order. Instead, users *switch their attention* between tasks, temporarily interrupting a primary activity (the job order) while completing a secondary requirement (the address entry), but returning to complete the first task at the conclusion of the second. If the user doesn't return to the original task, no real work gets done.

You can design your FoxPro application to model this real-life behavior. In FoxPro terms, the secondary activity is always modal; it should be completed and then the user should return to complete the original task. If you take this approach, the trick is simply to decide which secondary activities should be attached to which primary application jobs.

You discover activity connections by observing your users' work patterns carefully. Then you implement these patterns by correctly designing the application-specific portions of your menu. *Careful arrangement of menu options with appropriate enabling and disabling of menu tasks is the key to managing a FoxPro application's events.*

In the next section, you'll look at my design for AD*Vantage's application-specific menu components as an example of the way that you can implement this system.

Adding an Application-Specific Menu Outline

Just as you build the generic menu elements from several layers, you add application-specific menu options in several sections.

The first application-specific menu section includes options that should appear on the application menu throughout the application session.

In rare cases, an application may not have any such options. For example, APPSetup, which you used in Chapter 6, is an application that centers around only one major task. In APPSetup, I chose to show this task as buttons on a "switchboard" dialog, which is constantly present, representing the one purpose of the APPSetup application, rather than putting them on a pop-up menu. However, most applications should append one or more pads to the generic menu pads, using APPMPR.PRG to initialize these sections of the menu.

See Also

- Source Disk:Seed App (AD*Vantage developed) Folder

In the fully developed AD*Vantage application, the local APPMPR.PRG executes the statement `DO VANTAGE.MPR` to initialize this part of SYSMENU. (I used the name VANTAGE.MNX to make sure the menu file would have a legal file name when I ported the application to DOS. Although the project name and .APP file name, AD*VANTAGE, will cause DOS the same problems as the menu file name, I can rename both files in DOS with impunity. On the other hand, the .MNX file must be recognized by the Project Manager, as an included Project element, as well as by DOS. I prefer not to take any chances with this file name, to avoid confusing the Project Manager when I move the .PJX file between platforms.)

After the user chooses a particular application task, additional menu sections appear *in context* as the user moves from task to task. Think of this menu change as an emulation of the way the Screen Builder or the Menu Builder and other FoxPro system features cause tool-specific menu pads to appear and disappear as the tools gain and lose focus. The change appears natural to Macintosh users, who are used to seeing the system menu bar change as they move from one activity to the next.

You don't initialize task-specific menu sections in APPMPR, which is global to the application, just as you wouldn't include application-specific pads to MINIMAL.MNX. Instead, you introduce these sections as separate .MPRs, which you execute as part of the local Setup for a particular task. When the task is completed, you RELEASE the menu options that are no longer appropriate.

You can think of this technique as performing a local version of the exact scenario that you use in MAIN.PRG each time the user starts a new task within the application. First, you perform task-specific Setup, then you enter the task's local wait state, and then, when the user chooses to end the task, you perform task-specific Cleanup. Setup includes menu definition, just like MAIN.PRG's, by executing the task-specific .MPR file. The wait state is typically a FoxPro screen set you create by executing an .SPR file. The .SPR holds GET and WINDOW definitions followed by a READ statement. When the user finishes this activity by exiting the nested READ, the task-specific Cleanup includes removal of menu options, using the following syntax:

```
RELEASE PAD Job OF _MSYSMENU
RELEASE POPUP Job EXTENDED
```

This example is from the Jobs module. For the duration of this task, I added one pad to SYSMENU by executing the command `DO JOBS.MPR`, a separate menu layer from the VANTAGE.MPR menu definition during Setup procedures. The Jobs module Cleanup RELEASEs the Jobs-specific pad and pop-up. If the Jobs task added more than one pad and pop-up, I'd RELEASE them all in the task's Cleanup.

Notice that I RELEASE the PAD and its associated POPUP separately. If you just release the PAD, you may not be able to see its pop-up but any menu shortcuts DEFINEd for its options can still fire!

FOXPRO MAC HACK TIP

You may wonder why I use an explicit RELEASE <menu element> technique instead of FoxPro's PUSH and POP MENU syntax. These commands allow you to PUSH the current menu definition to a stack, redefine the menu for a particular task, and then POP the old menu definition back after completing the task. I use PUSH and POP MENU in the Setup and Cleanup sections of my generic MAIN.PRG code. Because you don't have to specify menu elements explicitly to use this syntax, PUSH and POP MENU are convenient for generic portions of your code.

However, PUSHing multiple levels of menu definitions to the menu stack uses memory rapidly. For that reason, I avoid PUSHing and POPping the menu in local Setup and Cleanup code. Instead, I append options to the menu and then explicitly RELEASE them by name when they're no longer needed.

See Also

- "FoxPro 2.6 and Beyond," Appendix E

CROSS-PLATFORM WARNING

You may have used the syntax SET SYSMENU SAVE in FoxPro for Windows or DOS. This syntax fixes the current state of the system menu as the version to which you'll return if you issue the command SET SYSMENU TO DEFAULT. (It's like a super version of PUSH/POPMENU.) Be warned that this command has a serious bug in the first shipping version of FoxPro Mac which may cause FoxPro to quit when the user accesses certain menu items. If you use SET SYSMENU SAVE, be sure to upgrade your copy of FoxPro Mac to 2.5c.

While working on the data structures for AD*Vantage, I determined that Jobs editing represented the most complex data-gathering task of this application, with the most complicated relationships to other application-specific tasks. Most other data entry tasks concerned either information subsidiary to a Job record (Inventory records and information in Inventory's child files) or providing lookups to Job records (such as Address, Employee, Department, or Rate information), so that a person performing the Jobs task might need to edit any, or all, of these files.

To begin designing AD*Vantage's global menu, VANTAGE.MNX, I created a Job-editing option. I then listed additional VANTAGE.MNX options that I thought the user should be able to access completely independent of Jobs: Payment and Receipt logging, Results, and a Maintenance choice with subchoices to allow the user to focus on editing each kind of lookup file (see figure 7.6).

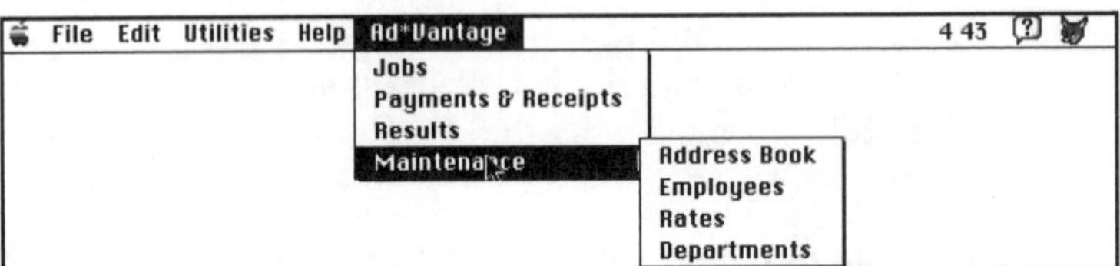

Figure 7.6. *AD*Vantage's application-global menu options.*

I decided that the Results options (querying and output tailored to the application) could wait until after data entry screens were available for users to begin creating test data, especially since my Utilities menu includes a simple Report Picker for interim use. By using the other parts of the application, users would get a better idea of how they wanted to pull Results out of their data, and I could make good use of their feedback. I wrote myself a note in the Comment field for this bar, as an informal "to do" list ("Create new reports, set filters, get counts, run output to printer"), to which I'd add after consulting users. At this point, I didn't even know whether Results would lead to a submenu of further choices or to a single dialog.

Payment and Receipt logging represented a discrete activity. After I'd designed the Jobs task's access to the Address Book, I knew I'd be able to create the same method of access in the Payment and Receipt module, so that users could enter new Client and Vendor information while logging checks in and out. This module didn't seem to require interaction with any other data entry tasks, and therefore posed no new challenges.

Having quickly sketched the rest of the application's modules, I focused my attention on the Jobs task. My next step was to create a Jobs-specific menu to demonstrate to users (and as notes for myself) which activities had to be available during Job editing.

In figure 7.7, you see the Jobs menu in the Menu Builder. I include options for access to the Address Book, along with three Jobs-specific activities (Cut, Copy, and Paste Inventory) requested by my ad agency clients.

I've omitted access to the other lookup files in this prototype because all such access will follow the same pattern set by the Address Book option. At this point, I want to gauge users' reactions to my system design, rather than putting a lot of effort into repeated motions.

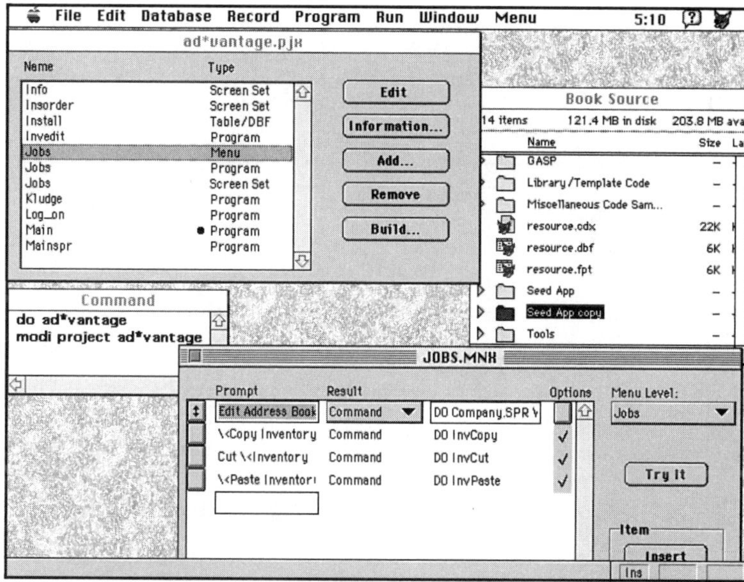

Figure 7.7. *Beginning to edit the Jobs-specific menu items.*

Similarly, you'll notice that I'm not discussing any code underlying all these options. On the main AD*Vantage menu, I added a default Command result (WAIT WINDOW "Feature not yet implemented!") to provide some quick feedback for any menu element to which I haven't yet attached code (see figure 7.8). On the Jobs menu, the Cut, Copy, and Paste Inventory options may lead only to program stubs with a RETURN statement in them.

The code isn't the point. Users can judge the layout of an application at an early stage without being able to see how each option is implemented. You don't want to waste time coding options if you find out you're proceeding in the wrong design direction.

Although you don't want to write the procedures underlying the menu options at this stage, you *can* create the SKIP FOR clauses that will show your intentions for the availability of menu options without writing complicated code. For example, the entire Vantage menu pad uses the following SKIP FOR clause to manage access to the application's major tasks:

```
EMPTY(m.user_id) OR RDLEVEL() > 1
```

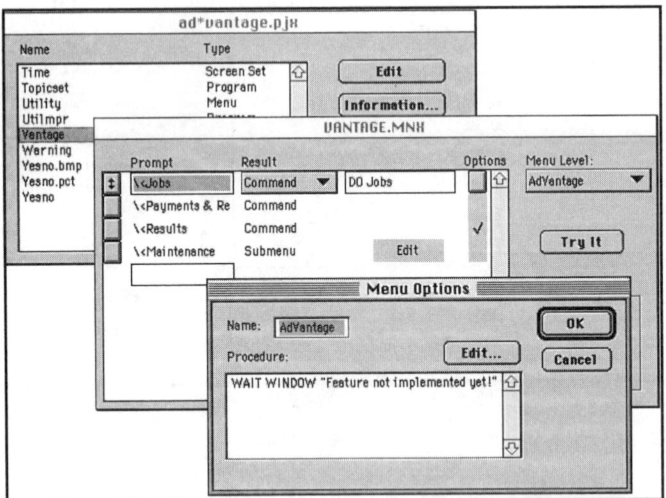

Figure 7.8. *Create a placeholder command for unfinished menu options while you work on the prototype.*

This expression disables the application's tasks when no user is logged in (EMPTY(m.user_id)) or when an application module is already in progress (RDLEVEL() > 1). Watching these options enable and disable will give users a good sense of the flow of the application.

The Jobs menu has a global SKIP FOR clause of RDLEVEL() > 2, so that the user cannot access any of its subsidiary actions if another one is already in progress. For example, the user can't Copy Inventory if s/he has accessed the Address Book and has focused attention on a new Client record rather than the current Job activity.

Each individual Jobs option has an additional, individual SKIP FOR clause. For example, you shouldn't be able to Paste an Inventory record into the current job if the current job isn't locked or if you haven't Cut or Copied any Inventory record previously.

You may not be able to implement such specific SKIP FOR clauses at this stage, but you should add notes about them as Comments as you investigate and propose this module's behavior. When you prototype the actual Jobs screen set in the next chapter, these conditions become easier to pinpoint, and you can return to your menu to include appropriate SKIP FOR evaluations.

In this manner, without writing much code, your work with the Menu Builder makes you familiar with the flow of information between different AD*Vantage data tables and the structure of the various AD*Vantage tasks. You can generate the AD*Vantage .APP with a skeletal, but working, menu at any point, using the template code foundation to supply standard application functions.

Chapter Wrap Up

The Menu Builder has brought you through the process of application design. In later chapters, you'll see how you can extend GENMENU and the Menu Builder for special tricks that make FoxPro menu objects even more powerful and capable of even more subtle adjustments to their runtime environment.

First, however, turn your attention to the Screen Builder in Chapter 8 to add application-specific, data-entry activities to the AD*Vantage prototype. The same attention that you pay to the dynamic access to menu elements serves you well as you design screen sets. In Chapter 9, a few demonstration queries and reports round out the prototype. Then, in Part III, you can write supporting program code and incorporate users' feedback into a refined version of your application model.

8

EXPAND THE PROTOTYPE: BEGIN DATA-HANDLING IN THE SCREEN BUILDER

by
Lisa Slater

When I wrote my first FoxPro books, I included a lot more information on the Screen Builder than on the Menu Builder. My experience on the beta test cycles of FoxPro for DOS 2.0 and FoxPro for Windows and DOS 2.5 taught me that the Screen Builder is by far the more complex tool to learn. People had difficulty figuring out how to choose among the different screen objects and how to attach code to each screen element's many associated events. These people had little trouble understanding the limited number of results available to menu pads, pop-ups, and bars.

Since then, however, my experience shows that the Menu Builder's impact on the *design phase* of application development is far more profound than the Screen Builder's influence, which is why the last chapter described the interlocking components of a FoxPro menu in considerable detail.

In this chapter, I recap the prototyping phase as it has proceeded so far. You need a checklist of the rapid development procedures you've taken with the AD*Vantage model application. I'll also discuss the use of the prototype as a working model that your users can understand.

You can use my template code and this checklist to begin designing any other application as you follow along.

Then I sketch an AD*Vantage screen with you and show you how to attach the screens to the AD*Vantage menu options. I'll point out some special features and quirks of the Screen Builder, where they're not covered in the documentation or aren't similar to other Macintosh layout and design tools. I'll give you hints for quickly producing screen prototypes that are both attractive and consistently designed—as well as workable—using GASP, a Screen Builder external tool created by Andy Griebel.

However, be aware that robust data entry screens require programming, mostly in the form of *validation code* that takes action based on the user's input. Your goal at this point is to use built-in code from a template model, which you will edit as little as possible to achieve a working result.

You also should realize that complex data entry tasks usually require more than one window, and that the Screen Builder lays out only one window at a time. The management of a multiple-window *screen set* is properly the purview of the Project Manager, not the Screen Builder.

In Part III, you learn Screen Builder techniques for creating reusable screen objects and for elaborating screen sets to satisfy the needs of a complicated and practical data entry system. The current prototype screen only provides a simple opportunity to get user feedback about the general application design.

Encourage users to *play* with the prototyped application, using both the nondestructive template options and your rudimentary data entry screens. Among the template dialogs, the Color Picker especially gives users the message that the application is theirs to design and adjust.

The file-maintenance code already built into the template code allows the users to specify data directories at will. Users can create "scratch data," erase data sets, and regenerate empty tables as often as they please as they wander through the system. You don't do harm by allowing the users free reign at this stage, and the more comfortable they feel, the more details they will recollect about the business rules and chronology of their own jobs. When you're ready to elaborate and validate the application-specific screen sets, you should keep all these valuable suggestions in mind.

Getting Design Mileage Out of Your Application Prototype

Remind your users that TeachText and other utilities are always at hand on the Macintosh, so they can jot down any suggestions or requests that come to mind while they work with your application. In FoxPro for Windows, they can use the Windows Notepad. You can add a Notepad option of your own on the Utilities menu, where even FoxPro for DOS users can access the feature, or users can put this information into the FoxPro Diary, already available on the template UTILITY.MNX Help pop-up (see figure 8.1).

FOXPRO MAC HACK TIP

To use the FoxPro Diary feature, an application must have a *resource* file in which FoxPro places the diary entries. This resource file is not the same as the *resource fork* Macintosh files often have; it's a normal FoxPro data table. As long as you don't specify the configuration option RESOURCE = OFF in your CONFIG.FPM file, FoxPro generates a default FOXUSER.DBF if one doesn't exist in the startup folder.

However, my INCLUDE.PRG turns off the resource file capability unless you edit INCLUDE.PRG to specify an application-specific resource file name. Many people don't need a resource file in their applications and don't want to bother with resource file management. If you want to use the Diary and you haven't established a resource file strategy for your applications yet, you can establish the environment's current resource file for the use of your application. Simply add the following line to INCLUDE.PRG in the same section as you establish the application's title and developer name:

```
m.resource = SET("RESOURCE",1)
```

Because the FoxPro resource file is a normal .DBF, a developer can USE this table and BROWSE it or create a REPORT FORM that lists all the diary entries in the file.

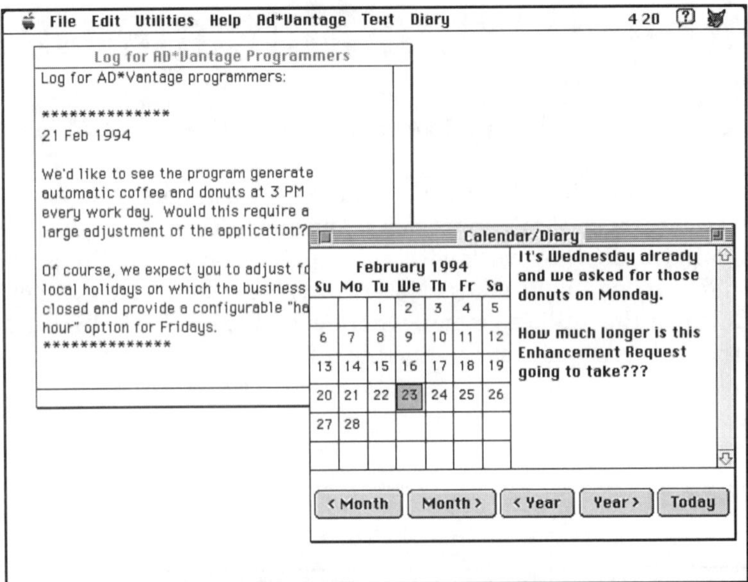

Figure 8.1 *A TeachText text file and the FoxPro Diary provide two methods by which users can record their wish lists and comments for your use.*

A notepad for suggestions shouldn't be a user's only method of communication with you. Show users the application's error logging system, too, *before* they encounter their first error, so they have an established routine with which to share their problems with you. If necessary, force an error to generate the first error log record, so that the relevant options become enabled on the Utilities pop-up menu. (Remember that INCLUDE.PRG provides an easy method of forcing a program error and then removing it.)

Even when an application is derived from 99 percent tested template code, the 1 percent application-specific code you wrote so far will still have a few errors—and the template code also may have some obscure bugs lurking within! You don't need to hide the possibility of problems from your users; just make sure they're prepared for it. As you can see in figure 8.2, the template error log utility provides plenty of room for them to describe the error in their own words, as well as a complete programmer's error record they can share with you.

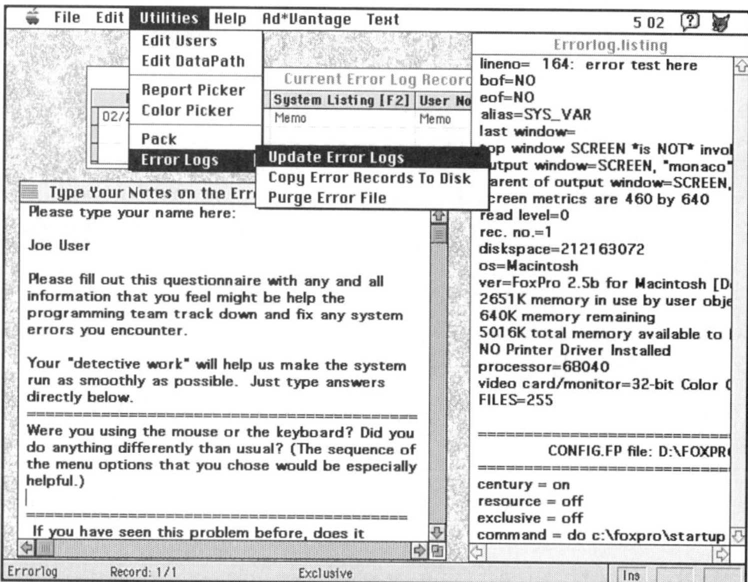

Figure 8.2 *The template error logging system provides a BROWSE of the current error log entries, a "survey" memo field for the user's comments on the problems, and a full programmer's log.*

> **FOXPRO MAC HACK TIP**
>
> In Appendix A, a list of FoxPro resources, you'll find a listing for CAPCON, a FoxPro project editing tool from Cascade Interactive Designs, Inc. CAPCON includes an integrated error-handling system that feeds user comments back into its reports so that management and developers can easily schedule further changes and enhancements. Take advantage of this capability, or any other methods available to you if you use additional FoxPro developer tools, to organize user feedback so that you can respond to suggestions—and complaints—constructively and quickly without undue effort.

Managing the Prototype Process

Now, review the steps you took to prototype this application so far and generalize these steps so that you can use them on your own development process.

Step 1: Design the Tables

First, you design the data structures. You may describe the application's tables in a CASE tool, or you may work on the structures in the FoxPro View window. If the application's data relationships are complex, as they are in AD*Vantage, you probably want to save a .VUE file that documents these relationships for future reference.

Put the tables in a DBFS folder nested in the folder that you intend to make your application's project location. If you create a .VUE file, place it in the main project folder and save it with DEFAULT SET to the project folder.

Step 2: Generate File Maintenance Code

Next, run APPSetup on your data structures. APPSetup expects a DBFS.DBF in the main project folder. You can create this file as you run APPSetup, or you can create the file earlier. Either way, the file lists each table in the application and the ALIAS under which the table is USEd. If you USE tables more than once with the AGAIN clause, create separate records for each USE, identifying each USE by the appropriate ALIAS.

Modify DBFS.DBF to include extra fields, either now or later, to describe additional attributes for your tables for any use that you find convenient. I use a Subform field for the AD*Vantage application to identify the different types of Inventory child files and a Parentkey field to identify file relationships.

Your source disk has a folder that contains all these application elements, including a .VUE file with the proper relationships and a DBFS.DBF file. You can make a copy of this folder and run APPSetup on it to begin the application-design process.

When you use APPSetup to generate code for your new application, it creates a nested PRGS folder with MAKEDBFS.PRG and MAKECDXS.PRG already included. (It also creates empty MENUS and SCREENS folders nested in the project folder.)

See Also

- Source Disk:Seed App (startup) Folder

Step 3: Build the New Project from Standard Components

Use the File New menu option, or the command MODIFY PROJECT in the Command window, to start the new application's project file in its home folder. You ordinarily indicate the project's main file first. As you did in Chapter 4, use the Library/Template Code folder's MAIN.PRG as the project's main file.

Add all system tables that the application will use as built-in, READ-only elements, because the Project Manager expects .DBFs to be external, editable objects except for any explicit exceptions you make. If you want to use the Color Picker, include it in the Library/Template Code folder. Include the DBFS.DBF file, too, because you may continue to edit this table but the user never needs to see it during production use of the .APP. You also may include the INSTALL.DBF, which you find in the Library/ Template Code folder. The template version of this file has just one entry: a subsidiary compiled file () used by some of my template programs. Subsidiary .APPs must exist separately on disk for FoxPro to use them, so INSTALL.DBF uses the procedure described in Chapter 5 to put copies of these kinds of files on disk as part of application startup.

MAIN.PRG skips this section of application startup procedures if INSTALL.DBF isn't available. Routines that use elements installed by this technique always do additional tests to make sure that the items are available. Any critical procedure that uses external files also has an alternative strategy if an external file has somehow disappeared from disk during the application session. (Remember, no generic object should depend on external help.) For this reason, your application won't fail if you forget INSTALL.DBF. However, including the file at this early point in development is a good habit, even if you prefer to use an empty copy as your template INSTALL.DBF and create local copies later when you're more aware of the application's needs.

See Also

- Source Disk:Library/ Template Code Folder: INSTALL.DBF

Step 4: Personalize the Project File

APPSetup created your application-specific INCLUDE.PRG in the main project folder. Add this program to your project and edit it with any application-specific features. In AD*Vantage, the INCLUDE.PRG changes include a test for disallowed versions of FoxPro, as follows:

```
m.disallowed = "(_DOS AND NOT '(X)' $ UPPER(VERSION(1)))"
```

I created this condition because the AD*Vantage program takes too many workareas for the Standard (non-Extended) version of FoxPro for DOS.

The only other changes you should make in AD*Vantage's INCLUDE.PRG at this point are the standard values for the application's title and developer:

```
* the following will provide
* the default password for the
* system, so change it to something
* you like!
m.developer = "FoxPro MAChete"
m.dev_id = "LCS"
m.app_title = "AD*Vantage"
* here's where you put
* m.resource = SET("RESOURCE",1)
* if you want RESOURCE SET ON but
* you haven't designated an
* application-specific resource table
* at this time
```

Step 5: Determine Application Data Flow Using Menus

The Project Manager now has the information needed to begin pulling in the rest of the application's generic pieces. As you saw in Chapter 7, you use a local copy of APPMPR.PRG to introduce your program's particular tasks to the generic framework, by defining some generic menu option's behavior in an application-specific way and by defining additional application-specific menu options. Here's the AD*Vantage copy, which leaves the application with a slender version of the File pop-up menu and adds the VANTAGE.MPR definition to SYSMENU:

```
* AD*Vantage APPMPR.PRG
 RELEASE BAR 1  OF file_popup && New
 RELEASE BAR 2  OF file_popup && Open
 RELEASE BAR 3  OF file_popup && --
 RELEASE BAR 4  OF file_popup && Save
 RELEASE BAR 5  OF file_popup && Save As
 RELEASE BAR 6  OF file_popup && Revert
 RELEASE BAR 7  OF file_popup && --

* the bars we're leaving on File menu
* remain in the file as comments:
* RELEASE BAR 8  OF file_popup && Log On or Off
* RELEASE BAR 9  OF file_popup && --
* RELEASE BAR 10 OF file_popup && Quit

IF _DOS
  RELEASE BAR _med_pstlk OF _medit
  RELEASE BAR _med_insob OF _medit
  RELEASE BAR _med_obj OF _medit
  RELEASE BAR _med_link OF _medit
  RELEASE BAR _med_cvtst OF _medit
  RELEASE BAR _med_sp300 OF _medit
ENDIF

IF NOT FILE("sys_var.dbf")
  * not using log on system...
  RELEASE BAR 8 OF file_popup
  RELEASE BAR 9 OF file_popup
ENDIF

* DO your app-specific appended pad here
DO VANTAGE.MPR
RETURN
```

You'll find a second copy of the AD*Vantage application in a Seed App Copy folder on your source disk. Its PRGS folder contains this version of APPMPR.PRG along with other files we will add to the project later.

See Also

- Source Disk:Seed App (AD*Vantage developed) Folder: PRGS: APPMPR.PRG

You can include APPMPR.PRG and the generated file maintenance PRGs in the Project explicitly if you like. This process ensures that your local versions take precedence over the generic placeholder programs in the Library/Template Code folder. You also can create a menu definition for the VANTAGE.MPR generated program that APPMPR.PRG executes, or you can use the VANTAGE.MNX you find on the source disk in the Seed App (AD*Vantage developed):MENUS folder.

However, you've now done quite enough work to Build the project and its compiled .APP file any time that you want. Figure 8.3 shows you the AD*VANTAGE.PJX container before you choose the Build option for the first time.

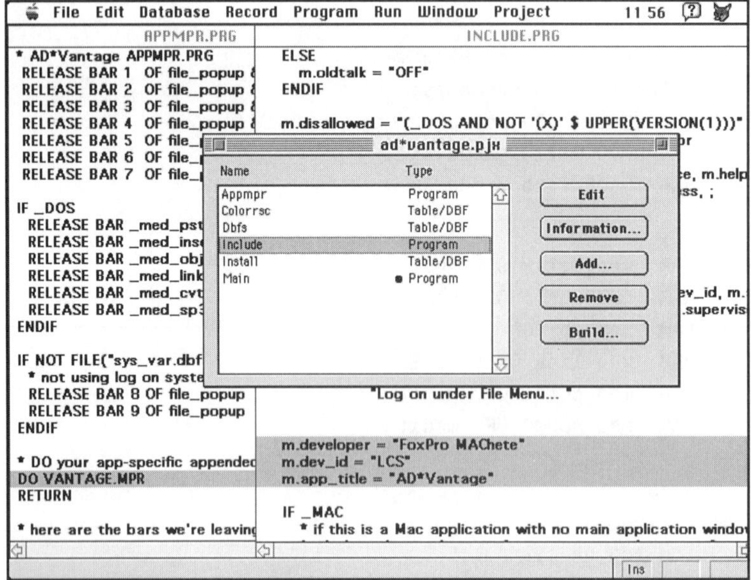

Figure 8.3 *The AD*Vantage project, with some explicitly included files, as it looks before you Build the project for the first time. The local APPMPR.PRG and INCLUDE.PRG that you see on-screen are the only programs you've edited directly at this point.*

Step 6: Build the Project and Continue Adding Application-Specific Elements

Whether you choose to Build the Project or to Build the Application in the Project Manager's Build dialog, a first Build process can take a long time. The Project Manager evaluates every program file in the system, including .SPRs from generic dialogs, looking for references to other programs. After the Build process, the AD*Vantage project file looks like the New project that you built quickly in Chapter 4.

Depending on whether you added a VANTAGE.MNX file at this stage, which might be from the Seed App (AD*Vantage developed) folder or from your experiments in the preceding chapter, you may get errors during the Build process. For example, your VANTAGE.MNX may have a menu option leading to the Command result `DO PURCHASE.SPR`. Because you haven't yet created a Purchase table editing screen, you get the Project Manager dialog shown in figure 8.4.

Figure 8.4. *The Project Manager warns you if your application-specific menu options are designed to call procedures or screen sets that you haven't created yet.*

You can choose to ignore these errors that disappear after you create the screens and serve as reminders of work you have yet to do. If you prefer not to have the errors, but you want to retain the appropriate lines of code in your menus, you can preface them with an asterisk like any other comment, as shown in figure 8.5. The way GENMENU generates the DEFINE BAR and PAD lines of code prevents this statement from being executed or investigated by the Project Manager.

In figure 8.6, you see a second technique for handling the code for the programs and screen sets called by a menu option. The Jobs task on the main AD*Vantage pop-up will require a complex screen set, so I choose to DO a JOBS.PRG from the menu option rather than DOing the JOBS.SPR directly. Then I can put the extensive Setup and Cleanup for this major task in a .PRG rather than hiding it in a Screen definition file with which it has little in common. I comment out the call to DO JOBS.SPR within the JOBS.PRG program.

As you learned in Chapter 7, a major application module usually follows the same structure, as the MAIN.PRG. JOBS.PRG is no exception. You will use this framing program to initialize variables as a Setup procedure for the READ, saving any environmental factors that you expect to change. Then you DO a special Jobs-context menu pad. You then issue the READ for this module (here, the DO JOBS.SPR commented out until it's available). After the READ, you RELEASE the Jobs context menu elements and proceed to additional Cleanup code.

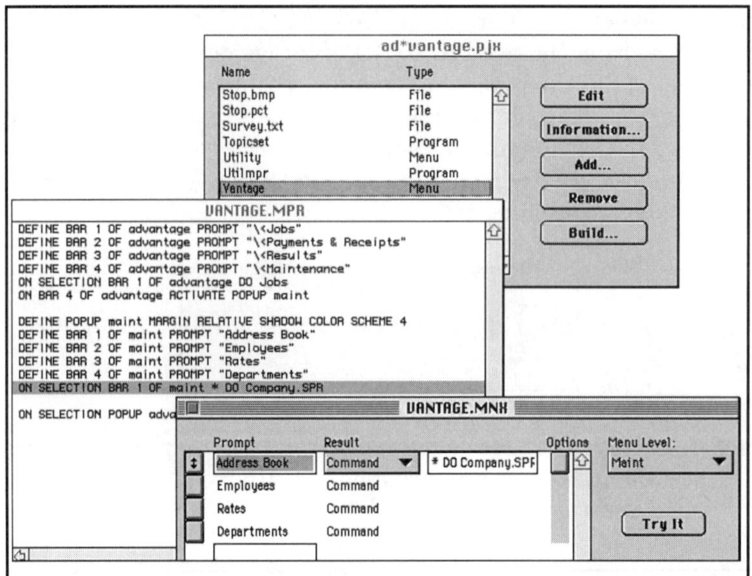

Figure 8.5 *You can place a line of code in the Menu Builder preceded by an asterisk, like a comment anywhere else in a program, when you haven't yet written the routine. The VANTAGE.MPR editing window shows the code GENMENU generates for such a line.*

In Chapter 7, your menu specifications established that the Jobs task allows options to access the address book as well as any other lookup files it uses, and that a user-requested feature, cutting and pasting Inventory records between jobs, also appears on the menu. Because these procedures are local to the Jobs task (no other module will use them), the JOBS.PRG is a good place to put them. Creating these procedures as simple PROCEDURE names and RETURN statements satisfies the Project Manager, and then you can safely add the names of these procedures as Command results of these menu bar options, as you can see in figure 8.6.

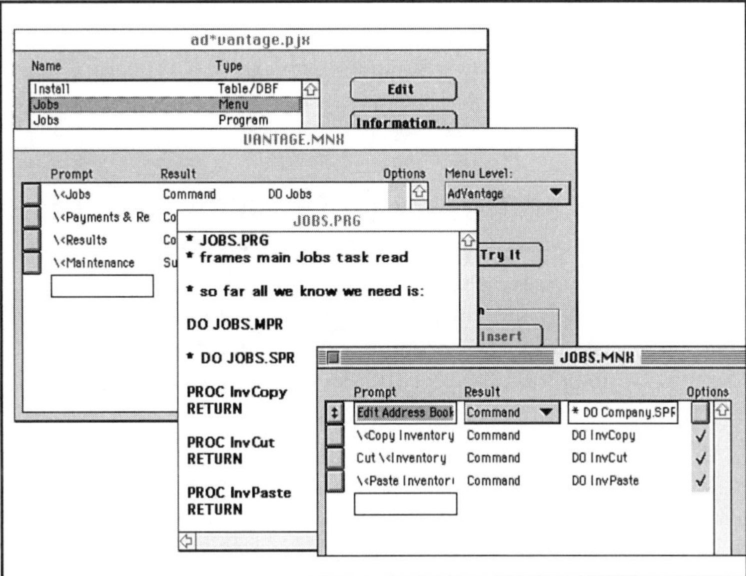

Figure 8.6 *The Jobs framing program called by VANTAGE.MNX's main pop-up sets up the Jobs subsidiary menu pad and adds a commented-out JOBS screen set. Then it provides empty placeholder procedures for the Jobs menu option results that you will write later.*

Prototyping Data Entry Screens

Now that you created menu items that execute screen sets, you can start building the screen sets in question. Remove the leading asterisks from the code executing each set as you build it, whether you placed that code in a framing program or directly in the Menu Builder. The prototype continues to accumulate executable features as you work.

Start with a simple screen layout. Remember that the Screen Builder constructs *one window at a time,* so that if the activity you're designing requires windows to work together, you have to write code or coordinate the windows in a screen set, using the Project Manager to do it, or put all the activity in one window temporarily.

The screen, which fills out the Company table, contains uncomplicated information that's used throughout the system, so it's a good idea to start adding sample records to it early. You'll use that table for the first exercise.

Start with the Template Data Entry Screen

You can place a new screen in the project by using the Project Add button and choosing New. However, this method starts the screen as a completely blank slate with default attributes that probably don't fit your working style. Instead, for a rapid development system, use a template screen to set up certain basic behavior according to your style and needs, and adapt it quickly to suit a particular data entry screen.

See Also

- Source Disk:Library/ Template Code Folder: TEMPLATE. SCX

You can find my template data entry screen () in the Library/Template Code Folder. Choose to edit this screen using SYSMENU's File Open option or using the MODIFY SCREEN command in the Command window. Then Save the template screen in the SCREENS folder APPSetup that's inside your main project folder.

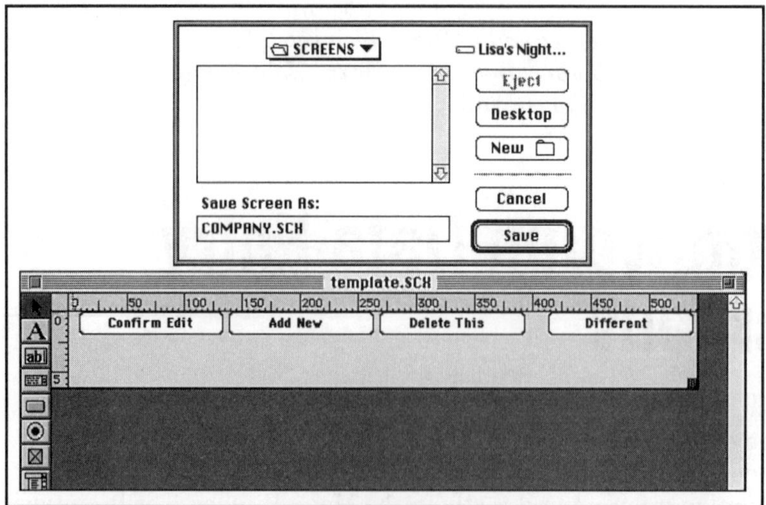

Figure 8.7. *Save the Template screen you find in the Library / Template Code Folder to the name COMPANY.SCX in the new project's SCREENS folder.*

As you can see in figure 8.7, the template screen layout is simple. It has a few buttons defined in it, already assigned default behavior. Its most valuable definitions are not apparent in the layout—they're hidden in the dialogs that provide basic attributes for the window and READ clauses assigned to this .SCX.

If you look in the dialog that you access from the Screen pop-up menu's Layout option and press the button for its subsidiary Code dialog, as shown in figure 8.8, you can see most of the attributes of TEMPLATE.SCX.

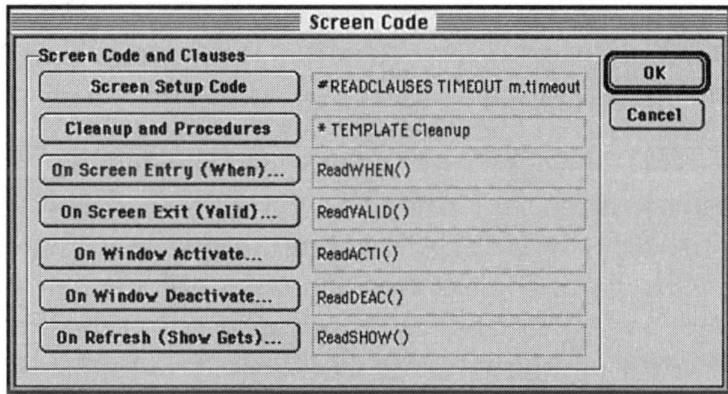

Figure 8.8 *The template screen starts with default READ clauses defined to speed your screen design process.*

The expressions that you see in the Code dialog are standard in my programs. These clauses represent an important part of my FoxPro implementation of OOP principles, which you learned about when you looked at menu procedures in Chapter 7. You saw menu objects *inheriting* behavior from global routines and then adding local routines of the same name to customize each *instance* of a menu option. In the same way, these READ clause expressions correspond to functions in MAIN.PRG. A particular screen can use these global functions, or countermand the global functions by including a local function of the same name. The local function can perform some specialized service and then, if necessary, delegate additional work to the global version.

For example, TEMPLATE.SCX contains some buttons with generic prompts. In each use of this screen, I use the READ WHEN clause to customize these prompts to correspond more closely to the file being edited, using a ReadWHEN() function local to this screen. This local function ends by calling the global ReadWHEN() function in MAIN.PRG to perform any tasks I want done in *every* READ WHEN clause:

See Also

- FUNCTION ReadWHEN, Source Disk:Library/ Template Code Folder: TEMPLATE. SCX Cleanup snippet

```
FUNCTION ReadWHEN
PRIVATE m.aliasname
m.aliasname = PROPER(ALIAS())
SHOW GET m.aliasact,2 ;
   PROMPT "Add New "+ m.aliasname
SHOW GET m.aliasact,3 ;
   PROMPT "Delete This "+ m.aliasname
SHOW GET m.pickalias,1 ;
   PROMPT "Different "+m.aliasname
DO ReadWHEN IN MAIN.PRG
RETURN .T.
```

The screens based on TEMPLATE.SCX are therefore a *subclass* of screens within my general system.

However, the COMPANY.SCX screen, a special *instance* of this subclass, takes further fine-tuning. The alias for the company file may be either Vendor or Client. You can SELECT the company file under either alias to perform address book editing—it won't make a difference. However, the user should focus on the *address book task* and not make distinctions between Clients and Vendors during this task. The COMPANY.SCX instance of the screen should be adjusted to use a prompt other than the usual prompt.

Making sure that you are editing your COMPANY.SCX copy of the template screen, rather than TEMPLATE.SCX, access the Setup and Cleanup code snippets for this screen. (Choose the Screen menu's Open All Snippets option or press ⌘-N.)

You find the ReadWHEN function in the Cleanup. Change the line that reads:

```
m.aliasname = PROPER(ALIAS())
```

To adjust for the special Address book task, this line should read:

```
m.aliasname = "Address"
```

A little further on in the Cleanup you find the local PickAlias and ReadSHOW functions for this screen. You don't have to understand this code right now; you are just going to make simple changes to match the change you just made in the button prompts. The PickAlias routine is executed when the user presses the "Different" button you see on the right side of the template screen, which brings up a BROWSE of records so that the user can choose a different record to edit. You see the following lines:

```
BROWSE ;
       TITLE "Pick "+m.wname+" Record to Edit" ;
       WHEN .F. NOMENU ;
       FONT "Geneva",10 ;
       COLOR SCHEME 10
```

Change the line to have a more appropriate title for the Address Book BROWSE:

```
BROWSE ;
       TITLE "Pick Address Book Record to Edit" ;
       WHEN .F. NOMENU ;
       FONT "Geneva",10 ;
       COLOR SCHEME 10
```

In the ReadSHOW function, you find this line:

```
   WAIT WINDOW NOWAIT ;
     "No existing "+PROPER(ALIAS())+ " records!"
```

Edit this line to read:

```
   WAIT WINDOW NOWAIT ;
     "No existing Address Book records!"
```

That's all the editing you need to do for the Cleanup code in this screen. All three changes are entirely cosmetic, occasioned by the unusual fact that the alias for the table won't mean much to users.

What's more, you could avoid the need for even these simple adjustments to your template code if you made your prompts and messages a little less explicit. For example, the WAIT WINDOW in the ReadSHOW function could say "No existing records!" and be appropriate for any file. However, little details like descriptive messages make the screen more meaningful to users, even during the prototyping stage, and these messages are fairly simple to tailor. They're worth the extra effort.

Turn your attention to the Setup snippet. You won't have to do much editing here, but you should understand some of the tricks in the Setup code for later use.

You see *generator directives* at the top of the code. These lines, which start with the # (pound sign, or hash), tell GENSCRN to perform some special actions at the time it generates your .SPR from this .SCX screen description file.

The first directive to GENSCRN in my template code is:

```
#READCLAUSES TIMEOUT m.timeout &readclauses
```

The directive tells GENSCRN to attach anything you type after it to the READ command generated, which provides a way to add completely variable contents to the READ command, including clauses (like TIMEOUT) that are not available elsewhere in the Screen Builder.

The second directive tells GENSCRN to attach anything that you type after it to the DEFINE WINDOW command. In the template screen, I use this directive to provide a window title and the keyword GROW:

```
#WCLAUSES TITLE "Edit "+PROPER(ALIAS())+" Record"  GROW
```

Once more, the template use of ALIAS() to provide a message to the user is inappropriate to the Address Book screen. Change this directive to read:

```
#WCLAUSES TITLE "Edit Address Book Record" GROW
```

FOXPRO MAC HACK TIP

The keyword GROW doesn't affect a READ window, which is why the Screen Builder provides no option for its use. However, GROW will affect any BROWSEs that take their attributes from this window. The template code includes a generic picklist BROWSE without a WINDOW clause of its own, because at this prototyping stage you're including only one DEFINEd WINDOW in a screen set. In this situation, when you're working on the full MACDESKTOP rather than within the main FoxPro application window, a FoxPro for Macintosh BROWSE will take on the attributes of the current READ window. You typically want to resize a BROWSE depending on the number of records that you want to see.

Unlike the TIMEOUT clause on READ or the GROW keyword on a DEFINE WINDOW statement, a window title is a standard Screen Builder feature. You find the window TITLE text box in the Screen Layout dialog. However, editing the window title in the Setup snippet is often more convenient than going into the Screen Layout window. Also, the Screen Layout dialog doesn't accept a variable or expression in the title box (rather than a simple literal title), unless you use the #ITSEXPRESSION generator directive. As a result, using the native feature instead of #WCLAUSES for the TITLE clause won't save you any work.

The next generator directive tells GENSCRN to place the code that follows it at the very top of the .SPR. You need this directive whenever you want to use a t, because a PARAMETER statement must always be the first line in a program. Without this statement, your Setup code appears after some of GENSCRN's own generated setup code, including the DEFINE WINDOW statements. With #SECTION 1 directing some Setup code to the top of the generated file, you can use to put other parts of the Setup code in its normal position. For example, my template code SETs READBORDER in #SECTION 2 because GENSCRN generates state-saving code before that point.

In this case, the template code uses the PARAMETER statement to receive the variable readclauses:

```
#SECTION 1
PARAMETER readclauses
```

CROSS-PLATFORM WARNING

If you design a screen to work on more than one platform, you must make sure that you edit each platform's version of the Setup code to contain the *same* PARAMETER statement. GENSCRN places other Setup code in platform-specific CASE statements, but generates a single PARAMETER statement before the DO CASE structure. (This isn't a bug; a program can have only *one* PARAMETER statement, so GENSCRN has no choice.) If the PARAMETER statements don't match on different platforms, GENSCRN refuses to generate your .SPR, with good reason.

If you continue reading the Setup code, you see that the template screen is a well-behaved object, testing to see if readclauses has been passed in this instance of the screen and assigning a default value for the TIMEOUT clause if none exists. The screen executes without an error if you never assign values to these variables.

See Also

- COMPANY. SCX Setup Code

However, this has significance in the prototype menu structure that you set up. When the Company-editing screen is called from within the Job task, through an option on the JOBS.MNX (Jobs-task-specific) menu pad, this nested task should be a MODAL read.

The checking clauses you assign to menu options prevent any harm from occurring if you forget this MODAL clause, and a user can't mistakenly access any of the Job GETs during the nested Address Book READ. The

MODAL clause goes a step further, preventing the user from bringing the Jobs window forward while the Address Book nested task takes place. This tactic prevents the user from being confused by the Jobs window and its temporarily inactive GETs.

See Also

- JOBS.MNX Setup code

If you use the MODAL clause with its attendant WITH <associated windows> clause, the user can move from the Address Book window, but only into windows you have specified. Currently, both the Maintenance pop-up on the AD*Vantage main menu of choices and the Jobs menu pop-up have a Command result: `DO Company.SPR`. Leave the Maintenance version alone, but change the Jobs version to read:

```
DO Company.SPR WITH "MODAL WITH  'Edit Numbers','Edit Contacts' "
```

The associated windows, Edit Numbers and Edit Contacts, are names of BROWSE windows for the child files for this READ. You haven't added the child BROWSEs into this prototype of the screen, but the associated windows list won't do any harm. (Remember that the AD*Vantage file relationships make Client and Vendor references vital to a Job record and its Inventory listings, but a personal contact name or number isn't required for each Job Client and/or Vendor for a valid Job record.)

See Also

- Template Window-RELEASing Cleanup Code

To match this change, the template code has a generic method of RELEASing the BROWSE windows at the conclusion of the READ whenever you define them. As in the READ MODAL WITH <associated windows clause>, RELEASE WINDOW code will not cause an error if the named windows don't exist.

As you continue to read through the rest of the Setup code, you see the following code:

```
* now you select the right file for this READ:

* SELECT aliasname
* SET initial ORDER here if you want to
GO TOP
```

This code SELECTs the focus table for the screen edit. Change the commented-out `* SELECT aliasname` to read as follows for the COMPANY.SCX instance of the template:

```
SELECT Vendor
```

(You also can use `SELECT Client` because both aliases refer to the same table.) After this line of code SELECTs the focus table, the code proceeds to set up a variable containing the table's alias, for use as the DEFINEd WINDOW's name, and to initialize the variables that the screen edits:

```
IF EMPTY(ALIAS()) && shouldn't ever happen
   m.wname = "dummy"
ELSE
   m.wname = ALIAS()
   SCATTER MEMVAR MEMO
ENDIF
```

If you look in the Screen Layout dialog's Name box, shown in figure 8.9, you see the trick I use to get a variable-named window into the Screen Builder. You have to use this exact form of the variable (a macro expression, surrounded by single quotation marks) to get the trick to work, because of the way GENSCRN generates the DEFINE WINDOW code.

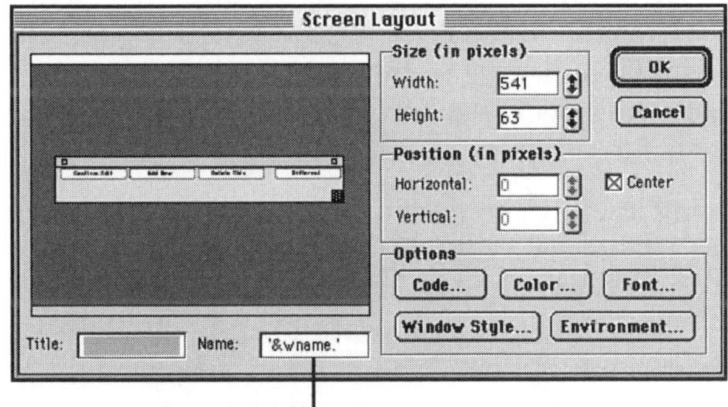

Use a macro expression surrounded by single quotation marks in the Name box.

Figure 8.9 *A trick in the Screen Layout dialog allows a variable window name.*

You can't use a variable expression in the name box instead of this trick, and you can't use the #WNAME generator directive (which *looks* as though it's supposed to do the same thing) to achieve this result. If you look through my template code, both the local READ clauses in the .SCX and the global READ clauses in the MAIN.PRG, you'll see very quickly why naming a window explicitly makes your code more portable and efficient. You *could* edit each instance of the template screen to have an explicit window name, but why would you want to do extra work?

So far, you've edited less than 10 lines of code, and, except for the crucial SELECT line that tells the screen what table it's editing, your edits have been inconsequential to the behavior of the screen. Template procedures have taken care of all the details of record maintenance.

The template leaves you free to handle the important business of properties of this screen that truly interest your users: the appearance and behavior of the GETs they use to collect their business' precious information.

Add GETs and Text Labels to the Screen

Before adding GETs to the layout, set up your interactive environment with the tables the .SPR needs, so that FoxPro can give you help setting up the GETs properly.

Using the template screen ensures that you never accidentally save the screen's *environment* (open tables, orders, and relationships) when you save the .SCX. After the first time you save a screen, you must explicitly choose the Screen Layout Environment option to change the first environment with which the screen was saved. TEMPLATE.SCX has been cleared of environment information.

Why avoid saving the environment of a screen? The screen environment enables GENSCRN to write file-opening, ordering, and relating code in the .SPR, but you want your own code to handle file management. It would be nice if you could leave this detail to GENSCRN. However, GENSCRN's generated code can't handle the variable data paths and indirect references appropriate to a distributed application—and especially appropriate to file-referencing on the Macintosh.

Although you don't want the .SCX to save the environment, you still can make good use of your .DBFs while you *design* screens to keep both you and the Screen Builder aware of the relevant data structures. Open any copy of COMPANY.DBF before continuing; the alias you use doesn't matter.

With the Company table open, you can ask the Screen Builder to perform a rough layout of GETs you need on this screen, using the Quick Screen option on the Screen pop-up menu . However, as you see in figure 8.10, this option works only when you start with any empty screen. The COMPANY.SCX already has buttons from the template. You remove these buttons temporarily to reenable Quick Screen.

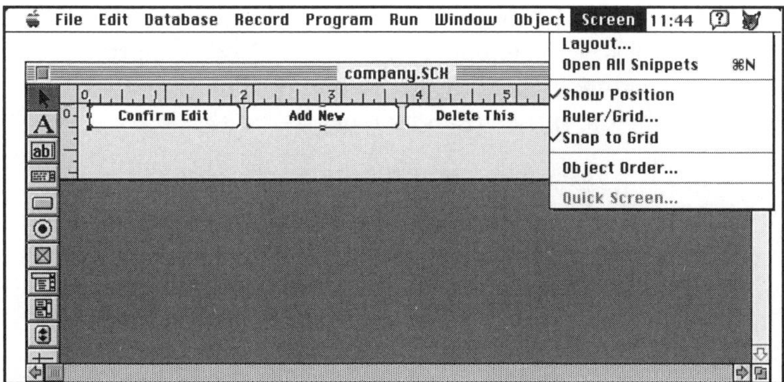

Figure 8.10 *The Quick Screen option is disabled if you already have GETs in the Screen Layout.*

Although you see four buttons, if you select them by clicking (or double-clicking to get to their dialogs), you'll find that two GETs actually are on the screen: a three-button set corresponding to the GET m.aliasact on the left, and a single button on the right, the GET m.pickalias. (The template screen code initialized both these variables during Setup.)

You can select both the objects on the screen, using shift-click to select multiple objects, or click-dragging a selection rectangle over both, or by pressing ⌘-A, the normal editing Select All key shortcut. Press Option-X to cut them from the layout, and Quick Screen is enabled on the Screen menu. In a moment you can use Quick Screen to place the Company GETs on the screen layout. Afterwards, use the Edit Paste option (⌘-V) to bring back the button objects.

Before doing a Quick Screen, resize the window to make room for all the GETs in the Company table. In the screen layout, drag the bottom right corner of the window image to resize. You also can resize the window in the Screen Layout dialog. Make the window larger than you think you'll need because you will have to repeat the Quick Screen process if all the GETs don't fit. You can make the window smaller after you finish rearranging the GETs.

In figure 8.11, you see the two dialogs. The main Quick Screen dialog, at the left, has a check box for memory variables, checked in the figure. This isn't the default value; by default, the Screen Builder creates *direct* READs to table fields, rather than memory variables.

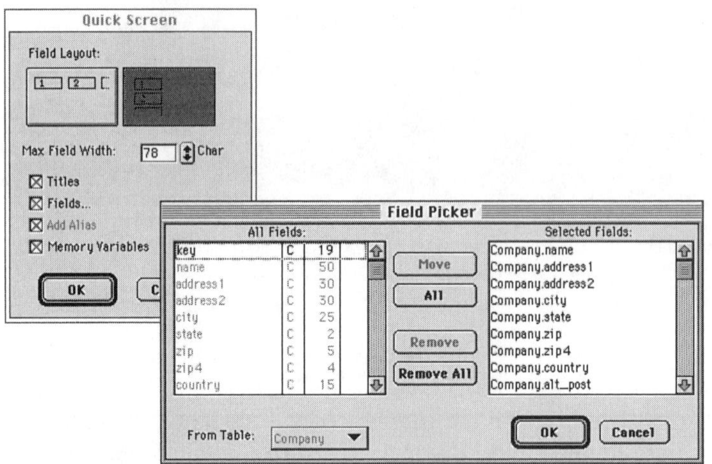

Figure 8.11 *The Quick Screen dialog and its subsidiary Field Picker dialog.*

All Xbase table editing either occurs directly on tables or to a temporary copy: memory variables, array elements, or a temporary table. No matter which method you choose, you create a temporary copy of all the data before you start the edit. (The template code used the line SCATTER MEMVAR MEMO in the screen Setup to initialize this copy, so the variables are available throughout the program.) In a direct edit, the user edits the table and you use the temporary copies of its values to cancel the user's work, if necessary. In an indirect edit, the user works the temporary copies and your code changes the values in the table to match the copies when the user confirms the edit.

You can choose either method, but all four authors of this book agree that indirect edits are safer in most circumstances. We remind you that programs sometimes crash in the middle of an edit, or the user turns off the computer! You don't always have a chance to cancel an edit explicitly.

FOXPRO MAC HACK TIP

Indirect edits are a little more complex, although safer to implement. The most significant difference is that FoxPro's automatic locking system provides no immediate multi-user protection unless you're using the actual tables. The template code in this book provides explicit locking instead, so you shouldn't have to put too much thought into the indirect edit alternatives. Whenever your procedures access the real data tables, MAIN.PRG's error handler gives a second layer of multi-user protection, in case your code lacks appropriate explicit locks, by providing an interface that kicks in at that moment.

You may not like my interpretation of the automatic locking in MAIN.PRG, or your application may require a different explicit locking strategy than I show in AD*Vantage. Locking strategies are highly dependent on the environment of a specific application. After reading the sections on network use later in this book and looking at the strategy, I chose AD*Vantage; you can decide what fits your own situation. Explicit locking, when performed on indirect READs, is therefore not only safer, but it also gives you wider latitude to handle different application needs.

When you choose to edit memory variables, the check box to Add Alias is checked and automatically disabled. Memory variables must have a prefix of "m." to distinguish them from table fields of the same name. If, for example, you have the Company table SELECTed, the command `WAIT WINDOW address1` shows you the contents of the address1 field. You can also say `WAIT WINDOW Company.address1` for the same result. (You *must* use the explicit alias if Company is open but not currently SELECTed.) To see the contents of a memory variable with the same name, you say `WAIT WINDOW m.address1`.

Although `address1` shows you the contents of the memory variable if there is no address1 field in the currently SELECTed table, you should still use the `m.` prefix for memory variables to be sure which value FoxPro will use, and to keep your code readable. GENSCRN automatically follows this rule (that's why the check box is disabled when you decide to edit memory variables in the Quick Screen).

There are two notable exceptions to the rule. First, you can't use the `m.` prefix when you macro-expand an expression, because the period is the macro terminator. If you place a character expression in the variable `mvar` and try to expand it by using `&m.mvar`, FoxPro looks for a variable `m` and tries to expand its contents. You must use `&mvar` instead. Second, you don't need to use the `m.` prefix for parameters in a function or procedure because these items are automatically variables. In fact, I find that leaving off the prefix for variables passed as parameters is a handy way of showing which values come from parameters in my code. The `readclauses` parameter in the template screen, used as a macro on the READ line, illustrates both exceptions.

After you opt to edit memory variables, you choose the Fields check box to edit the list of GETs that Quick Screen creates automatically. You see the field-picker dialog at the right side of figure 8.11. At first, all the fields in the currently SELECTed table show at the left side, and the box at the right is empty. Don't worry about the fact that the fields show with aliases instead of m. prefixes; they still are created as memory variables.

If you use the Move All button, all the fields move to the right box. Then you decide which fields you don't need to see in the screen and double-click on them—or Move them with the Move button—back to the left side.

You usually don't want GETs in the screen if the user doesn't edit this information directly. In the AD*Vantage system, each record has a unique key value generated by the system, used to establish file relationships. The user never needs to be aware of this information. As you see in figure 8.11, I opted not to show the key at all.

Sometimes, the user *should* see information and still not edit it directly. The table often contains one or more foreign keys that links this record to look up information. Although the Company table doesn't have such a lookup, the Job records hold key values for the commissioning Client name. You don't want the user to see (or edit) the Client key; you want to place the Client's *name* on the screen for confirmation. In Chapter 10, you see how to accomplish this task efficiently.

You follow the same procedure for the parent key values in a child file. While editing an Inventory record, for example, you don't display the key for the parent Job record as a GET, although you do make sure the user has some visual confirmation of the current Job while working on the Inventory.

While prototyping the Job screen, however, you may want to add this GET representing the Client's name to the screen and disable it, to remind you that you must provide a method of changing and displaying this value at a later time. If you have the Company table open along with Job, you can use the pop-up at the bottom to choose fields from other open tables.

When you are satisfied with your fields list, close the subsidiary field picker and choose OK in the Quick Screen dialog. You'll return to the screen layout, with a screen looking something like figure 8.12.

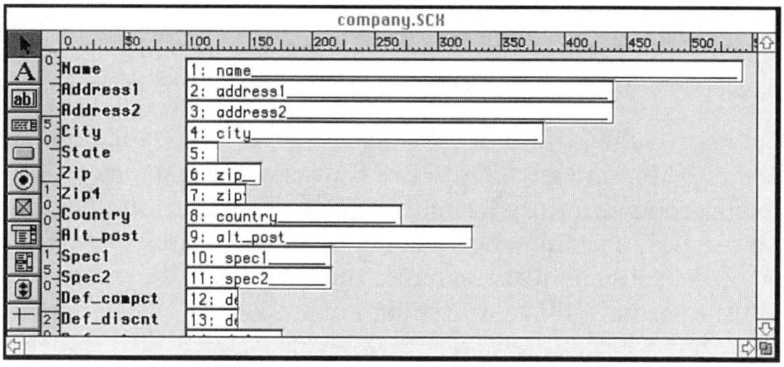

Figure 8.12 *The Company Quick Screen.*

Replace the buttons on the screen before you do anything else. It doesn't matter where you place these buttons, but they should be in a consistent position for all your data entry screens of a similar type. You may want to Select All the Quick Screen objects and position them to leave room *before* you Paste the buttons back on the screen.

FOXPRO MAC HACK TIP

If you copied something else to the clipboard in the meantime, you may not be able to paste the buttons. Don't worry. You can always replace the buttons from the template screen because you can copy and paste items between screen layouts. Remember, you haven't edited the template versions of these buttons or their code in any way since creating the Company copy of the template screen.

Enhance the GETs and Text

Your GETs are now on the screen, but you probably want to change the way this window looks before declaring the prototype ready for your users to see.

One change you will make is to the *type* of GET for each object. The Company table has no logical fields, but, if it did, you probably would want to exchange the default text box for a field box. A field that holds a choice between a few limited entries (for example, an Invoice schedule field which can hold the values Weekly, Monthly, or Quarterly) usually appears as a set of radio buttons. In these cases, the Quick Screen GETs serve as initial reminders of manual layout work you have to do.

In the Company table, you find two memo fields (Spec1 and Spec2) that Quick Screen automatically created as Edit regions instead of Text boxes. Edit regions are appropriate for memo fields, which contain free-form text, but these two GETs should be resized more appropriately. After you size the Spec1 Edit, you may want to make the Spec2 Edit the same size. You can resize the second Edit by watching the status bar closely for its dimensions, but a better method is to delete the Spec2 Edit, copy the Spec1 Edit, and paste a new copy of the Spec1 Edit into the layout. Double-click the new Spec2 Edit to access its Edit Region dialog and change its input value to `m.spec2`, as you see in figure 8.13.

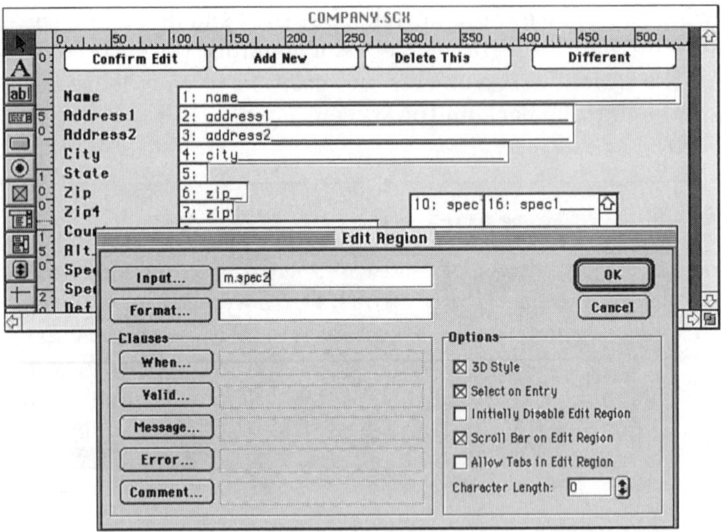

Figure 8.13 *Editing an Edit Region GET...*

Edit regions have a few quirks. Figure 8.13 shows the Edit Region dialog's Select On Entry checked, the default setting. This choice is not really appropriate to Edits because users may be annoyed when they start typing and wipe out all the notes they made earlier. Uncheck this box in the Edit Region dialog.

> **FOXPRO MAC HACK TIP**
>
> Although this attribute also is an interface standard for text boxes, I don't think Select on Entry is appropriate to all text boxes. You may want to change this attribute for additional GETs on your screens, unless your local Interface Cops object strenuously.

The Edit regions in figure 8.13 have scroll bars (by default, this option is checked in the Edit Region dialog as well). However, you may create an Edit Region with a scroll bar in the Screen Builder but the scroll bar doesn't show up in the screen when you execute the .SPR. You may even find that the EDIT has a scroll bar and then suddenly loses the bar when you change this GET's font.

This problem is not due to an error of the Screen Builder's or a mistake in the way GENSCRN generated the code. Although the *image* of the Edit always has a scroll bar in the Screen Builder layout, an actual EDIT GET object only has a scroll bar if it has sufficient height. The reason the object sometimes loses its scroll bar when you change its font is that the Screen Builder resized it vertically to have the same number of lines in the new, smaller font as it did in the original font. If you resize the object to have more lines than it did before, the scroll bar will re-appear in the executed screen.

Microsoft specifies a height of 48 pixels as the minimum size for an EDIT with a scroll bar on the FoxPro for Macintosh screen. You can be sure to follow this rule if you watch the status bar when you size an EDIT. The template screen is set up to show the position of the mouse cursor or selected object in pixels. If you start with a different screen, be sure to turn on the Show Position attribute from the Screen pop-up menu and use the Ruler/Grid dialog on the Screen pop-up menu to set the Ruler to pixels, as shown in figure 8.14. Once more, the default Screen Builder values are *not* the most useful. Using either a template screen or Andy Griebel's GASP utility, as you see later in the chapter, you can set up Screen defaults that save you time and frustration.

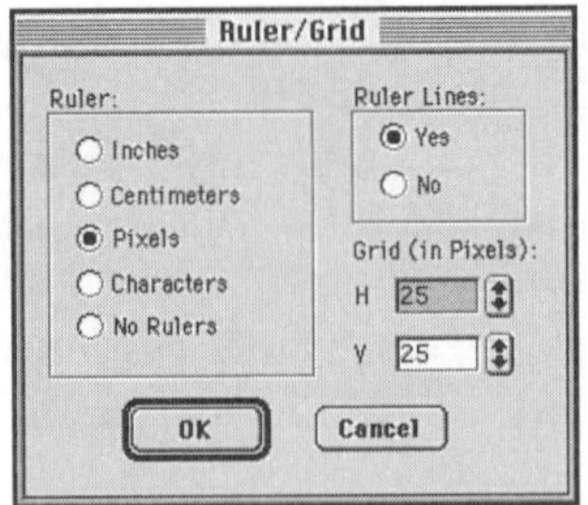

Figure 8.14 *...to some non-default values for more efficient screen work.*

> **FOXPRO MAC HACK TIP**
>
> I return to discussing GET objects and their properties in Chapter 10. Before leaving the subject of EDITs, however, there's an additional trick that you need so that you can use this special GET type. As you see in the Edit Region dialog, an EDIT can be *initially disabled*, like any other GET. However, unlike other GETs, EDITs can't be read properly unless you can scroll through their contents. If you have an EDIT that should be READ-only, you can use the expression `.T. NOMODIFY` in the EDIT's WHEN snippet to achieve this effect. You can even have two EDITs superimposed on each other in the layout, one with this WHEN expression and one without, to change the EDIT's state from editable to unmodifiable while the screen runs. In Chapter 10, you'll use the SHOW GET command to change the state of the GETs in this way and many others. (You've already seen this command briefly in the template screen's READ WHEN code, where it changes the button prompts to screen-specific text strings.)

Beyond changing the types of GETs in the original Quick Screen, you probably want to change the descriptive text labels next to them. These labels are the actual field names when Quick Screen creates them, but in the screen versions aren't limited to the length and legal characters characteristic of field names. For example, the `def_compct`, `def_rate`, and `def_discnt` fields communicate their purpose better if they show the labels `commission %`, `rate`, and `discount`, all grouped under the word `Default`. You also might add a box around these fields to group them logically in the user's mind.

You also move the GETs and associated labels around in the layout until they follow a more meaningful pattern than they did in their linear Quick Screen arrangement.

In FoxPro for Macintosh, like most Mac programs, you do initial placement and sizing of objects with the mouse. You'll find that fine adjustments, however, are easier to make with cursor keys, "nudging" objects into place one pixel at a time. You use the Shift key with cursor keys to adjust objects' size.

FOXPRO MAC HACK TIP

In FoxPro for Macintosh, you have a second special way to use the cursor keys. Check your Control Panel folder for the control, which comes with System 7. This Control panel is designed to help people who have physical difficulty using a mouse and other computer controls. However, the Easy Access feature offers an opportunity for everyone to fine-tune a layout using the cursor keys. Mouse Keys has two aspects you won't find in the native FoxPro for Macintosh cursor-key handling: when you turn it on, you can *select* an object or a tool bar button using the cursor keys (a real boon), and you can also achieve diagonal movement with the cursor keys. Anybody who's tried to move multiple selected objects in a Screen or Report layout will appreciate the difference.

Turn on Mouse Keys with the keypress ⌘-Shift-End. (The End key is on the numeric keypad.) Then turn on the numeric keys to move the mouse. You press 5 to click the mouse (press twice to double-click). To lock the mouse button when you want to drag (for example, to make an extended selection), press 0. To unlock the button when you're finished dragging, press . or 5.

Press End whenever you want to turn off Mouse Keys. Use the Easy Access control panel to adjust the speed with which the keys move the mouse cursor.

After you have the GETs in their final position, you should *reorder* the GETs to mirror the usual sequence in which users want to enter information. Quick Screen determined original GET order by the order of the fields in the table, which may not be appropriate, and your changes to the screen (such as deleting a memo field and adding a second copy) may have changed the GET order since the Quick Screen. Access the Object Order dialog from the Screen pop-up menu, as shown in figure 8.15, and simply drag the entries for GETs into the order that makes sense to you.

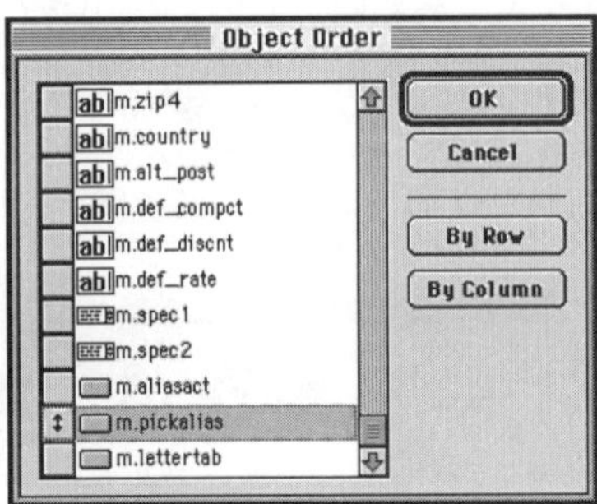

Figure 8.15 *Reorder the GETs to match a logical data entry sequence.*

The order isn't important to habitual mouse users, who click around the screen in any order they like. Consider, however, that your entry screen may be used by high-speed typists entering multiple records. These people are keyboard jockeys who use the Tab key to move between GETs without watching the screen. They appreciate a logical sequence that doesn't make them look up at the screen to see where they are.

FOXPRO MAC HACK TIP

For the needs of the same typists, I think you should always leave Object Order ON in a complex data entry screen, so that FoxPro doesn't move automatically to the next GET without an explicit Tab keypress (or press Enter, in FoxPro for DOS) expressing a desire to move on. For this reason, my MAIN.PRG provides this default.

You can change this default in MAIN.PRG's SaveSets procedure, if you disagree, or you can provide an option for your users to choose which way they prefer data entry. However, if you SET CONFIRM OFF for data entry, you should always SET BELL ON, so the fast typists have *audible* feedback when FoxPro automatically moves them to a new field.

The order of GETs has one consequence even for people who use the mouse to move between fields: it determines the *first* data entry GET in which the cursor is placed when a READ starts, and the default order in which GETs are refreshed on the screen. You learn more about the significance of this order in Chapter 10.

Creating a Consistent, Useful, and Pleasing Interface

Keeping a high-level perspective on the general impression the screen makes is important. Sometimes it's hard to see the effect of your design work in the layout window, usually because your window is large and you can't see the entire layout at once. Use the Screen Layout dialog's sketch of the screen to see the effect of the design as you work.

> **FOXPRO MAC HACK TIP**
>
> If you work with a very small main application FoxPro window and MODIFY the SCREEN IN MACDESKTOP (the default), sometimes you can't even size the Screen Layout dialog to be big enough to access its whole left-size toolbar. This limit probably is a bug. If it happens to you, close your .SCX file, resize your main application window after choosing Screen from the Window pop-up menu, and open the .SCX again.

Take time to consider what enhancement you can make to increase the attractiveness of the screen and its connection with the Address Book metaphor that you want to present. You will see my attempt to embody this metaphor in a screen image in the figures that end this chapter. I used rounded rectangles and some border lines to create the illusion of a spiral notebook.

I could add additional graphics. You may decide the image of a clipped-on note is appropriate for one of the memo fields, like an attachment to the notebook page.

Remember, however, to keep your design uncluttered. One of the most troubling aspects of a graphical interface is the tendency for extraneous images to overwhelm the information the user really wants to see. In addition, you have a limited amount of space on the screen in which to work. Don't force yourself to use tiny fonts for your GETs, which are frustrating to the user, simply because you cluttered the screen with extra design elements.

The buttons on this screen might have pictures on them rather than word prompts. Often, however, words have more clarity than pictures. The words "Different Address" on the m.pickalias button require less interpretation than any picture I can imagine, no matter what the user's background. You could design attractive screens that *include* a word (such as a large check mark with the word "Confirm" next to it), but remember that this approach limits your ability to *refresh* the prompt to reflect the user's choices. You can use the SHOW GET PROMPT trick you already saw in the READ WHEN clause of the Address screen to change the picture on the button, but you can't change the word in the picture dynamically, as you did with a character prompt.

Prototype Additional Features

Your concern for the appearance and features of the screen should focus on utility rather than pure aesthetics. The prototype screen is missing some features the user wants in the finished module. For example, the Address Book doesn't let the user access the contacts associated with each company yet. You can add a temporary button that brings up a "features not implemented" screen, as an EDIT or MODIFY MEMO. Alternatively, just add a reminder of these features in the READ WHEN, such as in the following line:

```
WAIT WINDOW NOWAIT ;
         "This Screen should allow access to "+ ;
         "Contacts and their Contact Numbers " + ;
         "for the current record!"
```

I made one additional change to this screen to provide additional utility, as well as to emphasize the Address Book metaphor. Buttons such as the tabs on dividers in the notebook permit the user to go quickly to a particular letter of the alphabet. From there, the user can access the "Different Address" button and BROWSE the file from a position close to his or her eventual target, just as they would do with a paper notebook.

You don't need to provide this feature in the prototype, if you're not ready to write the code. You can simply design the buttons and have the button VALID run a WAIT WINDOW that explains to the user what the buttons are supposed to do. You might want to ask users if these buttons should automatically bring up the Address BROWSE at the appropriate letter. They might prefer to see the GETs for the first record matching the letter they selected immediately. They'll still have the option of choosing the BROWSE separately from the button themselves if they want to scroll through the surrounding entries.

However you provide information and visual clues to the user, make sure your design is consistent. Don't use a WAIT WINDOW in the READ WHEN clause on one screen and a "Press here to learn about features not implemented" button on the next.

Use GASP To Enhance the Screen Design Process

You already saw that the template screen can provide a degree of consistency without thought on your part, by starting your screen with window attributes and default button behavior. If you use Andy Greibel's GASP, you can extend that consistency to the three-dimensional enhancements that many designers like to use in dialog design. By generating the 3D effects for you, GASP also prevents your having to lay out these effects separately for each GET, which is probably the most tedious part of standard FoxPro screen design sessions.

To use GASP, place the files you find in the source disk's GASP folder in your FoxPro home directory. Then you can add GASP to SYSMENU by executing the following statement:

See Also

- Source Disk:GASP Folder

```
DO SYS(2004)+"GASP.MPR"
```

You'll find a GASP.TXT and GASPHELP.TXT files in the GASP folder, with additional information on how to customize your GASP installation.

With GASP installed, use its menu option to set up your own preferences for 3D effects, as shown in figure 8.16. As you see in the dialog, you can set some other preferences, such as the Ruler, so that you don't have to adjust the screen manually even when you don't start from a template.

GASP works best if you start from 2D objects, rather than the Screen Builder's default of 3D GETs. In figure 8.17, you see the Address screen layout after GASP has affected its elements (in accordance with the preferences you saw in figure 8.16), and a second copy of the screen with its original objects. All the adjustments GASP makes are WYSIWYG (you can see them directly in the layout, without having to generate and run the .SPR).

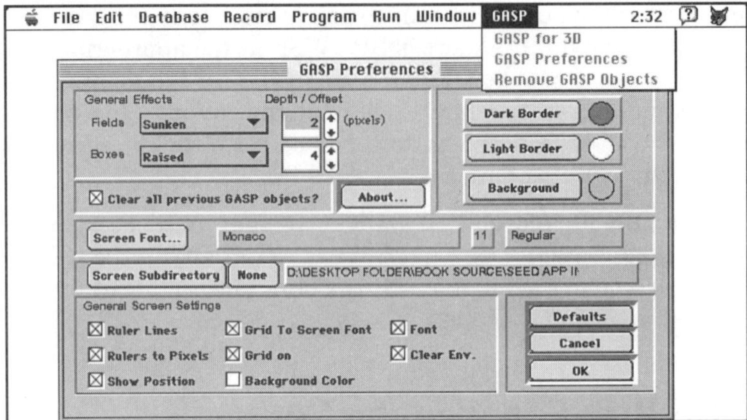

Figure 8.16 *Set up screen effects and Screen Builder defaults through GASP for consistent design.*

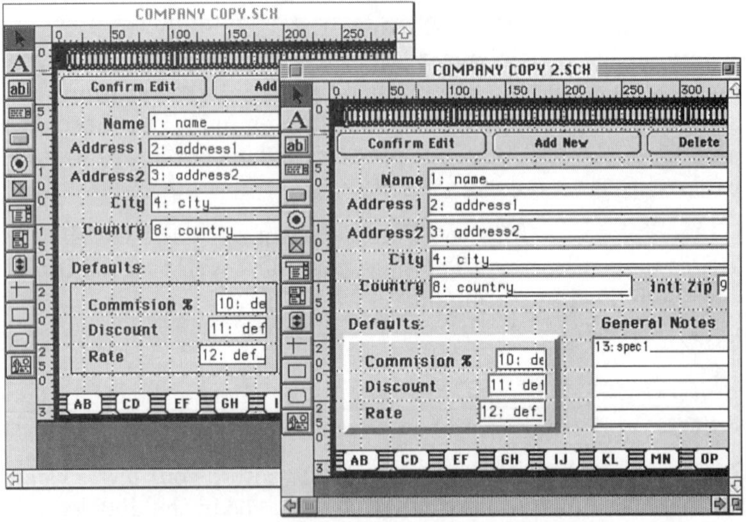

Figure 8.17 *"Before" and "After" copies of the Company screen, with its original 2D objects and after having been GASPed.*

GASP can assign special effects to individual objects, either accruing to your chosen default effects or replacing them with instructions you place in the objects' Comment fields. I rarely use this kind of instruction because my goal is a consistent design. In fact, for the Address Book metaphor I want to use for this screen, I'm not convinced that *any* 3D effects are appropriate, whether they're GASP's or the standard Screen Builder 3D. (You can see the standard 3D effects in figure 8.19 at the end of the chapter.) Fortunately, GASP is completely nondestructive. Use the Remove GASP Objects menu option to return to the native Screen Builder objects at any time. Continue to experiment until you're satisfied.

Be Aware of Font Problems

Any attempt to provide a consistent interface should take into account the fonts in the screen, both for text the user should read and GETs into which the user types.

The Company screen has inherited one more critical behavior from the template, not visible until you began to place GETs in the layout: the font for this window is Monaco, a standard Macintosh monospace font. Text GETs always should be in a monospace font. Otherwise, the entry space bears no relation to the number of characters the user can put in the field.

When you use memory variables, you encounter an additional problem: the size of the GET may allow the user to type far more characters than the field eventually permits, and the entry is truncated when you save the edit to the table. To avoid allowing extra characters, you can use the Picture clause, or Format option in the GET's Field dialog. In figure 8.18, for example, you see the two `A`'s in the Format template, restricting the State entry to two characters (the `@!` automatically makes the entry upper case).

Using Format on all your GETs definitely makes data entry easier for users, but they still need the visual clue of a properly sized GET, only possible with monospace fonts. If you make the window's base font monospace in the size and style you want for text GETs, the GETs will share the font attributes of the window automatically. Assuming the table from which the GETs are derived is open, the Screen Builder makes these GETs the correct size when you use Quick Screen.

If you're not using the template screen or another template of your own design, the window's base font will *not* be monospace automatically. Use the Layout dialog's Font option to choose a monospace font before you choose the Quick Screen option.

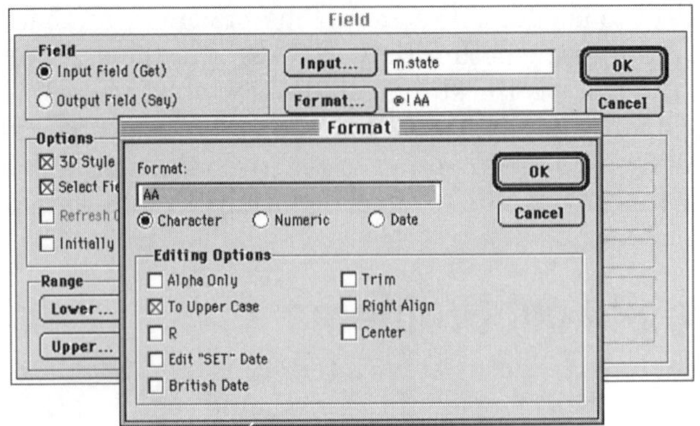

Figure 8.18 *A Format or Picture template safeguards user entry without complex validation techniques.*

Sometimes, you want a GET to be a different size or font from the other GETs. The GET starts out in the same font as the others, of course (the base font for the window). When you use the Object menu option to change its font attributes, the Screen Builder adjusts the GET for point size, but not for width. It's no longer automatically the right size for the information it will contain.

You have two possible methods to make sure this GET is the right width. First, you can change the base window font temporarily to the font attributes you want for this GET and then create the new GET. The new attributes will affect the new GET, but not the GETs previously created. Afterward, change the base window font back to its usual state. Second, you can create a text label with the font attributes you want and with the right number of characters. Size this special GET to the same size, watching the number of pixels closely in the status bar, as you did for the Edit regions in the preceding section. (Remember that neither method works unless you use a monospace font.)

See Also

- "Evaluating MACDESKTOP Metrics," Chapter 1

Neither text labels nor EDIT regions have to be monospaced. You can select these objects in the layout and assign them a more attractive font, either one at a time or as a group, using the Object menu pop-up's Font option.

You return to the problem of fonts several times in this book, from different perspectives. If you're a FoxPro for DOS programmer, new to GUIs, you have a lot to learn. Even seasoned Macintosh developers find that FoxPro's use of fonts has some unusual aspects.

Generate and Check the Prototype

The AD*Vantage main application-specific menu pad (VANTAGE.MNX and its generated VANTAGE.MPR) has a Maintenance pop-up with an option to edit the Address Book. The option's Command result is DO COMPANY.SPR. If you created your own copy of VANTAGE.MNX and commented out this result before creating COMPANY.SCX, remove the commenting asterisk now. Re-Build the AD*Vantage project, and COMPANY.SPR is generated when the Project Manager encounters the reference to this file in the menu.

See Also

- "Portable and Not-So-Portable Fonts, Graphics, and Screens," Chapter 1
- "Handle Windows and FONTS: The Unique MACDESKTOP," Chapter 12

When you execute the AD*Vantage.APP again, your Address Book option summons the new screen. You can add records and move around in the table using the "Different Address" button to BROWSE existing records. In figure 8.19 you can see that the BROWSE shows the generated unique key values the template code creates in the file, even though this field is never editable in the screen. While you enjoy having this confirmation of the unique keys in the BROWSE now, the final BROWSE statement you use in this screen set probably will have a FIELDS list, omitting the key in favor of the fields that the user understands and uses to search for records.

As figure 8.19 shows you, the Address Book's BROWSE automatically has the functionality of a Find dialog, using the native Edit Find option (shortcut ⌘-F) on SYSMENU. This handy option searches across *any* character, numeric, and date fields and requires absolutely no programming from you. (The source disk includes a replacement dialog () I wrote, which allows BROWSE searches that check memo fields along with the other field types. But the native Edit Find option is very powerful on its own.)

See Also

- Source Disk:Resource Folder: BFIND.SCX

Notice the alphabet "tabs" at the bottom of the Address Book window, for which I used 2D push buttons. If you use the Color Picker on the Utilities pop-up menu and then access the Address Book screen again, you see the difference between the color-behavior of 2D buttons and the 3D buttons at the top of the Address Book screen. If you check the COMPANY.SCX copy you find in the Seed App Copy version of the AD*Vantage application on the source disk, you will find the code I used to make the 2D buttons match the current color scheme in the buttons' WHEN clause. You learn more about invoking the FoxPro color system in Chapter 14.

See Also

- Source DIsk:Seed App (AD*Vantage developed): Screens Folder: COMPANY.SCX
- "Reference Colors Indirectly," Chapter 15

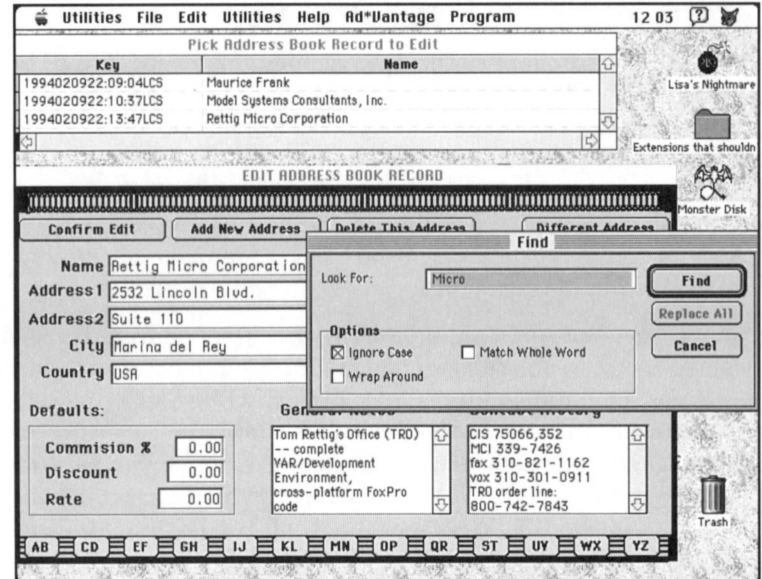

Figure 8.19 *The Address Book editing screen. The user has pressed the "Different Address" button, summoning a BROWSE to pick a record, and then uses the native Edit Find dialog to search the BROWSE for information.*

If you check the Seed App (AD*Vantage developed) version of COMPANY.SCX, you'll see the code I used to implement the alphabet tabs. The code is straightforward and uses some very powerful FoxPro techniques.

As you see in figure 8.20, I also placed this code directly in a procedure snippet for the button, rather than using an expression, explicitly naming the function, and placing the function in the screen Cleanup. Right now, this code is not generic. It specifies the field and tag needed to search the Company table and relies on the prompts of the associated buttons to know what letter the user wants. If I want to use this lookup code for a different purpose, I can copy and then paste the buttons into a new screen. The snippets follow the button set as a self-contained object. I can edit the code for the new screen by accessing the snippet again, rather than copying the associated function from the Cleanup code to the new screen as a separate action.

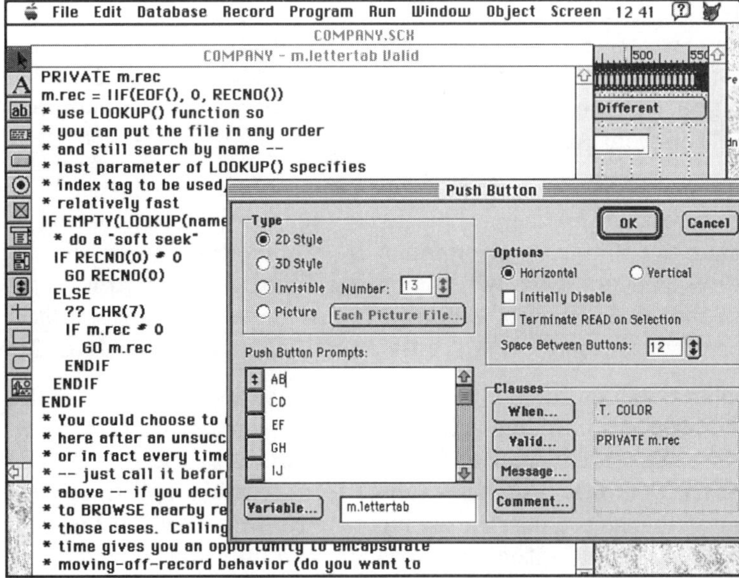

Figure 8.20 *The VALID procedure snippet for the alphabet tab button set.*

Eventually, I will improve this function so that the code doesn't require editing for each new use and works for other "soft seek" lookup situations. I'll migrate the code out of the snippet, either into the template cleanup code, or as a separate .PRG in my template folder. By staying aware of opportunities to make your code more flexible, you enhance your library of functions and procedures—and your rapid development methods—as you work.

Chapter Wrap Up

Running the prototype gives you a chance to think about validation needs without actually writing validation code. Just as event-handling in FoxPro depends on you intelligently disabling and enabling menu options, validation in FoxPro depends to a large extent on the intelligent enabling and disabling of GETs in a screen. All the READ objects should respond to changes the user makes.

As an example, watch the buttons change prompts and become selectively disabled as the user opts to Add rather than Edit. If you can enable file sharing on your machine for two FoxPro sessions or if you run FoxPro on a network, watch the way the GETs behave when the record displayed is already under edit at another station. The screen shows all the relevant information, but the only GETs the user can access are the alphabet tabs and the "Different Address" button.

You may not think of this responsiveness as *validation* because it doesn't involve correcting the user's choice. However, the job of validation is more comprehensive than correcting input. Its real purpose is to *prevent user frustration* on every level, which means guiding the user through procedures so that valid entries become easier to make, not waiting until the user does something that may cause a problem and then scolding about it.

I'll develop this idea further in Chapter 12. Meanwhile, keep looking for ways that you can implement the basic principles as you run the prototype. For example, consider adding *default values* to different fields in the records. Could the Company table's Country field default to a user-specified value, so the user rarely has to enter this information? Can you fill out the state field if the user adds zip code information first?

You can create prototypes of the other lookup tables in the AD*Vantage application (Rates, Employees, and Departments) by using the template screen. You even can create a quick version of the Jobs module using these techniques, although the complex relationships and multiple windows in that module will take more work to manage, as you will see in Chapter 10. As you develop the prototype, continue re-Building and running each new version to see where you can make improvements.

9

PROVIDE QUICK RESULTS: EASY REWARDS FROM THE RQBE AND THE REPORT WRITER

by
Lisa Slater

Having come this far with the prototype, you can add additional single data entry screens, such as the Employee and Rate maintenance screens, with little trouble. So far, you haven't seen how to make these screens work together in a single READ. You also haven't investigated the behind-the-scenes responses by FoxPro programs that validate and calculate data based on user input.

You're going to work on this aspect of applications development in the next part of this book. But you don't need perfect validation, or even screens for each table, before you start building some practice data sets and pulling out results.

At this stage, you should be more concerned about giving users a feel for the types of information the system contains than for its final appearance. The more exposure users have to the system, the more thoroughly you test the validity of your assumptions about the data structures. Even the complex set of Job relationships can be portrayed as a group of related, editable BROWSEs. Just throw in some rudimentary validation to stamp records with primary and parent keys (using the BROWSE WHEN and VALID clauses) if you can't figure out the screen sets yet.

Users help you test data structures as they enter the practice data set because they notice missing data items. For example, the Time table has a single Hours field. You've decided the agency estimates on a per-service basis, but they bill based on actual hours spent on the job. If a user comes to you with a question such as, "How do I show estimated versus actual hours?", you know you have to change the single Hours field to two (perhaps Est_hours and Act_hours), which you then use to calculate estimated and actual net. If nobody complains, your original assumption stands.

The most important test of your assumptions comes when users tell you what they expect to *do* with the data. Users need to produce management reports, bills, labels, and other written output. Sometimes they need to verify information on the screen in a specific arrangement, or to export it to other programs for further use.

I use the term *results* for what users expect to do with data, to underscore the fact that this objective can be achieved by many different methods, not just by written reports. Since results are the ultimate goal of the data model, results are also the model's ultimate test. You start designing results early to perform this test.

Categorizing the Components of FoxPro Results

Although results come in many forms, FoxPro result-getting has two main components: choosing the records to be part of the *result set*, and choosing the method of *presentation*, or output, for those records.

In the final section of Chapter 4, you saw a rudimentary Report Picker dialog, part of the template code for this book. This dialog executed a version of the FoxPro sample code's Browser dialog, which I adapted to provide reports with filtering conditions (see figure 9.1). You can think of the adapted Browser dialog as a simple embodiment of the first part of result-getting (selection criteria). Its parent Report Picker dialog represents the second component (output form).

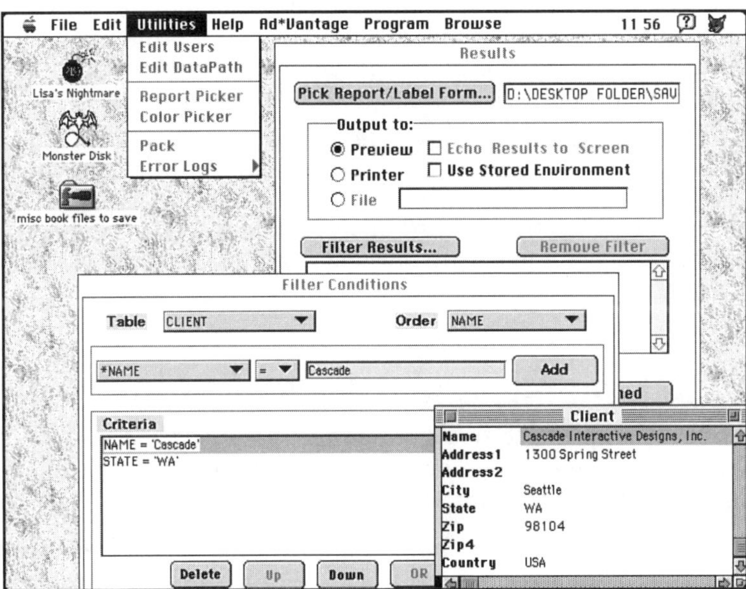

Figure 9.1 *The Browser/Filter dialog picks records and the Report Picker dialog provides presentation options, the two main components of FoxPro results.*

You'll look at a revised version of the Report Picker dialog in the final section of this chapter. No matter how you make the choices available and what methods you use to fulfill them, these two aspects—record selection and presentation format—form the basis of your results system. The next two sections of this chapter examine each of these aspects in turn.

Choosing the Result Set

Just as you can divide result-getting into two components, you can divide FoxPro results into two major types:

- Results presenting data from actual database tables
- Results presenting temporary tables that you create by manipulating the actual database tables

Both temporary tables and real tables may present data using the full range of FoxPro result commands (REPORT and LABEL FORM, COUNT, LIST, BROWSE, and so on). Both types may be filtered to show only some records, using logical conditions that take this general form:

```
<condition expression> <comparison operator> <constant value expres-
sion>
```

As you see in this chapter, this one general form can be used in many different FoxPro commands with varying degrees of efficiency and tremendous flexibility.

Using Commands and Clauses To Filter a Table

Except when you want the result to show all records, the first type of result requires placing a filter or filtering conditions on the tables in the database. The result command then acts only on the records you want.

If your selection criterion matches the active ORDER, or index expression, of the controlling table for the result, you can SEEK the first record that matches your criterion and then use the WHILE clause to process the records with a result command. For example, if you want to process all jobs for one client, you can `SELECT` the Job file, `SET ORDER TO client_key`, `SEEK` the key value for the client you want, and then `LIST WHILE Client_key = <the key for client you want>`.

This method doesn't preclude an additional order for the records you show. For example, suppose you want to show the jobs for this client in the order of their due dates. You could use an index expression of `Client_key+DTOS(Date_due)` on the Job table and still SEEK the first part of the expression (the key value for the client), assuming you have SET EXACT OFF, its default value. Because of the *composite* key expression, the records show up in order by date within the group of records for the one client.

> **FOXPRO MAC HACK TIP**
>
> Notice the use of the DTOS() function in the composite key expression above. When you concatenate expressions in FoxPro, you have to convert them between data types so they are all the same type. In this case, you're turning a date into its string equivalent, to match the data type of the client_key field. The DTOS() function uses the format YYYYMMDD, no matter what format DATE is SET to, so it's safer than the older date-to-character DTOC() function.

Using SEEK on the active index and then processing records WHILE the record set matches your criteria is always the fastest way to obtain results in FoxPro. Often, however, you can't rely on the active order of a table to match your selection criteria.

For example, you may want to list all Clients in order of revenues received, but you want to limit the list to states in a certain salesperson's territory. You might ask, "Why not just create an index based on a composite of the payment and state factors?" It's not practical to keep a composite index for every possible set of criteria and orders you might need. Instead, you SET FILTER on the table or use a FOR clause on the result command acting on the table to set complex criteria. You'll learn more about creating these filtering conditions later in the chapter.

Creating a Temporary Result Table

When you get results from a temporary table, you commonly use a FoxPro SQL SELECT command to process the real tables into a target table containing only the required records. The result command then acts on the new, temporary table. This table may have additional filters placed on it, using the same methods as you'd use on the real database.

The temporary table may be a physical table on disk you erase after use, but it's usually a *cursor* (SQL shorthand for "current set of records"). FoxPro disposes of cursors automatically when you close them.

FoxPro creates a disk image of the cursor while you use it, or, if it can, it maintains the cursor entirely in memory as a set of pointers to the original table. You usually don't have to worry about how or when FoxPro makes this choice. There are times, however, when a query *must* create a file on disk to have usable results. For example, if you want to create a result set and APPEND FROM those records into a different .DBF, the APPEND FROM command works only from a file on disk. If you want to check the real name of the file on disk for a cursor, the DBF() function returns a temporary table name when FoxPro creates a disk file. The DBF() function returns the original table name when FoxPro doesn't need to create a temporary table "underneath" the cursor. If there is no temporary table, the subsequent APPEND FROM will get all the records in the original table — not your filtered set.

> **FOXPRO MAC HACK TIP**
>
> If you want to force a file on disk, simply add a constant to the SELECT fields list so that the cursor no longer exactly matches the structure of the original table.

Deciding between Real and Temporary Tables for Results

How should you decide when to use a cursor or other temporary table, and when to get results from the real database? You can't limit yourself to one of the two types in most FoxPro applications. This section considers the different strengths and issues associated with both types of results.

SELECTs Bring Together Information from Many Tables.

The SELECT statement allows you to *join* tables using a WHERE condition. For example, `SELECT <fields> FROM Client, Job INTO CURSOR CurrJobs WHERE Client.Key = Job.Client_key` shows job information with associated client information. Add additional tables to the FROM clauses and additional WHERE conditions to indicate the linking fields, and the cursor can hold all the inventory for these jobs, along with the inventory child records, such as Broadcasts.

The <fields> list can be an asterisk (`SELECT *`) if you want all the fields in one or all of the source tables. However, you usually pick out only the fields you need to see. Sometimes it's easier to report on a single *flat file* like this without requiring relationships.

SELECTs Summarize Information Effectively.

The following query shows you the total collected from each client, with one record for each Client, because of the `GROUP BY` clause:

```
SELECT ;
Client.*, SUM(Receipt.amount) ;
   FROM Client, Receipt ;
   WHERE Receipt.Client_key = Client.key ;
   GROUP BY Client.key
```

Add the clause `HAVING SUM(Receipt.amount) > 25000`, and you see only records for big accounts. You can make this query a lot more complicated:

```
SELECT ;
Client.*, SUM(Receipt.amount), SUM(Inventory.act_gross);
    FROM COMPANY Client, Receipt, Job, Inventory;
    WHERE Receipt.client_key = Client.key;
      AND Job.client_key = Client.key;
      AND Inventory.job_key = Job.key;
      AND Client.state = "CA";
    GROUP BY Client.key;
    HAVING SUM(Inventory.act_gross) > SUM(Receipt.amount)+10000
```

Now the query joins four files to show all clients in the state of California who owe more than $10,000 (total gross billed is over $10,000 more than total received). Since I used SELECT Client.*, obtaining all the address fields in the Company table, the result set is ideal for creating a "dunning" list for mail merge.

I haven't specified the target format for the results of this query. I might create a cursor to process the letters in the Report Writer. I might also export the data from the cursor with a separate command or program to a format my word processor understands. As a third alternative, I could write the results to disk as a table immediately if my word processor can handle a .DBF file.

FOXPRO MAC HACK TIP

Don't be surprised that I suggest moving the data out of FoxPro to produce final results. You should use every program you own for what it does best. As a DBMS, FoxPro has unparalleled ability to sort, select, and format *data*. These capabilities may be built into your word processor, but they'll be handled less flexibly and much more slowly.

On the other hand, you can only get a certain amount of *text*-formatting out of the FoxPro Report Writer, which you investigate later in this chapter. If your requirements exceed FoxPro's capabilities, sometimes you'd be better off switching to a desktop publisher or word processor for output.

Isn't graceful integration of different programs one of the reasons you use a Mac?

Cursors Are an Efficient Way To View a Small Subset of a Large, Complex Matrix of Information.

In the last query, you see the WHERE clause providing three join conditions, linking the files by their key fields. The last WHERE clause (`WHERE Client.state = "CA"`) provides a filtering condition, rather than a join. The query might have many more filtering conditions, joined with ANDs and ORs, nested with parentheses.

The more accurately you can pinpoint a small result set out of a mass of data, the more useful cursors become. Instead of traversing the full record set during the result command (such as REPORT FORM or BROWSE) and evaluating each record to see if it matches the criteria, FoxPro evaluates the conditions *once* when it creates a cursor. The cursor presents the results more quickly thereafter.

You may think that this rule is subject to the rules of FoxPro *optimization*, as described later in this chapter, but optimization (or lack thereof) of a filter condition applies equally to cursors and real tables.

SELECTs Are Designed To Express Complicated Selection Criteria Simply. They're Easy To Learn To Write and Encourage You To Experiment.

In spite of the seeming complexity of the last query you saw, you don't have to know how to phrase the SELECT statement to write these queries. Figure 9.2 shows you the last query as I designed it in the RQBE dialog. I USEd tables with the aliases they need in the AD*Vantage application before starting to write the query. Different sections of the jam-packed RQBE dialog provide easy ways to pick the source tables, fields list, target formats, and other clauses of the SELECT command. In the figure, you see the HAVING clause under construction.

As you write a query, the dialog builds the SELECT statement, getting ready to write the .QPR file. You can read the SELECT syntax as you work (press the SEE SQL button to get the text window containing the query).

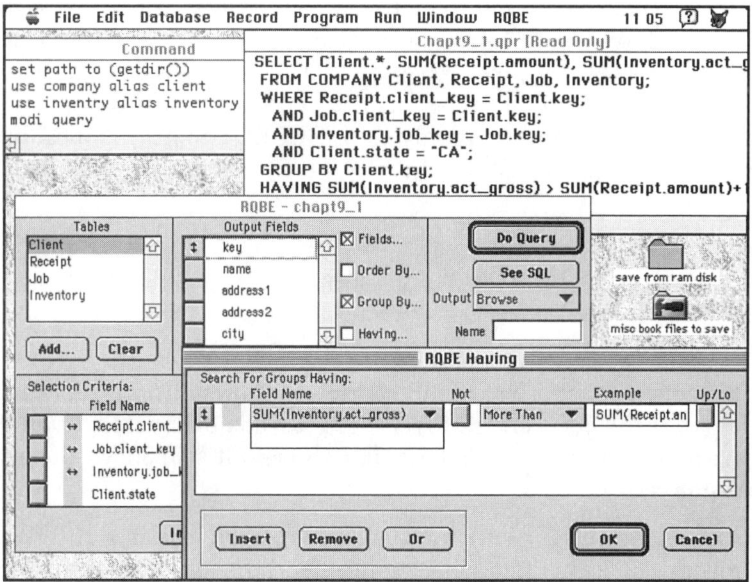

Figure 9.2 *The RQBE dialog can write complicated queries. The See SQL button lets you see the syntax as you build it.*

Notice that I can type a complex expression into the right side of the HAVING expression, not just a literal value to be compared with the expression on the left. If you create a complex .QPR on your own, the RQBE properly recognizes such expressions and puts them in the dialog. You can do the same thing with expressions on the right side of the WHERE box.

SQL SELECT was a new command in FoxPro 2.0. With all its wonderful capabilities to explore, some developers gave up on real tables for reports all together. They soon found out, however, that there are some situations in which a SELECT is not the answer.

Outer Joins Are More Natural with Real Tables in Relationship Than with a SELECTed Set.

Outer Join is a SQL term for a join in which some records on one side of the join have no matches on the other side. For example, the agency might want a listing of all Jobs and their Inventory records, but some existing Jobs may not have any Inventory recorded yet. The SQL SELECT statement `SELECT * FROM Job, Inventory WHERE Job.Key = Inventory.Job_Key` skips the new Jobs with no Inventory. As you see in the next section, you *can* write a complex (and relatively slow) SELECT to list all Jobs, but an outer join requirement is fulfilled easily with the following standard FoxPro code:

```
USE Job
USE Inventory ALIAS Inventory IN 0 ORDER job_key
SET RELATION TO key INTO Inventory
SET SKIP TO Inventory.
```

With this setup, any FoxPro result command shows *virtual records* for each Job until the Job's entire Inventory record is exhausted. Even if there are *no* Inventory records for a Job, the result still shows one record for each Job record.

Figure 9.3 shows you the way these virtual records look in a BROWSE of job numbers, the associated client names, and the jobs' current inventory lines. The shaded pattern indicates extra BROWSE lines FoxPro adds for each Job record because it has many Inventory records. The middle job listed, for the client Peirse & Peirse, has no Inventory yet, but it still has a single BROWSE line. The same virtual listing of records would occur in a report, or even a SCAN/ENDSCAN of the Job file.

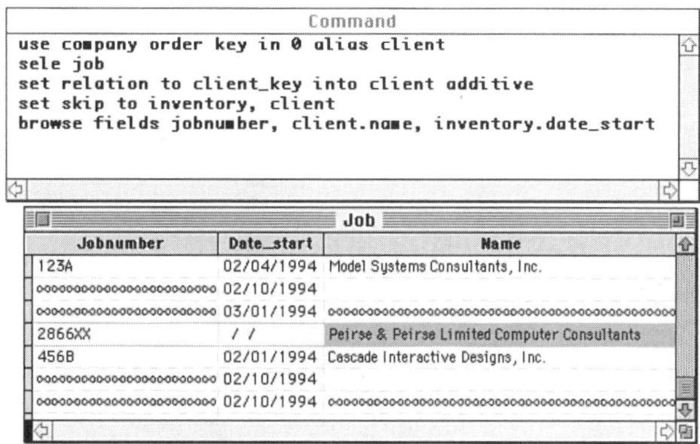
```
use company order key in 0 alias client
sele job
set relation to client_key into client additive
set skip to inventory, client
browse fields jobnumber, client.name, inventory.date_start
```

Jobnumber	Date_start	Name
123A	02/04/1994	Model Systems Consultants, Inc.
	02/10/1994	
	03/01/1994	
2866XX	/ /	Peirse & Peirse Limited Computer Consultants
456B	02/01/1994	Cascade Interactive Designs, Inc.
	02/10/1994	
	02/10/1994	

Figure 9.3 *A SET SKIP BROWSE, showing a one-to-many relationship between jobs and inventory lines, represents the FoxPro equivalent of a SQL outer join.*

FOXPRO MAC HACK TIP

Each job has one and only one client associated with it, but I SET SKIP TO Inventory, Client rather than just Inventory for figure 9.3, so you could see the interesting and anomalous shaded block pattern you get in the Client.name listing. If you try SET SKIP TO Inventory only, you'll see the Client.name repeated for each virtual Job record, which would have made the one-to-many pattern much more difficult to read in the figure. Neither behavior seems appropriate to me; I would have expected shaded patterns under each Client.name, matching the fields from the Job file. This peculiarity of a SET SKIP BROWSE doesn't affect the effectiveness of the SET SKIP technique, especially for reports.

Cursors Created by a SELECT Statement Are Read-Only.

You can use the `CREATE CURSOR` command to build an empty temporary table, just like the `CREATE TABLE` command APPSETUP generates in MAKEDBFS.PRG to create all the .DBFs in your database. A CREATEd CURSOR is editable just like the tables. However, when you SELECT records INTO a CURSOR, the cursor represents a read-only result set. If you want to edit results, you can SELECT unique keys into a cursor and then relate the cursor back into the real table. This technique allows you to filter the editable records—but you are still editing the real table. Similarly, you can SELECT into an editable TABLE rather than a CURSOR, but you're still left with the problem of updating the real file.

Queries Are Inefficient with Large Subsets of the Original Files.

Remember when I said that FoxPro decides when it can maintain a CURSOR in memory and when it must create a temporary table of its own underneath? Suppose you run a large agency, and you want to run a total on the inventory gross and net for all jobs except for jobs of a particular, obscure classification. You could easily have a database containing information about 5,000 jobs, only a few of which are in this classification, and most of which have over 10 inventory detail lines each.

If you create a SELECT to filter and join this data, your result set contains almost 50,000 records. If it doesn't fit in memory, FoxPro has to write this 50,000 record table out to disk before you can start working with the cursor. If you're working on a network and assign your temporary files to go to your local drive, as you usually do, think about all those records being pulled over the network!

In contrast, a normal one-to-many relationship in the database, plus a simple filter for the job classification which will omit few records from consideration, handles this large result set more naturally. Yes, the records still have to be pulled over the network, but usually not all at once, and the operation may appear smoother to the user.

Experimenting with SELECT Statements

Eventually your experimentation with SELECTs will take you to syntax the RQBE dialog can't handle. For example, you might prefer to express the last query a little more legibly by giving the SUMmed columns new names, using the AS clause to provide column-level aliases:

```
SELECT ;
   Client.name, ;
   SUM(Receipt.amount) as receipts, ;
   SUM(Inventory.act_gross) as billed;
```

```
 FROM COMPANY Client, Receipt, Job, Inventory;
 WHERE Receipt.client_key = Client.key;
   AND Job.client_key = Client.key;
   AND Inventory.job_key = Job.key;
 GROUP BY Client.key;
 HAVING billed > receipts + 10000
```

If you create a .QPR like this yourself as a regular program file, you may find that the RQBE reads it beautifully. But when you start making changes to the query in the RQBE dialog, the dialog gets confused. If you've previously run the query interactively, the RQBE may recognize the HAVING clause as legal because it "knows" about the billed and receipts columns. You can even stuff the AS clause into the Expression text box of the Fields dialog in the RQBE. But the RQBE may spontaneously remove the AS clauses from the fields list when you save or re-edit the file, producing erroneous results. (If you haven't run the query previously during this FoxPro session and you try to edit the HAVING clause, you get a "SQL Column not found" error.)

As you get more comfortable with SELECTs, you *can* write them yourself and then import them into the RQBE dialog. However, don't use any features of the SQL SELECT command that the RQBE doesn't know how to create itself— even when it looks as though it's handling the clauses well— or you may have an unpleasant surprise later.

Legibility is not your only reason for designing queries beyond the scope of the RQBE. In the last section, you learned about an outer join, which you produce easily with an Xbase SET RELATION. The equivalent SELECT statement requires a UNION and a nested SELECT, which you can't use in the RQBE. The following SELECT literally says, "Give me all Jobs and their Inventories, plus all Jobs that don't have any Inventory:"

```
SELECT Job.Jobnumber, Inventory.date_due ;
   FROM Job, Inventory ;
   WHERE Job.Key = Inventory.Job_key ;
UNION ;
SELECT Job.Jobnumber, {} ;
   FROM Job ;
  WHERE Job.Key NOT IN ;
      (SELECT Inventory.Job_key FROM Inventory)
```

FOXPRO MAC HACK TIP

This query technically represents a *left outer join*. An outer join on the *right* side would mean a check for Inventory records that had no matching Jobs added to the list of Inventory records and their jobs. In Xbase, we call such Inventory records *orphaned children*. Your programming should take steps to make sure that no such records exist. For example, Randy's CasDel procedure in MAIN.PRG, used to delete Jobs in the Job screen set in the next chapter, will *cascade* a Job deletion to include deletions of all its child and grandchild records.

Notice the use of curly braces ({}), the FoxPro method of supplying an empty value of date type in the SELECT statement above. This value is necessary as a placeholder because the SELECTs on either side of the UNION keyword must contain matching field lists so the SELECTs can be joined into one set of rows and columns.

You should be aware that a SELECT's fields list doesn't have to contain fields only; the list can include complex, formatted expressions as well as constants. For example, if you wanted to modify the structure of a table programmatically, adding a character field of length 30, you could write a query like this:

```
SELECT *,SPACE(30) FROM <source> INTO TABLE <target>
```

Similarly, in a query designed to result in a mail merge, you could format items in the fields list to be appropriate for use in letters, like this:

```
SELECT ;
   PADR(ALLTRIM(first)+" "+ALLTRIM(last), 50), ;
   IIF(EMPTY(greet),first, greet), ;
    <additional fields>...
```

Notice that the first item in this example is *padded* to the maximum length you need for the full name. Without this precaution, the column width of the result may be determined by a short name in the first SELECTed record, and all other results will be truncated to match. The second item performs some conditional logic for a letter salutation using the IIF() function. You know you want to use the `greet` field containing a more personal form of the person's name instead of the `first` field in the salutation whenever the `greet` field contains an entry. In this situation, you have no reason to force your result command (or the external program producing the letter) to do this evaluation. The SELECT takes care of this requirement with dispatch.

The setup code for the Jobs screen set you investigate in the next chapter contains two additional examples of queries you can't design in the RQBE. The first one uses a nested query of the DBFS table to determine which tables are child tables of the different kinds of Inventory tables. The DBFS.Subform field keeps this information. You can't express this query in the RQBE dialog because, like the outer join, it has a nested SELECT to find out which tables have parents whose parent, in turn, is the Inventory table:

```
SELECT aliasname, subform ;
   FROM DBFS ;
   INTO CURSOR subtypes ;
       WHERE subform IN ;
       (SELECT aliasname FROM DBFS ;
             WHERE subform = "INVENTORY")
```

The second Jobs screen setup query is simpler than the preceding one, but it doesn't fit the RQBE because its result is an *array,* rather than one of the result types offered by the RQBE Output popup control. When the user opts to add a new Inventory line in the Job screen set, this array provides the user's choices of available Inventory items.

```
SELECT aliasname, tablename ;
   FROM DBFS ;
   INTO ARRAY invtypes ;
       WHERE subform = "INVENTORY"
```

After the user chooses an inventory line type from a pop-up control based on the Invtypes array, the inventory item-editing procedure uses the Subtypes cursor to figure out which child tables are affected. This method allows the Job screen and its subsidiary INVEDIT.PRG routines to edit as-yet unspecified Inventory items. The programs don't have to change; you just add new records, describing the new Inventory items, to DBFS.DBF.

From the last two SELECTs, you learn another important fact about FoxPro results: sometimes they don't have any visible output at all. A subset of records is often useful in your programs even when the user is completely unaware of the result.

Refining and Optimizing Result Set Conditions

You've already seen that criteria for a SELECT-created temporary table are expressed as a WHERE clause on the SELECT statement. To filter a real database table's records, you use FOR clauses on the result commands, or add a SET FILTER command before the result command, using the same general format of `<condition expression> <comparison operator> <value expression>`. You can't learn about these conditions in the RQBE, but you can learn about them in FoxPro's Expression Builder instead.

Figure 9.4 shows the Expression Builder called from the Database Count option on the interactive menu. I've checked the Count dialog's For box, and I'm building the FOR clause of the COUNT command in the Expression Builder dialog.

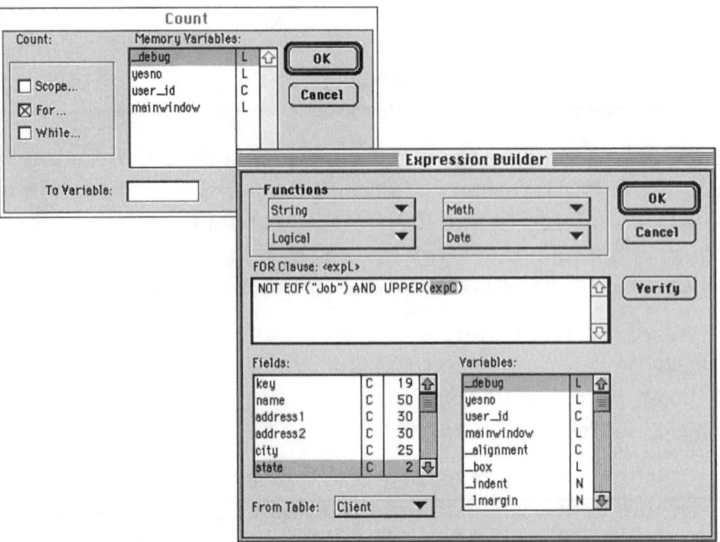

Figure 9.4 *Learn about FoxPro filter expressions in the Expression Builder dialog.*

You can access this dialog from almost every menu option that executes a result command in the interactive FoxPro environment, because all the result commands take FOR clauses. Expression building also figures heavily in the Report Writer, which you investigate in the next section. You can even include this dialog in distributed applications by using the `GETEXPR` command to summon it, if you think it's appropriate to the application's users. (For most users, an adapted version of BROWSER is a better choice.)

Use the Expression Builder to build filter conditions from the wide variety of functions available for different data types in FoxPro. In the figure, I've used the String pop-up to select the UPPER() function. The function is automatically placed in the text box in which you build the filter.

You see that `expC` is highlighted. If I now double-click on the word `state` in the fields list on the lower left, `state` replaces `expC` in the text box. The Expression Builder controls' effect on the expression in the text box has a logic opposite to the Macintosh's norm, which is to select an object, and then act on it. In this dialog, you pick an action (a function), and then you select the item on which you wish to act (a field or memory variable from the lists). Some people find this behavior confusing, and you also can't use the controls to produce the full variety of complex expressions you can write in FoxPro. You're often better off typing the expression in the text box.

When you practice creating expressions, use the Verify button to make sure you've created a valid expression of the type you need (logical, for filter conditions). If I press Verify on the expression shown in figure 9.4, I get an error because I'm only part way through creating the filter. In figure 9.5, you see the completed filter expression, which I designed to get a result of all companies in the state of California that have at least one job record on file. The Verify button will approve this expression now, assuming I have the Job table open along with Client.

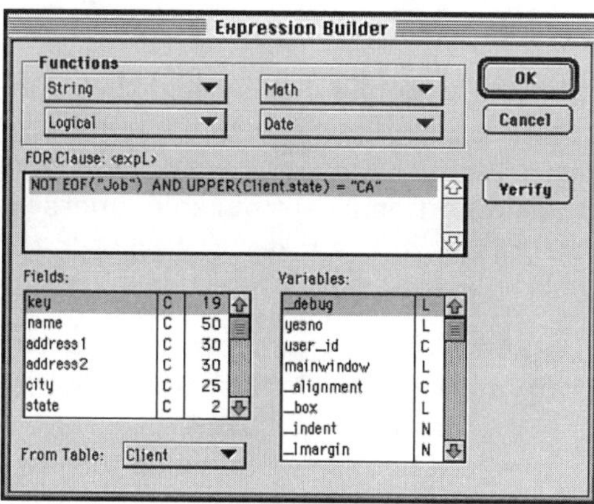

Figure 9.5 *A completed, verifiable filter expression must be Boolean or logical in type.*

As you practice creating SELECTs and filter expressions, you are probably using a small sample set of records, such as the Tutorial folder tables from the FoxPro for Macintosh installation disks. You're probably aware, however, that FoxPro's real strength is in using these same commands to query extremely large databases quickly, using its patented Rushmore technology, a form of *optimization* of filtering databases.

You also may know that you can't always count on Rushmore technology to work with a particular filter condition. You often will hear FoxPro developers talk about structuring a query to optimize it or about a condition that is not optimizable.

How does Rushmore work, and when is a filter condition optimizable?

Rushmore uses available index expressions in your tables' structure index files and any other index files you've opened along with the tables. It compares your conditions to index expressions it knows about. If it finds an index expression that matches your condition, it can check the index file for the records it needs, which is a much faster operation than checking the table.

The filter may be a WHERE clause on a SELECT, a SET FILTER, or a FOR clause and be equally accessible to Rushmore. (You can probably see, however, that the efficient SEEK WHILE strategy described earlier doesn't use or need Rushmore, since this method already relies on the use of an index for its record selection.)

The match must be an *exact* match for Rushmore to work. Rushmore isn't a human being who can reason that two expressions are functionally equivalent or that one expression is a subset of another.

Earlier in the chapter, for example, I suggested the expression `Client_key + DTOS(Date_due)` for an index. If you decided to maintain this index and you wanted to create a result for a particular Client_key, Rushmore wouldn't recognize the condition as optimizable unless you expressed it as `Client_key+DTOS(Date_due) = <client key value>`, even though you didn't need the date half of the expression.

For a more typical example, if the user typed in a client name, you may want to initiate a case-insensitive search of the table by checking for `UPPER(Client.Name) = m.name`, having formatted the user's input in all uppercase. Rushmore would not use an index on the `name` field for this operation; you need an index on `UPPER(Name)`.

Because the requirement for case-insensitive searches is so common, Andy Griebel and I decided to place tags on UPPER() versions of character fields in the structural of the AD*Vantage tables (see figure 9.6).

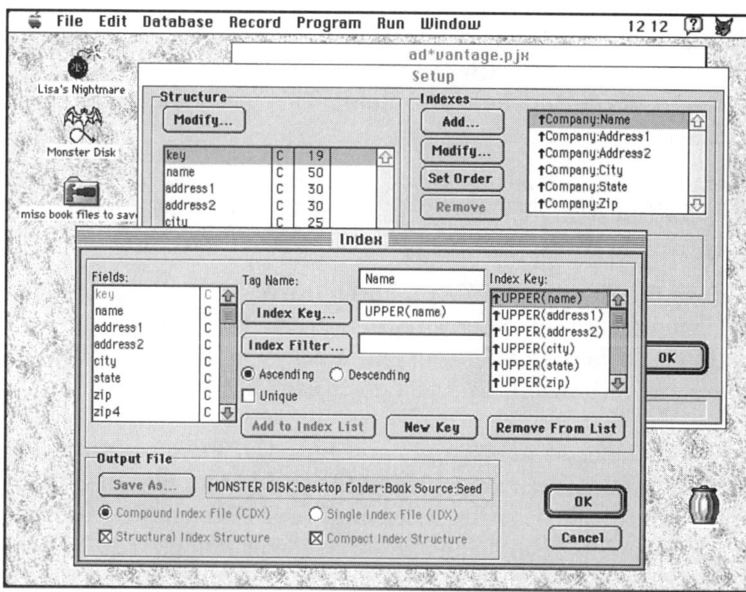

Figure 9.6 *The AD*Vantage table fields are indexed on UPPER() versions of their character fields to allow optimized case-insensitive searches of their contents.*

This strategy presents a problem for optimizing queries that use the BROWSER screen because the dialog automatically presents fieldnames, rather than key expressions, for the left side of filter expressions. In fact, BROWSER mistakenly thinks our index keys and its fieldname pop-up control produce optimizable expressions. BROWSER places an asterisk in front of all the fields in its pop-up that it believes have matching indexes, but its code checks for optimization by looking at tag *names,* rather than key *expressions.*

If you only use some form of BROWSER to allow users quick practice queries during the prototyping period, this problem isn't serious. However, if you want to address the problem, you have several options:

- Change the SetTags procedure in BROWSER to create an array of key expressions (using SYS(14) rather than TAG()). This method just gets rid of misleading asterisks; it doesn't make the results optimizable.
- Change the tag names for UPPER() versions of fieldnames to make sure they don't match the fieldnames exactly (for example, U_Name instead of Name for the Name field). This method also doesn't make results optimizable.
- Change the tag names as above, and also add new tags and expressions for the straight fieldnames. This is a lot of excess baggage to carry around just to create optimizable results in BROWSER!
- Change the Add button VALID procedure in BROWSER to automatically create the filter condition on the UPPER() version of the fieldname when the field is of character type. Now the BROWSER filters are optimizable and you don't need extra tags.

If you agree with the strategy Andy and I use (UPPER() versions of all character fields for index expressions), the last option is your best solution. It also provides a good illustration of the *consistency* necessary to ensure that your filter conditions and index expressions match throughout different modules and different applications, if you want to be sure of optimization as often as possible.

> **FOXPRO MAC HACK TIP**
>
> The same rapid development principles apply here as elsewhere in your programs: standardize your techniques so that you're certain you know how they work and that they're well tested. Then avoid duplicating techniques in different procedures to call the same action. If you always call one engine procedure to generate filters, for example, you find it easy to make sure that all evaluations of character fields use the UPPER() function.

Matching index expressions exactly allows Rushmore optimization for a simple comparison of one expression to one value. However, there are a few more restrictions.

First, the index expression must not contain aliased fields from related tables, and should not be *conditional* (`INDEX ON <expression> FOR <condition>`) or *negative* (`INDEX ON NOT <expression>`).

Second, the comparison operator must be one of the optimizable operators: `=, <, > , <=, >=, #, <>, or !=`. Since the last three operators mean "not equal," you can see that the restriction against `INDEX ON NOT <expression>` for optimizable expressions is not onerous.

Third, make sure to take the SETting of DELETED into account. My template MAIN.PRG SETs DELETED ON, because this is a convenient setting for many applications. (You can change it in PROCEDURE SaveSets if you disagree, or you can countermand it in INCLUDE.PRG for any specific application.) When you SET DELETED ON, FoxPro checks to see whether records are deleted before deciding that they fit a filter condition. Simply add a tag on DELETED() to all your tables, as shown in figure 9.7, and this unstated part of all your filters is optimized (FoxPro doesn't have to check the real table for this information.)

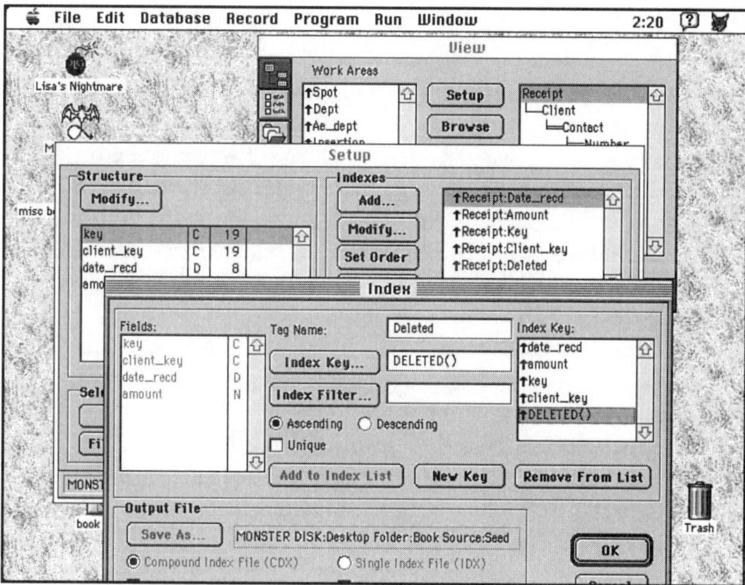

Figure 9.7 *Creating an index tag on DELETED() for each table is critical for filter optimization in applications that SET DELETED ON.*

FOXPRO MAC HACK TIP

As you increase your understanding of optimization in FoxPro, you may change your mind about the tags and index expressions you should maintain many times. *Be careful not to re-create the same index tag over and over using the INDEX ON TAG command.* Because structural indexes maintain many tags in the same file, and because the INDEX ON command can't know in advance how much space your latest use requires within the .CDX, this command abandons the space it used before and creates the new version of the tag at the end of the file. Re-creating the index repeatedly, therefore, leads to the file growing enormously, a condition FoxPro people call *index bloat*.

A command such as PACK or REINDEX that readjusts the whole table takes care of index bloat, but you should also have a mechanism to re-create indexes in case something happens to the index file. This mechanism should *not* rely on REINDEX because the index file header may be corrupt or the file may be missing entirely. Your index re-creation routine *must* use INDEX ON.

Fortunately, if you're using APPSETUP, the necessary index re-creation routines are generated for you, as MAKECDXs.PRG. If you examine this program, you see the trick to index re-creation without index bloat: start the routine with a DELETE TAG ALL, bringing the size of the .CDX down to nothing before you begin. While you're working interactively and adjusting table structures in the design period, simply check to see whether an index tag already exists before you re-create this tag.

There's nothing really mysterious about the rules of optimization in FoxPro. After you understand the simple principles above, you can compose complex criteria of different comparisons linked by ANDs and ORs. Understanding optimization of these complex filters takes only a little more work.

As a general rule, remember that conditions linked by ANDs form a gradually narrowed result set, with each condition working on the result of the one FoxPro evaluated before it. If you filter for all clients in California AND all outstanding balances greater than $25,000, then FoxPro can get one subset of all clients based on the state filter and look *only within that subset* for all balances that fit the second condition. If you link conditions by OR, however, FoxPro has to go back to check the entire original record set for each condition.

FoxPro is smart about which condition to evaluate first; it doesn't always go from left to right. If you link optimizable conditions with non-optimizable conditions, it will use the optimizable part of the filter to find a small subset first, and then do the non-optimizable comparison on this subset instead of the whole file. For example, the $ comparison operator (which compares a string to see if it is *contained in* another string) isn't optimizable. When FoxPro sees the condition "Tod" $ Name AND State = "CA" in a filter on the Client file, FoxPro looks only in the subset of Client records in the state of California for records with a Name field containing "Tod."

Now that you know the basic optimization rules, you can experiment with your own data structures to see how best to express filter conditions for the results your application needs. Don't neglect the simple SEEK WHILE approach where the indexed order is appropriate to your results.

FOXPRO MAC HACK TIP

When you have conditions that are completely non-optimizable, like substring searches with the $ operator, sometimes you can take an entirely different approach with a *conditional index*. Although conditional indexes aren't accessible to Rushmore for normal optimization, sometimes you can create a temporary index by using `INDEX ON <order expression> FOR <non-optimizable, possibly complex expression>` for fast output. FoxPro takes a little time to create the index on-the-fly, but execution of the result command afterwards is extremely fast.

If you often have need for temporary indexes of this nature, don't create separate temporary .IDX files each time you create an index. Instead, assign a file name for a second *compound* index file (.CDX) besides the structural .CDX for each table in your system that requires temporary indexes. Use the SYS(3) or SYS(2015) to assign tag names to each tag in this second .CDX as you create them. Now you only have to ERASE one .CDX for each table when your application performs Cleanup chores before it QUITs.

Fortified with the ability to cull record selections from your database tables, and to create temporary result sets with SQL SELECT, you next look at FoxPro's primary mechanism for delivering those results to the user: the REPORT FORM command, its underlying .FRX table definition, and the Report Writer tool in which you lay out the reports.

Presenting Results with the Report Writer

Result-getting in FoxPro is a Zen-like experience: most of the enlightenment of the journey occurs during the journey itself, not upon arrival. When you put together the various capabilities you have for filtering and ordering a database, you see that FoxPro is capable of queries that are precise, intricate, and elegant as well as fast. When you go to the Report Writer to present those queries, however, you may find the mechanism relatively clumsy and lacking in the fine control you expect from programs providing professional-quality output on the Macintosh.

Don't get me wrong. The Report Writer can easily satisfy many people's demands for DBMS output. In this section, you see the way the Report Writer works and learn about some of the special features you can use to fulfill unusual requirements with FoxPro report forms. Just remember that, if you need a desktop publisher, FoxPro isn't one, but you're not *stuck* because FoxPro isn't one.

I've already suggested using the results of a query in a format suitable to another Macintosh application for a mail merge. Later in the chapter, I'll suggest several ways to export FoxPro result sets to other formats. Part of learning to use the Report Writer wisely is learning when not to contort the tool beyond endurance (yours or FoxPro's!). However, the Report Writer bends quite extensively before it breaks.

Report Writer Layout Components

The Report Writer is a graphical design tool similar to the Screen Builder. You create objects and assign attributes to them, and assign certain global attributes to the report in a Layout dialog. You can store an Environment with the .FRX definition table, you can create a Quick Report using features similar to the Screen Builder's Quick Screen, and of course you can set up a template report (like a template screen) to match your custom working style.

There are two major differences between the Screen Builder and the Report Writer, beyond the obvious fact that one provides display on the monitor and the other is designed primarily for printed output.

First, the Report Writer does not have a matching generator program like GENSCRN to take the .FRX table and turn it into executable code. FoxPro executes REPORT FORM commands by acting directly on the .FRX table. This fact has an important consequence: users of a distributed application can MODIFY and CREATE REPORTs because the resulting .FRXs don't need code generated and compiled before the report will run.

Second, while the Screen Builder presents one set of fields or memory variables at a time in a window by default, a report form is designed specifically to handle multiple records in a repeating, or periodic, format. To handle this requirement, the Report Writer uses a *banded* layout. Each type of band repeats on a different schedule:

- *The detail band* contains elements you want to repeat and evaluate for each movement of the record pointer (each record) in the controlling table of your result set (whether the result is a cursor or a real table in your database).
- *The page header and footer bands* contain elements you want to repeat and evaluate once per page, at the page's top and bottom.
- *The title and summary bands* contain elements you want to repeat and evaluate once per report, at the report's beginning and end.
- *The column header and footer bands* contain elements you want to repeat and evaluate once per report, if you choose to have more than one column on a page.
- *The group header and footer bands* contain elements you want to repeat once per group, or *control break*. You define groups using expressions similar to the GROUP BY clause in a SELECT statement. They usually correspond to the ORDER of the controlling table. For example, a report of jobs for each client might be ordered by `Client_key + DTOS(Date_due)`, as suggested earlier in this chapter. A group on the expression `Client_key` would allow group header and footer information, including subtotals and other calculated figures, for each client.

See Also

- Source Disk:Seed App (AD*Vantage developed): Results: CHAP9_1.FRX

The report layout in figure 9.8 shows these bands as they're used in a report layout, designed to produce a letter to vendors. Although this layout is simple, its bands and the elements they contain serve as a good introduction to Report Writer features.

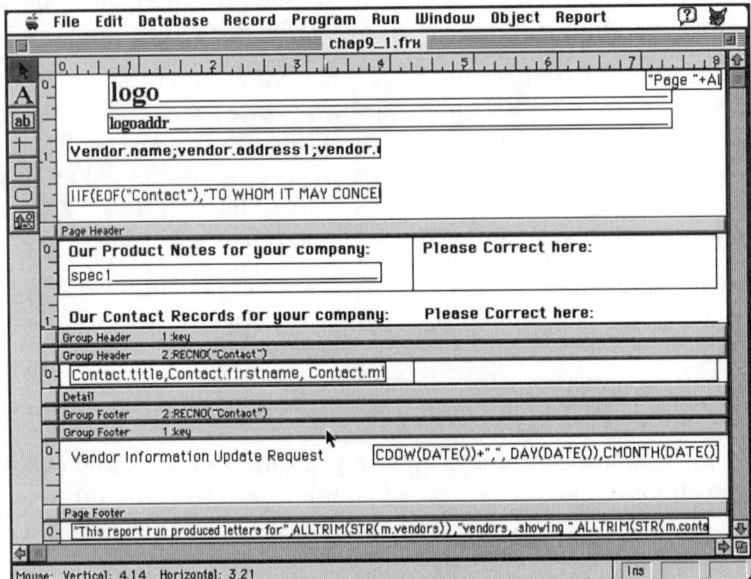

Figure 9.8 *The Report Writer Layout window shows the design of a Vendor Information Request letter.*

This particular report has no Title band. Title, summary, column, and group bands only appear in the layout if you choose them. Every report has page header, page footer, and detail bands, although these bands may be empty and they may take up no space.

The detail band, in the center of the layout, is the "nerve center" of a report because it holds the elements that are repeated for each record in the result set. This report's detail holds a vertical and horizontal line to set off each *detail instance*, and one other report object. When you double-click on it, you see the dialog in the background of figure 9.9. If you click the Expression button, you see immediately that the expression held by this report object is not like other Xbase expressions you may have written:

```
Contact.title,Contact.firstname, Contact.midname, Contact.lastname,
IIF(EMPTY( Contact.greetname),"","("+ALLTRIM(Contact.greetname)+")");
Contact.jobtitle
```

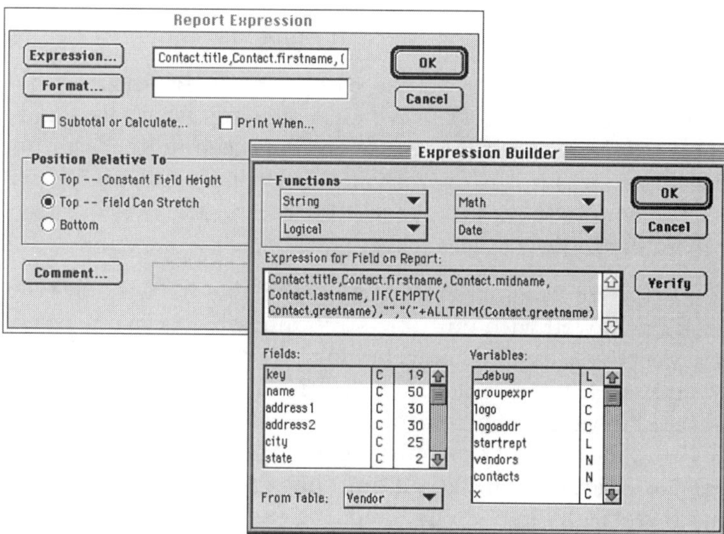

Figure 9.9 *When you build a Report Expression, commas and semi-colons have different meanings than they do in normal Xbase syntax.*

Report expressions may be concatenated with commas and semicolons along with the usual Xbase + sign. The different segments of the expression don't even have to be of the same data type! Concatenating two expressions with a comma trims all trailing spaces from the first expression and links the two expressions by exactly one space. Concatenating two expressions with a semicolon forces a line break between them.

As you see in the Report Expression dialog in figure 9.9, I chose the option to Position this report object Relative To the Top of its band but allowed to Stretch, so the entire expression shows in the report with its several line breaks, not just the one line it occupies in the layout.

The Expression Builder is designed for normal Xbase syntax. If you try to Verify the expression in figure 9.9, the Expression Builder tells you the syntax is invalid. If this worries you, you can obtain the same results from a valid expression by concatenation with +'s, `TRIM()`ing and converting expression components between data types, and concatenating `CHR(13)`'s (carriage returns) between expression components to force line breaks. This process is almost always a lot more work, however. I also find it's difficult to make sure that I've concatenated exactly one space between components in proportional fonts.

The use of a line break within an expression may be confusing to you. Why didn't I just make the different lines of this expression into different report objects? Using the line breaks within one object ensures that each line has exactly the right *leading* (vertical spacing) for its font and point size, relative to the rest of the expression. This technique also automatically closes up spaces in the expression (for example, in an address listing, if there is no `address2` data for a particular record, the `city, state, zip` line immediately follows `address1`).

Also, the FoxPro for Macintosh Report Writer, like its Windows counterpart, doesn't deal well with multiple stretching objects in one band. Although report expressions move to make room for other objects that stretch, you have limited options for additional report elements, such as pictures, text labels, and horizontal lines. These elements can only be "anchored" to the top or bottom of the band; they don't "float" within the band space (see figure 9.10). You'll find that the fewer objects you have to deal with vertically in a single band, the easier it is to manage their positioning.

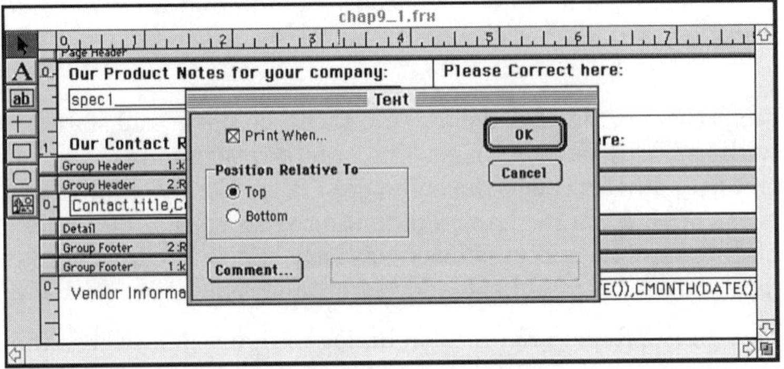

Figure 9.10 *Text labels, such as this report contains in its group header band, are always anchored to the top or bottom of their band.*

In fact, as a rule, you should try to confine *all* vertically aligned expressions in a single band to a single expression with this exception: elements that require different fonts or other object attributes (color, alignment, or mode) *must* be formatted as separate objects to receive these attributes.

The page header band includes objects vertically positioned in separate objects for precisely this reason. The page header objects demand special treatment as visual report elements because they form the letterhead of the report.

The AD*Vantage application runs for multiple advertising agencies, so the letterhead isn't always the same. You learn how these elements get their variable contents later in the chapter. Right now, you should understand the letterhead's relationship to the report bands to see how its display is suppressed for all but the first page of each Vendor's records. The trick is a control break, or group, on the Vendor table's unique key field, with instructions to start a new page on group and reset the page number to 1 for each group (see figure 9.11). This decision makes sense because each group is actually a separate letter to be sent to a separate company. (The concatenated report expression in the page header, which you looked at before, is the address for a window envelope.)

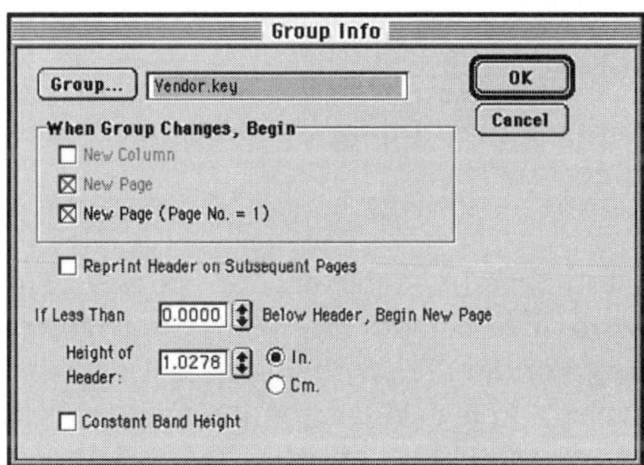

Figure 9.11 *You specify the control break expression for a Group in the Group Info dialog, and also indicate the attributes of the group band.*

Now you can use the Print When option on the items you want to appear only at the beginning of a group. You access this feature from a checkbox in the Report Expression dialog. Notice in figure 9.12 that the Print When dialog has a wealth of options of its own. In this case, you use it to access the Expression Builder again, using its Print Only When Expression Is True checkbox, and you enter the simple expression `_PAGENO = 1` for your "letterhead" elements.

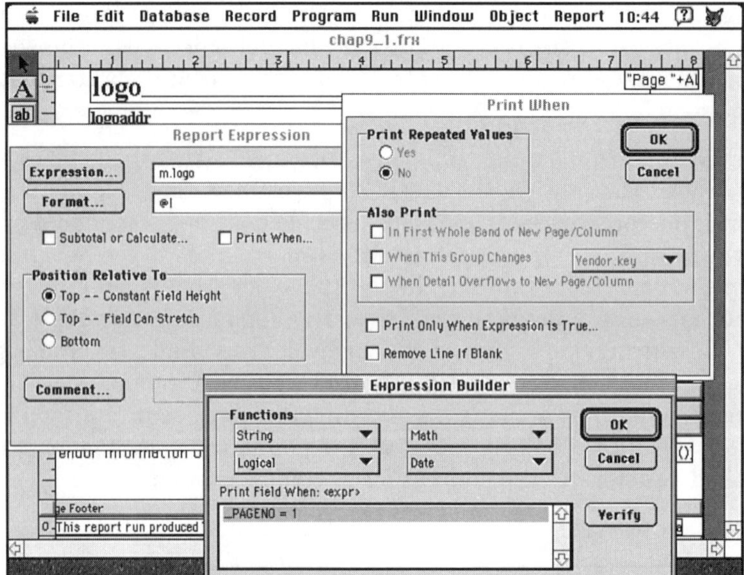

Figure 9.12 *The Print When dialog is an extremely powerful feature of the Report Writer.*

You notice an overlaid page header object at the right side of the figure. This figure provides a page number element for pages following the first page for any Vendor's letter. This report expression is `"Page "+ALLTRIM(STR(_PAGENO))`, and I've assigned it the Print When expression `_PAGENO # 1`. You can see that I was perfectly safe in overlapping it with the logo because the two Print When expressions are mutually exclusive and therefore the two report elements never conflict.

Report Writer Layout Tips

Notice that the page-numbering expression uses the traditional Xbase concatenation techniques (the + connector and the transformation of `_PAGENO` to character type to match the `Page` label). I couldn't use a comma here because that special method of concatenation won't trim the leading spaces from the second object, leaving an unsightly gap between the label and the number. A second way to handle the juxtaposition of the two elements would be to use separate report objects for each. You could then format `_PAGENO` as left-aligned.

> **CROSS-PLATFORM WARNING**
>
> When you align objects in the Report Writer, always use the options on the Object pop-up menu rather than the Report Expression Format alignment check boxes, which are retained for reports transported from FoxPro for DOS. When the Report Writer needs to, it translates your Object pop-up menu alignment choices to Format entries by itself.

I mentioned that the logo or letterhead elements for this report change for different advertising agencies. The agency names and addresses will have different lengths. Properly centering variable-length elements such as these requires several steps. First, make the objects wide enough to hold all their eventual contents. If possible, make them the full width of the report, but often you have other report elements that share the same line. Next, use the Object menu option to Text Align these expressions to Center. This technique *centers the variable-length contents of the expression within the report object*. Finally, use the Object menu option to Center the *report object itself* within the report layout. Figure 9.13 shows you one of the logo objects selected and the Object pop-up menu options that affect it.

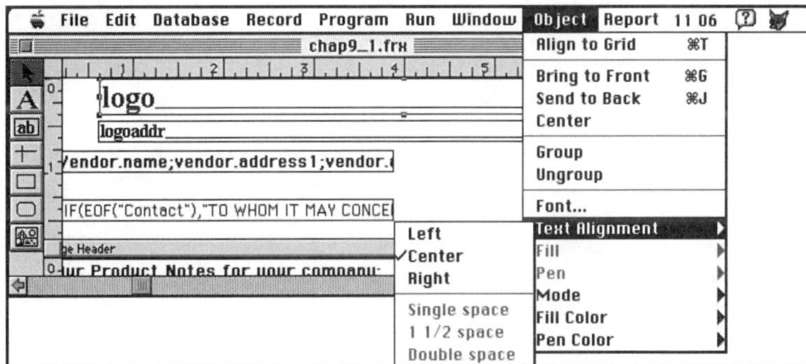

Figure 9.13 *Center a variable-length object using both Center options on the Object pop-up menu.*

Formatting and laying out objects within a graphical report design is an art. If you aren't trained in graphics design or desktop publishing yourself, try to get advice from other people with an expert eye. Along with general expertise, the FoxPro Mac Report Writer requires specific *practice* to get the hang of its various layout elements and their relationship to FoxPro expressions and tables. Investigate the sample reports that I've created thoroughly, but also use the *Getting Started* tutorial volume of your FoxPro documentation for examples of more standard reports.

CROSS-PLATFORM WARNING

Although the tutorial is a good introduction to FoxPro report creation, the documentation includes instructions that are highly unfortunate for Mac users. Some of the queries and reports display their results to the main application window by default. If you're a Mac user, rather than a convert from FoxPro DOS or Windows, you've probably closed or hidden that window and won't see any results!

If you have problems with the tutorial instructions, this may be why. You can either adapt the instructions to send the results to a more reasonable target display (perhaps PREVIEW or a WINDOW that you DEFINE for this purpose), or you can hunt around for your missing main application window. For Mac people who switch between different-sized monitors, this is no easy task!

First, use the Window pop-up menu to select Screen from the list of available windows. Screen may already be checked on the list; reselect it anyway. If you see your main application window now, resize it appropriately so that it can display your report.

If you still can't find it, Screen may be off-screen (FoxPro truth is, as usual, stranger than fiction!). Enter the following lines in your Command window:

```
MOVE WINDOW SCREEN CENTER
ACTIVATE WINDOW SCREEN
```

This method should bring your main application back within bounds. If you can't find your Command window (this also happens to people with dual monitors occasionally), you can still type these lines into it (carefully!). Just make the Command window active (sight unseen) with ⌘ - F2 or the Window pop-up menu before entering the commands.

> Use these instructions if you can't make your Report Layout window the size you want, too. Similar to the Screen Builder, the Report Writer is "bound" to the size of the main application window, even though you've SET MACDESKTOP ON.

As you practice in the Report Writer, you'll find that the layout techniques you used in the Screen Builder are useful in the Report Layout screen, too, including the Easy Access MouseKeys trick you learned about in Chapter 8. You'll probably find that you use the mouse with Snap to Grid turned on for quick layout (you can always countermand Snap to Grid for the mouse by holding down the Ctrl or ⌘ key), and then make final, precise adjustments with the keyboard.

Advanced Reporting Techniques

This section investigates some more Report Writer options that don't directly affect a report's appearance, although they materially increase a report form's capability to produce complex results.

See Also

- "Enhance the GETs and Text," Chapter 8

While you're working with the techniques you learn here, you have to use the report Preview option (shortcut ⌘-I) frequently to check the results of your formatting and additions to the layout. Be aware that the Preview option in FoxPro Mac requires a lot of memory and sometimes fails. In marginal memory situations, it may work but provide inaccurate results. This doesn't happen very often, but if you get Preview results you can't explain any other way, try restarting FoxPro Mac and accessing the report again.

The first shipping version of FoxPro Mac has a memory leak that affects any use of the REPORT FORM command distinct from the PREVIEW problem. You'll see this leak if you issue repeated individual REPORT FORM commands rather than a single REPORT FORM command scoped to act on many records in one pass. Since the scoped, single REPORT FORM command is always more efficient anyway, this is a good strategy to follow.

The report you are investigating in this chapter, grouped by vendor with page breaks by group rather than separate REPORT FORMs for individual vendors, is an example of this strategy.

> **CROSS-PLATFORM WARNING**
>
> Although upgrades to FoxPro for Macintosh have reduced reports' memory leaks, problems remain. Always check the VERSION(1) function and then inquire at Microsoft to make sure that you have the latest update when you suspect problems with FoxPro.

Both my original Report Picker and the revision you review at the end of this chapter use a special error-handling code to compensate for the fact that they can't know in advance whether the reports they run are intact, or if there is sufficient memory available to run them. Even without bugs in the product, you can't always guard against errors of this kind. Your best bet is to inform the user gracefully when the error occurs.

```
PROCEDURE rpterror
PRIVATE m.msg
m.msg = ;
   "The report or label you chose "+ ;
   "may not correspond to your current data or filter, "+ ;
   "or you may have a memory problem."
* very possibly a memory problem if m.device = 1
DO WARNING.SPR WITH  m.msg,"Error producing report!"
IF NOT EMPTY(ALIAS())
   GO BOTTOMENDIF
RETURN
```

Notice that this error-handling code *interrupts the report* by using the command `GO BOTTOM` to get to the end of the current REPORT FORM scope as soon as possible. When an error occurs in a report, whether it's because of limited memory, a missing function, or for any other reason, a user or a program can do little to fix the error and continue without impairing calculations, unless it's a printing error. If you like, you can expand this error-handler to give a separate message for printing problems and RETURN without changing the scope.

> **FOXPRO MAC HACK TIP**
>
> You can use the same `GO BOTTOM` trick to interrupt a report at the user's request, using a key press assigned to an ON KEY LABEL command, for example, even when no error occurs. To use this trick, however, make sure the report contains at least one user-defined

function, even if you have to write a bogus one, that simply RETURNs "", in the page header of the report. (The page header is a good place to put such a function because you don't want to evaluate an unnecessary UDF in every instance of the detail band on the page.)

Without a UDF, the ON KEY LABEL keypress will not execute its command until after the REPORT FORM command concludes (the report will not be interrupted). ON KEY LABELs can only execute between other lines of executing code. Because a REPORT FORM command is technically only one line of code that executes for a long time, you need the UDF to provide the "spaces" between commands in which the ON KEY LABEL can act.

To increase the capability of a report to handle scopes with flexibility, you sometimes can design a report to give results for both a real database table and its SELECTed temporary subset. Just omit the aliases from the report expressions derived from table fields, so that the expressions can refer equally to the original table and the cursor.

This technique won't work for a report that must contain aliased fields from non-SELECTed work areas, of course, until you can relate the original table and the cursor to the other tables in exactly the same way. You can't transpose a report meant for a table in RELATION to many others to a cursor that contains a flat file, joined version of these many tables.

FOXPRO MAC HACK TIP

People sometimes use a real table to design a report form and forget that they eventually mean to use the report with a cursor result. They add aliases to expressions, SELECT to a cursor, and then wonder why the REPORT FORM command shows them as many detail instances as they have cursor records, but with the *same* information repeated in each instance! Of course, because the expressions are aliased to the real table, and because the record pointer isn't moving in that table, the report form is showing information for the current record in the real table over and over.

If this happens to you, you may find editing the report layout to remove every alias a tedious exercise. Instead, remember that an .FRX is just a database table like any other. You can USE this table and remove the aliases from the Expr memo field, which holds the report expressions.

Returning to the example report layout you've been investigating, you notice that there is a group control break *inside* the vendor group on RECNO(). Since this group doesn't have any header or footer information, you may be wondering why I included it. I wanted to specify a minimum amount of room for the next instance of the detail band on the page or force a page break. The instructions for this group provide that specification, using the `If Less Than ___ Below Header, Begin New Page` option, as you see in figure 9.14.

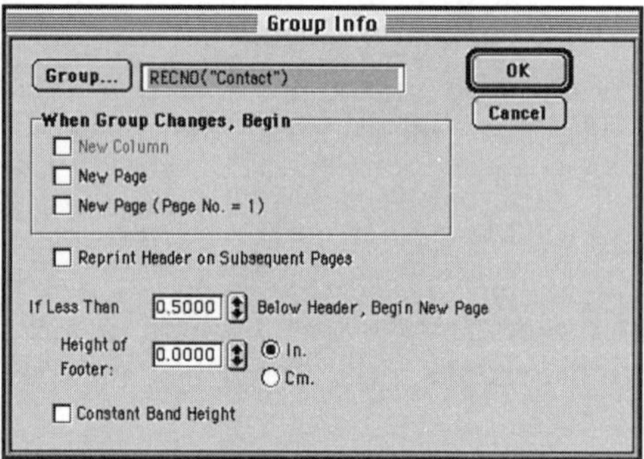

Figure 9.14 *Instructions to Begin a New Page when a group header has less than a specified space below it helps preserve the integrity of the detail band if you group on each instance of the detail band.*

Special groups are enormously useful. You can, for example, group using a numeric variable as a control break. This group can be assigned the "new page on new group" attribute. Then you use a user defined function (UDF) *at any point in the report* to increment the variable, thus forcing a new group and a page break.

Although this trick is valuable, it isn't a perfect answer to the problem of windows and orphans in the Report Writer. There *isn't* a perfect answer to this problem, in fact, especially if you deal with stretching report objects that may span more than one page. I deliberately inflated the `spec1` field of one Vendor record to show you what happens when the contents of a group header can't fit on one page. As you see at the bottom of figure 9.15, the group header actually overflows the page footer. If you looked at the report's next page, you'd see that the bottom of the bordering box for this group header occurs there, and that the first instance of this group's detail band (in this case, its only instance) does not appear.

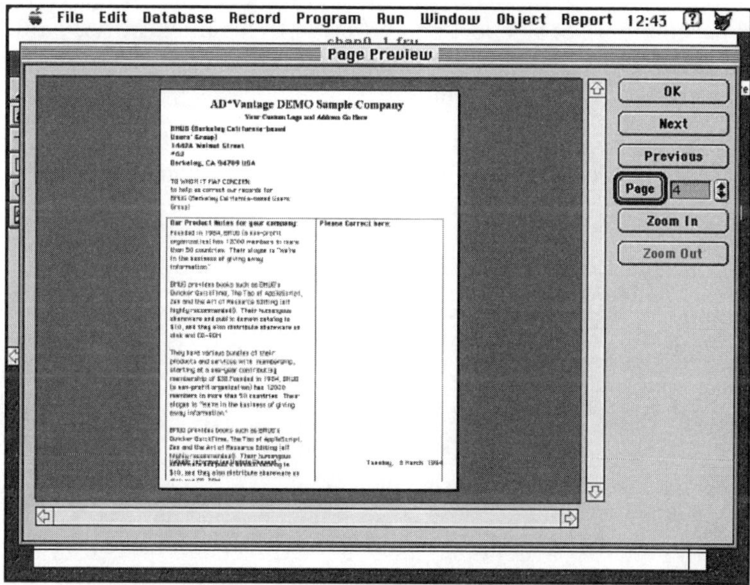

Figure 9.15 *Stretching memo fields that are longer than a single page overwhelms the Report Writer.*

If your application deals with voluminous memo fields and other large quantities of text, you will find FoxPro adept at managing and massaging your data. However, between its inability to separately format individual items within a report object such as a memo field, and the limitation I've just described, you may want to export your results to another program more equipped to deal with text for final output.

The final special tricks in this report all use a feature of the Report Writer that Fox Software first introduced in FoxPro 2.0: *report variables*. Report variables are special variables that you define within a report, giving each a special *initial value* at the beginning of the report. Each variable's initial value can be restored at either a group or page break. Each variable is reevaluated by FoxPro, using a formula you provide as its *value to store*, in a precise sequence, every time the REPORT FORM command moves the record pointer to a new instance of the detail band.

Variables can undergo *calculation*, such as summing or averaging, as the REPORT FORM command evaluates their value to store. The variables can be used in various combinations in report expressions where they can undergo further calculations, or they can appear nowhere in the report. (As you'll see, they often provide conditions you evaluate when you decide what *other* elements of a report should print.) Variables' initial values and their values to store may be user-defined functions of any type, as well as complex native FoxPro expressions.

Unless you choose to have the variables retained after the report, FoxPro automatically releases report variables upon conclusion of the REPORT FORM command.

CROSS-PLATFORM WARNING

You should be aware that report variables are declared PUBLIC by FoxPro. Since the capability to retain these variables after the REPORT FORM command requires making a variable from a subprocedure visible to its calling procedure, the FoxPro development team may not have had a choice about this decision. However, the unpleasant side effect is that you should never use report variables named with variable names you also use outside reports, as these outer variables may change their values or even their data types when you run a report!

Also, don't use report variable names that are longer than the significant number of characters allowed for a variable (10 characters). FoxPro for Windows handles long-named variables easily, and they add to the legibility of your report code. However, the DOS Report Writer can't use such variable names, which means that any variables you choose to retain after the report can't be evaluated with the same names by both versions unless they are 10 characters or under. Even worse, the first release of FoxPro for Mac bombs completely (with an "unexpected application error") if you use a long variable name, even though it permits you to type one in the dialog. This problem should be fixed eventually, but the only answer is not to use long variable names even in Windows, or a transported report may cause you grief!

The first two report variables in the sample report store their own names to themselves after they receive their initial value. FoxPro really never evaluates them at all, as you can see in figure 9.16.

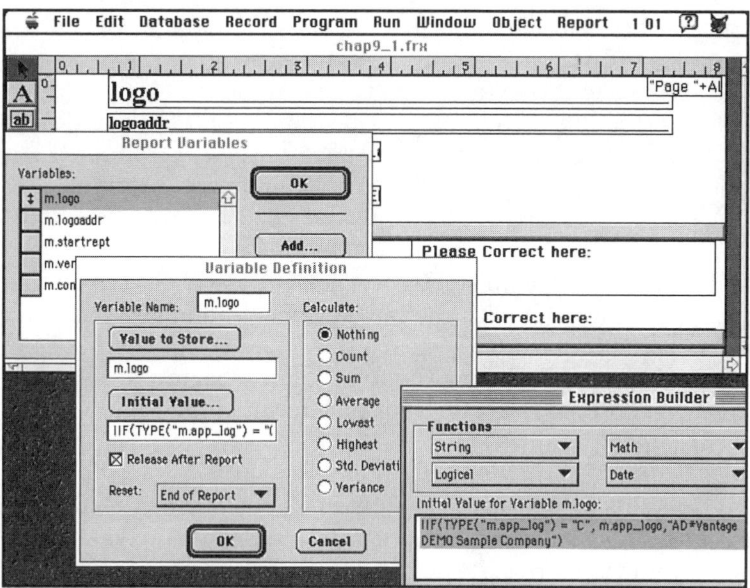

Figure 9.16 *Assigning values to report variables.*

The initial values of m.logo and m.logoaddr provide the default versions of the letterhead objects, using a TYPE() check of an outside variable to see if these objects are given overriding values elsewhere in the environment:

```
IIF(TYPE("m.app_log") = "C", m.app_logo,"AD*Vantage DEMO Sample Com-
pany")
```

```
IIF(TYPE("m.app_addr") = "C",m.app_addr, "Your Custom Logo and Address
Go Here")
```

This strategy prevents the report from crashing when I test it interactively or use the Preview option from within the Report Writer. More importantly, it makes the report a more robust object, able to handle itself without errors no matter what the calling environment, just as similar TYPE() checks and default assignments in Setup strengthen generic menu and screen objects.

FOXPRO MAC HACK TIP

The default values I've chosen for these objects also make it easy for you to provide a demonstration version of your program to prospective buyers. You can add custom values for m.app_log and m.app_addr to INCLUDE.PRG, "branding" a copy of the program just before a recompile, when somebody decides to buy. You can even provide these values in a separate subsidiary .APP or .FXP file called by INCLUDE.PRG, so that you only need to compile and redeliver a very small program to accomplish the branding procedure.

The third report variable, m.startrept, doesn't appear directly in the report at all. It starts out with the initial value .T. and gets the value .F. assigned as value to store. This means that m.startrept is only .T. for a very short period of time during the report, at its beginning. The fourth variable, m.vendors, uses m.startrept to determine its initial value:

```
IIF(m.startrept,1,m.vendors+1)
```

The first time this expression is evaluated, at the beginning of the report, m.startrept is .T. and m.vendors is therefore assigned the value 1. M.vendors' value to store is its own name, like the logo variables, but this variable is reset on the vendor group level. After the first group, therefore, m.startrept is .F. and m.vendors receives the alternative value in the IIF() construct above, incrementing its previous value by one for each group. This method allows a count of groups throughout a report.

You can rely on this method to work because the variables in a report receive their initial values as well as their values to store *in the same order they appear in the report variable dialog list*. Looking back at figure 9.16, you can see that m.startrept occurs before m.vendors in the list, so you know that m.startrept has a value and the value is .T. before m.vendors gets its first initial value. This reliable sequence allows you to have report variables work in combination, referencing each other and their evaluated, changed values in countless ways.

Compared to this relatively sophisticated trick to provide a count of groups, counting detail instances is a simple task for the Report Writer. You probably think you'd use the native report variable Calculate: Count option. In this report, the detail band displays contact names. However, there's a catch: some Vendors don't have any contact listings yet. They still get a single detail instance, which means that the final count of detail instances would be wrong by the number of Vendors without contact records if I used the native Count feature.

Instead, I create what I call a *conditional count*, using the method you see in figure 9.17. M.contacts, the variable providing this count, gets the initial value 0, and stores `IIF(EOF("contact"),0,1)`. Now I use the Calculate:Sum feature to add together all the 1's that occur when the Contact table is not at EOF() (end-of-file).

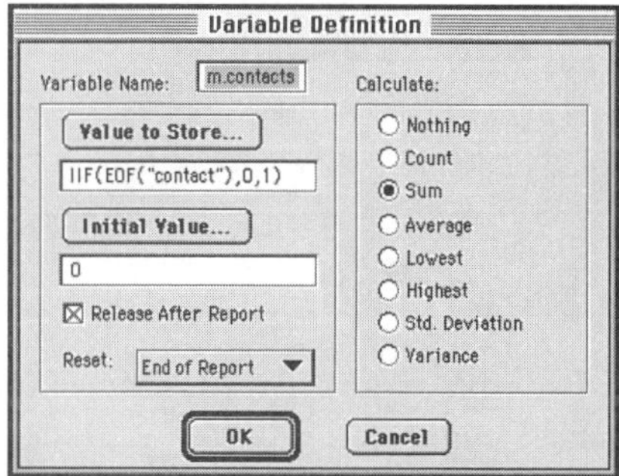

Figure 9.17 *Creating a conditional count means using a sum, rather than the count, for report variables.*

The two counts appear in a report object in the summary band of the report, using the following expression:

```
"This report run produced letters
for",ALLTRIM(STR(m.vendors)),"vendors,  showing
",ALLTRIM(STR(m.contacts))," contacts."
```

I have only scratched the surface of report variables' capabilities with these examples—and I have yet to use a single, user-defined function (UDF) in a report. To continue exploring the Report Writer, start looking at a second sample layout, which you see in figure 9.18.

- Source Disk:Seed App (AD*Vantage developed): Results: CHAP9_2.FRX

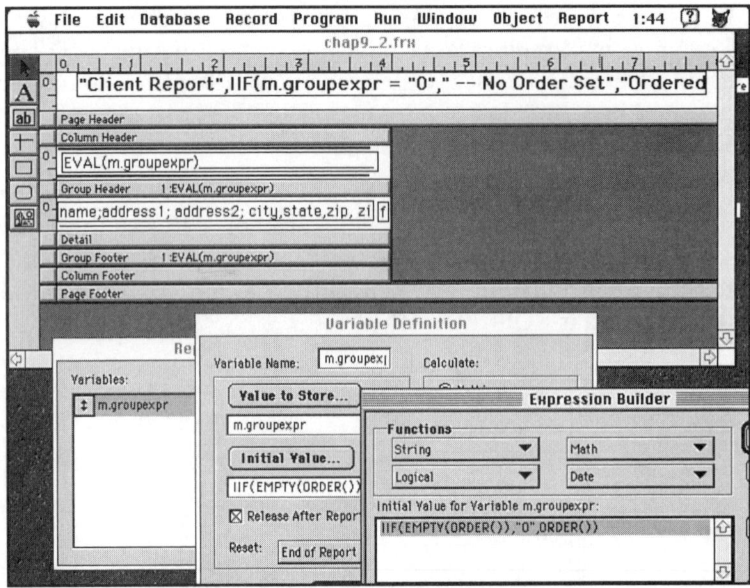

Figure 9.18 *A second sample report layout allows multiple columns and dynamically evaluated groups.*

You immediately see one difference between this layout and its predecessor: this report is designed by using more than one column. You make this choice in the Page Layout dialog that you access by using the Report pop-up menu. As you see in figure 9.19, the columns feature permits records to "snake" down and then across in the report layout, or to go across first and then down. The second layout is designed for mailing labels, and therefore is implemented with fixed-width bands (otherwise the label text might not be properly positioned on the physical forms).

The more profound innovation in this layout, however, is its use of the EVAL() expression in the group control break. As you see in figure 9.18, the report creates a report variable, `m.groupexpr`, using the initial value `IIF(EMPTY(ORDER()),"0",ORDER())`. This value remains constant throughout the report, once again through the device of using the report variable's own name as its value to store. M.groupexpr holds information about the *current table order* for the report. The control break on `EVAL(m.groupexpr)` uses this information to determine control breaks based on the current index value, effectively matching the groups to the index order at run time.

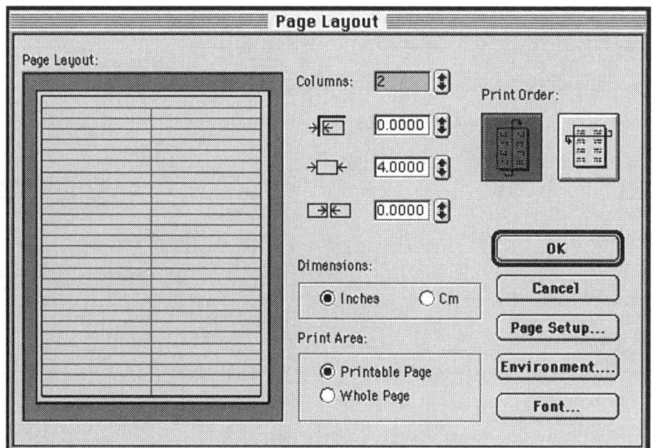

Figure 9.19 *The Page Layout dialog permits columns of data to flow in two different formats.*

This technique gives you the ability to use one report with many different orders or no order at all. A comparison of the report's behavior with ORDER set to 0 and ORDER set to State shows in figures 9.20 and 9.21. I used the Print When expression `m.groupexpr # "0"` and `Remove Line If Blank` on all group-defining layout elements to suppress these objects when the table is natural order.

You may wonder why I bothered to store the value of ORDER() into a report variable rather than evaluating the function throughout the report as necessary. The answer is simply that the value I want (the current order) never changes throughout the report. Therefore, it's a waste of FoxPro's processing energy to call the function more than once. You can use this as a general rule in report design.

This report has one more noteworthy aspect—it gave me an opportunity to show you a UDF in a report. Because the Client table is in a SET SKIP (one to many) relationship with the Contacts field, this report would have multiple detail instances (virtual records) for any Client with more than one listed Contact, not the desired result of this layout.

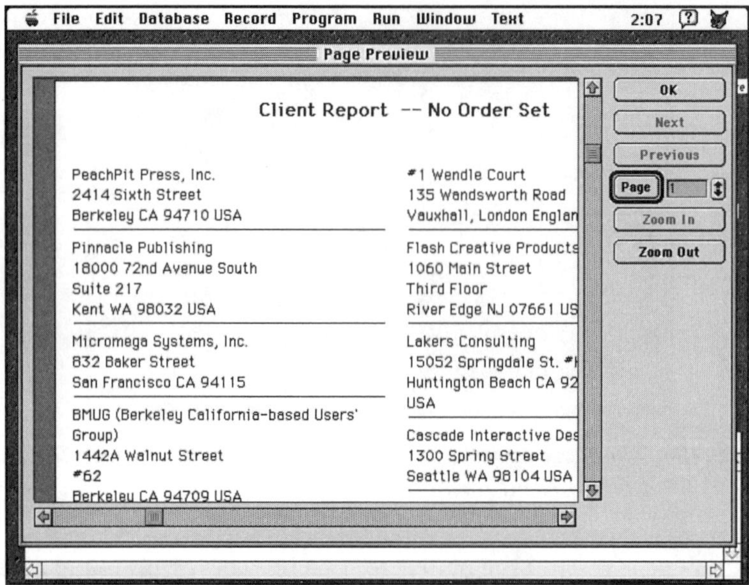

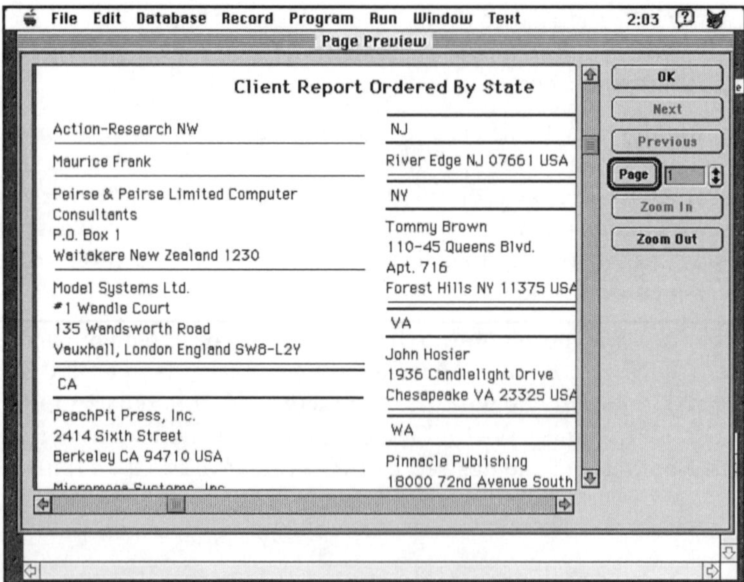

Figures 9.20 and 9.21 *Results of the dynamically grouped report.*

In a program that knows about the reports it calls, you can just `SET SKIP TO <nothing>` at the beginning of the report and turn on the one-to-many relationship again at the end of the report. The next section should give you some ideas of how to accomplish this feat even when you don't know what reports a program runs, or whether they need SET SKIP. However, this situation can also be handled *within* a report, by a UDF, illustrating both the way you "install" the UDF within the report layout and also the fact that your code can manipulate the record pointer (if you're careful) to change the scope of a REPORT FORM command while it executes.

A UDF can appear in any band of the report, or as one of the expressions that define a report variable. The job of this UDF is to decide whether the record pointer should skip virtual instances of the Client data for additional Contact records after the first time the Client data appears. Here's the simple program that does the job:

```
* FixSkip.PRG
IF EMPTY(SET("SKIP"))
   * no need to adjust pointer in this case!
   RETURN ""
ENDIF
PRIVATE m.rec
m.rec = RECNO()
SCAN WHILE RECNO() = m.rec
ENDSCAN
SKIP -1
* let the RW do its normal SKIP now
RETURN ""
```

Now you just have to determine at exactly what point in the report this UDF must work. In this case, since you want the record pointer evaluated after the first appearance of the Client data, which appears in the detail band, you should place the UDF at the *end* of the detail band. Objects in a band, including UDFs, are evaluated in the same order in which they appear in the band. If two objects overlap, the one that starts further up or further to the left is evaluated first. If two objects occupy the same space, then FoxPro evaluates the object in back before the object in front.

You place the UDF in the report like any other report expression. First, you indicate its position in the layout. Then you type the name of the UDF in the Report Expression dialog, just like a native FoxPro expression, as you see in figure 9.22. In the code run by the UDF, listed above, note that the RETURN value of the function is `""` (the null string), so nothing shows up in the report as a result of this code. If you choose, of course, you could return a value, which would then print as the report expression. You may, for example, want to provide a count of contacts in each Client's listing. You could adjust the FixSkip's SCAN code to provide that count.

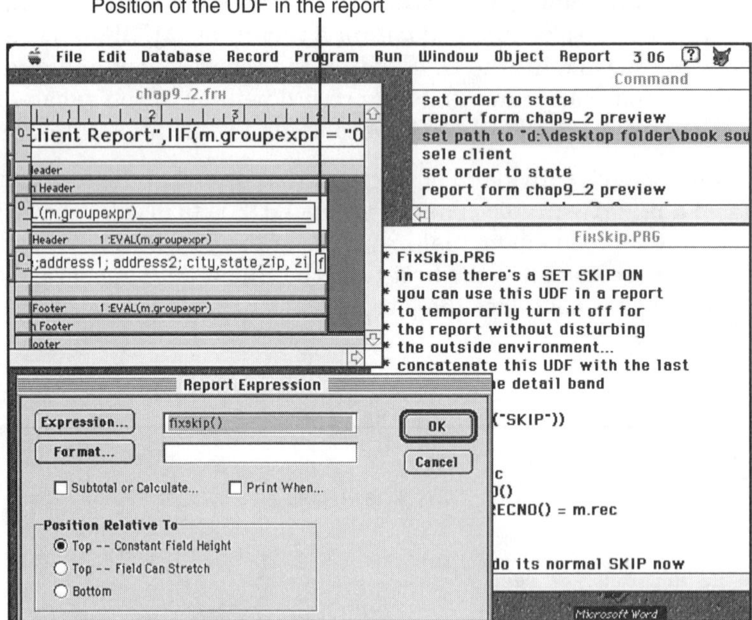

Figure 9.22 *Placing a UDF in a report layout requires no more work in the report than any other report expression using native functions—but you provide the executed code in .PRG form.*

Notice that I used the SET PATH command in the Command window in figure 9.22. FoxPro must be able to find your UDFs when it runs a report that includes UDFs. When you use the Project Manager to compile an .APP, this isn't a problem (the Project Manager coordinates UDFs along with all the other programs your application calls). However, you do need to help FoxPro find these functions while you test the report interactively.

Because UDFs are external programs, they slow down a REPORT FORM command. Before you resort to a UDF in any report, try using report variables in combination to accomplish the same task. When you do need UDFs, however, you can assign a single UDF multiple tasks to avoid going out of the report more times than necessary. For example, a single UDF can establish initial values for many report variables during one SCAN of a lookup table, even though you call it in the initial value evaluation of just one of the variables. Just call the UDF in the initial value for the *last* report variable on the list, having used a throw-away or placeholder value for the other report variables' official initial values.

> **CROSS-PLATFORM WARNING**
>
> You see that the exact position of the UDF and the sequence in which FoxPro evaluates it with respect to the rest of the report elements is critical to using UDFs, just as the sequence of evaluation is critical to report variables. You should be aware that report elements don't necessarily evaluate in the same sequence cross-platform. This problem is partially unavoidable, because the DOS Report Writer and the Windows and Mac Report Writers don't have the same sequence of events to evaluate! The DOS Report Writer makes calls to printer drivers that Windows and the Mac don't use, and the latter two platforms have Print When evaluations, which may contain UDFs, while DOS does not.
>
> There are other differences between the platforms that are apparently just matters of chance, and not so forgivable. For instance, report variables reset on group receive their new values at the end of the previous group in DOS, while they don't receive their new value until the new group header in Windows and on the Mac. If you use the "new page on new group" feature, this means these variables don't contain the same values in the page header of the group's first page on each platform.
>
> You should be very careful to test *all* complex calculations in reports you transport between platforms, especially if the calculations rely on different report elements referencing each other.

Expanding the Results Available

Now that you know something about selecting result sets and designing their appearance, you need to think about making the results accessible in applications. At the beginning of this chapter, I promised you a revision of the template Report Picker dialog with some significant new features.

Figure 9.23 shows you this second version. You see that the dialog provides a pop-up from which to pick available results, rather than FoxPro's native GETFILE() dialog. You also notice that the Environment check box is gone, replaced by an option to receive a count rather than a report.

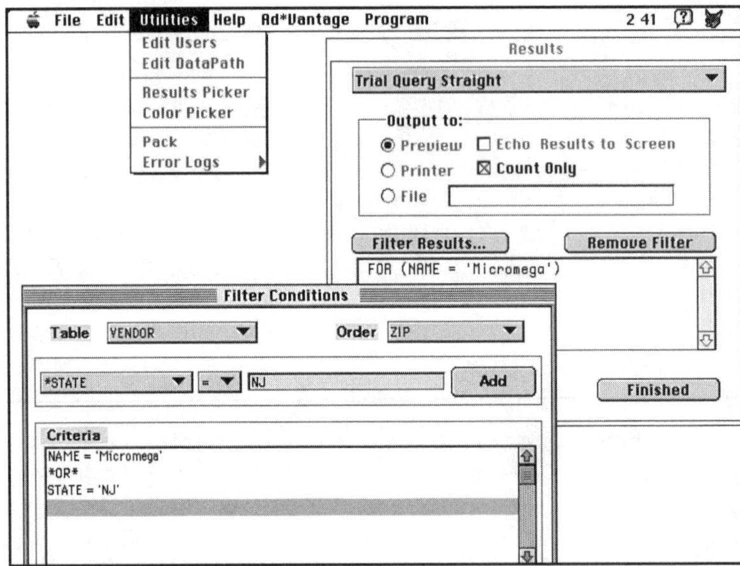

Figure 9.23 *The revised Results Dialog provides more control over reports the user may run, but still allows the user to filter data on-the-fly.*

- Source Disk:Library/ Template Code Folder: REPORTS1.SCX
- Source Disk:Library/ Template Code Folder: REPORTS2.SCX
- Source Disk:Library/ Template Code Folder: UTILITY.MNX

The Utilities menu option, which currently reads `Results Picker` rather than `Report Picker`, runs this new dialog in place of the Report Picker that you saw earlier. I didn't change the menu file to provide this alternative; the UTILITY.MNX cleanup code checks for the presence of a new RESULTS.DBF to decide which dialog is appropriate. The changed prompt and activity are more examples of the polymorphic menu behavior you learned about in Chapter 7.

The RESULTS table has a field, `Queryfirst`, designed to specify the name of a .QPR file REPORTS2 executes. Although the RQBE (*FoxPro's Relational Query By Example dialog*) usually creates .QPRs, these files are just text files, like any program, with a special extension. You can create a .QPR with any instructions you want, although it will typically filter the data among its other activities. One result may require a specific filter before they run, so the .QPR creates that filter automatically. Another result employs a .QPR that runs a complex dialog to ask the user to specify selection criteria at run time.

For the dynamically grouped report you saw earlier, the associated .QPR in the RESULTS.DBF, could even call an ORDER.SCX dialog for the user to set the order at that point. (The screens that ship with the FOXAPP source code contain a dialog that you can use for this purpose.)

The RESULTS.DBF on your source disk has an entry for the dynamically grouped report, another entry for the first report you designed in this chapter, and a third entry for a simple query-plus-report combination, so that you can see how this result-getting system works.

After running a .QPR if RESULTS.DBF specifies a query, REPORTS2 runs the report whose name you place in the `Whatreport` field, to achieve the final output.

See Also

- FoxPro Home Folder: FOXAPP: SCREENS: GETORDER. SCX

> **FOXPRO MAC HACK TIP**
>
> Don't forget to place the names of your .QPRs and report forms (.FRXs) in INCLUDE.PRG's IF .F. construct, as described in Chapter 5. REPORTS2 executes these files using an indirect reference, like this one:
>
> ```
> DO(ALLTRIM(pickform(formfile,4))+".qpr")
> ```
>
> Pickform() is an array holding the contents of the RESULTS.DBF file. Its first column creates the descriptive text for the pop-up control, using the character field `result` in RESULTS.DBF. Its fourth column holds the query file name. You need a direct reference in INCLUDE.PRG (such as `DO TRIAL.QPR`), to ensure that the Project Manager builds each required file into the .APP.
>
> When you want an editable report form, the .APP can COPY the Included .FRX and .FRT to disk. Your program can USE the .FRX as a table to modify it, or the user can edit the report layout in the Report Writer when your program issues a MODIFY REPORT command.

See Also

- Source Disk: Seed App (AD*Vantage developed): RESULTS.DBF
- Source Disk: Seed App (AD*Vantage developed): RESULTS: CHAP9_3.FRX and CHAP9_3.QPR

Along with the complex instructions executed by the .QPR, this Results dialog still allows the user to filter any open files by calling the modified BROWSER. You should create simple reports for every table in your database, without attached `queryfirst` instructions, so that users have a way to list information quickly, assigning their own ad hoc criteria at runtime in BROWSER.

RESULTS.DBF has a `selectwhat` field to match up each report with the alias of the table the report needs. This method is more appropriate to a distributed application than the report form's stored Environment, just as the screen tables' stored Environment is an inappropriate way to open and relate tables in your applications.

REPORTS2 checks to make sure that the user hasn't accessed BROWSER to SELECT an inappropriate table before running a report, although of course BROWSER can *display* any available data in its BROWSE window no matter what report result is the current pop-up. If the user just wants a record count, rather than a report, REPORTS2.SCX allows free table selection in BROWSER.

You can see that this version of the dialog executes the first job of result-getting (choosing records) more flexibly than REPORTS1.SCX. It allows some flexibility in its options for the second component (presentation), too. The .QPR can even create or edit the .FRX file before the REPORT FORM command runs.

Output to Non-REPORT FORM Presentation

Add more fields to RESULTS.DBF and more options to the REPORTS2 dialog, and you can take this concept much further, even when no native FoxPro presentation method suits your needs.

For example, change the `Output To` radio buttons to a scrollable list including both output devices and export file types. A `fields list` field in RESULTS.DBF, or even a list of fields specified by the user at run time, can provide the information necessary for a programmatic `CREATE REPORT <name> FROM <file> FIELDS &whichfields` command or a `COPY TO <export file> TYPE <export type> FIELDS &whichfields` statement, instead of the `REPORT FORM` statement. Figure 9.24 shows you the interactive SYSMENU COPY TO dialog (on the Database pop-up menu), with its many foreign file type choices. The alternative command, EXPORT, shows in a help listing in the background of the figure.

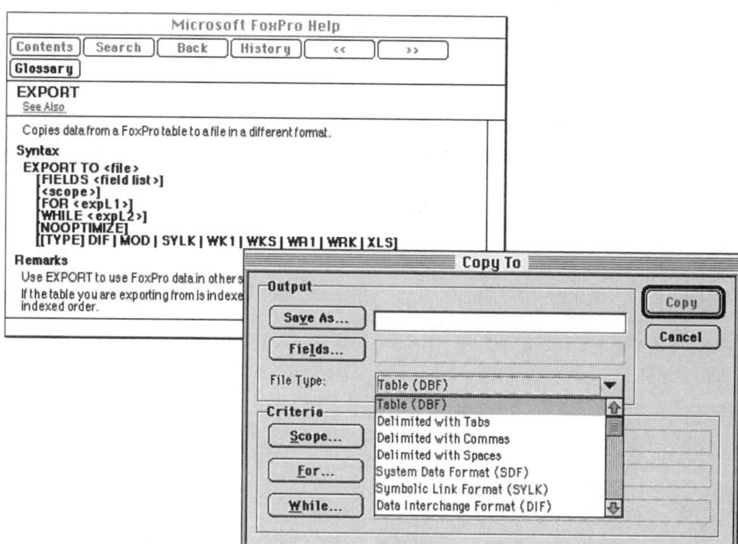

Figure 9.24 *The COPY TO and EXPORT commands, shown in a system dialog and help entry, provide you with a wide variety of non-FoxPro result types.*

CROSS-PLATFORM WARNING

I used SET KEYCOMP TO WINDOWS to make the screen capture for figure 9.24 with the list of file types "popped open." If you have KEYCOMP at its default MAC SETting, you'll notice that the list looks as if it's created using a completely separate object in the Mac programming toolbox. Several, although not all, of the native system dialogs show this difference in pop-up controls.

I mention this odd difference to reassure you about two facts. One, this book is *not* written using a beta or unreliable version of the FoxPro Mac product, even when the screen shots look different from what you see on your monitor. Two, Microsoft Fox Team is good, but they make mistakes like everybody else when they work with multiple copies of the same routine. The more you work with generic objects, and the fewer adjustments you make to *instances* of those objects, the more likely you are to make your program consistent and error-free.

Even the venerable LIST command may be an appropriate method of exporting information. As you see later in the chapter, printing a report to a file is limited to PostScript in FoxPro Mac (and problematic for other reasons in Windows), but LIST easily provides a straight ASCII textfile. You can use either a fields list or a complex, formatted set of expressions with LIST.

> **CROSS-PLATFORM WARNING**
>
> When you provide output as an ASCII text file, either through LIST or a COPY TO command, be aware that FoxPro Mac appends line feed characters to each line of the file, for compatibility with its DOS and Windows versions. Macintosh programs don't want these characters. The FoxPro low-level functions provide a method for you to write text files without these characters or you can use FxStripLF(), a function in FOXTOOLS, to strip them after creating the file by another method. Chapter 6 includes an example of low-level function file-handling.

See Also

- "Extrapolate from the CASE Model to FoxPro Code," Chapter 6

Besides the types of files listed for each result command, many desktop publishing programs accept PostScript as an import format. The REPORT FORM command's ability to write a PostScript file to disk can therefore provide an initial text-formatting step for this programming. In the next section, you see how the REPORTS dialogs handle this requirement.

When you send data out to other programs in a foreign file format, the user can choose what happens to it after the file appears on the desktop. Alternatively, your program can send instructions to the target application, using an AppleScript whose name is stored in yet another RESULTS.DBF field. Similarly, you can use another Mac application to call FoxPro to process a query and provide a set of results. In Part IV, Randy Brown shows you examples of this approach, using AppleScript to tie the two applications together.

See Also

- "Communicate with the other Mac Application:Apple Events and AppleScript," Chapter 18

Output Printed to File

Printing a report to file is probably the least cross-platform-worthy operation you can perform in FoxPro. Character-based FoxPro for DOS prints to file the same way it prints to the printer: one ASCII character at a time. FoxPro for Windows only prints readable text to file if you use the Windows Generic Text (TTY) printer driver, which circumvents the graphical page-description approach that the other Windows drivers use and prints like DOS. FoxPro for Macintosh only prints to file if you have a PostScript driver installed, which doesn't produce immediately readable output.

"This is a mess," you're probably thinking (and you're right). The next logical question is: *Why does anybody bother printing to file in the first place?* Can't we just skip the subject? I'd love to, but printing to file provides a host of valuable capabilities.

Files on disk provide the opportunity for custom spooling on a schedule you determine in a program, or perhaps on a "slave" print server machine elsewhere on the network.

You can APPEND print files into memo fields of an ARCHIVE.DBF, matched to datestamps and descriptive fields, providing a "snapshot" of the exact status of the data at any point in time. Such a snapshot is often more acceptable to accountants as a record of financial data than recalculating the data based on a range of dates in the live data tables, because they feel it's too easy for some of the old records to be adjusted later.

If you're printing to file on the Mac, you are using PostScript, which is as close to a universal standard for graphical printing on PCs as exists today. A PostScript print file may be taken physically to another printer, perhaps a color printer not connected to everyone's Mac or not even at the same site. The print site doesn't need FoxPro to print the file. You can even transfer the same PostScript file to a PC attached to a PostScript printer, where it's printable straight from DOS (using the `COPY /B` command).

Finally, as mentioned in the previous section, if you own an application capable of interpreting PostScript, this program may provide further formatting enhancements, either on the PC or Mac platform. If the program is an AppleScriptable Mac application, this interpreter even may serve as a superior Preview mechanism for FoxPro Mac.

Both my Report Picker dialogs implement FoxPro Mac printing to file using the same code, which illustrates my recommended approach to this problem on the Macintosh. Before beginning a print-to-file operation, the dialogs call a function to check the active print device. In the following code, I reprinted sections of the FUNCTION CheckPrt(), which implements part of the approach, using an XCMD, PrinterType, written by Dave Lingwood. I've interspersed the code with comments to show you my rationale for the method I use.

See Also

- Source Disk:Library/ Template Code: CHECKPRT. PRG
- Source Disk:Library/ Template Code:Printer Type
- Source Disk:Library/ Template Code:Printer Type DOC

```
* checkprt.prg
* FPMac-specific...
IF NOT _MAC
   RETURN
ENDIF
```

This function is Mac-specific. If this function is called from another environment, the call is made in error. Print-to-file solutions are platform-specific and should be in bracketed CASEs that test for each platform.

```
IF NOT FILE("Printertype")
    DO Warning.SPR with ;
         "Can't check Chooser device",;
        "'PrinterType' File Missing"
   RETURN .F.
ENDIF
```

The preceding code is a second level of check because your printing dialog should test for the availability of this file on the Mac and disable the print-to-file option if it's not found. It never hurts to check again, within the function, in case some code in the dialog accidentally re-enables the option. Next, you load the XCMD, which is actually an XFCN in this case, but (as you'll learn in Part IV) there's little practical difference.

See Also

- "Use External Commands and Functions (XCMDs and XFCNs): Access to Macintosh Capabilities," Chapter 16

```
PRIVATE m.xx, m.oldxcmd
m.oldxcmd = SET("XCMDFILE",1)
SET XCMDFILE TO PRINTERTYPE
LOAD ptrType FUNCTION
```

Again, note that the code shown here is an abbreviated version of the function, highlighting the aspects of Checkprt() of significance to result-getting, the subject of this chapter. The full function, which you'll find on your source disk, has additional error-checking for the proper installation of the PrinterType file. I discuss this aspect of the Checkprt() function in more detail in Appendix B.

See Also

- "FoxPro's Use of File Extensions and Macintosh File Types," Appendix B

If PrinterType is properly loaded and the XFCN ptrType can be properly CALLEd, Checkprt() performs the following initial check for a PostScript driver.

```
CALL "ptrType" TO xx
IF NOT (UPPER(m.xx) == "LASERWRITER") \
 * has to be exact because other Laserwriter drivers
 * are not PS, just the plain one is
   DO WARNING.SPR WITH ;
```

```
      "Your current printer driver may not be PostScript; "+;
      "if so, it won't print to file...  "+CHR(13)+;
      "You may wish to "+;
      "use the Chooser to change your printer device "+;
      "before continuing.", ;
      "Possible Chooser Device Conflict:"
```

Now perform a second check of the Chooser device. It's possible that the user took your advice and changed the Chooser device as a result of the alert:

```
   CALL "ptrType" TO m.xx
   DO INFO.SPR WITH ;
      IIF(UPPER(m.xx) == "LASERWRITER", ;
      "Thanks for changing your driver!",;
      "If your driver isn't PostScript, the file "+;
      "won't be created."), ;
      "Proceeding with Print-to-File job..."ENDIF
```

Finally, reset the environment and return success or failure to the calling program:

```
IF EMPTY(m.oldxcmd)
   SET XCMDFILE TO
ELSE
   SET XCMDFILE TO (m.oldxcmd)
ENDIF
RETURN UPPER(m.xx) == "LASERWRITER"
```

The 64-dollar question here is what does a RETURN of .F. from this function mean to the calling program? What's the appropriate action at that point? You might think that the print-to-file operation should be aborted immediately, but that isn't a reasonable response. The function has determined that, for one reason or another, it was *unable to confirm* that the current print device was PostScript. It doesn't know for certain that the current driver isn't PostScript. There may be a proprietary PostScript driver available of whose name the function is unaware (which would be true no matter how many PostScript driver names you added to this function).

Additionally, there are Macintosh programs that *override* the Chooser device, such as Print Juggler by Sonic Systems. The user chooses the print-to-file option, presumably with appropriate documentation of the way it works. If the user wants to override your warning, it's very possible that the user knows more about the current print device than your function does.

Therefore, a RETURN of .F. from this function doesn't force an immediate end to the operation, but rather a polite warning that a problem *may* exist and that the print file *may not* be created. A REPORT FORM command to file doesn't result in a terrible disaster if the driver is not PostScript; the output just does not occur. Any code you write to use the print file after creation should take appropriate precautions, in case that file does not exist.

You may wonder why I don't use an XCMD or XFCN to simply *change* the chooser device to a PostScript driver if I don't find one. As I've already mentioned, it's possible that the Chooser is overridden in the user's environment by a control panel or other Mac program to handle drivers. It's also remotely possible that no relevant driver is actually installed on the Mac.

My most important reason, however, is that the Mac—like Windows—is a task-switching environment in which other applications may be printing while FoxPro runs. In this kind of environment, you are unsafe and unwise to change the system defaults programmatically.

Instead, the Mac is designed to keep the user in charge. Your programming strategy should follow this lead. With sufficient information from your dialogs, the user should be able to make the necessary choice to comply with your request — or decide that other activities, including other print jobs in progress, are more pressing at the moment.

Similarly, you may design a report that requires Landscape orientation or other special characteristics, separate from print-to-file requirements. Instead of finding a way to control this throughout your program, simply tell the user about it. The RESULTS.DBF includes a `Special` field in which you can place these instructions. REPORTS2.SCX puts the contents of `Special` into a message to the user and then provides the user with an opportunity to adjust the driver with the new Mac-specific SYS(1037) function.

In figure 9.25, you see SYS(1037) summoning the Macintosh Print Setup dialog interactively. You can use this function or the REPORT FORM's PROMPT clause, which also works in FoxPro for Windows, in your programs.

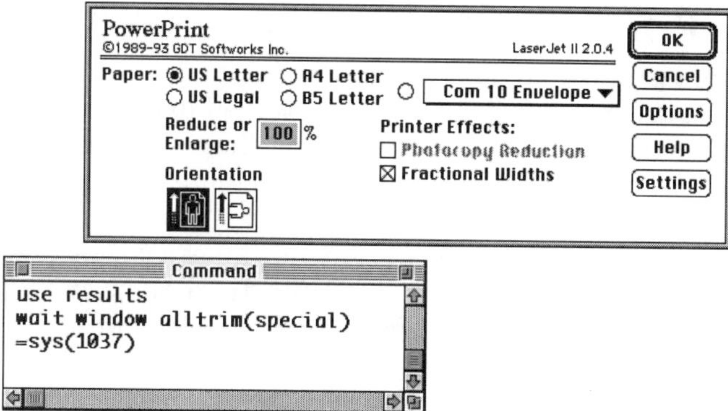

Figure 9.25 *Provide appropriate information about the requirements of your report and then offer the Mac Print Setup dialog so that the user can adjust the printing environment accordingly.*

If you are writing a Macintosh-only application, you have an alternative to the PostScript file approach.

You'll find the shareware Chooser extension Print2Pict on your source disk for this book. Randy found this marvelous utility a little too late to give it the space it deserved in his chapter on Third Party Tools and Extensions in Part IV. However, its significance to enhanced FoxPro Mac output made Print2Pict too good to ignore entirely.

Print2Pict is a printer driver that sends output to a PICT file rather than to the printer. After choosing this driver in the Mac Chooser, you (or your users) can use it as a sophisticated PREVIEW option for *all* FoxPro result commands. The resulting PICT can appear as a file on disk or on the Mac clipboard, from which it can be pasted into other Macintosh applications. The image can even be saved as a "postcard," which is a stand-alone application other people can display without any additional display program on their Macs.

For the purposes of print-to-file operations, you can use Print2Pict to extract the text portion of a report and to send results to an ASCII text file! Be sure to follow the Print2Pict instructions for specifying a path to its drivers or you may have trouble getting this option to work. However, after you've properly installed this utility, you'll find uses for many other clever Print2Pict features, along with this ASCII file option within FoxPro. Please register your copy of Print2Pict if you decide to use this terrific program and drop a line to its author, Baudouin Raoult, to thank him for sharing it with us, too.

A Cross-Platform Print-to-File Alternative

See Also

- Source Disk:Tools: Print2Pict Folder
- "Additional Resources," Appendix A

The PostScript print-to-file approach using CheckPrt() illustrated in the last section is, in my opinion, far superior to the FoxPro for Windows Generic Text driver method of providing text files, and it also has an advantage over Print2Pict's save-to-ASCII capability. PostScript files aren't immediately readable with a FoxPro `MODIFY COMMAND <filename> command`, like plain text files, but they provide an exact copy of the *graphical* report layout you'd get if you printed directly to the printer, and both DOS and Mac environments have programs capable of interpreting these files.

However, many people still want a non-graphical, straight ASCII report that FoxPro can view without outside intervention. I've already mentioned that you can use other FoxPro commands besides the REPORT FORM to generate straight ASCII output (TEXTMERGE, LIST, and the low level functions among others). You also have the option of running a FoxPro for DOS .FRX form that contains *no Mac platform information* within FoxPro for Macintosh. Since this type of REPORT FORM generates a straight ASCII listing, it's ideal for viewing as a file — as long as you don't expect it to look anything like a Macintosh report, or to edit it in the FoxPro Mac Report Writer.

You have a sample of this type of report on your Source disk with a program to illustrate the way the technique works. Unlike the PostScript file option, which works with a `REPORT FORM TO <filename>` syntax, this method requires the alternative `SET PRINT TO <filename>`. Figure 9.26 shows you the file output, a glimpse of the code that provides the output, and the special DOS-style REPORT PREVIEW mode that FoxPro Mac provides for DOS-only reports.

I can't show you the character-based DOS report in the Report Writer, of course, because the moment I tried to MODIFY this REPORT on the Macintosh, FoxPro's Transporter would kick in and create Mac-equivalent objects for the DOS elements of the report. After that, the report would run as a normal Macintosh REPORT FORM unless you USEd the .FRX and `DELETE`d all the records `FOR PLATFORM # "DOS"` to turn it back into a DOS-only report.

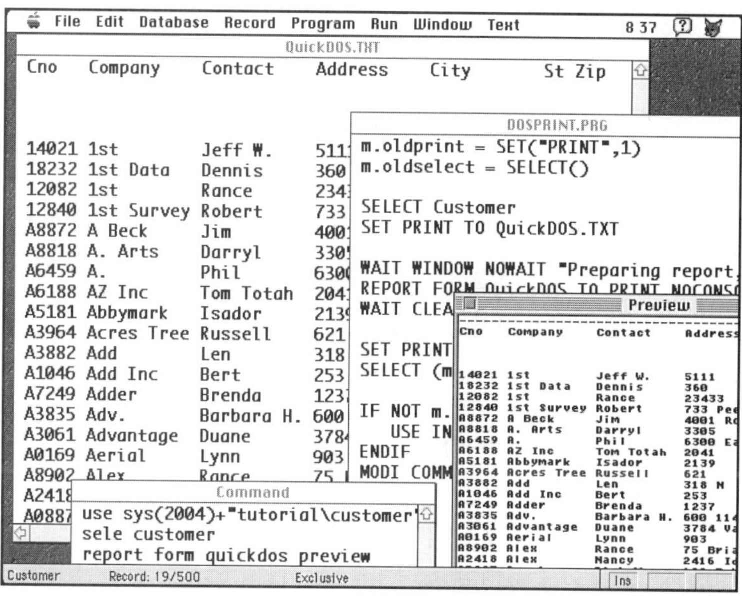

Figure 9.26 *Working with DOS-style, character-based reports on the Mac.*

See Also

- Source Disk: Miscellaneous Code Samples: DOSPRINT.PRG
- Source Disk: Miscellaneous Code Samples: QUICKDOS.FRX

CROSS-PLATFORM WARNING

The capability to execute DOS report forms appears to exact an especially severe toll on FoxPro, with reference to the memory leak I mentioned earlier. You have a second problem of how to procure the DOS reports if you opt to use this method.

You can edit FoxPro's Transporter program (TRANSPRT.PRG) so that it takes a Macintosh report form and creates a DOS equivalent from within the Mac environment, but this solution doesn't allow you to check the results of the Transport. Transporting from a GUI report to a character-based report rarely goes exactly as you expect, even if you consider appearance alone. Besides, as I stressed in the section on report variables, all calculations done in the Mac REPORT FORM may require adjustments for execution as a DOS REPORT FORM.

You are better off creating DOS reports in FoxPro DOS, if you have the opportunity, so that you can check the results of your work.

After you create the ASCII text file through a DOS REPORT FORM command, a LIST command, or other method, you may eventually want to send the straight ASCII output to the printer. FoxPro for Macintosh allows you to send characters directly to a port by using the `SET PRINTER TO COM1` command, discussed in the Readme File that you find in the FoxPro home directory. This file also contains extensive information on adjusting the FoxPro PREC resource for custom page sizes, using ResEdit.

These adjustments are beyond the scope of this chapter. As you see, the issues of printing from FoxPro are complex, and, especially if addressed cross-platform, could easily fill a book of their own.

Chapter Wrap Up

The second Report Picker dialog I've created as part of the template code for this book, and the RESULTS.DBF on which it depends, provides a *data driven* application component, like the DBFS table and COLORRSC table you've seen in previous chapters. This dialog, however, only begins to explore the information about results you can store in FoxPro tables.

I've already suggested some extensions you could make to RESULTS.DBF, but the possibilities far outrun what most developers want to encompass with their own code (if they'd wanted to *build* their own DBMS, they wouldn't have bought FoxPro!). Similarly, my adjusted version of BROWSER doesn't give users a chance to use the full range of FoxPro result selection criteria at runtime. This point is crucial, because the RQBE dialog (unlike the MODIFY REPORT command) cannot be used in a distributed application. You need to develop a plan for dynamic record selection that you can use in diverse applications (distributed applications) that allows multiple forms of presentation.

For a rapid development strategy, use available tools rather than trying to write your own code whenever possible. To this end, consider using a third-party result tool such as FoxFire! by MicroMega. This FoxPro program (see figure 9.27) fulfills the criteria of a rapid development system and can be configured to suit almost any application.

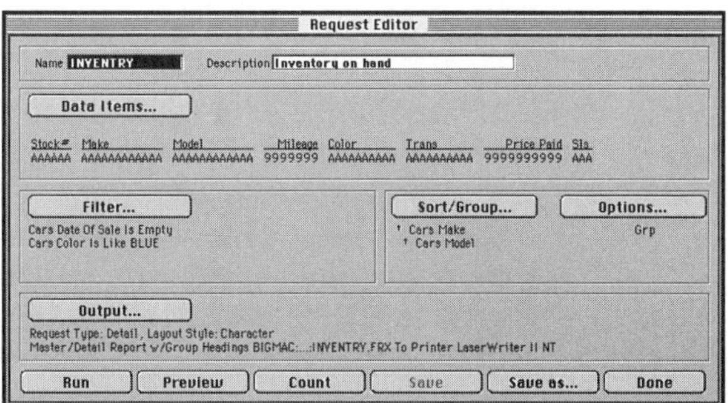

See Also

- "FoxPro for Macintosh Resource List," Appendix A

Figure 9.27 *The FoxFire! Request Editor screen illustrates the record selection portion of FoxPro result-getting...*

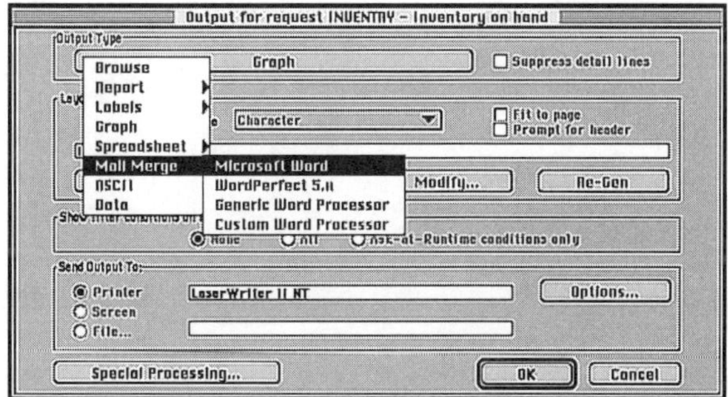

Figure 9.28 *...and its Output Options dialog fulfills the presentation component of the result process.*

This chapter concludes Part II and your introduction to the PoxPro design tools, appropriately with the suggestion that the tool set can and should be extended by additional aids wherever you find them. In Part III, you'll continue to explore ways to work smarter and faster in FoxPro using the extensive Fox programming language that supports the tools.

PART III

SUPPORT THE APPLICATION SURFACE: FOXPRO CODE

Chapter 9 introduced you to the SQL SELECT command and some of the complex expressions that you can write in FoxPro. You learned to express filtering conditions on result commands and to create complex formatted objects and user-defined functions in the Report Writer.

By now, you probably realize that no matter how good its tools are, FoxPro often requires extensive code beneath the layout or design surface to bring your work to a satisfactory conclusion.

Rapid development techniques minimize the code that you have to write, and the template code for this book gives you a lot of solid code on which you can build.

But we can't teach you all about Xbase structured programming techniques, or even all about the programming concepts specific to FoxPro in this book.

Fortunately, a lot of other books about FoxPro can teach you these techniques. They're not FoxPro-Mac-specific, but they don't need to be. The Mac version differs most from the FoxPro's for other platforms in the code that handle the interface for each platform, as you'd probably expect. The underlying code, and the theory behind the code, remain the same cross-platform.

Part III of this book concentrates on some important forms of sophisticated control of FoxPro, control that you can achieve *only* through programming. We chose subjects for inclusion here either because there were Mac-specific aspects to the subject you need to know, or because there was something we could add to the subject from a rapid development perspective that hasn't been published elsewhere.

Chapter 10 returns to the Screen Builder and techniques for building complex screen sets out of separate .SCX definitions and other FoxPro windows for multi-table data entry sessions. Chapter 11 covers additional aspects of robust menu and screen design with the aim of raising the comfort-level and preserving the sanity of both developers and users. Chapter 12 delves into some fundamental window- and font-relationships required for GUI programming. Chapter 13 alerts you to the sophisticated techniques that you need to master if you distribute your program internationally. Finally, Chapter 14 reviews some of the minor tools and features that FoxPro provides for fine-tuning applications.

After you emerge from Chapter 14, Part IV investigates the aspects of FoxPro for Macintosh that distinguish it from its cross-platform cousins. We think you'll have some well-deserved fun!

10

ASSEMBLE APPLICATION MODULES: MULTIPLE FOXPRO ELEMENTS IN A READ CYCLE

by
Lisa Slater

You added application-specific elements to a FoxPro development template in the chapters in Part II. As you've seen, this process starts with an initial design phase, in which you identify the database entities (related tables) and the data flow (user tasks and other operations) relevant to the application. To implement the design, you describe the database tables' fields, orders, and relationships in FoxPro code. You describe the database tasks, or processes, in menu options and screen sets.

Real-life business events are complicated, and the FoxPro procedures you design to mirror these events have to be complicated, too. This chapter shows you how to integrate complicated events into a FoxPro Mac event-handling system.

Evaluating FoxPro Events, Macintosh Style

Before the Macintosh, people typically wrote programs in which the user performs actions in a structured, rigid sequence. Each section of the program might interpret the user's actions according to a different set of rules. A set of rules to interpret the user's actions is commonly known as a *mode*; for example, the user might be in *view mode* or *edit mode*, but not both.

See Also

- *Apple Human Interface Guidelines: The Apple Desktop Interface*, Addison-Wesley Publishing Company
- "Modality and Event-Driven Programming," Chapter 12

Both the rigid sequence and the modality of old-style conventional programming are unacceptable on a Macintosh. In fact, you'd have a hard time finding a present-day personal computer environment in which they are acceptable. Certainly, FoxPro programs written for DOS and Windows should follow the same principles of event-handling the Macintosh interface standards and Apple's Human Interface Guidelines require. Users deserve the widest possible latitude to change their minds or back out of an activity, to perform multiple activities at once, and to leave some activities incomplete while they initiate others.

Your challenge is to implement these principles in FoxPro. In Chapter 7, I mentioned that the Microsoft FoxPro sample programs EX1 and EX2 suggest an approach to modeless programming that involves moving in and out of many simple activities. The user remains unaware of the fact that each activity proceeds independently of all other tasks, and that, as he or she clicks between windows, each activity actually cancels the one in progress before it.

See Also

- "Exploring Menu-Based Event Handling," Chapter 7

FOXPRO MAC HACK TIP

Mac folks often spell *modeless* as *modaless* to stress that the word means *the opposite of modal* rather than *having no modes*. You'll see both spellings, but in this book we've chosen *modeless* to follow Apple's practice in their *Human Interface Guidelines*.

This approach only *imitates* modelessness. Each limited task becomes a mode of its own (editing the customer file is separate from editing the inventory file). If you don't want to completely forgo the advantages of Macintosh-style programming, in which the user is encouraged to leave tasks in progress and pick them up later, you have to save the state of all unfinished tasks so that you can restore them transparently when the user comes back to finish a job.

Apple's Guidelines, however, suggest another approach to the problem. They describe an acceptable form of modality, known as *long-term modes,* noting that each application is a mode in which a *complex* activity different from all other applications takes place.

Think of each major task of your FoxPro application, or module, as an application on its own. Instead of designing a host of separate event loops and switching between them, cram a lot of activity into one event loop just as a Mac application does and stay in that one loop as long as possible. Make your programs respond gracefully as the user clicks between windows—*without* ending the activity and needing to re-initiate it later behind the user's back.

This chapter shows you some methods by which you maintain a single READ CYCLE, FoxPro's most important wait state, as an event loop for complex events. First, I'll show you the way the READ command's various clauses maintain control over this CYCLE or loop. Then you'll look at different modules, showcasing different FoxPro capabilities, built with a single READ CYCLE.

A single menu option initiates each complex READ module. In essence, each module is a stand-alone application, although different modules are coordinated on one menu. Within one FoxPro session, the user can't access more than one module at once, but if the modules are properly designed and sufficiently elaborate, the user doesn't see this as a restriction.

FOXPRO MAC HACK TIP

To enable more than one complex module, you can design the modules as separate FoxPro applications, each launched individually from the Finder. In the Standard version of FoxPro, you must have two copies of FoxPro installed to accomplish this trick. However, using the Distribution Kit in the professional version of FoxPro for Macintosh, you can create *stand-alone executable* applications and launch each application separately. Either way, you'll need as much memory for each module as you ordinarily use to launch FoxPro.

Your applications must still differentiate between the freewheeling, complex activity that characterizes their modules and some truly modal interruptions. For example, if the user chooses a customer record currently under edit at another workstation, you have to give this user *read only* access (a view mode) to the record. Two people can't edit the same record at once. Similarly, alert dialogs, which cause the user to make a choice before continuing with other activities, are modal by definition.

The Guidelines acknowledge each of these possibilities as a justifiable modal state. Such states are allowable as part of the Mac paradigm if you differentiate between them with clear visual clues from the application's normal behavior. In the case of a view-only, (unlocked) record, you dim all GETs except the ones allowing movement off the record to show that you've disabled editing for these GETs. For an alert dialog, you use distinctive colors, sounds, images, and borders. I'll show you a trick to add a dynamic image to a window, to indicate a locked or unlocked state or any other pair of states. You get additional ideas for making these changes throughout the chapters in Part III.

Guidelines not withstanding, there is no single right way to design a database application for the Macintosh. My goal is to give you the assortment of tools you need to design complex events in FoxPro. You start from generic components and template code, as you have done throughout this book, but you'll find the opportunities for customization are limitless.

If there is no single right way according to the Guidelines, you may wonder why I haven't relied on the FoxPro Wizards and FOXAPP, the applications generator that ships with FoxPro for Macintosh, preferring to write my own template code. The Wizards and FOXAPP are both applications written in FoxPro, like APPSETUP, which Microsoft ships with the product to make aspects of application design proceed more smoothly. (You access them both from the Run pad on the default system menu.)

You can certainly use the Wizards (with or without the addition of my template code) to start your visual design process. The Screen Wizard, shown in figure 10.1, is particularly well-designed. You can build a rapid application method *around* the results you get from the Wizards, using the techniques you learn in this chapter. (Be careful to change the fonts in the Report Wizard's output, however, if you intend to distribute applications. The fonts in these reports are TrueType fonts; your user must be licensed for these fonts if you distribute them.)

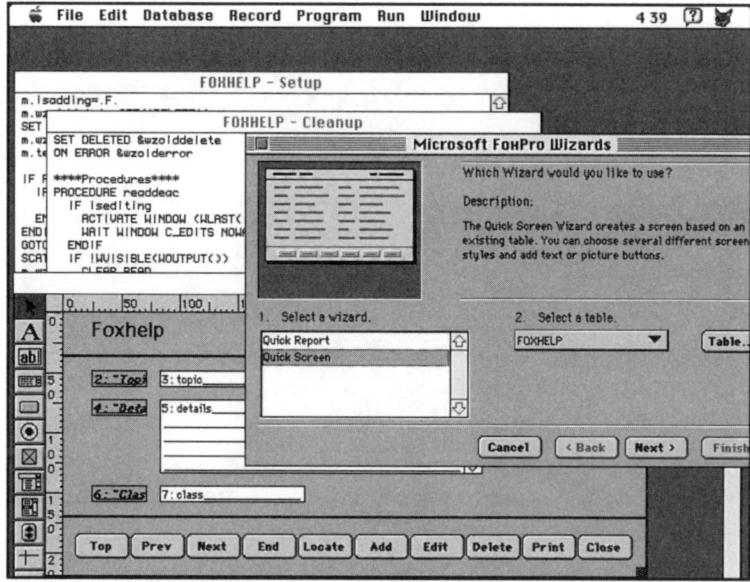

Figure 10.1 *The Screen Wizard can provide components of a rapidly developed FoxPro application.*

You can also borrow many generic application elements from FOXAPP. For example, in the last chapter I suggested that you borrow the GETORDER screen from FOXAPP's stock objects to enable the user to choose a record order before running a dynamically-ordered report. You've already seen my adaptation of the BROWSER screen from other Microsoft sample files. You can use the techniques you learn in this book to assess and improve FOXAPP menu and screen elements. Then you add them to your own library of template routines.

FOXAPP includes many thoughtful touches, such as the capability to specify cascading delete for a child table (see figure 10.2). Its generated product, shown in figure 10.3, not only includes generic features such as searching and ordering gracefully, but also provides a simple model of the complex screen set, using BROWSEs of tables related to the file you specify as the project's main data entry event.

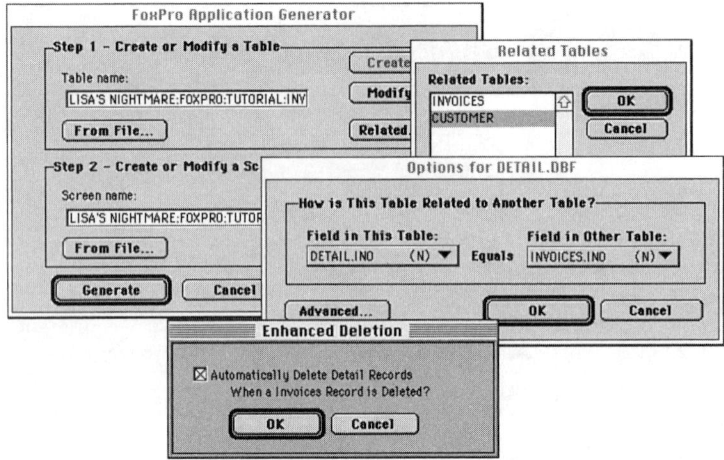

Figure 10.2 *FoxApp, FoxPro's included application generator, can create a simple but complete seed project.*

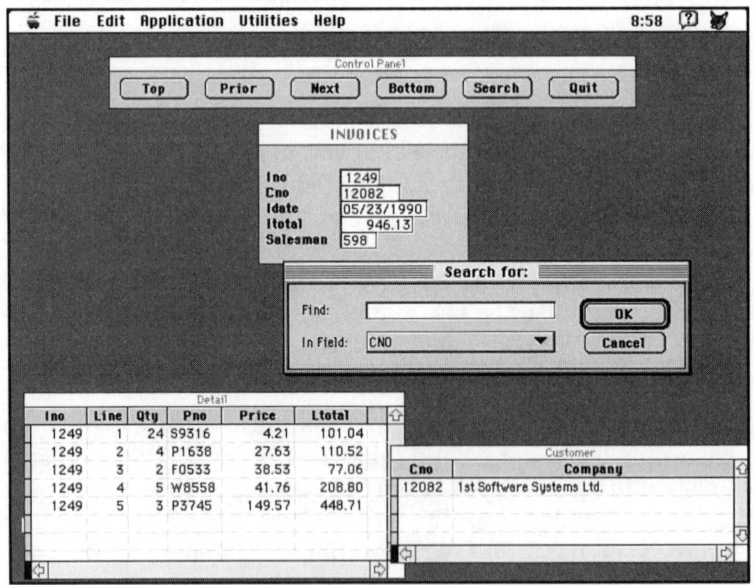

Figure 10.3 *A FoxApp-generated application shows related tables and a useful modal Search dialog that you can use in your own projects.*

Useful as its individual elements are, however, a full FoxApp-generated application does not provide an easily extended model for robust FoxPro applications on the Macintosh. It relies on direct READs to its tables, including editable BROWSEs, and FoxPro's implicit or automatic locking system. If you try to include indirect READs or additional data entry screens to the screen set created by FOXAPP, you'll give up quickly.

The approaches I model in this chapter require more supporting code and, admittedly, more work on your part, but they take you quite a bit further in the direction of an appropriate FoxPro for Macintosh event system. Remember that there's always a trade-off between ease of use and functionality in application development.

Controlling the READ

While using the Screen Builder, you may become aware of the snippets designed to hold the procedures or expressions for each clause, but you may have no idea how to separate your programs into these various elements. If you're still bewildered by this system, take heart—your condition is perfectly normal.

While I was writing this book, FoxPro Mac users read *Using FoxPro 2.5 for Windows*, written by Steven E. Arnott and me for Que Corporation, to get started with the Macintosh version of the product. Many readers communicated with me on CompuServe's FoxForum, giving me valuable feedback for a Mac book. (I wish I could thank all of you individually! If I fulfilled all the suggestions I got, this book would repeat everything I've already written *and* amplify a number of topics—and you'd be holding a 2,000-page tome.)

The one subject about which *all* these new FoxPro users were confused, however, and for which they all requested more information, was the way the various READ and GET clauses work to manage FoxPro events. Users usually express this question by saying, "How do I know what goes in each code snippet?"

In this section I go through the different parts of a READ CYCLE. I show you how my template code uses each clause to give you an idea of the uses you might find for it in your own programs.

The Basic READ CYCLE

FoxPro permits your program to communicate with the user through a variety of *wait states* in which you collect user information. For example, the GETEXPR command summons the Expression Builder, the user types an expression, and GETEXPR places the expression into a variable of your choice. WAIT WINDOW and ACCEPT both take a TO <memvar> clause, two more ways you can collect the user's response into a variable.

The READ command is the most flexible of FoxPro wait states. It permits you to accept user input into a window or multiple windows of GET controls, much like the objects in FoxPro's native system dialogs and other dialogs you see on the Macintosh. These GET objects may be text input boxes, radio or push buttons, check boxes, pop-ups, scrollable lists, or free-form text description fields. After "painting" an input screen with these GETs, you activate the GETs with the READ command.

In FoxPro, you usually create these GETs by laying out a screen or screens in the Screen Builder. GENSCRN generates the GET statements, followed by a READ command to activate them.

In early versions of Xbase, the user accessed the GETs in a strict sequence, from the first to the last, and the READ ended after entry to the last GET. In FoxPro 1.0x, users could use the mouse to click between GETs, obviating the READ's strict sequence. In FoxPro 2.0, Fox Software added the CYCLE keyword to the READ command, which prevents the READ from ending after the last GET. If the user enters input into the last GET, the first GET becomes available for editing again.

The CYCLE keyword is the critical component that allows the READ state to function as an event-handling mechanism in FoxPro, similar to the loop you use in other Macintosh programs. The program remains in the READ state until the user exits the READ using a terminating button or keystroke, or until you explicitly CLEAR the READ programmatically.

Within a READ, you can associate code with each individual GET, using the GET WHEN and VALID clauses. Code you place in a GET WHEN clause runs before the user accesses the GET, and code in the VALID runs after the user makes an entry to the GET.

In the Screen Builder, you make this code a *Procedure* if you want GENSCRN to place the code in a function and automatically generate a unique function name. Alternatively, you can make this code an *Expression* of logical type, which may contain any mixture of native FoxPro functions, memory variables, and user defined functions.

Figure 10.4 illustrates the difference between a code snippet designated as a Procedure and one containing an Expression. I find that code snippets naming Expressions are more flexible for rapid development, because you can call a UDF you've written generically. You can place this reusable function in the screen's Cleanup, save it as a standalone .PRG, or include it in any of the programs along the calling chain that leads to this .SPR. By contrast, GENSCRN always places the Procedure's code in the Cleanup section of the .SPR, where it's not easily accessible from other programs in the system.

You'll find the same distinction applies to the READ clauses you learn about in this section, along with any other snippets (such as the GET MESSAGE clause) the Screen Builder offers.

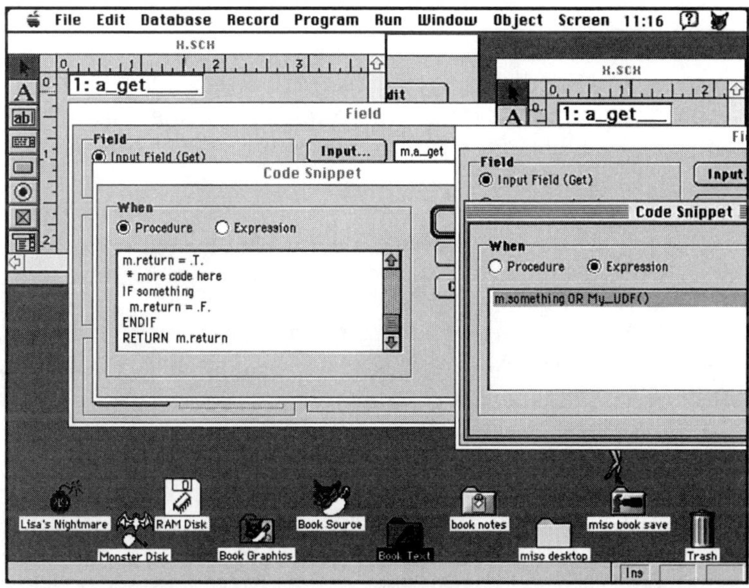

Figure 10.4 *Two GET WHEN clauses in development show the difference between using a snippet as a Procedure or as an Expression.*

Although users can move at will between GETs, in typical Macintosh style, GETs within a READ retain a numeric sequence that corresponds to the order in which they were painted onscreen. FoxPro maintains awareness of what GET is current using the function VARREAD(), which holds the name of the current GET, and also through a system variable called _CUROBJ, which holds the GET's sequence number. You can derive the object number of any GET onscreen using the function OBJNUM(<get name>). Your program can assign this number to _CUROBJ, if you need to direct the user's attention to a particular GET. _CUROBJ is FoxPro's way of indicating the READ's *focus*.

You can ENABLE and DISABLE GETs by name to dynamically influence the entries the user can make. For example, a checkbox for `Married` status might use its VALID to direct the user's attention to a spousal name GET:

```
* VALID clause for Married checkbox
IF m.married
   SHOW GET m.spousename ENABLE
   _CUROBJ = OBJNUM(m.spousename)
ELSE
   SHOW GET m.spousename DISABLE
ENDIF
```

As you work on FoxPro dialogs and data entry screens, you'll find that much of your programmatic intervention consists of lines such as these that intelligently enable and disable options in response to a user's previous choice.

CROSS-PLATFORM WARNING

Be careful about assigning _CUROBJ to a GET other than a text box or scrolling list object. You may be accustomed to assigning the focus to a push button or other control in FoxPro for DOS or Windows, but the Macintosh interface doesn't permit a button to retain focus. Buttons are only accessible with the mouse. If you port programs that routinely assign focus to buttons, or if your FoxPro DOS and Windows programs expect READ windows to stay active when they have no GETs other than buttons, you must `SET KEYCOMP TO WINDOWS` to have the programs work the same way they do on the other platforms. In most cases, you should rewrite the programs to function the Macintosh way.

Sometimes a GET is composed of multiple objects, such as multiple radio buttons issued as a single GET command. In this case, each object within the set has its own sequence number. For example, in a radio button set, the third button's number is OBJNUM(<the radio button GET variable>) + 2. You can ENABLE or DISABLE single objects with a GET by using the SHOW OBJECT <number> command. The SHOW OBJECT command has the same keywords available for use on the SHOW GET command.

CROSS-PLATFORM WARNING

FoxPro 2.6 for DOS and Windows contains some significant enhancements to allow your programs to manipulate GETs while a program executes. A new function, OBJVAR(), serves as a superior version of VARREAD(). Using its first argument, you can derive the GET name from any object number (use _CUROBJ as the argument if you want the current GET's name). Unlike VARREAD(), OBJVAR() prefaces the GET name with `m.` to represent a memory variable or the alias of the field if the GET is a direct READ. OBJVAR also has a second argument which allows you to specify the *READ level* of the GET name you derive. For example, you could use `OBJVAR(1,RDLEVEL()-1)` to discover the first GET in a READ that called a current nested READ MODAL dialog.

FoxPro 2.6 also adds two undocumented GENSCRN directives, `*# USERPRECOMMAND` and `*# USERPOSTCOMMAND`. You place these directives in a GET's Comment field, followed by code you want placed before and after the statement that GENSCRN generates to create the GET. By surrounding a GET with an IF/ENDIF construct using these directives, you can decide whether the GET should exist for a given instance of the screen at runtime.

You can't use FoxPro 2.6-specific commands and functions, such as OBJVAR(), in the initial release version of FoxPro for Macintosh. Upgrade to 2.6 while you're waiting, or at any time during which your FoxPro versions are out of synch, you can replace FoxPro for Macintosh's GENSCRN.PRG and GENMENU.PRG with a version bearing a later date from any other version of FoxPro, to get fixes, new generator directives, and any other enhancements Microsoft has added to the generator programs.

You can enhance GENSCRN by adding your own improvements to Microsoft's code, as you see in the next chapter. You can also take advantage of improvements other people make available for the generator programs. GENSCRNX.PRG is a public domain program, written by Ken Levy, that provides enhancements similar to these new generator directives and much more. Ken's approach to the Screen Builder gives you a comprehensive method of implementing object orientation in FoxPro screens. SCXs and elements within an SCX can inherit behavior from a template when they're processed by GENSCRNX, and they can also deviate from that behavior to exhibit

> polymorphism. You'll find GENSCRNX, and many example programs and drivers people have written for GENSCRNX, in the Third-Party Library of CompuServe's FoxForum.

See Also

- GENSCR.ZIP and other files with the keyword GENSCRNX on CompuServe: GO FOXFORUM, Library 10

Later in this chapter, you see how to add more than one window to a READ CYCLE. The numeric sequence of GETs and GET objects continues throughout all the windows in a READ. When you move past the last GET on the first window, you automatically move to the next window. You can page up and down through all the windows in the cycle. The window containing the _CUROBJ, and thus the READ focus, automatically moves to the top of the window stack and comes forward of other FoxPro windows, as you move through the sequence of GETs. If you page down past the last window of a READ CYCLE, the focus moves to the first GET, and therefore the first window comes back on top. The WONTOP() function is FoxPro's method of telling you which window currently has focus.

So far, you've seen that the WHEN and VALID clauses of a specific GET can interrupt this sequence to allow your programs to evaluate conditions and send the user to a specific GET as needed. The READ clauses that you learn about in the rest of this section each provide a different way of interrupting the sequence for more global control as the user moves through the actions of the READ. The Screen Builder permits you to attach these clauses to an .SCX using the Layout Screen Code dialog that you see in figure 10.5. You should realize, however, that even when you have multiple windows (and thus multiple .SCXs) involved in a READ, *the READ has only one of each of the clauses, and these clauses remain in effect throughout the life of the READ*. You don't have separate READ clauses for each window, in spite of the confusing way the Screen Builder attaches the clauses to individual windows.

As you see in the template code examples, you can provide different behavior for different windows by evaluating the current window in the clauses. You should follow the method I've used in the template, however, and make these evaluations as generic as possible, so that you don't have to adjust the clauses for each new window you add to a READ.

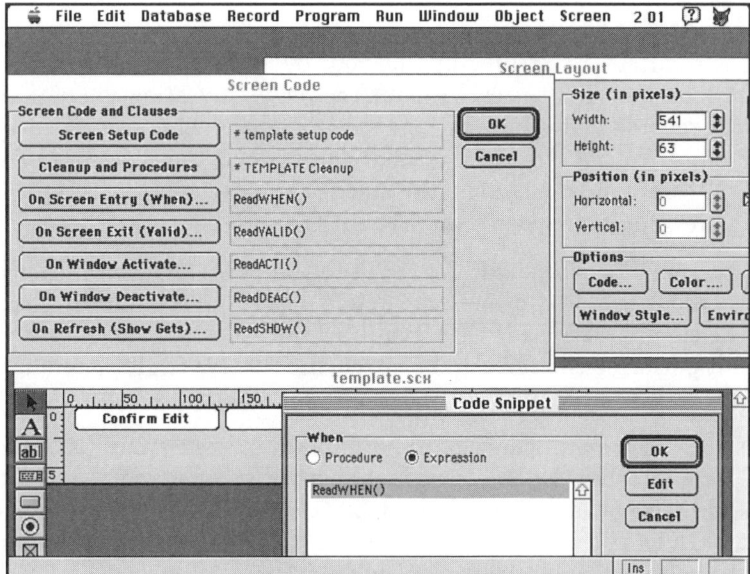

Figure 10.5 *The Screen Builder attaches READ clauses to the .SCX in the Screen Code dialog.*

FOXPRO MAC HACK TIP

If you add separate snippets for the same READ clauses of two .SCXs in the same READ, GENSCRN treats them differently, depending on whether you've used Expressions or Procedures. GENSCRN concatenates snippets of Procedure code together into one function, usually with results that are not what you expect if you're not aware of this behavior. If you've used Expressions, GENSCRN takes the first one it finds and ignores the rest. If you've used Procedures and Expressions inconsistently for the same clause, the results will vary depending on which type GENSCRN sees first.

The best strategy is to consolidate *all* READ-level clauses into one master clause, usually in the first window in the set. I use TEMPLATE.SCX to provide the controlling window's behavior and minimize the code in all other windows in a set.

READ SHOW

Because the READ CYCLE remains your event loop for the duration of an application's activity, the cycle spans the user's investigation of many different records as well as the user's confirmation of many different record edits. You've already seen that you can use the SHOW GET and OBJECT commands to change the status of a particular READ element, toggling its availability with the ENABLE and DISABLE keywords.

You often need to refresh all the GETs in the READ with new information because the user has chosen to move to a different record or to add a new one. The command SHOW GETS (plural) refreshes all GETs at once. Before it performs the refresh, however, the SHOW GETS command *also runs any code you place in the READ SHOW clause.*

Think about the significance of the capability of the SHOW GETS command for a moment. No matter which method you use to allow users to navigate between records during a READ CYCLE, you need to synchronize the GETs and the memory variables that control the screen whenever users move to a different record. You can issue a single SHOW GETS command, placing the necessary navigational chores in the SHOW clause, and the code executes just when you need it.

The template SHOW clause code is a call to FUNCTION ReadSHOW. I placed the ReadSHOW function in the TEMPLATE.SCX cleanup, rather than in MAIN.PRG, because this code is specifically designed to work together with the rest of the code in the template screen.

```
FUNCTION ReadSHOW
IF EOF()
   WAIT WINDOW NOWAIT "No existing "+;
        PROPER(ALIAS())+ " records!"
   m.aliasadd = .T.
ENDIF
UNLOCK ALL && because we've moved
m.aliaslock = .F.
IF NOT m.aliasadd
   IF RLOCK()
      m.aliaslock = .T.
      SHOW GETS ONLY ENABLE
      SHOW GET m.aliasact, 1 ;
           PROMPT "Confirm Edit"
   ELSE
      WAIT WINDOW ;
      "Sorry — Someone else is "+;
       "editing this record!"
```

```
      SHOW GETS ONLY DISABLE
      SHOW GET m.pickalias ENABLE
      IF WEXIST("Toolbar")
         PRIVATE m.wchild
         m.wchild = WCHILD("Toolbar",0)
         SHOW GETS ONLY ;
              WINDOW (m.wchild) ENABLE
         m.wchild = WCHILD("Toolbar",1)
         DO WHILE NOT EMPTY(m.wchild)
            SHOW GETS ONLY ;
                 WINDOW (m.wchild) ENABLE
            m.wchild = WCHILD("Toolbar",1)
         ENDDO
      ENDIF
   ENDIF
   SCATTER MEMVAR MEMO
ELSE
   SCATTER MEMVAR BLANK MEMO
   SHOW GET m.aliasact DISABLE
   SHOW GET m.aliasact,1 ENABLE ;
        PROMPT "Confirm Add"
ENDIF
DO Show_Children WITH m.aliasadd
RETURN
```

This code performs several critical tasks. First, it checks to see whether there are any available records to edit. If not, the clause sets up the screen for adding a new record. Next, it releases any lock the screen may have placed on a record before this call (during a previous edit). If the user is not adding a record, the code must try for a lock on the current record.

See Also

- FUNCTION ReadSHOW, Source Disk:Library/ Template Code Folder: TEMPLATE.SCX

If the new lock is successful, the clause uses the SHOW GETS ONLY ENABLE command to make sure all GETs are available for editing. Notice the ONLY keyword, which tells FoxPro to refresh the state of the GETS but *not* to call the SHOW clause. Whenever you use the SHOW GETS command within the SHOW clause, you use this keyword to prevent calling the clause again recursively. Outside the SHOW clause, you can use this keyword any time you want to refresh GETs without running the code. You can also use the OFF keyword on the SHOW GETS command any time you want to call the clause without automatically refreshing all GETS.

When setting up the edit of a duly locked record, the code uses a `SHOW GET m.aliasact,1` command with the PROMPT clause on the template screen's push buttons to change the first button to read `Confirm Edit`; it may have read `Confirm Add` for the last action. Notice the `,1` attached to the GET's variable name to indicate the first button object in this GET. The `,1` is required with the PROMPT clause even when the GET's button set contains only one button.

If the record cannot be locked, the code informs the user and issues a `SHOW GETS ONLY DISABLE` to limit access to the data entry GETs without knowing the names of any of the GETs in this particular READ. After the global DISABLE, you turn on any specific GETs you need to retain for navigation or choosing a new action. In the template, I ENABLE the button that calls a navigational BROWSE of the table (`m.pickalias`), followed by a check for any toolbar window objects in this screen set. I'll explain how the toolbar works with the template in the section on the Employee screen later in the chapter.

Whether the record is locked or not, the code for an existing record SCATTERs MEMVAR MEMO so the memory variables hold the correct information before the SHOW GETS call does its automatic refresh of the GETs. As you continue to read the rest of this code, you see that you use a `BLANK` keyword on the SCATTER command when you want to set up the GETs for adding instead of editing.

The final action in the template SHOW clause is a call to a second procedure, Show_Children. This procedure handles the refresh procedures for child tables on the main table for the READ, using an array you create in Setup to tell the template about the child tables you want to receive this treatment. You learn more about how you integrate these additional windows into the READ in the section of this chapter covering the expanded Address Book screen set you created in Chapter 8.

At this point, however, be aware that the procedure checks to see whether the screen is currently editing a valid parent record or adding a new one. If the user is editing an existing parent record, PROCEDURE Show_Children makes sure BROWSEs of the appropriate child records are onscreen. If this screen set has also set up data entry windows for each child, it enables the elements of these windows appropriately. If the user is creating a new parent record, PROCEDURE Show_Children removes both the BROWSEs and the data entry windows, both to provide a visual clue and to prevent the possibility of orphaned child records if the user doesn't confirm the addition of this parent:

```
PROCEDURE Show_Children
PARAMETER adding
IF TYPE("childfiles(1,1)") # "C"
  RETURN
ENDIF
```

```
PRIVATE m.xx, m.oldselect
m.oldselect = SELECT()
IF adding
  FOR m.xx = 1 TO ALEN(childfiles,1)
    SELECT (childfiles(m.xx,1))
    IF WEXIST("Edit "+ALIAS())
      HIDE WINDOW ("Edit "+ALIAS())
    ENDIF
    IF WEXIST(ALIAS())
      SCATTER MEMVAR BLANK
      SHOW GETS ONLY WINDOW (ALIAS()) DISABLE
      HIDE WINDOW (ALIAS())
    ENDIF
  ENDFOR
ELSE
  FOR m.xx = 1 TO ALEN(childfiles,1)
    SELECT (childfiles(m.xx,1))
    IF WEXIST("Edit "+ALIAS())
      SHOW WINDOW ("Edit "+ALIAS()) SAME
    ELSE
      IF NOT EMPTY(childfiles(m.xx,2))
        BROWSE WHEN Do_SHOW() NOMENU NOWAIT NODELETE;
         TITLE "Edit "+;
                PROPER(childfiles(m.xx,1)) ;
         FIELDS &childfiles(m.xx,2) ;
         COLOR SCHEME 10 &inparent
      ENDIF
    ENDIF
    IF WEXIST(ALIAS())
      IF EOF()
        STORE .T. TO ;
              ("m."+childfiles(m.xx,3)+"add")
        SCATTER MEMVAR BLANK
      ELSE
        SCATTER MEMVAR
      ENDIF
      IF m.aliaslock
        SHOW GETS ONLY WINDOW (ALIAS()) ;
          ENABLE
        IF EOF()
          SHOW GET ;
            ("m."+childfiles(m.xx,3)+"act") ;
             DISABLE
```

```
            SHOW GET ;
              ("m."+childfiles(m.xx,3)+"act"),1 ;
               ENABLE ;
               PROMPT "Confirm Add"
          ELSE
            SHOW GET ;
              ("m."+childfiles(m.xx,3)+"act"),1 ;
               ENABLE ;
               PROMPT "Confirm Edit"
          ENDIF
        ELSE
          SHOW GETS ONLY WINDOW (ALIAS()) DISABLE
        ENDIF
        IF NOT WVISIBLE(ALIAS())
          SHOW WINDOW (ALIAS()) SAME
        ENDIF
      ENDIF
    ENDFOR
  ENDIF
  SELECT (m.oldselect)
  RETURN
```

Because this code is part of a generic template, it may seem unnecessarily careful and complex. For example, the code references the buttons in each child window indirectly (`SHOW GET ("m."+childfiles(m.xx,3)+"act")`) because the template doesn't know the names of the buttons. It also uses the WEXIST() function to check for the existence of each window on which it acts because the template doesn't know if you've created data entry windows for the children or just show BROWSEs of the children onscreen (you see examples of both techniques in the Company and Job screen sets in this chapter).

Your code can be much simpler—without these checks—if you settle on a consistent representation of child tables in your screen sets. However, there is one technique used in this procedure that is highly significant, no matter which system you use: By using the SHOW GETS ONLY DISABLE command with the WINDOW clause, I remove all the GETs from a single window from consideration during the READ CYCLE until I re-ENABLE the window's GETs. Once no GET in a window can become _CUROBJ, I can use the command HIDE WINDOW <window name> to make the window vanish from the READ.

> **CROSS-PLATFORM WARNING**
>
> Before FoxPro for Macintosh, I taught people to make READ windows vanish by moving them off the screen to negative coordinates (you can use the MOVE WINDOW command in #SECTION 2 of Setup, after GENSCRN's generated DEFINE WINDOW commands). This method is inappropriate on the Macintosh because a window at negative coordinates may be visible on a second monitor. You can use the SHOW GETS WINDOW <name> DISABLE/HIDE WINDOW <name> technique successfully cross-platform.

The locking technique you see here (using a lock on the parent record to indicate "ownership" of all children) may not be the best technique for every application, but it is widely used. In Chapter 15, Doc Livingston shows you a more robust, semaphore-based method of flagging locks in a multi-user environment, but you will find that his general strategy corresponds well with the habits you learn here.

Alternatives to READ SHOW

The WINDOW clause of the SHOW GETS command has another important use. During the READ, the user may move through the child records of the current parent, without changing parent records. When the user takes this action, your program shouldn't run the SHOW clause meant to refresh the entire screen for a new parent record with a global SHOW GETS command. Instead, you can imitate the global actions of the SHOW GETS command with a custom procedure designed to refresh only the child table:

```
PROCEDURE SubSHOW
PRIVATE m.xx, m.subaddvar, m.subactvar
IF TYPE("childfiles(1,1)") # "C"
  RETURN
ENDIF
m.xx = ASUBSCRIPT(childfiles, ;
   ASCAN(childfiles,ALIAS()),1)
m.subaddvar = "m."+childfiles(m.xx,3)+"add"
m.subactvar = "m."+childfiles(m.xx,3)+"act"
IF EOF()
   * you may want to add:
   * WAIT WINDOW NOWAIT ;
```

```
   "No existing "+PROPER(ALIAS())+ " records!"
   STORE .T. TO (m.subaddvar)
ENDIF
* don't have to worry about locking subform
* records because parent is locked,
* and all child records are only editable
* when the parent record is lockable,
* because of code run in Show_Children
IF NOT EVAL(m.subaddvar)
   SHOW GET (m.subactvar) ENABLE
   SHOW GET(m.subactvar), 1 ;
        PROMPT "Confirm Edit"
   SCATTER MEMVAR MEMO
ELSE
   SCATTER MEMVAR BLANK MEMO
   SHOW GET (m.subactvar) DISABLE
   SHOW GET (m.subactvar),1 ENABLE ;
        PROMPT "Confirm Add"
ENDIF
SHOW GETS ONLY WINDOW (ALIAS())
RETURN
```

When the user navigates through a child table, you `DO SubShow` rather than using the command `SHOW GETS`. PROCEDURE SubShow runs the relevant code, ending with the command `SHOW GETS ONLY WINDOW <name>` to take the place of the SHOW GETS command's automatic refresh capability.

You may wonder why I bother to design a separate procedure for child tables, rather than adding such code into the SHOW clause and checking within the SHOW clause to see if the user has moved between records in the parent or only in the child. I limit calls to the SHOW clause to global changes in the screen set because the global READShow code is complicated enough already!

In addition, the dual responsibility of the SHOW clause — to run the code and refresh all GETs—means that it can run more code than you need, and it can run slowly. You have other situations besides the navigation of a child table in which you should be cautious about relying on this clause.

Most significantly, the Screen Builder permits you to use a Refresh option on SAYs for non-editable text elements in the screen. This option, however, forces you to issue a global SHOW GETS command. In the Employee screen, for example, the user can pick a Department assignment for the current Employee, but the user never edits the department name directly. You could use a refreshed SAY for the department name, as shown in figure 10.6. Notice in the figure that the colors for a SAY are clearly distinguishable from the editable GETs onscreen (you use the Transparent mode on this object to achieve this effect).

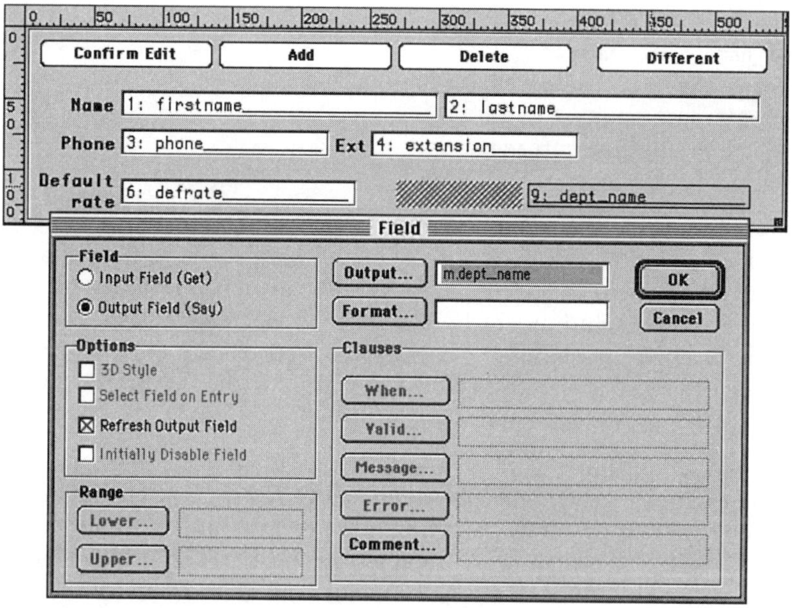

Figure 10.6 *A SAY label onscreen can be Refreshed...*

To refresh a SAY you must issue the global SHOW GETS command because GENSCRN generates the code for the SAY in the SHOW clause to accomplish the refresh. You can see that running the entire SHOW clause and refreshing all the GETs onscreen when the user picks a new department—just because you want to confirm this one choice—is inefficient. *Avoid refreshing SAYs!* Instead, use a GET for the text object, storing the value you want in a variable that you initialize in Setup and adjust whenever the user picks a new department, like this:

```
FUNCTION pickdept
SELECT Dept
BROWSE NOMENU NODELETE TITLE ;
       "Pick Department for this Employee"
SELECT Employee
* store the key value to the variable
* that will eventually be GATHERed to the
```

```
* employee record
m.dept_key = Dept.key
* store the descriptive character
* version of the department information
* to another variable
m.dept_name = Dept.descr
* refresh the description on screen
SHOW GET m.dept_name
_CUROBJ = OBJNUM(m.firstname)
RETURN
```

This function runs as the VALID of an invisible button behind the Department text label in the Employee screen, enabling the user to pick a department by clicking on this label. The Job screen contains additional examples of this technique for handling lookups. In each case, the command SHOW GET <memvar> allows you to refresh the label and nothing else after the user chooses a new lookup value, without running the global SHOW GETS.

As you can see in figure 10.7, I've initially disabled the m.dept_name GET so that I can see its difference from normal GETs in the Screen Builder. But I don't rely on this initial disabling to keep the label unmodifiable because I'd have to redisable all such lookup labels explicitly whenever my code issued a SHOW GETS ENABLE command globally or for this window. Instead, I use the WHEN expression .F. so the user can never edit this GET whether it's been ENABLEd or not.

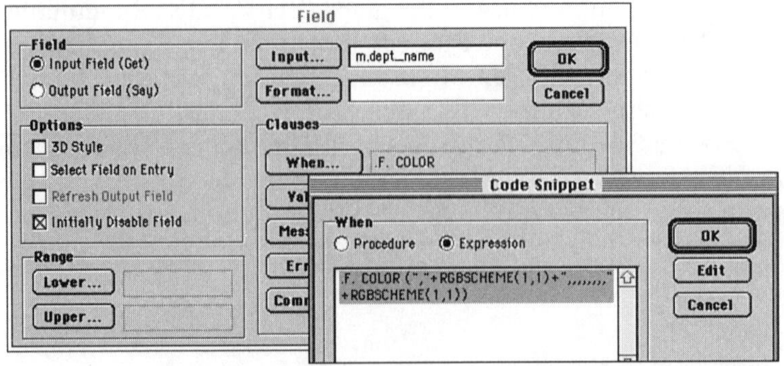

Figure 10.7 *... but a GET WHEN .F. is more efficient.*

FOXPRO MAC HACK TIP

Figure 10.7 also shows you the COLOR clause I've stuffed into the WHEN clause after the .F. expression (GENSCRN just generates this clause along with the rest of the GET command, without knowing what it is). This clause provides the same colors for this unmodifiable GET as you get by default for a normal SAY. You learn more about the FoxPro color system and how to perform tricks like this one in Chapter 14.

READ ACTIVATE and DEACTIVATE

The SHOW clause on a READ receives much of the burden of event-handling in the READ CYCLE because it is the *only* clause your program can force FoxPro to execute by using the SHOW GETS command. The other READ clauses trigger automatically when the user initiates an action during the READ, so that your code in these clauses is primarily a response to the user's choice. You'll be relieved to see that the necessary code is simple in comparison to SHOW code. Keeping your reactions to the user's actions simple is vital if you want your code to cope appropriately with actions you haven't imagined.

FoxPro triggers the READ ACTIVATE clause when the user moves *into a window containing GETs that participate in the current READ*, and the DEACTIVATE clause when the user moves *away* from a window containing GETs that participate in the current READ. Notice that I haven't said "when the user clicks into a different window, any window on the screen." The ACTIVATE and DEACTIVATE clauses only handle GET windows in the current READ, using the precise rule I have just stated. Keep their limitations in mind when you design the roles of these clauses in your screen sets.

Here's my template code for the ACTIVATE clause:

```
FUNCTION ReadACTI
IF UPPER(WPARENT(WONTOP())) ;
   == "TOOLBAR"
   PRIVATE m.oldrec
   m.oldrec = RECNO()
   DO (WONTOP())
   ACTIVATE WINDOW (WLAST())
   * was this the kind of Toolbar tool
```

```
   * that navigates?  If so...
   IF RECNO() # m.oldrec
       SHOW GETS
   ENDIF
   _CUROBJ = 1
ELSE
   DO ReadACTI IN MAIN
ENDIF
RETURN
```

This code uses the WONTOP() function to check the newly-activated window. It makes a special exception for windows that belong to the Toolbar, if one exists in this READ, with results you'll discover in the section on the Employee screen set. Then it inherits the behavior of my generic READACTI procedure in MAIN.PRG, which contains the code I run in the ACTIVATE clause even when I'm not using this template:

```
FUNCTION ReadACTI
IF USED(WONTOP())
   SELECT (WONTOP())
ENDIF
RETURN
```

This code makes use of my naming convention for READ windows: each window uses the ALIAS() of the table it edits for its window name. A complex READ can involve many different tables, each of which must be SELECTed appropriately before a GATHER MEMVAR and other table-handling code acts on the correct set of fields. This simple code uses the window name to recognize which table to SELECT at all times.

FOXPRO MAC HACK TIP

You already know that all windows do not call the ACTIVATE clause; for example, when you click into a BROWSE window, ACTIVATE doesn't fire because a BROWSE doesn't have GETs in it. However, FoxPro *automatically* SELECTs the proper table when a BROWSE gets the focus. My ACTIVATE clause just synchronizes the behavior of GET windows to this automatic feature of the BROWSE.

The DEACTIVATE clause is not a perfect parallel to the ACTIVATE clause in FoxPro. While FoxPro ignores the RETURN value of an ACTIVATE clause, the DEACTIVATE clause's RETURN value is its *raison d'être*. A RETURN of .T. from the DEACTIVATE clause causes FoxPro to

CLEAR the current READ. This attribute permits your program to handle a feature of FoxPro and Macintosh windows otherwise overlooked completely by FoxPro's READ system: the window Close Box. If the user clicks on the close box, the DEACTIVATE clause fires. You can evaluate this possibility using the same naming convention for windows that I use in my generic ACTIVATE clause:

```
FUNCTION ReadDEAC
RETURN NOT WVISIBLE(ALIAS())
```

The template screen contains no DEACTIVATE code at all, relying on this simple ReadDEAC function in MAIN.PRG to do its entire job.

READ WHEN and READ VALID

Just as READ ACTIVATE and DEACTIVATE clauses allow your code to respond to the user's movements between windows, the READ WHEN and VALID clauses give your program a moment to interrupt the action of the READ as the user begins and ends the READ.

The WHEN clause triggers when all the GETs have been painted into their respective windows. Use it to execute code that you only need once in the READ that must affect the current GETs. Before WHEN runs, GETs don't have object numbers or status in the new READ. You can't SHOW individual GETs with new prompts or set _CUROBJ to a number you get by evaluating OBJNUM(<the get name>, until the READ WHEN clause runs.

The template ReadWHEN function sets the prompts for the main window's buttons and the prompts for any subordinate windows (using the same array to handle the subordinate windows that were used in the SHOW clause):

```
FUNCTION ReadWHEN
PRIVATE m.aliasname, m.xx
m.aliasname = PROPER(ALIAS())
SHOW GET m.aliasact,2 ;
     PROMPT "Add New "+m.aliasname
SHOW GET m.aliasact,3 ;
     PROMPT "Delete This "+ m.aliasname
SHOW GET m.pickalias,1 PROMPT ;
     "Different "+m.aliasname
IF TYPE("childfiles(1,1)") = "C"
  FOR m.xx = 1 TO ALEN(childfiles,1)
   IF EOF(childfiles(m.xx,1))
```

```
      STORE .T. TO ;
       ("m."+childfiles(m.xx,3)+"add")
      SHOW GET ;
       ("m."+childfiles(m.xx,3)+"act"),1 ;
        ENABLE PROMPT  "Confirm Add"
      SHOW GET ;
       ("m."+childfiles(m.xx,3)+"act"),2 ;
        DISABLE ;
        PROMPT "Add "+PROPER(childfiles(m.xx,1))
      SHOW GET ;
       ("m."+childfiles(m.xx,3)+"act"),3 ;
       DISABLE ;
       PROMPT "Delete "+PROPER(childfiles(m.xx,1))
    ELSE
      STORE .F. TO (;
        "m."+childfiles(m.xx,3)+"add")
      SHOW GET ("m."+childfiles(m.xx,3)+"act"),1 ;
        ENABLE PROMPT "Confirm Edit"
      SHOW GET ;
       ("m."+childfiles(m.xx,3)+"act"),2 ;
        ENABLE ;
        PROMPT "Add "+PROPER(childfiles(m.xx,1))
      SHOW GET ;
       ("m."+childfiles(m.xx,3)+"act"),3 ;
       ENABLE ;
       PROMPT "Delete "+PROPER(childfiles(m.xx,1))
    ENDIF
  ENDFOR
ENDIF
DO ReadWHEN IN MAIN.PRG
RETURN .T.
```

Although this function ends with a call to ReadWHEN IN MAIN.PRG, the main program holds only an empty placeholder WHEN function at present.

If your WHEN clause RETURNs .F., the READ never allows user input at all. However, when the WHEN clause fires, from FoxPro's point of view, the READ has officially begun (that's why the GETs already have sequence numbers).

Because the READ has started, you can use the WHEN clause to override FoxPro's automatic menu disabling in a READ MODAL. If you have a limited menu that should be available during a modal READ, DO a special, limited .MPR file in the READ WHEN, and this menu will not be disabled.

CROSS-PLATFORM WARNING

You may object to menu items being available during a modal READ because this concept goes against Macintosh interface principles for a modal dialog. You should definitely *not* create a menu pad for an alert or other normal modal dialog!

As you saw in Chapter 7, however, you can use the READ MODAL keyword and its attendant WITH <window names> clause to limit a complex READ's access to certain specified windows onscreen. For example, when you call the Company screen set during a Job edit, you don't want the user inadvertently clicking on Job windows because those windows' GETs belong to a different READ and are inactive at that point. As you'll see in the next section, the Company screen set is a complex activity, and not modal from the user's point of view, even though you use the MODAL keyword in your code. It's perfectly appropriate for the Company screen set to append a module-specific menu pad to the menu, if you want one.

At the beginning of a READ, the WHEN clause executes, followed by the ACTIVATE clause for the window containing the first GET that gets the READ focus, followed by the SHOW clause. Finally, the first GET's WHEN clause executes (if any), and the normal, user-initiated activity of the READ begins.

FOXPRO MAC HACK TIP

The Setup for my TEMPLATE.SCX and the SUBFORM.SCX code for subsidiary READ windows in the screen set SCATTERs MEMVAR for all the tables involved in the READ, along with initializing any other necessary variables, such as the m.dept_name text table I described earlier. You may think this is wasted effort because the SHOW clause executes immediately after Setup at the beginning of a READ. The SHOW clause's code re-initializes everything in the same way as it gives these variables new values when the user moves to a new record later in the READ.

Unfortunately, you can't skip the Setup code. You need these variables initialized on the top level of the program. If you omit the Setup, the automatic DEFAULT clauses on the GETs generated by GENSCRN will assign values to each variable—but these default values may not be the right values, or even the right data type, for the use you plan to make of each GET.

The READ VALID clause runs at the conclusion of a READ, just as the WHEN runs at its beginning. If you RETURN .F. from the VALID clause, the user must remain in the READ. Your VALID clause typically evaluates the activities in progress when the user chooses to end the READ, RETURNing .F. if something critical is left undone, often giving the user a modal dialog that provides a choice to cancel the activity underway. The clause often sets _CUROBJ to direct the user's attention appropriately before a RETURN .F.

The template code contains only an empty placeholder ReadVALID function in MAIN.PRG because I have no generic way of deciding what code the VALID clause should run.

Continuing To Explore READ Clauses

The READ WHEN and VALID clauses complete the major interrupt points your code can use during the user-centered READ wait state. Additional clauses that control the READ state include the TIMEOUT <number> clause, which sets a time limit, in seconds, that a READ can remain idle before CLEARing automatically, and an OBJECT <number>, which sets _CUROBJ at the beginning of a READ. These two clauses aren't available through the Screen Builder. You saw how to add a timeout value to the READ command by using the #READCLAUSES generator directive in Chapter 8. The OBJECT clause can't evaluate GET sequence numbers properly because it executes before the WHEN; you should avoid this clause and set _CUROBJ in the WHEN clause instead.

FoxPro offers a LOCK and NOLOCK set of keywords on the READ, but these capabilities aren't useful with indirect READs (FoxPro doesn't know which record to lock unless you edit a table field directly). Because these keywords only take effect when the READ begins, if you use READ LOCK or NOLOCK on a direct READ, you use SHOW GETS LOCK and NOLOCK commands as conditions change during a READ CYCLE.

The READ clauses and interrupt points give you the flexibility to control the READ state and react to the user's actions—but you have to understand when and how they execute. You especially have to learn the *sequence* in which they execute in situations where multiple clauses fire.

When you have a question about how a particular READ event works, write a simple model program to discover FoxPro's behavior. For example, you might ask the questions, "Does the READ WHEN precede or follow the SHOW clause when the READ begins? Does a CLEAR READ execute the READ VALID clause? Does a SHOW GETS command with the WINDOW clause issue the READ SHOW clause code just as a global SHOW GETS command executes it?"

You could run the following sample program to find the answers:

```
* READTEST.PRG
* adjust any way you like to
* answer questions about READ and GET
* clause behavior
DEFINE WINDOW x FROM 1,1 TO 20,20
ACTI WINDOW x
DEFINE WINDOW y FROM 21,1 TO 30,30
@ 1,1 GET someget DEFA 1111
@ 2,2 GET otherget DEFA 2222
ACTI WINDOW y
@ 1,1 GET thirdget DEFA 3333

PUSH KEY CLEAR
ON KEY LABEL F10 SHOW GETS OFF WINDOW y
ON KEY LABEL F9 CLEAR READ
READ CYCLE ;
     WHEN udf() SHOW udf1() VALID udf2()
RELEASE WINDOW x,y
POP KEY

FUNC udf
_CUROBJ = OBJNUM(otherget)
RETURN

FUNC udf1
?? CHR(7)+CHR(7)
WAIT WINDOW NOWAIT ;
   "during SHOW clause, _CUROBJ = "+ ;
    ALLTRIM(STR(_CUROBJ))
RETURN

FUNC udf2
?? CHR(7)
RETURN
```

Execute the program, press the hotkeys you defined to initiate certain actions and listen for the CHR(7) (which sounds the bell in FoxPro), look for the WAIT WINDOW, or check for the other results you provided in the UDFs each clause calls. As you think of more questions, it's easy to adjust the test program to provide the answers.

See Also

- Source Disk: Miscellaneous Code Samples: TEST.PRG

FOXPRO MAC HACK TIP

Leave TEST.PRG onscreen and execute it as you edit it, using the menu shortcut ⌘-E (Program Execute). When a program editing window has the focus, this option appears on the Program drop-down menu, as you see in figure 10.8.

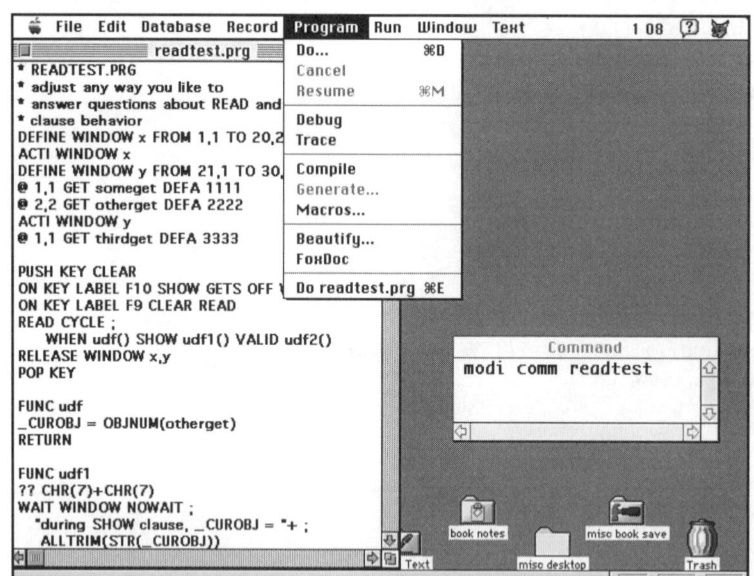

Figure 10.8 Experimenting with short test programs is easy to do in FoxPro, and it's one of the best ways to learn about READ CYCLEs.

Developing a Complex READ

Now that you understand how a READ CYCLE operates, this section provides a closer look at three complex screen sets that exploit the features of this wait state. First, you revisit the Address Book screen set (COMPANY.SPR) that you designed in Chapter 8, adding additional windows to edit individuals associated with a company record and their contact numbers, which the AD*Vantage application stores in related Contact and Number tables. The screen set provides BROWSEs to show the many child records related to the current Company address onscreen, as well as READ windows in which the current record for each child table may be edited.

Next, you look at a different design, employing a toolbar similar to the control windows in the examples shipped with Microsoft FoxPro. My toolbar concept uses the READ clauses to provide a flexible way to add tools to any READ, suitable to a rapid development system. This example focuses on the Employee table.

The third and final example is the complex Job editing screen set. This set doesn't rely on the template code, although you will see similar principles at work. This data entry model includes a data entry window for the table with focus (Job) and BROWSEs for navigation among the child records (Change Orders and Inventory). However, the set doesn't include READ windows for the child records. Instead, when you decide to edit a child record, the set launches a nested modal READ for that record.

You wouldn't ordinarily have modules navigate between records by using different methods in one application, as I do in these three examples. I chose these examples to show you a wide variety of approaches. Decide what you like, and make sure that your application's interface is more internally consistent than the collection of techniques I used here!

Why and How To Use BROWSEs in Screen Sets

The BROWSEs in these examples fall into two basic categories. You already used a BROWSE executed from a push button in the Chapter 8 version of the Address Book edit. I call this type of BROWSE a *modal BROWSE* because you summon it from the button and, once you are in the BROWSE, you can't return to the rest of the windows onscreen without the BROWSE disappearing. (The BROWSE closes automatically when you bring another window on top by any method.)

In the screen sets that you see in this section, many BROWSEs are executed with SAVE NOWAIT keywords, which bring the BROWSEs onscreen, and then continue with the READ without closing the BROWSE window. These BROWSEs can exist for the duration of the READ, and they can be freely entered and exited like other windows that participate in the READ. I call this type a *participating BROWSE*. While a modal BROWSE is appropriate for choosing the record on which the READ focuses, I think participating BROWSEs, which constantly show their contents during the edit, are more appropriate for navigation of the focus table's many child records.

The BROWSE image gives the user a graphical way to visualize the one-to-many relationship, much as spreadsheet grids allow users to see data in a format that truly represents the information the spreadsheet edits. In FoxPro, you also can use the native Find function, on the Edit menu, within a BROWSE. In a BROWSE window, Find can locate information across all numeric and character fields, which makes the Find dialog and its associated menu shortcut, ⌘-F, ideal for quick navigational purposes.

Figure 10.9 shows you the native Find dialog at work in a BROWSE of Contacts in the Address Book screen set. On the source disk, I included a Find dialog I wrote (BFIND.SCX) that imitates the native dialog but adds memo fields to the data that you can search in a BROWSE with ⌘-F.

When you use a participating BROWSE and also show a data entry window for the table at the same time, you want the data entry GETs synchronized with the BROWSE as the user scrolls through the available records. BROWSEs have a WHEN clause, just like GETs and READs, and this clause is executed each time the record pointer moves in the BROWSE. The WHEN clause is therefore ideal for satisfying this requirement. Here's the BROWSE WHEN function in MAIN.PRG I use on every participating BROWSE:

```
FUNCTION Do_Show && in MAIN.PRG
* for BROWSE WHEN clauses
* that drive a data entry
* window
IF WEXIST(ALIAS())
  * is there an associated READ window
  * for this file?
  SCATTER MEMVAR MEMO
  SHOW GETS ONLY WINDOW (ALIAS())
ENDIF
RETURN .F.
```

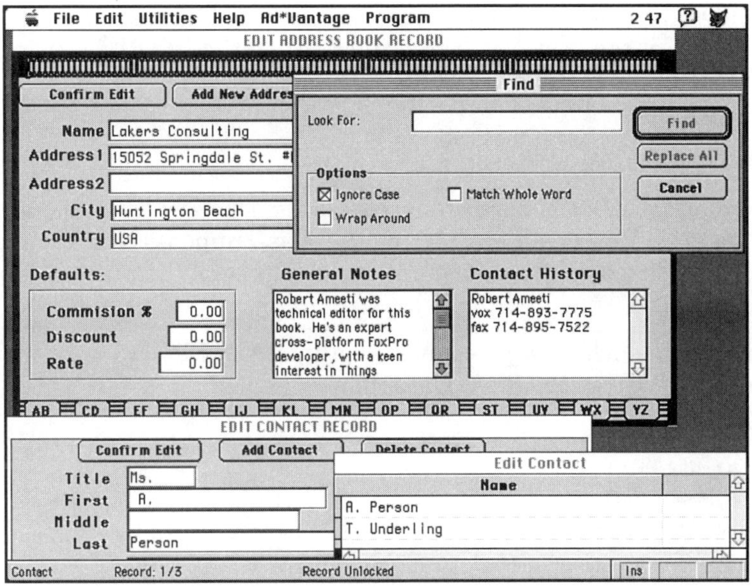

Figure 10.9 *The Find Dialog is a native FoxPro feature that makes BROWSEs especially suitable for record navigation.*

The template code calls this generic function from a local copy of FUNCTION Do_show and then synchronizes the other child files using a function (Show_Children) local to the template, which you've already seen called by the SHOW clause:

```
FUNCTION Do_show && local to the template cleanup
* BROWSE WHEN clause
* in case you have local instructions
* put them here, followed by
DO Do_Show IN MAIN
* to do universal instructions, then:
DO Show_Children WITH .F.
RETURN .F.
```

FUNCTION Do_Show calls Show_Children with the parameter .F. to tell Show_Children that the user is not in the process of adding a record. Because the BROWSEs are essentially pick lists of existing records, the user can't be adding while scrolling the contents of the BROWSE. Notice that these BROWSE WHEN functions have a RETURN value of .F., which ensures that the user cannot edit records in the BROWSE.

You need one more technique to standardize BROWSE-handling in a complex READ – a method to return from the BROWSE to an editable data entry window for the current record. I chose to use an ENTER keypress to let the user pick a record for edit in the BROWSE, using this setup code in the template:

```
PUSH KEY CLEAR
ON KEY LABEL ENTER DO PickBrow
```

The `PUSH KEY CLEAR` command removes all previous key assignments on their way into the screen set, placing these assignments on a key *stack*. A matching `POP KEY` in the Cleanup code brings back the previous key assignments.

I designed the PickBrow procedure, kept in MAIN.PRG, to work with any type of BROWSE in the READ, as follows:

```
PROCEDURE Pickbrow
PUSH KEY CLEAR
PRIVATE m.whichwind
m.whichwind = UPPER(WONTOP())
DO CASE
CASE m.whichwind = "PICK"
  * in a modal browse
  KEYBOARD "{CTRL-W}"
CASE m.whichwind = "EDIT" AND WONTOP() # WOUTPUT()
  * in a non-modal browse
  * in this READ
  IF WEXIST(ALIAS())
     ACTIVATE WINDOW (ALIAS())
  ENDIF
CASE WREAD(m.whichwind)
  * in a READ window for this READ
  KEYBOARD "{ENTER}" PLAIN
OTHERWISE
  KEYBOARD "{ENTER}" PLAIN
ENDCASE
POP KEY
RETURN
```

This code evaluates the current window and processes the user's Enter keystroke accordingly. The code relies on some naming conventions for the different types of BROWSEs I use. If the current window name starts with PICK, I know the user is in a modal BROWSE. I KEYBOARD "{CTRL-W}" to exit the BROWSE, and the procedure that summoned the modal BROWSE continues from there. In Chapter 14, you learn how to take care of the same requirement when the user double-clicks the mouse in a BROWSE.

If the current window name uses the word EDIT, a participating browse may have focus. I add a second check to make sure the window is BROWSE type: `WONTOP() # WOUTPUT()`. WONTOP(), as you've already seen, represents the current window with focus, which may be the BROWSE. WOUTPUT(), by contrast, represents the current *output* window (the window in which text would be displayed or GETs would be painted if you issued an @... SAY or @.. GET command, and in which other text would be echoed). A BROWSE can never be the current output window.

The participating BROWSE may or may not be matched with a data entry window for the same table, so I check WEXIST(ALIAS()) for the data entry window's existence before attempting to ACTIVATE the appropriate window.

See Also

- "Handle Keys and the Mouse," Chapter 14
- PROCEDURE MouseBrow, Source Disk:Library/ Template Code:MAIN.PRG

FOXPRO MAC HACK TIP

As you investigate the template code, you see a correspondence between the *titles* I give to each BROWSE window (using the BROWSE TITLE clause) and the *name* with which I refer to the BROWSE window to manipulate it (to RELEASE it, evaluate whether it has focus, and so on). A BROWSE gets its programmatic name from the title you see in its title bar. Don't be confused and use the name of a DEFINEd window you may have used to give the BROWSE attributes, using the BROWSE WINDOW clause. For example, look at the following BROWSE:

```
DEFINE WINDOW X FROM 1,1 TO 20,20 ;
       TITLE "This is a Window" ;
       FONT "Geneva" COLOR SCHEME 10
BROWSE WINDOW X TITLE "My Browse"
```

This BROWSE has the programmatic name "My Browse" because that's the BROWSE title. If you didn't use the TITLE clause on the BROWSE, its title would be the same as the title on the DEFINEd window (X) you used to give this BROWSE its position, color scheme, and font attributes, so the BROWSE's programmatic name would now be "This is a Window." The BROWSE's name would never be X; if you RELEASE WINDOW X, you release the DEFINEd WINDOW X, *not* the BROWSE.

If the window with focus is neither type of BROWSE, I KEYBOARD the "{ENTER}" keystroke with the PLAIN keyword, which simply passes the keystroke on for normal data entry purposes.

Notice that the PickBrow procedure begins with a `PUSH KEY CLEAR` and ends with a `POP KEY`. This precaution prevents the procedure from being called recursively if the user holds the Enter key down.

I don't change these functions for each BROWSE or even each type of screen set. These simple techniques handle all the BROWSEs most of the time, although I add some special cases and cosmetic improvements to the code in the Job screen set. Once you figure the techniques out, using BROWSEs in screen sets becomes an easy, routine procedure.

You must still decide what kinds of BROWSEs to use, and when it's appropriate to use the BROWSEs. I've already suggested that you use BROWSEs as a natural database metaphor for the one-to-many relationships of certain tables in the current module. In addition, you may want to hold the total number of windows in the screen set to a manageable maximum. Not only do multiple windows require FoxPro to use more memory to set up the screen set, but the screen can become too cluttered for the user to manage. If you have several child tables for a particular module, you may want modal BROWSEs, called by push buttons, for each child rather than participating BROWSEs. You may even HIDE the child windows not directly under edit, using the technique you saw in PROCEDURE Show_Children earlier.

FOXPRO MAC HACK TIP

While considering the design of the screen set, and a reasonable maximum for the number of windows with which the user contends at one time, don't forget that not all users have the same size monitor. To simulate a Mac Classic-sized monitor, try turning MACDESKTOP OFF temporarily and sizing your main FoxPro window to approximate a Classic monitor. When you run your screen set under these conditions, can the user access all windows easily? How cluttered does the screen look?

The next sections show you practical examples that integrate BROWSEs, multiple tables, and READ windows in different types of screen sets.

Editing COMPANY.DBF in a Complex Version of the Address Book Screen Set

First, change your previous COMPANY.SCX from its current state, editing the Address records only, to a complex set that edits the Vendor/ Client child records. You'll see that very little code accomplishes this task.

Then, change COMPANY.SCX's Setup code to alert the template to the child tables that you want to incorporate in the set. Before the Setup line that SELECTs the Vendor alias, add the following code:

```
PRIVATE childfiles(1), m.xx

DIME childfiles(2,4)
childfiles(1,1) = "CONTACT"
childfiles(1,2) = ;
   "name = ALLTRIM(firstname)+' '+lastname"
childfiles(1,3) = "con"
childfiles(2,1) = "NUMBER"
childfiles(2,2) = "type :H ='Contact Type'"
childfiles(2,3) = "num"
```

You're creating an array the rest of the COMPANY.SCX code uses to handle the child tables without explicit references to each table. In this array, one row refers to each child table. The first array column holds the alias for the child file. The second column holds the field or other expression that you want to use for the participating BROWSE for this table. If you don't want a BROWSE, you leave this element empty. The third column holds a three-letter prefix that you'll add to each child table's action button variable and add-record flag variable.

The template code fills out the fourth column as it runs, saving SET SKIP information in Setup for restoration in Cleanup. Although the SET SKIP method of showing one-to-many relationships is useful elsewhere in your application, the template uses separate BROWSEs for each child table. The multiple levels of one-to-many relationships in a parent-child-grandchild relationship, such as the Vendor-Contact-Number relationship you see in this screen set, are more clearly expressed without the virtual records of SET SKIP when you use separate BROWSEs for each table.

Here's the template Setup code that fills out the fourth column. You don't need to edit this code, but it shows you the general method by which the template uses the array you just created. First, the template code checks to see whether you've initialized the array, using a TYPE() check, and then it loops through the array rows to do its job for each table:

```
IF TYPE("childfiles(1,1)") = "C"
   FOR m.xx = 1 TO ALEN(childfiles,1)
      SELECT (childfiles(m.xx,1))
      childfiles(m.xx,4) = SET("SKIP")
      SET SKIP TO
   ENDFOR
ENDIF
RELEASE m.xx
```

When you looked at the Read SHOW clause earlier, you saw similar loops through the childfiles() array in PROCEDURE Show_Children to set the memory variables, BROWSEs, and the prompts for buttons in each child table's READ window. The template Cleanup code contains many such loops through the array. Thanks to the array, you don't have to make a single change to the extensive Cleanup code in the template to include the child files.

However, you added one additional custom feature to the Company screen: the `m.lettertab` button set that imitates the alphabetic divider tabs on a physical address book, shown in figure 10.10. If you haven't done so earlier, you should initialize this GET in the Setup to a character value because GENSCRN's generated DEFAULT clause on the GET will otherwise initialize it to numeric type.

```
m.lettertab = ""
```

Declare this variable PRIVATE along with the other screen-specific variables you initialize in Setup. Next, turn to the SHOW clause in the Cleanup of the COMPANY.SCX. The section of the ReadSHOW code that handles a failed record lock DISABLEs all the GETs except `m.pickalias`, so the user can look at this record and use the browsing button to move to another record. Since `m.lettertab` represents another way for the user to move to other records rather than editing data, you should add an explicit `SHOW GET m.lettertab` to this section of the SHOW code for this screen's instance of the template code.

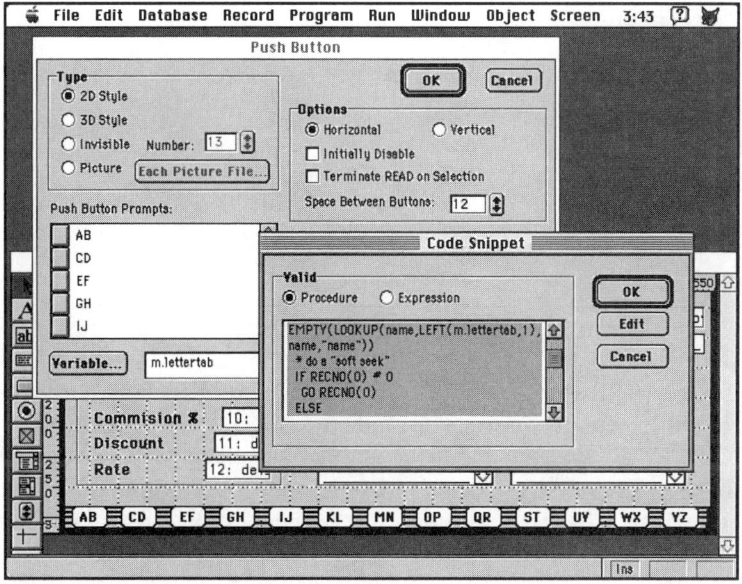

Figure 10.10 *Designing the lettertab button set object in the Address Book.*

Here's the code you write for the VALID of `m.lettertab` for the desired effect:

```
* m.lettertab VALID
PRIVATE m.rec
m.rec = IIF(EOF(), 0, RECNO())
* use LOOKUP() function so
* you can put the file in any order
* and still search by name —
* last parameter of LOOKUP() specifies
* index tag to be used, making it
* relatively fast
IF EMPTY(LOOKUP(name,LEFT(m.lettertab,1),;
         name,"name"))
  * do a "soft seek"
  IF RECNO(0) # 0
    GO RECNO(0)
  ELSE
    ?? CHR(7)
    IF m.rec # 0
       GO m.rec
```

```
    ENDIF
  ENDIF
ENDIF
IF RECNO() # m.rec
   DO NewParentRec
   SHOW GETS
ENDIF
RETURN .T.
```

FOXPRO MAC HACK TIP

As figure 10.10 shows, I've left the VALID code for `m.lettertab` attached to the buttons as a procedure, contrary to my usual practice. Although the lettertab code is not yet generic enough to be used with other tables, the concept of the lettertab buttons is inherently useful. I think I will continue to work on this function and consider its behavior carefully. For example, should the search automatically call FUNCTION *pickalias*, showing a BROWSE, after moving the user to the chosen letter? Should an unsuccessful search result in a *soft seek*, as the code currently does, or move the user to the top of the file? How can I change the LOOKUP() call so the buttons use other tables besides the Company table?

Once I'm sure I like the lettertab behavior, I can use the lettertab button set as an object, copying it to other screens. Leaving the code attached in a VALID procedure snippet ensures that the code will travel with the buttons when I paste them. Eventually, I may generalize the function and move it to MAIN.PRG, so the function works with buttons of different visual appearance and can be edited for all instances with one change.

You proceed to create the data entry windows for each child table. For these windows, you don't start from TEMPLATE.SCX, which contains all the READ-global information. For each child table's READ window, you begin with a secondary template, named SUBFORM.SCX, which you find in the Library/Template Code folder. As before, you Save the screen As a new name for each instance of the model screen you need (Contact and Number, in this case) in the application's SCREENS subfolder.

As you see in figure 10.11, SUBFORM.SCX is a simple screen with buttons and Setup code. It doesn' t have TEMPLATE.SCX's elaborate Cleanup code. You can customize the copy of SUBFORM with some minimal edits before an instance of the screen is ready for use in your screen set.

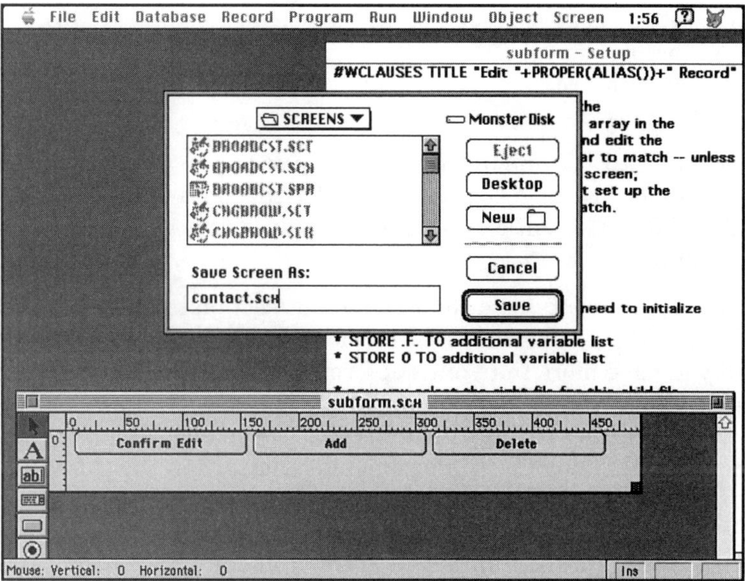

Figure 10.11 *The SUBFORM.SCX template gives you a head start on designing the subsidiary READ windows for each child table in a complex READ.*

Start by editing the Setup code in each copy of SUBFORM that you're going to use. The Setup starts with a #WCLAUSES generator directive, like TEMPLATE.SCX, followed by initialization of some variables:

```
#WCLAUSES TITLE "Edit "+PROPER(ALIAS())+" Record" GROW
PRIVATE m.subadd, m.subact
STORE .F. TO m.subadd
STORE 0 TO m.subact
* STORE "" TO any variables you need to initialize
* to character type here
* STORE .F. TO additional variable list
* STORE 0 TO additional variable list
```

You need to edit the TITLE line in the subform because the ALIAS() of the currently SELECTed table will be the main table in the screen, not this child table, at the time when the DEFINE WINDOW code is executed. If you have only one subform in use for the READ, you can leave the rest of the code above as you find it, and use the three-letter prefix `sub` for the third column in the array that you create in the main screen's Setup code. However, if you have more than one subform, you assign variable name prefixes for each subform separately. In the case of the Contact screen, for example, you used the prefix `con`, so the code above becomes:

```
#WCLAUSES TITLE "Edit Contact Record" GROW
PRIVATE m.conadd, m.conact
STORE .F. TO m.conadd
STORE 0 TO m.conact
```

You edit the SELECT line in the subform, just as you did in the main table's Setup, to SELECT the right table for this data entry window before the SCATTER MEMVAR MEMO line initializes variables (`SELECT Contact`, in this example).

The subform code contains a commented-out section to initialize an *sname* variable to hold the subform's ALIAS() for use in the window name, but, again, if you have more than one subform you can't use this trick. Instead, use the Screen Layout dialog to change the `'&sname.'` window name to explicitly match the alias for this table (`contact` in one subform, `number` in the other). Finally, double-click on the push buttons in the subform screen and change the m.subact variable for this GET to match the three-letter prefix you used for this child file. As you see in figure 10.12, the variable becomes `m.conact` for the Contact subform. You don't have to edit the call to FUNCTION Subaction in the push button's VALID clause; however, each child button set calls the same function.

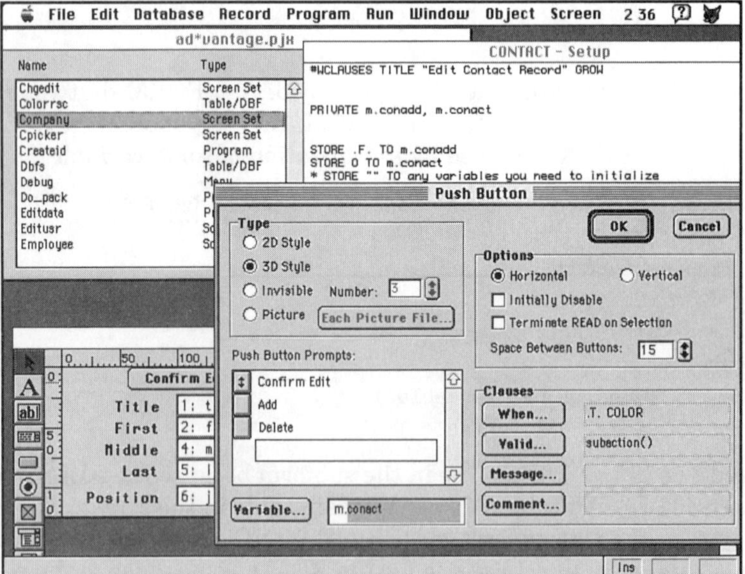

Figure 10.12 *Customize the variables and action button for each subform that you include in the READ.*

> **FOXPRO MAC HACK TIP**
>
> If you're tempted to avoid customizing the subforms' button names by using the FoxPro REGIONAL designation to maintain several copies of the `m.sname` and `m.subact` variables, don't waste your time. You need to use these variables globally in the screen set, and FoxPro can't associate the variables with their appropriate regions (local windows) at all the necessary points. The SUBFORM template still saves you development time.

Your final task is to add the Contact- and Number-specific GETs for each window. Using the same procedure as you did for the Company .SCX layout earlier, Cut the buttons out of the layout temporarily (⌘X). Do a Quick Screen, omitting the primary and parent key fields for this table (the template code takes care of them automatically). Edit the labels for the GETs, modify the labels' fonts, rearrange the GETs in the layout, and Order the GETs so their sequence matches a logical data entry order. Then paste the buttons back into the layout. Add any cosmetic improvements you like, using GASP or manually adjusting the layout.

> **FOXPRO MAC HACK TIP**
>
> To avoid the buttons getting focus, even with KEYCOMP set to MAC, you should make sure that the buttons aren't the first GETs in the screen. You can easily make them the *last objects* in the GET sequence by selecting the buttons and choosing the Bring to Front option from the Object pop-up menu.

You're ready to create the complex screen set.

Your AD*Vantage project currently has a Company screen set. You added the menu command DO Company.SPR in Chapter 7. When you re-Build the .APP after adding that menu option and creating the Company screen in Chapter 8, the Project Manager automatically added this screen set to AD*Vantage. However, the project record currently doesn't include information about the child tables.

Double-click on the Company screen set record in the AD*Vantage project and use the Add button in the Edit Screen Set dialog to add the CONTACT.SCX and NUMBER.SCX screens to the list of screen files in this set. Press the Arrange button to summon the dialog that you see in figure 10.13 and move the three GET windows around until you like their arrangement.

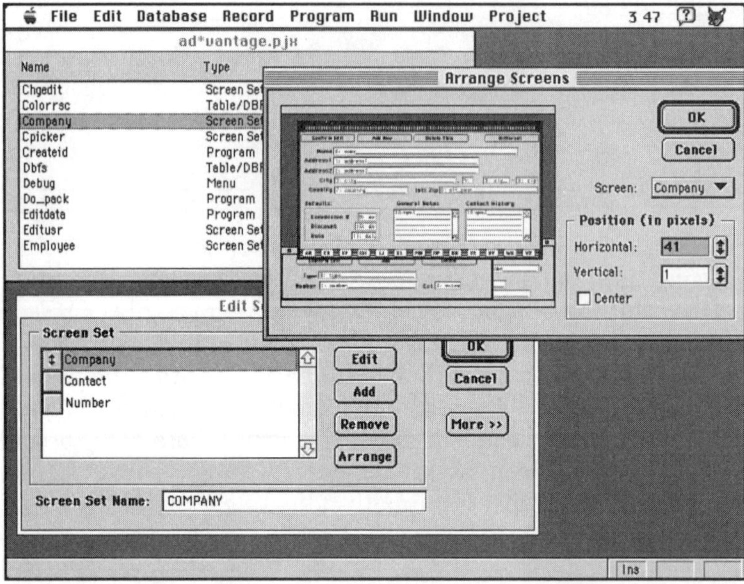

Figure 10.13 *Add the new subsidiary .SCXs to the Project's screen set record and arrange the screen set's windows.*

FOXPRO MAC HACK TIP

The arrangement of windows in a set manifests itself in the DEFINE WINDOW coordinates generated by GENSCRN. These coordinates are *relative to the parent window and the parent window's font*. The parent window whose attributes GENSCRN uses to figure out the Arranged coordinates for a window is the FoxPro main application window (SCREEN), even though on a Macintosh you have SET MACDESKTOP ON and you're not using the screen at all. It's vital that you make sure the screen font attributes that GENSCRN used at generation time are the same attributes with which the window coordinates are evaluated at runtime. Chapter 11 provides you with a trick to help synchronize these attributes with a simple change to GENSCRN. Chapter 12 teaches you more about the fontmetric issues that make the trick necessary.

Now you're ready to re-Build the AD*Vantage application and try the new screen set. When you access the Address Book option, either from the AD*Vantage Maintenance group of lookup data entry screens or modally from the Job module's menu, you should see a screen something like figure 10.14.

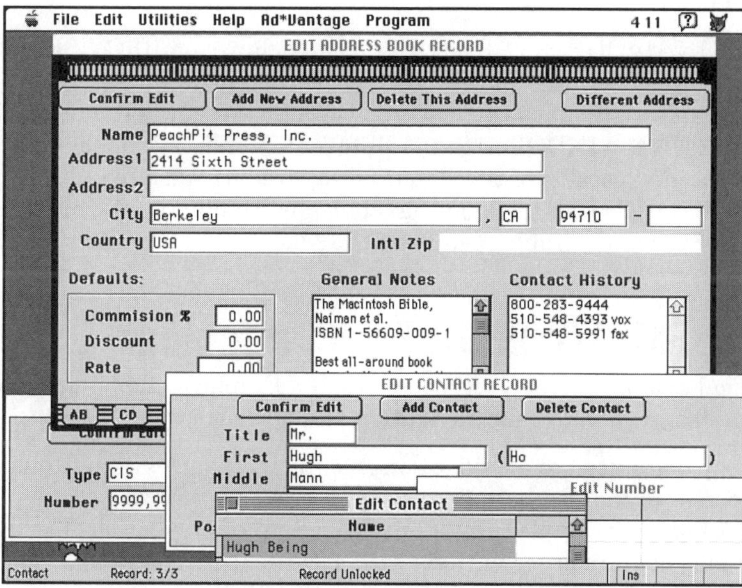

Figure 10.14 *Executing the complex Address Book screen set.*

You should be able to navigate through the parent (Company or Address) records and watch the child BROWSEs and data entry screens change to match. If you choose to Add a new address, the child BROWSEs and data entry screens disappear until you confirm the new parent record.

Try the different options in the screen set and note any behavior you'd like to change. Concentrate on the *level* at which you want to make the change; is this change something that should be limited to the Address Book screen set, or should you make the change to the template, where it can be inherited by all your screen sets?

You'll immediately notice that the BROWSEs for the Contact and Numbers tables show up onscreen in an inappropriate size and position. To simplify the template and this initial example, I've left these BROWSEs without defining their various attributes carefully. The user is free to resize and reposition these windows at will.

The Job screen set shows you how to control BROWSEs' appearances in a screen set more exactly.

When you look at the generic template code for the BROWSEs, however, you see one macro-expanded clause that requires a little extra explanation: an &inparent variable. I declare the variable `m.inparent` in the Setup function of MAIN.PRG, as follows:

```
PUBLIC m.inparent
m.inparent = IIF(_MAC, "IN MACDESKTOP", "IN SCREEN")
```

Using the IN MACDESKTOP or IN SCREEN clause on BROWSEs is a simple way to make sure that the BROWSEs don't end up taking on the attributes and positions of the last ACTIVATEd window without explicitly using a DEFINE WINDOW (via the BROWSE WINDOW clause). The macro-expanded version of the clause is required because IN MACDESKTOP doesn't work on the other FoxPro platforms while IN SCREEN gives undesirable results on the Mac.

Editing EMPLOYEE.DBF with a Toolbar

The second example screen set focuses on the Employee table, using a *toolbar accessory window* for navigation and other common tasks.

Many people are used to a navigational *control window* with buttons to send the user to the top, bottom, next, and previous records because the Microsoft FoxPro example projects use this form of navigation. The control window may contain other buttons with other features as well, such as a Quit button for the screen or access to the BROWSER generic dialog.

In my template code and in this section, I refer to a generic screen of this type as a *toolbar* rather than a control window, following Macintosh usage. Mac users are accustomed to programs with toolbars and *palette windows* to accompany the document windows in which they edit. A palette typically floats free onscreen in front of the document window (for example, a selection of brush styles in a paint program), whereas a toolbar is fixed at the edge of the screen (for example, the toolbar on the left edge of the FoxPro Screen Builder). Neither type of window ever retains focus; you make a choice and are returned immediately to edit your document.

Although I prefer BROWSEs for navigation, for reasons I stated earlier in the chapter, I still like the idea of generic accessory windows for other tasks. My template is designed to allow you to create any type of toolbar elements you like—and to attach them to template screens without writing additional code.

FOXPRO MAC HACK TIP

When I decided to include this functionality in my template code, I found it easier to integrate a toolbar with other READ windows than a palette. Allowing FoxPro for Macintosh windows to float requires a title bar on the windows—and the user may click on the title bar, giving the palette focus. Although I could trap for this problem in code, often it's better to consider FoxPro's natural behavior and work within that behavior, rather than fighting the program for every last drop of interface flexibility.

Palettes didn't provide significant additional functionality over toolbars, so my choice was easily, and happily, made.

The moral of this story: *There is no particular merit in making your programming life difficult for any reason, and there is no shame in taking the easy way out occasionally!*

You can start creating the set just as you created CUSTOMER.SCX: Open the TEMPLATE.SCX in the Screen Builder, Save the screen As EMPLOYEE.SCX in your AD*Vantage SCREENS subfolder, edit the Setup code to SELECT Employee as the table with focus in this screen, and add initialization for the onscreen confirmation of the lookup you learned about earlier, with the following line:

```
STORE "" TO m.dept_name
```

In figure 10.15, you see an invisible button under the Department text label. The user clicks on the label for lookups throughout the AD*Vantage system to edit the lookup, which is not editable directly. Earlier in the chapter, you saw the code executed by the VALID of the invisible button (FUNCTION PickDept), which presents the user with a modal BROWSE from which to pick a department.

FOXPRO MAC HACK TIP

You could decide to provide pop-up controls for the lookups in your system, instead of BROWSEs, but be aware that pop-ups and scrollable lists cost memory. If you have a lookup which may eventually show hundreds of choices, a BROWSE runs much more quickly.

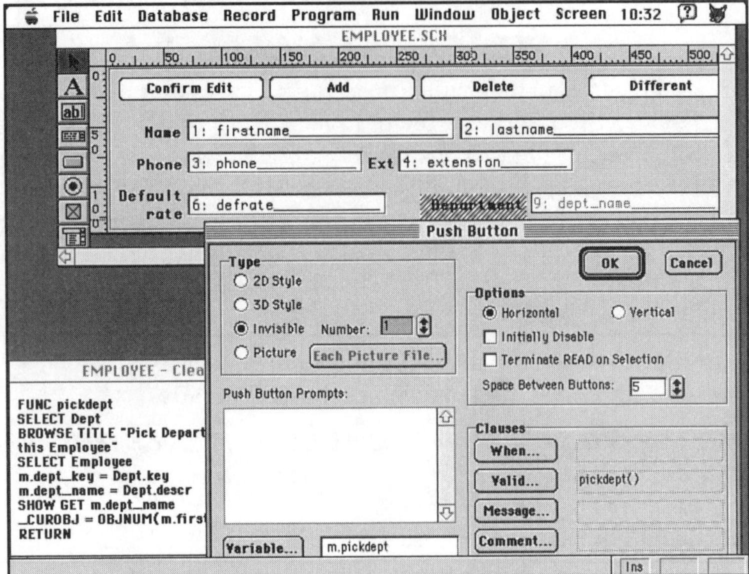

Figure 10.15 *Add an invisible button to the Employee screen to edit a lookup field (Department).*

Besides this invisible button, the Employee screen is not noteworthy in itself. *You don't need to make any other changes to the template code for this screen besides adding the two lines of Setup and the screen-specific FUNCTION PickDept to Cleanup.* You're ready to add the toolbar elements and generate the new screen set.

If you haven't already done so, add an option to the main AD*Vantage menu, under Maintenance, to edit Employees using the Command result `DO EMPLOYEE.SPR`. Add the EMPLOYEE.SCX to the AD*Vantage project as a screen set, and access the Edit Screen Set dialog from the project.

You'll find the various toolbar elements I've created in the Library/Template Code folder; they're all .SCXs with names beginning with TOOL. Choose to Add all six of these elements to the Employee screen set, as shown in figure 10.16, arranging them in the screen set list after the Employee screen, in the order you'd like them to appear on the toolbar. Although you arrange their order logically in the screen list, *don't bother arranging these screens visually in the Arrange dialog.*

That's it! You can re-Build AD*Vantage.APP and try out the new screen set. You should see the results in figure 10.17, and you should be able to add Employee records and try out the toolbar items.

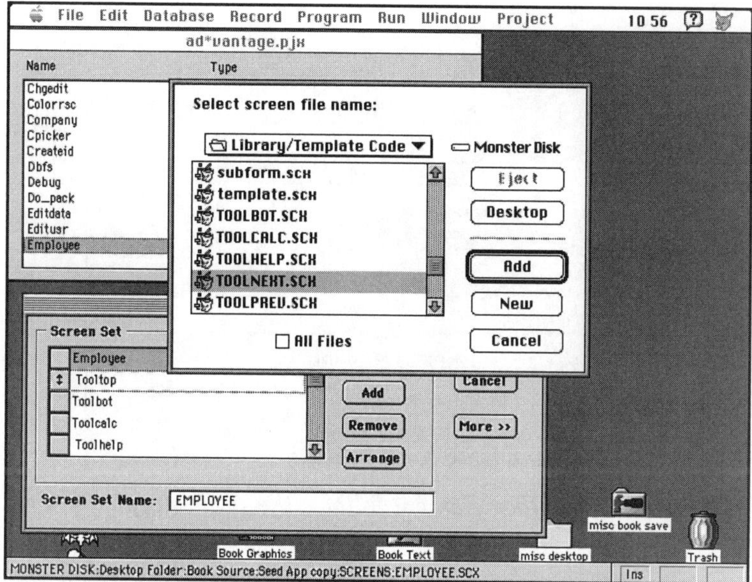

Figure 10.16 *Add toolbar elements to the Employee Screen Set.*

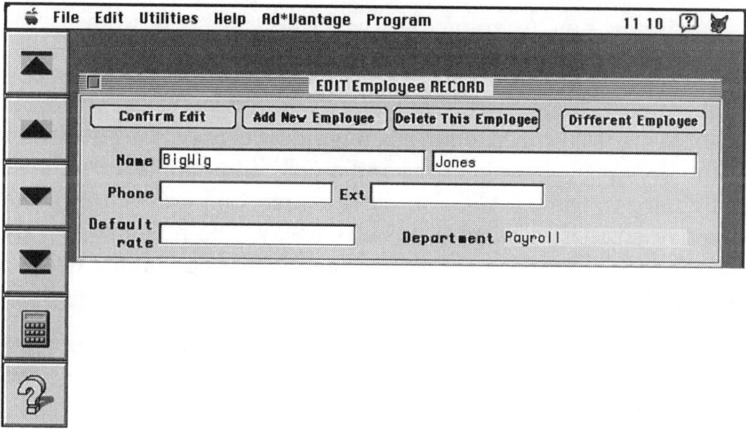

Figure 10.17 *The Employee screen set uses a generic toolbar.*

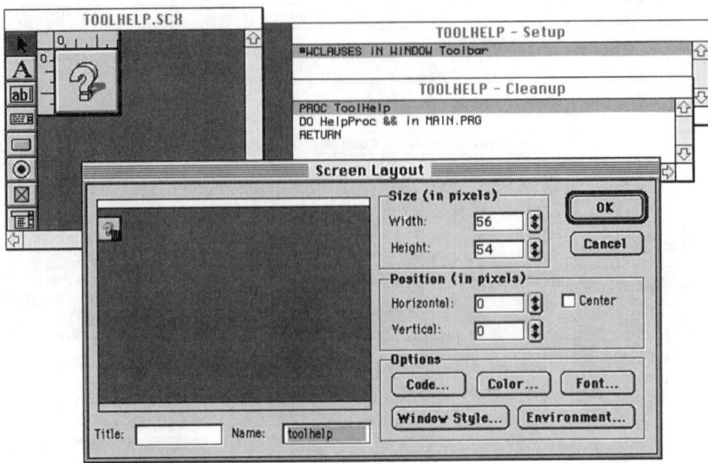

Figure 10.18 *Each toolbar element follows the same simple pattern.*

Exit from the AD*Vantage application and investigate the TOOL*.SCX files. You will find that all of these files contain the following factors (highlighted in figure 10.18):

- Each window has *the single Setup line* `#WCLAUSES IN WINDOW ToolBar`, making each tool a child window of ToolBar.
- Each window has *a procedure in its Cleanup code* that performs the action for this tool. Although each window contains a button, the button only provides a picture and a GET to make the window a participant in the READ. You don't attach this procedure to the button or edit the button in any other way. The memory variable edited by the button can be named anything you want; I use `m.tool` for *all* of them.
- Each window has *the same window name as its Cleanup procedure*. (I named each .SCX the same way, but this isn't a required factor.)

Although you can't see it in the figure, each window also has FoxFont *as its base font* for convenience in figuring out its size and position in the template code.

If you incorporate these factors into additional windows of approximately the same size, you can collect as many different tools as you want, and you can mix and match them in screen sets with no more effort than you used here.

How does the template incorporate these windows? If you examine TEMPLATE.SCX's Setup and Cleanup code, you find that the Setup DEFINEs a WINDOW named Toolbar with no border, using FoxFont, in #Section 1, before GENSCRN's generated window definitions. #Section 2 of Setup, which executes *after* GENSCRN's window definitions, contains code to RELEASE the Toolbar window, if no child windows are DEFINEd for Toolbar, or to size the Toolbar window and position its child windows properly, if you have added Toolbar elements to this READ:

```
PRIVATE m.xx, m.yy, m.pchildren, m.prows, ;
        m.pcols, m.pchild, m.oldattrib
m.pchildren = WCHILD("Toolbar")
* did we use a Toolbar window in this READ?
IF m.pchildren = 0
   * Toolbar not used
   RELEASE WINDOW Toolbar
ELSE
   IF_MAC OR _WINDOWS
      m.oldattrib = [FONT "]+WFONT(1,"")+;
                    [", ]+ALLTR(STR(WFONT(2,"")))+;
                    [ STYLE "]+WFONT(3,"")+["]
      MODI WINDOW SCREEN FONT "FOXFONT", 9 STYLE N
   ENDIF
   * start off the stack of child windows,
   * one button to a window
   m.pchild = WCHILD("Toolbar",0)
   m.prows = WROWS(m.pchild)
   m.pcols = WCOLS(m.pchild)
   * read the rest of the stack:
   MOVE WINDOW (m.pchild) TO 0,0
   FOR m.xx = 1 TO m.pchildren - 1
      m.pchild = WCHILD("Toolbar",1)
      * all the buttons should actually
      * have the same dimensions,
      * but just in case
      MOVE WINDOW (m.pchild) TO m.prows,0
      m.pcols = MAX(WCOLS(m.pchild),m.pcols)
      m.prows = WROWS(m.pchild) + m.prows
   ENDFOR
   ZOOM WINDOW Toolbar NORM AT 0,0 SIZE m.prows,m.pcols
   SHOW WINDOW Toolbar SAME
```

```
   IF _MAC OR _WINDOWS
      MODI WINDOW SCREEN &oldattrib
   ENDIF
ENDIF
RELEASE m.xx, m.yy, m.pchildren, m.prows, ;
        m.pcols, m.pchild, m.oldattrib
```

The WCHILD() function is critical to this code. You call this function with a second parameter of 0 to find the first child window in a stack for any given parent; then you call it with a second parameter of 0 to find each child window in succession until the stack is exhausted.

Notice that this code sets the main application window (SCREEN) font to FoxFont in order to synchronize its row and column calculations with Toolbar's and those of the Toolbar child windows. It immediately restores the font attributes of the main application window, so this step shouldn't affect your screens in any way.

The Cleanup code for TEMPLATE.SCX RELEASEs WINDOW Toolbar explicitly. The child windows will be RELEASEd by GENSCRN's generated code, but GENSCRN didn't DEFINE WINDOW Toolbar and can't RELEASE it. If Toolbar was RELEASEd earlier because this screen set incorporates no toolbar elements, this second RELEASE doesn't cause an error. Now the Cleanup's ReadACTI function adds the real toolbar trick: If a newly-ACTIVATEd window is a child of Toolbar, ReadACTI executes a function *with the same name as the current window* and then sets focus back to the previously active window using the following code:

```
FUNCTION ReadACTI
IF UPPER(WPARENT(WONTOP())) == "TOOLBAR"
   PRIVATE m.oldrec
   m.oldrec = RECNO()
   DO (WONTOP())
   ACTIVATE WINDOW (WLAST())
   * was this the kind of Toolbar tool
   * that navigates?  If so...
   IF RECNO() # m.oldrec
       SHOW GETS
   ENDIF
   _CUROBJ = 1
ELSE
   DO ReadACTI IN MAIN
ENDIF
RETURN
```

The other READ clauses and generic template functions make a few additional adjustments to take care of toolbar elements as a special class. Each function uses the check for WPARENT() to see if a toolbar element window is involved in an operation. The SHOW clause explicitly re-ENABLEs toolbar windows after DISABLEing GETs for a record that can't be locked, just as you explicitly re-ENABLEd the `m.lettertab` navigational GET in COMPANY.SCX. Although a Mac toolbar should never gain focus and accept keystrokes, the ON KEY LABEL ENTER procedure, `PickBrow`, takes care of cross platform use of the toolbar by checking to see if it has received an Enter press in a toolbar window. If so, it KEYBOARDs "{ENTER}" PLAIN, passing on the keystroke to the button, which is an appropriate selection mechanism in FoxPro for DOS and Windows.

CROSS-PLATFORM WARNING

The check for the possibility of a keystroke in the toolbar uses the following expression:

```
CASE WPARENT(m.whichwind) == "TOOLBAR" ;
     AND (_DOS OR SET("KEYCOMP") # "MAC")
```

I check SET("KEYCOMP") rather than the platform variables _MAC, _WINDOWS, _UNIX, or _DOS, because you may have `SET KEYCOMP TO DOS` or `TO WINDOWS` on the Mac (much as I despise the thought). If you have KEYCOMP SET to emulate DOS or Windows, you need this CASE on the Mac as well.

You may wonder why I precede the SET("KEYCOMP") check with a check for _DOS. The SET("KEYCOMP") function causes an `invalid SET expression` error in FoxPro for DOS 2.5 and 2.6. Since KEYCOMP can only be SET to DOS on the DOS platform, the second check isn't necessary in DOS. The OR Boolean connector prevents the second condition from being evaluated and causing an error on the DOS platform. FoxPro doesn't evaluate an expression following the OR connector if the expression preceding the OR evaluates to .T.

I describe the template handling of a Toolbar *class* of windows because this technique represents a good use of the READ clauses and solid programming practice. However, you can forget about how it works and concentrate on building interesting tools by thinking up new generic procedures your toolbar windows can run.

When you look at the procedures for my sample toolbar elements, you'll notice that the tool summoning the calculator uses the following code to imitate the keystrokes the user would type to bring the calculator into the group of available windows: `KEYBOARD "{F10}hl"`. If your version of SYSMENU gives the Calculator a different position than the Help pad, or a different hotkey on the pop-up menu, of course you should adjust this code to match. In fact, you can materially improve the performance of this tool by adding a menu shortcut for the Calculator, and KEYBOARDing that single key combination rather than the three steps required here.

FOXPRO MAC HACK TIP

You can add menu option equivalents for *all* your tools if you want, and even create a separate Tool menu pad that appears automatically when you're using a toolbar. Just add a `DO TOOLBAR.MPR` command to the section of Setup's #SECTION 2 that executes if WINDOW Toolbar has one or more children. Give the special Tool pop-up menu an option for every tool element that you use and RELEASE unnecessary BARs in the menu Cleanup, as you learned to do in Chapter 7 by checking WEXIST() for all the tool elements. If each Tool menu item has a related menu shortcut, you can perform any option programmatically by KEYBOARDing its shortcut.

A toolbar is a specialized way to collect and present generic objects. Once you understand the way windows interact in a FoxPro READ and learn to evaluate the window the user chooses while in the READ state, you'll think of additional ways to exploit this information.

Editing JOB.DBF in a Tailored Screen Set with Multiple READ Levels

You remember from Chapter 6 that the Job table caused much head-scratching as Andy and I worked on the data structures for AD*Vantage. This table also caused my most intensive and complex efforts when I designed the application's data entry modules.

The Job screen set's components evolved as I grappled with the special nature of the Inventory file. You remember that the AD*Vantage data model requires each Inventory record to have a one-to-one relationship with a record in another child file (Broadcast, Purchase, and others) that describes the special nature of these Inventory line items. The child tables may in turn have a one-to-many relationship with additional tables (Broadcast has child Spot records, an Insertion Order has multiple Insertions).

I decided to keep these changing entry requirements off the screen until the user opts to add or edit an Inventory record. This approach means there's less screen-refreshing as the user investigates the Job records, and also makes the screen much less confusing for the user.

The screen set presents the Job table data on the "outside" of a file folder, much as this information might be written or typed on a file folder containing all the records for a single job (see figure 10.19). The user-assigned Job number, unlike the system's internal primary key for the Job, appears "typed" on a "label" on the file folder's index tab. The set presents lists of Change Orders and Inventory records, like summary sheets pulled from the job folder, as participating BROWSEs below the GET window.

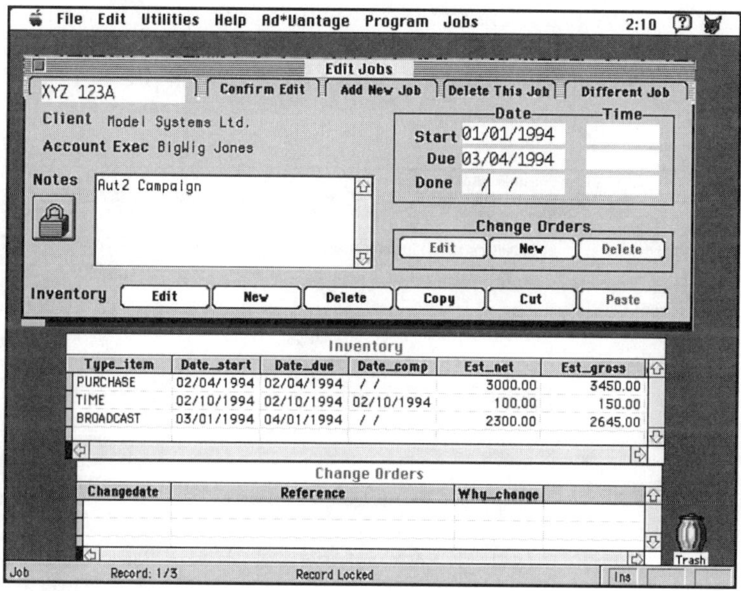

Figure 10.19 *The initial presentation of the Job screen set.*

Many of the elements of this screen are already familiar to you: The action buttons (to confirm edits, add Job records, and summon a modal BROWSE to pick a different Job) work exactly like the analogous buttons in screens you've investigated previously.

When you look at the Job screen in the Screen Builder, you'll see dummy GETs in front of these buttons masking their lower edge, so that the buttons appear more like file tabs. The buttons show their lower edge briefly when "pressed," as if this tab has been brought forward, and then a `SHOW GET m.dummy` brings the character GETs masking the edge forward again. The dummy GETs use the same WHEN .F. COLOR trick that you saw used for lookup text in the other screen set. The Job set contains two more such lookups for the names of the Job's account executive (derived from the Employee file) and the Job's client (derived from the Client-aliased version of the Company table). The labels for these lookups and the associated invisible buttons work the same way as the Department lookup you saw in the Employee screen.

When the user chooses to edit a Change Order or Inventory line for this job, either by pressing the appropriate button or by pressing Enter on a line in the Change Order or Inventory BROWSE, the child item appears in a nested READ MODAL for the edit.

If you choose to create a *new* Inventory line, the Job screen has to know which type of Inventory line to create because each type of Inventory line has a separate modal screen set with different business rules and GETs. You see the modal dialog visible in figure 10.20, which presents you with a list of available Inventory types.

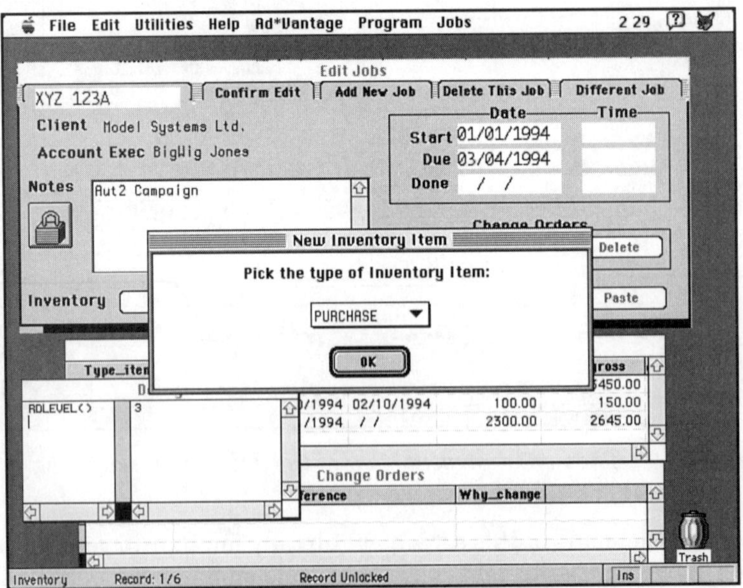

Figure 10.20 *The user must pick a type for a new Inventory item from a data-driven, generic dialog.*

FOXPRO MAC HACK TIP

If you set `_DEBUG = .T.` interactively, before running the AD*Vantage application, you get access to the Program pad visible in figure 10.19. Access the Debug window from the Program menu and type RDLEVEL() on the left side of the window, as shown in figure 10.20. When you are not engaged in an AD*Vantage application task, the Debug window evaluates RDLEVEL() as 1, because the application waits in the foundation READ. When you start to edit Jobs, you'll see the READ level move to 2. When you edit an Inventory or Change Order for the Job, the nested modal READ brings the level to 3. When you add an Inventory record, the modal dialog in which you choose an Inventory type brings the level to 3, also.

At no time, however, is this READ activity out of control. Recall that FoxPro allows a maximum of 5 READ levels. The modal dialog exits, bringing the level back to 2 before the code executes the nested Inventory line item screen set. Menu items that would nest additional READ activities are appropriately disabled while such a nested modal READ takes place.

The dialog that allows the user to choose an Inventory type receives its information from a SELECT statement that you saw briefly in Chapter 9:

```
SELECT aliasname, tablename ;
       FROM DBFS INTO ARRAY invtypes ;
       WHERE subform = "INVENTORY"
```

Driving the dialog from the DBFS table like this permits additional Inventory types to be added to the application without changing the Job screen set. The dialog itself is not custom-designed for this task; it's actually a special instance of the generic ASK.SCX that my template code uses to ask for a user log-on and a host of other standard application questions. The syntax for this instance of the dialog is:

```
m.type_item = Invtypes(1,1)
DO ASK.SPR WITH ;
        "Pick the type of Inventory Item:",;
         m.type_item, ;
         "FROM Invtypes FUNCTION '^' ", ;
         "New Inventory Item"
```

ASK.SCX notes the `FUNCTION '^'` syntax and creates the appropriate pop-up control GET.

See Also

- Source Disk:Library/ Template Code Folder:ASK.SCX

When you begin to investigate this and other aspects of the complex code that drives the Job screen set, you will probably open the Job screen in the Screen Builder and wonder where all the code went! The objects in this screen are very complicated, and I rarely need to edit the layout at the same time as I work on the underlying code. Instead of attaching the code to the screen, I've enclosed the command executing the .SPR in a *framing program*, JOBS.PRG, that includes all the code for the screen and is easier to open and modify without disturbing the graphical screen objects.

You'll find the framing program is very similar to MAIN.PRG: It initializes variables and sets up a menu and other conditions for the module, executes its .SPR as the module's wait state, performs cleanup routines and RETURNs. After its RETURN statement, JOBS.PRG concludes with a long list of local UDFs and procedures called only within this module. Although JOBS.PRG doesn't use the TEMPLATE.SCX procedures at all, the logic in its READ-handling and table-handling procedures is very similar to the template.

Because the Inventory editing procedures are so specialized, I segregated them in a separate program, INVEDIT.PRG, called by various procedures in JOBS.PRG. You'll find the call to ASK.PRG just described in INVEDIT.PRG.

See Also

- Source Disk:Seed App Copy: PRGS: JOBS.PRG
- Source Disk:SeedApp Copy: PRGS: INVEDIT.PRG

Whether the user opts to add a new Inventory record or picks an existing Inventory record to edit, INVEDIT.PRG checks the table name associated with this alias using the invtypes array and executes the appropriate .SPR for this type of Inventory item, using an indirect reference:

```
DO (m.whichdbf+".SPR")
```

CROSS-PLATFORM WARNING

I use the table name rather than the alias name to link the generated screen program (.SPR) to the Inventory item because all the table names in the AD*Vantage database are legal DOS file names. Aliases, by contrast, can be longer than 8 characters. If I port AD*Vantage to FoxPro DOS or Windows and used aliases, my .SPR-naming system wouldn't work.

FOXPRO MAC HACK TIP

Because I reference the .SPRs in the system indirectly, the Project Manager won't automatically include the appropriate screen sets. Use the IF .F. construct in INCLUDE.PRG to add explicit references to each .SPR:

```
DO Broadcst.SPR
DO InsOrder.SPR
DO Time.SPR
DO Purchase.SPR
```

I've also placed the statement `PUBLIC InvTypes(1)` in INCLUDE.PRG's IF .F. construct because this array is referenced in all the programs called by INVEDIT.PRG. (Because it's surrounded by an IF .F., the array doesn't actually get declared PUBLIC.) This reference in INCLUDE.PRG allows me to call InvTypes() without adding an EXTERNAL ARRAY advisory to the Project Manager in each program—besides INVEDIT.PRG—that uses the array. Without the PUBLIC declaration or an EXTERNAL ARRAY directive, the Project Manager thinks references to array elements may be calls to a UDF it can't locate.

All the .SPRs called by INVEDIT.PRG use the same confirm/cancel set of buttons with variables initialized in INVEDIT's setup code. Rather than performing the alteration of the inventory line upon confirm in the child READ, I've chosen to make these buttons Terminating, so they return control to INVEDIT. INVEDIT holds the code for all the child READs' confirm or cancel, as follows:

See Also

- Source Disk:Seed App Copy: INCLUDE.PRG

```
IF m.confirm = "Cancel"
   IF m.invadd AND ;
      NOT EMPTY(m.whichsub) AND ;
      SEEK(m.itemkey,m.whichsub)
      * they added child records
      * and then cancelled the whole
      * inventory line add
      SELECT (m.whichsub)
      DELETE WHILE &foreignkey = m.itemkey
   ENDIF
```

```
ELSE
   IF m.invadd
      m.job_key = Job.key
      INSERT INTO Inventory FROM MEMVAR
      SELECT Inventory
      REPLACE key WITH CreateID()
      m.invent_key = key
      m.key = m.itemkey
      INSERT INTO (m.type_item) FROM MEMVAR
   ELSE
      SELECT (m.type_item)
      m.key = key
      GATHER MEMVAR MEMO
      SELECT Inventory
      m.key = key
      GATHER MEMVAR MEMO
   ENDIF
   SHOW WINDOW ("Inventory") REFRESH SAME
ENDIF
```

If the edit or add is confirmed, you'll notice several lines that set `m.key = key`. All the tables in the AD*Vantage database use the field name `key` for their primary key field. I've used the repeating field name to my benefit in the template code in order to help determine the parent key value for new child table records, but repeating field names also cause problems. In INVEDIT, I'm forced to resynchronize key values for different tables just before I alter table records because a previous SCATTER MEMVAR may have overwritten the key value with a different m.key from another table.

FOXPRO MAC HACK TIP

When I have a choice, I avoid repeating field names, and I recommend that you do the same. You have other ways to determine key field values in a database application, many of which I use in the template and JOBS.PRG code. You can restrict the parent key to a particular field position in the table structure, you can use a repeating field name with a unique identifier for each table appended to it, or you can store the key field name in a table such as DBFS and look up the name when you need it.

In AD*Vantage, repeating names both in the key fields and elsewhere caused numerous problems, but I didn't change the field names. There *are* situations in which your table structures are set by

> forces beyond your control, and I wanted you to see that you can surmount this obstacle with a little extra code if necessary. For example, the Inventory child tables had memofields with the name `notes`. When I used the SCATTER MEMVAR MEMO command, `m.notes` conflicted with the memory variable editing the Job table memo field with the same name. Because the child tables are edited in a separate nested READ, I solved this problem by declaring `m.notes` PRIVATE in INVEDIT, hiding the Job table's `m.notes` memory variable while the child table edit proceeded.

The child edits for each type of Inventory lines are little more than prototypes as provided on your disk. They even open the READ with a WAIT WINDOW NOWAIT announcing to the user that the screens are not in their final form. Half-finished screens are perfectly appropriate at this stage of application development, especially because these screens require highly specialized validation to calculate the final values in the Inventory record from each type of Inventory data. You need the user's help to finish writing these screens!

You'll learn more about validation and other ways to refine these screens in the next chapter, and you should already have ideas for improving them from what you've learned so far. For example, you could split the Inventory header information from the subsidiary fields derived from Broadcast and the other child tables, affording the user a clearer view of the database information and affording yourself a generic Inventory .SCX that you could use in *each* of the child screen sets.

However rudimentary the child screen sets still are, the Job screen set includes other sophisticated features worthy of comment here. Some of these features are a direct result of previous requests from users—you get most of your good design ideas that way, if you listen carefully.

While I was working on the screen set, Andy was working on Chapter 3 and comparing the features of other Macintosh DBMSs such as Filemaker Pro and 4th Dimension to FoxPro for Macintosh. He particularly liked one capability he felt was lacking in FoxPro: the capability to cut and paste child records between one parent and another. Andy asked, "Hey Lisa, can we add this feature to the Job screen set?"

There's nothing like a challenge from a rival database system to get me to work (I suspect Andy knows this), so of course the answer had to be "yes." The results are the buttons on the Job screen that allow you to Cut, Copy, and Paste Inventory records as you move between Job records. I added Job menu options for these features, too, so you could use them when you were in the Job BROWSE as well as the screen. Implementing this requirement proved possible with the help of arrays to hold the contents of the child records. Each procedure has to keep track of possible multiple children for an Inventory line, without directly referencing the tables in any way, to fulfill the objective of keeping the Job screen independent of the Inventory child table structure and contents. For example, the procedure to cut an Inventory line from an existing record uses the following code:

```
PROCEDURE InvCut
PRIVATE m.oldselect, m.thiskey, m.thisfield
m.oldselect = SELECT()
SELECT SubTypes
LOCATE FOR Subform = Inventory.Type_Item
IF FOUND()
   m.thiskey = EVAL(ALLTRIM(Subform)+".Key")
   m.thisfield = FIELD(2,ALLTRIM(Aliasname))
   SELECT * FROM (ALLTRIM(Aliasname)) ;
            INTO ARRAY SubItems ;
            WHERE &thisfield = m.thiskey
   IF _TALLY # 0
      SELECT (ALLTRIM(SubTypes.Aliasname))
      SEEK m.thiskey
      DELETE WHILE &thisfield = m.thiskey
   ELSE
      DIME SubItems(1,1)
   ENDIF
ELSE
   DIME SubItems(1,1)
ENDIF
SELECT (ALLTRIM(Inventory.Type_Item))
SCATTER MEMO TO PasteItem
DELETE
SELECT Inventory
SCATTER MEMO TO PasteInv
DELETE
SELECT (m.oldselect)
SHOW WINDOW "Inventory" SAME REFRESH
IF m.joblock
   SHOW GET m.invact, 6 ENABLE
ENDIF
RETURN
```

(You'll find all the relevant procedures in JOBS.PRG.)

Part of the challenge in this requirement was figuring out exactly when each feature was appropriate. If you refer back to figure 10.19, you'll see that the Paste button is disabled. In imitation of the Edit menu pad Paste option, I disable this button and the corresponding menu bar when the array that represents my "Inventory clipboard" has no contents. Paste and Cut must also be unavailable when the current Job record isn't locked, while the Copy option is appropriate even for an unlocked record. You'll find these conditions reflected in the menu options' SKIP FOR clauses as well as the button enabling and disabling code in JOBS.PRG.

> **FOXPRO MAC HACK TIP**
>
> Although I used SKIP FOR clauses on the menu options, this situation is a good candidate for SET SKIP OF <menu element> commands instead. As you learned in Chapter 7, these menu commands aren't dynamic like the SKIP FOR clauses on DEFINE <menu element> commands, but my code already has to ENABLE and DISABLE buttons explicitly in many places. I may as well add the SET SKIP menu commands in the same routines that handle the buttons.

As I found myself paying extra attention to the locked or unlocked state of the Job record, I decided some special visual clue might be helpful to the user because fields may dim for other reasons than an unlocked state. The result is the picture of a padlock that you see in figure 10.19. The image is actually a picture button with another WHEN .F. clause (this GET doesn't do anything but provide a picture). Although the Screen Builder only permits you to associate one picture with each button, the SHOW GET command permits you to associate *three* pictures to a button: one for its ENABLEd state, one for its depressed state, and one for its DISABLEd state. I use the following command in the READ WHEN clause to associate a second picture for the DISABLEd state of this button:

```
SHOW GET m.secure,1 ;
   PROMPT "secur02b.pct,,secur02a.pct"
```

An extra comma in the command holds the place for the depressed-state picture, since I don't need to assign a picture to that state.

Now my SHOW clause can SHOW the button DISABLEd to exhibit an alternative picture (an unlocked padlock), or SHOW the button ENABLEd to exhibit the picture that you see in the figure.

FOXPRO MAC HACK TIP

If you need to display pictures dynamically, you may need to display more pictures than the three states of a button allow. I have an alternative trick that allows you to place as many different pictures in the same location as you like. Use a regular SAY instead of the picture tool to place and size the picture. Mark this SAY Refresh in the SAY/GET dialog and use an indirect reference to a filename, followed by the word BITMAP (and any additional clauses) as the SAY expression! For example, type (m.pictfile) BITMAP in the SAY expression text box.

Initialize the variable to the name of an appropriate file (with a line of code such as m.pictfile = "INFO.PCT") in the Setup of the screen. Whenever you have to change the picture, issue a SHOW GETS. Have the SHOW clause change the value of m.pictfile; the code automatically generated to Refresh the SAY will do the rest!

As an additional enhancement, I mentioned earlier that the Job screen set maintains tighter control over the initial participating BROWSE attributes than you saw in the Address Book screen. The secret is a WINDOW clause on each BROWSE, naming a window that you design in the Screen Builder. These additional windows in the Job screen set are completely empty; they have a #WCLAUSES directive to permit them to GROW (a useful attribute for BROWSE windows, not permitted for GET windows, and therefore not available directly in the Screen Builder). You size them the way you'd like the BROWSE to look, and you give each one an explicit name, so that you can use the name in the BROWSE WINDOW clause. I created one of these *attribute windows* for the Inventory and Change Order participating BROWSEs, and used a standard window I name GenBrow for the Job-picking modal BROWSE.

As you see in figure 10.21, you can include these attribute windows in the Project Manager's screen set record for the Job module and arrange the windows with the Job screen as you would any other window. DEACTIVATE these attribute windows in the READ WHEN clause, so they don't accidentally show up during the READ. When you issue the BROWSEs with the WINDOW clause, you see the BROWSEs properly positioned and sized according to the attributes of the DEFINEd WINDOW you designated for it.

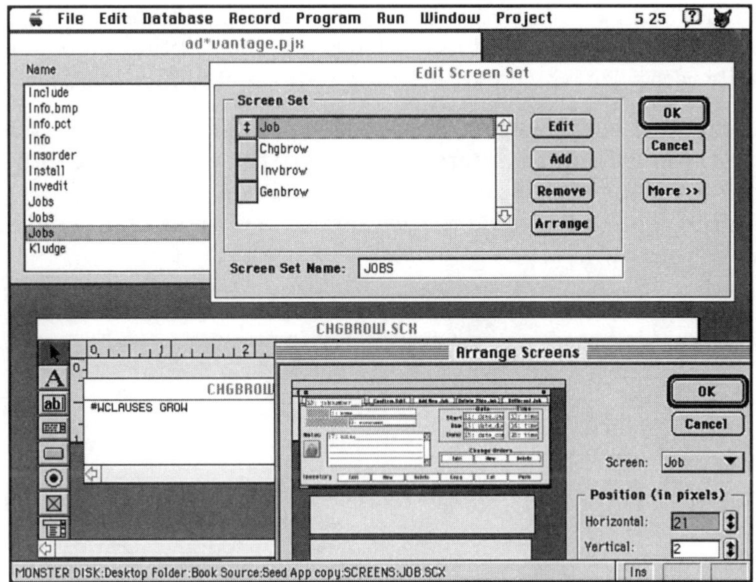

Figure 10.21 *Attribute windows in a screen set give you more control over the appearance of BROWSEs in a screen set.*

Chapter Wrap Up

JOBS.PRG, INVEDIT.PRG, and the Jobs screen set deserve your careful study. Although you have progressed from basic READ-handling techniques to some very sophisticated GET-and-window juggling in this chapter, you need practice before you'll have a feel for the flow of READs.

I can only compare this difficulty with learning physics—or at least it compares with the difficulties I had learning physics! You receive a series of word problems, and you have to match these problems with a set of equations that you've learned should be applied in different situations. The problem is that all the problems and the equations use the same set of variables in different combinations. How do you figure out which equation applies to which problem?

Data entry requirements are like the word problems you had in physics, and the READ clauses, GET clauses, and window-handling techniques are the uniform components that you use to solve *all* the problems. By repetition and example, you learn to see patterns in the solutions, and you gradually recognize which pattern fits a new set of requirements.

In this chapter, you've walked through some complex screen sets that use the READ components in different combinations and in some depth. You haven't seen every possible combination, but I hope you've gotten a good sense of the depth, giving you the confidence to work on additional combinations of your own.

11

ASSURE COMFORT FOR DEVELOPERS AND USERS: CROSS-PLATFORM USABILITY AND THOUGHTFUL DESIGN

by
Lisa Slater

This chapter considers a host of underlying programming issues with critical implications for application design in FoxPro for Macintosh.

When you look at the section titles herein, you may think they're entirely unrelated. In FoxPro, however, no issue or command stands entirely on its own. Some people say learning the single BROWSE command involves consideration of over 50 percent of the FoxPro language!

The best solution to any FoxPro problem requires considering that problem *in its wider FoxPro and Macintosh perspective*. Typically, you solve a problem by thinking about its relationship to:

- Efficient use of FoxPro syntax. Because many commands perform the same job with minor variations, which variation works best in your case?
- Effective use of FoxPro design tools. Are you *avoiding* code as much as possible? Besides limiting the potential for programming errors, this tactic gives FoxPro and the Project Manager a chance to coordinate the elements of your application as they were designed to do.
- Anticipation of difficulties on different hardware configurations and platforms. How flexible is your solution when faced with different environments?
- Fulfillment of users' interface expectations. Are you giving the application its best chance to succeed by designing behavior that your users understand and enjoy and to which they will respond appropriately?

All these criteria boil down to one rapid-development goal: *maximum benefit for minimum effort.*

In pursuit of this goal, you really can't separate coding problems from underlying interface design assumptions, just as you can't properly consider the graphical design tools without considering their supporting code generators.

I'm not going to be able to *remove* every obstacle you encounter on the road to a specific application objective. Think of this chapter as a series of signposts to help you *surmount* some of the obstacles in your path.

Considering Generic Object Design

As you try to streamline your work and create results with less effort, you bring all your previous experience to bear on each new dilemma. Have you solved a similar problem before, and can you build on work already performed? Is there a system function or third-party tool that does the job *without* additional work on your part? If not, when you invent a new solution, how generic and re-usable is your solution? How do you avoid the same work next time?

Throughout your investigation of the template code for this book, you've seen generic solutions in action. These solutions are embodied in the following:

- Menu options that pass messages instead of running code directly
- Dialogs that take cues from their environment
- Data-driven code that flexes to incorporate new options or unknown table structures

Your goal is to develop standards for these solutions that require little or no modification to their code each time you use them.

In this section, you take a closer look at the process of developing your library of standard objects and procedures, using some of my template dialogs as examples.

Code Standards for Generic Dialogs and Procedures

Start with the About screen from the template code. You can edit this screen through the AD*Vantage model project. Remember that all projects that use this screen will read the same copy of APPABOUT.SCX for their information, so any change you make to the dialog ripples through all your work. Alternatively, you can MODIFY the SCREEN by opening it directly in its home folder.

See Also

- Source Disk:Library/ Template Code Folder: APPABOUT. SCX
- Source Disk:Library/ Template Code Folder: APPABOUT. PRG

As figure 11.1 shows, the About dialog is very simple in layout. The only formatting or other adjustment to the screen objects not shown in the figure is formatting for the SAYs that hold the information.

CROSS-PLATFORM WARNING

I've used `@TI` formatting for these SAYs to center them. You'll find that this formatting doesn't work properly on the DOS platform, and it also doesn't work with monospaced fonts on the Window platform. For generic objects' visual characteristics, you often have to build in separate attributes to get the best effect on each platform. Refer to the section on cross-platform code later in this chapter, and the discussion of #WCLAUSES in this section for some useful examples.

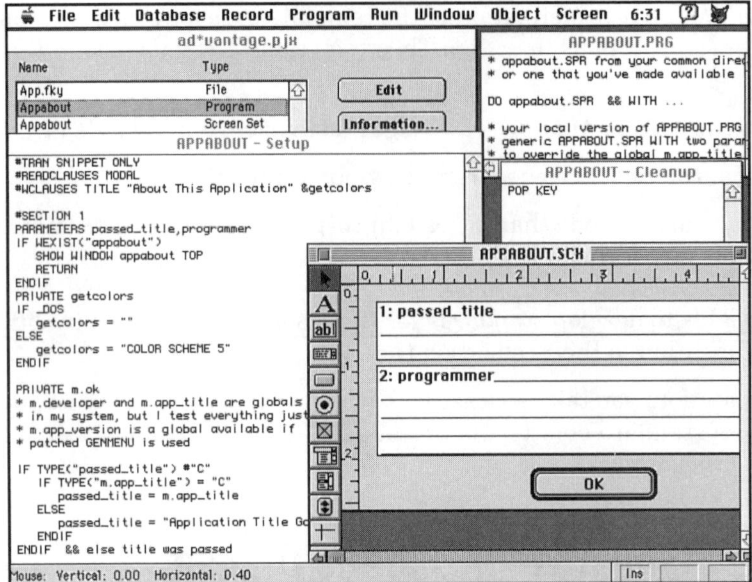

Figure 11.1 *Anatomy of a generic dialog: do almost all the work in Setup code.*

The .SCX takes care of all customization for each instance or appearance of this dialog's layout in its Setup snippet, as follows:

```
#TRAN SNIPPET ONLY
#READCLAUSES MODAL
#WCLAUSES  &getclauses
```

The Setup begins with three generator directives. The instruction #TRAN SNIPPET ONLY tells the cross-platform Transporter program not to make any cosmetic changes while synchronizing code differences for existing objects when I port the dialog back and forth between platforms. The #READCLAUSES directive, which you've seen in earlier chapters, tells GENSCRN to attach the MODAL clause to the READ command.

If I didn't use #READCLAUSES, I'd have to edit every appearance of this dialog in every project to add the MODAL keyword to its Screen Set options. *You don't want generic objects to depend on the Project Manager or the .PJX file for their constant attributes.* Each appearance of the object in a project file is an instance of the object; you should never have to tell an instance about basic behavior it should inherit from the master object.

Because of this rule, I always call generic screens with the DO <procedure> syntax rather than as a UDF:

```
err_ask = "RETRY "
DO ASK.SPR WITH ;
    "The printer is not ready; "+;
    "RETRY or CANCEL?",;
     err_ask,"@M  RETRY, CANCEL"
* rather than
err_ask = ;
   ASK("The printer is not ready; "+ ;
        "RETRY or CANCEL?",;
        "RETRY", "@M RETRY,CANCEL")
```

To use a screen file as a UDF requires GENSCRN to use a .PRG extension for the generated output of the .SCX file. I'd have to specify this .PRG extension for each instance of each generic dialog for each project.

FOXPRO MAC HACK TIP

If you use the GENSCRNX pre- and post-processor for GENSCRN, which I described briefly in the last chapter, you can use a GENSCRNX directive to specify a .PRG extension. After you attach these instructions *to the .SCX file*, where it works for every instance of the dialog, I will have no further objections to the UDF syntax.

Following the #READCLAUSES directive, you see a macro expression, `getclauses`, in the #WCLAUSES directive. This variable, which receives its value later in the Setup code, handles the TITLE and COLOR SCHEME clauses for the dialog. (Don't get confused because I seem to be assigning the variable a value after I use it. The #WCLAUSES instructions aren't used until GENSCRN DEFINEs the WINDOW—*after* #SECTION 1 of the Setup code.)

As you will see in the section on FoxPro color use in Chapter 14, dialogs use COLOR SCHEME 5 in FoxPro by default. I use the default color schemes for each type of system object to ensure color consistency throughout the application.

However, I specify User Window type (by default COLOR SCHEME 1) rather than Dialog in the Screen Builder because the unorthodox Dialog-type window settings in the Screen Layout Window Style dialog don't work as well on the Macintosh. Among other problems, the close box and "moveable" attributes force a title bar on the dialog. The User Window setting lets you specify window attributes more accurately (see figures 11.2 and 11.3). Using the #WCLAUSES directive, I override the default color scheme for a User Window definition with an explicit COLOR SCHEME 5 clause befitting a dialog.

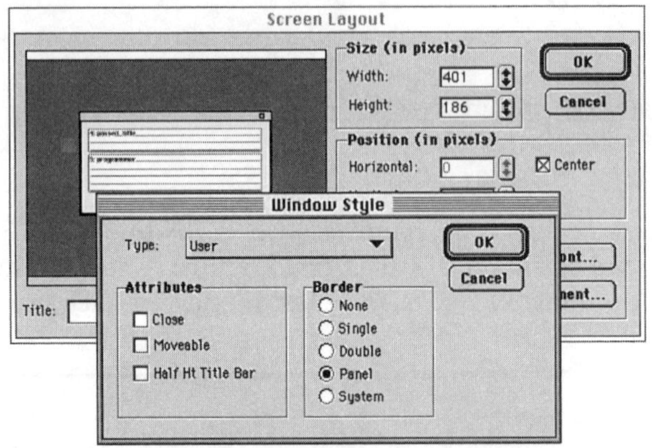

Figure 11.2 *The Window Style dialog's User type lets you pick appropriate attributes for a Macintosh dialog...*

You'd probably expect an explicit `#WCLAUSES COLOR SCHEME 5` in this situation. In fact, that's the way I originally wrote this code. Unfortunately, in the DOS version of the product, the User Window type generates a COLOR SCHEME clause automatically, and two COLOR SCHEME clauses on the window definition cause an error. Since the Dialog type attributes specified in the DOS Screen Builder don't clash with any DOS interface standards for dialogs, I use Dialog type in DOS and User type (with explicit attributes and SCHEME) in Windows and on the Macintosh.

Similarly, the dialog should have a title in Windows and DOS, but a title of any type, like close box, creates a title bar on a Macintosh window. That's why `getclauses` makes sure there is *no* TITLE clause on the dialog's window definition on the Mac platform. (Isn't cross-platform development fun?)

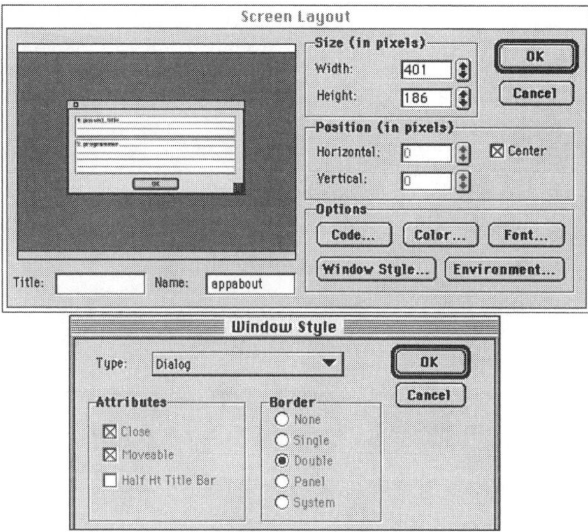

Figure 11.3 *... while the Dialog style requires an inappropriate title bar because of the close box (note the dimmed radio buttons, fixing the window attributes for this type).*

> **FOXPRO MAC HACK TIP**
>
> Even a null string in the TITLE clause will force the title bar; that's why I don't use #ITSEXPRESSION and an expression in the Screen Layout Title text box for this requirement. I also simply prefer to type the title in Setup, where I can see its full length easily, rather than using the cramped text box in the Screen Layout dialog—so I sometimes use `#WCLAUSES TITLE <string>` even when the title is a constant.

After the directives, #SECTION 1 of the real Setup code begins with a PARAMETERS statement. Next, a critical WEXIST( ) checks only for an item that appears on the Macintosh Apple menu using FoxPro's SET APLABOUT command. The Apple menu isn't subject to a SKIP FOR RDLEVEL( ) check, like other menu options on FoxPro's SYSMENU. It also doesn't become unavailable when you use the READ MODAL statement, unlike other menu options on FoxPro's SYSMENU.

By checking to see if the dialog window already exists, I prevent the user using the About option repeatedly and nesting READ statements beyond my program's control:

```
#SECTION 1
PARAMETERS passed_title,programmer
IF WEXIST("appabout")
   SHOW WINDOW appabout TOP
   * don't go on to issue the GETs and READ!
   RETURN
ENDIF
```

CROSS-PLATFORM WARNING

Cross-platform FoxPro developers have never faced this situation before. You may not use my About system, but whatever dialog or other program you attach to the Apple About feature will have a similar problem. You *must* include code that ensures appropriate modality *within the code called by your About object* because your normal event-handling strategy will not work.

Simply put, the problem is this: ON APLABOUT, the command that permits Fox programmers to change the native Apple About feature, does not allow a SKIP FOR clause. It probably should!

The Setup code continues, assigning a value to the `getclauses` variable, and performing checks for each outside variable required by the dialog. If a parameter or outside value hasn't been passed, or isn't available in the environment, I assign a default value:

```
PRIVATE getclauses
IF _DOS
   getclauses = ""
ELSE
   getclauses = "COLOR SCHEME 5"
ENDIF
IF NOT _MAC
   getclauses = getclauses + ;
      "TITLE 'About This Application'"
ENDIF
PRIVATE m.ok
```

```
IF TYPE("passed_title") #"C"
   IF TYPE("m.app_title") = "C"
      passed_title = m.app_title
   ELSE
      passed_title = ;
          "Application Title Goes Here"
   ENDIF
ENDIF  && else title was passed

IF TYPE("programmer") # "C"
   IF TYPE("m.developer") = "C"
      programmer = IIF(_DOS,"(C) ","©  ")
      programmer = ;
         programmer + m.developer + ;
         CHR(13)+CHR(13)+"All rights reserved."
   ELSE
      programmer = ;
         "Programmer's Name and Copyright"+ ;
         CHR(13)+"Goes Here"

   ENDIF
* else special programmer string was passed
ENDIF

IF TYPE("m.app_version") = "C"
    passed_title = passed_title + ;
                CHR(13)+ ;
                "Version "+m.app_version
ENDIF

PUSH KEY CLEAR
```

You have already seen the `m.developer` and `m.app_title` variables at work in the template code. They're derived from INCLUDE.PRG, where you can customize them for each application, but where they receive default values if you forget to customize them. It's highly unlikely that these global variables will *not* have default values by the time these dialogs use them, but I check anyway. After all, the dialogs should be (and are) sturdy enough to be taken out of the template framework and used in an entirely different system.

The `m.app_version` variable, on the other hand, often doesn't exist. It's a version stamp, only created if the application uses my patched version of GENMENU. Later in the chapter, you'll see how this trick works and what difference it makes to the dialog's appearance. Again, the dialog operates smoothly whether it finds this variable in the environment or not.

The final line of the Setup code uses the `PUSH KEY CLEAR` command to avoid any ON KEY LABEL key-mapping in the calling program to inappropriately affect this dialog. The Cleanup code contains a single line, `POP KEY`, restoring those key assignments, if any, from the stack.

The flexibility of the About option is further enhanced by a calling program, APPABOUT.PRG. This "frame" exists in the Library/Template Code folder and consists of the single line DO APPABOUT.SPR. You can override the library version with a local APPABOUT.PRG for any application that needs a custom approach to the About feature, or simply to specify APPABOUT.SPR's optional parameters with application-specific strings that depart from the default m.developer and m.app_title versions.

This menu option belongs to the Utilities menu, on the Help pop-up menu, by default. However, the dynamic behavior of the menu object itself provides yet another level of flexibility. The option that calls APPABOUT.PRG is RELEASEd by its menu cleanup on the Macintosh platform because the template's MAIN.PRG puts the About option on the Macintosh-native Apple menu instead, where it belongs, using the following code:

```
* from PROCEDURE SaveSets in MAIN.PRG
IF _MAC
   *...
   Savesets(13,1) = ;
                 "SET APLABOUT "+ ;
                  SET("APLABOUT")
   Savesets(13,2) = ;
                 [SET APLABOUT PROMPT "]+;
                  SET("APLABOUT",1)+["]
   SET APLABOUT ENABLED
   SET APLABOUT PROMPT ;
        "About "+IIF(EMPTY(m.app_title), ;
        "this application... ",m.app_title+"...")
   *...
   Savesets(15,1) = "ON APLABOUT "+ON("APLABOUT")
   ON APLABOUT DO appabout
ENDIF
```

Fail-Safe Techniques for Generic Dialogs and Procedures

As you review the last code sample, notice that I check for the existence of `m.app_title` even within the template code, just in case, substituting a default phrase if the developer has forgotten to edit this item in INCLUDE.PRG or isn't using a properly written INCLUDE.PRG with the template. APPSETUP generates a default INCLUDE.PRG with default strings for these variables, so this failure is very unlikely, but I still check. *Every generic object or procedure that depends on outer elements should fall back on a second approach when the tie-in to the outer element somehow fails.* The extra time the program spends executing this code is inconsequential in comparison to the extra grace the code adds.

Yes, it's more work to make a dialog or procedure handle errors gracefully and respond dynamically to different situations, but the payback for the time you spend in the design should be apparent to you: neither this code nor the .SCX requires adjustment for any FoxPro system after you think it through *once*, properly and thoroughly.

In some situations, assigning a default value to a parameter that hasn't been passed, or correcting any other error condition and moving forward with the business of the dialog (or object-procedure) isn't the right approach. Instead, an object can set an error flag or RETURN an error code to indicate that it was improperly called. The object still handles its own errors, rather than relying on your standard error handler, because the program (or the programmer) will get more specific and helpful feedback from the object on what went wrong. For example:

```
IF TYPE("my_param") # "N" OR ABS(my_param) # my_param
  m.got_error = .T.
  IF TYPE("n,show_err") = "L" AND m.show_err
     * you could use the _DEBUG variable
     * that I use to enable the Program
     * bar on the menu as your m.show_err test
     WAIT WINDOW ;
      "You must pass a positive number "+ ;
      "as the second parameter!"
  ENDIF
ENDIF
IF FCOUNT( ) < 5
  m.got_error = .T.
  IF TYPE("n,show_err") = "L" AND m.show_err
     WAIT WINDOW ;
```

```
      "You can't use this function " + ;
      "with less than 5 fields in the table!"
  ENDIF
ENDIF
IF m.goterror
   RETURN .F. && or check m.got_error,
              && a global variable, in
              && the calling program —
              && RETURN a more specific
              && error string and store
              && the results if you like
ENDIF
```

Each dialog knows its requirements and expresses them; your standard error handler doesn't maintain information of this nature about every object in your system.

When you think about it, you've experienced the difference between these two types of error handling in FoxPro when you misuse a system function. In some cases, you get a generic failure error from the general FoxPro error handler, and in others you find out much more specifically what you did wrong (see figures 11.4 and 11.5). Which kind of error message do you prefer?

> **FOXPRO MAC HACK TIP**
>
> Think of your error handling techniques as part of your technical documentation or help system. Generic dialogs must be more than capable and ingenious. For programmers to use them, the dialogs must also be forgiving of mistakes and easy to understand as programming objects, just as your general interface must have those characteristics for users. You should provide yourself with as much help as possible in this manner, and you should also look ahead to your work's use by other people. These other programmers may be members of your own programming team or developers who need to maintain your programs as VARs.
>
> I often see large programming teams in which every member of the staff has his or her own set of supposedly "re-usable" objects because nobody knows how to use anybody else's objects. Rapid-development procedures require a more sensible approach.

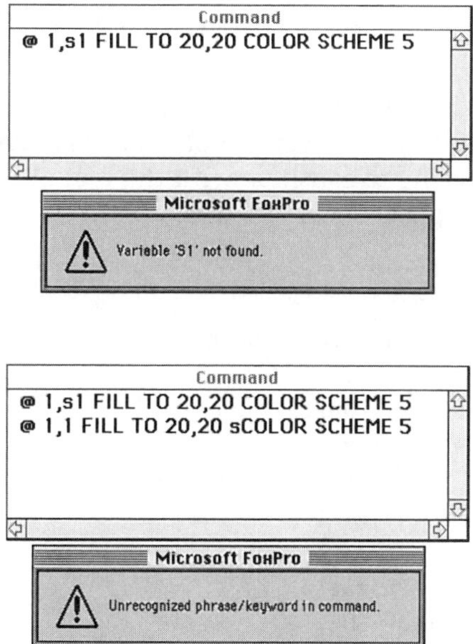
Command
@ 1,s1 FILL TO 20,20 COLOR SCHEME 5
Microsoft FoxPro
Variable 'S1' not found.
Command
@ 1,s1 FILL TO 20,20 COLOR SCHEME 5
@ 1,1 FILL TO 20,20 sCOLOR SCHEME 5
Microsoft FoxPro
Unrecognized phrase/keyword in command.

Figures 11.4 and 11.5 *Sometimes FoxPro's error messages are more helpful than others. Make your generic dialogs and procedures give the most intelligent error messages they can.*

Visual Clues in Standard Dialogs

Turning to additional template dialogs to look at other examples of generic dialog design, you'll find a trio of alerts (INFO.SCX, WARNING.SCX, and YESNO.SCX) in the Library/Template Code directory.

All three dialogs follow a similar strategy. They receive passed values for the strings in the dialog. YESNO.SCX receives a default value for its "yes" and "no" buttons as well. Each dialog creates default strings if it doesn't receive appropriate parameters.

On the Macintosh platform, the dialogs check to see if the FOXTOOLS library is loaded. You may recall that the template Setup procedures load this library automatically on the Mac, but its loading is not critical to the workings of the application as a whole. The library may have failed to load (in which case the user got an error notice, but the application didn't

QUIT), or you may have RELEASEd it in Section 2 of the INCLUDE.PRG, because you want to save memory.

If the dialogs find FOXTOOLS available, each dialog uses the FxAlert( ) library function to call the appropriate Mac toolbox alert and then RETURN without bothering to continue with the rest of the screen set. The code (in the Setup snippet) looks like this:

```
* From the YESNO.SCX Setup
IF _MAC
   * using the getclauses trick you've
   * already seen, the Mac dialog
   * doesn't have a title, while the
   * other platforms' dialogs do —
   * so I place the title information
   * into the body of the dialog on the
   * Mac platform:
   m.question = ALLTRIM(m.title) ;
                + CHR(13)+CHR(13)+ ;
                ALLTRIM(m.question)
   IF "FOXTOOLS" $ UPPER(SET("LIBRARY",1))
      IF m.default
         m.answerbutton = ;
          FxAlert(2,265,0,0,m.question)
         m.default = ;
           IIF(m.answerbutton = 1, .T., .F.)
      ELSE
         m.answerbutton = ;
          FxAlert(2,266,0,0,m.question)
         m.default = ;
          IIF(m.answerbutton = 1, .F., .T.)
      ENDIF
      RETURN m.default
   ENDIF
ENDIF  && FoxTools not loaded, or not Mac —
       && READ continues here...
```

You'll find the FxAlert( ) function and the rest of the FOXTOOLS functions documented in a text file in the Goodies:Misc Folder of your FoxPro installation files.

In figure 11.6, you can see that the dialog layout and design I use when FoxTools isn't loaded and the .SPR runs its normal course. The appearance is strikingly similar to the native alert, also showing in the figure. (Remember that the Screen Builder doesn't show the actual colors of the window; the Layout window isn't aware that my code overrides the default color scheme for a User defined window.) The FoxPro version even sounds an alert tone that matches the standard Mac alert sound.

See Also

- FoxPro Home Directory: Goodies: Misc:FoxTools Readme
- Table 12.3, "FxAlert() function," Chapter 12

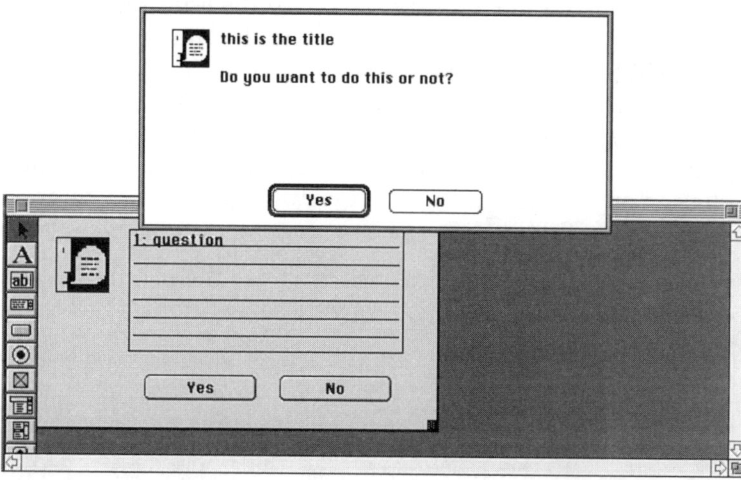

Figure 11.6 *The FxAlert( ) shows with the Screen Builder layout for its FoxPro alert equivalent.*

The icon *should* look exactly like the standard picture you see in the FoxTools version—it's a copy of the same picture! Whenever possible, you should use the images with which people are familiar from the Macintosh environment and other programs.

FOXPRO MAC HACK TIP

Using standard pictures makes your programs easier to maintain with less documentation because your users easily understand your visual clues. Equally significant, this practice also decreases your development time. *Creating visual elements from scratch is the single biggest time-sink in FoxPro development*, and in every other form of GUI development I've encountered.

See Also

- "Modifying the GETFILE Dialog Using ResEdit," Chapter 12

Where do you find these picture resources? They exist in the *resource fork* of the various applications you use on the Macintosh. In the case of the picture you see in the figure, you can find it in the System file itself. If you've never investigated Macintosh resources using ResEdit, Apple's resource-editing utility, this section gives you a simple and painless introduction to the technique.

Make a copy of the System file, or the FoxPro executable application file, or any other file you decide to investigate with ResEdit. Launch ResEdit and Open the *copy* of the file. The file opens to the window you see in the background of figure 11.7. There are many different types of resources, many of which have their own associated ResEdit editor. You'll find a number of icon-type resources in the file; double-clicking on any one of them opens the list of pictures it contains in a second window. When you double-click on one of the pictures, that picture opens in an editor, shown in the foreground of figure 11.7.

Your FoxPro for Macintosh applications can't use the pictures in applications' resource forks directly, so you copy these pictures and save them to separate PICT files on disk.

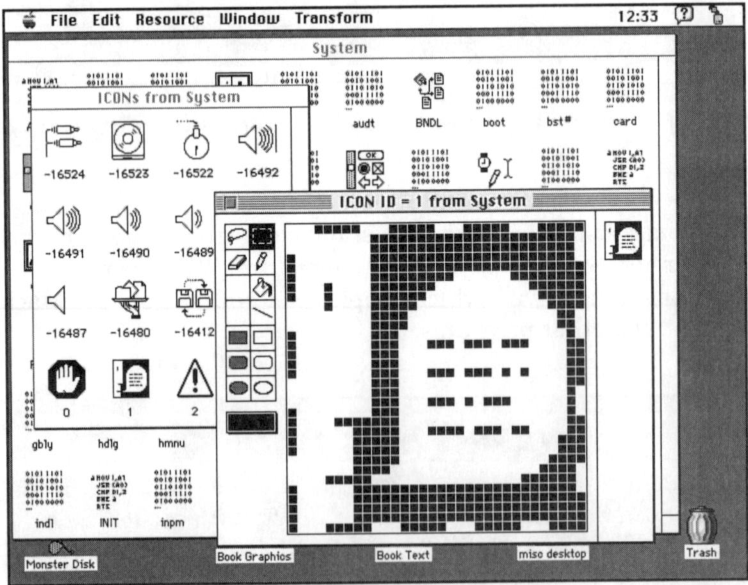

Figure 11.7 *Open a copy of the System file in ResEdit and find the picture you want to use in FoxPro.*

Use the Edit menu's Select All and Copy options to place a copy of the picture on the Macintosh Clipboard. Now you can open a drawing program, such as MacDraw, Paste the contents of the clipboard to a document there, and Save the document As a PICT-type file.

The FOXTOOLS library has a special function, Pict2File( ), that you can use instead of ResEdit to extract picture resources from application resource forks to separate PICT files. This function appears to be limited to three types of icon resources of the many types of icon resources available. If you choose to use Pict2File( ), here's an example of the syntax because the Foxtools Readme file example isn't very clear:

```
=pict2file;
  ("my disk:temp:system copy", ;
   "ICN#", -3996,"my disk:apps:app.pct")
```

The first argument is the name of the file from which you're extracting the resource. Notice that this syntax requires the native Macintosh method of referring to a file's location; you can't use FoxPro-style backslashes or your SET VOLUME-shorthand to a path. If you're not sure what the actual Macintosh notation for a file name is because you're using the result of a FoxPro function such as GETFILE( ) to obtain the file name, use `SYS(2027, <file name>)` to get its fully qualified Mac name.

The second argument is the resource type containing the picture you want. Pict2file( )'s third argument is the *resource number*, within the specified type, for the picture you want to copy to a file. Since you need to use ResEdit to obtain this number in the first place, I can't see the advantage to using Pict2file( ) to grab the copy, rather than copying the image directly in ResEdit.

Once you have the PICT file on disk, you can use this separate file as a graphical element in the Screen Builder, either as the prompt on a Picture Button or as Picture, as you see in figure 11.8.

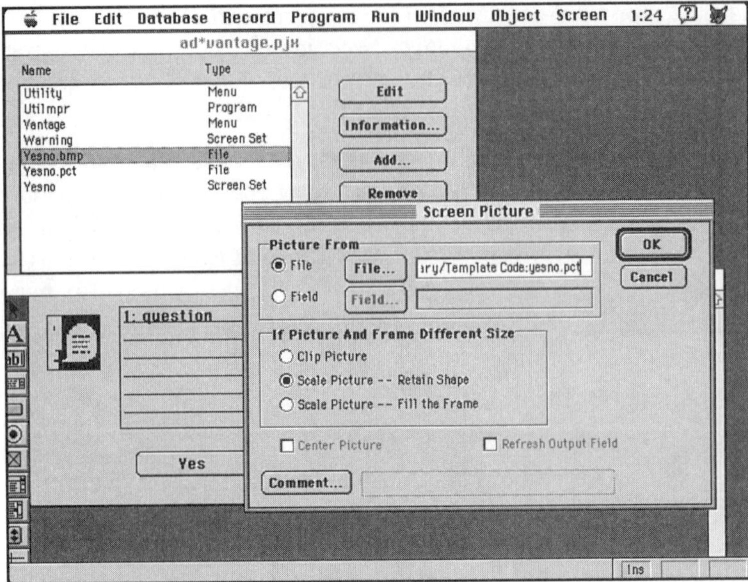

Figure 11.8 *FoxPro for Macintosh can use PICT-type files and Windows-style Bitmaps in the Screen Builder.*

CROSS-PLATFORM WARNING

The open AD*Vantage project file in figure 11.8 shows you that the PICT-type file I used in this dialog (YESNO.PCT) has a matching Microsoft Windows-style Bitmap file (YESNO.BMP). FoxPro for Macintosh can display either PICTs or Bitmaps; the native PICT format displays slightly faster, so I use it when it's available. FoxPro for Windows, however, can't use the PICT. FoxPro ships with a utility (Pict To Bmp) to convert the Macintosh format for use in FoxPro for Windows, but this utility is very limited in the size and complexity of the PICTs it can handle. (If you use Pict To Bmp, be sure to increase its Preferred Size in the Finder's Get Info dialog for this application, or it has a hard time handling even the simplest pictures.)

If you are already using a conversion utility such as MacLink PC to move files between platforms, the utility probably has a preference option to translate between graphics formats. Otherwise, there are numerous utilities and drawing programs on the Macintosh that export to the .BMP file format.

See Also

- FoxPro Home Folder:Goodies: Misc:Pict To Bmp
- "Third Party Tools and Extensions," Chapter 19

Additional Object Resources

Look closely at the FOXTOOLS functions to see what else you can borrow and avoid re-inventing by using this library. Chapters 16 and 17 show you how to use available resources from compiled libraries and XCMDs. Don't limit your borrowing to non-FoxPro sources, however. You can incorporate fully developed FoxPro utility applications as subsidiary modules in your programs. If they're well designed, you don't need to know how they work internally; just like a normal FoxPro function, you just need to know their calling syntax.

For example, my template code uses PICKER.APP by John Hosier. This useful double-scrollable list dialog takes elements of one array and allows the user to place multiple selected elements into another array. I've integrated PICKER.APP into several of the template code features, including the Packing option as shown in figure 11.9. Having satisfied myself that PICKER.APP is a robust utility, I don't concern myself further with its internal workings. In fact, the version you see in the figure has never been ported to the Macintosh; I simply moved the .APP form of the utility from FoxPro for Windows.

The full syntax for John's dialog shows you how easy and how flexible this object is to use:

```
DO Picker WITH ;
   SourceArray, TargetArray, Title, ;
   SourceTitle, TargetTitle, SourceMsg, ;
   TargetMsg, SortArray

*or:

#_of_rows_in_TargetArray = ;
   Picker( @SourceArray, @TargetArray, Title, ;
           SourceTitle, TargetTitle, SourceMsg, ;
           TargetMsg, SortArray)
```

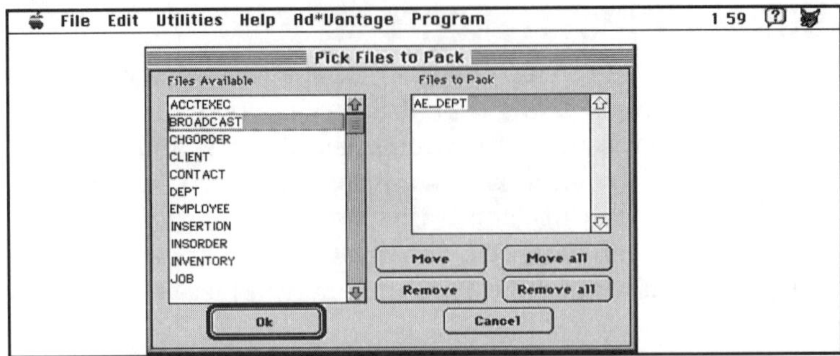

Figure 11.9 *John Hosier's PICKER.APP is a double-picklist "mover" utility incorporated into the template code.*

See Also

- Source Disk:Library/ Template Code Folder: PICKER.APP
- Source Disk:Library/ Template Code Folder: PICKER.TXT

Along with the numerous shareware and public domain programs you find available for the Macintosh, and which you learn about in Part IV, you'll find many FoxPro developers like John Hosier willing to share their work and teach you additional tricks to speed your work. Thank you once again, John, and thanks to all the readers and CompuServe FoxForum regulars who contribute ideas and techniques.

Complying with the Apple Human Interface Guidelines

In the last section, you saw a situation (assigning default dialog window attributes) in which FoxPro standards don't match Mac interface design guidelines and user expectations. In many cases, you have to do some extra work to change FoxPro defaults for greater interface consistency. *Doing this work does not go against rapid development principles*. Matching user expectations and keeping to a rigorous design standard eventually saves you time and effort.

FoxPro gives you many coding methods to reach similar results. Remain aware of interface details, not just ease of implementation, when deciding which method to use.

For example, in the last chapter I implemented a toolbar, rather than a palette, in the template code. (You saw it in the Employee screen set, but it's designed for easy incorporation into a variety of screen sets.) I preferred a palette originally, but creating a window that is always on top yet never has focus is extraordinarily difficult in FoxPro. I regretfully concluded, after discussions with Randy, that a palette without the appropriate attributes was worse than no palette at all. By contrast, I didn't have to sacrifice basic toolbar attributes to achieve a toolbar effect in FoxPro.

Because Apple and the Macintosh environment have a sound set of interface guidelines, you don't have to work hard to figure out what kind of interface you should build. Set your interface goals to match the *Human Interface Guidelines*, and you're way ahead of the game at the start. However, you haven't finished playing, much less won the game.

The guidelines don't free you from the need to think creatively about your interface. Extrapolating from the Macintosh standard to the best possible behavior for a data entry screen set is not an automatic process. You won't end up with the same conclusions as I do, or as the next developer does, although we are all conscientiously striving for the same goal.

Sometimes earnest Macintosh developers focus on complying with the details of the Guidelines but miss the big picture. I call these folks the Interface Cops—they have Windows analogs I think of as the Jazz Police. These people mean well, and they are extremely knowledgeable. Don't ignore their advice, just take their advice with a grain of salt. The Macintosh standard isn't really defined by what a default button or dialog border looks like. The standard is defined by a constant objective *to make the user as happy working on the Macintosh as possible*.

Familiarity and orthodox appearance are vital components of the guidelines, but they're just a means to this objective.

I realize that the position I've just stated may not be popular with Mac developers, but it's important to remember that even Apple's interpretation of its own guidelines has evolved over time. Don't mistake slavish devotion to interface attributes for a real devotion to the standards, or to the Mac community the standards are designed to serve.

What's the practical result of this advice?

First, when you design FoxPro dialogs and generic objects, it's not particularly important that you decide to use 2-dimensional buttons versus 3-dimensional buttons. It's more important that dialogs of a particular type always have the *same* style of buttons, that default buttons always occur in one place, and that prompts for buttons that perform a particular action remain consistent in different windows.

The template screens for this book use a system with consistent verbs on the buttons, to which use SHOW GET PROMPT commands add appropriate noun-objects for a particular window or instance of the button. This system guarantees button prompt-consistency to some extent.

I hope you notice the occasions on which FoxPro for Macintosh's own dialogs violate this advice! In particular, be aware of how irritating it is when "Yes" and "No" buttons switch positions, and when one dialog responds when you press "Y" to indicate "Yes" but the next dialog does not. The more sensitive you are to your own problems with the interface, the more critically you approach the applications you use, and the better your own designs will be.

Figures 11.10 and 11.11 show you two dialogs in FoxPro for Macintosh that caution you before you change an existing file on disk. The two dialogs look completely different; presumably one comes from the Mac system tool kit and the other is Fox-specific. Figure 11.10 shows you the "overwrite" dialog that you get if you choose to BUILD an APP from the Project Manager to a file name that already exists. The non-destructive option (Cancel) is on the left. Pressing "C" or "B" doesn't initiate the Cancel or Build button action. Figure 11.11, on the other hand, shows you the "cancel changes" dialog you get if you press Esc while editing a text file. The non-destructive option (No) is on the right. If you press "Y" or "N" you initiate the Yes or No options.

I guess I should be grateful that the non-destructive option is the default option in both dialogs. However, for your own dialogs, find a single method of displaying and coding such buttons, and stick to it.

Second, be amenable to slight excursions from visual orthodoxy, where your application uses screen elements in an unusual way. Just handle these changes consistently and document them well.

In the last section, you saw that I'm willing to do extra work to make sure that standard modal alert dialogs don't have an inappropriate title bar on the Macintosh. However, I have *complex* dialogs, such as a password screen or report-picking dialog, to which the "no title, no float" rule does not apply, although these activities are modal.

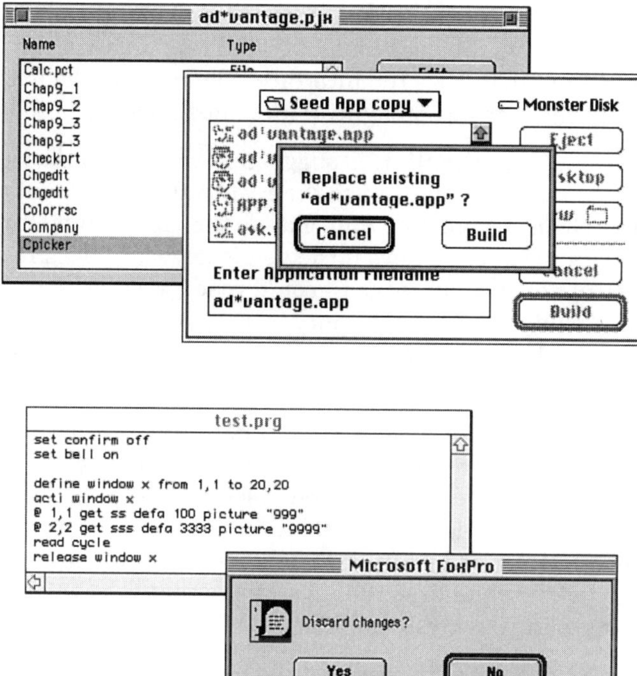

Figures 11.10 and 11.11 *FoxPro for Macintosh uses different styles of dialogs to accomplish similar tasks – don't try this at home.*

Apple instituted this type of *moveable modal dialog*, which can be dragged around on the desktop by its title bar in System 7. Previously, there was no such object in the Macintosh lexicon. You now see similar dialogs in the Finder's own Find option and word processing dialogs (such as Find or Create Envelope) that are well-served by being moveable.

With this new set of attributes, the user can make intelligent reference to other screen elements otherwise obscured by the dialog window, while entering the appropriate responses into the otherwise-modal dialog. Clearly, the interface guidelines are not static. The interface is open to changes that materially improve the user's ability to get work done—so you should keep your mind open, too.

Third, the objective of the guidelines suggests that you constantly seek *additional* ways to give the user control of and rapport with the interface, rather than seeking to impose the interface's defaults on the user. This is the essense and the spirit of thoughtful Macintosh design.

In some cases, you comply with this suggestion without fanfare or user awareness. For example, you can use the FKMAX( ) function or the FoxTools FxKeyboard( ) function and change the labels on menu shortcuts to reflect the lack of function keys if the user's keyboard doesn't support them. A label that ordinarily reads `F1` could read `[AB]1` instead. A label that ordinarily reads `[AB]F1` could read `control[AB]1`. The section on altering GENMENU later in this chapter shows you how to accomplish this task without separate menu files.

The user should feel encouraged to make other interface decisions explicitly, perhaps through a Preferences option on the Utilities pad. You already have a record for each registered user of an application, in the application's SYS_VAR.DBF control table, created and maintained by the template code. You can add additional fields to this table to store user preferences, much like the Preferences settings that FoxPro and other applications store in your System folder.

Memofields in SYS_VAR.DBF can hold the user's last-selected color set as indicated through the template color picker dialog and preferred style of help file (.DBF or .HLP). You can use the SAVE MACROS TO MEMO <field name> to maintain a personal set of macros for each user without littering the disk with extra .FKY files. Users can set the value of _DBLCLICK, the system variable that indicates how much time occurs between mouse clicks before FoxPro decides the second click is no longer associated with the first, perhaps by using a sliding control as a visual scale rather than absolute numbers. (You learn more about all these FoxPro capabilities in Chapter 14.)

Users may prefer silent alerts or they may want to adjust SET BELL and SET CONFIRM. You may want to provide some intelligent guidance for these settings. For instance, if they SET CONFIRM OFF, so they are automatically moved from one GET to the next when they completely fill a field, you may want to require BELL to be ON, so they receive a clue that they moved between fields.

Depending on the type of data entry or the background of the user, even an option to SET KEYCOMP TO DOS or WINDOWS as well as MAC may be welcomed. (I added this option to the developer's Color Tutor dialog you see in Chapter 14, so you can see how it works.) Satisfying your users is always more important than bowing to the Interface Cops—or to anybody else.

Establishing a Validation Strategy

As part of creating sensible and usable data entry modules and dialogs, you add *validation* conditions that examine users' input and evaluate and respond to it. This section reviews validation design as an integral part of your general interface plan.

Make Your Validation as Permissive as Possible

As a developer, you're responsible to make sure that only valid information finds its way into the application's database. Sometimes you need to reject the user's input (politely) because the information doesn't correspond to the application's business rules. Making sure data is correct is only one part of the job of validation, however. Other forms of validation simply adjust the values of other fields and other GETs on-screen based on the new information.

Both forms of validation commonly occur when the user changes the contents of a GET and opts to leave the GET. At this point FoxPro executes the GET's VALID clause, if you've written one.

You rarely submit a prototype application with all validation in place. For example, the subsidiary Job screens for different types of Inventory records you find in the AD*Vantage application aren't finished in this respect. As you see in the Broadcast-editing module shown in figure 11.12, I've simply indicated onscreen that some figures eventually depend on others.

When this screen set is finished, estimated gross and net will be calculated using the total information about the Spots for this Broadcast order, plus default rates attached to this client's record. Actual gross and net will be supplied by the validation routines as equivalent to estimated, initially, after which the user can adjust these figures manually. The actual figures can, in turn, be subject to additional validation; for example, the agency may want to keep adjustments within certain percentage limits, or at least bring excessive adjustments to the attention of the operator.

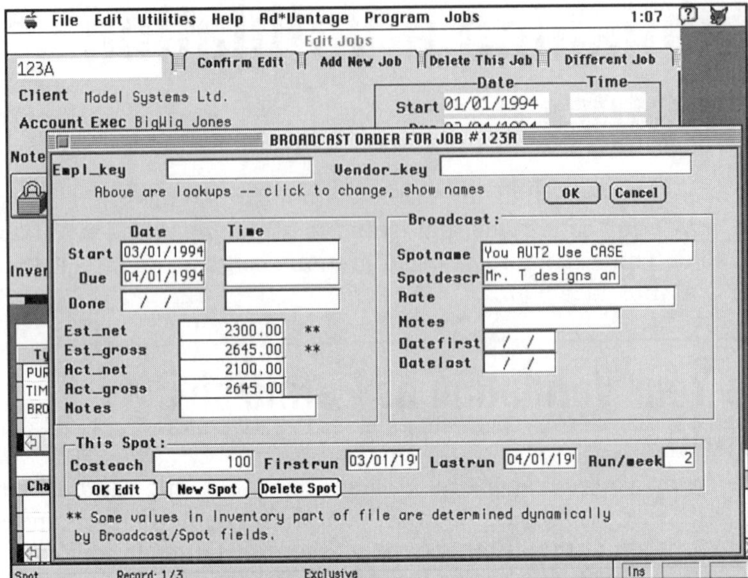

Figure 11.12 *The prototype Broadcast editing screen does not include lookups or validation as of yet.*

The prototype screen, *sans* validation, is actually not far removed from the original Quick Screen with which I started its design. As you see, I didn't even supply the simple lookup BROWSEs for the agency employee and the media vendor responsible for this order. The screen currently shows the key values for these fields, with a note indicating how the screen will eventually work. The user knows how such lookups operate from the Client and Account Exec lookups on the master Job screen and can visualize this feature without difficulty.

Lookups are a special form of validation. They avoid any possibility of the user entering invalid data, and any necessity to reject the user's action. Adjusting calculated fields on the basis of other fields, as you do when you multiply gross by a percentage to get net, is another example of what I call *permissive validation*.

Cast in FoxPro terminology, permissive validation consists of VALID clauses (responses to user input), which never RETURN .F. (tell the user the input is unacceptable). A *restrictive* VALID (a VALID that RETURNs .F.) constrains the user to remain in the GET he or she has just tried to leave.

As you work to design validation in FoxPro for Macintosh, your goal does not change from your general interface objective. You want to tell the user "no" as little as possible and facilitate what the user wants to do as long as the user's desire is safe. This leads you to an inescapable conclusion and a very clear plan: *the best validation strategy is the one that provides safe and accurate data while RETURNing .F. as little as possible.*

You can start following this plan by using GET controls such as radio buttons and pop-ups whenever feasible. Since you provide all the choices in these GET controls, you can make sure the user's choice is never invalid. In fact, where only one choice is appropriate, you can DISABLE the GET control after making the correct choice for the user. The dimmed GET, which still reflects the choice you've selected, is a response to, and corroborates, some previous decision by the user.

For example, in the template's two REPORTS dialogs, if you check the Counts Only checkbox, the Output radio buttons (Preview, Printer, and File) become disabled. The user's previous Output choice is still selected, in case the user wants output after receiving the count. Similarly, if the user unchecks a Married checkbox on a data entry screen, you may dim a text box that holds the spouse's name.

Only free-form text entries have the potential to contain invalid data and thus need restrictive validation. Therefore, correlative to the decision to avoid RETURNing .F. from validation is a second conclusion: *avoid text box GETs for data with rigid requirements.* When you have to use text box GETs, remember to use the Format option to add PICTURE templates to transform the user's entries as they occur in order to further limit the times you must correct users' input after entry.

Sometimes a free-form text GET is unavoidable, yet it requires validation. For example, the agency determines the job number for each Job.DBF record according to a personal notation system you don't know, and that they may change frequently. The agency doesn't want your code to regulate this job number, which is entirely separate from the internal key field your program uses to maintain database relationships. However, you still need to ensure that each new job number is unique.

For a properly forgiving, Mac-like interface, *don't attach the validation which must RETURN .F. to the GET.* You can permit the user to enter an incomplete or a non-unique job number, dash over to check a vendor address, add a job start-date, and *then* return to finish the job number GET if necessary. You don't need to ensure the job number's uniqueness until the user chooses to confirm the addition of the new job or the edit of the existing job.

As a general rule, I'm suggesting that you concentrate all restrictive validation to the VALID of the Confirm or Save button. This idea may be completely new to those of you who wrote procedural Xbase code in the past, but it has several important advantages.

First, along with permitting the user to complete information in any order, this method allows graceful cancellation of the whole operation.

If a VALID clause RETURNs .F., it keeps the user in that GET, so if the user left the GET to click a cancellation button, the focus returns to the GET with the VALID clause. You can avoid this problem by setting up the cancellation button as an "Escape" button (using `\?` in the button prompt) and checking for an Esc press in the VALID clause, like this:

```
* FUNCTION My_Valid
IF LASTKEY( ) = 27  && escape press
  RETURN
ENDIF
PRIVATE m.return
m.return = .T.
* continue with validation here
RETURN m.return
```

However, this solution is tedious to implement (you have to use it in every VALID function you write), and it's only partially successful. If the user chooses a menu option to end an operation rather than a cancellation button, the VALID is obviated altogether, whether you want it to run or not. If the user chooses the close box on the window, the GET VALID runs and the LASTKEY() check for an Esc press won't work to avoid it.

FOXPRO MAC HACK TIP

The fact that a VALID "holds" the user in the current GET until FoxPro knows for certain that the VALID RETURNs .T. has a very important corollary: you can't ACTIVATE another WINDOW within a VALID because the current GET is still _CUROBJ, and _CUROBJ will "pull" its own window back on top.

For example, you might try to get a button's VALID to bring a participating BROWSE forward by using the command `ACTIVATE WINDOW <browse window>`. You notice that the BROWSE seems to flash forward for an instant, and then the GET window gets focus again. Instead of ACTIVATEing the BROWSE window within the VALID, create a menu shortcut for this window that executes the same command. Then you can KEYBOARD the menu shortcut in the VALID code. The KEYBOARDed keystrokes occur *after the VALID clause RETURNs to the READ wait state*, so the BROWSE can be ACTIVATEd at that point. When you use this trick, you're also giving users a keyboard shortcut to bring the BROWSE forward whenever they want to—a nice plus!

As a second benefit, if you centralize all your important validation in *one* function, rather than scattered throughout the GET VALIDs, you document all the business rules for the module in one place. Now your cancellation button, your menu option to quit the READ, your DEACTIVATE code for the READ, and any other ways the user might CLEAR the READ, such as a true Esc press or a ⌘ press, can all summon the same function.

The master validation function can make certain standard decisions if the entry isn't finished or if some data is not correct. You can offer the user a choice to abandon the entry or to return and fix the problem. You recall from the last chapter that you can set the system variable _CUROBJ to direct the user's attention to the problem GET. The master validation function therefore contains a series of checks, in whatever order or priority you set, each one of which has the opportunity to show an informative and specific error message before SETting _CUROBJ to the offending GET and RETURNing .F.

At first glance, you might think that this strategy of reserving validation for the last moment can't work with direct READs to fields, rather than my preferred indirect READs to memory variables. In reality, I recommend the same strategy for both types of READs. In both cases, you need a mechanism to cancel or confirm the user's changes as you learned in Chapter 8. The only difference is whether you take action because they *confirm* an edit (in indirect READs) or when they *cancel the edit* (in direct READs)—and in how safe the actual data tables are in the event of a system crash.

Consider Additional Validation Refinements

The template code simply cancels unconfirmed changes-in-progress when he or she navigates to a different record. This is a safe option when the user is only editing memory variables (you just discard the edited memory variables by SCATTERing a new set of MEMVARs from the next-chosen record), but I recommend that you add some confirmation to this process.

You can maintain a second, pristine copy of the original record contents by SCATTERing to an ARRAY. If the user opts to move off the record, you can check for changes by comparing the two copies in memory. You can attach your master validation function to any button or other feature that allows navigation, just as you attach it to any option that CLEARs the READ. If the array and memory variables show a change, you validate first, and then give the user appropriate choices before allowing navigation.

This method of comparison assumes that you're locking the record at the beginning of the edit, as my template code does, and as you'll find Doc Livingston advises in his review of FoxPro multi-user strategy in Chapter 15. Locking a record throughout the editing process is known as *pessimistic locking*; locking only when the user is ready to save changes is called *optimistic locking*. If you follow an optimistic locking strategy, you need a second array that you SCATTER from the record when you're ready to commit the edit to disk—to compare to the first array in case some other user has edited the record since this edit began. If the record was updated since this edit began, you have to decide whose changes take precedence, or you have to give the user that decision. This problem can get very complicated, and Doc and I agree that it's more trouble to implement than it's worth.

As you continue to think about ways to improve validation and to make your screen sets more robust, you may also want to substitute editing in a CREATEd CURSOR for editing memory variables created with SCATTER MEMVAR, especially if your database contains memofields with extensive text. As you recall from Chapter 9, FoxPro maintains a cursor in memory if there's room in memory for the cursor's contents. If necessary, FoxPro uses a temporary file on disk for the cursor instead of memory. This process is transparent, so you don't have to worry about the size of the memofield, as you do with SCATTER MEMVAR MEMO.

The use of a cursor also facilitates editing General (OLE) fields in temporary copies, a feature you can't provide with SCATTER MEMVAR MEMO. If the user confirms an edit, you DELETE the original record and APPEND FROM the cursor to get the new General field into the table. Recall from Chapter 9 that you need to use the DBF( ) function to get the name of the temporary table on disk to use as the source in the APPEND FROM command.

The AD*Vantage application doesn't contain any General fields; OLE is not as widely used a standard on the Macintosh as it is in Microsoft Windows. Appendix D gives you a brief introduction to OLE and General field use.

Enhancing the Code Generators

As you create increasingly complex modules with multiple FoxPro menu and screen files, you realize that the FoxPro language is sometimes more flexible than the results you can get from the graphical design tools. Resist the temptation to edit the generated code (.MPRs and .SPRs) to get the results that you want! Instead, realize that the generator programs supporting the design tools are FoxPro programs. If you don't like the results of the tools, edit GENSCRN.PRG and GENMENU.PRG, the generator programs, until you're satisfied with what they produce.

Often, the additional flexibility you require comes as a result of the differences between the different platforms FoxPro supports. For example, in Chapter 7 you saw that the menu definition can support a variable string, rather than a literal, to take care of the different platforms' appropriate "quit" prompts on the menu:

```
"+IIF(_WINDOWS,"E\<xit","\<Quit")+"
```

As you recall, GENMENU creates a DEFINE BAR statement with a PROMPT clause which surrounds the string above with another set of quotation marks, so the end result is a legal FoxPro character expression that changes from Exit to Quit depending on the platform. However, if you want to extend this change to menu shortcuts, you can't use a comparable trick in the Menu Builder.

The menu shortcut problem has two components: the key combination for the shortcut itself, and the way this shortcut shows up on the pop-up menu. For example, if you wanted a menu shortcut for this Quit option, you might want Ctrl-Q or ⌘-Q for DOS and the Mac, but the *key label* in the menu for this shortcut should show as `^Q` in DOS and `_-Q` on the Mac. Meanwhile, the Windows shortcut combination should be Ctrl, and its menu prompt should read `Ctrl+X`.

The Menu Builder's Options dialog for each menu element doesn't give you a place to attach platform-specific properties to the element. You could create separate bars for each platform and then RELEASE the ones you don't need at runtime, but this method is wasteful and causes you to have up to four times as many bars to edit any time you make a change to your menu results.

Instead, get a modified GENMENU to generate the code more flexibly, using platform-specific instructions that you place in the Comment field for a particular menu option with platform-specific key shortcuts and labels (don't use the Options shortcut feature at all). The Comment instructions you use should take the following form:

```
*&*KEYWIN CTRL-X, "CTRL+X"*&*KEYWIN
*&*KEYDOS CTRL-Q, "^Q"*&*KEYDOS
*&*KEYMAC CTRL+Q, "CTRL+Q"*&*KEYMAC
```

In this notation, you delimit what you'd like to appear in the KEY clause with `*&*KEY<platform>`, where <platform> is either `WIN`, `DOS`, `MAC`, or `UNIX`. You don't need carriage returns between the platform segments of these instructions.

FOXPRO MAC HACK TIP

You may balk at this rather verbose delimiter pattern, but many other people use the Comment field for different effects; it's important to remember that your Comment instructions are clearly delineated from anybody else's.

CROSS-PLATFORM WARNING

You can use an underscore, a plus sign, or a hyphen in the first part of the KEY notation, representing the key assignment, whether in my instructions or when you're defining menu elements by other methods. However, you *must* use a plus sign in the second part with quotation marks, representing the key label, when you want the CTRL section of the label to show up as a ⌘ symbol on the FoxPro for Macintosh menu. The other concatenators and symbols (such as ^ for the DOS menu, representing the DOS Ctrl shift key) show up exactly as you type them—including capitalization—so be careful to follow the interface standards of each platform!

The Comment example is taken from a TEST.MNX that you find in the source disk's Miscellaneous Code Samples folder along with my modified LGENMENU.PRG. This sample handles the differences between the different Quit menu shortcut characteristics you want. An additional bar on TEST.MNX shows you how you'd use the Comment syntax to change the key label on a Macintosh keyboard without function keys, where the user can use ⌘ plus the digits on the keyboard to issue the same instructions. In this case, only the label changes; the actual KEY assignment stays the same:

```
*&*KEYWIN CTRL-F2, "CTRL+F2"*&*KEYWIN
*&*KEYDOS CTRL-F2, "^F2"*&*KEYDOS
*&*KEYMAC CTRL+F2,
 IIF(FKMAX( )>1,"CTRL+F2","CTRL+CTRL+2")*&*KEYMAC
```

You can see the results of this notation in figures 11.13 and 11.14, changed to match the evaluation of the condition you set. Notice that the double CTRL+CTRL in the key label code is translated as the ⌘ plus the Ctrl shift keys, which is appropriate; a plain F2 maps to ⌘-2 on a Mac without function keys, so Ctrl-F2 or ⌘-F2 maps to a double-shifted press of the number key.

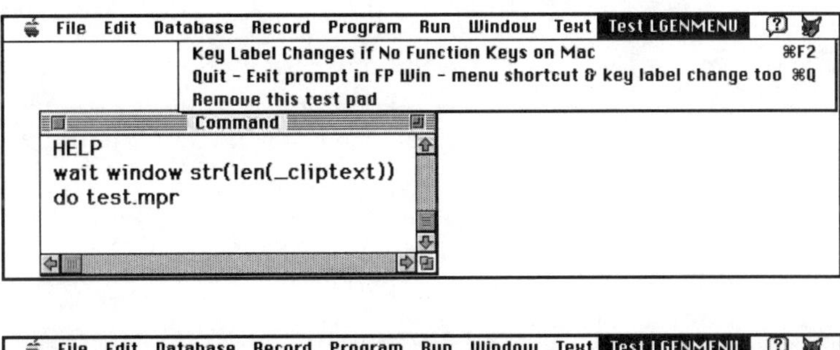

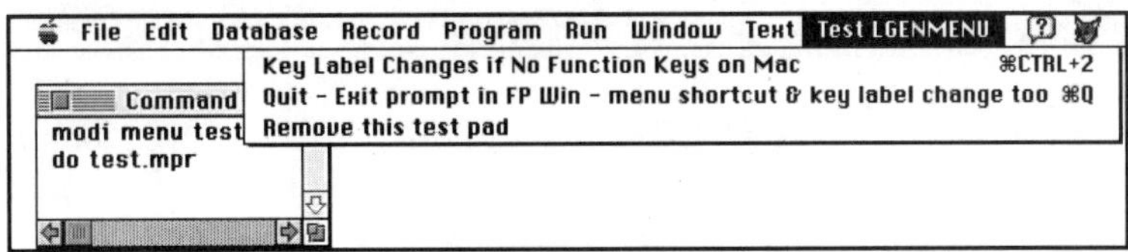

Figures 11.13 and 11.14 *The same menu gives different effects with dynamic KEY clauses generated by LGENMENU.PRG.*

You're probably wondering how the Comment field gets translated into usable FoxPro code by the altered generator program. If you want to see the generator create the results using TEST.MNX or another menu file, make LGENMENU the active generator program by storing its full path and name to the system variable _GENMENU. To return the generator to its default state, issue this command:

```
_GENMENU = SYS(2004)+"GENMENU"
```

FOXPRO MAC HACK TIP

If you find you like my altered program for permanent use, you can put the fully pathed file name for LGENMENU into your CONFIG.FPM file, using this syntax:

```
_GENMENU = [<pathed file name>]
```

You can use the same assignment form for _GENSCRN and _TRANSPRT, the Transporter program. Be sure to use delimiters, either the brackets shown above or single- or double- quotation marks, even if you have not used them in FoxPro for Windows or FoxPro for DOS in your configuration files, in case the Mac path or file name contains spaces or other DOS-illegal characters. FoxPro recognizes VOLUME = assignments you've made in the CONFIG.FPM file as part of these file name designations. If you make the assignment incorrectly and FoxPro can't find the file you name, the system variable will have a null value when you load FoxPro. Figure 11.15 shows a check of the value of _GENMENU, using a WAIT WINDOW, and a check of the contents of the CONFIG.FPM, using the function SYS(2019), which contains the location and full name of this file.

To find my adjustments to GENMENU in LGENMENU.PRG, look for the comments preceded by the symbols `*&*`. For instance, near the top of the program, you'll find a single added global variable definition:

```
*&* >L< added
m.g_usekeyprop = .F.
*&* end >L< additions
```

In the procedures that generate the lines for DEFINE BARs and DEFINE PADs, you'll find the addition of this subroutine call:

```
*&* >L< added
      DO genkeyprop
*&* end >L<
```

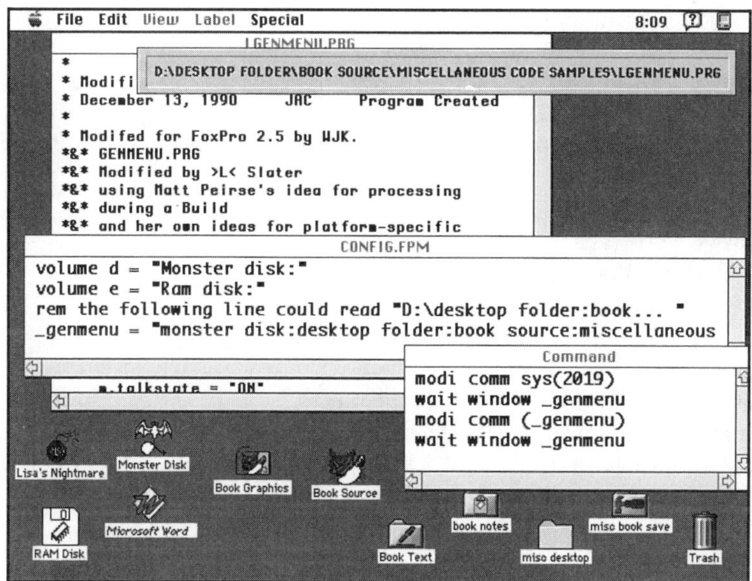

Figure 11.15 *Edit the contents of the FoxPro for Macintosh configuration file using the SYS(2019) function and edit the name and location of the menu generator program using the system variable _GENMENU.*

This routine checks to see if my special instructions for key shortcuts are in the Comment field for the pad, pop-up, or bar, and, if so, generates menu code that parses out the Comment field contents, as follows:

```
*&* >L< added
PROCEDURE genkeyprop
m.g_usekeyprop = EMPTY(Keyname) AND ATC("*&*KEY",Comment) > 0
IF m.g_usekeyprop
   PRIVATE m.front, m.back, m.keypropvalue
   \DO CASE
   \CASE _WINDOWS
    m.front = ATC("*&*KEYWIN",Comment)+9
    m.back = ATC("*&*KEYWIN",Comment,2)
```

```
    m.keypropvalue = ;
      SUBSTR(Comment,m.front, m.back-m.front)
    \   m.keyproperty = [<<m.keypropvalue>>]
    \CASE _MAC
    m.front = ATC("*&*KEYMAC",Comment)+9
    m.back = ATC("*&*KEYMAC",Comment,2)
    m.keypropvalue = ;
      SUBSTR(Comment,m.front, m.back-m.front)
    \   m.keyproperty = [<<m.keypropvalue>>]
    \CASE _DOS
    m.front = ATC("*&*KEYDOS",Comment)+9
    m.back = ATC("*&*KEYDOS",Comment,2)
    m.keypropvalue = ;
      SUBSTR(Comment,m.front, m.back-m.front)
    \   m.keyproperty = [<<m.keypropvalue>>]
    \CASE _UNIX
    m.front = ATC("*&*KEYUNIX",Comment)+10
    m.back = ATC("*&*KEYUNIX",Comment,2)
    m.keypropvalue = ;
      SUBSTR(Comment,m.front, m.back-m.front)
    \   m.keyproperty = [<<m.keypropvalue>>]
    \ENDCASE
ENDIF
RETURN
```

This code may be your first view of FoxPro's TEXTMERGE capability. When TEXTMERGE is ON, as it is SET in the generator programs, characters preceded by the instructions `\` are output to the destination you've SET TEXTMERGE TO (a window or a file name) starting with a carriage return and linefeed. Characters preceded by the instructions `\\` go to the destination without the preceding carriage return and linefeed.

This output is very similar to the Xbase `?` and `??` output instructions with one important difference: *the characters you send after the \ and \\ instructions go as literal characters, except when the characters are enclosed in delimiters forcing FoxPro to evaluate them as an expression*. The default TEXTMERGE delimiters are `<< >>`, so the `m.keypropvalue` variable name enclosed in the delimiters isn't outputted. Instead, the generated code includes the *value* of this variable. In the code above, the lines are output to the .MPR file like this:

```
DO CASE
CASE _WINDOWS
   m.keyproperty = [ CTRL-X, "CTRL+X"]
CASE _MAC
   m.keyproperty = [ CTRL+Q, "CTRL+Q"]
CASE _DOS
   m.keyproperty = [ CTRL-Q, "^Q"]
CASE _UNIX
   m.keyproperty = []
ENDCASE
```

These lines precede the actual pad, pop-up, or bar definition in the .MPR. I altered the procedure in GENMENU that generates the KEY clause on the actual DEFINE PAD, POPUP, or BAR line to make use of the `m.keyproperty` variable, as follows:

```
PROCEDURE addkey
    IF NOT EMPTY(keyname)
        \\ ;
        \      KEY <<Keyname>>, "<<Keylabel>>"
    *&* >L< added
    ELSE
        IF m.g_usekeyprop
           \\  ;
           \    KEY &keyproperty
        ENDIF
    *&* end >L<
    ENDIF
```

This change gives the DEFINE line in the .MPR a `KEY &keyproperty` clause to use the value just assigned to `keyproperty` in the preceding CASE statement when appropriate, instead of the normal KEY clause. The only other change I made to GENMENU to support this capability was a PRIVATE definition of the `m.keyproperty` variable to the header section of the .MPR.

This change materially extends the usefulness of your .MPRs by stopping the limitation of the generator program GENMENU from obstructing the real flexibility of the FoxPro menu syntax. If you study GENMENU and GENSCRN closely, even though you may prefer not to edit them, you get a better idea of how your menu and screen definitions turn into FoxPro code—and therefore a much clearer idea of the most efficient way to manipulate the Menu Builder and Screen Builder design tools.

If you look closely at GENSCRN, for example, you see that it generates CASE statements for *the entire .SPR sequence* for each platform with records in the .SCX. Whether you agree that such all-encompassing bracketing is appropriate or not (as you see in the next section, I think more limited bracketing would be a better policy), GENSCRN must make an exception for the PARAMETERS statement you may have put in #SECTION 1 of the Setup code snippet. No program can have more than one PARAMETERS statement, so separate PARAMETERS simply can't be placed in CASEs.

This fact gives you two immediately useful pieces of information: it explains why GENSCRN refuses to generate your .SPR if you have Setup snippets with different PARAMETERS statements on different platforms; and it tells you that PROCEDURE GenParameter in GENSCRN is a very good place to change GENSCRN if you have code you want to run cross-platform.

LGENSCRN.PRG, which you find in the Miscellaneous Code Samples folder with LGENMENU.PRG, contains the following altered parameter-generating procedure:

```
PROCEDURE genparameter
*)
*) GENPARAMETER - Generate the PARAMETER statement
*)
IF !EMPTY(m.g_parameter)
   \PARAMETERS <<m.g_parameter>>
ENDIF

\
\*&* >L< added
\IF _WINDOWS OR _MAC
\    MODIFY WINDOW SCREEN FONT "<<WFONT(1,"")>>", <<WFONT(2,"")>> STYLE
"<<WFONT(3,"")>>"
\ENDIF
\*&*
\
RETURN
```

This change puts a MODIFY WINDOW SCREEN line in the header of an .SPR that exactly matches the main FoxPro window screen conditions that were in force at the moment GENSCRN generated the .SPR. This trick solves many window-arrangement conditions because the window coordinates that GENSCRN uses for DEFINE WINDOW statements are dependent on the DEFINEd WINDOW's parent font *as calculated at generation and window-arrangement time on the developer's machine.* The main application window, or SCREEN, is usually the parent for the DEFINEd WINDOWs for the purpose of determining the parent font, even when you SET MACDESKTOP ON.

Again, the change to the generator program materially extends the capabilities of the generated program, as well as enhancing your knowledge of the design tools' behavior and capabilities. You also find that it's possible to change the generator programs to provide additional services that don't show up anywhere in the generated code.

Matt Peirse, an excellent New Zealand FoxPro developer, came up with a modification to GENMENU that uses a special menu to run some additional code to provide a version stamp for your applications. When the modified GENMENU sees this special menu name, it doesn't create a normal .MPR file. I extended Matt's idea a bit to allow the special menu to run additional, unspecified code you place in the Comment field of the special menu's one item. Here's the way the additional change looks in LGENMENU.PRG:

```
FUNCTION buildenable
    PRIVATE m.stat
    m.stat = opendb(g_mnxfile[1]) AND openfile( )
    IF m.stat
        SET TEXTMERGE ON        *&* >L< added, using Matt Peirse's
        *&* AUTO_VER technique, and
        *&* adding more project processing
        *&* via Comment memo field:
        IF g_mnxfile[2] = "AUTO_VER"
           LOCATE FOR objtype = 3
           REPLACE prompt WITH ;
                   LTRIM(STR(1+VAL(prompt)))
           \<<procedure>>
           IF NOT EMPTY(comment)
              *&* you can add additional stuff
              *&* to do in here!!
              PRIVATE m.proc, m.olderr
              m.proc = SYS(3)+".PRG"
              DO WHILE FILE(m.proc)
                 *&* highly unlikely, but <g>...
                 m.proc = SYS(3)+".PRG"
              ENDDO
```

```
                COPY MEMO comment TO (m.proc)
                m.olderr = ON("ERROR")
                ON ERROR RETURN TO Buildenable
                DO (m.proc)
                IF FILE(STRTRAN(m.proc,"PRG","ERR"))
                   ERASE ;
                    (STRTRAN(m.proc,"PRG", "ERR"))
                   WAIT WINDOW ;
                    "Custom Build procedure "+ ;
                     "had errors!"
                   *&* yes, there are other the
                   *&* procedure can fail,
                   *&* but the proc itself
                   *&* can and should handle
                   *&* its own errors...
                ENDIF
                ERASE (m.proc)
                ERASE (STRTRAN(m.proc,"PRG","FXP"))
                ON ERROR &olderr
             ENDIF
             DO builddisable
             RETURN .F.
          *&* end >L< additions
          ENDIF
      ENDIF
      RETURN m.stat
```

The components of the matching AUTO_VER.MNX, which you find in the Miscellaneous Code Samples folder, are shown in figure 11.16. I've used the Append attribute for this menu, assigned the pad a name, and explicitly RELEASEd this PAD in the menu cleanup, as shown in figure 11.16, so you can put a call to DO AUTO_VER.MPR into your main program without worrying about whether you've got the right menu generator loaded.

You give the AUTO_VER menu a single pad with a number in the prompt, which the custom GENMENU procedure increments before creating the special .MPR in the AUTO_VER procedure. Instead of creating a menu option, the AUTO_VER result procedure creates a public variable, which I've called `m.app_version`, and assigns a value to this variable.

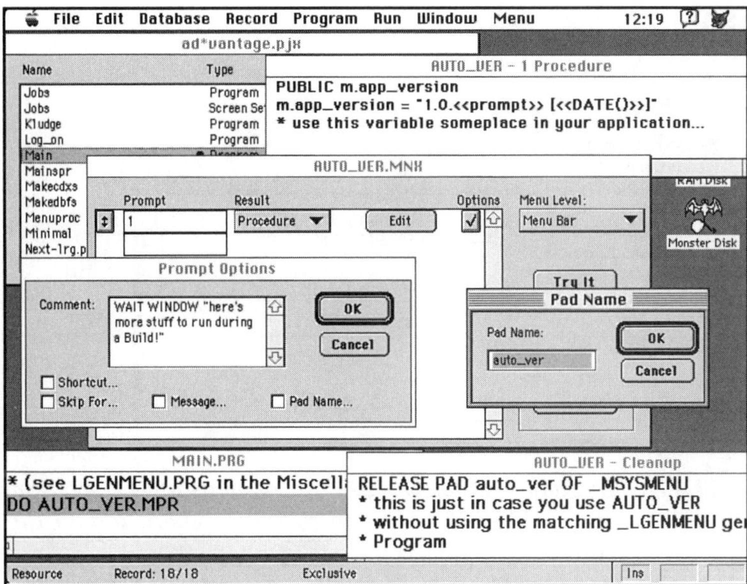

Figure 11.16 *AUTO_MENU.MNX provides a version stamp and a method to add additional processing to the Project Manager's Build process.*

You've seen the variable in the APPABOUT.SCX dialog setup code earlier in this chapter. If the variable doesn't exist, the About dialog doesn't include a version stamp. If I build an application using LGENMENU, the resulting About dialog looks like figure 11.17.

When the special LGENMENU procedure increments the prompt by REPLACEing a field in the AUTO_VER table, it doesn't merely increment the version number. This action changes the date on the AUTO_VER.MNX file, ensuring that *the Project Manager processes AUTO_VER.MNX with the menu generator every time you do a Build.* This is the true brilliance of Matt's approach. Because I can rely on the procedures in AUTO_VER to run during every build, I added code to add some extra processing to the Project Manager. If you place extra lines of code in the Comment field, the special AUTO_VER processing writes that code to disk and executes the resulting program.

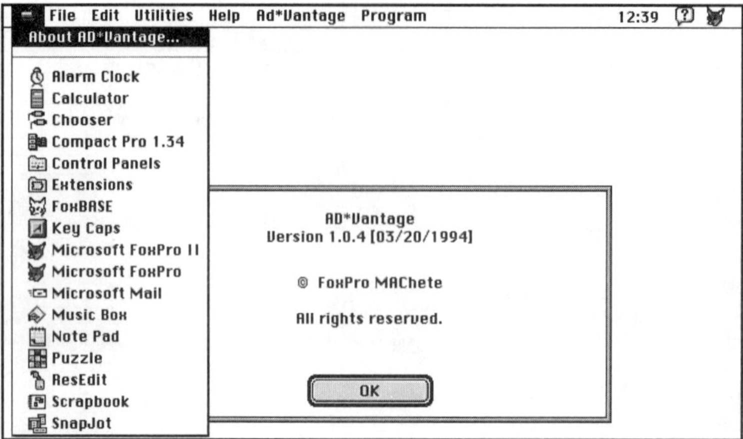

Figure 11.17 *The About dialog in AD*Vantage has a version stamp when LGENMENU handles menu generation for the Build process.*

You can use this trick to adjust the project file itself during the Build process. For example, a number of files you may want to Include in the Project routinely are not added automatically to the .PJX file by the Project Manager. The template code makes use of some read-only tables (DBFS.DBF, INSTALL.DBF, COLORRSC.DBF, and RESULTS.DBF) and a number of additional read-only files (notably the macros-definition file APP.FKY you learn about in Chapter 14 and a SURVEY.TXT form for the error handler). Rather than manually including these files in the Project, you can write AUTO_VER Comment code that checks the PJX for records for these files and adds additional .PJX records for the ones it doesn't find.

FOXPRO MAC HACK TIP

Because the generator programs are FoxPro code, and because the elements of a FoxPro application are defined by normal FoxPro data structures, your opportunities to manipulate the application-building process are limitless. Two companies (Flash and Cascade) have created multi-programmer versions of the ordinarily single-user Project Manager (MUPET and CAPCON), thereby addressing its most serious shortcoming. MUPET and CAPCON can succeed in manipulating the project and its components because the .PJX is a regular FoxPro table. I mentioned CAPCON's capability to add feedback to the development process, along with coordinating multiple programmers' use of a project, in Chapter 8. MUPET adds a pre- and post- processing feature to the Build, similar to the "hook" we've provided using GENMENU.

You should look at the other written-in-FoxPro system programs provided by Microsoft, even if you don't choose to modify them. When you understand how they work, you can get the best possible results from these programs. Along with the generators, investigate GENXTAB.PRG, which creates crosstab queries, and TRANSPRT.PRG, the program that manages the cross-platform conversion process.

• "Guide to Resources," Appendix A

FOXPRO MAC HACK TIP

Explore the FoxPro system programs for fun as well as profit. If you do nothing else to figure out the Transporter, be sure to investigate FUNCTION Transprmpt, shown in figure 11.18! If you want to see its effects, comment out the first CASE (CASE _MAC) and change your System Date and Time control panel to read between 11 PM and midnight on Saturday.

Don't forget to reset your Date and Time afterwards, and don't leave the Transporter in this condition unless you shorten the prompt in the OTHERWISE case (it's too long for the Mac button).

Bracketing Code For Cross-Platform Applications

Throughout this chapter you have seen attention to the details of cross-platform development. Despite Microsoft's valiant attempt to provide a FoxPro that works transparently in different environments, many adjustments must be made for the interface conventions and underlying operating systems of each platform.

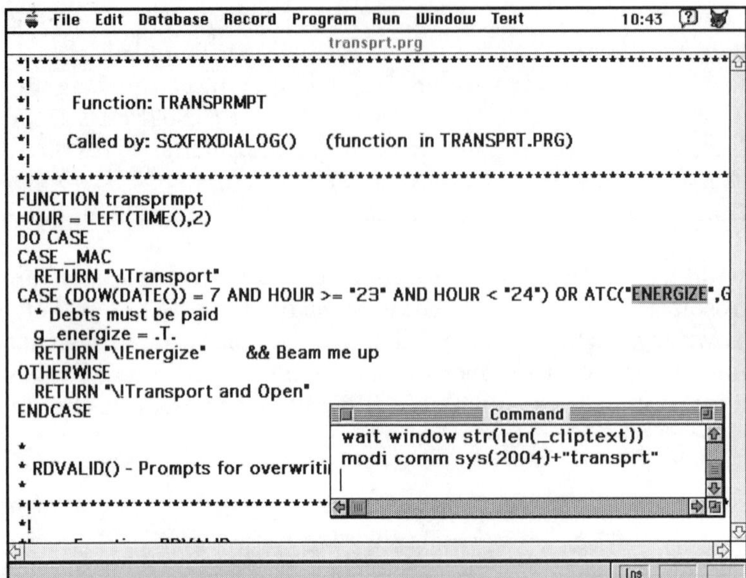
File Edit Database Record Program Run Window Text 10:43
transprt.prg
*!
*! Function: TRANSPRMPT
*!
*! Called by: SCXFRXDIALOG() (function in TRANSPRT.PRG)
*!
FUNCTION transprmpt
HOUR = LEFT(TIME(),2)
DO CASE
CASE _MAC
RETURN "\!Transport"
CASE (DOW(DATE()) = 7 AND HOUR >= "23" AND HOUR < "24") OR ATC("ENERGIZE",G
* Debts must be paid
g_energize = .T.
RETURN "\!Energize" && Beam me up
OTHERWISE
RETURN "\!Transport and Open"
ENDCASE
* RDVALID() - Prompts for overwriti
Command
wait window str(len(_cliptext))
modi comm sys(2004)+"transprt"
Ins

Figure 11.18 *Proof positive that Microsoft FoxPro Team developers are human—or at least Vulcan!*

You could write a cross-platform application by having a top-level MAIN.PRG that checked FoxPro's platform system variables like this:

```
DO CASE
CASE _MAC
   DO mac_ver
CASE _UNIX
   DO unix_ver
CASE _DOS
   DO dos_ver
CASE _WINDOWS
   DO win_ver
RETURN
```

Underneath MAIN.PRG, you'd have completely different sets of code for each platform. However, much of this code would be identical across platforms. As you already know, writing code more than once is worse than a waste of time—it's a potential maintenance nightmare. Instead, for rapid development, you always write code as broadly as possible, and you write specific CASEs only when you get down to the specific events that require special distinctions.

In FoxPro, the special distinctions you make for platform-specific situations are known as *bracketed* code. Bracketed code falls into two main types:

- A four-way CASE statement for each platform, as shown in the last code sample
- A two-way separation between the GUI-based FoxPro versions and the character-based versions:

```
IF _UNIX OR _DOS && char-based
   DO char_ver
ELSE
   DO gui_ver
ENDIF
```

> **FOXPRO MAC HACK TIP**
>
> Don't try to use the _PLATFORM version variables in #IF/#ENDIF preprocessor directives because the variables don't contain the right values at compile time. Instead, to use the preprocessors with platform-specific code, use a check for #IF <version string> $ VERSION(1). Remember that if you use such a check you're limiting the resulting code to a particular platform because the rest of the code (for the other platforms) won't be included in the object file.

GENSCRN generates code bracketing the entire business of the .SPR, after the common PARAMETERS statement, as I showed you earlier in this chapter. *Don't fall into this trap in your own code.* Even in an .SPR, where you're painting objects on a screen that may look entirely different on the DOS and Macintosh platforms, much of your programming work is cross-platform, such as initialization of variables and validation functions. Don't use separate snippets or separate functions for each platform, just add the CASE statement or IF/ENDIF construct for the *single element* within the function that may need a different treatment on each platform.

For example, the button that creates output in REPORTS1.SCX and REPORTS2.SCX calls the same VALID function on each platform, but the function determines its print-to-file strategy based on the current platform. This means that I only have one function to change if I decide to add extra features to the output button.

Avoid Cross-Platform Errors

Bracketing does more than add platform specific behavior; it also prevents program errors where a command you use is not suitable to the current environment.

Some commands have no meaning in an environment and FoxPro simply ignores them. For example, if you DEFINE a WINDOW with the FONT clause in DOS, you don't get an error. However, if you issue the MODIFY WINDOW command in DOS, you get a "Feature not available"; that's why my modification to GENSCRN, which you saw in the last section, surrounds the MODIFY WINDOW line with an IF\ENDIF construction in the generated code.

Similarly, calling the ASCII and Special Character desk accessories available in FoxPro for DOS from FoxPro for Macintosh results in a "Feature not available" error.

As you see in figure 11.19, you can trap for this error, which carries the number 1001. By flagging this error number, your error handler should provide you with the information you need to edit any platform-specific code that you mistakenly left unbracketed.

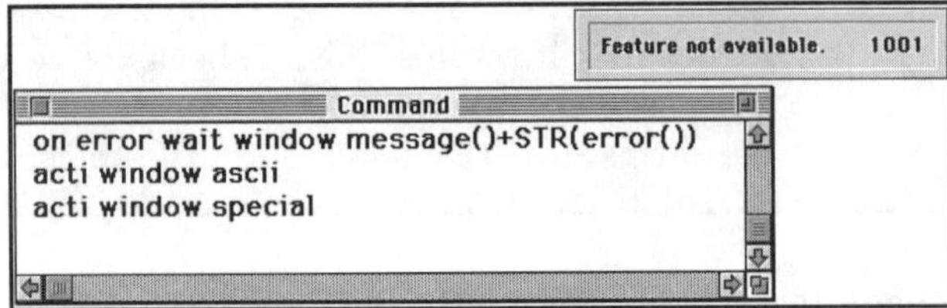
Feature not available. 1001
Command
on error wait window message()+STR(error())
acti window ascii
acti window special

Figure 11.19 *Some FoxPro code that's inappropriate to the Macintosh causes error # 1001, the "feature not available" error.*

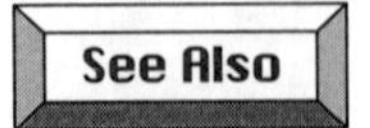
See Also

- PROCEDURE AppError, Source Disk: Library/ Template Code: MAIN.PRG

Unfortunately, commands being ignored or presenting the "Feature not available" error are not the only two possible results of cross-platform code programs. Some commands also provide *compile-time* errors. For example, the ON SHUTDOWN command causes a syntax error from the compiler in FoxPro for DOS. If you have FoxPro for Windows or DOS 2.5, you should upgrade to 2.6 to avoid getting errors (both from the compiler and at runtime) from such Macintosh-specific syntax as SET APLABOUT. On the other side, the shipping version of FoxPro for Macintosh does not understand the new syntax added to FoxPro for DOS and Windows 2.6.

You can't bracket to avoid compile-time errors, in the sense that the compiler runs through all the constructs in the program whether they're platform-appropriate or not. You look through the .ERR text file the Compile or Build procedure creates and verify that each one of these syntax errors is, in reality, enclosed properly in a bracket for the right platform in your program.

Microsoft rectifies these problems as it finds them and when it releases new versions of each FoxPro product. The next edition of FoxPro for Macintosh will probably use the new OBJVAR( ) function added to 2.6 FoxPro for Windows and DOS, for instance, rather than this function causing an error. If the next release of FoxPro Mac comes across a 2.6 feature that's inappropriate to the Mac platform (perhaps the PRTINFO() function), presumably it will ignore the feature rather than present an error.

However, the plain fact is that the versions may always be slightly out-of-synch. Your error handler is the only real protection you have against problems of this kind.

Specific Areas of Cross-Platform Incompatibility

Handling the inconsistencies between platforms can make good use of the localization techniques Randy teaches you in Chapter 13 because the problems of writing for different platforms and different languages are very similar in scope and resolution. You want to use each environment to its best advantage, rather than writing for the lowest common denominator, so you have to *organize* the departures from a standard so they're easy to maintain.

I suggest you stick with the lowest common denominator in one respect: use standard DOS-acceptable names and extensions for your FoxPro file names. Although you can evaluate Macintosh file types in FoxPro for Macintosh, instead of extensions, this method severely limits your ability to work cross-platform. File types also have the following limitations:

- Some FoxPro functions have been enhanced to be aware of file types as well as extensions, but their use of file types may be flawed. For example, GETFILE( ) allows you to specify a file type using a new optional parameter in FoxPro for Macintosh, but this parameter doesn't let you specify *multiple* filetypes for the picklist, which you can do with multiple extensions.

- Evaluating file types within FoxPro requires FOXTOOLS. It's possible that your programs will encounter low memory situations or distribution situations in which you don't want to assume FOXTOOLS is always loaded.
- Evaluating file types becomes code that must be mirrored on other platforms with extension-evaluating code, adding enormously to the amount of code you must bracket.

Save your awareness of Macintosh file types for points at which the user will notice a real difference. For example, the installation procedures in MAIN.PRG copy the contents of INSTALL.DBF/FPT out to disk, and adjust their creator and file types afterwards. Similarly, APPSETUP fixes the creator and filetypes of the .PRGs it generates. In both cases, I ensure the user's ability to launch these files properly from the Finder.

Your users can still assign Mac-style folders and file names for the files they create because you address files using the indirect reference form of reference you learned early in this book.

See Also

- "FoxPro File Types," Appendix B

Library and XCMD use presents another thorny cross-platform issue. You don't always know that equivalent functionality is available on each platform. In general, use compiled libraries (.MLBs) and XCMDs in situations where the code is bracketed to begin with. For example, I use a SET XCMDFILE call in my Macintosh print-to-file procedures because I know that the code to print to file is completely on each platform anyway. I don't have to find an equivalent DOS .PLB or Windows .FLL to match the XCMD.

CROSS-PLATFORM WARNING

Although most people prefer to use .PLBs and .FLLs in DOS and Windows, sometimes an old-style .BIN file (LOAD MODULE) works best when you have a need for a DOS and Windows operating system call and no equivalent need on the Macintosh. For instance, I prefer to use the ISDISKIN.BIN file in FoxPro for DOS and Windows than equivalent .PLB and .FLL library functions. The .BIN file can be Included as a File in the .APP, unlike .FLLs, and I can rest assured that the need to check whether a disk drive has a disk in it is obviated on the Macintosh. In FoxPro for Macintosh, you check mounted volumes using FOXTOOLS's FxGVolume( ) to fulfill a completely different need at the same point in the program.

Where a need is truly ubiquitous, and where you can't run a program without fulfilling it, try to fulfill it in FoxPro code rather than through libraries if possible. You may pay a small speed penalty, but you'll know that the feature will work exactly the same way on each platform. For example, FOXTOOLS.MLB, FOXTOOLS.FLL, and FPATH.PLB, libraries that are included respectively with the Macintosh, Windows, and DOS versions of FoxPro, all contain some string-handling and file name-handling functions such as StripPath( ), StripCR( ), and JustStem( ). However, these functions have some subtle differences in how they handle a missing or incorrectly typed argument, and how they RETURN a failure.

You can easily write generic versions of these functions in FoxPro, avoiding the library differences. In fact, you can *find* generic FoxPro versions of most of these functions appended as subroutines in GENSCRN.PRG!

Along with the different functionality that libraries provide on different platforms, the act of establishing a library (using the SET LIBRARY command) is, in itself, a cross-platform can of worms. Each Library Construction Kit is different in order to handle the needs of the different operating systems. A failure of the SET LIBRARY command requires a different response on each platform. When you refer to the SetLib( ) function in MAIN.PRG, through which my template code funnels all SET LIBRARY requests, you find that the code is almost entirely bracketed:

```
FUNCTION SetLib
* This important generic function
* loads a library or returns string that,
* by being empty, provides an indication
* that the library wasn't found or,
* by reading "loaded !", that
* the library was already available
* to the program in the environment or
* what the fullpathname of the loaded library is
* — information you need to RELEASE it later.
*
* If no param is passed it defaults to the
* generic FPATH/FOXTOOLS libraries, looking for
* them in their expected-installed places but
* letting the user look for them elsewhere if
* necessary.
*
* You can pass a version of the FPATH/FOXTOOLS
```

```
* file name that points to a "local" version
* if necessary.
*
* Note that in FoxPro 2.5 libraries have to be on
* disk (not bound into the app) and (again)
* that to be SET or RELEASEd a library *must*
* be specified by full path and file name.

PARAMETER whichlib
IF TYPE("whichlib") # "C" OR EMPTY(whichlib)
   * by default look for standard library to call
   DO CASE
   CASE _DOS
      IF FILE("FPATH.PLB")
          m.whichlib = "FPATH.PLB"
      ELSE
          m.whichlib = ;
            SYS(2004)+"FOXAPP\LIBS\FPATH.PLB"
      ENDIF
   CASE _WINDOWS
      IF FILE("FOXTOOLS.FLL")
         m.whichlib = "FOXTOOLS.FLL"
      ELSE
         m.whichlib = ;
           SYS(2004)+"FOXTOOLS.FLL"
      ENDIF
   CASE _UNIX
      m.whichlib = ""
   CASE _MAC
      m.whichlib = "FOXTOOLS.MLB"
   ENDCASE
ELSE
   m.whichlib = UPPER(m.whichlib)
   IF NOT "." $ m.whichlib
      DO CASE
      CASE _DOS
         m.whichlib = TRIM(m.whichlib)+".PLB"
      CASE _WINDOWS
         m.whichlib = TRIM(m.whichlib)+".FLL"
      CASE _UNIX
      CASE _MAC
         m.whichlib = TRIM(m.whichlib)+".MLB"
```

```
      ENDCASE
   ENDIF
ENDIF
DO CASE
CASE EMPTY(m.whichlib)
     && if this is called
     && by accident in _UNIX
     && and we don't have appropriate
     && libraries to match FOXTOOLS/FPATH
   SET COLOR OF SCHEME 5 TO SCHEME 7
   WAIT WINDOW NOWAIT ;
      "We don't have the library we need yet!"
   SET COLOR OF SCHEME 5 TO
CASE m.whichlib $ UPPER(SET("LIBRARY",1))
   m.whichlib = "loaded !"
CASE FILE(m.whichlib) AND NOT _MAC
   SET LIBRARY TO (m.whichlib) ADDITIVE
CASE NOT FILE(m.whichlib) AND NOT _MAC
   m.whichlib = ;
    GETFILE("PLB¦FLL",;
            "Where's library: "+m.whichlib+"?")
   IF EMPTY(m.whichlib) OR NOT FILE(m.whichlib)
      SET COLOR OF SCHEME 5 TO SCHEME 7
      WAIT WINDOW "We can't find library!" NOWAIT
      SET COLOR OF SCHEME 5 TO
   ELSE
      SET LIBRARY TO (m.whichlib) ADDITIVE
   ENDIF
CASE _MAC
   PRIVATE m.olderror, m.goterror
   m.olderror = ON("ERROR")
   m.goterror = .F.
   ON ERROR m.goterror = .T.
   SET LIBRARY TO (m.whichlib) ADDITIVE
   IF m.goterror
      DO MultiWait ;
       WITH  ;
      "Serious problem! "+CHR(13)+ ;
      "Can't load shared library file — "+;
       CHR(13)+ ;
      "check your installation of "+m.whichlib+;
       CHR(13)+ ;
```

```
        "and the Apple Shared Library Manager"+;
         CHR(13)+;
        "in your System Extensions Folder!"
        m.whichlib = ""
   ENDIF   ON ERROR &olderror
ENDCASERETURN m.whichlib
```

In the preceding code, pay close attention to the final CASE, in which the actual SET LIBRARY command is executed for the Macintosh platform. The proper loading and availability of the ASLM (Apple Shared Library Manager) is an issue that doesn't occur on the other platforms. Whether you use SetLib( )'s approach or not, you will have to find some way to handle the possibility of the ASLM being missing when your programs run.

Cross Platform Application Elements

See Also

- "Use External Commands and Functions (XCMDs and XFCNs)," Chapter 16
- "Add Functionality with Libraries," Chapater 17

You're thinking, "That has to be the last issue, right? We're through with this daunting laundry list of problems to watch out for in cross-platform design and development." Not quite.

I mentioned the Transporter several times in this chapter, and you know that Microsoft has designed FoxPro menu, screen, and report definition tables to give satisfactory results cross-platform with the help of this conversion program. However, each type of application element requires some additional thought from you. The Microsoft goals of "unmodified" cross-platform application execution, and the limited conversion options offered by the Transporter simply don't match exacting developer standards without additional work.

To cover all the vagaries of the Transporter process and its relationship to cross-platform design and development is beyond the scope of this chapter. I urge you to read Nancy Jacobsen's treatise on this subject, *Developing Cross-Platform Applications in FoxPro 2.5*, in Pinnacle Publishing's *Pros Talk Fox Series 2.5*. Although it was written before FoxPro for Macintosh, it gives you a much better understanding of the Transporter than I can hope to provide here.

To what Nancy has written, this section adds a few points pertinent to FoxPro for Macintosh.

I already mentioned that menu definition tables (.MNXs) don't have platform-specific properties, and you've seen how to provide these interface niceties with a change to GENMENU. By contrast, screen and report files (.SCXs and .FRXs) maintain separate sets of records for each platform. Objects that you place in the screen and report layouts receive unique identifiers that are matched across the different records for an object on each platform. The records are timestamped, so that when you make a change to an object on one platform, the Transporter can intervene the next time you edit that object on another platform, to ask if you want this platform's record updated as well.

The first time you MODIFY a screen or report on a new platform, you'll see the main Transporter dialog, shown at the upper left in figure 11.20. The Transporter has to add a basic set of Macintosh objects based on the layout and snippets of the objects you created on another platform. You can access the font button in this dialog to transport the objects with a specific base font. Just as you used a monospace base font for your GETs and your template screen when creating it from scratch, be sure to use a font appropriate to most of the objects on your screen when you Transport. Then you can adjust individual objects with special font needs afterwards.

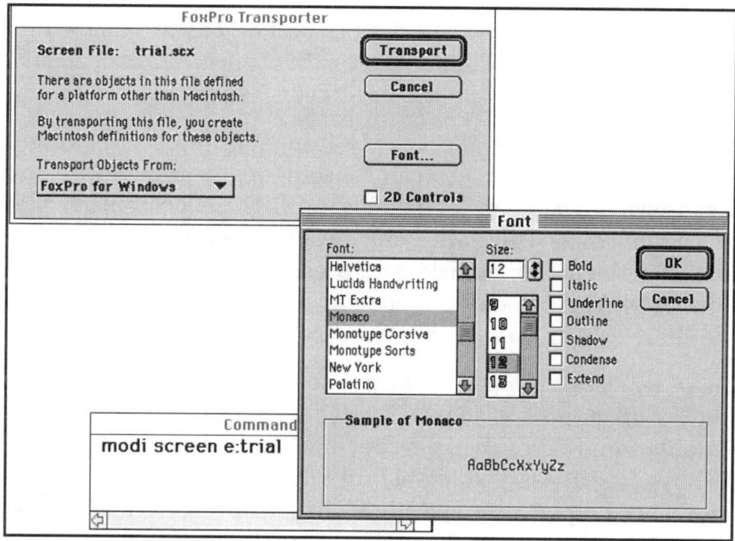

Figure 11.20 *The initial Transport dialogs.*

As shown in the figure, use a standard Mac font in FoxPro for Macintosh. Using the Transporter's mapping of TrueType fonts will give you neither accurate nor distributable results.

I gave you a brief glimpse of Randy's Cosmic Converter, a better solution, in Chapter 1, and Randy gives you an extensive review of font issues on the Macintosh in Chapter 12. However, once you've disposed of font questions, you have a few more issues to address when you convert screens and reports across platforms.

Although appearance issues resolve themselves smoothly as a rule between the two GUI platforms (Windows and Macintosh), you run into trouble with pictures in a few cases. When you transport Windows screens to the Mac, the Mac can use the included bitmaps (.BMPs), but you may prefer to provide PICT versions for greater speed. If you Transport from the Mac to Windows, you have to explicitly assign bitmaps to your picture displays because FoxPro for Windows can't use PICTs.

If you are writing cross-platform applications that include at least one character-based platform (DOS) as well as one of the GUIs, do your development in the character-based layout tool, make sure your validation and other code works properly, and then port "up" to the more complex GUI screens. You'll find that it's much more difficult to translate a Windows or Macintosh screen to DOS than the other way around — and the DOS product generates and builds faster than the other two, so it's perfect for prototyping and addressing the basic code issues.

After you've created an initial set of platform-specific records in an .SCX by running the Transporter, you can concentrate on appearance standards for each platform. When you MODIFY the SCREEN on another platform again, the Transporter will notice any outdated objects, by checking timestamps for the object records, and present you with a list of changed screen elements. You can opt to transport all changes, no changes, or select the changes you want to make cross-platform.

If you make cosmetic changes, you can use the `#TRAN SNIPPET ONLY` directive in the Setup snippet of the .SCX so the Transporter will only alert you to code changes and leave the layout changes unremarked. However, the Transporter will still ask you about any *new* objects you add to the screen, unless you placed a platform-specific transporter directive (such as `#MACOBJ` for a Macintosh-only object) in the new object's Comment field.

> **FOXPRO MAC HACK TIP**
>
> If you're like me, you may get tired of having the Transporter intervene in your work for any reason. I get the code as stable as I can before I Transport even once. After initial transport, I use the `#TRAN SNIPPET ONLY` directive for many of my screens because I may continue to fuss with the layout or window attributes on each platform and don't want the Transporter dialog's interference. If I need to change the code after this initial period, I don't MODIFY the SCREEN because the Screen Builder only gives me access to the current platform's instance of the objects and their attached code. Instead, I USE the SCX and change the snippet *for each platform's instance of the object* at the same time. For example, if I have to initialize a new variable in the Setup snippet, I make this change to each platform's header record in the SCX, distinguished as the record with the value of 1 in the objtype field. The Setup code memo field in this record contains the Setup snippet.
>
> To *completely* avoid the Transporter, USE the .SCX file, store the value of the timestamp field in a variable, and then `REPLACE ALL timestamp WITH <memvar>`.

Your last cross-platform challenge is reports. Here, as I suggested in Chapter 9, you should be very careful to check the results of calculations after Transport because the character-based and GUI Report Writers don't function with exactly the same sequence of evaluation. The benefit of Transporting reports is also limited from an appearance standpoint.

If you work cross-platform, you may be well-advised to maintain a DOS report version useful for printing to file and designing a GUI report form in Windows or on the Macintosh from scratch. Even making allowances for the differences fonts, pictures and styles make, the resulting reports will not achieve exactly the same format. Concentrate on accuracy and legibility of your results, and don't be overly concerned with getting the other attributes of your printed output to match exactly.

Your final cross-platform challenge is how you *physically* Transport the development files from one environment to the next. If you've never had to do this before and are concerned that it may prove difficult to read your FoxPro files as you move from one machine to the next, you'll find the files themselves are completely readable. As for how the files manage to migrate from one hard disk to the next, take heart—this is a problem that has faced developers throughout the history of computers, and you'll find a number of DOS/Windows-to-Mac-and-back utilities and solutions discussed in Part IV.

Chapter Wrap Up

See Also

- "Enhance the Development Process: Third Party Tools and Extensions," Chapter 19

The methods and advice presented in this chapter, like my template code, aren't meant to show you the "only way" to design or to program in FoxPro. They're meant to give you a head start, and a consistent plan, for rapid development.

The goal is to *analyze and isolate* design and programming decisions, so that you can change your techniques easily and globally. You fulfill this goal in many different ways:

- You make interface design decisions once and stick to them.
- You figure out a cross-platform development strategy you can use throughout your work.
- You design a robust generic dialog or procedure and find a standard way to call it throughout your code.

For example, my code calls a CreateID( ) function that creates a 19-character, date-time-user stamp. You may not like this method of creating IDs, but you can easily substitute another function named CreateID( ) in your version of MAIN.PRG that RETURNs an entirely different result to the rest of the template code—and the template code should behave just the same way as it did before.

Think of these techniques as signposts, not just for FoxPro 2.x, but for whatever versions of FoxPro lie beyond. Develop good habits and learn pertinent concepts now. The object oriented Xbases of tomorrow will present you with new syntax, but not with an overwhelming challenge.

12

Handle Windows and Fonts: The Unique MacDesktop

by
Randy Brown

Some people might claim that FoxPro for Macintosh ignores the Human Interface Guidelines as published by Apple Computer. In the strictest sense, this statement is accurate. However, to Microsoft's credit, these violations were necessary for the FoxPro products to maintain a common code base and for FoxPro to function cross-platform.

In many circumstances, Microsoft FoxPro uses its own internal interface objects (such as radio buttons and check boxes) instead of defining the objects through the Macintosh operating system. They look the same visually. Because of these objects' departure from standards, many third-party add-ons such as QuicKeys, which modify or accentuate these interface objects, will not work as expected with FoxPro.

To no one's surprise, Microsoft also rolls their own windows to a degree in FoxPro for Macintosh. FoxPro handles much of the dirty work of creating and manipulating windows for you, and many additional details are managed by the code that you generate from your screen files. However, you also need to know how to handle windows within your applications for occasional special requirements.

In this chapter, you'll learn about FoxPro's windows, starting with a review of Macintosh event-driven programming as it pertains to a windowed interface. The second half of this chapter zooms in on the often overlooked topic of *fontmetrics*. As you will see, fonts can play a key role in various aspects of a FoxPro window.

Modality and Event-Driven Programming

Windows are the heart and soul of the Macintosh. They are so important that Microsoft felt it necessary to capture that same essence for PCs. As a comprehensive database development platform, FoxPro offers a fairly extensive set of windowing options, but the product didn't start out that way.

I can remember when Fox Software first came out with FoxPro 1.0 for DOS machines. The attendees at the first Fox Developers Conference in Toledo sat in total amazement as Dr. Dave moved and resized a window. No big deal for us Mac folks in attendance since we already had this stuff in FoxBASE+/Mac, but to the vast DOS-oriented audience it was a major innovation. Unbeknownst to most there, these capabilities established the foundation for doing event-driven programming in FoxPro.

Most Mac users are already familiar with event-driven applications. As opposed to a menu-driven system, which limits a user to specific actions (i.e., those off of a menu), event-driven programs are meant to offer the user maximum flexibility. A typical menu-driven system usually restricts the user to working in one window at a time, limited to a specific set of actions. Each limited activity is known as a *mode*. A *modeless* or modaless condition, as defined pertaining to a windowed interface, exists if the user is not restricted to switching between windows. This is a key requirement for an event-driven program. If your window is modal, you are limiting the user's next action. Obviously, there are circumstances where users should be in a modal state, such as an Alert dialog.

CROSS-PLATFORM WARNING

FoxPro has strong cross-platform support. You might feel that a simple port from DOS is all that is necessary to move one of your applications over to the Macintosh, but be very careful. Mac users expect event-driven applications without a lot of modal windows. If your application looks menu-driven and you port it without modification, you can expect resistance from Mac users.

Even FoxBASE+/Mac users may not have programmed using event-driven techniques previously because an event-driven program was very difficult to manage in FoxBASE. Now's the time to change!

Whether a FoxPro window is modal or modeless is not controlled by the window definition. Rather it is handled by the READ statement. As you have already seen, the READ statement plays a major role in defining the events commonly associated with event-driven programming.

FoxPro Window Types

FoxPro makes extensive use of windows throughout the product. As a developer, you will most likely use the screen builder to create your application windows, but you can also use FoxPro's rich language directly.

```
DEFINE WINDOW mywind FROM 1,1 to 30,50 ;
  SYSTEM FLOAT CLOSE ZOOM GROW MINIMIZE
ACTIVATE WINDOW mywind
```

This simple code snippet creates a window that can be moved, resized, closed, and zoomed. Although there is a MINIMIZE keyword included in the sample code, FoxPro ignores it on the Macintosh. The MINIMIZE option enables the window to shrink down to an icon (FoxPro for Windows) or a title bar (FoxPro for DOS).

FOXPRO MAC HACK TIP

A third-party shareware product called WindowShade 1.2 lets you shrink a window to the title bar. While it works in FoxPro, FoxPro itself does not recognize the new window state as being minimized (WMIN()), thus limiting its programmatic functionality.

See Also

• "Third Party Tools and Extensions," Chapter 19

A window defined without an accompanying READ can have both GROW and ZOOM attributes. Non-READ windows such as BROWSEs, MODIFY MEMOs, and MODIFY FILEs can be resized/zoomed even under a READ. In Chapter 10, you saw that you could add these keywords to a window definition in the Screen Builder, using the #WCLAUSES directive, when you want to arrange BROWSEs or other system windows in a screen set.

The design tool for creating a FoxPro window is the Screen Builder. Remember that this power tool is simply a design surface. You are responsible for all objects placed on-screen and handling their actions. In addition, you need to control the windows modality because this is tied to the READ statement and not the window definition.

You can create the following types of windows using the Screen Builder:

Alert	This window is always modal and notifies or prompts the user for an immediate response. For example, you might use an Alert to reaffirm a user's intent to delete a record. Unlike other types of windows, the Alert does not include a close box in the upper-left corner.
Dialog	This dialog can either be modal or modeless. It is used when the user needs to make several choices before performing some action. For example, the common print dialog offers the user a number of options before the actual process of printing a document begins.
System	The system window is virtually equivalent to the dialog in FoxPro for Macintosh. It does vary on other platforms where borders can differ, but not on the Macintosh. You might use a System window for a data input screen.
User	This is the most flexible window type because it is user-defined. FoxPro allows you to specify the border and various window attributes (close box, half-height title bar, and moveable).

Figure 12.1 shows the four types of windows that you can create using the Screen Builder's standard settings. You specify the type by selecting the Window Style option in the Screen Layout dialog.

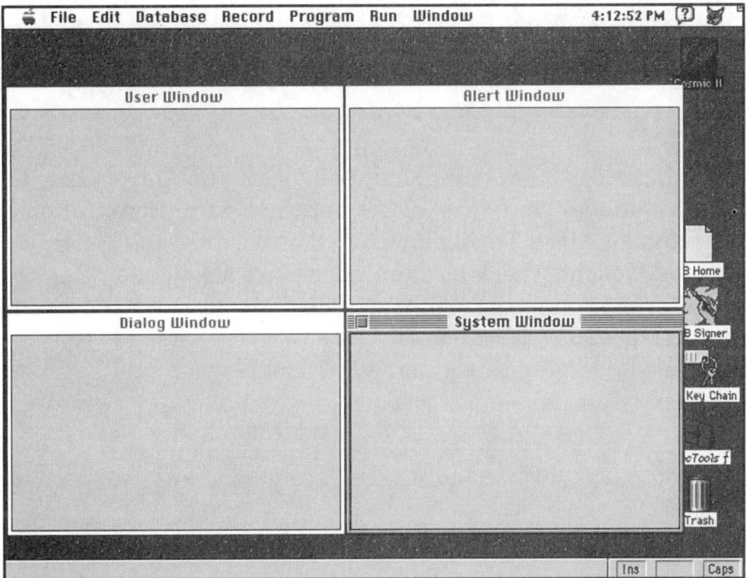

Figure 12.1 *Common FoxPro windows created in Screen Builder.*

Notice that there is one screen type left out: the Desktop type. The Desktop screen simply uses the main FoxPro screen itself. If you look at the GENSCRN output (SPR file) from a window created of this type, you will see a MODIFY WINDOW SCREEN command. The desktop screen is simply altered to your specifications.

FOXPRO MAC HACK TIP

It's possible to use a Desktop-type window to create a *switchboard*-style dialog application, as described in Chapter 5. In this interface a set of buttons giving the user further choices takes the place of a standard GETless Foundation READ. However, the present version of GENSCRN doesn't do a good job of handling Desktop windows on the Macintosh. It doesn't ensure the main application window (SCREEN) is visible, and it doesn't properly ACTIVATE this window.

> If you want to design a main switchboard window for your FoxPro Mac applications, you should use a user-defined window and hide the SCREEN window as you normally do. If you decide you do want to use the SCREEN window, you can prevent the template code from automatically hiding this window by setting the `m.mainwindow` switch in your INCLUDE.PRG.

Typically, Macintosh Alerts and Modal dialogs do not have a title bar. The illustration of an alert in figure 12.2 is not the best representation of a proper Macintosh Alert. To display a window without a title bar, you must uncheck the Moveable check box and make sure the window has no title. Since the Alert option in the Window Style dialog doesn't allow you to uncheck the Moveable check box, as you saw in Chapter 11, you use the User Defined style and pick the correct attributes yourself.

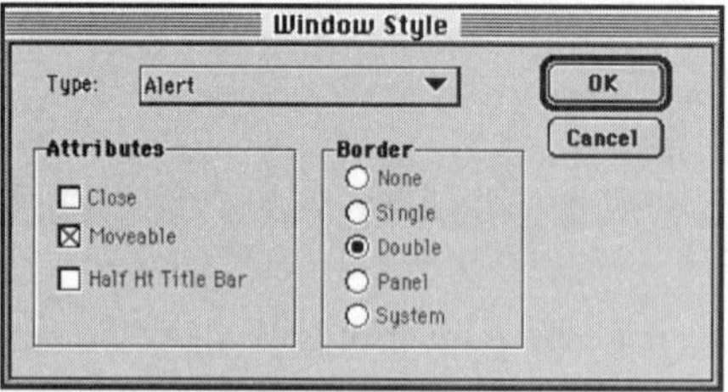

Figure 12.2 *Alert setting in Window Style dialog.*

I said earlier that FoxPro defines windows from its own unique internal code base rather than the more common Macintosh operating system (Toolbox), but this is not consistently true. There are some dialogs for which FoxPro does rely on the Macintosh. In the next section, I will explore these two window sources and the options that you have with each.

Doing Windows the FoxPro Way

Take a look at the GETFILE() dialog in figure 12.3. If you have been using FoxPro for awhile, it probably looks a little different than some of the other dialogs (for example, the Font dialog). What is going on here?

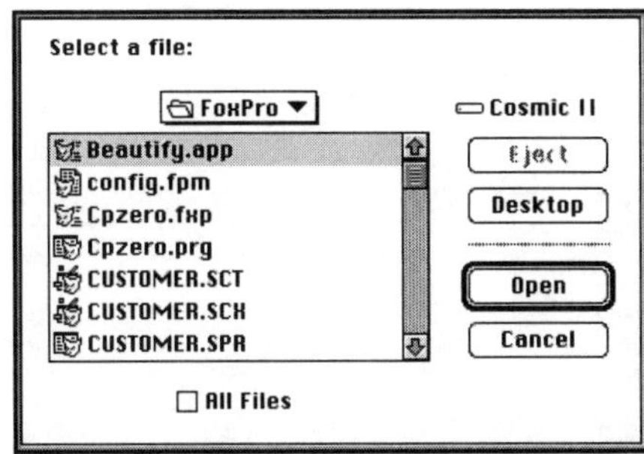

Figure 12.3 *GETFILE() dialog showing typical Macintosh dialog from a resource.*

GETFILE() comes from the Macintosh operating system. Most Macintosh software uses standard dialogs (and alerts) in a similar fashion. Other windows in FoxPro come from FoxPro's internal window structures. Table 12.1 illustrates the primary differences between the two.

Table 12.1

Comparison of FoxPro vs. Macintosh Dialogs Used by FoxPro

Window Source	*Font*	*Font Size*	*3D Effects*
FoxPro	Geneva	10	Yes
Macintosh	Chicago	12	No

Why does FoxPro depart from the standard dialog attributes on the Macintosh? As you become more familiar with the product, you notice some rather complex dialogs, such as the RQBE. During development of FoxPro for Macintosh, Microsoft needed to come up with an alternative to the standard Chicago,12 dialog because some dialogs were too large to fit on a 9" Macintosh Classic. The smaller font window proved to be the best solution. To add a little spice, they added 3D effects to the controls.

FoxPro relies on Macintosh internal windows for file and folder dialogs such as those associated with GETDIR(), GETFILE(), LOCFILE(), and PUTFILE() functions. Like other Macintosh applications, FoxPro for Macintosh has a resource fork containing all of the application resources needed by FoxPro itself. The file/folder dialog resources are stored in this fork. (You looked at the resources stored in your Mac System file in Chapter 11.)

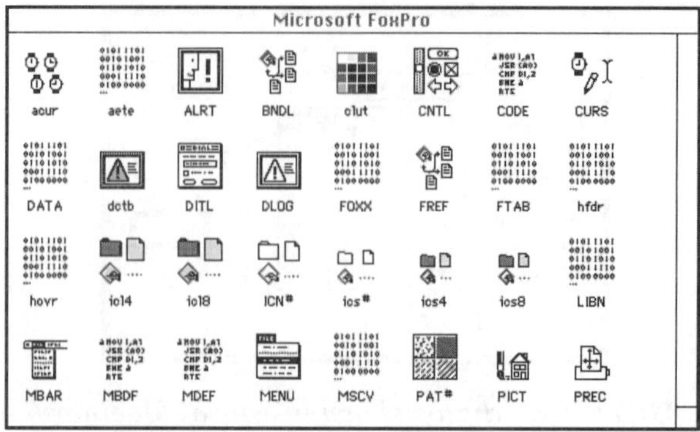

Figure 12.4 *FoxPro opened up in ResEdit.*

If you have a copy of ResEdit, you can open up FoxPro and take a peek at its resources (see figure 12.4). As I mentioned earlier, FoxPro uses a common code base, but certain Macintosh conventions, such as the unique Mac resources, cannot be ignored no matter how common Microsoft wants to make the code base and how foreign these concepts are to DOS and Windows.

CROSS-PLATFORM WARNING

You should always work on a backup copy of FoxPro before you start using ResEdit because you can accidentally destroy resources. ResEdit has a set of built-in template editors for use with a variety of resources such as ICON, ALRT, CICN, PICT, and so on. Some resources are just binary code and cannot be edited through a template using ResEdit. Under no circumstances should you attempt to change these resources.

With most Macintosh software, there are five common resources used for handling windows. As you see in table 12.2, FoxPro does not use the WIND resource because it relies on its own. This is defined internally and from the WDEF resource, which is non-editable code.

Table 12.2

Macintosh Resources Devoted to Windows, Alerts, and Dialogs

Resource	*Description*	*Editable*	*Used by FoxPro*
ALRT	Alert template	☒	☒
DLOG	Dialog template	☒	☒
WIND	Window template	☒	
DITL	Dialog items list	☒	☒
WDEF	Window definition		☒

Because Microsoft has exposed some of their dialogs through Macintosh resources, you now have additional flexibility not available through the DOS and Windows products. Let's look at one of the tricks you can do using ResEdit on FoxPro.

Modifying the GETFILE dialog using ResEdit

FoxPro uses a combination of DLOG and DITL resources to display the standard GETFILE() dialog (see figure 12.5). I am going to show how you can modify this dialog to disable the `All Files` check box. Why do this? As you may know, with GETFILE() you can pass a file skeleton to limit the display of files for a certain extension. For example, you may want to limit the user to a list of DBF files to choose from. With the `All Files` check box, the user can bypass this DBF-only list and select another type of file, probably one you wouldn't want him to select. This trick disables the check box so that the user cannot click on it. Here is a list of steps to take:

1. Open a backup copy of Microsoft FoxPro in ResEdit.
2. Double-click on the DLOG resource icon.
3. Select and open resource id #129, the GetFile dialog.
4. Open the associated DITL resource.
5. Select and open the check box dialog item.
6. Uncheck the enabled check box.
7. Save FoxPro and close ResEdit.

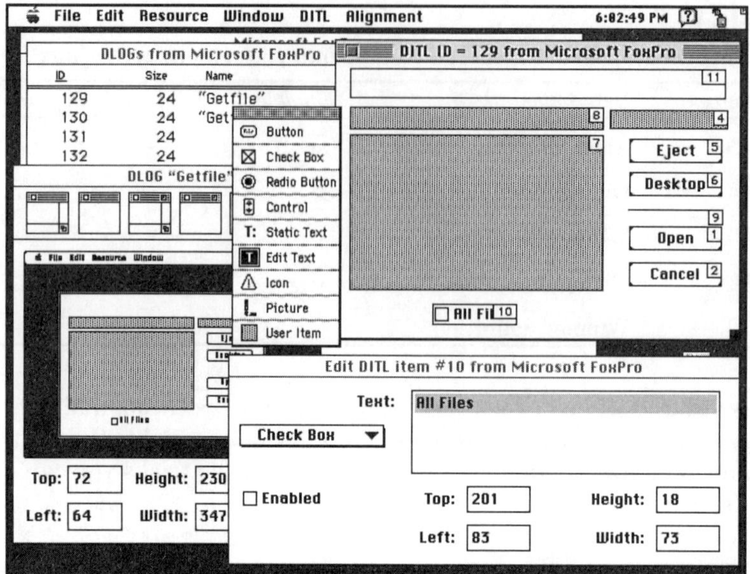

Figure 12.5 *GETFILE() dialog opened up in ResEdit.*

It is important that you do not delete the `All Files` check box because FoxPro references it internally by number. You can play around with this dialog and others, but remember that each dialog item is probably referenced somehow by FoxPro. You might want to try changing the item type or static text contents, and, as I mentioned earlier, you should try this first on a backup copy.

This GETFILE() trick is best suited for distributed applications because you probably wouldn't want to limit yourself to file restrictions during development. Remember, if you plan on porting this application over to FoxPro for Windows or FoxPro for DOS, you will not be able to use this same trick on a PC, so you must include additional code to check for the file extension. Also, whenever you make a resource modification like this one, be sure to thoroughly test it because FoxPro might choke on the change.

Using Macintosh Alerts

The FxAlert() function contained in the FOXTOOLS.MLB library uses true Macintosh ALRT resources. Instead of having to create your own alerts from FoxPro's screen builder, you can use this function instead. Those of you using FoxPro for Windows probably know about the similar MsgBox() function in the FOXTOOLS.FLL library, which accesses the Windows operating system standard alerts.

Should you use FxAlert() or create your own with the Screen Builder? With FoxPro for Windows, I usually recommend using MsgBox() because it dynamically resizes the alert window for the text message. However, I am a little reluctant to do this with FxAlert(). One of the problems with using FxAlert() and MsgBox() is that neither allows you to specify text for the buttons. You are limited to standard prompts such as `OK`, `Cancel`, `Yes`, and `No`. With FoxPro for Macintosh, you have another more serious problem. Since you cannot distribute Apple's ASLM system extension (unless you purchase a distribution license from Apple), you will not be able to ship the FOXTOOLS.MLB library with your distributed applications.

> **CROSS-PLATFORM WARNING**
>
> The XCMD chapter shows an XCMD with similar functionality to the FxAlert() function. In addition to the 12 standard dialogs supported by FxAlert, the Xalert XCMD also allows for custom alerts.

Regardless of these setbacks, it is a good idea to maintain interface standards as much as possible, and using FxAlert() helps do this. Those of you familiar with FoxBASE+/Macs ALERT NOTE command immediately recognize the similarity. In fact, Microsoft added FxAlert() primarily for backward compatibility. Here's the full FxAlert() syntax:

```
FxAlert(<expN1>, <expN2>, <expN3>, <expN4>[, <expC1>][,
<expC2>][, <expC3>][, <expC4>])

ex. m.retval=FxAlert(1,259,-1,-1,;
  "Do you want to delete record?")

<expN1> - number of icon displayed on the alert (0=CAUTION,1=STOP,
2=NOTE).
<expN2> - resource id of dialog (see table below).
<expN3>, <expN4> - coordinates in pixels from the top left of the
screen. Use default values of -1 to center dialog.
<expC1>...<expC4> - text that will appear on the alert.
```

Table 12.3 shows the push buttons displayed on each of the 12 alerts with the default push button noted by an asterisk.

Table 12.3

FxAlert() Function (in FOXTOOLS.MLB Library) Dialog Resources

Resource ID	*Button 1*	*Button 2*	*Button 3*	*Misc*
257	Continue*			
258	OK*			
259	Yes*	No		
260	Yes	No*		
261	Yes*	No	Cancel	
262	Yes	No*	Cancel	
263	Continue*			Large 257
264	OK*			Large 258
265	Yes*	No		Large 259
266	Yes	No*		Large 260
267	Yes*	No	Cancel	Large 261
268	Yes	No*	Cancel	Large 262

** default button*

This table lists the resource ids of DLOG resources referenced by the FxAlert() function. As with the GETFILE() dialog example shown earlier, you can use ResEdit to make modifications to the dialogs and items. You might want to change the button prompts or resize the dialog.

The Unique MACDESKTOP

I can remember speaking with the FoxPro team at Microsoft prior to final development of their Macintosh version. They faced a dilemma: their DOS and Windows products didn't quite address the unique Macintosh multi-tasking windowing environment. Multi-tasking was never an issue with the DOS product because the DOS operating system by itself is not a multi-tasking platform. Microsoft Windows is multi-tasking, but all application windows exist within that application's main window. This parent-child concept is what Microsoft calls a *Multiple Document Interface* (MDI).

If you are serious about using the Macintosh, you should forget about this parent-child paradigm. Visually, it is a *serious* violation of Macintosh interface standards. Technically, as we will see shortly, it can be used in a variety of ways to get around FoxPro limitations.

Microsoft hasn't forgotten those folks who want to port their DOS and Windows applications over to the Macintosh. They have addressed this multi-tasking windowing issue with the new *MACDESKTOP* setting. Just remember, Mac purists expect application windows to exist at any level of the Mac desktop. FoxPro for Macintosh does have a main application screen like FoxPro for Windows' main window, but all other windows are free to exist in front or behind that one. The MACDESKTOP setting addresses the relationship of these windows.

By default, FoxPro sets MACDESKTOP ON so that windows exist in a true Mac manner. If for some reason you want your Macintosh to act like a Windows product, you can SET MACDESKTOP OFF. (You can also set `MACDESKTOP = OFF` in the CONFIG.FPM file.) You might want to do this if you are working on a cross-platform application.

As someone who has been using a Macintosh since its roots, I can tell you that Mac users are extremely particular when it comes to interfaces. Look what happened to Lotus and WordPerfect when they decided to do a port of their popular DOS products without consideration for the Mac interface. If you do decide to do a simple port of your Windows/DOS application without addressing the MACDESKTOP issue, you are truly shorting your endusers. To capture the true essence of the Mac, the authors of this book agree that your FoxPro applications should have MACDESKTOP set ON. All the template code for this book is written with this interface goal in mind.

CROSS-PLATFORM WARNING

Beware of PC FoxPro gurus disguised as Mac zealots telling you that it is fine to SET MACDESKTOP OFF so that your Mac will emulate Microsoft Windows.

If you still insist on ignoring our advice and SET MACDESKTOP OFF, consider the following consequences of your decision:

- Windows are limited in size to that of the main FoxPro screen.
- Windows can become clipped or partially obscured from view.
- Windows can't be minimized, or iconified, as they can in Microsoft Windows.
- The main FoxPro screen must always be visible.
- Windows cannot be spread across multiple monitors unless the main FoxPro screen extends to the other monitors.

As a developer, you may want to keep all of your FoxPro development tools within the FoxPro screen. It can become quite a nuisance when you accidentally click on the FoxPro screen and the Command window disappears behind it. I move the Command window to the side a bit so that it can never be fully obscured. You may, however, want to activate this window within the FoxPro screen so that it always stays on top. The following command will handle this:

```
ACTIVATE WINDOW Command IN Screen
```

This next command reverts the window back to its original state:

```
ACTIVATE WINDOW Command IN MACDESKTOP
```

You can do this same trick with other developer windows such as Trace, Debug, and View, as you can see in figure 12.6. If you are using FoxPro for Windows, note that closing the main FoxPro screen in the Mac product doesn't terminate FoxPro. The screen is just hidden. You can redisplay the screen by selecting the Screen option under the Window menu. Note also that the RELEASE WINDOW SCREEN command only hides the screen and does not actually release it. You can prove this with a simple test:

```
RELEASE WINDOW SCREENWAIT WINDOW "Main Window (SCREEN) ";
   IIF(WEXIST(""), ;
      "still exists!", ;
       "is really gone!")
```

In this code, notice that you refer to the main application window using the null string in all FoxPro window-handling functions, such as WEXIST().

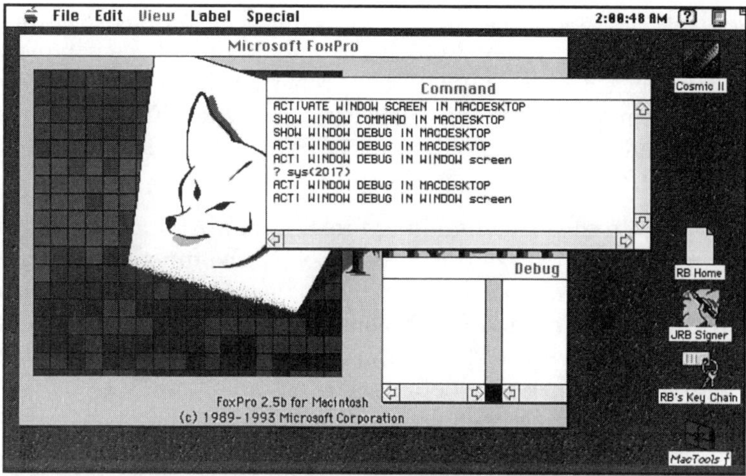

Figure 12.6 *Command window floating in MACDESKTOP and Debug window clipped to FoxPro main application window, or SCREEN.*

Windoids

Macintosh people call them floating palettes. Windows users call them Always-On-Tops. Fox folks call them IN DESKTOP windows. Whatever you want to call these critters, their behavior is always the same: this type of window always stays on top of other windows. They can only be covered up by other IN DESKTOP windows. Most interface guidelines state that these windows should have a half-height title bar. This is not a strict requirement. FoxPro's spell checker is an IN DESKTOP window with a normal title bar.

If you are not familiar with floating palettes, take a look at another software package that uses them (such as graphics software). Windoids often serve as palettes of tools, colors, or other options to assist in working with the main window. With most software, they act independently and only influence changes to the front window.

FoxPro offers an IN DESKTOP type window, which you might be inclined to implement as a windoid in your applications. Using FoxPro's current event-driven tools, it is very difficult to simulate true Mac-like windoids. The main obstacle that you face is determining which window is currently active. WONTOP() returns the topmost window. However, if you are trying to implement a windoid, the value returned by WONTOP() will be the IN DESKTOP one — not the one you want. The WCHILD() function can be used with FoxPro for Windows to get a list of all the windows in the window stack. However, WCHILD() relies on these windows being children of the main FoxPro SCREEN. In most cases, FoxPro for Macintosh windows aren't children of the SCREEN, unless you've SET MACDESKTOP OFF.

If you investigate the error-handling function in MAIN.PRG (PROCEDURE AppError), you'll see that WPARENT(), the function telling you the name of a window's parent window, is smart enough to return "MACDESKTOP" to normal FoxPro for Macintosh windows. However, if you use WCHILD() with "MACDESKTOP" as an argument to find out which windows are currently defined, you get an error ("WINDOW 'MACDESKTOP' has not been defined").

Microsoft has indicated that these window types will be better supported in the future.

Parent-Child Windows

By now, you probably know how I feel about parent-child windows. They don't belong on the Mac! On the other hand, I have found occasion to use them under special circumstances. Take a look at the Cosmic Converter utility included with the source code disk (see figure 12.7). I had to use a child window within the main window so that I could display the selected font and have it clipped if it was too large for the display region (that is, child window).

Figure 12.7 *Cosmic Converter shareware utility by Randy Brown showing parent-child window used to display a sample font.*

You've seen the WCHILD() function and child windows put to good use in the template code's toolbar code in Chapter 10. An invisible parent window holds the various elements of the toolbar together and tells your application which windows are part of the toolbar. Similarly, parent-child windows can be useful for BROWSEs. By defining your BROWSE window within a previously defined, smaller window, you can mask the BROWSE title bar or scroll bars, and you can make a BROWSE look like an integral part of a data entry screen.

FOXPRO MAC HACK TIP

If you try this trick with child-window BROWSEs, make sure to paint your GETs in *another* child window of the same parent, rather than in the parent itself. Otherwise, the parent window comes forward, obscuring the BROWSE when the GET objects receive focus in the READ.

All of these tricks do not give the user the impression that there is any sort of parent-child relationship involved. It is important to understand this concept when developing Macintosh applications: *you can use parent-child windows as long as your users don't know you're using them.*

Cross-Platform Screen Development

Maybe I should call this section "The Tao of Fontmetrics." For most developers, fontmetrics is one subject they would rather not touch. If you plan on transporting your screens (and reports) between a PC and a Mac, you will need to be somewhat familiar with fontmetrics, and to spend some time creating an efficient font strategy.

There's no such thing as a free lunch, even in FoxPro. It's not possible to move software effortlessly from one platform to another—particularly when it comes to user interfaces. You've already received some advice on cross-platform problems and solutions in Chapter 11. In this section, I present some tried and tested strategies for cross-platform screen development, focusing in particular on screen objects and font characteristics.

Early in my cross-platform development efforts, I made a conscious decision to isolate screen code into two basic components:

- Interface design, or platform-specific, code (SCX files)
- Database operation, or platform-transparent, code (PRG files)

When code is generated for screen files (SCX/SCT), *code snippets* and interface/environment code are simultaneously generated. These snippets (screen setup, cleanup and object valids, and so on), which are embedded directly within screen files, define how the application handles typical database operations, such as record movement, printing, or deletion. In essence the screen, with all its objects and their functionality, can be entirely self-contained. When a screen file is opened on another platform, FoxPro's Transporter intercedes to create a duplicate set of screen objects specifically for that platform. And when you regenerate screen code, often twice as much code is created, much of it being redundant. Consequently, I avoid using snippets with my screen files.

Code snippets are merely expressions with calls to procedures/functions in the same or higher calling program (PRG). These files contain mostly platform-transparent database operation code. The SCX/SCT files, on the other hand, hold the platform-specific interface code. Editing a PRG is usually quicker and doesn't require GENSCRN each time a change is made. If you are storing code in your screen snippets, you must ensure that any change is also made to those same objects for all other platforms in the SCX/SCT file.

In general, porting between FoxPro for Macintosh and FoxPro for Windows is relatively easy because both support virtually the same set of screen objects. While FoxPro for DOS makes use of many GUI-like controls, as shown in table 12.4, it doesn't include many of the options supported by FoxPro for Windows and FoxPro for Macintosh. (There are third-party tools available, such as Espia from Devices Inc., which provide true graphics feeling to FoxPro for DOS applications.)

Table 12.4

FoxPro Screen Objects by Platform

Screen Object	*DOS*	*Windows*	*Macintosh*
Static Text	☒	☒	☒
Fields	☒	☒	☒

Screen Object	*DOS*	*Windows*	*Macintosh*
Lines	☒	☒	☒
Boxes	☒	☒	☒
Rounded Rectangles		☒	☒
Push Buttons	☒	☒	☒
Invisible Buttons	☒	☒	☒
Picture Buttons		☒	☒
Radio Buttons	☒	☒	☒
Picture Radio Buttons		☒	☒
Check Boxes	☒	☒	☒
Picture Check Boxes		☒	☒
Popups	☒	☒	☒
Lists	☒	☒	☒
Edit Regions	☒	☒	☒
Spinners		☒	☒
3D Effects			☒
OLE Objects		☒	☒
Pictures		BMP	BMP,PICT

Although it's easy to say "only use objects supported by all platforms being used," I don't adopt this strategy or want to be limited in my development. There is no reason why FoxPro for Windows shouldn't be able to use picture buttons and FoxPro for DOS use normal push buttons.

This isn't to say there aren't limitations. People still use monochrome Macs, and Apple still makes 640×400 PowerBooks and Macs with 9-inch, 512×384 displays.

When a screen is ported to another platform and opened for the first time, FoxPro invokes the *transporter*—a program (TRANSPRT.PRG) that creates new platform screen objects from those already existing. As you might imagine, some complex heuristics are involved in mapping an object from a character-based coordinate system (FoxPro for DOS) to a graphical one (FoxPro for Windows or FoxPro for Macintosh). Topping the list of these calculations is font handling. Transporting between FoxPro for

Macintosh and FoxPro for Windows, however, is simply a matter of remapping fonts with similar characteristics—fontmetrics. In fact, it is likely that less than 10 percent of the almost 400K TRANSPRT.PRG file is devoted to GUI transports.

The Transporter does an adequate job of transporting files between FoxPro for Windows and FoxPro for Macintosh. Still, at the present time, it is nearly impossible to come up with an identical-looking screen. You should expect to make minor adjustments to both position and size of many objects. After a screen is converted, however, the Transporter does an excellent job of keeping objects synched when you modify the screen and re-Transport between platforms.

The Cosmic Converter utility included on the source code disk provides an alternative, yet basic, transporter for converting a screen. The main advantage of this alternative program over the FoxPro Transporter is that it gives you the ability to specify both default screen and object fonts.

Font Use and FontMetrics

To understand what is happening in the Transporter, you need to understand how fonts work in FoxPro. One of the dilemmas Microsoft faced when developing FoxPro for Windows was how to address object size and positioning. The company wanted software to be compatible on both GUI and character-based platforms. The solution was a unit of measurement known as a *foxel*, which is a cross between a pixel and a FoxPro row/column. The following FoxPro command displays an input field on a screen at coordinates of 9.063,40.125:

```
@ 9.063,40.125 GET m.state ;
   SIZE 1.000,3.200 ;
   DEFAULT " " ;
   FONT "Geneva", 9 ;
   PICTURE "@K XX" ;
   COLOR ,RGB(,,,255,255,255)
```

These coordinates are actually based on rows and columns of the screen itself. They are not, however, controlled by the object's font (Geneva,9,Normal), but are based entirely on the default font (Geneva,13,Normal) for the window in which the object occurs. The window font is set by a window definition shown on the following page (Note: Both code examples are GENSCRN output from a sample screen file):

```
IF NOT WEXIST("_qls1cbchi")
   DEFINE WINDOW _qls1cbchi ;
      AT  0.000, 0.000  ;
      SIZE 18.188,62.500 ;
      TITLE "Customer" ;
      FONT "Geneva", 13 ;
      FLOAT ;
      COLOR RGB(,,,192,192,192)
   MOVE WINDOW _qls1cbchi CENTER
ENDIF
```

> **CROSS-PLATFORM WARNING**
>
> The window definition from a GENSCRN output SPR file creates absolute coordinates for the window location (the AT clause). Notice in the code example, that there is a MOVE WINDOW CENTER command following. This is good practice because the location of the screen is based on the font of the main FoxPro screen, which as you know is subject to change. This is an anomaly in FoxPro. You have two options if you don't want to center the window. One is to always restore the main FoxPro screen to the one you had at the time GENSCRN was run. Chapter 11 shows you a way to alter GENSCRN to provide this information automatically in the .SPR. The other option is to use complex formulas for these coordinates.

Each font has its own unique set of attributes commonly known as *fontmetrics*. These values are always measured in pixels in both FoxPro for Macintosh and FoxPro for Windows. FoxPro has a FONTMETRIC() function that returns 20 various dimensional characteristics of a font. The values I'll examine here primarily affect the font's height and width dimensions:

- FONTMETRIC(1) Character height in pixels.
- FONTMETRIC(5) Extra leading in pixels (not available in FoxPro for Macintosh).
- FONTMETRIC(6) Average character width in pixels.

Now we can jump back to this mystical unit known as a foxel. The following formulas yield the single foxel row and column values as well as the calculations of the example field's position.

1 Foxel Row = FONTMETRIC(1) + FONTMETRIC(5)

1 Foxel Column = FONTMETRIC(6)

Calculation of example:

1 Foxel Row = FONTMETRIC(1,'Geneva',13) + FONTMETRIC(5,'Geneva',13)

= 16 pixels

1 Foxel Column = FONTMETRIC(6,'Geneva',13)

= 8 pixels

The location of the @..GET field:

= number of rows * pixels per foxel row

= 9.063 * 16 = 145

= number of columns * pixels per foxel col

= 40.125 * 8 = 321

The pixel values of 145,321 represent the coordinate position of the field from the upper left corner of the defined window. The field's size (1.000,3.200) is based on the fontmetric values of the object font itself (Geneva,9). As you might expect, the foxel values for the object are smaller.

1 Foxel Row = FONTMETRIC(1,'Geneva',9) + FONTMETRIC(5,'Geneva',9)

= 12 pixels

1 Foxel Column = FONTMETRIC(6,'Geneva',9)

= 5 pixels

When you take another look at the DEFINE WINDOW command (see above) for the screen definition, you see a similar analogy. SIZE coordinates are based on the window's own font, but the AT coordinates are based on the global FoxPro default font. FoxPro works with multiple coordinate systems. All objects within a single screen are based on the local coordinate system of that screen, while the screen itself is based on a more global coordinate screen. Each coordinate system varies because of the differences in foxel values.

Let's revisit the Transporter now that you understand how different fonts affect position and size of objects. You'll notice immediately that the Transporter only allows an option for one font. And guess which font this is? That's right, the object font! I fully expect Microsoft to address this issue soon, but right now there are no accommodations for specifying the default, or base, font used in the window definition. In fact, Microsoft defaults to the two fonts shown in table 12.5 when transporting between the platforms.

Table 12.5

Default Screen Fonts and Their Fontmetric Values

Platform	*Default Screen Font*	*FONTMETRIC(1)*	*FONTMETRIC(6)*
Windows	MS Sans Serif,8	13	5
Macintosh	Geneva,10	12	6

It is virtually impossible to obtain an identical-looking screen when you first transport. Because of these single pixel differences in fontmetrics of the platforms, two critical components of the transport process are affected. First, the position of objects will be off because their coordinate system is based on a font with different dimensions. Second, the size of the window is altered because its definition is based on this same font. It is much more crucial that the fontmetrics of base window fonts match than that those of object fonts match.

It just so happens that the above two fonts are also the default fonts used when a new .SCX is created (using the CREATE SCREEN command). Most programmers don't bother changing the default screen font because it doesn't visually impact the look of a screen (since each object can have its own font). If you've been following instructions in this book, however, you know that the base font for the window is critical.

The key to a truly successful transport is finding default fonts with exact fontmetrics. Table 12.6 shows my preferences for default fonts.

Table 12.6

Suggested Screen Fonts with Identical Fontmetric Values to Facilitate Better Transporting Between Platforms

Platform	*Default Screen Font*	*FONTMETRIC(1)*	*FONTMETRIC(6)*
Windows	MS Sans Serif,10,B	16	8
Macintosh	Geneva,13,N	16	8

I chose these fonts because they are both common system fonts for their respective platforms. (Note: You need to use the Cosmic Converter utility to port the screens because FoxPro's Transporter doesn't allow you to alter the window font.) No doubt, there are countless combinations of fonts with similar matching values. If possible, you should use common fonts that you know exist on the computers running your screens. This is especially important if you plan to distribute your applications to additional users.

There is more room for variations in fontmetrics of the object fonts than base window fonts because most people leave extra space onscreen. The Transporter is actually quite smart in how it handles object fonts. You can specify a single object font for all objects to convert. If you choose, however, not to specify an object font and instead use the default transporter font (Geneva,10,B for FoxPro for Macintosh), both font size and style are retained. With FoxPro for Macintosh, the font used will either be Geneva or Chicago depending on which font is found in the FoxPro for Windows objects. The transporter even transports controls, such as push buttons, to default system fonts.

The window's look and feel is strictly at your discretion. If you're looking for a simple cross-platform font strategy for objects, you may want to try the fonts in table 12.7, which have a similar look and feel on their respective platforms and are close in fontmetrics. In addition, these are common Windows and Mac system fonts.

Table 12.7

Suggested Fonts for Objects with Similar Fontmetrics

Platform	*Default Screen Font*	*FONTMETRIC(1)*	*FONTMETRIC(6)*
Windows	MS Sans Serif,8	13	5
Macintosh	Geneva,9	12	5

See Also

- Source Disk: Miscellaneous Code Samples: CONVERT.PRG

As an alternative to the Cosmic Converter utility, you may want to try a more simplistic approach, as shown in the next program. This program has only the basic conversion code, which is similar to that of the Cosmic Converter:

```
* CONVERT.PRG
* This simple program converts a screen file
* (SCX/SCT) between GUI platforms (Mac and
* Windows). You can provide the fonts at the
* top of the program.
```

```
PRIVATE objfont,objfsize,objfstyle
PRIVATE scrnfont,scrnfsize,scrnfstyle
PRIVATE nosize,nostyle,SysControl
PRIVATE mystamp,splatform,splatform2
PRIVATE tmparr,tmpcurs,tmpalias,scrnfile

* Select fonts you want to use for
* transporting
DO CASE
CASE _MAC
  * default screen font
  scrnfont='Geneva'
  scrnfsize=13
  scrnfstyle=0
  * object font
  objfont='Geneva'
  objfsize=9
  objfstyle=0
CASE _WINDOWS
  * default screen font
  scrnfont='MS Sans Serif'
  scrnfsize=10
  scrnfstyle=1
  * object font
  objfont='MS Sans Serif'
  objfsize=8
  objfstyle=0
ENDCASE

splatform = IIF(_MAC,'MAC','WINDOWS')
splatform2 = IIF(_MAC,'WINDOWS','MAC')

m.nosize = .F.     &&retain original font style
m.nostyle = .T.    &&retain original font size
m.SysControl = .F. &&use system font for controls

* Select screen file to transport
m.scrnfile=GETFILE('SCX','Select Screen File:')
IF !'.SCX'$UPPER(m.scrnfile)
  RETURN
ENDIF
```

```
* If the file already has platform objects
* it is kicked out. You can manually delete
* these objects and retransport.
m.tmpalias='_'+LEFT(SYS(3),7)
SELECT 0
USE (m.scrnfile) ALIAS (m.tmpalias) EXCLUSIVE
LOCATE FOR platform=m.splatform
IF FOUND()
  WAIT WINDOW 'File has already been transported.'
  USE IN (m.tmpalias)
  RETURN
ENDIF

WAIT WINDOW 'Transporting Screen...' NOWAIT

* Create cursor of new platform objects
* to be appended to original file later.
=AFIELDS(tmparr)
m.tmpcurs='_'+LEFT(SYS(3),7)
CREATE CURSOR (m.tmpcurs) FROM ARRAY tmparr
APPEND FROM DBF(tmpalias) ;
  FOR platform = m.splatform2

* Add new platform
REPLACE ALL platform WITH m.splatform

* Handle porting of objects
DO CASE
CASE m.nostyle AND m.nosize  && only fontface
  REPLACE ALL fontface WITH m.objfont;
    FOR INLIST(objtype,5,11,12,13,14,15,16,22,23)
CASE m.nostyle    &&dont' change fontstyle
  REPLACE ALL fontface WITH m.objfont,;
    fontsize WITH m.objfsize;
    FOR INLIST(objtype,5,11,12,13,14,15,16,22,23)
CASE m.nosize     &&dont' change fontsize
  REPLACE ALL fontface WITH m.objfont,;
    fontstyle WITH m.objfstyle;
    FOR INLIST(objtype,5,11,12,13,14,15,16,22,23)
OTHERWISE
  REPLACE ALL fontface WITH m.objfont,;
```

```
    fontsize WITH m.objfsize,;
    fontstyle WITH m.objfstyle;
    FOR INLIST(objtype,5,11,12,13,14,15,16,22,23)
ENDCASE

* Add system fonts for controls if option set
IF m.SysControl
  DO CASE
  CASE _MAC
    * use Geneva,10,N for controls
    REPLACE ALL fontface WITH 'Geneva',;
      fontsize WITH 10,fontstyle WITH 0;
      FOR INLIST(objtype,11,13,14,16,22)
    * use Geneva,10,B for text buttons
    REPLACE ALL fontface WITH 'Geneva',;
      fontsize WITH 10,fontstyle WITH 1;
      FOR objtype=12
  CASE _WINDOWS
    * use MS Sans Serif,8,B for controls
    REPLACE ALL fontface WITH 'MS Sans Serif',;
      fontsize WITH 8,fontstyle WITH 1;
      FOR INLIST(objtype,12,13,14,16,22)
    * use MS Sans Serif,8,N for lists
    REPLACE ALL fontface WITH 'MS Sans Serif',;
      fontsize WITH 8,;
      fontstyle WITH 0 FOR objtype=11
  ENDCASE
ENDIF

* Handle screen default font objects
*   - picture buttons, invisible buttons
*   - picture check boxes, picture radios
REPLACE ALL fontface WITH m.scrnfont,;
  fontsize WITH m.scrnfsize,;
  fontstyle WITH m.scrnfstyle ;
  FOR INLIST(objtype,1,20) OR '@*B'$picture OR ;
  '@*RB'$picture OR '@*CB'$picture

* Note: can add code here to
* replace objtype 23 info

* Cleanup a little
```

```
SELECT (m.tmpalias)
APPEND FROM DBF(m.tmpcurs)
USE IN (m.tmpalias)
USE IN (m.tmpcurs)
WAIT CLEAR
MODIFY SCREEN (m.scrnfile) NOWAIT
RETURN
```

Fonts on the Mac

I wrote this section originally as a brief overview on fonts. After reading it, I thought it just lacked—not *something*, it just lacked. I decided to cover a little more technical side of fonts, something you definitely won't see in any other FoxPro book.

If you have been using a Macintosh for awhile, you probably know that fonts come in two flavors: TrueType (TT) and bitmap (let's consider PostScript fonts as part of the TT category). And maybe that's all you know. If you're the kind of person who views fonts (and maybe printer drivers) as elements that should work *without* being understood, you may want to do a quick SCAN ENDSCAN of the finer points (no pun intended) of this section.

What is a font? Let's get a few definitions straight so that we are on common speaking terms:

- *Font* A set of typographical characters with a consistent look (such as Helvetica).
- *Character* The smallest element in a font (such as a,3,*).
- *Glyph* The distinct visual representation of a character(s).
- *Ligature* Multi-character representation of a single glyph (such as a Æ).
- *Typeface* The font name (such as Helvetica).
- *Font style* Bold, italic, and so on.

Most folks are used to talking about characters and glyphs as one and the same, but in reality they are separate concepts. Think of a character as the generic letter C and one glyph as the letter C in Chicago,12 on a color monitor. The visual representation of this one letter varies on the display device and its font representation; hence the need for a separate term—*glyph*.

Traditional bitmap fonts only exist in specified sizes. For example, you might have a bitmap font for Helvetica,12 point. The collection of all fonts for a given typeface is called a *font family*. The Macintosh relies on font families to speed up font rendering and maintain visual consistency.

TrueType fonts, which were developed by Apple and Microsoft, have only been around since System 7. PostScript and TT fonts are functionally similar in that the characteristics for any font size are determined from mathematical font vector formulas. These are commonly referred to more generally as *outline fonts* because their formulas are really an outline representation of the glyph. With an outline font, you can change the font size to any desirable point size and still have the same pretty look.

This concept of changing a font from one size to another is known as Font Scaling. Since bitmap fonts are not scalable, when you switch to a non-supported size, they appear with jagged edges onscreen. In addition, these jaggies represented problems for folks printing on non-laser printers (remember ImageWriters?). Because of these issues, Adobe Systems introduced Adobe Type Manager and saved the day. It was partly a response to Apple's pending TT technology at the time.

FOXPRO MAC HACK TIP

If your computer has both a TrueType and bitmap version of the same font, the TrueType font takes precedence in FoxPro. This is not always the case. Most other software packages default to the bitmap font to avoid problems with documents made on other machines not containing the equivalent TT font.

As with most Macintosh interface objects, fonts are stored as resources. Table 12.8 shows the resources commonly associated with fonts. Since FoxPro uses standard methods for accessing fonts, you can embed fonts directly into your applications for distribution. Just remember, fonts are just like other software, so make sure you pay any required distribution royalties.

Table 12.8
Standard Macintosh Font Resources

Resource	*Type*	*Description*
FONT	bitmap	basic font definition
NFNT	bitmap	stylistic variations
sfnt	outline	scalable font like TrueType
FOND	bitmap, outline	font family information

FoxPro uses the AFONT() function to return supported font and size information. The AFONT() function populates an array of all the available Font Typefaces (e.g., Helvetica, Geneva, Monaco, Chicago, and so on). In addition, you can use it for some other useful tests. First, you can see if a particular font exists by passing its typeface name as the second parameter.

```
DIMENSION tmparr[1]
IF  AFONT(tmparr,"Monaco")
  * do some commands here
ELSE
  WAIT WINDOW "Font does not exist"
ENDIF
```

Using this same function, you can also test to see if you have a scalable (TrueType) font on your hands. The array will be a single-element array returning a value of -1.

```
DIMENSION tmparr[1]
IF  AFONT(tmparr,"Monaco") AND tmparr = -1
  WAIT WINDOW "Scalable font."
ENDIF
```

Fonts are traditionally measured in *points*. Each point on a Macintosh equals 1/72 of an inch. On a Mac screen, it happens that this amount is equal to one pixel (that is, a screen resolution of 72 dots per inch or dpi). I put together the masterpiece in figure 12.8 to illustrate some of the dimensions associated with fonts. It should be self-evident.

The key to deciphering font dimensions is to start all calculations from the Base line. Recalling that all of the measurements for a font, such as those shown here, are called its fontmetrics, you should now have a better understanding of what the following FoxPro FONTMETRIC() functions represent:

- FONTMETRIC(2) Character ascent (units above Base line) in pixels.
- FONTMETRIC(3) Character descent (units below Base line) in pixels.

From these values, you can probably deduce that a character's height, FONTMETRIC(1), is the combination of its ascent and descent. FoxPro's FONTMETRIC() values can play a crucial part in cross-platform development as you have already seen. Remember, all the values returned are in pixels, not foxels.

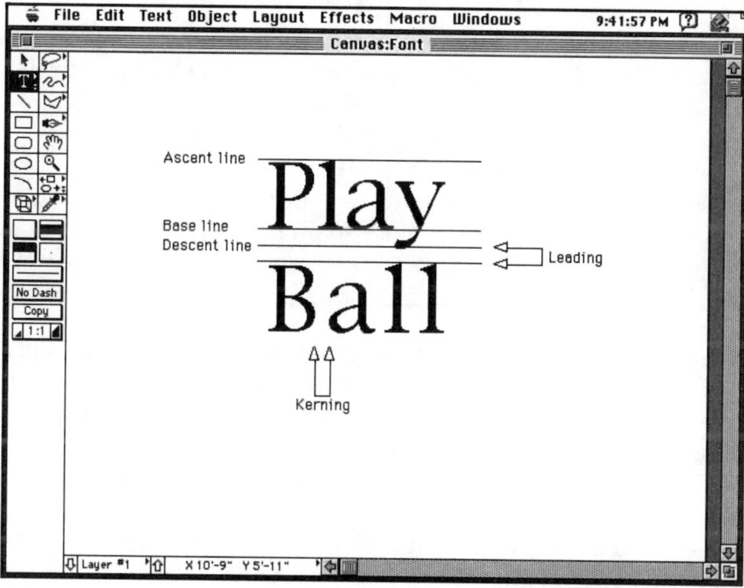

Figure 12.8 *Illustration of standard font characteristics.*

Another important dimension to a character is its width. FoxPro's FONTMETRIC() function uses two important width-related dimensions, which play an important role for sizing fields in screens.

- FONTMETRIC(6) Average character width in pixels.
- FONTMETRIC(7) Maximum character width in pixels.

Probably the first time you tried to add a field (@...GET) to a screen, you found out later that not all the letters you wanted to type fit into this field. For example, maybe you have a five-character ZIP code field in which the field size does not quite fit right. Chances are that you have a sizing problem due to proportional fonts. Take a look at the text on this page. It is a proportional font. Notice that the width of the letter W is much wider than the letter i. With monospace fonts, such as those used in FoxPro for DOS, the width of all characters are the same. Character-based platforms rely exclusively on monospace fonts. On GUI platforms, however, fonts can also be proportional.

CROSS-PLATFORM WARNING

You might assume a sure-fire test for monospace fonts would be to see if FONTMETRIC(6) = FONTMETRIC(7). You should not rely on this measurement because FoxPro will surely fail you, due to an apparent anomaly in the FONTMETRIC() function. FoxPro for Windows seems to be more reliable than FoxPro for Macintosh for this test. Your best bet is to have a list of known monospace fonts that you can check against (such as FoxFont, Courier, or Courier New).

The Screen Wizard is fairly smart about sizing fields, basing a field's size on the average width of a representative character. If the field is very small, the Wizard uses the largest character (W) so that all typed letters will appear. As it turns out, this is a good approach to use in your own screens. The TXTWIDTH() function returns the width in foxels of a particular string or character. Table 12.9 illustrates a simple letter guide you can use to base your field widths (for example, you should size a seven-character field so that it can fit AAAAAAA).

Table 12.9

Recommended Letters to Use for Determining Field Widths Using Proportional Fonts

Width of Field	*Letter*
5 or less	W
6 to 12	A
above 12	O

With most fonts, you find that the width of all numbers (1,2,0,5,9) is the same, regardless of whether the font is proportional or monospace. Keep this in mind when you size, number, and date fields.

Adobe Type Manager

Many Mac users have ATM loaded in their system at startup. It is quite popular and does not appear to cause any conflicts with FoxPro. You should, however, understand how ATM works and can affect FONTMETRIC() values returned by FoxPro. As mentioned before, ATM helps smooth out the jaggies of bitmap fonts so that they can be displayed both onscreen and in print in a more visually appealing manner. To do this, ATM traps and alters the font dimensions internally. ATM only affects bitmap fonts and will not touch scalable fonts.

If you are developing applications that you plan to redistribute or run on other machines, it is important that you not make assumptions regarding FONTMETRIC() values of various bitmap fonts you might have. Because ATM traps and alters their dimensions, the FONTMETRIC() values returned on a machine with ATM and one without might not be the same for an identical font. Therefore, be careful not to hardcode any of these values unless absolutely necessary.

Fonts and Screen Resolution

If you develop cross-platform applications for Macs and Windows, be sure you take into account video drivers, which impact screen resolution. An important pitfall to watch out for is that non-scalable fonts often have varying FONTMETRIC() values based on the video driver. Take, for example, the following two Windows drivers:

514/a:

FONTMETRIC(1,'MS SANS SERIF',8) = 16

8514/A (Small fonts):

FONTMETRIC(1,'MS SANS SERIF',8) = 13

Notice that the character heights differ even though both are being displayed in a 1024×768 screen resolution. You should always test fonts you plan to use in your distributable applications. Scalable fonts usually retain their FONTMETRIC() values regardless of video drivers.

Chapter Wrap Up

Had enough? During most FoxPro development, you don't need to think about the window and font problems described here. Even for cross-platform work, you settle on a strategy that works, make that strategy part of your routine, and forget about it. However, this chapter should give you the confidence to know that you can face any such problems that arise and deliver a FoxPro application with a satisfying, Mac-like appearance and style.

13

INTERNATIONAL APPLICATIONS: LOCALIZATION STRATEGIES AND CODE PAGES

by
Randy Brown

Localization is the process of transforming software from one language (dialect) to another. When you think of porting your FoxPro application to another language for the first time, what comes to mind first? That's right. Strings! Strings! Strings! What's a language except a lot of words, right?

There is a lot more to localization than just changing words. I'll start with some of the mechanics associated with successful localization projects. What should be your goals? What are the priorities? Who is doing the localizing? You should consider all these things up front.

FOXPRO MAC HACK TIP

Many of the concepts presented here should not be thought of solely for their localization impact on FoxPro applications. Top programmers use methods that reduce code and simplify development. You can incorporate most localization concepts into your everyday coding practices to strengthen your overall rapid development approach.

The next time you embark on a new FoxPro project, consider the amount of work you need to do to allow a French-speaking user to enjoy the fruits of your efforts. Now take this thought a step further. What if you had to let *someone else* make all the necessary changes? Not every FoxPro developer speaks French, German, and Portuguese. To add another log to this fire, consider the situation where the localizer knows little about FoxPro. Are you going to trust this person to change your .PRGs? If your current development method and applications can hold up to these tests, you probably can skip the rest of this chapter.

Your strategies in localizing a FoxPro application should consist of several important goals, which I'll discuss in turn:

- Minimize effort of localizer.
- Minimize number of files being touched.
- Consolidate localization of strings.
- Ease accessibility to strings.

Program Files

As a general rule of thumb, do *not* put strings in .PRG files. Sure, we all do it, but consider the situation where our friendly localizer knows nothing about FoxPro. Are you going to trust this person to edit your code? In a minute, I will show you a strategy that leaves your .PRG files free of strings.

FoxPro has a compiler directive, #DEFINE, which is the localizer's friend. Many developers have started using this directive in their program files.

The most common practice is to place all the #DEFINEs at the top of the file because the compiler can't use #DEFINEs placed in one .PRG to affect any other program. (#DEFINEs don't affect subroutines called by a program, unlike variables, which are visible to the subroutines of the program that initialized them.) Remember, #DEFINEs are not limited to strings; they also can hold numeric constants. The FoxPro compiler simply substitutes the contents of the #DEFINE assignment for the label you specify.

```
* MYFILE.PRG

#DEFINE C_MESSAGE1 ;
  'You have entered an invalid number.'
#DEFINE C_MESSAGE2  ;
  "This program can only be run on a Mac."
.
.
IF !_MAC
  WAIT WINDOW C_MESSAGE2
  RETURN
ENDIF
```

The preceding code snippet shows you how to localize by placing all your strings at the top of your program. Evaluated in terms of the goals suggested at the beginning of this chapter, this method certainly fulfills the ease of accessibility factor. All the localizer needs now are located at the top of the file. What about the other goals? What if you are building the mother of all FoxPro applications (not to be confused with the mother of all READs—more commonly referred to as MOAR by folks at one with the Fox)? Your application can easily have 20 files. OK, make it 100 files. All right, if it truly is the monster of all FoxPro applications, we'll assume 500 files. Do you really want your localizer hitting the top of each of these files to change the #DEFINEs?

If you are dealing with a small application, you can get away with placing #DEFINEs at the top of files. There may be other circumstances where you want to do this, even in a sizable application. Again, try to avoid putting strings in programs. I can't emphasize this point enough because it is the kind of decision you will want to make *before* you begin a project. Once you have started working on an application, converting everything to another method can be a real pain.

> **FOXPRO MAC HACK TIP**
>
> While I am on the subject of using #DEFINEs with strings, take another look at the preceding sample code listing. Notice that the `C_MESSAGE1` constant has single quotes delimiting the string, while the other one has double quotes. You should always use double quotes if possible. Remember, the person doing the localization is going to change only what is between the delimiters. If the string to localize has single quotes around it and the localizer adds an apostrophe to the string, *the program will bomb*. FoxPro also offers another alternative for string delimiters. You can use square brackets ([ ]).

The approaches I am going to show you also use #DEFINEs at the top of files. The #DEFINEs are not for strings, but instead are for numbers that refer to strings. With this technique, you place a reference number to a string at the top of a file and forget about it—localizers never need to touch the file. There are several benefits to this method.

- All of the strings can be localized from one convenient location—one file—which is the only file you need to give to the localizer. If you feel the text needs improvement in the grammar, it's easy to hand off one file versus many.
- Because strings now are centrally located, you can avoid having redundant strings throughout your application. How often have you made a change to text only to find later that it wasn't entirely fixed because you forgot to make the change universally?

What magical reference file holds the strings? The file that serves as your localizable string file can be either a FoxPro table (.DBF) or a program file (.PRG). You can even avoid the file approach entirely and use arrays exclusively to hold your strings. The best bet, however, is to use a combination of the two, based on the purpose of strings. Table 13.1 shows you some differences between the three storage methods.

Table 13.1

Comparison of localization techniques for storing strings

Database Table	*Program File*	*Array*
Moderate access because it has to look up references in table.	Fast access because program may be loaded in memory.	Fastest access because everything is stored in RAM.

Database Table	*Program File*	*Array*
Consumes extra workarea, which may be a problem if user has access to View window.	Large control statement and program file.	Consumes memory, which may affect performance on machines with limited memory.
Memo fields make it attractive for long strings.	May have calling conflicts if working with multiple applications.	Bad element order in array may cause problems.

When you choose a method for storing strings, consider the type of string being localized. Here are recommendations for various types:

- *Error messages*. Recommendation: Table. These strings can be quite lengthy depending on the message. Because the performance associated with displaying an error message is not critical, you do not need to consume valuable memory by placing strings in an array.
- *Text prompts*. Recommendation: Array. Because text prompts are used in a variety of interface objects, the timing of their display is crucial. Also, they tend to be very small. These prompts include strings in FoxPro dialogs such as in LOCFILE(), GETFILE(), or PUTFILE().
- *Window Titles*. Recommendation: Array. These tend to be small and timing is a factor.
- *Dialog prompts*. Recommendation: Table. As with error messages, program execution essentially halts while waiting for user input, so these strings can be stored in a table.

Strategies for Using Tables

A database lookup table is ideal for storing dialog prompts and error messages. The following source listing is just an example of a method you can use to look up strings in a FoxPro DBF table. The obvious advantage of using a DBF file is that the localizer needs to touch only the records in the database, not look at code.

When you create your string table, you may want to have an associated index file (CDX) to speed up the LOOKUP function if your table becomes large. Because the content of the table is fairly static, you can bind it directly into your FoxPro application (.APP file).

Remember the problem with conflicting delimiters and #DEFINEs that I mentioned previously in this chapter? You shouldn't have to worry about this as much because you won't need to include delimiters inside the character or memo field.

```
* MYFILE.PRG
* This is a sample program which calls
* the Getstr function to lookup a string.
#DEFINE C_MESSAGE1  21
  **You have entered an invalid number.
#DEFINE C_MESSAGE2  32
  **This program can only be run on a Mac.
.
IF !_MAC
  WAIT WINDOW getstr(C_MESSAGE2)
  RETURN
ENDIF

* GETSTR.PRG
* This is a generic routine which
* looks up a string specified by
* the passed parameter.
* Note: this assumes that you have
* a DBF string file which has two of
* the following fields:
*    strfkd - char or memo containing string
*    numfld - number field with reference code
PARAMETER strnum
PRIVATE getstr,oldarea
m.oldarea = SELECT()
IF USED(strdbf)
  SELECT strdbf
ELSE
  SELECT 0
  USE strdbf AGAIN ALIAS strdbf
ENDIF
m.getstr = LOOKUP(strfld,m.strnum,numfld)
SELECT (m.oldarea)
RETURN m.getstr
```

You may have a situation in which you want to include a variable in your string. You can handle this with several methods. You can always concatenate the lookup string with the variable, which may be a headache especially if the wording of the message changes. Here is a neat trick you can use to include variables in your strings:

```
The file "&getfile." is missing. Please choose another.
```

The macro substitution operator can be used in a variety of places, including database string lookup tables, as shown here. In this example, the string stored in either a character or memo field contains a reference to a memory variable named `getfile`.

> **CROSS-PLATFORM WARNING**
>
> When working with the macro substitution operator "&" and memvars, you cannot precede the name of the variable with an "m."—otherwise FoxPro will return an error (for example, do not use "&m.getfile." in the preceding string).

The #DEFINEs above use numbers, which are the best choice if you use arrays instead of a lookup table using the approach shown below. As an alternative, you might want to play with using a descriptive string for the lookup.

Strategies for Using Arrays

Take another look at the sample program. Modifying it to use arrays instead of tables is easier than you might think. Notice in the variation below that there's now an array element in the WAIT WINDOW prompt. In this example, the #DEFINEs actually refer to array element numbers.

```
* MYFILE.PRG
* This is a sample program which calls
* the Getstr function to lookup a string.
#DEFINE C_MESSAGE1  21
  **You have entered an invalid number.
#DEFINE C_MESSAGE2  32
  **This program can only be run on a Mac.
.
```

```
IF !_MAC
  WAIT WINDOW strarr[C_MESSAGE2]
  RETURN
ENDIF
```

The hardest part of using this system is coming up with an approach for creating the array. The method presented in the following code uses the same database file as shown in the preceding code. You just SELECT the text field straight into an array. This approach, as you may notice, requires that the `Numfld` numeric field contains the same value as RECNO(). Because you are SELECTing into an array, the records are inserted sequentially. Therefore, you cannot omit a number. As an alternative, you may want to consider selecting both `Numfld` and `Strfld` into a two-dimensional array. Using this strategy, you need to have a lookup routine that makes use of the ASCAN() function.

```
* MSTRARR.PRG
* This program creates the message array
USE strdbf AGAIN IN 0 ALIAS strdbf
SELECT * FROM strdbf ;
  WHERE numfld # RECNO() ;
  INTO ARRAY tmparr
IF _TALLY=0
    WAIT WINDOW "The message array is broken!"
    * insert error handling here
ELSE
    SELECT strfld FROM strdbf INTO ARRAY strarr
ENDIF
USE IN strdbf
RELEASE tmparr
```

To reiterate, you may want to have two string tables for your localization. The first table is your main lookup, which contains the longer strings such as error messages. To minimize memory consumption, use the table approach for these strings. The second table can be used to insert smaller strings into an array, as you've just seen. These strings would be used for prompts such as in GETFILE() dialogs.

Looking down the road a bit, Microsoft has indicated that they may include an #INCLUDE directive in their next release (FoxPro 3.0). This action will greatly speed localization efforts. An #INCLUDE directive is used to specify a file that gets incorporated into the current file at compilation time. The #INCLUDE file can include a common set of #DEFINEs. Currently, a #DEFINE is only recognized in the program in which it is contained. You cannot place a #DEFINE in a top level program and have it recognized by programs called after.

> **CROSS-PLATFORM WARNING**
>
> Watch out for #DEFINEs you place in the Setup of a cross-platform .SCX, unless this #DEFINE is the same for each platform. With multiple #DEFINE statements for the same constant, only the first #DEFINE counts, even if the various definitions occur in different CASE statements as they might in the platform-specific CASE statements that GENSCRN emits in the SPR. The #DEFINE that counts is the #DEFINE in the first CASE statement, and which CASE that happens to be can change from Build to Build, depending on the platform from which you execute the Build.

Screens

Screen localization can be easy or difficult, depending on your approach. You should address two issues: the screen code contained within the code snippets and the objects on the screen (buttons, fields, text, lists, and so on).

You know that the Screen Builder offers the capability to attach code to various screen objects (including the generated READ statement) through editable code snippets. Most code snippets (with the exception of the Setup and Cleanup snippets) allow either a procedure or an expression. If you choose the expression, you are creating a UDF that references a routine located either in the Cleanup snippet or in another program outside the screen itself.

Although I expressed my preference for expressions in the previous chapter, whether or not to put procedures in snippets or just expressions referring to code in the snippets is a personal choice. In fact, you will find top FoxPro developers who sit in both camps. However, if you are developing an application that may someday need localization, you should probably choose *not* to use procedure snippets because you might have strings located in the procedures. A localizer unfamiliar with a FoxPro screen will have trouble manipulating FoxPro's maze of dialogs just to get to a specific code snippet.

FoxPro offers a variety of screen objects, including radio buttons, check boxes, lists, pop-ups, fields, and static text. Each of these objects has a prompt or text that is a candidate for localization. You can make your localizer's life a lot happier if you follow a few simple rules.

First, leave lots of extra space. The length of English words often doubles when translated to another language. It is a good practice to leave enough space in the objects for 1.5 to 2 times the length of the current English expression.

You also should follow the WYSIWYG (What You See Is What You Get) rule. It is much easier for the localizer to change and possibly realign screen objects that contain localizable strings if they can see what they are working with. Although this may not be the most efficient method, it can lead to less confusion for localization. For example, you can use `&memvar` expressions in radio button prompts. The localizer cannot see what the final outcome looks like until the code is generated and run. If the newly localized text prompts exceed the boundaries of the radio button set or the screen size, part of the string may be cut off when displayed.

FOXPRO MAC HACK TIP

Steven Black's INTL Toolkit differs a bit from the WYSIWYG approach. He includes an option to specify the prompts through a lookup function at run-time. One benefit of using functions to display prompts is that you can have an application that you can distribute as a single international version. All the data is self-contained (localized strings for each country) within the one application. As you can imagine, there are also some disadvantages to hiding the prompts from the developer in this way, so INTL Toolkit also allows you to have a WYSIWYG compile-time driven localization.

See Also

- "FoxPro for Macintosh Resource List," Appendix A

If you follow these simple rules, you should encounter fewer problems, but FoxPro's diversity does hold a few more potential "gotchas." For example, if you are including high ASCII characters (greater than 128), you may be surprised to see a new character displayed under a different code page. Again, if you are using the WYSIWYG approach, the localizer will see this problem immediately and make the necessary conversion to a different character.

Another possible localization issue to look out for is list/pop-up variables. FoxPro allows the variables to which these GETs store a value to be either character or numeric type. If you are setting these variables to character type, then the value returned is that of the item in the list/pop-up. You will have a localization problem if you are trying to compare this character type variable to a specific hardcoded string.

Finally, I thought it would be neat to show you a trick that simplifies the localization of common screens. A typical FoxPro application has many common screens. By this, I mean screens with common elements, such as a set of push buttons for edit screens (see figures 13.1 and 13.2).

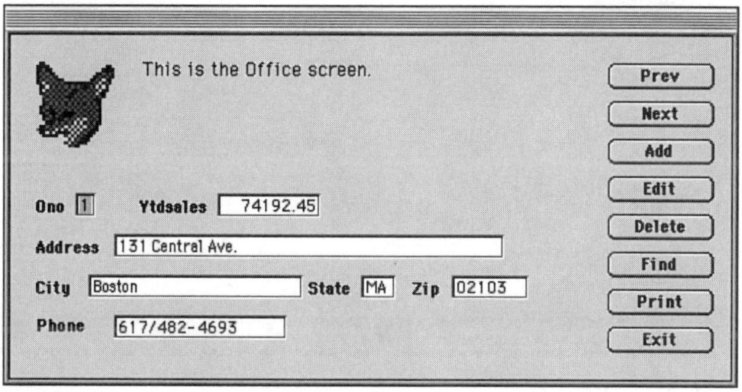

This is the Office screen.

Ono 1 Ytdsales 74192.45

Address 131 Central Ave.

City Boston State MA Zip 02103

Phone 617/482-4693

Prev Next Add Edit Delete Find Print Exit

Figure 13.1 *Input screen for Office table.*

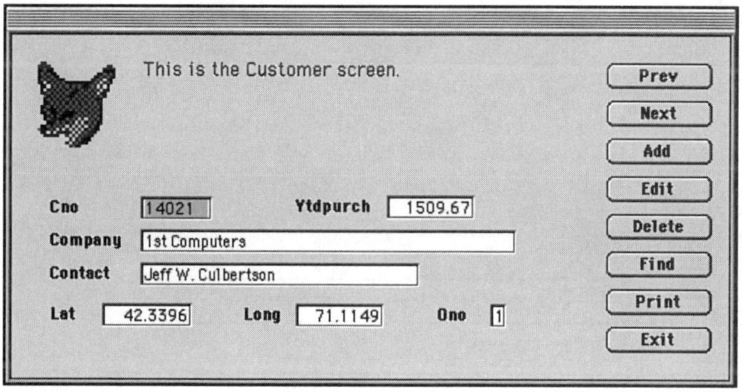

This is the Customer screen.

Cno 14021 Ytdpurch 1509.67

Company 1st Computers

Contact Jeff W. Culbertson

Lat 42.3396 Long 71.1149 Ono 1

Prev Next Add Edit Delete Find Print Exit

Figure 13.2 *Input screen for Customer table.*

Both of these screens have similar objects: top picture, top text, and buttons. The only other objects on the screen are edit fields, which are unique to the specific databases being edited. Now, look at two of the screens in the Screen Builder, as shown in figures 13.3 and 13.4. They probably don't look the way you expected.

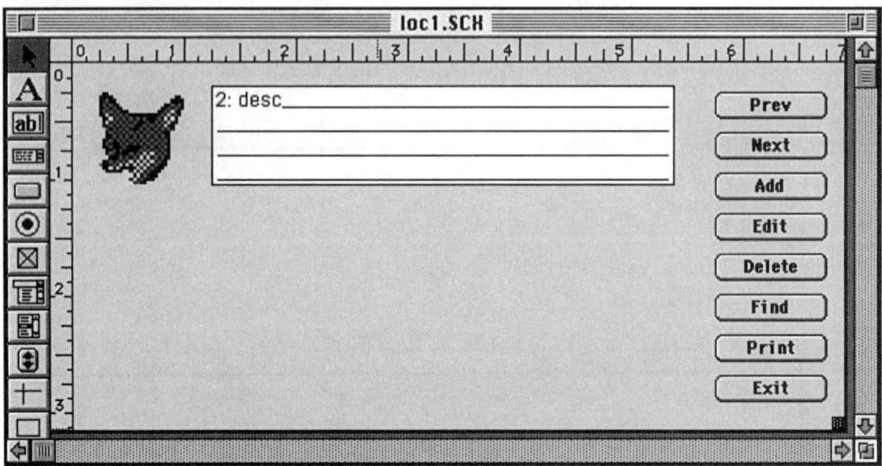

Figure 13.3 *SCX with common interface objects appears in the Screen Builder Layout window.*

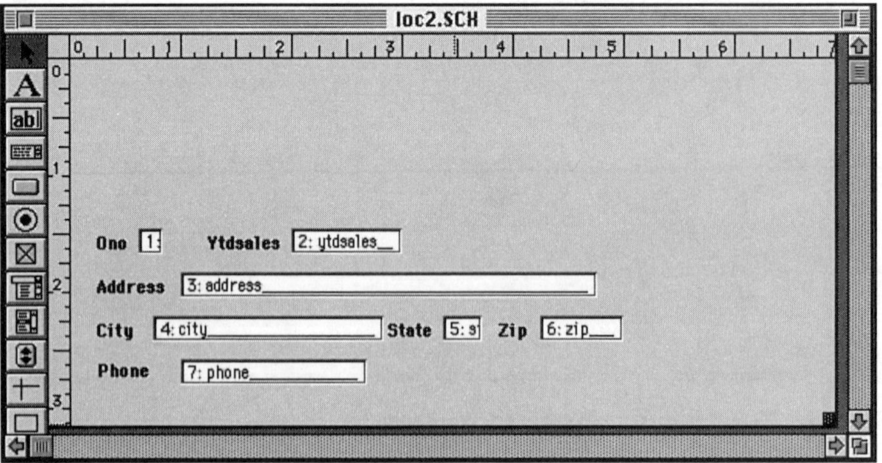

Figure 13.4 *SCX for fields in Office table.*

You see that we are combining elements of multiple screens. How can we do that? FoxPro has a screen directive, #NOREAD PLAIN, which can be placed in the Setup snippet of any FoxPro screen. This directive causes GENSCRN to create code that only contains the @..GET/SAY statements of objects on the screen. No code is generated for the window or READ. The following lines show the Setup snippets for the two screens. (Notice the embedded string in the setup snippet of LOC2.SCX. Bad idea!)

```
*setup snippet of common object screen (LOC1.SCX)
#NOREAD PLAIN

*setup snippet of Office screen (LOC2.SCX)
m.buttons = 1
m.desc = "This is the Office screen."
#WNAME "thiswin"
ACTIVATE WINDOW "thiswin" NOSHOW
DO loc1.spr
```

FOXPRO MAC HACK TIP

You will find the #NOREAD PLAIN technique useful to refresh large numbers of SAYs on a screen, too. Lisa uses it in both Color Picker applications (refer to Chapter 14) to provide the onscreen displays of sample objects that change dynamically as you try out or create color sets. You also can use this directive to provide different button sets for a generic dialog.

Menus

If you aren't using FoxPro's Menu Builder, you should. Menus are one of the first places a localizer will look for strings. If the localizer needs to search through a number of programs to change menu prompts, you risk having that code corrupted. The Menu Builder serves to isolate the menu objects from the menu code.

As with the Screen Builder, the Menu Builder contains access to several code snippets where code can be added. Again, my recommendation for localization purposes is not to use code snippets, but instead to have expressions (UDFs) refer to routines external to the menu. If for some reason you choose to use snippets, make sure that strings are stored elsewhere (in a table or array) and inform the localizer not to touch the snippets.

You will probably hand the menu off to a localizer to make changes. Make sure to inform this person about the hotkey meta-characters so that she/he can choose an appropriate replacement. Also, this will prevent him or her from having two hotkeys that are the same.

With the techniques you saw in Chapters 7 and 11, you can give menus variable prompts and hotkeys. You can easily have the variable prompts defined by UDFs, the prompts can include array elements, or they can include variables that receive their string values from a lookup to a localization string table in the menu's Setup code.

Do you use PRMBAR(), PRMPAD(), POPUP(), and PROMPT() functions to obtain the character strings of your menus, pop-ups, and bars? You should take precautions if you do so. Look at the code below and you will see why.

```
IF PROMPT() = "Open File..."

ENDIF
```

In this case, I am hardcoding the string, but even if I had an array such as described earlier, chances are the string in the array may not equal that of the menu bar string. A better alternative is to use a function such as BAR(), which returns a numeric value of the menu bar. If you use the message-handling system described in this book (`DO Menuproc WITH "Open"`), you don't need to worry. In this case, the message ("Open") remains the same no matter what language the menu uses for the prompt.

Reports and Labels

Reports are fairly easy to localize. For the most part, the only places that localizers should touch are the objects on the reports themselves. FoxPro does not generate code for the reports. However, there are a few report elements that can contain code that you might want to recheck.

- *Report Fields*. Most of the time, a report expression consists of a field name or memory variable. However, FoxPro allows any valid expression in a report object. Make sure that these expressions are free of any strings. You can use a lookup array method discussed earlier. Many developers like to include both the field label and field in an expression (for example, First Name: +fname). This practice might make life a bit difficult for a localizer unfamiliar with FoxPro.

- *UDFs*. FoxPro allows you to include UDFs in your report fields. Make sure these UDFs do not have strings embedded in them. If you do need to include strings, use the approach mentioned above in the Program Files section.
- *Report Variables*. Think of handling report variables as a problem similar to report field management. Try to leave out the strings.

Chances are the localizer will need to make changes to the static text contained on the report. In addition, she/he also may need to change the date and time display format to coincide with standards for that particular country. Make sure that you leave enough space in case the strings need to be lengthened. Finally, don't forget about that "Page:" string which is ubiquitous to most reports.

International Versions of FoxPro

The process of localization becomes somewhat more complex when you begin to use international versions of FoxPro. Internally, FoxPro has a resource file that contains strings translated to the language of that version. Remember, you can run a localized application in the U.S. version of FoxPro. As long as the user doesn't know this, it won't matter. International versions, however, are often preferred because development can be done by a foreign FoxPro developer who may not know the English language well.

It is always a good idea to have code at the top of your program that checks for an international version. You can use the VERSION() function for this. For example, the French FoxPro version returns the following:

? VERSION()

FoxPro 2.5c pour Macintosh

While testing for a certain language specific word, such as `pour`, will suffice for most occasions, you can also use the VERSION(1) function for more accuracy. This function returns something like:

? VERSION(1)

FoxPro 2.5b for Macintosh [Dec 4 1993 10:38:29] Serial # 00-215-0255-56103085

A relatively unknown fact to many experienced FoxPro developers is that Microsoft uses specific serial number country codes for their various international versions (that is, the first two numbers of **00-215-0255-xxxxxxxx** represent the country code). You could easily parse out the serial number using FoxPro string functions to check for a specific international version. Note: With FoxPro 2.6 and all future Microsoft releases, the serialization process has changed. A new 17-digit code is used in which the first five numbers now contain information for the country version (for example, **22080-065-xxxxxxx**).

Look for spots in your code where you might compare a function to a string that is probably localized in an international version. For example, the CMONTH(DATE()) function may return "January" in the English language, but in French it may be "Janvier."

Another issue to contend with on international versions is *capitalization*. Capitalized words in the English language tend to be either all capitals or capital. Foreign languages can and often have capital letters embedded in the middle of words. Use the PROPER() function with care.

Ligatures is a term referring to characters that contain two joined letters. Many foreign languages use ligatures. Some examples of ligatures are ßÆ (in German, the character ß is identical to the letter pair "ss"). When you are doing substring searches and letter comparisons, make sure your program is flexible in handling ligatures.

Code Pages and Collation Sequences

Computers represent all characters internally as numbers. Traditionally, microcomputers have used the ASCII character set as the basis for the first 128 characters. In addition, there are 128 additional characters that differ based on computer and/or language. The entire 256 character set representation is referred to as a *code page*. Different code pages have different character sets. Table 13.2 shows the common code pages for the popular U.S. platforms.

Table 13.2
Standard default US Code Pages for common FoxPro platforms

U.S. Computer	*Code Page*
Macintosh	10000
Windows	1252
MS DOS	437

Microsoft first added support for code pages in FoxPro 2.5a. Finally, German users could have a version that contained all the accented diacritical characters that their language supports. With code pages, FoxPro can now do automatic translation of characters for a number of foreign languages. When you open a program file (.PRG), FoxPro does an automatic translation on-the-fly.

Code pages are set in the CONFIG.FPM file, which gets loaded at startup. There is no SET command that you can issue in a program. You must set the code page in the configuration file. Here are a few examples:

- CODEPAGE = 10007 (Russian Macintosh)
- CODEPAGE = AUTO

Microsoft recommends setting the code page to AUTO. With CODEPAGE = AUTO, when you open a table on a platform different than the platform on which the table was created, accented characters are AUTOmatically translated. For example, if the letter ä is entered in a table created in a U.S. version of FoxPro for MS-DOS (`code page #437`) and is then displayed in FoxPro for Macintosh (`code page 10000`), FoxPro for Macintosh performs the translation necessary to display the letter as ä. When data is added to the table in FoxPro for Macintosh, it is automatically translated and stored in the table written in `code page #437`. This is because the DBF has been tagged with a `code page #437`. FoxPro tags database files (DBF, SCX, MNX, FRX, and so on) in the current code page.

FOXPRO MAC HACK TIP

Because programs (PRGs) are simple text files, there is no way to tag one of these files. This presents a problem when transporting your files between various platforms using differing code pages. Microsoft

> has addressed this issue in FoxPro 2.6 with several new commands. A new SET CPCOMPILE TO command and modified COMPILE command allow you to tag the compiled program (FXP, SPX, MPX, APP, and so on).

In addition to code pages, international users needed a way to sort character fields correctly based on their character set. FoxPro added *collation sequences* to keep track of the order of characters. For example, the GENERAL sequence orders ä< z, but in the NORDAN (Norwegian) sequence ä > z. As you can see, the collation sequence plays a major role in FoxPro indexing.

One of the drawbacks of using collation sequences is that SEEKs do not take into account diacritical marks. When you issue the command `SEEK "äbc"`, you may end up at a record with "abc." Microsoft chose to ignore diacritical marks in SEEKs for performance reasons.

You determine collation sequence, like code pages, in the CONFIG.FPM file.

- COLLATE = DUTCH
- COLLATE = GENERAL
- COLLATE = MACHINE (default)

FoxPro has a SET COLLATE function so that you can change the sequence within your programs. (The View window also has a pop-up to change this interactively.) Whereas code page numbers attach to databases, collation sequences attach to indexes.

FoxPro has a number of commands and functions devoted to using the new international code pages and collation sequences. Before you begin working on an international application, be sure to read the materials provided in the FoxPro documentation and help files.

Resources

There are a number of valuable resources you should investigate if you are at all serious about international development. Microsoft has a number of books available on international software design. These books cover everything from commonly used messages and button prompts to interface design. In addition, the Microsoft Developer's Network (MSDN) puts out periodic CDs that contain international reference materials.

Steven Black's INTL Toolkit, which I mentioned earlier in the chapter, is a great FoxPro resource for international developers. This toolkit works in conjunction with Ken Levy's GENSCRNX and Steven Black/Andrew Ross MacNeil's GENMENUX programs (both freeware) to assist you in rapid screen and menu translation. INTL allows you to produce either run-time or generate-time (that is, compiled hard code) localizations.

Chapter Wrap Up

Normally, a localizer goes through an entire project and touches only those areas containing strings that need translation. This can be a tedious job for the localizer if there is no road map through the application components. Consider including a text file in your project describing the project from the perspective of a localizer. Mark this file as Excluded so it doesn't get compiled into the application.

If you develop an application in tandem with localization efforts, you will need some sort of log so the localizers will know if they need to redo some of their earlier efforts. Again, this illustrates how important it is to avoid including strings in your program files. If you are constantly making changes to fix bugs, the localizer will need to update its localized version of the file each time.

You may have only skimmed through this chapter because you are saying to yourself, "I'll never need to localize any of my applications." That may be the case, but as I mentioned earlier, these recommendations enhance your everyday development practices as well. Think of them as normal coding methods to make your project developments more efficient—and then, should you ever have to localize an application, you'll be ready.

14

TAKE ADVANTAGE OF DEVELOPER RESOURCES: COLORS, HELP SYSTEMS, AND BEYOND

by Lisa Slater

In Part II, you used FoxPro's suite of power tools to prototype effective, professional applications. In Part III you were introduced to coding techniques that support these applications, from READ clauses through localization strategy.

Once you have these aspects of application development under control, turn your attention to the host of amenities that FoxPro provides to enrich the lives of developers and end-users alike. I won't cover *all* the minor FoxPro resources in this chapter, but I will highlight items that offer you unique opportunities to polish your applications.

Resource Files

FoxPro resource files deserve a special mention in a Macintosh book because they are modelled after and yet are utterly unlike anything Mac people are accustomed to calling a "resource." FoxBASE+/Mac people may be especially confused because FoxBASE used the usual Macintosh resources in a normal Macintosh way.

FoxPro resource files are .DBFs. Like other FoxPro files, these files have no Macintosh resource fork at all and are composed strictly of data. Each resource file record contains information that FoxPro uses to manage the appearance and behavior of its elements, just as real Macintosh resources perform this service in other applications. (Of course, the executable FoxPro file has a real Macintosh resource fork, as you know from your work in Chapter 12, but Fox Software created the resource table alternative for FoxPro's other platforms.)

If you don't change any defaults, you should find that FoxPro creates a resource file named FOXUSER.DBF in the FoxPro startup directory. You can examine this file's structure and contents by using the command `USE SET("RESOURCE",1) AGAIN`.

The resource file records store window positions, diary entries, the standard label layouts that the FoxPro Report Writer uses when you indicate that you want to design a new label, FoxApp application generator and Wizard specifications you've created, and other preferences (see figure 14.1).

If you USE this file, you see the temporary index that Fox creates (on the expression `Type+Name+ID` fields) so that it can search the resources quickly. The default resource file for your interactive work in FoxPro can grow quickly, as you open different design windows. Even with the index, you may want to purge the file periodically (for example, deleting all records `FOR Id = "WINDMODIFY")` to limit the table's size and to increase FoxPro's speed.

You can designate a resource file for use by your applications, by issuing the command `SET RESOURCE TO <filename>`, if the table you name has the correct structure. Limit this table to the records your application really needs; perhaps you should start it with an empty seed file for each user.

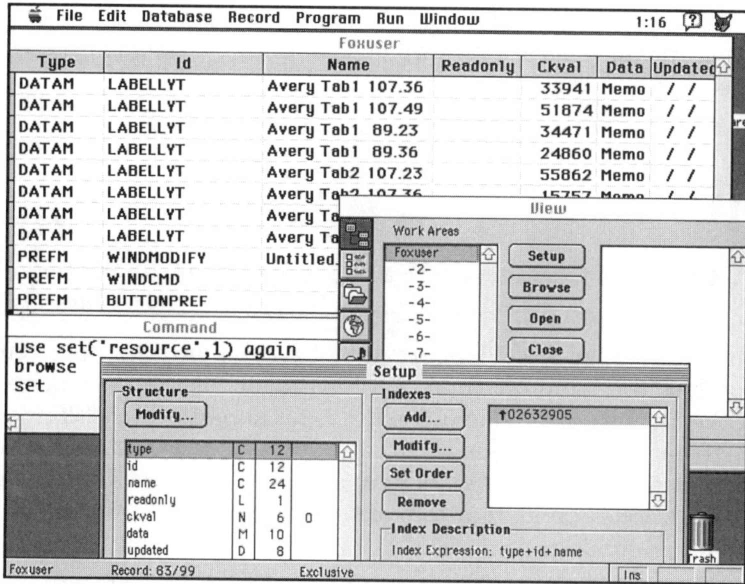

Figure 14.1 *Investigate FoxPro's Resource file.*

If the table is read-only, users can share one resource file. Designate the file Read-only by marking it Locked in the Finder, Read-only in FoxPro's Filer utility, or by binding the table into your application by Including it in the Project.

Unless you allow users of an application to create labels, or your application issues BROWSEs without WINDOW clauses that determine position and size, resource files seem somewhat less useful to me in FoxPro for Macintosh applications than on the other FoxPro platforms. Unlike FoxPro, DOS and Windows, FoxPro for Macintosh can't use color sets stored in the resource file (you get an alternative in this chapter). Unlike FoxPro for DOS, FoxPro for Macintosh doesn't need resource printer setups. The diary feature in FoxPro is nice, but you can't share diary entries among users unless you create a utility to merge the entries to one central table from users' individual resource file entries.

You need to know about resource files so that you can manage their use, even if all you decide to do is SET RESOURCE OFF. You also have the opportunity to create your own application Types and IDs and add them to the resource file, to take the place of my template code's SYS_VAR.DBF or another system table of your own design. Both FoxApp and the Wizards take this approach to storing their required information.

Colors

Colour is its own reward, the chiming of the perfect chord.
Crowded House, "Fingers of Love," *Together Alone*

I was amused to read a *MacWeek* review of FoxPro for Macintosh complaining that "the Windows version of FoxPro includes better color tools." In fact, the Macintosh version of FoxPro is far superior to the Windows version, if you rate the products on color control. It's true that FoxPro for Macintosh can't use color sets stored in a normal resource file. It's also true, as the article stated, that color control in FoxPro for Macintosh requires programming.

However, the end result of working with colors in FoxPro Mac is more complete and more satisfying than the results you get in Windows. Windows' native color-handling frustrates and overrides FoxPro's work at various points. For example, in Windows, push button colors can't be altered inside FoxPro, where Macintosh (2D-style) push buttons follow the normal FoxPro color rules in FoxPro Mac. I use this fact to good effect in the AD*Vantage Job and Address Book screens, where the file folder and address book divider "tabs," actually 2D push buttons, change color to suit the rest of the dialog.

Because color control requires programming, remember our rapid development goal: *when you have a standard requirement, find a way to do the work once, not every time you develop an application.* This principle certainly applies to the complex problem of color handling. Luckily, I've done the work, and you can use the results in your applications.

First, however, examine the requirement: why adjust colors at all? You can reference the quotation with which I begin this section if you want to know my personal answer—but even if you don't enjoy playing with color for color's sake, you have two main reasons to adjust color defaults:

- You want to create special screen effects, perhaps to perform some magic of which the user is never aware.

- You want the user to be able to customize the environment. Color changes are non-destructive and fun! More importantly, they encourage the user to explore other aspects of the application because of the immediate, pleasurable feedback they provide.

Both these reasons are worthwhile, and they both require that you manipulate the FoxPro color system. This system is extremely detailed, but not especially complicated. Once you understand its organization, you can set up a simple strategy to handle your FoxPro color needs.

Get To Know the FoxPro Color System

First, you need to get rid of misconceptions you may have about the right way to proceed.

FoxPro appears to have a simple way to set colors built into the Screen Builder. The Screen Builder provides explicit color settings for objects and for screen backgrounds, giving you 16 color choices. You can see the Object menu's display of these choices in figure 14.2 and the Window Color dialog in figure 14.3.

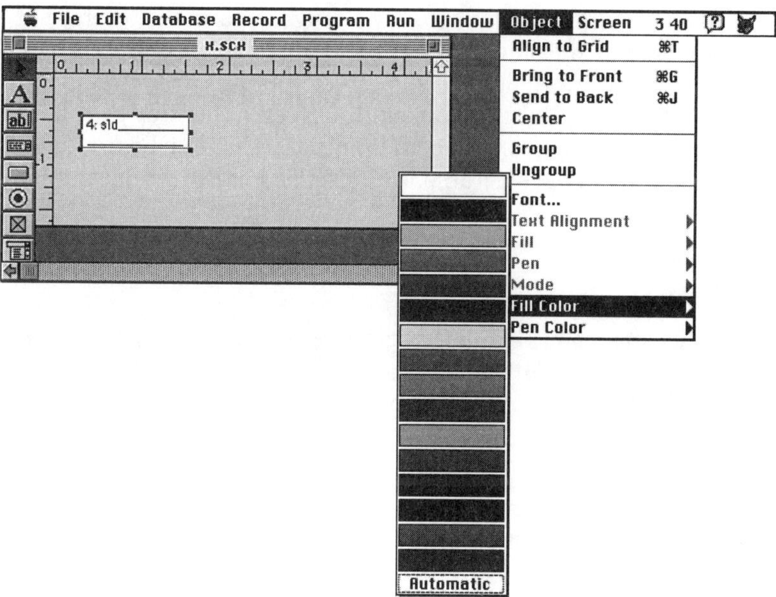

Figure 14.2 *Coloring a screen object.*

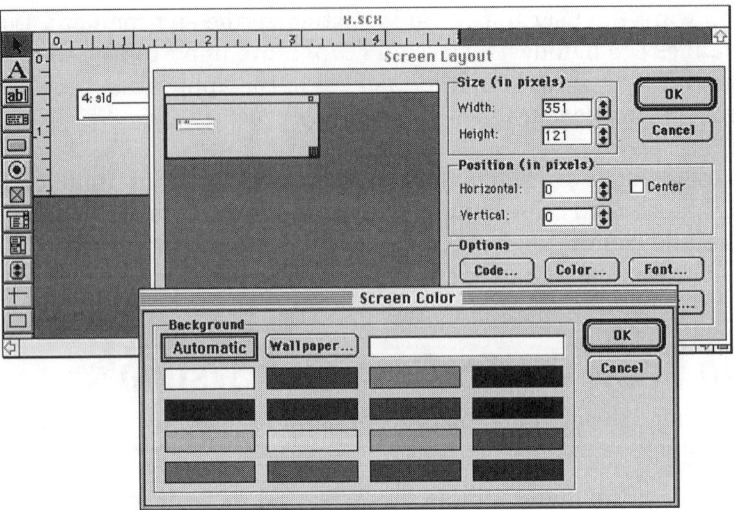

Figure 14.3 *Coloring a screen background.*

Using these explicit choices is an extremely wrong-headed idea. The 16 available colors may not look anything like what the user wants to see, and they also may clash with any color changes you make for special effects. They may also look different depending on the color depth of the user's system. Text that looks dark green to you may or may not be distinguishable from a light gray background on a monitor that has four shades of gray for its display. The mapping process that FoxPro goes through is not entirely predictable. (I'll discuss FoxPro's color mapping later in this section.)

Always leave these settings at the default of `Automatic`, as shown in the figures.

Instead of choosing colors *explicitly*, get to know the way that FoxPro defines color setting for different interface objects and their component elements. Refer to the appropriate color settings, rather than the explicit colors, in your code.

Reference Colors Indirectly

This approach is known as *indirect color referencing*. You don't need to know what the colors are, and you can still change specific settings so they match or contrast with other elements of the color system. You can provide users with the opportunity to change all the settings at once, to have a completely different screen appearance, without fear that some of your color choices will disappear onscreen.

The key to indirect referencing is FoxPro's color *set, scheme, and pair* assignment system. Every interface element has a foreground and background color assignment. Related interface elements work together in a combination of 10 pairs, which FoxPro calls a single color scheme. At any time, there are 24 available color schemes in force, working together in a single color set.

FoxPro represents each color pair assignment as a series of six RGB values separated by commas (a red, green, and blue value for the foreground, followed by the red, green, and blue values for the background). The pairs link together in a scheme assignment that shows all 10 pairs' RGB values in a string separated by commas.

The RGB notation may be either Macintosh-style 5-digit numbers or Windows-style 3-digit numbers, or even DOS-style character codes. You'll find that using the Windows-style notation gives the most accurate results onscreen. In this notation system, for example, the values RGB (0,0,0,255,255,255) represent a color pair with a black foreground on a white background. The colors on a monitor mix in equal proportions in the same way colored lights do, so the first three 0's represent the absence of red, green, or blue (black foreground), while the last three 255's (the highest value available) create a high intensity white when taken together. (Equal values between, such as three 192's, create different shades of gray.)

I've written a Color Tutor utility that you can use to see these values at work onscreen, as well as their relationship to Macintosh-style notation. You'll learn more about that utility later in this section. However, you never have to refer to these RGB values explicitly, or to know what they look like in *any* notation in your programs. Instead, you refer to the values of a particular pair of a particular scheme, indirectly, using the RGBSCHEME() function.

How does this work in practice? You DEFINE a WINDOW with a COLOR SCHEME <expN> clause, in effect assigning it a group of 10 pairs for its attributes, and for the defaults of any objects that you define within the window.

In Chapter 11, you learned how to use the #WCLAUSES directive to take a User Defined-type window, usually scheme 1, and change its scheme to a different scheme to represent a Dialog (scheme 5) or Alert type of window (scheme 7) according to FoxPro's conventions. After you add the appropriate COLOR SCHEME clause to a DEFINE WINDOW command, you've defined the default values for almost all the objects the window can contain. (I say "almost" because each type of window has a second associated scheme to handle the attributes of pop-ups within the window. You have to take care of these objects a little differently, as you'll see shortly.)

A SAY uses the first pair of the current scheme, so a SAY in a window defined with COLOR SCHEME 5 uses the first pair of scheme 5. The background of this pair represents the background of the SAY, and by extension the background color of the window itself. The foreground is the text of the SAY. A GET uses color pair 2 of the scheme when enabled and color pair 10 when disabled.

Interface elements such as SAYs and GETs *always use the same pair of their assigned scheme*. You can still change their default assignments, overriding their window's color scheme, by adding COLOR and COLOR SCHEME clauses to the object-painting code.

For example, in Chapter 10, you saw GETs with a WHEN .F. clause take the place of Refreshed SAYs for onscreen confirmation of lookup values. Using the GET allows you to refresh the onscreen value by saying SHOW GET (singular) rather than SHOW GETS (plural), which runs the whole SAY clause to refresh a measly label. You don't want this GET to look like a GET, however; you want it to match other unmodifiable elements of your screen (text labels, lines, and so on).

To make this never-edited GET look like a SAY, you attach a COLOR clause to the GET. Because there isn't any place to put the COLOR SCHEME clause in the Screen Builder dialog for the object, I stuff it into the WHEN expression, along with the WHEN's .F. value, as you can see in figure 14.4.

In the WHEN expression, following the .F., you see the COLOR keyword, followed by an indirect reference: `(","+RGBSCHEME(1,1)+",,,,,,,,"+RGBSCHEME(1,1))`. The RGBSCHEME(1,1) function gives you the color notation for the first scheme's first color pair, used for the SAYs in this window, since the window was designed using the default User-Defined COLOR SCHEME 1. The expression I've specified uses a placeholder comma to represent the first pair and then substitutes the RGBSCHEME(1,1) SAYs value for the *second* pair, used for enabled GETs. After some more placeholder commas for the intervening pairs, I substitute the RGBSCHEME(1,1) value for the *tenth* pair, used for disabled GETs. The net effect of this expression is to tell the GET to use SAY colors, whether it's enabled or disabled.

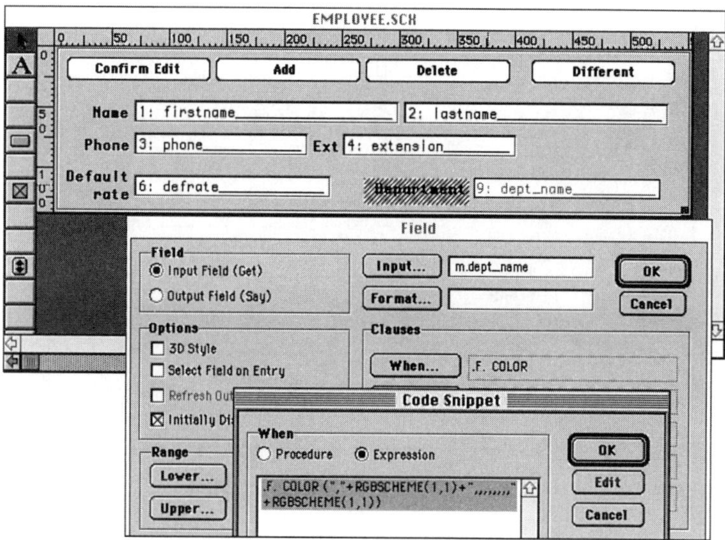

Figure 14.4 *Add a COLOR clause to a GET.*

Figure 14.5 shows you a similar trick to make a SAY use colors reserved for other interface elements. This screen comes from my application Color Picker, which uses SAYs to show examples of all types of interface elements. As you can see in the figure, I can stuff the COLOR clause directly into the SAY expression, instead of the WHEN. The clause `COLOR (RGBSCHEME(1,10))` tells the SAY (which is supposed to represent a disabled GET in the Color Picker screen) to use the *tenth* pair values, associated with disabled GETs, by putting these values into the *first* (SAY) pair of the window's scheme.

Use the COLOR SCHEME clause, rather than a list of pairs with the COLOR clause, to make an interface element use the attributes of a different scheme entirely. For example, suppose I want a SAY indicating "hot prospect" status to use Alert colors, even though the rest of the window is defined with normal User-Defined color scheme 1. The SAY can have the clause COLOR SCHEME 7, the scheme associated with Alerts. Automatically, the SAY has the attributes of SAYs in the new scheme.

To redefine the colors of a pop-up, be sure to use COLOR SCHEME with two arguments: the first argument for its main scheme and the second for the second scheme in which the pop-up elements show when the pop-up list opens.

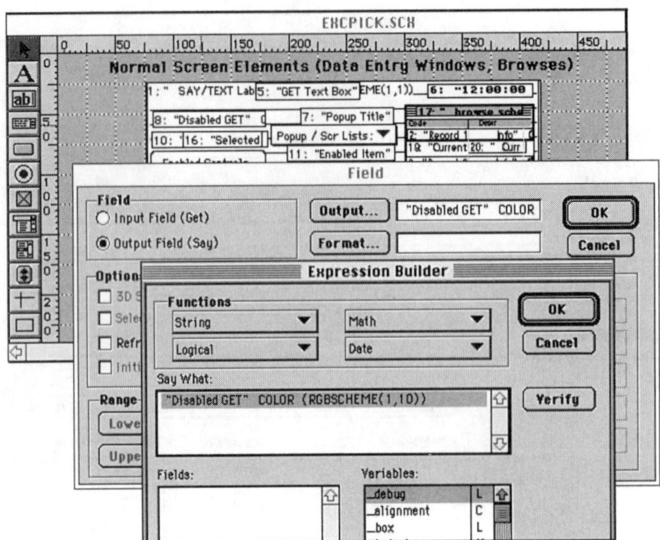

Figure 14.5 Add a COLOR clause to a SAY.

Notice, again, that I don't know or care what any of the colors actually are when I use this indirect notation. The method will work no matter what color set (assortment of color schemes) fits the user and his or her monitor.

Use the Color System without Pain

To see the system at work, you can use the application Color Picker in AD*Vantage. Access the "About this Application" window and note its colors. Use the Color Picker to change the working color set and then access the "About this Application" option once more (see figure 14.6). This window was defined with COLOR SCHEME 5 to represent a dialog. Notice that its look has changed to reflect the new color set when you use the option the second time. If you set a new color set in this dialog and then use the Job menu option, you'll see that the entire Job screen changes to match the User-Defined window colors of the new set.

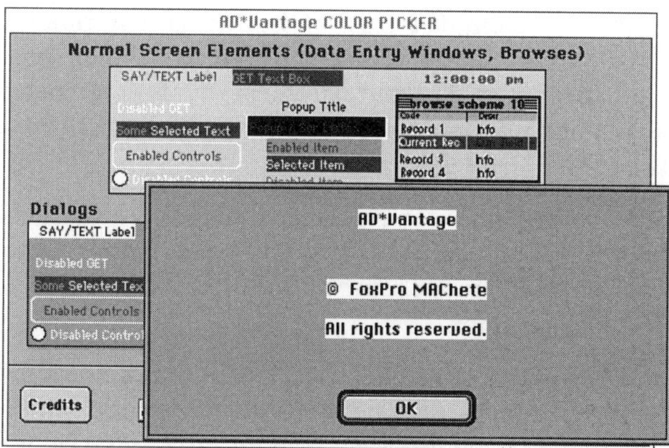

Figure 14.6 *The About window changes to match the Dialog colors in the current ("Accordian") color set.*

To use the system yourself, you provide the Color Picker in your applications, giving the users control over general application colors. You then can reduce your color control programming to a couple of simple rules:

- Use appropriate COLOR SCHEME clauses on your window definitions, in order to represent a visual interface clue to the different types of windows.
- Override your windows' COLOR SCHEME clauses occasionally with COLOR and COLOR SCHEME clauses on objects that need colors that don't follow the defaults.
- Use the RGBSCHEME() function to reference colors without finding out what the colors are. Don't ever assign explicit colors instead.

As you saw in Chapter 7, you give the users a chance to use the Color Picker simply by Including the COLORRSC.DBF in your application. This file holds available color sets. If you examine the table, you'll find that it isn't the normal resource table structure. I mentioned earlier that FoxPro for Macintosh can't use "native" FoxPro color sets stored in the resource file with the CREATE COLOR SET command, or restore sets created on the other platforms using the SET COLOR SET command. COLORRSC.DBF is my custom resource file to store color sets in a way that can be stored and restored using relatively few lines of FoxPro code. You can use COLORRSC color sets on all three platforms, if you want, using the code I show you in this section.

See Also

- "Adaptable Utility Menu Options," Chapter 7
- Source Disk:Library/Template Code Folder:COLORSRSC.DBF

I personally have no patience for creating color sets at all! Most of the sets you find in the seed COLORRSC.DBF started out in one of two places: a file on CompuServe and a great color-handling utility—both of which were designed for FoxPro for DOS.

The file on CompuServe, COLORS.ZIP in FoxForum's library, included color sets written by Nancy Jacobsen and Sue Cunningham, two of the most helpful members of the FoxForum community. The color utility, *The Harless Color Sets*, was written by Wayne Harless, who can be termed, without exaggeration, the father of all knowledge about Fox colors. I also brought in sets that started life in a group of color sets that Fox Software shipped with FoxPro 1.0 as well as in PROCOLOR, the color utility that shipped with FoxPro 2.0, written by Blaise Mitsutama.

You can create additional COLORRSC records from existing DOS 2.5 or Windows color set records in your own resource file. Here's a quick-and dirty program you can use to import native color sets from either environment to COLORRSC form:

```
* crea_col.prg

IF NOT (_DOS OR _WINDOWS)
   WAIT WINDOW ;
     "Need to be in FP DOS or Win!"
   RETURN
ENDIF
CREATE TABLE ColorRsc ;
     (SCHEME1  M, SCHEME2  M, ;
      SCHEME3  M, SCHEME4  M, ;
      SCHEME5  M, SCHEME6  M, ;
      SCHEME7  M, SCHEME8  M, ;
      SCHEME9  M, SCHEME10 M, ;
      SCHEME11 M, SCHEME12 M, ;
      NAME C(24), ;
      READONLY L(1))
* set your resource file to the
* one that contains the color sets
* you wish to convert
* before you run this code
```

```
IF SET("RESO") = "OFF"
   SET RESOURCE ON
ENDIF
SELE 0
USE SET("RESO",1) AGAIN ALIAS RealSets

SCAN FOR ALLTRIM(ID) == "COLORSET" AND ;
          TYPE = IIF(_DOS,"PREF2.5","PREFW")
   SET COLOR SET TO (ALLTRIM(RealSets.Name))
   SELE ColorRsc
   DO NewRec WITH RealSets.Name
   WAIT WINDOW ALLTRIM(RealSets.Name)+"... "
ENDSCAN
INDEX ON name TAG name
RETURN

PROC NewRec
PARAMETERS prefname
APPEND BLANK
REPLACE Name WITH prefname
DO SetMemos
RETURN

PROC SetMemos
PRIVATE m.xx
FOR m.xx = 1 TO 12
   REPLACE ("Scheme"+ALLTRIM(STR(m.xx))) ;
             WITH RGBSCHEME(m.xx)
ENDFOR
RETURN
```

When you use COLORRSC.DBF in your own application, you may want to restore color sets programmatically without the user accessing the Color Picker. For example, as I suggested in Chapter 11, you may save the user's color preferences in SYS_VAR.DBF or even the native FoxPro resource file and restore this preference when a user logs in. Here's a sample procedure you might use to accomplish this task:

```
DO CASE
CASE _UNIX
  * who knows??? <g>
CASE _DOS or _WIN
```

```
  * use real resource file
  * or you may prefer to use my COLORRSC.DBF
  * for all platforms:
  SET COLOR SET TO <color set name>
CASE _MAC
  * use our custom resources:
  PRIVATE m.oldselect
  m.oldselect = SELECT()
  IF NOT USED("ColorRsc")
     USE ColorRsc AGAIN ALIAS ColorRsc IN 0
  ENDIF
  SELECT ColorRsc
  LOCATE FOR Name = <Mac color set name>
  PRIVATE m.xx, m.yy, m.zz
  WAIT WINDOW NOWAIT ;
      "SETting COLOR SCHEMEs for "+;
       ALLTRIM(ColorRsc.Name)+" Set... "
  FOR m.xx = 1 TO 12
     * get the contents of this scheme's memo:
     m.zz = ;
      EVAL("ColorRsc.Scheme"+ALLTR(STR(m.xx)))
     * find beginning of 6th set of RGB values:
     m.yy = ATC("R",m.zz,6)
     * set the scheme in two sections, to avoid
     * a problem with strings that are too long
     * for SET COLOR OF SCHEME to use either as
     * a macro or an indirect reference
     SET COLOR OF SCHEME m.xx TO ;
        (SUBSTR(m.zz,1,m.yy-1))
     SET COLOR OF SCHEME m.xx TO ;
        (",,,,,"+SUBSTR(m.zz,m.yy))
  ENDFOR
  WAIT CLEAR
  SELECT (m.oldselect)
ENDCASE
RETURN
```

In FoxPro for Macintosh, you can use final procedures (NewRec and Set Memos) in CREA_COL.PRG, the color set creation code above, to create COLORRSC records interactively, while you use SET COLOR OF SCHEME <expN> TO <pair definitions> to adjust your working color set. (If you create color sets that you like, either using my Mac-initiated cross-platform system, or as native FoxPro for DOS or Windows color sets, consider adding to the general wealth by posting your sets on FoxForum, as Sue and Nancy did!). However, I've provided a utility application to help you create COLORRSC.DBF records on the Macintosh and to learn about the FoxPro for Macintosh color system in detail.

Use the FoxPro Mac Color Tutor to Learn More about the Color System

You'll find the complete source code for my Color Tutor on the Source Disk. When you DO COLORS.APP, you see the complex dialog shown in figure 14.7.

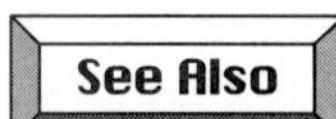

- Source Disk:Color Tutor Folder

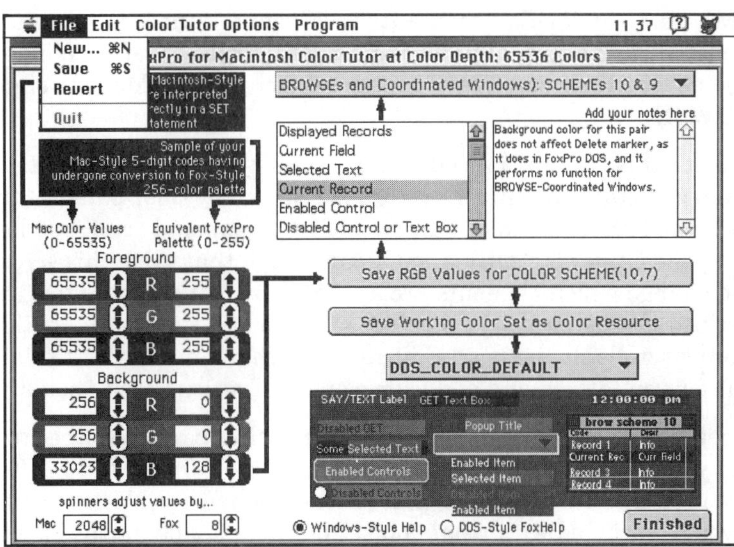

Figure 14.7 *The FoxPro Mac Color Tutor dialog.*

The Color Tutor has a lot going on, so you may be confused about what some of its elements do at first, but its operation is actually straightforward. The constant redisplay of various elements in response to any changes you make should make the relationships between the elements clear as you work.

On the left side of the dialog are two sets of RGB values (foreground and background each for Mac 5-digit system and Windows 3-digit system) addressed as “spinners” (they’re not actually Fox spinners, but that’s what they look like). Adjusting the figures in either notation will cause the other notation’s values to change to reflect your change and the two SAYs at the top left to show you what the current foreground and background looks like, in both notations.

All of this notation pertains to just one pair of one scheme.

At the top right, you see a pop-up that shows you which interface object you’re currently editing and which schemes pertain to this object. For example, in figure 14.7, the editable object is BROWSEs and windows defined in the same scheme as the BROWSE scheme to coordinate with the BROWSEs. BROWSEs use scheme 10, and I’ve chosen scheme 9 as the secondary scheme for any window pop-ups DEFINEd in COLOR SCHEME 10. (BROWSEs’ scheme 10 and System Windows, scheme 8, are almost always practically the same color pair list. System Windows use scheme 9 as their secondary pop-up scheme, so I’ve done the same for BROWSEs.)

Underneath this pop-up, a scrollable list shows you which elements of the object you can edit. The current record is affected by color pair 7 of the main scheme (10) for Browse windows. (The pop-up and scrollable list represent the OBJECTS.DBF and CPAIRS.DBF that drive this screen. You can change which elements are available by editing these two tables, as described in Customizing Color Tutor in the application’s help file.) Next to the scrollable list is an Edit region with my notes about this element for you to read and add your own observations to my notes.

Underneath the scrollable list and edit region that pertain to the current element you’re modifying is a `Save RGB Values for...` push button. The button’s prompt confirms which pair of which scheme you’re working on. When you’re satisfied with what you see on the left side, push this button, and the appropriate pair of the appropriate scheme in the working color set will change. You’ll see this change reflected in one element of the examples at the bottom right of the dialog.

The full example at the bottom right pertains to just one linked pair of schemes at a time, representing the one interface object that the top pop-up indicates. So if you change the pop-up from BROWSEs and Coordinated Windows to Dialogs (Modal) SCHEMEs 5 & 6, the entire bottom right corner will change to show you a new set of values for the new schemes. (In the Macintosh startup color set, these schemes may look the same, but they’re still different schemes.)

When you like the look of all the elements in all the types of interface objects you can edit, you can push the middle push button (`Save Working Color Set as Color Resource`). This will either change the values in the current COLORRSC.DBF record, as shown in the pop-up right above the examples, or (if the pop-up reads `_New Color Resource_`) you'll be prompted for the name of a new color resource record.

You may want to start your new set based on one of the current sets in COLORRSC.DBF, rather than starting from the defaults. The File menu has a Revert option, if you want to return the working set to its defaults while you're playing with existing sets. Using this option when you are editing a _New Color Resource_ will bring you back to FoxPro for Macintosh defaults.

Note that the COLORRSC.DBF has a READ-only field that I'm not currently using, for color sets you want to protect from modification.

Beyond the creation of color sets, however, use the Color Tutor to watch the interactions of the two RGB coordinate systems and to think further about the FoxPro color schemes and the pairs assigned to objects and elements in this system. I wrote a help file for the Color Tutor, which is far more extensive than the text in this section of the book, to help you go forward in your understanding of FoxPro colors (see figures 14.8 and 14.9). You can use both the FoxPro .DBF and Windows-style .HLP files outside the Color Tutor to investigate advanced color topics.

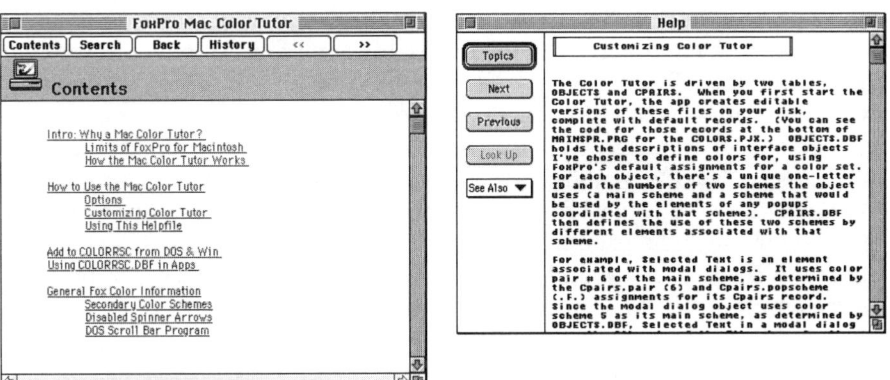

Figures 14.8 and 14.9. *CTUTOR.HLP and CTUTOR.DBF provide advanced help for color topics.*

Use the Color Tutor Source Code to Learn More about FoxPro

The Color Tutor's source code, like APPSETUP, also provides a good look at the flexibility of my template system and a model for data-driven dialogs. Color Tutor is driven by a pair of tables, OBJECTS.DBF and CPAIRS.DBF, which you'll find described in the Customizing Color Tutor help topic. Color Tutor places an editable version of these tables on your disk. You can adjust the pairs and schemes you edit in the Tutor by adjusting these tables.

In addition, Color Tutor performs a host of interesting FoxPro tricks you won't find used in many other places. All the code is contained in COLORS.PJX's MAINSPR.PRG; it is highly modular and heavily commented.

Probably the dialog's most striking visual trick is the use of a second .SPR containing only SAYs and uneditable GETs, EXAMPLES.SPR, with a #NOREAD PLAIN directive, to refresh the bottom right corner of the display. This corner is actually empty in COLORS.SCX itself, as you see in figure 14.10. I do EXAMPLES.SPR whenever I've changed values in the working color set or need to display a different interface object. This is a very extended form of the trick that Randy uses to display font samples in the Cosmic Converter.

When you examine the COLORS.SCX layout, you'll see that the spinners you see when you run the utility aren't really spinners. I wanted you to be able to push the spinner buttons and see an immediate change, in the same way that a WHEN on a scrollable list fires as you move through the available values in the list, but this doesn't happen with spinner objects. Instead of real spinners, each apparent spinner is a host of small arrows and lines on top of invisible buttons—a total of 24 invisible buttons in all (6 RGB fore-and-background * 2 coordinate systems * 2 up-and-down buttons for each). As is appropriate for spinners, you can also edit the figures in the text boxes directly rather than "spinning" the controls. Andy uses a similar trick to handle color values in GASP.

All 24 buttons and their 12 associated text boxes use the same code, with indirect references and EVAL()s accounting for the individual object being affected. For example, both buttons and text boxes in the ersatz spinners share the following single UDF as a MESSAGE clause:

```
FUNCTION rgbmsg
* MESSAGE clause for all RGB value
```

```
* and spinner GETs
PRIVATE m.var
m.var = UPPER(VARREAD())
IF INLIST(RIGHT(m.var,2),"_U","_D")
  && we're in a spinner...
  m.var = LEFT(m.var, LEN(m.var) - 2)
ENDIF
RETURN ;
   "Set the value for the "+;
    SUBSTR(m.var,2,LEN(m.var)-3)+;
   " component of the "+ ;
     IIF(LEFT(m.var,1) = "F",;
           "foreground", "background")+;
    " color in the "+ ;
     IIF(RIGHT(m.var,1) = "F", ;
          "256-value Fox system", ;
          "65535-value Mac system")
```

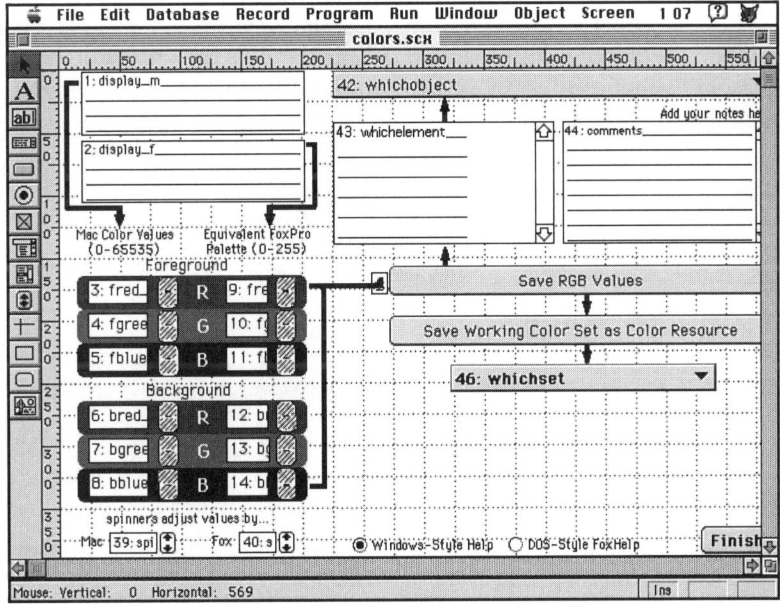

Figure 14.10 *The COLORS.SCX dialog layout may look different from what you expect in the Screen Builder. The bottom right corner is empty, and the RGB spinners on the left aren't really spinners at all.*

When you look at this function, you'll see that the strategy I use to make the code work for all the objects is a strict naming convention for the associated memory variables. An initial "f" or "b" denotes" "foreground" or "background". A final "_u" or "_d" denotes a spinner button (up or down).

The letters "_d", "_f ", and "_m" within a screen element's name are used to denote the color notation system to which it belongs. There are screen elements and associated variables for all three notation systems (DOS, FoxPro/Windows, and Macintosh native), although all the DOS objects are commented out in this code. Read the comments in the source code to see how to easily add DOS color notation samples to the Macintosh and Windows samples already available in the dialog.

Learn More about Macintosh Colors from FoxPro

You'll notice that the Color Tutor tells you what *color depth* is currently available in its dialog title. I use FOXTOOLS.MLB's FxGDepth() function to provide this information. It's important to know the color depth because the number of colors available on your Mac display, as set in the Monitors control panel shown in figure 14.11, materially affects the way FoxPro can display your color choices.

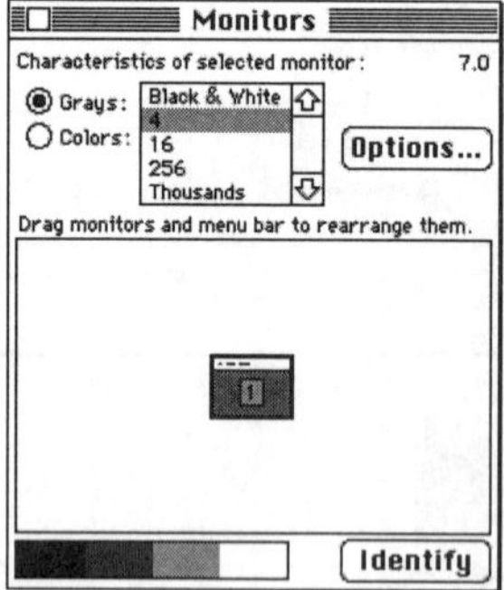

Figure 14.11 *Changing your Macintosh color depth in the Monitors control panel.*

FOXPRO MAC HACK TIP

When you're playing with colors, you may want to change the Monitors control panel setting and try the Color Tutor again. You should quit Fox and come back in each time that you use the Monitors control panel to change the number of colors available to FoxPro. FoxPro checks color depth only on startup, so it's not a good idea to change your system setup "behind FoxPro's back." If you simply leave the dialog, remain in FoxPro, and restart this application with a different number of available colors or grays, you may notice anomalous results as you specify colors afterward.

When you change color depth, you realize that your carefully-wrought color sets change radically with the display mode. For example, on a 4-color grayscale display, the pure red and pure green values (128,0,0 and 0,128,0) may be matching grays, while the pure blue (0,0,128) is black. In 16 grays, the same green may be represented by black, but now red and blue are almost identical grays.

FoxPro DOS and Windows users will recognize this problem as similar to what we face when we design color sets for laptop use. It seems that every monochrome and grayscale display adaptor maps colors differently.

This is why one of the best reasons to use Mac Color Tutor is to find groups of color sets that work well with different Macs. Your application can present choices based on a table of likely prospects after checking FxGDepth() for the current display mode.

I've noted that the default (SET COLOR SET TO <nothing> to reset to defaults) is often the best idea with limited numbers of grays or colors. Mac Color Tutor will reset to this default when you start up the dialog, giving you a place to begin your experiments. Generally, for limited numbers of color or gray values, you may want to use a default color set with one or two particular interface elements (like the BROWSE current record) tweaked a little more exactly.

FoxPro for Macintosh works with a 256-color palette, regardless of the number of colors available to your display. Apple uses "16-bit color," in which actually the first 15 bits produce colors (5 bits each for the 5-digits of the red, green, and blue values, with the 16th bit producing special effects such as transparency). 16-bit color allows thousands of colors, from which applications specify their palettes. As you switch among applications on the Macintosh, you may notice your colors flashing as the Mac switches among palettes each application specifies.

Applications use a `clut` or `pltt` type resource to specify their 256 colors out of the colors available. Figure 14.12 shows you FoxPro's clut resource in ResEdit. Because FoxPro doesn't use a pltt-type resource, which forces color mapping to the specified values, you may find that colors in FoxPro are partially dependent on the application you used just before FoxPro.

> **CROSS-PLATFORM WARNING**
>
> FoxPro for Windows users should be aware that the SET PALETTE OFF command has no effect in FoxPro for Macintosh.

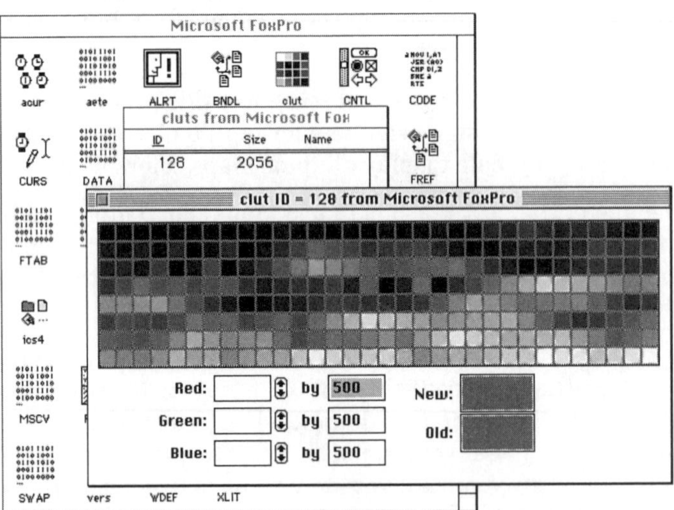

Figure 14.12 *FoxPro's color resource open in ResEdit.*

If you have fewer colors available than 256 on your Mac display, FoxPro has to decide how to map its 256 colors to your color set. As I mentioned earlier, its formulae for performing this mapping are slightly unpredictable. However, if you set up your system at different color depths and create COLORRSC records that provide good contrasts at each depth, you should be able to find color combinations that satisfy everybody to whom you distribute applications.

Help Systems

The help system I created for the Color Tutor exists in two versions (FoxPro .DBF and Microsoft Windows-style .HLP) that are both produced by one master table, CMASTER.DBF, so the text for the two versions always stays synchronized. (I used a beta copy of a new utility called GenHelp, by Cornerstone Software Limited, to produce the final versions from the master table). Use whichever help file you prefer, as you continue to learn about the FoxPro color system, and pay attention to the help file format, too.

Evaluate Help Styles

When you create help systems for FoxPro for Macintosh applications, it's a good idea to give users a choice between help styles. They both have limitations from the Mac point of view. The .DBF version is marred by its use of FoxFont, necessitated by the line-drawing characters in the body of its text, and it doesn't have all the bells-and-whistles of Windows-style help. However, the .DBF style help is much more useful when you want to search information in a long help topic or to copy and paste help information. The .DBF-style help is also the only version you can use in FoxPro for DOS, so it's essential to three-platform applications.

The Macintosh version of the Microsoft Help Engine is very slow and hogs memory unmercifully. Users will not enjoy watching its buttons repaint several times every time they call the help system, and you won't enjoy figuring out which features of the help engine aren't supported on the Macintosh. You find some of the limitations documented in the *Distribution Kit User's Guide*, included as part of the FoxPro for Macintosh Professional Version, but other errors seem to appear almost randomly.

In figure 14.13, you see a typical Help engine error that doesn't occur when the same .HLP file is subjected to the same user actions in the Windows environment. The Help file in question is Microsoft FoxPro's installed FOXHELP.HLP—so the error in question isn't mine.

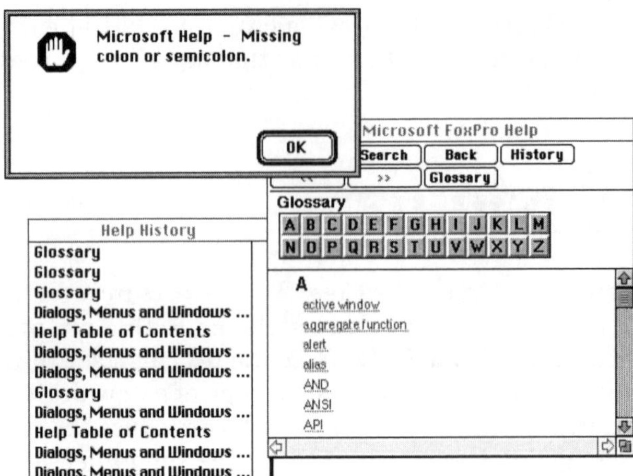

Figure 14.13 *The Macintosh version of the Microsoft Windows Help engine sometimes gives spurious errors, even when you use FoxPro's own help file.*

The Microsoft Help Engine compiler is part of the FoxPro for Macintosh Professional version, but if you have the Standard version of FoxPro Mac, you still have this compiler if you own the Windows version of the FoxPro Distribution Kit. If not, you can download the compiler from various Microsoft forum libraries on CompuServe (search for files with the name HC*.EXE). The compiler itself doesn't run on the Macintosh; you must create the .HLP file on a DOS machine.

Set Up Your Application for Efficient Help Systems

My template code takes care of setting up your chosen help file on the Apple Help menu, as well as the normal chores of saving and restoring an existing help file. You can use the template's INSTALL.DBF to place a copy of the .HLP on disk (you'll find that COLORS.APP installs CTUTOR.HLP as it runs) because the .HLP is a document belonging to a separate application, the Microsoft Help Engine. Although the .HLP can't execute while bound into the FoxPro .APP or .EXE file, you generally include the .DBF-style help in your .APP or .EXE.

If you have both types of help files available with the same name, you'll find that SET HELP TO <filename> with no extension defaults to the Windows-style help file.

After your help file is installed and SET, create a procedure to evaluate current conditions and SET TOPIC TO an appropriate topic, in order to provide context-sensitive help.

The SET TOPIC TO command was originally designed to allow you to specify a logical condition that stayed in force for the life of your application. This method doesn't work with the .HLP style files, and has quirks even with the .DBF style help system. Instead, create a custom help procedure that runs whenever the user presses a help key or uses a help menu option. The procedure SETs TOPIC at the instant the user needs the help and then issues the HELP command.

Your custom help procedure can evaluate the current GET, the current window, the currently SELECTed table, or any other factors you want to decide how to SET TOPIC TO <expression>. The expression you set should be the topic name you want to display, or, for the .DBF-style help system, a logical expression which will result in the appropriate topic being displayed. The topic name is always the first field in the .DBF-style help file, which must be a character field (the field name is usually Topic, but can be anything you want).

Following the character field with the Topic name, the .DBF-style help file has a memo field (usually named Details) that stores the actual topic information. After these two required fields, the .DBF-style help file can have as many additional fields as you like, all of which can participate in your evaluation of conditions to execute a SET TOPIC TO <logical expression> command (The FOXHELP.DBF table has a Class field FoxPro uses internally for this purpose, as you see in figure 14.14.)

If you use the .HLP-style help file but maintain a master .DBF table for both help versions, you can USE the master table in a normal workarea and evaluate the current conditions in your custom help procedure. Use a LOCATE or SEEK to match the evaluation you do in the complex SET TOPIC TO <logical expression> you use for the .DBF-style help. Then SET TOPIC TO the topic name as a character expression, as the result of your evaluation, and finally issue the HELP command.

You may find it convenient to use this technique to evaluate topics for both help file versions. With appropriate indexes on the master table to optimize your conditions, evaluating the conditions yourself isn't appreciably slower than SETting TOPIC TO <logical expression> for the .DBF version of the help file.

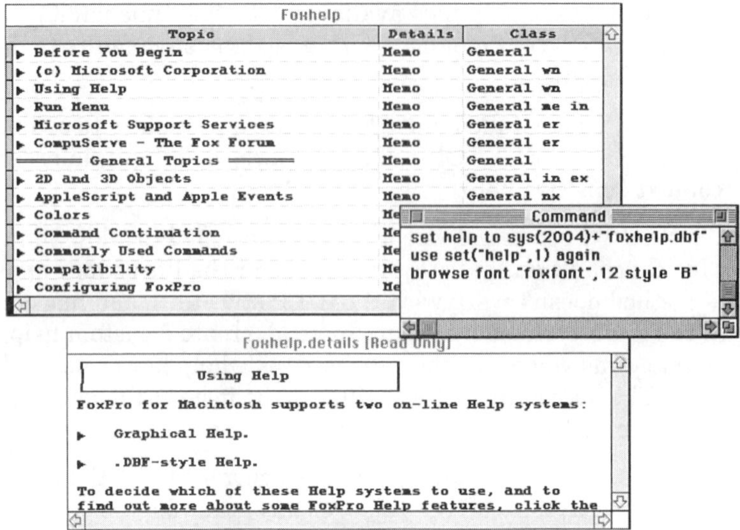

Figure 14.14 *Explore the .DBF-style help system.*

> **CROSS-PLATFORM WARNING**
>
> For efficient cross-platform and cross-helpfile-version development, you may also want to avoid SET HELPFILTER. This very handy feature of the .DBF-style help causes an error if you've SET HELP TO an .HLP file.

While you're creating your help system, don't neglect other ways that are available in FoxPro to document and prompt your users. You've already seen a use of the MESSAGE clause in this chapter. You can create a prompt in the status bar for every GET and menu option if you create MESSAGE clauses for each item. In addition, menu options can use Macintosh Balloon Help. You add balloon information into the menu options' MESSAGE clause!

You may think that Balloon Help is useless; many Mac people dislike it. However, new users can turn on the Balloon Help feature and get a quick tour of the entire application with Balloon Help explanations, simply by moving the mouse over unfamiliar menu options. Then they can turn off the feature so that it never obstructs their work. Users can do something similar, but extremely slow, if they press Option-Ctrl-F1 or Option-Ctrl-click, the Macintosh equivalent of Alt-F1 or Alt-click. With Balloon Help, however, they don't have to work at all. Also, although they can use the regular help system, it's quite difficult to get context-sensitive help to work well for menu options—and sometimes the full help text is overkill anyway.

Below is the template code procedure that I use to provide Balloon Help with some additional notes on its cross-platform use and font-handling. This function code is bracketed to only add the Balloon Help message where appropriate—on the Mac, that is. However, if you're interested in trying it, the status bar font and equivalent calculation will work to push the balloon message out of the status bar in Windows and in DOS, too, if you use the status bar system font in Windows, MS Sans Serif 9.

Instead of wasting effort, BALLOON.PRG brackets code at the *lowest* point possible, as you learned in Chapter 11. In this case, that means the function only passes back the balloon help and does the necessary "message padding" for the platform that can use it.

Notice as always that params are checked for proper type and availability, and that I don't even bother to do the padding on the *Mac* platform if I haven't gotten a balloon message on this call to the function.

```
* FUNCTION balloon
* used in the MESSAGE clause of FoxPro menus

PARAM m.msg, m.balloonmsg

IF TYPE("m.msg") # "C"
   m.msg = ""
ENDIF
IF _MAC AND TYPE("m.balloonmsg") = "C" ;
   AND NOT EMPTY(m.balloonmsg)

   * what the calculation actually does
   * to figure out the number of spaces:

   * take the number of pixels across the full
   * width of the display, subtract the length
   * in pixels of the current non-balloon
   * message you want to show up in the space bar
   * Divide the full pixel width by the width in
```

```
* pixels of a single space so you now have
* padding in numbers of spaces to push
* the balloon message to the full length of
* the status bar
* Subtract the column position of the status
* bar indicators, so you now have the number
* of spaces to get to that position

* SCOLS() only "knows about" the main
* application window in terms of the font it
* uses to return a number of screen columns
* and the status bar is always written
* in Geneva 10, not main application window
* font.  Besides, SCOLS() may refer to either
* display width or main application window,
* depending on whether MACDESKTOP is ON or OFF.
* That's why we use SYSMETRIC() pixel-width
* information against the Geneva FONTMETRICs
* instead to figure out the necessary padding.


* The calculation starts out a little extra-
* generous, because it uses the whole display
* width so it pushes the balloon information
* out past the end of the status bar rather than
* just "underneath" the status bar area of
* Ins/Numlock/Capslock indicators.  I add -40
* so that we push the balloon message only as
* necessary. If you unbracketed Balloon(),
* the -40 would be a different value for Win
* and removed for DOS, where the message row
* goes all the way across.

* It's necessary to trim over-generous spaces:
* there's limit to the MESSAGE clause of 254
* characters, unfortunately <sigh> — we don't
* want to waste characters on the padding.  If
* a too-long balloon, the function returns only
* first 254 characters to avoid a "string too
* long to fit" error.
```

```
   * Only padding right side (done with a REPL(),
   * but you could also use with PADR) will work!
   * If you use this function without bracketing,
   * padding and concatenating with Balloon Help
   * even for the platforms that don't use the
   * Balloon, the message would still be centered
   * in DOS, although but Balloon() still works:
   * if it weren't, you'd see your additional
   * balloon stuff tacked on the end, including
   * little musical notes for the CHR(13)s <g>.
   * FP DOS apparently trims spaces from messages
   * and then centers what's left.

   m.msg = m.msg +  ;
           REPL(" ", ;
           ( SYSMETRIC(1) - ;
           ( TXTWIDTH(m.msg,"geneva",10,"N") * ;
             FONTMETRIC(6,"geneva",10,"N") ) )/;
            ( FONTMETRIC(6,"geneva",10,"N") * ;
              TXTWIDTH(" ","geneva",10,"N") ) ;
             - 40 ) ;
      + CHR(13)+CHR(13)+ ;
      m.balloonmsg
ENDIF
RETURN LEFT(m.msg,254)
```

Handle Keys and Mouse with ON KEY LABEL, Macros, and Menu Shortcuts

Although Randy has written an Appendix on QuicKeys, a Macintosh utility that is a far superior macro-handler to FoxPro macros, the FoxPro macro system is still a good cross-platform feature you can offer your users. You can SAVE MACROS TO a MEMO field, allowing each user to have an application-set of personal macros as one of the amenities of your application.

If you prefer, don't use macros yourself and don't offer any access to them for your users. `SET MACKEY TO <nothing>` so there's no way for users to record a macro. However, FoxPro has a default set of macros built in that you should still know about and that you *must* handle in your programs.

See Also

- "QuicKeys: Mac Developer's Tool," Appendix C

Most people don't realize that FoxPro uses macros to implement the command function key settings (such as `SET` when you press F2).These macros are in force when FoxPro starts up and no DEFAULT.FKY macro file is available at all; these macros are internal to FoxPro.

At the very least, your applications should CLEAR MACROS at the start, to eliminate the possibility of Fox keywords such as SET and DISPLAY being played back inappropriately when the user touches the function keys. However, I prefer to RESTORE MACROS FROM an APP.FKY file I build into the application, so that I can retain the shifted numeric keypad editing macros I've added to my default macro set. Figure 14.15 shows you the way FoxPro's macro facility implements these editing keystrokes. You still have to CLEAR MACROS first because RESTORE MACROS is an additive operation.

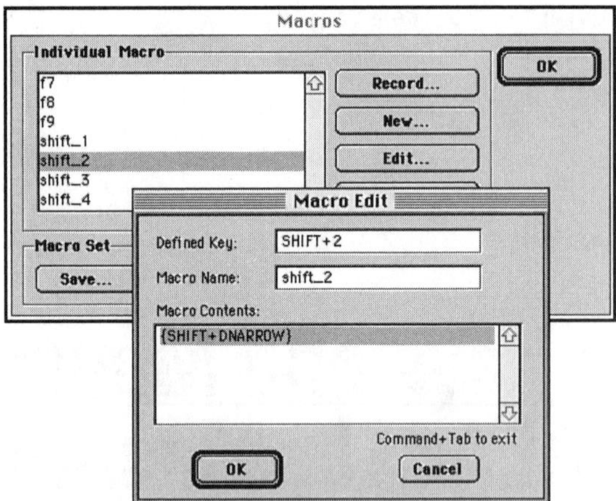

Figure 14.15 *FoxPro has default macros built in, and you can add others to your DEFAULT.FKY file for convenience.*

The template code takes care of this detail for you, as well as restoring the old macros when your application cleans up. As always, the template will respond appropriately whether or not it finds an APP.FKY file available, and you have the option of using a local APP.FKY instead of the template file for any application with special macro needs. The template APP.FKY includes the shifted numeric keypad editing macros and nothing else.

Macros are only one way of several that FoxPro allows you to control the keyboard. You have seen menu shortcuts as you worked with the Menu Builder, and you worked with the ON KEY LABEL ENTER command in the template code to allow a press of the (Return) key to select a record in a BROWSE for editing.

The KEYBOARD PLAIN command allows you to override both ON KEY LABEL and macro-setting for keys with assignment; the ON KEY LABEL ENTER procedure used `KEYBOARD "{ENTER}" PLAIN` when it evaluated the current window and found the user wasn't in a BROWSE. KEYBOARD PLAIN, however, does not obviate a menu shortcut assignment.

If you mistakenly assign different meanings to a single key combination, a menu shortcut is overruled by a macro, and both are superseded by an ON KEY LABEL. If you use a `KEYBOARD the_key PLAIN` statement for a key with all three assignments, the PLAIN obviates the macro and ON KEY LABEL assignments, leaving the key behavior back at the menu shortcut level.

You often KEYBOARD a key without the PLAIN keyword to play out keystrokes that the user might have taken, or that the user took and you temporarily intercepted. You saw an example of that technique in X_ASCII.PRG at the end of Chapter 1, in which I intercepted keystrokes with an INKEY() wait state and evaluated these strokes before passing them on. You can use INKEY() in a similar technique in the WHEN of a GET, to determine whether the user needs a pop-up of choices or is typing in a valid code. If you receive a function key press, or if the user prepares to leave the GET with a navigation key, such as a (Tab), you ACTIVATE the POPUP. If, on the other hand, you receive a valid character, you KEYBOARD the character you've received right into the GET and let data entry proceed.

Both KEYBOARD and its close cousin PLAY MACRO send keystrokes to the *keyboard buffer*, where FoxPro holds them until you have returned from the procedure sending the keystrokes back into the wait state in which the program is receptive to user keystrokes. You can remove this input by using the command `CLEAR TYPEAHEAD`, if necessary.

Except for macros, which ignore the mouse, these commands all have a special relationship with the mouse. You can even KEYBOARD a "{LEFTMOUSE}", although it's important to realize that the click may not end up where you expect it to go.

You can use ON KEY LABEL LEFTMOUSE to great effect, as you'll see shortly. This command is different from other ON KEY LABEL assignments in that the mouse-trapping doesn't "eat the click" (the click still occurs in its original location after the ON KEY LABEL procedure RETURNs). If you want to trap the click and remove it from the events FoxPro will process, you can execute the command `=INKEY("M")` to "eat the click" explicitly within your ON KEY LABEL LEFTMOUSE procedure.

CROSS-PLATFORM WARNING

Notice the use of the key label LEFTMOUSE. Most special keys in FoxPro can be referenced in macros, ON KEY LABEL assignments, and KEYBOARDs using a key label of this type (such as {TAB} or {SPACEBAR}). You enclose the key labels in curly braces when you KEYBOARD them or include them in a macro set of keystrokes. Because the braces are delimiters for key labels, if you want to indicate the braces themselves, you use the key labels {LBRACE} and {RBRACE}.

For the Macintosh, the commands ON KEY LABEL LEFTMOUSE and MOUSE are identical, but you should use LEFTMOUSE to avoid any cross-platform problems. Be warned that the documentation talks about a special ON KEY LABEL RIGHTMOUSE emulation feature built into FoxPro for Macintosh, but this capability doesn't exist. It was removed early in the Beta process, and somehow remains in the documentation.

When you assign an ON KEY LABEL "{LEFTMOUSE}" procedure, you often want to evaluate the position of the mouse within the procedure, using the MCOL(), MROW(), or MWINDOW() functions. *Be sure to pass these values to the procedure as arguments*, rather than evaluating them within the procedure, because the user may move the mouse after the click occurs.

FoxPro contains a few other special mouse-handling facilities. The system variable _DBLCLICK, which defaults to the value of .49 seconds, tells

FoxPro how long a user can pause between two clicks before the clicks will be interpreted as separate events, rather than a double-click. You may want to let your users adjust this setting.

> **FOXPRO MAC HACK TIP**
>
> The _DBLCLICK variable also tells FoxPro how long between keystrokes is allowed before FoxPro abandons an incremental search in a pop-up to start a new search string. If you're unable to duplicate the effect of increment search in a pop-up, and a single keystroke serves to deactivate the pop-up as if you've made a selection, SET CONFIRM ON to solve the problem.

The _DBLCLICK value is useful to your programs, as well as internally to FoxPro, when you want to determine whether a double click has occurred. Unfortunately, the examples given in the documentation don't work as advertised! If you look in MAIN.PRG, I've integrated one of the most-requested double-click capabilities into the template: the use of a double click to select a record in a BROWSE. To use it, the template screen set Setup includes these lines along with the ON KEY LABEL ENTER assignment that performs the same function:

```
PRIVATE m.gotclick
m.gotclick = 0
ON KEY LABEL LEFTMOUSE ;
   DO MouseBrow WITH ;
      MROW(WONTOP()), MCOL(WONTOP()), ;
      UPPER(MWINDOW()), SECONDS()
```

Notice that I'm passing the return values of all the mouse-evaluating functions I need, as I've advised you to do. The procedure called by this ON KEY LABEL assignment follows:

```
PROCEDURE MouseBrow
PARAMETERS mwrow, mwcol, mwind, mtime
PUSH KEY CLEAR
IF mtime <= m.gotclick + _DBLCLICK ;
   AND  mwind # UPPER(WOUTPUT())  ;
   AND mwrow # -1 AND mwcol # -1
```

```
   KEYBOARD "{ENTER}"
   && selection keystroke for BROWSEs
ELSE
   m.gotclick = mtime
   * pass the key on
ENDIF
POP KEY
RETURN
```

In this procedure, the critical section is the condition in the IF/ENDIF construct. The first condition checks the click against the last click and evaluates a possible double-click condition, using _DBLCLICK. If a double-click condition exists, the second condition checks to see if the mouse is in a browse, and the third condition checks to see that they haven't clicked *outside* the current window.

> **CROSS-PLATFORM WARNING**
>
> If you've used MDOWN() to determine if the mouse button is down in FoxPro before, you should be warned that this function has some serious timing problems that are more obvious on the Macintosh than in other versions of FoxPro—although you can see the problems in any version. Avoid using this function.

When you work with ON KEY LABEL assignments of important keys like the Enter key and the mouse, you may get into a situation that handles a keystroke inappropriately if you crash. For example, you may end up at the Command window with your ON KEY LABEL ENTER command still set to close a browse. You may also not be able to get to normal menu functions because Cleanup didn't get a chance to restore your usual system menu. If there's an ON SHUTDOWN routine in force, you may not be able to QUIT or even Restart your Mac.

If this happens to you, don't panic and throw the power switch! If you can reach the Program menu's Do option or the Trace window, you can execute a small program to null out all the critical assignments and at least get you in a position to issue a normal QUIT. Remember that the Trace window is available in a template application on the Program menu if you've initialized a variable named _DEBUG to .T. in your interactive environment before running the application. (You can set this condition to any other condition you like by changing the line evaluating _DEBUG in MAIN.PRG.)

As you can see in figure 14.16, my small "cut-me-loose" program is named PANIC.PRG. You'll find it in the Library/Template Code folder; edit it to contain any additional entries that you deem necessary. Make sure that you know how to find it *before* you need it.

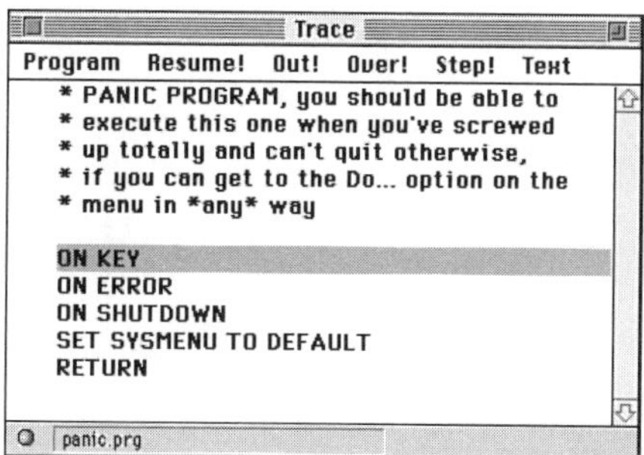

Figure 14.16 *Keep a PANIC.PRG around for emergencies and access it through the Program Do option or the Trace window when you've crashed.*

Chapter Wrap Up

Among the wealth of minor FoxPro features (I've only discussed a few in this chapter), I've tried to focus on those capabilities of special value to application developers. I hope you continue to discover other features, such as the Filer, in the interactive environment. The Fox tool set is full of obscure goodies and tricks that you can use to improve your working habits and enhance your rapid development techniques.

PART IV

INTEGRATE FOXPRO APPLICATIONS: THE MACINTOSH ENVIRONMENT

When you use the techniques for rapid development in this book, the applications that you build are good citizens of the cross-platform FoxPro world. Wherever necessary, you've written platform-specific code, but you've concentrated on making applications platform-independent.

The applications are also good citizens of the network world, with code that incorporates sound multi-user safeguards throughout. You learned FoxPro techniques that make your applications portable and easily extended.

There's more to writing an application for Macintosh than simply writing a good, generalized application. You already saw how each programming step you take must be matched with awareness of the Mac interface design decisions it entails. You've tangled with some facts of life about the Macintosh operating system that impact on what you can do with FoxPro.

In Part IV of the book, you'll focus on special features and requirements of the Mac environment. You'll go beyond what you can do on other FoxPro platforms to address exclusive needs and benefits of working on the

Macintosh. Many of the tools and approaches considered here are incommensurable with their DOS and Windows counterparts, if counterparts even exist.

You'll start by considering network issues more closely than you have elsewhere in the book. Doc Livingston gives you a masterly overview of networking and performance that you *can* learn from for multi-user work based on any platform. You will find, however, that his analysis is drawn from a thoroughly Macintosh perspective.

You'll continue with additional essays by Doc and Randy Brown that show the true meaning of *extensiblility* in Macintosh—the unique way in which applications and tools can work together. Although compiled external libraries exist in FoxPro DOS and Windows, there is no analog in other environments for Mac XCMDs and Apple Events. Neither is the rich world of Macintosh third party tools and extensions matched on other platforms.

PowerPCs are becoming available with their even-handed approach to applications based in different operating systems. With this change in mind, some people will have difficulty understanding why a developer would choose one primary platform over another, given the thoroughly cross-platform aspects of a DBMS like FoxPro. This section of the book reminds you *why* you chose to work on Macintosh—and expands your understanding of the benefits of this choice.

15

POSITION FOXPRO FOR MACINTOSH IN A NETWORK ENVIRONMENT: INTEGRITY, CONFIGURATION, AND PERFORMANCE

by
John R. "Doc" Livingston

Business information is far more valuable when many people can see and update the information at the same time. Consider an order-entry system for a company that sells products by phone. Many customers call to place orders at the same time. Each customer needs to know the availability and price of all items of interest. When the customer commits to the order, the items must be allocated to that customer's order. When the order ships, the amount of inventory on hand decreases. When new stock comes in, the amount of inventory on hand increases. The results of all of these activities, and others, must become available to everyone involved as soon as possible. All parties must carry out their tasks with as little hindrance from the system as practical.

You can imagine how chaotic this situation becomes if only one computer can process or view transactions. Customer service representatives, order pickers, and accounting personnel would have to queue up to post transactions. The value of the information system is clearly much greater if each concerned party can simultaneously call up and update information from a central database at his or her own desktop computer.

The development of real time business applications requires a clear head, a steady hand, and a sharp set of tools. In this chapter, you'll learn to unleash the potential of FoxPro Mac to build powerful multi-user applications. You will understand how:

- To think multi-user
- FoxPro works on a network
- Multi-user FoxPro differs from other database products
- To select, design, and install a local area network that will best support your FoxPro Mac application
- To install and configure FoxPro for Macintosh on your network
- To design and write your applications to best take advantage of FoxPro Mac's multi-user features
- To deal with FoxPro applications that support DOS, Mac, and Windows clients simultaneously

Multi-User Fundamentals

The database is a shared resource. What your application does affects other users and their applications. To optimize your design, you need to understand basic multi-user design considerations. These considerations often conflict with each other. You should consider the items described in this section and their relative priorities as you design your application.

Concurrency

A database has a high level of *concurrency* when changes posted to the database by writers of data are available very quickly to all other readers of data. Concurrency is a fundamental design consideration for a multi-user database.

The amount of concurrency that you want is paid for by being a bit more or less demanding in your other application goals. A pick list of valid sales persons, for example, may be cached in your application at startup in an array, and then used later to validate the sales person entered by a user. This approach gives better system performance, as you investigate in the following section, but it validates sales persons from a potentially out-of-date list. Another approach is to validate the sales person from the sales person table at the time of the user's entry of the data. This approach guarantees concurrency, but results in slower system performance and increases network congestion.

Like most application goals, absolute concurrency is impossible to achieve. More importantly, buying more concurrency after a certain point always results in substantial decreases in other performance metrics.

System Performance and Throughput

System performance is the system's responsiveness as seen by an individual user. For example, the time your system needs to post transactions, validate user input with a pick list, or run a customer inquiry all fall into this category.

System throughput is the sheer amount of work that your system can perform during a given time. Typical metrics include number of sales orders shipped, the number of cash receipts posted, and the number of vendor purchase orders received.

FOXPRO MAC HACK TIP

There is no free lunch with multi-user FoxPro for Macintosh or with any other multi-user database system. Increasing the performance of a multi-user application in one way generally reduces the application's performance in some other way or ways.

There can be no deficit spending here. For example, design choices made with the goal of increasing an application's concurrency must generally be paid for with reduced integrity, reduced application maintainability, decreased system performance, or other penalties.

Data Integrity

Data integrity is the extent to which your application enforces and adheres to business rules. These business rules include primary key integrity, foreign key integrity, and transaction integrity.

The relational model dictates that every record in any given data table be uniquely identified by a *primary key*. This objective also is known as entity integrity. A primary key is a field, or set of fields, within a table that you use to identify a record. For example, you meet the object of primary key integrity by requiring that customers have unique customer numbers. The physical location of the records within the table (the record number) is not sufficient to guarantee primary key integrity. Often, the values contained in a field or set of fields also must agree with the values contained in records from another table. For example, an invoice is always identified by an invoice number, but it also might need to contain the customer number of a valid customer. This kind of integrity is know as *foreign key*, or *referential*, integrity.

> **CROSS-PLATFORM WARNING**
>
> FoxPro does not directly support primary key or foreign key integrity. It is your responsibility to write FoxPro code that supports the data integrity requirements of the application.

Transaction integrity refers to the common requirement for a series of operations, also known as a *logical transaction*, to either occur as a complete unit or not occur at all. Consider the posting of an invoice. You must insert a new record into the invoice master table, insert a record for each line item into the invoice line item table, update inventory on hand, update the customer's balance, and post debit and credit transactions to the general ledger. If only a portion of this transaction occurs, then the database will be in an inconsistent state.

Data integrity is a crucial item of interest to the developer. In many cases, it takes absolute priority over other design goals.

Usability

Application usability is becoming a goal of ever-increasing importance to the developer. Mac users want to click and drag, drag and drop, and double-click their way through applications intuitively. The realities of other system design goals sometimes make this ideal impossible.

A good example of the issues involved is the design of your data input screens. Should you emphasize more Mac-like pop-ups and buttons or plain, old, keyboard-style entry? New users will almost always find that they can become productive more quickly using the more graphical approach, but once a user becomes familiar with the application, the keyboard approach yields greater productivity.

An extremely Mac-like approach may often extract a disproportionate toll on data integrity, system throughput, and concurrency. Some sort of a trade-off between the two extremes is usually the most appropriate approach. Make sure that you have a clear understanding of the importance of usability versus other multi-user design goals before you get started with your FoxPro Mac application.

Application Maintenance

As you reach for maximum performance in your multi-user FoxPro Mac application, it is sometimes tempting to give short shrift to thinking about and sticking to a consistent system architecture and coding style. The result is a spaghetti code-laden application that you may find is very difficult to modify a few months down the road.

Realize that bug fixes and program enhancements always will be a requirement. You cannot simply code up your application, throw it over the wall, and walk away, feigning that your work is a creative masterpiece.

Recognize that there is a trade-off between application maintainability and performance. In general, you should establish a multi-user architecture prior to starting your FoxPro Mac project. Stick to it, even if you have to give up a bit of performance. Once you are up and running, you can identify bottlenecks. In some cases, you can then opt to selectively violate your rules when the performance benefits are justified. Later in this chapter, you learn one systemic approach to multi-user FoxPro programming.

Decision Support Versus Online Transaction Processing Applications

Most database applications can be classified as either *Decision Support* (DS) or *Online Transaction Processing* (OLTP). OLTP applications are designed to maximize system performance and throughput. DS applications are tailored to the requirements of *ad hoc* reporting. An online customer support system falls squarely in OLTP territory. A marketing database allowing analysts to cull trends in sales would be a decision support application.

OLTP applications are characterized by many small "look up" type queries and a significant number of writes. DS applications are more likely to conduct a relatively small number of compute-intensive queries and almost no writes. In many cases, DS databases are populated with data drawn from OLTP databases.

Consider whether your FoxPro Mac application is more OLTP-like or DS-like before you begin its design. For example, a multi-user OLTP database will probably have fewer indexes than a DS database.

Collisions and Resource Locking

Collisions occur when the actions of one user interfere with the actions of another user. In the context of a multi-user database system, this generally means that two or more users are attempting to write to the same system resource simultaneously.

Collisions are a fact of life in multi-user applications. As a developer, you are responsible for designing your application in such a way that collisions are resolved gracefully. To resolve collisions, all multi-user database systems provide *resource locking* features. These features usually are evoked either explicitly (directly from your application code) or implicitly (automatically by the database management system). When an application locks a resource, it prevents any other users from writing to that resource or acquiring a conflicting resource lock.

Most database management systems provide record, or row-level, locking features. During a record lock, only the user who has the lock on the record may update or delete that record. Additionally, most systems also provide file, or table level, locking features. During a file lock, only the user who has the lock on the table may write to it. An active file lock also prevents any record locks within the data table. Likewise, an active record lock prevents others from obtaining a file lock on that table. FoxPro Mac gives you tools to lock resources at both the record and file levels.

When a resource is written to, it must be locked. However, during the time a resource is locked, there can only be one writer to it. As a result, you must carefully manage how you lock resources and weigh the impact of your resource locking activities on other multi-user design goals. Because a resource lock reduces system performance, throughput, and concurrency, it is usually best to lock resources as briefly as possible and at the lowest possible level.

> **FOXPRO MAC HACK TIP**
>
> *From single- to multi-user, effortlessly!* Many database products try to broaden their markets by telling customers that their products require no, or at least very minimal, special programming to handle multi-user operations. This message is reinforced by adding features that "automatically" or "seamlessly" handle the details of multi-user application development. While many of these features are indeed very nice, you should not be seduced into believing that anything less than a complete grasp of multi-user development fundamentals will be sufficient for you to successfully deploy a FoxPro Mac multi-user application. You should be particularly wary of features that will lock your database's resources automatically. Locking a record or table makes that record or table unavailable for other users to write to. Reliance on automatic locking features significantly reduces your ability to detect and resolve collisions in your application.

Multi-User Engineering Tradeoffs

Table 15.1 summarizes the multi-user application considerations outlined above. Generally, you will find that moving an application from some base case toward improvement in one area comes only at the cost of some other desirable attribute. Make sure that you have a clear understanding of these considerations and how they translate into costs and benefits on your multi-user FoxPro Mac application before you begin your project.

Table 15.1
Multi-user application design summary

Design Consideration	*Meaning or Design Goal*
Concurrency	Changes made by writers are available immediately to readers.
System Performance	Application responds immediately to the user.
System Throughput	Number of transactions moving through a system during a given period of time. Goal is a relatively large number of transactions during the period in question.
Data Integrity	Data is written to the database only in accordance with business rules.
Usability	Is the application easy to learn and enjoyable to use? Does the application add to the user's productivity? How much?
Application Maintenance	How easy is the application to maintain?
DS versus OLTP	Is the application best classified as Decision Support or Online Transaction Processing? DS applications are optimized for a relatively small number of complex, ad-hoc queries. OLTP applications are optimized for a relatively large number of short validation queries and a large number of writes.
Collision Resolution	Application and DBMS must gracefully resolve table insert, update, and delete conflicts. Goal is to resolve collisions at the lowest cost.

How Multi-User FoxPro Mac Works

In this section, you'll explore:

- Multi-user FoxPro Mac communications basics
- FoxPro Mac's Multi-user architecture
- How FoxPro applications communicate with each other
- How DOS, Windows, and Mac clients interact in a multi-user setting
- The importance of the network and the network operating system

Up and Down the Protocol Stack

Clear communication requires proper etiquette. For example, when we communicate with each other via speech, we form words and sentences in accordance with the rules of our language. At another level, our vocal cords vibrate between certain frequencies, and the air transmits sounds between the mouth of the speaker to the ear of the listener. At yet another level, we conduct polite conversations with only one person speaking at any given time.

The Open Systems Interconnection (OSI) model generalizes these communications rules, or protocols, into a model consisting of 7 layers: the physical, data link, network, transport, session, presentation, and application layers (see figure 15.1). Communications originating at higher layers are handed off to lower protocol layers. When communications finally arrive at the physical layer, they move back up to their destination at the higher layers of the model. Because communications logically move up and down, the layers of the OSI model are sometimes called a *protocol stack*. We can use this model to conceptualize any sort of communications process, whether between people, animals, or computers.

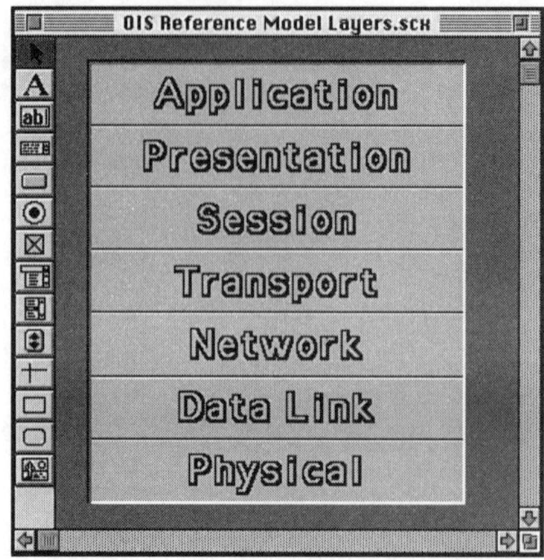

Figure 15.1 *Layers of the OSI model.*

AppleTalk is the communications protocol that you will most often use in your multi-user FoxPro Mac application. Apple originally designed the AppleTalk protocol to allow Macintosh users to share LaserWriter printers, which were quite expensive at the time. The first implementation of AppleTalk is now known as LocalTalk. LocalTalk is generally considered too slow to support a multi-user, file-sharing database system such as FoxPro Mac.

Apple's engineers were quite clever when they developed AppleTalk. They designed it to be modular and extensible. This has enabled Apple and other vendors to "swap out" the original physical and data link layers of LocalTalk in favor of other implementations. Current AppleTalk implementations now include EtherTalk (AppleTalk over Ethernet) and TokenTalk (AppleTalk over Token Ring). These newer AppleTalk implementations have made high-bandwidth, multi-user database applications for the Macintosh a reality.

Although you will most likely use the AppleTalk protocol suite to provide LAN connectivity for your FoxPro Mac application, there are a number of other options. Two popular alternative protocols are IPX/SPX and TCP/IP.

IPX/SPX (often referred to as simply IPX) stands for Internetwork Packet Exchange/Sequenced Packet Exchange. This protocol suite is Novell's approach to linking the physical and data link layers with the upper layers of the OSI model. IPX is the most common protocol in use on LANs today. If you are using a DOS or Windows workstation that is connected to a local area network, it is most likely that you are using IPX. However, it is still quite rare to see Mac machines connected to a LAN via IPX.

TCP/IP (Transmission Control Protocol/Internet Protocol) was first popularized by the UNIX community. Partly because of its association with open systems, TCP/IP has become a sort of *lingua franca* in the LAN industry. A product known as Mac TCP is often used to provide TCP/IP connectivity for Macintosh clients. Mac TCP can run at the same time and over the same cabling as EtherTalk.

FoxPro's File-Sharing Architecture

When you use FoxPro to read data from or write data to your database tables, FoxPro directly opens, reads, and updates the physical files that represent those objects. When many users are running an application simultaneously, each instance of FoxPro accesses the same data files. Because users communicate at the level of shared files, this architecture is often referred to as *file-sharing*.

When a file-sharing database application runs over a local area network, each node on the network does its own processing. For example, if your application issues a LOCATE FOR command without the aid of indexes, FoxPro Mac walks through each record of the table over the network until it finds a record matching your criteria, or comes to end of file. When many users are online, this type of architecture can lead to very high levels of network traffic.

File-sharing contrasts with the client-server database model. In a client-server application, each node connects to one or more database servers. Client applications communicate with the database server using higher level protocols. Only questions from clients and answers from the database server are transmitted over the network. Because the database server does the actual data processing, network traffic is reduced. This reduction in network traffic is achieved at the expense of increased congestion in the CPU and internal buses of the database server.

The client-server model offers several advantages over the file-sharing approach. However, a file-sharing application will often turn out to be less expensive and run faster than a client-server application. A file-sharing database such as FoxPro is often best-suited for departmental applications. As Microsoft continues to add power to FoxPro, it becomes a better choice for larger and larger projects.

Recognize that FoxPro uses a file-sharing, and not client-server, architecture. Later in this chapter, you will learn how to write FoxPro applications that take advantage of file-sharing's strengths and minimize file-sharing's weaknesses.

FoxPro Inter-Application Communications

FoxPro has very limited inter-application communications capabilities. To send messages between applications, you are limited to reading and writing data to and from shared files. Although the AppleTalk protocol stack built into your Mac allows applications to communicate, you would have to develop your own functions, perhaps using the FoxPro Mac Library Construction Kit, to tap into AppleTalk. Even then, you would still have to deal with DOS and Windows clients separately, since they would generally not have access to AppleTalk services.

In FoxPro, the developer is responsible for constructing a system for any required inter-application communications. FoxPro data tables are the most logical mechanism to use for this purpose.

Multi-Platform Issues

Using FoxPro for Macintosh, DOS, and Windows, you can develop multi-user, *multi-platform* applications. In this situation, your application shares the same data tables and indexes, while potentially running in three environments at the same time. You need to understand how FoxPro functions in this setting.

File Sharing Requirements

In a multi-user, multi-platform environment, your Network Operating System (NOS) plays a key role. As a minimum, your NOS will need to be able to handle logins using the communications protocols of each type of client. In most cases, this means support for AppleTalk for Macs and IPX for PCs. In addition, the NOS must support FoxPro's basic resource sharing requirements: access to a shared filing system, file locking, and record locking.

File Name Differences

Macintosh file names may be up to 31 characters long, and they may contain characters that DOS reserves for other purposes. DOS file names are limited to 8 characters and a 3 character extension. It will make your life a lot easier if you restrict all file names used in your systems to the DOS file name conventions. If you choose not to do this, these objects will have different names on each platform, and you will have to spend a lot of time putting logic into your application to handle the different names.

Filing System Differences

DOS files store all data in only one portion of the file: the data fork. On the other hand, Mac files may contain both a data and a resource fork. Because the DOS file system, as currently implemented, does not support the notion of a resource fork, files created by a Mac and moved to a DOS machine will lose any data contained in the resource fork of the file. This issue is generally not, however, a problem in FoxPro Mac/DOS integration projects because the shared resources (data tables, indexes, reports, etc.) all depend almost entirely on the data fork of the file.

The Importance of the Network and the Network Operating System

In your multi-user FoxPro Mac file-sharing application, the network plays a key role. The file server must provide speedy and reliable access to FoxPro files for many users. In addition, the cable plant must be reliable while facilitating the free flow of large amounts of data. Finally, the network operating system itself may need to provide support for clients communicating via not only AppleTalk, but also with IPX or TCP/IP. Selecting the most appropriate network solution is at least as important as a sound FoxPro application design.

Multi-User FoxPro for Macintosh and other Macintosh Multi-User Database Systems

It is useful to understand how FoxPro for Macintosh compares with other multi-user Macintosh database management systems. This section presents an overview of FoxPro Mac's most direct competitors: 4th Dimension and Omnis 7^2.

4th Dimension and Omnis both contain application development environments integrated with their own proprietary database management systems. Both systems contain *data dictionaries*, allowing other system utilities to be aware of all data structures and indexes. In recent years, these products have diverged fairly radically.

What's a Data Dictionary?

Many database management systems include a data dictionary, or system catalog. A data dictionary contains *meta data*, or data about data, for the entire database. At a minimum, a data dictionary includes symbolic descriptions for each table, each field in each table, each index, and the physical location of each tracked item. Many data dictionaries also include information that relates tables within the system to each other, as well as descriptive information for each table, field, and index for the reference of all the developers working on the project.

There are pros and cons to having an integrated data dictionary in your database management system. The negatives include the fact that each vendor takes a proprietary approach to its data dictionary, so that in many cases you cannot easily work with the data dictionary except in the way that the vendor has provided. In addition, if you prefer to design and maintain your database outside of the vendor's design environment with a third-party design tool, you face the task of synchronizing the third-party tool with the vendor's proprietary data dictionary.

The positives of a data dictionary, however, are compelling. The data dictionary clearly separates the task of designing the database from the operations of applications. The system catalog also clearly establishes the system design for everyone concerned, allows for system-level tools that guarantee the integrity of the entire database, and permits the database itself to do such things as optimize queries and prevent deadlocks. Finally, most data dictionaries will help you to enforce basic design rules, and can help to prevent you from making some truly awful mistakes during the design process. Most developers would agree that data dictionaries are a good thing.

4th Dimension and Omnis have integrated data dictionaries. FoxPro does not. Microsoft says that it will be adding one in the future. For the present, you have three choices: live without one, "roll your own," or purchase a FoxPro application development shell that contains a data dictionary. If you prefer the latter choice, you may want to consider either TRO (Tom Retting's Office), from Tom Retting Associates, or the SBT Accounting Systems Professional Series Developer's Platform, from SBT Accounting Systems. TRO is a more general tool, while SBT's offering is focused on the development of accounting applications.

4th Dimension

4th Dimension combines a Pascal-like procedural language with an elegant user interface and powerful application development tools. However, 4th Dimension has often been criticized for its slow multi-user performance. In some cases, FoxBASE+/Mac and FoxPro have been observed to complete equivalent multi-user database operations several orders of magnitude faster than 4th Dimension. ACI, the developers of 4th Dimension, identified raw multi-user performance as their most pressing problem. To address this issue, ACI developed the 4D Server. 4D Server is a database server designed specifically to support multi-user 4th Dimension operations. Although 4th Dimension continues to contain a local database, this database no longer supports multi-user operations. The developer must plug into a 4D Server when he or she is ready to move into a multi-user environment. The 4D Server runs only on Macintosh hardware. It supports connections from non-4th Dimension applications, but only with an application programming interface that is sold separately.

Omnis 7[2]

Omnis has always been highly regarded for its cross-platform features. Mac and Windows versions of the application function nearly identically, and the effort to maintain a system that runs on both platforms is relatively minimal. Omnis is organized internally as a network, rather than a relational database, resulting in good multi-user performance. Although Omnis' multi-user performance has always been well regarded, most developers who have compared it with FoxBASE+/Mac or FoxPro would agree that it is generally slower than Microsoft's offerings. In recent years, the developers of Omnis have chosen to position their product as a cross-platform client-server development tool. Although the local database lives on, Omnis now emphasizes client-server connectivity features.

Network Selection, Design and Installation

Before you can field your multi-user FoxPro Mac application, you need a LAN in place that can support your application's demanding requirements. A common situation is to work all of the way to the acceptance testing phase of your project, only to find that an existing LAN is not suitable for your application. You need to take a proactive approach with the LAN, since it may very well make or break your FoxPro project. You should ensure that LAN design issues are addressed at the same time that you are designing the rest of your database application. It is important to take a quantitative approach to the LAN analysis and design process.

In many cases, a network may already be in place. Here you need to identify the network's *baseline*, or beginning, condition. This process includes listing the type and configuration of all existing file servers, as well as identifying the configuration of the cabling plant and network protocols in use. You also need to determine how heavily the current servers and network are utilized. By adding the requirements of your application to the baseline case, you can determine what changes, if any, are needed.

If you are lucky, you can design a network from scratch at the same time that you design your application. In this case, you will be able to take more of a "no compromises" approach, designing the network specifically to meet the needs of your application.

In either case, your approach is nearly the same:

- Identify basic multi-user requirements
- Identify the required communications protocols
- Determine the best lower-layer implementations (physical and data link layers) for those communications protocols
- Select the best NOS and network hardware
- Design and install the network, or implement any required changes on top of your existing network

FOXPRO MAC HACK TIP

A *protocol analyzer* is a tool that can help you to baseline and forecast network utilization. Protocol analyzers come in one of two flavors: software-based or hardware-based. Hardware-based protocol analyzers include proprietary boards that can, among other things, transmit and respond to signals very quickly. Hardware-based systems are often very costly, and may be overkill for a simple baselining or forecasting project. Software-based protocol analyzers operate on generic personal computers and generally don't have special hardware requirements. They communicate with the network using a conventional network adapter operating in *promiscuous mode*. While software-based analyzers lack some high-end features, they are often more than adequate. Common features include user-configurable *alarms, macro statistics, packet filtering,* and *packet decoding.*

As protocol analyzers have become less expensive, they have become more viable as tools for occasional use by application developers. If you invest some time in learning and using an analyzer, you will take an important step in the process of tailoring your LAN to your multi-user FoxPro Mac application.

Identify Basic Multi-User Requirements

The first step in tailoring the LAN to your FoxPro application is to identify the essential multi-user needs of your application. You need to determine the scope of the application, the intensity of the expected multi-user environment, and the client computer mix. The *scope* of the application is how many users will be using the application, how many users you expect to have online at once, and how important the application will be to the organization's mission. *Intensity* refers to the average data throughput, peak data throughput, and number of transactions that you expect to flow through the system. Finally, *client mix* means the expected blend of client front end systems, such as Mac only, or Mac and PC clients.

Remember that the FoxPro file-sharing architecture makes substantial demands on the LAN. A protocol analyzer can be very useful in estimating average and peak demands of your application under full user load.

Identify Communication Protocols

If your user mix is exclusively Mac, you probably only need to connect clients via AppleTalk. If your application supports both Macs and PCs, it is likely that you will have to provide both AppleTalk and IPX protocol support. Multi-protocol support requires a more sophisticated LAN approach.

FOXPRO MAC HACK TIP

You do not have to use IPX to connect a PC to your LAN. If you prefer, you can gain access to AppleTalk using PhoneNet PC.

PhoneNet PC is a software product that gives your PC access to the AppleTalk protocol stack. It allows the PC to log in to an AppleShare file server, share files on the server with other computers, and select AppleTalk network-visible entities through a DOS version of the Chooser.

There are several disadvantages to this approach. First, PhoneNet PC takes up a rather large amount of conventional memory, much more than Novell's IPX stack. For all practical purposes, when PhoneNet PC is loaded into your computer's memory, it prevents your PC from entering the IPX world. In addition, PhoneNet PC generally operates more slowly than a direct PC IPX connection.

For these reasons, PhoneNet PC is most appropriate for networks that are nearly all Mac and need to support a small number of PCs. It can also be useful if you need to allow PCs normally connecting via another protocol to occasionally attach to an AppleShare file server, or use other AppleTalk services.

Determine the Best Physical and Data Link Implementations for the Required Protocols

AppleTalk most commonly runs over LocalTalk, Ethernet, Token Ring, and Arcnet. IPX is also available in these, and other, formats. As you choose the best implementation, you will need to consider the following factors: previous wiring decisions, performance, multi-protocol support, and reliability. In many cases, you can opt to run these protocols over 2-, 4-, or 8-cable telephone wiring, permitting connection through modular phone jacks.

LocalTalk

Both IPX and AppleTalk can run over Apple's LocalTalk cabling. In addition, these protocols have been implemented over a single pair of telephone wires. Both formats are now known as LocalTalk. You will probably find LocalTalk unacceptable for a multi-user database application, since you will be limited to 230 kbit/sec of bandwidth.

Arcnet

A number of protocols, including AppleTalk or IPX, can be run over Arcnet. Arcnet once had a certain amount of appeal because of its low cost relative to Ethernet. However, as Ethernet and Arcnet have become comparable in price, Arcnet's more limited capabilities and generally poor market acceptance have become an issue. In general, you should not choose Arcnet unless it has already been established as the lower-layer protocol implementation for your application.

Ethernet

Ethernet is today's most popular choice, and increasingly the preferred Ethernet implementation is 10BASET Ethernet. 10BASET Ethernet runs over 2 pairs of wire and can be integrated into your telephone wiring system. Both AppleTalk and IPX can run over the same cable at the same time, permitting connections from both Macintoshes and PCs. Like LocalTalk, Ethernet is a logical bus, meaning that all clients communicate over a single shared data pipeline. Ethernet uses a technique known as *collision detection* to resolve conflicts along the data bus. This keeps practical throughput well below its 10 mbit/sec theoretical capacity. Additionally, collision detection prevents Ethernet from guaranteeing a slice of time to any particular network node.

Token Ring

Token Ring is a popular alternative to Ethernet. However, its current market share is still far below that of Ethernet. Token Ring is a logical ring, but is implemented physically as a star. It supports both AppleTalk and IPX. Network access is controlled by the passing of a token between nodes, guaranteeing each node a slice of time. This feature is a requirement in certain factory automation and financial applications. Another advantage of Token Ring vis à vis Ethernet is that the deterministic token passing mechanism allows for a smoother response to increasing network loading. Finally, Token Ring has the ability to detect and correct breaks in the logical ring using processes known as *beaconing* and *closing the ring*. Ethernet has no such fault detection capabilities. These advantages come at the cost of much greater hardware expense and fewer vendor and product choices. Token Ring is available in 4 mbit/sec and 16 mbit/sec variants.

Select the Network Operating System and Network Hardware

Once you understand the demands of your application and agree on client connectivity options, you can select the NOS, the server hardware, and the rest of the network's physical infrastructure. It is more than likely that you will select either AppleShare or NetWare as your NOS. Popular choices for communications include AppleTalk and IPX running over 10BASET Ethernet, AppleTalk, and IPX running over 10BASE2 "Thin Net," and AppleTalk and IPX running over Token Ring.

As you select an NOS and file server, consider the following factors:

- *Protocol support*. How well does the NOS support the protocols used by all potential clients? If you will be using both Mac and DOS/Windows, you may well need to provide not only AppleTalk connectivity for Mac clients, but also IPX connectivity for DOS/Windows clients.
- *Resource locking features*. The NOS needs to reliably support FoxPro's resource locking features. Potential file access conflicts need to be resolved between clients, potentially attached using different protocols.
- *Performance*. The NOS needs to provide speedy access to the file system for all clients. Recall that file-sharing applications are not really very compute-intensive at the file server. The overriding concerns are how fast files can be read and written, how quickly resource conflicts are resolved, and how well the NOS and server hardware respond as more and more clients make requests. Effectively caching reads and writes, while getting requests and responses on and off the wire quickly, will help to pump up performance numbers.
- *Reliability and fault tolerance*. The NOS and server hardware should perform with a high degree of reliability. In the event of software and hardware failures, system recovery features should be available to allow your application to come back online as soon as possible, and with as little disruption as possible.
- *Administrative costs*. Many advanced features cost dearly to administer. Carefully evaluate the cost/benefit tradeoffs of these features.

In most cases, the NOS decision will come down to AppleShare versus NetWare.

AppleShare

AppleShare is Apple Computer's NOS software. You can run it on any Macintosh. It is fairly easy to set up and maintain. AppleShare supports AppleTalk connections, but it does not support IPX. In addition, the relatively poor performance of AppleShare has long been a sore point for many database developers.

Apple now offers AppleShare installed on specially-tuned hardware bundles known as *Apple Workgroup Servers*. The most expensive of these machines, the Workgroup Server 95, runs a special version of AppleShare on top of Apple UNIX. The Workgroup Servers have helped to boost the performance of AppleShare from snail-like to acceptable. However, AppleShare running on a Workgroup Server still lacks many of the core features of a serious business network operating system.

AppleShare is easy to administer and it runs on Macintosh hardware. These features are paid for with limited connectivity, limited hardware flexibility, and less-than-spectacular performance. Thus, AppleShare is most appropriate when your application will have a relatively small number of Mac-only clients.

NetWare

NetWare is Novell's network operating system. Although generally associated with the Intel platform, NetWare actually runs on a number of non-Intel platforms.

NetWare is known for its zippy performance, reliability, fault tolerance, high degree of hardware independence, and nearly unlimited connectivity options. Working with NetWare for Macintosh, NetWare can provide connectivity to PCs via IPX and Macs via a complete implementation of the AppleTalk protocol stack. Macintosh users logged on to a NetWare server running NetWare for Macintosh notice very few differences between the NetWare server and an Apple-branded Macintosh server.

There are a number of disadvantages to selecting NetWare as the NOS for your FoxPro Mac application. First, NetWare is more costly to administer than AppleShare. In addition, many Mac installations report a dearth of trained support staff that can deal with the integration issues involved with NetWare servers and Mac clients. Finally, some critics find NetWare's non-preemptive multi-tasking architecture objectionable.

The bottom line on NetWare is that it gives you very good performance, reliability, fault tolerance, hardware flexibility, and connectivity features relative to AppleShare. The cost of these advantages is greater administrative complexity. NetWare is most appropriate for your multi-user FoxPro Mac project if you plan to have many clients running the application, if the application will be reading and writing a lot of data over the LAN, or if you plan to have both Mac and PC clients.

Apple-Labeled NetWare

In May of 1993 Apple announced that it would offer a version of NetWare that had been ported to the Macintosh platform. Initial indications are that it will run on top of the Macintosh OS, rather than Apple UNIX. Apparently, Apple will ship this product as a bundled unit with NetWare pre-installed, much like the Workgroup Servers.

This development has attracted some interest in the LAN community. However, one needs to carefully consider the case for this product. If you want to use NetWare anyway, it is hard to see why you would opt for the Apple-labeled version of NetWare installed on a proprietary Apple box. And the third-party support now available for NetWare in the Intel-compatible world will not be available on this platform for a long time, if ever.

Configuration of FoxPro Mac on a Local Area Network

In this section, you'll learn how to install and configure FoxPro for Macintosh on your local area network. You'll first learn system requirements and how to select an installation strategy. Next, you will install FoxPro Mac on the network and install the Apple Shared Library Manager. You will then learn how to configure FoxPro Mac for network operations by configuring FoxPro's memory partition, setting up the CONFIG.FPM file, and establishing appropriate network access privileges.

System Requirements

To run multi-user FoxPro Mac, you will need:

- A Macintosh equipped with a Motorola 68020 or higher CPU
- 4 MB RAM; 8 MB RAM is the recommended minimum
- Macintosh System 7.0 or later
- Access to a local area network

Installation Strategy

To install FoxPro Mac on your network, first determine whether you want to install a copy of FoxPro on each user's machine (local installation), or a single, shared copy of FoxPro on the network for all Mac users (network installation). There are advantages and disadvantages to each approach.

A local installation strategy gives users more flexibility, but costs more in terms of up-front installation time. Additionally, when you need to upgrade FoxPro Mac, you will be required to upgrade the installation on each client machine. In general, local installation is more appropriate for smaller, multi-user projects.

A network installation approach requires less up-front time, and less time when you are ready to upgrade FoxPro. The downside to network installations is that they are less flexible, require more careful configuration, and must be conducted by someone who has a clear understanding of the network operating system. As you might expect, network installation of FoxPro Mac is better for projects with a larger number of Mac clients.

Installing FoxPro Mac

After you have determined your installation strategy, a multi-user installation of FoxPro Mac is fairly straightforward. Follow these steps:

1. If you will be installing a shared copy of FoxPro Mac on the network (network installation), log on to the network as the Supervisor, or someone with equivalent access privileges.
2. Create a destination folder for FoxPro and all of its associated files and folders, either on the file server or on the local computer.
3. Insert the FoxPro Mac "Disk - 1 Setup" floppy disk into your Macintosh. Double-click on the "Microsoft FoxPro Mac Setup" icon, shown in figure 15.2.

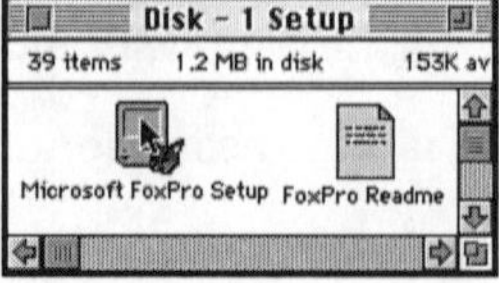

Figure 15.2 *Starting up FoxPro Mac Installation Program.*

4. You will be presented with a dialog allowing you to select your installation options, as shown in figure 15.3. Select "Complete" to conduct a normal, complete installation of FoxPro for Macintosh, all of FoxPro's associated tools, and all of the tutorial and example files. Select "Custom" to select only certain of these items for installation. Select "Minimum" to select only the parts of FoxPro required for the program itself to execute. Select "Network" to place the installation files on the network, allowing you to install FoxPro onto other client workstations without floppy disks later. Select "Quit" to abandon the installation process. Do not confuse the "Network" button with the network installation strategy discussed above.

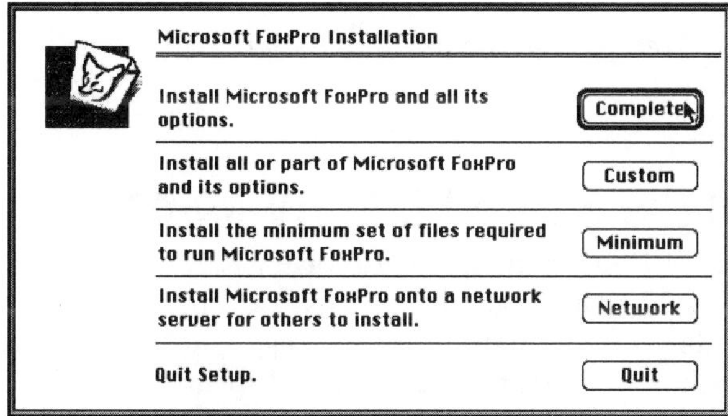

Figure 15.3 *Selecting the installation program options.*

5. After selecting the installation options, select the destination folder for your FoxPro Mac installation and confirm by selecting the "Setup" button. To abort the installation, click on "Quit" (see figure 15.4). The installation program prompts you to insert all required disks. After a few minutes, the process is complete.

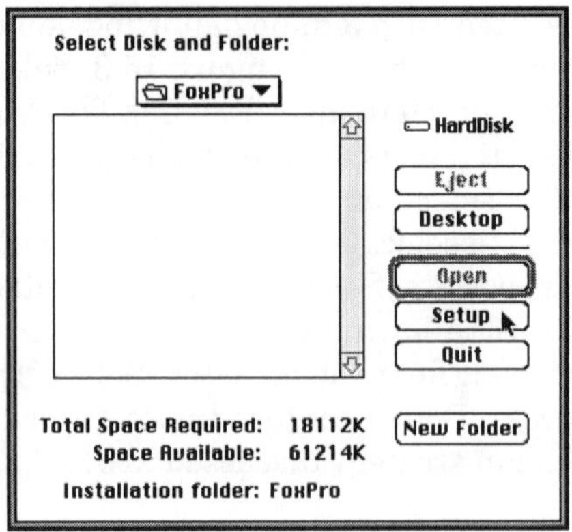

Figure 15.4 *Selecting the Installation folder.*

Installing the Shared Library Manager

You need to install the Apple Shared Library Manager (ASLM) to run custom functions developed using the FoxPro Library Construction Kit (LCK). Regardless of the installation strategy you have selected for FoxPro, you will need to install the Shared Library Manager on each Macintosh client. Follow the steps below to install the ASLM:

1. Insert the "ASLM Installer" disk into your floppy disk drive. Double-click on the "Installer" icon (see figure 15.5).

Figure 15.5 *Starting up ASLM Installation Program.*

2. Select installation options from the ASLM installation options dialog (see figure 15.6). Click on "Install" to install the ASLM on your computer using default settings. Select "Switch Disk" to select a different disk for installation. Click on "Eject Disk" to eject the current disk from your floppy drive, allowing you to insert and select a different disk for ASLM installation. Click on "Customize" to override system defaults for Apple System 6 versus Apple System 7 for this installation. Select "Help" to see online installation instructions. Click on "Quit" to abandon ASLM installation.

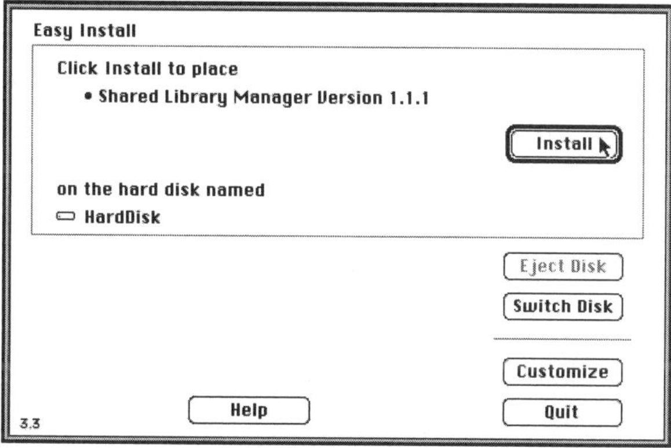

Figure 15.6 *Selecting ASLM installation options.*

FOXPRO MAC HACK TIP

Make sure that you install the Apple Shared Library Manager (ASLM) on each Macintosh that will be running your application. Mac clients need the ASLM to run functions that you develop using the FoxPro Mac Library Construction Kit. ASLM installation is separate from the installation of the FoxPro Mac product. In addition, the architecture of ASLM dictates that you must install it on each Mac separately, even if you opted to install only one shared copy of FoxPro Mac on the LAN.

Configuring FoxPro's Memory Partition

The next step in your multi-user FoxPro Mac installation is to set FoxPro's memory partition size. You can modify FoxPro's memory settings by using the "Get Info" item from the "File" menu of the Finder. To change FoxPro's memory settings:

1. Make sure that FoxPro is not running.
2. Go to the Macintosh Finder and select "Get Info" from the File menu with the FoxPro Mac application highlighted.
3. In the Get Info dialog, note three important settings: Suggested Size, Minimum Size, and Preferred Size (see figure 15.7). You cannot change Microsoft's Suggested Size. You can, however, change the Minimum and Preferred Sizes using this dialog. The Preferred Size setting is available only in Apple System 7.1 or greater.

   If you have enough memory in your Macintosh, set the Preferred Size to the Suggested Size or greater. If enough memory is available, FoxPro will use up to this amount on startup.

   Also note the Minimum Size. If your computer does not have at least this much memory available when you start up FoxPro, the program will not run. You can reduce this setting, but this will reduce performance. Below about 2.5 MB, you are risking abnormal termination of the program. In computers running pre-System 7.1, you must use the minimum setting to control the desired memory partition size. This is one good reason to upgrade to Apple System 7.1 as soon as possible.

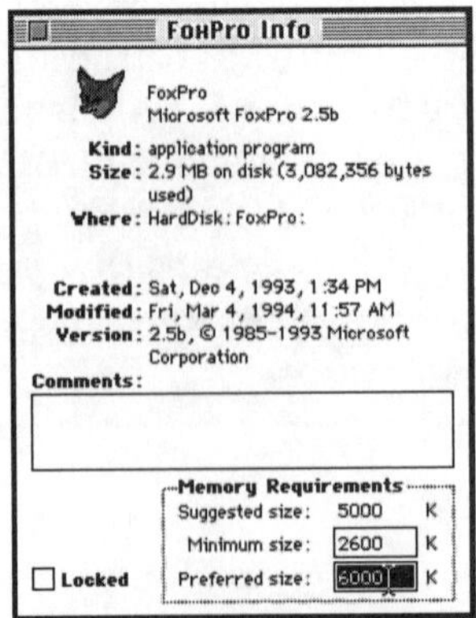

Figure 15.7 *Changing FoxPro's memory settings.*

Setting Up the CONFIG.FPM File

Use the CONFIG.FPM file to customize your FoxPro Mac working environment. You can create this file with any text editor, including the editor that comes with FoxPro. The entries in the CONFIG.FPM file are of the general format:

```
<item> = <value>
```

Entries in the CONFIG.FPM file fall into two general categories: entries that are equivalent to FoxPro's SET commands and entries that have no SET command equivalent. CONFIG.FPM options that have no FoxPro SET command equivalent can only be established using the CONFIG.FPM file. If a CONFIG.FPM setting does have a SET equivalent, you set the parameter in question using either the CONFIG.FPM file or the equivalent FoxPro Mac SET command.

Not all FoxPro SET commands have CONFIG.FPM equivalents. You'll find a complete listing of all valid CONFIG.FPM settings in the FoxPro *Installation and Macintosh Features Guide.*

Several CONFIG.FPM settings are especially useful in a multi-user, multi-platform application. The EDITWORK, SORTWORK, PROGWORK, and TMPFILES options direct FoxPro's temporary files to folders of your choice. Use EDITWORK to direct FoxPro's temporary text editor files to any desired folder. Use the SORTWORK option to specify a location for FoxPro's temporary database manipulation files, such as those used during the execution of SQL-SELECT, INDEX, and SORT commands. Use the PROGWORK setting to specify a location for the temporary program cache files. If you would like all of FoxPro's temporary files to go to the same location, use the TMPFILES option.

In general, the best location for all of these temporary work files is the user's local hard drive. If you use the file server hard drive, FoxPro will have to move the data from the file server to the CPU of the local computer and back to the file server again, traversing the network cable twice. If you use a local hard disk, the data will only need to travel over the network once, effectively cutting traffic in half. However, the SORTWORK files in particular can grow very large when substantial FoxPro data tables and indexes are processed, so use the temporary file options in CONFIG.FPM with care.

One other important CONFIG.FPM option is VOLUME. Use VOLUME to map DOS volume names to Macintosh volume names in a multi-platform environment.

The following listing is a sample CONFIG.FPM file appropriate for multi-user, multi-platform applications. Table 15.2 explains each setting in this file.

```
CLOCK = STATUS
EDITWORK = HARDDISK:
EXCLUSIVE = OFF
HOURS = 24
INDEX = NDX
MVCOUNT = 2048
PROGWORK = HARDDISK:
REPROCESS = 1
RESOURCE = OFF
TALK = OFF
TYPEAHEAD = 128
SORTWORK = HARDDISK:
VOLUME C: = HARDDISK:
```

See Also

- Source Disk:Network & Config: CONFIG.FPM

Table 15.2

Explanation of the sample multi-user CONFIG.FPM file

CONFIG.FPM Setting	*Explanation*
CLOCK = STATUS	Display system clock in the status bar.
EDITWORK = HARDDISK:	Place text editor files on the HARDDISK volume, at the root of the volume.
EXCLUSIVE = OFF	Open data tables SHARED by default.
HOURS = 24	Display system clock in 24-hour mode.
INDEX = NDX	Use .NDX extension for single-tag, conventional indexes. Indexes are still constructed using FoxPro index technology.
MVCOUNT = 2048	Set maximum number of memory variables available for FoxPro to 2048.
PROGWORK = HARDDISK:	Place temporary program cache files on the HARDDISK volume, at the root of the volume.
REPROCESS = 1	Retry an unsuccessful record or file lock one time only. This setting effectively disables automatic locking.

CONFIG.FPM Setting	*Explanation*
RESOURCE = OFF	Changes made to the FoxPro environment are not to be saved to a FoxPro resource file. This setting is selected to avoid possible conflicts with the FoxPro resource file in a multi-user setting.
TALK = OFF	Disable display of the diagnostic feedback normally displayed during certain commands.
TYPEAHEAD = 128	Maximize the number of characters that can be stuffed into the keyboard buffer.
SORTWORK = HARDDISK:	Place the files generated by internal FoxPro data manipulation commands on Mac volume HARDDISK, at the root of the volume.
VOLUME C: = HARDDISK:	Map volume token C:\ to volume token HARDDISK:.

If you do not use the correct syntax in your CONFIG.FPM file, the incorrect line of the file is ignored. To confirm that your CONFIG.FPM settings are being interpreted correctly by FoxPro, use the LIST STATUS or DISPLAY STATUS commands.

FOXPRO MAC HACK TIP

FoxPro generates no diagnostic output during the interpretation of the CONFIG.FPM file. The only way to find out whether your CONFIG.FPM file is being interpreted correctly, or if FoxPro is even finding it, is to examine the status of the SET commands in question.

If you distribute applications, you have to make sure that your network-based application includes a procedure to help the administrator write appropriate CONFIG.FPMs for each station on the network. Unlike a DOS-only application, your program's installation techniques can't rely on the designation C:\ for a local disk for most users (discounting the possibility of diskless workstations for a moment). You can use the VOLUME setting to map the user's boot volume to the C:\ designation—but only after your installation routine knows what the name of the volume is.

See Also

- Source Disk:Network & Config: INSTALLER. PJX

FOXPRO MAC HACK TIP

The Source disk includes a bare-bones INSTALLER.PJX to give you an idea of how you might write a routine to help the adminstrator create the local CONFIG.FPMs. The INSTALLER.APP asks the adminstrator which workstation disks should get a copy of the FoxPro application and uses TEXTMERGE to write a CONFIG.FPM file to those locations, complete with TMPFILES designations that specify the workstation volumes. As shown in the INSTALLER.PJX, you can include a small starter .APP file *as a File, not as an Application*, and copy out the small .APP to the user's local drive along with the CONFIG.FPM. This approach allows the user to double-click on an .APP file with the name of your choice to start the program (the CONFIG.FPM cannot be renamed.)

Because the small .APP and the local CONFIG.FPM are in the same folder, this approach also ensures that the *right* CONFIG.FPM, with the settings you've specified, is read by FoxPro as the program starts. Remember that your users may have multiple FoxPro applications and multiple CONFIG.FPMs on their systems. More details and extensions to this suggestion are included in the INSTALLER.PJX as an INSTALLER.TXT file.

Establishing Appropriate Access to Folders and Files

When you install FoxPro Mac on your LAN, you need to give users appropriate access to the FoxPro application and enclosed folders. In addition, you must give users access to the folders containing any shared data tables, indexes, and any other shared application objects, such as program files and reports. AppleShare and NetWare use somewhat different approaches to the problem of controlling access to folders and files.

AppleShare: Access Privileges

In AppleShare, you control access to a folder by granting privileges to the folder's owner, any specified user or group, and/or all defined users (everyone). The privileges granted are See Folders, See Files, and Make Changes.

In a network FoxPro installation you will almost always have to grant See Folders, See Files, and Make Changes to an appropriate group, or to everyone, in the network FoxPro home directory. To see the folders installed with FoxPro, your users will need See Folders privileges. To see the FoxPro Files, they also need to See Files. And unless there are no files requiring update within the FoxPro folder, your users will need Make Changes privileges. If you are very careful about setting up the CONFIG.FPM file, it may be possible to avoid granting Make Changes. Note that granting Make Changes makes it possible for users to delete FoxPro itself.

Locate your data tables, indexes, and application objects in a folder or folders separate from the network FoxPro directory. As a minimum, users need See Files and Make Changes privileges in any folders containing data tables and indexes. For users simply running applications, you may be able to get away with only See Files in directories containing application objects, but it is safer to also grant users Make Changes privileges in these folders, too.

NetWare: Trustee Assignments

NetWare provides a more fine-tuned mechanism to control access to folders and files. Any users and groups defined in the bindery are referred to as *trustees*. You may grant or revoke *rights* to trustees for any selected directory. The listing of all rights granted to a trustee at any time is known as a *trustee assignment*. The rights that you may grant to any trustee are Read (R), Write (W), Create (C), Erase (E), Modify (M), File Scan (F), Access Control (A), and Supervisory (S). Rights that are set within a folder in NetWare cascade down through all enclosed folders, unless revoked through the use of the *inherited rights fitter*.

You can set NetWare trustee assignments from either a Mac or PC client. From a Mac, use the NetWare Control Center (NCC) application. NCC comes with the NetWare for Macintosh disks. From a PC, you may use either GRANT or REVOKE (DOS command line utilities), or FILER (a DOS menu-driven utility).

In the NetWare environment, the recommended approach for the network FoxPro folder is to GRANT R W C E M F to any trustees that you want to use FoxPro. Again, if you are clever, you can configure your system such that only R F are needed in this folder. In network data table and index folders, you will probably want to GRANT R W C E M F also.

In the NetWare environment, each file is also assigned a series of attributes. These attributes have priority over trustee assignments in determining how a file behaves. When you first copy files to a NetWare server, each file is assigned a default set of attributes. In many cases, you will need to override these defaults to permit shared access of a file. The process of setting a file's attributes is known as *flagging* the file.

You can flag files from either a Mac or PC client. From a Mac, use the NetWare Control Center (NCC) application. NCC comes with NetWare for Macintosh. From a PC, you may use either FLAG (a DOS command line utility) or FILER (a DOS menu-driven utility).

CROSS-PLATFORM WARNING

If you opt to use the NetWare DOS-based FLAG or FILER utilities to work with Macintosh files, remember that these utilities access Macintosh files using DOS naming conventions, even though both the Mac and DOS names point to the same file. For example, the default name that Microsoft uses for FoxPro Mac at the time of installation is "Microsoft FoxPro." For a DOS client, this file will probably be named "MICROSOF." If you have any difficulties determining the DOS names for the Mac files that you want to flag, try using the NetWare FILER utility to see the DOS and Mac names for the files in question.

Whether you decide to use NCC, FLAG, or FILER, make sure that you flag the FoxPro Mac executable files Read Only (Ro) and Shareable (S). If you do not, any time a second user attempts to start up a copy of FoxPro Mac over the LAN, that user will receive a FILE IS IN USE BY ANOTHER error message. Execution of FoxPro then terminates.

FoxPro for Mac's Multi-User Features

FoxPro Mac provides a rich set of multi-user tools. You need to understand each multi-user command and function, and how these commands and functions interact, in order to develop and implement a sound multi-user programming strategy.

In this section, you'll learn each of FoxPro Mac's multi-user commands and functions. You'll also learn how to use these tools to manage user collisions in your application. Table 15.3 lists and provides an overview of each of FoxPro Mac's most important multi-user commands and functions.

Table 15.3

FoxPro Mac multi-user commands and functions

Command or Function	*Description*	*Comments*
ERROR()	Returns the most recent error number (Appendix B of *FoxPro Mac Developer's Guide*).	ON ERROR must be active.
FLOCK()	Attempts to lock a database table. Returns .T. if the lock is successful.	Use SET REPROCESS to automatically retry a failed FLOCK().
LOCK()	Attempts to lock one or more table records.	Alternative token for RLOCK().
MESSAGE()	Returns the most recent error message (see Appendix A of *FoxPro MacDeveloper's Guide*).	Optional argument 1 returns the offending source code.
ON ERROR	Execute a command file when an error occurs.	Good ON ERROR routines are vital for recovering from unexpected situations.
RETRY	Re-executes the previous command.	Use in ON ERROR routines.
RLOCK()	Attempts to lock one or more table records.	Use SET REPROCESS to automatically retry a failed RLOCK(). Use SET MULTILOCKS to permit the locking of more than one record in a table simultaneously.
SET EXCLUSIVE	Specifies whether tables are opened for exclusive or shared use by default.	

continues

Table 15.3
Continued

Command or Function	*Description*	*Comments*
SET MULTILOCKS	Enables or disables the locking of multiple records within one table.	
SET REFRESH	Changes settings affecting how often updates made by other users are posted to the BROWSE, CHANGE or EDIT windows.	
SET REPROCESS TO	Specifies how FoxPro deals with unsuccessful setting record or file locks.	SET REPROCESS TO 1 effectively disables implicit record locking.
SYS(2011)	Returns the current record or file locking status.	
UNLOCK	Removes locks from files or records.	
USE	Closes a FoxPro data table.	Implicitly removes any file or record locks on the affected table.
USE...EXCLUSIVE	Attempts to open a table for exclusive use.	Overrides SET EXCLUSIVE OFF status.
USE...SHARED	Attempts to open a table for shared use.	Overrides SET EXCLUSIVE ON status.

Each of the FoxPro Mac multi-user commands and functions listed in table 15.3 can be classified by the type of service provided:

- Resource access
- Resource locking
- Concurrency management
- Error management

In the following sections, you will learn how each of FoxPro Mac's multi-user commands and functions render these multi-user services.

Resource Access

FoxPro Mac can open data tables for either shared access or exclusive access. The following commands are employed to control access to data tables: SET EXCLUSIVE (OFF/ON), USE, USE <table> EXCLUSIVE, and USE <table> SHARED.

SET EXCLUSIVE establishes the default access method for tables. By default, EXCLUSIVE is set ON at the time FoxPro starts. When EXCLUSIVE is ON, your application attempts to USE <table> with exclusive access. When EXCLUSIVE is OFF, your application attempts to USE <table> with shared access. You may override the default by explicitly issuing the commands USE <table> SHARED, or USE <table> EXCLUSIVE. To change the access method currently in effect for an open data table, you must first close the table and then attempt to reopen it using the desired access method. The USE command without any modifiers simply closes the table.

If any user has a table open and another user attempts to open the table with exclusive access, the exclusive access attempt will fail, and a FoxPro error is returned to the application. Likewise, if any user has a table open with exclusive access, any other user attempting to open the table is denied access, and an error is also returned to the application. The possible outcomes of USE EXCLUSIVE and USE SHARED are summarized in table 15.4.

Table 15.4

Multi-user access Truth Table

	User 2 attempts to USE table SHARED	*User 2 attempts to USE table EXCLUSIVE*
User 1 is currently using table SHARED	No Conflict.	User 2 cannot access table.
User 1 is currently using table EXCLUSIVE	User 2 cannot access table.	User 2 cannot access table.

It is important for you to understand the implications of shared and exclusive USE of data tables. In general, you should avoid exclusive access to shared data tables because this action completely blocks access of the table to other users. However, there are some cases where you may want to create temporary, non-shared tables in your application and open these tables for exclusive access. For example, you might create a temporary table for a report, erasing the file once the report is completed. In this case, exclusive access to the temporary table would probably improve the speed of the report.

In addition, there are some FoxPro commands that will fail unless you have exclusive access to the data table involved. These are commands that cause significant physical reorganization of data tables and indexes, and are usually run when you perform system maintenance activities. The FoxPro commands requiring exclusive access are outlined in table 15.5.

Table 15.5

FoxPro commands requiring exclusive access to data tables

FoxPro Command	*Description*	*Comment*
INDEX ON (compound index tag)	Create, rebuild, or destroy a compound index tag.	
INSERT BLANK	Insert blank record into database table.	Old xBASE artifact. Do not use this command in a production system.
MODIFY STRUCTURE	Interactively change the structure of a FoxPro data table.	
PACK	Remove all records marked for deletion.	
REINDEX	Rebuild all indexes currently attached to a database table.	
ZAP	Physically remove all records from the current database table.	Use with greatest caution.

Resource Locking

FoxPro has several commands and functions that you can use to lock files and records, unlock files and records, and control automatic resource locking: FLOCK(), LOCK(), RLOCK(), SET REPROCESS, SYS(2011), UNLOCK, and SET MULTILOCKS.

FLOCK(), LOCK(), and RLOCK()

FLOCK(), LOCK(), and RLOCK() are functions returning logical values that also act as commands. Use FLOCK() to ask FoxPro to lock an entire data table. If FoxPro is able to lock the table, FLOCK() returns .T. and locks the table. If FoxPro is not able to lock the table, FLOCK() simply returns .F.. Use RLOCK(), or its synonym LOCK(), to ask FoxPro to lock one or more records within a table. If FoxPro is able to lock the record, RLOCK() or LOCK() return .T.; otherwise these functions return .F..

If two or more users have a data table open for shared use, only one user may have the table locked at any given time. While the table is locked, no other users may lock either the table or any records within the table. Likewise, only one user may lock a given record at a time. A record lock also blocks any file locking attempts by other users on the same table. The possible outcomes of file and record locking attempts are summarized in table 15.6.

Table 15.6

FoxPro file and record locking Truth Table

User 1 is USEing table SHARED and currently has the following lock status:	*User 2 is USEing table SHARED and attempts the following:*		
	No Lock	*RLOCK()*	*FLOCK()*
No Lock	No Conflict	No Conflict	No Conflict
RLOCK()	No Conflict	Possible conflict if attempting to RLOCK() the same record	FLOCK() denied
FLOCK()	No Conflict	RLOCK() denied to User 2	FLOCK() denied to User 2

SYS(2011)

SYS(2011) returns a diagnostic character string indicating table access status or file lock status. Fox example, if you currently have a table locked, UPPER(SYS(2011)) returns "FILE LOCKED." Unlike the locking functions described above, SYS(2011) does not change the lock status of a data table or record.

SET MULTILOCKS

SET MULTILOCKS <ON/OFF> permits or denies your application to lock multiple records within one data table. With SET MULTILOCKS ON, you may lock as many records within a table as you wish. With SET MULTILOCKS OFF, FoxPro only permits one record to be locked within a table by any user at any point in time.

UNLOCK

UNLOCK is a command you can use to release any pending record or file locks. It is good programming practice to follow any FLOCK(), LOCK(), or RLOCK() calls with an explicit UNLOCK command as soon as the activities requiring the resource lock are completed. However, closing a data table with the USE command automatically releases any file or record locks that your application has established on the table in question.

SET REPROCESS

SET REPROCESS controls how many times, or for how long, FoxPro is to retry an unsuccessful locking attempt before reporting an error condition. SET REPROCESS, ON ERROR, and an appropriate error handler work together to allow you to take advantage of FoxPro's automatic (implicit) resource locking features.

Specifying SET REPROCESS TO 0 causes FoxPro to attempt to relock indefinitely, but allows the user to press the escape key to abort the relocking attempt. However, if an ON ERROR routine has been defined, the error handler fires and takes precedence. SET REPROCESS TO -1 also tells FoxPro to attempt to relock indefinitely, but does not permit abortion of the attempt through either the escape key or an ON ERROR routine.

SET REPROCESS TO <retry attempts> specifies the number of attempts that FoxPro is to make in the event of a resource locking failure. If attempts to lock the resource fail after the specified number of retries, any defined ON ERROR routine fires. However, an explicit locking attempt (FLOCK(), LOCK(), or RLOCK()) does not cause an ON ERROR routine to execute, and the calling function simply returns .F.. Alternatively, you can specify SET REPROCESS TO <retry delay> SECONDS to specify an amount of time, rather than a number of times, to retry a failed lock attempt.

SET REPROCESS TO 1 effectively disables implicit resource locking features in FoxPro Mac.

Explicit versus Implicit Resource Locking

FoxPro Mac allows you to either explicitly or implicitly (automatically) lock resources. Consider the following technique:

```
IF RLOCK()
  REPLACE company WITH f_company
  UNLOCK
ENDIF
```

You need to REPLACE the current value of company contained in a field of a data table with a new value, contained in the memory variable f_company. FoxPro needs to lock the record in order for the REPLACE to succeed. You choose to explicitly ask for the RLOCK() before attempting to perform the REPLACE. Because you are detecting whether a resource lock is available in advance, your application can take actions based on whether the lock attempt has been successful or unsuccessful. The explicit technique also enforces a certain measure of discipline as you write the program because it forces you to deal with the possibility of a resource locking failure up front.

FoxPro also permits implicit resource locking. If you choose this approach, the equivalent program code would simply be:

```
REPLACE company WITH f_company
```

In this case, you allow FoxPro to attempt to automatically lock the record. If FoxPro cannot obtain a record lock, a FoxPro error ensues, and your generic ON ERROR routine must deal with the situation. It should be evident that automatic, or implicit, resource locking features cause you to lose a certain measure of control over the process of managing collisions.

Explicit Resource Locking

If you choose to lock resources explicitly, you need to use FLOCK(), LOCK(), or RLOCK() before using a number of FoxPro commands. In addition, good programming practice requires explicit resource locking in a number of cases that the FoxPro language does not strictly require. To implement explicit resource locking, you need to understand when record and file locks are required, and when they are not required. Tables 15.7 and 15.8 summarize these locking requirements. Table 15.7 lists the FoxPro commands requiring a record lock. Table 15.8 lists the FoxPro commands and programming situations where a file lock is required.

Table 15.7

FoxPro commands requiring record locks

Operation	*Description*	*Comment*
DELETE	Marks the current record for deletion.	Record is not physically removed until PACK or COPY TO FOR .NOT. DELETED() are completed.
REPLACE	Updates selected fields in current record to new values.	
RECALL	Release deletion marker on the current record.	

Table 15.8

FoxPro commands and programming situations requiring file locks

Operation	*Description*	*Comment*
APPEND FROM	Inserts new records into the current data table from another table.	FLOCKing a table prior to APPEND FROM is the only way to use APPEND FROM reliably in a multi-user application.
APPEND BLANK	Inserts a new, blank record into the current data table.	FLOCKing a table prior to APPEND BLANK is the only way to use APPEND BLANK reliably in a multi-user application.

Operation	*Description*	*Comment*
DELETE (with scope)	Marks records identified by <scope> for deletion.	Record is not physically removed until PACK or COPY TO FOR .NOT. DELETED() are completed.
INSERT INTO	Inserts new record into data table and updates selected fields to new values.	
REPLACE (with scope)	Updates selected fields in records identified by <scope> to new values.	
RECALL	Releases deletion marker on the current record.	
UPDATE	Updates fields in current data table with related fields from another data table.	Do not confuse FoxPro UPDATE with SQL UPDATE. This is an older command and is rarely used today.
When checking for a primary key.	To prevent users from accidentally using a primary key twice, it is necessary to FLOCK() the data table, confirm that the key is not used, insert the new record, and UNLOCK the table.	
When read consistency is mandatory.	Read consistency is required when your applicatation needs to report on a table or tables as a single, unchanging entity.	An accounting general ledger report falls into this category.

Implicit Resource Locking

Alternatively, you may choose to rely on FoxPro Mac's implicit, or automatic, resource locking features to manage collisions. In this case, you need to understand which objects FoxPro attempts to lock so that your ON

ERROR routine can handle collisions gracefully. Table 15.9 lists every FoxPro command that can evoke implicit record and file locking. In each case, the command and options that generate the automatic resource locking are listed, and the scope of the locked resource is defined.

Table 15.9

FoxPro commands that perform automatic locking

FoxPro Command	*Scope of Implicit Resource Lock*
APPEND	Selected table
APPEND BLANK	Header of selected table*
APPEND FROM	Selected table
APPEND FROM ARRAY	Header of selected table*
APPEND GENERAL	Selected record
APPEND MEMO	Selected record
BROWSE	Selected record, records in any related tables
CHANGE	Selected record, records in any related tables
DELETE	Selected record
DELETE NEXT 1	Selected record
DELETE RECORD n	Selected record n
DELETE (scope > 1)	Selected table
EDIT	Selected record, records in any related tables
GATHER	Selected record
INSERT (SQL)	Header of selected table*
MODIFY MEMO	Selected record
READ (w/GET(s) on selected data tables(s) in effect)	Selected record, records in any related tables
RECALL	Selected record
RECALL NEXT 1	Selected record
RECALL RECORD n	Selected record n
RECALL (scope > 1)	Selected table

FoxPro Command	*Scope of Implicit Resource Lock*
REPLACE	Selected record
REPLACE NEXT 1	Selected record
REPLACE RECORD n	Selected record n
REPLACE (scope > 1)	Selected table
SHOW GETS	Selected record, records in any related tables
UPDATE	Selected table

*If 2 or more users attempt to execute APPEND BLANK, APPEND FROM ARRAY, or INSERT (SQL) at the same time, FoxPro will return the message "File is in use by another." Executing an explicit FLOCK() prior to executing these commands is one way to avoid this problem.

Concurrency Management

FoxPro provides one SET statement to control whether and how changes made to records by one user are displayed on the screens of other users: SET REFRESH TO <screen update interval>, <buffer update interval>.

Use the <screen update interval> argument of SET REFRESH to specify how many seconds elapse between updates of BROWSE, EDIT, or CHANGE windows over the network. A <screen update interval> of 0 disables screen updating over the network. The default <screen update interval> is 0.

The optional <buffer update interval> setting specifies how often local data buffers are updated over the network. The default <buffer update interval> is 5 seconds. A setting of 0 disables this feature.

In general, lower SET REFRESH settings decrease application performance because updating occurs more often over the network. SET REFRESH TO 0,0 disables both screen and buffer updating, resulting in the best performance.

Error Management

ERROR(), MESSAGE(), ON ERROR, and RETRY manage the error detection and resolution process. In FoxPro for Macintosh, you can establish an *error handler* command file that automatically "fires" whenever

FoxPro encounters an error condition. In addition to simply handling and resolving the error gracefully, a good error handler also provides feedback to the developer and user concerning what happened. Good feedback is necessary in order to fix problems and tune the application. Your error handler fires in the event of any FoxPro error, so it must handle both multi-user and non-multi-user errors.

See Also

- PROCEDURE AppError, Source Disk:Library/ Template Code: MAIN.PRG

To activate your error handler, issue the ON ERROR DO <error handler>, where <error handler> is the name of your ON ERROR command file. When an error occurs, this command file runs. In your error handler routine, you can use ERROR() to return the error numbers and MESSAGE to return the text of the error messages contained in Appendix B of the *FoxPro Developer's Guide*. Use RETRY in your error handler to try the offending command or function again. RETRY is useful if RLOCK() or FLOCK() fail, but you want your application to continue to try to gain a resource lock.

Keep in mind that certain activities may generate an error in one case, and yet not generate an error in another case, simply because of multi-user interactions. If you make use of FoxPro's implicit resource locking features, you will have to be especially careful of this sort of situation.

Multi-User FoxPro Mac Application Strategy

Now that you understand FoxPro Mac's multi-user features, you need to understand how to put them to work. In this section, you'll learn FoxPro Mac multi-user programming strategies and specific techniques and rules for implementing these strategies. These guidelines permit you to develop applications consistent with the objectives of concurrency, performance, throughput, and data integrity in an online, transaction-processing environment. You will understand how:

- To use memory variables and temporary tables to control the adding and editing of records
- To best control access to your FoxPro data structures
- To gracefully lock and unlock resources using explicit locking
- To tell the difference between physical and logical locking
- To implement and use physical locking and logical locking

- To tell the difference between static and dynamic locking
- To implement and use static and dynamic locking
- To use Rushmore to speed multi-user queries

Memory Variables and Temporary Files

FoxPro permits direct editing of data tables using, among other things, the BROWSE command. BROWSE is very powerful. When used in conjunction with VALID, BROWSE presents an appealing approach to FoxPro data entry and editing.

While BROWSE is a useful technique for presenting information to readers of data, do not use BROWSE or any of FoxPro's table entry and edit commands to directly edit data in shared FoxPro tables. FoxPro does not permit transaction rollback, so directly editing data creates a very risky situation.

Throughout this book, you'll learn to use memory variables and temporary data tables to edit and validate data before committing that data to live FoxPro data tables. The example screen sets use numerous BROWSEs, but always as READ-only picklists.

Using memory variables and temporary data tables for *indirect reads* allow you to manage the worst aspects of the lack of transaction rollback. When you are editing or adding a new record, copy fields to memory variables, edit the memory variables, validate the user's input, and finally update the underlying data tables with the new data. When you are editing more than one record from a table, or adding more than one record to a table, copy records to a temporary data table, and then edit each record using memory variables. After you have checked the integrity of the records in the temporary table, update the live FoxPro table from the temporary table.

Memory Variables

Memory variables are distinguished from data table field variables in that while memory variables have program-dependent scope, field variables have table-dependent scope. To edit fields in a data table, you should first copy the values of each field to a memory variable.

FoxPro has very simple rules for creating and assigning memory variables. You do not have to explicitly declare variables or variable types, and you can change variable types on the fly. This flexibility presents a challenge to the application developer: You have to provide the structure that other compilers and languages often enforce more strictly.

One basic road map for FoxPro memory and field variable naming follows. Although these conventions are not specifically required for multi-user applications, and are not employed in the sample code from other parts of this book, using *some* variable naming strategy provides important structure as you develop your application.

- *Field and memory variable names.* Use data table field names beginning with the letters a-z. Use all lowercase letters to refer to field and memory variable names in your application code. Use all uppercase letters for FoxPro commands and functions. Use field and variable names that logically relate a field name to the object that it represents. For example, you may want to use 'city' to represent the customer's city name, rather than 'xyz.'
- *Field and memory variable name lengths.* Limit FoxPro data table field names to 7 characters or less. Limit memory variable names to 10 characters or less.

FOXPRO MAC HACK TIP

FoxPro limits all variable names (field and memory variables) to 10 characters. If you attempt to create a memory variable in excess of 10 characters long, FoxPro truncates the name at the 10 character limit. If the abbreviated name conflicts with an existing name, the older variable name is overwritten. In either case, FoxPro reports no errors.

This can be a big problem when you copy the contents of database fields to temporary memory variables for editing. For example, if you have a field named first_name and try to copy it to a variable named f_first_name, FoxPro will reference the variable using the name f_first_na. As a result, you probably want to limit data table field names to 7 or fewer characters.

- *Variable scope naming conventions.* In this chapter, conventions distinguish the scope of a memory variable. This naming convention is completely optional and serves only to increase program clarity. Use f_<var_name> for variables copied from data table fields, g_<var_name> for global (public) variables, l_<var_name> for local program variables, and p_<var_name> for parameters passed to a user-defined function. FoxPro also supports the #REGION compiler directive, and REGIONAL variables that are unique within the defined region. Use r_<var_name> to refer to such variables.

- *Variable type naming conventions.* It is also useful to distinguish variable types (i.e., character, date, general, float, logical, memo, number, or picture) with a variable type naming convention. Although a variable type naming strategy is not used here, you may want to develop one to add clarity to your FoxPro programs.

To edit a record, copy the fields that you want the user to edit to memory variables (f_<var_name>), call a screen that you have created with the screen builder to allow the user to edit the memory variables, and then update the original record with the new values provided by the user. In order to create a new record, create memory variables with default values, call the screen to edit the memory variables, and then insert a new record into the table using the memory variables. The following listing illustrates these techniques:

```
* — Set up client table
CREATE TABLE CLIENTS (clientno  N(15,0), ;
                      company   C(35), ;
                      addr1     C(30), ;
                      addr2     C(30), ;
                      city      C(20), ;
                      state     C(10), ;
                      zip       C(10), ;
                      country   C(15), ;
                      phone     C(20);
                      )

* — Set up indexes for the table
USE CLIENTS EXCLUSIVE;
INDEX ON clientno TAG clientno
INDEX ON company  TAG company
INDEX ON city     TAG city
INDEX ON state    TAG state
INDEX ON zip      TAG zip
INDEX ON phone    TAG phone
SET ORDER TO 0

* — Insert two records into the table
* — NOTE: Table is open EXCLUSIVE;
```

```
* — no locking required
INSERT INTO CLIENTS (clientno, ;
                     company, ;
                     addr1, ;
                     addr2, ;
                     city, ;
                     state, ;
                     zip, ;
                     country, ;
                     phone;
                     ) ;
             VALUES  (1, ;
                      'Freight Movers, Inc.', ;
                      '123 North First Street', ;
                      'Suite 123', ;
                      'Palo Alto', ;
                      'CA', ;
                      '94301', ;
                      SPACE(0), ;
                      '415/999-9999';
                      )
INSERT INTO CLIENTS (clientno, ;
                     company, ;
                     addr1, ;
                     addr2, ;
                     city, ;
                     state, ;
                     zip, ;
                     country, ;
                     phone;
                     ) ;
             VALUES  (2, ;
                      'Print Masters Printing', ;
                      '789 South Second Road', ;
                      'Suite 789', ;
                      'Stanford', ;
                      'CA', ;
                      '94305', ;
                      SPACE(0), ;
                      '415/172-9999';
                      )
```

```
* — Here is an abbreviated example
* — of editing an existing record
LOCATE FOR clientno = 1
f_clientno = clientno
f_company  = company
f_addr1    = addr1
f_addr2    = addr2
f_city     = city
f_state    = state
f_zip      = zip
f_country  = country
f_phone    = phone
* — Call screen to edit f_ memory variables here
* — If the data is OK, update old values
* — with new values like this
* — NOTE: Table is open EXCLUSIVE;
* — no locking required
LOCATE FOR clientno = f_clientno
REPLACE company WITH f_company, ;
        addr1   WITH f_addr1, ;
        addr2   WITH f_addr2, ;
        city    WITH f_city, ;
        state   WITH f_state, ;
        zip     WITH f_zip, ;
        country WITH f_country, ;
        phone   WITH f_phone

* — Here is an abbreviated example of
* — adding a new record
SET ORDER TO clientno
GO BOTTOMf_clientno = clientno + 1
* — Use blank record at end of file to
* — initialize f_ memory variables
SKIPf_company  = company
f_addr1    = addr1
f_addr2    = addr2
f_city     = city
f_state    = state
f_zip      = zip
f_country  = country
f_phone    = phone
SET ORDER TO 0
* — Call screen to edit f_ memory variables here
* — If the data is OK and user wants to save
```

```
* — add a new record like this
* — NOTE: Table is open EXCLUSIVE;
* — no locking required
DO WHILE .t.
  LOCATE FOR clientno = f_clientno
  IF FOUND()
    f_clientno = f_clientno + 1
  ELSE
    EXIT
  ENDIF
ENDDO
INSERT INTO CLIENTS (clientno, ;
                     company, ;
                     addr1, ;
                     addr2, ;
                     city, ;
                     state, ;
                     zip, ;
                     country, ;
                     phone;
                     ) ;
             VALUES  (f_clientno, ;
                      f_company, ;
                      f_addr1, ;
                      f_addr2, ;
                      f_city, ;
                      f_state, ;
                      f_zip, ;
                      f_country, ;
                      f_phone;
                      )
```

Temporary Tables

When you need to edit more than one record, copy the records to a temporary table with the same structure as the original table. When you need to create a batch of records for insertion into a table, copy the structure of that table to a temporary table and add records to the temporary table. As you add or edit records in a temporary table, use the memory variable techniques discussed above.

Before you can open up a temporary table in your multi-user application, you need to be sure that the file name you want to use will not conflict with any file names used by other users. The following listing shows how to create temporary file names that will be unique. You can use this program to create temporary file names in your programs.

```
* ———————————————————————
* — TmpFiles
* — (Procedure)
* — Description:
* — This procedure sets up ten memory
* — variables pointing to ten unique file names.
* — Run this procedure during your application's
* — startup process to establish file handles
* — Parameters Passed:
* — (None)
* — Returned values:
* — (None)
* — Example procedure usage at startup time:
* — DO TmpFiles
* —
* — Example usage of environment created:
* — CREATE TABLE (g_tmpf0) (DEMO C(1))
* — USE (g_tmpf0) EXCLUSIVE ALIAS temp0
* ———————————————————————
PROCEDURE TmpFiles
* — Set up private variable l_seed to hold
* — unique seed file name
PRIVATE l_seed
l_seed = SPACE(0)
* — Define temp file variables 0 through 9
* — Use these variables to create unique
* — temporary files later in your application
RELEASE g_tmpf0, ;
        g_tmpf1, ;
        g_tmpf2, ;
        g_tmpf3, ;
        g_tmpf4, ;
        g_tmpf5, ;
        g_tmpf6, ;
        g_tmpf7, ;
        g_tmpf8, ;
        g_tmpf9
PUBLIC  g_tmpf0, ;
        g_tmpf1, ;
```

```
        g_tmpf2, ;
        g_tmpf3, ;
        g_tmpf4, ;
        g_tmpf5, ;
        g_tmpf6, ;
        g_tmpf7, ;
        g_tmpf8, ;
        g_tmpf9
STORE SPACE(0) TO g_tmpf0, ;
                  g_tmpf1, ;
                  g_tmpf2, ;
                  g_tmpf3, ;
                  g_tmpf4, ;
                  g_tmpf5, ;
                  g_tmpf6, ;
                  g_tmpf7, ;
                  g_tmpf8, ;
                  g_tmpf9

* — Set up 7-character seed variable
l_seed = SUBSTR((SYS(3) + "00000000"), 1, 7)
* — Generate unique file names
g_tmpf0 = l_seed + "0"
g_tmpf1 = l_seed + "1"
g_tmpf2 = l_seed + "2"
g_tmpf3 = l_seed + "3"
g_tmpf4 = l_seed + "4"
g_tmpf5 = l_seed + "5"
g_tmpf6 = l_seed + "6"
g_tmpf7 = l_seed + "7"
g_tmpf8 = l_seed + "8"
g_tmpf9 = l_seed + "9"
RETURN
```

See Also

- Source Disk:Network & Config: TMPFILES.PRG

You will want to open temporary tables using exclusive access to enhance performance. Exclusive access also negates the need to lock the temporary table during insert and update operations.

You can also use temporary tables to enhance the performance of reports and decrease concurrency issues at report run time. For example, locking a general ledger entries table, copying that table to a temporary table, and then immediately unlocking the original table will release the shared table to other users rapidly while providing a consistent data set for the report using the temporary table.

FOXPRO MAC HACK TIP

FoxPro provides some alternatives to the techniques outlined above.

One alternative to explicitly copying fields to memory variables is SCATTER MEMVAR. SCATTER MEMVAR automatically copies all fields of the current record to memory variables named m.<field>, where field is the literal field name from the data table. For example, if you had a table with one character field named "company", SCATTER MEMVAR would create a memory variable named "m.company" and copy the contents of the company field to that variable. I prefer the approach of explicitly copying fields to memory variables because it makes the program easier to read while enforcing my rules for memory variable naming conventions.

Some programmers also prefer to use arrays instead of temporary data tables. COPY TO ARRAY copies one or more records from a table to an array, and FoxPro has a number of commands for manipulating data within arrays and copying the data from arrays back into live data tables. There are a number of problems with using arrays to simulate data tables. First, the size of arrays is limited by FoxPro's memory, so the number of records that you can copy into an array is limited. In addition, the commands and functions that work with arrays are far more limited than those that work with FoxPro data tables.

Resource Access

Opening a data table for exclusive use blocks both read and write access to the table. However, exclusive access does improve performance because FoxPro can safely cache large amounts of data. In addition, when exclusive access is gained, there is no need to use records or table locks. Finally, exclusive access is required for several FoxPro commands to function.

In general, you should open data tables in your multi-user FoxPro Mac application using shared access. SET EXCLUSIVE OFF, either in your CONFIG.FPM file or in your application before any data tables are opened. When you do need EXCLUSIVE access to files, avoid changing the default access mode using SET EXCLUSIVE ON. Instead, issue the USE <table> EXCLUSIVE command.

There are at least two exceptions to the shared access rule. USE <table> EXCLUSIVE when:

- You are reorganizing data and index files during a system maintenance procedure that requires PACK, ZAP, or INDEX ON (to rebuild existing indexes). Here, USE EXCLUSIVE is mandatory.
- You are opening temporary data tables. In this case, exclusive access is desirable, but not mandatory. Since there is no need to share temporary tables, it is generally best to open them using exclusive access.

Resource Locking Strategy

Use the record and file locking functions RLOCK() and FLOCK() to lock a record or file explicitly before changing existing records in or adding new records to FoxPro data tables. Do not rely on implicit, or automatic, locking features.

If you cannot obtain the required resource lock, you may want to give the user the option to retry the failed lock attempt. Take this approach when you are conducting a simple, single-write transaction, such as changing the address of a customer. In the event that the user opts to abort such an attempted lock, causing the insert or update operation to fail, inform the user that the write request was unsuccessful.

At other times, if you are not immediately able to lock a record or file, you may wish to continue trying for a lock until you can obtain one, and not give the user the option of aborting the transaction. Use this technique after you have begun a complex transaction requiring that all writes be completed.

See Also

- Source Disk:Network &Config: LOCKR.PRG, LOCKF.PRG, RETRYLCK. PRG, and NOTE.PRG

Lock resources at the lowest level possible (i.e., lock at the record level instead of the file level if you can get away with it). Lock resources for the shortest duration possible.

The following listing contains four user defined functions that you may find useful for explicit resource locking. LockR() adds features to the basic RLOCK() function. Similarly, LockF() adds features to the basic FLOCK() function. RetryLck() and Note() provide a simple means for you to get feedback from your user and to keep the user informed about how your program is resolving user collisions. LockR() and LockF() optionally call RetryLck() to ask if the user would like to continue trying to lock the resource. You can use Note() to notify the user that the resource lock attempt has failed.

```
* ————————————————————————
* — LockR
* — This function will try to lock
* — the selected record
* — in a data table in the currently
* — selected work area
* — Parameters Passed:
* — p_retry - # of times to retry lock
* —           -1 to retry lock indefinitely
* — Returned values:
* — l_return - .t. if lock succeeded
* —          - .f. if lock failed
* — Example usage:
* — IF RLOCK() .OR. LockR(500)
* —   REPLACE phone WITH f_phone
* —   UNLOCK
* — ENDIF
* ————————————————————————
FUNCTION LockR
PARAMETERS p_retry
PRIVATE l_counter, l_return
l_counter = 0
l_return = .f.
DO CASE
  CASE .NOT. USED()
    * —  No table selected for record locking
    l_return = .f.
  CASE EOF()
    * — At end of file
    l_return = .f.
  CASE UPPER(SYS(2011)) = "EXCLUSIVE"
    * — Table currently open for exclusive use
    l_return = .t.
  OTHERWISE    * — Lock the file
    l_return =  RLOCK()
    DO WHILE .NOT. l_return
      * — Retry the lock
      l_counter = ;
         IIF(p_retry <> -1, p_retry, 5000)
      DO WHILE l_counter > 0 .AND. .NOT. l_return
        l_return = RLOCK()
        l_counter = l_counter - 1
```

```
      ENDDO
      DO CASE
        CASE .NOT. l_return .AND. p_retry = -1
          LOOP
        CASE .NOT. l_return
          * — CALL RetryLck function to see
          * — if user wants to keep trying...
          IF RetryLck("Record in " + DBF() + ;
             " is locked by another user.  " + ;
             "Retry lock?") = 1
            LOOP          ELSE
            EXIT
          ENDIF
      ENDCASE
    ENDDO
ENDCASE
RETURN l_return
* ————————————————————————
* ————————————————————————
* — LockF
* — (Function)
* — This function tries to lock data table in
* —  the currently selected work area
* — Parameters Passed:
* — p_retry - # of times to retry lock
* —           -1 to retry lock indefinitely
* — Returned values:
* — l_return - .t. if lock succeeded
* —          - .f. if lock failed
* — Example usage:
* — IF FLOCK() .OR. LockF(500)
* —   APPEND FROM (g_tmpf0)
* —   UNLOCK
* — ENDIF
* ————————————————————————
FUNCTION LockF
PARAMETERS p_retry
PRIVATE l_counter, l_return
l_counter = 0
l_return = .f.
DO CASE
  CASE .NOT. USED()
```

```
    * — No table selected for record locking
    l_return = .f.
  CASE UPPER(SYS(2011)) = "EXCLUSIVE"
    * — Table currently open for exclusive use
    l_return = .t.
  OTHERWISE
    * — Lock the file
    l_return =  FLOCK()
    DO WHILE .NOT. l_return
      * — Retry the lock
      l_counter = IIF(p_retry <> -1,p_retry,5000)
      DO WHILE l_counter > 0 .AND. .NOT. l_return
        l_return = FLOCK()
        l_counter = l_counter - 1
      ENDDO
      DO CASE
        CASE .NOT. l_return .AND. p_retry = -1
          LOOP
        CASE .NOT. l_return
          * — CALL RetryLck function to see
          * — if user wants to keep trying...
          IF RetryLck("Table " + DBF() + ;
           " is locked by another user.  " + ;
           " Retry lock?") = 1
            LOOP
          ELSE
            EXIT              ENDIF       ENDCASE
    ENDDO
ENDCASE
RETURN l_return
* — — — — — — — — — — — — — — — — — — — — — —
* — — — — — — — — — — — — — — — — — — — — — —

* — RetryLck
* — (Function)
* — Description:
* — This function will display a message
* — that you select to tell the
* — user that a resource is locked and
* — allows the user to retry
* — or abort the lock retry attempt
```

```
* — Parameters Passed:
* — p_message - The message you want
* — displayed on screen
* — Returned values:
* — l_retval - 1 = user wants to keep trying
* —          - 2 = user aborts lock retry
* — Example usage:
* — ?RetryLck("Table " + DBF() + " ;
* —           "is locked by another user.  " + ;
* —           "Retry lock?")
* ————————————————————————
FUNCTION RetryLck
PARAMETERS p_message
PRIVATE l_retval,l_talkstat,l_compstat,l_rborder
IF SET("TALK") = "ON"
  SET TALK OFF  l_talkstat = "ON"
ELSE
  l_talkstat = "OFF"
ENDIF
l_compstat = SET("COMPATIBLE")
SET COMPATIBLE FOXPLUS
l_rborder = SET("READBORDER")
SET READBORDER OFF
* — Define alert window
IF NOT WEXIST("locked") ;
  OR UPPER(WTITLE("LOCKED")) == "LOCKED.PJX" ;
  OR UPPER(WTITLE("LOCKED")) == "LOCKED.SCX" ;
  OR UPPER(WTITLE("LOCKED")) == "LOCKED.MNX" ;
  OR UPPER(WTITLE("LOCKED")) == "LOCKED.PRG" ;
  OR UPPER(WTITLE("LOCKED")) == "LOCKED.FRX" ;
  OR UPPER(WTITLE("LOCKED")) == "LOCKED.QPR"
  DEFINE WINDOW locked ;
              AT  7.778, 17.857  ;
              SIZE 11.000,53.667 ;
              TITLE "Locked Resource" ;
              FONT "Geneva", 10 ;
              NOFLOAT ;
              NOCLOSE ;
              DOUBLE
  MOVE WINDOW locked CENTER
ENDIF
* — Display alert window, get response from user
```

```
IF WVISIBLE("locked")
  ACTIVATE WINDOW locked SAME
ELSE
  ACTIVATE WINDOW locked NOSHOW
ENDIF
@ 0.667,3.333 SAY p_message ;
              SIZE 7.000,47.333 ;
              FONT "Geneva", 10
@ 8.500,3.000 GET l_retval ;
              PICTURE "@*HT3 \!Yes;No" ;
              SIZE 1.500,10.429,1.143 ;
              DEFAULT 1 ;
              FONT "Geneva", 10 ;
              STYLE "B"
IF NOT WVISIBLE("locked")
  ACTIVATE WINDOW locked
ENDIF
READ MODALRELEASE WINDOW locked
* — Restore old settings
SET READBORDER &l_rborder
IF l_talkstat = "ON"
  SET TALK ONENDIF
IF l_compstat = "ON"
  SET COMPATIBLE ON
ENDIF
* — Return result to calling program
RETURN l_retval
* ————————————————————————
* ————————————————————————
* — Note
* — (Function)
* — Description:
* — This function displays a message you select.
* — Parameters Passed:
* — p_message - The message you want displayed
* — Returned values:
* — l_retval - 1 (always)
* — Example usage:
* — ?Note(DBF() + " is totally corrupted.  "+ ;
* —       "You'd better call the data doctor!")
* ————————————————————————
```

```
FUNCTION Note
PARAMETERS p_message
PRIVATE l_retval,l_talkstat,l_compstat,l_rborder
IF SET("TALK") = "ON"
  SET TALK OFF
  l_talkstat = "ON"
ELSE
  l_talkstat = "OFF"
ENDIF
l_compstat = SET("COMPATIBLE")
SET COMPATIBLE FOXPLUS
l_rborder = SET("READBORDER")
SET READBORDER OFF
* — Define alert window
IF NOT WEXIST("Note") ;
  OR UPPER(WTITLE("NOTE")) == "NOTE.PJX" ;
  OR UPPER(WTITLE("NOTE")) == "NOTE.SCX" ;
  OR UPPER(WTITLE("NOTE")) == "NOTE.MNX" ;
  OR UPPER(WTITLE("NOTE")) == "NOTE.PRG" ;
  OR UPPER(WTITLE("NOTE")) == "NOTE.FRX" ;
  OR UPPER(WTITLE("NOTE")) == "NOTE.QPR"
  DEFINE WINDOW Note ;
              AT  7.778, 17.857  ;
              SIZE 11.000,53.667 ;
              TITLE " Note " ;
              FONT "Geneva", 10 ;
              NOFLOAT ;
              NOCLOSE ;
              DOUBLE
  MOVE WINDOW Note CENTER
ENDIF
* — Display alert window, get response from user
IF WVISIBLE("Note")
  ACTIVATE WINDOW Note SAME
ELSE
  ACTIVATE WINDOW Note NOSHOW
ENDIF
@ 0.667,3.333 SAY p_message ;
              SIZE 7.000,47.333 ;
              FONT "Geneva", 10
```

```
@ 8.500,3.000 GET l_retval ;
              PICTURE "@*HT3 \!OK" ;
              SIZE 1.500,10.429,1.143 ;
              DEFAULT 1 ;
              FONT "Geneva", 10 ;
              STYLE "B"
IF NOT WVISIBLE("Note")
  ACTIVATE WINDOW Note
ENDIF
READ MODAL
RELEASE WINDOW Note
* — Restore old settings
SET READBORDER &l_rborder
IF l_talkstat = "ON"
  SET TALK ON
ENDIF
IF l_compstat = "ON"
  SET COMPATIBLE ON
ENDIF
* — Return result to calling program
RETURN l_retval
* ----------------------------
* ----------------------------
```

Use LockR() to control explicit record locking requests as in the following example:

```
IF RLOCK() .OR. LockR(500)
  REPLACE phone WITH f_phone
  UNLOCK
ELSE
  ??Note("Cannot lock record.  Update canceled...")
ENDIF
```

Similarly, use LockF() to control explicit file locking requests:

```
IF FLOCK() .OR. LockF(500)
  APPEND FROM (g_tmpf0)
  UNLOCK
ELSE
  ??Note("Cannot lock file.  New invoice not saved...")
ENDIF
```

FOXPRO MAC HACK TIP

FoxPro allows expressions to *short circuit*. As soon as FoxPro can determine the result of a logical expression, the evaluation of the expression stops. Consider the following expression:

```
? (1 = 1 .OR. EOF())
```

Since 1 equals 1, the expression evaluates to true. And since 1 = 1 is evaluated first, the FoxPro function EOF() is not evaluated at all.

You can short circuit FoxPro to your advantage. In many cases, your application will call both an internal FoxPro function and a user-defined function. Internal functions run much faster than user-defined functions. Ensuring that the internal functions evaluate first in these cases will help to turbo-charge your multi-user FoxPro Mac application.

In this chapter, I have recommended an explicit locking strategy. To implement this strategy, you will need to have custom record and file locking functions. However, short-circuiting allows you to call these custom functions only when the standard, built-in FoxPro locking functions fail to return a lock. That is why my suggested syntax always looks like this

```
IF RLOCK() .OR. LockR(500)
  REPLACE company WITH f_company
  UNLOCK
ENDIF
```

and not:

```
IF LockR(500)
  REPLACE company WITH f_company
  UNLOCK
ENDIF
```

Call LockR() or LockF() with the -1 argument to continue attempting to retry the lock attempt indefinitely. If you choose to call LockR() or LockF() with a positive argument, you allow the user to interact with the lock resolution process in the event of a failed lock attempt. In this case, both functions call RetryLck(). RetryLck() presents the user the choice to abandon or retry the attempt to lock, as you see in figure 15.8.

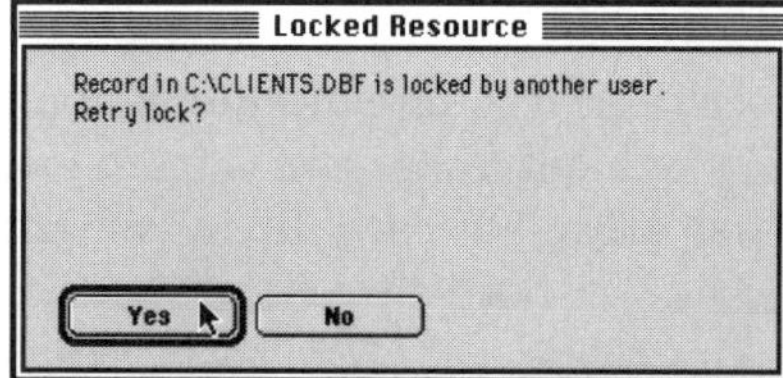

Figure 15.8 *RetryLck() in action.*

If a lock attempt fails, use Note() to tell the user that the update or insert operation has failed. Figure 15.9 shows Note() in action:

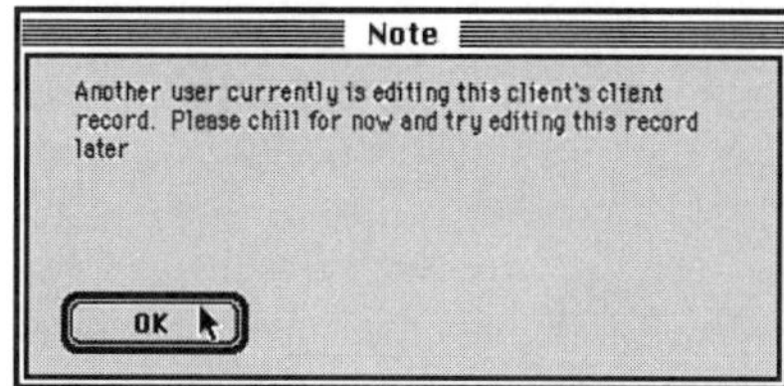

Figure 15.9 *Note() in action.*

Physical Locking, Logical Locking, and Lock Duration

FoxPro's raw tools for resource locking—RLOCK() and FLOCK()—allow you to use the network operating system to control access to a record or file. Because these tools operate at the relatively low level of files and byte ranges within files, they can be said to control physical locking processes. While necessary in many parts of your application, physical locking suffers from several drawbacks.

In contrast to physical locking, logical locking schemes are implemented using custom data structures, custom function calls, and specialized logic that you build into your application. In many cases, you will need to supplement physical locks with logical locks. You need to understand when physical or logical locks are more appropriate and how to apply each locking technique.

Physical Locking Issues

Physical locks are indiscriminate. For example, when you lock a file before using APPEND FROM, you block other users from locking records. Likewise, if an application locks a record during an editing operation, no other users can lock the file. In both cases, there is no real conflict between these users. The limitations of physical locking cause the only problem.

Physical locks are also not natural devices for controlling complex data structures and processes. For example, you probably want only one user at a time to be able to cut checks in an accounts payable application. It is difficult to satisfy this requirement by using only physical locks without placing persistent locks on many resources, and thus blocking all users from doing any other accounts payable activities.

Logical Locks

Since it is hard to control multi-user operations using only physical locking, you need to develop alternative locking procedures. In the FoxPro Mac environment, you can accomplish this by adding logical locking data structures and adhering to certain rules when reading from and writing to these data structures. You alone are responsible for creating and maintaining a coherent logical locking scheme. FoxPro provides neither commands nor functions to specifically support logical locking.

Your data structures form the foundation for logical locking. Therefore, you need to think about logical locking requirements as you design the data structures of your FoxPro application. In the case of simple objects, you may need to add only a single field to a table to support logical locking. In the case of complex objects or processes, you may need to establish separate tables.

Because FoxPro interapplication communications are generally limited to passing messages through data tables, FoxPro logical locking is a passive process. Your application polls data tables to determine an object's status. Because you are using data tables to signal the status of a process, this type of logical locking is also known as *semaphore* locking.

When you are ready to conduct a logical locking operation, you first check the value of a field or fields to see if there is a conflict. If there is not a conflict, update the field or fields to indicate that you are conducting a privileged operation. When you are done with your work, release the logical lock.

Lock Duration: Dynamic vs. Static Locking

A *static* lock is a lock whose duration is dependent on user input. For example, using RLOCK() on a record while a user is editing the record to prevent others from editing the record is a static lock. A *dynamic* lock is a lock made completely under program control, independent of user input from beginning to end. In a dynamic lock, once a resource is locked, changes are written to the database and the resource is immediately unlocked.

Do not use physical locking to support static locking requirements. If you find that you need to lock a resource during user input, you probably need to add data structures to support logical locking.

> **FOXPRO MAC HACK TIP**
>
> Logical locks are maintained by reading and writing values from data tables. It is possible for a user to leave a resource in a logical static lock because of hardware or software failures, preventing others from working with the resource. To deal with this situation, you add features into your system maintenance routines that release all logical locks globally.

Implementing Physical and Logical Locking

The most effective way for you to understand how physical, logical, dynamic, and static locking techniques are used in FoxPro Mac is to see some examples. The following section outlines approaches for controlling three common multi-user problems:

- A simple one-record, one-table object
- A more complex multi-record, multi-table object
- A complex process spanning a number of data tables

Implementing a complete system for physical and logical locking is an involved process entailing the careful consideration of engineering tradeoffs. The approaches below are tailored to OLTP applications requiring a high degree of data integrity and concurrency. These techniques may not be the best ones for your application. Nevertheless, they should prove a useful starting point as you work to develop your own strategy.

Simple Objects

Consider the problem of controlling access to single records within the simple client data table discussed earlier. You need to control multi-user editing and updating for each record within this table while permitting new records to be added.

One approach to this problem is to reserve a record for editing with the RLOCK() function. Before allowing an editing session to begin, you schedule the record for editing by asking for a record lock. If a lock is obtained, you allow the user to begin editing the record. Once the user is ready to commit changes to the table, you update the record and release the record lock.

This approach violates the rule against static physical locking. A static physical record lock prevents other users from locking both the affected record and the data table. You need to add a data structure to support logical locking for this one record object.

The following listing presents a solution to this problem. Add a new field to the client table called `objstat (C(1))`. Use objstat to reserve the record for editing and to signal that an edit is in progress to other users.

```
* — Set up clients table
* — objstat field supports object locking
CREATE TABLE CLIENTS (clientno   N(15,0), ;
                      company    C(35), ;
                      addr1      C(30), ;
                      addr2      C(30), ;
                      city       C(20), ;
                      state      C(10), ;
                      zip        C(10), ;
                      country    C(15), ;
                      phone      C(20), ;
                      objstat    C(1);
                      )
* — Set up indexes for the table
USE CLIENTS EXCLUSIVEINDEX ON clientno TAG clientno
INDEX ON company  TAG company
INDEX ON city     TAG city
INDEX ON state    TAG state
INDEX ON zip      TAG zip
INDEX ON phone    TAG phone
SET ORDER TO 0
* — Insert two records into the table
```

```
* — NOTE: Table is open EXCLUSIVE;
* — no locking required
INSERT INTO CLIENTS (clientno, ;
                     company, ;
                     addr1, ;
                     addr2, ;
                     city, ;
                     state, ;
                     zip, ;
                     country, ;
                     phone, ;
                     objstat;
                     ) ;
              VALUES (1, ;
                      'Freight Movers, Inc.', ;
                      '123 North First Street', ;
                      'Suite 123', ;
                      'Palo Alto', ;
                      'CA', ;
                      '94301', ;
                      SPACE(0), ;
                      '415/999-9999', ;
                      SPACE(0);
                      )
INSERT INTO CLIENTS (clientno, ;
                     company, ;
                     addr1, ;
                     addr2, ;
                     city, ;
                     state, ;
                     zip, ;
                     country, ;
                     phone, ;
                     objstat;
                     ) ;
              VALUES (2, ;
                      'Print Masters Printing', ;
                      '789 South Second Road', ;
                      'Suite 789', ;
                      'Stanford', ;
                      'CA', ;
                      '94305', ;
                      SPACE(0), ;
```

```
                    '415/172-9999', ;
                    SPACE(0);
                    )
* — Here is an abbreviated example
* — of editing using object locks
* — Note physical locking only done dynamically
* — Note logical locking supports static locks
USE CLIENTS SHAREDSET ORDER TO 0
LOCATE FOR clientno = 1
f_clientno = clientno
* — In this example, possible actions are:
* —  "READ" (display record in non-edit mode)
* —  "EDIT" (display record in editable mode)
* —  "SAVE" (write changes out to database)
* —  "DONE" (done working with this record)
l_action   = "READ"
DO WHILE .t.
  SET ORDER TO 0
  LOCATE FOR clientno = f_clientno
  IF FOUND()
    * — Initialize field variables
    f_company  = company
    f_addr1    = addr1
    f_addr2    = addr2
    f_city     = city
    f_state    = state
    f_zip      = zip
    f_country  = country
    f_phone    = phone
    f_objstat  = objstat
  ELSE
    EXIT
  ENDIF
  * — Call screen program
  * — Screen program allows for record display,
  * — record editing, and returns the actions
  * — that the user selected to perform

  DO CLIENTSC.PRG WITH l_action
  * — l_action passed by reference
  * — Note: CLIENTSC causes update of l_action
  DO CASE    CASE l_action = "READ"
```

```
  * — User wants to read values in record

CASE l_action = "EDIT"
  * — User wants to edit record
  * — Place object lock and update mem vars
  * — If object lock is not possible, loop
  l_action = "READ"
  SET ORDER TO 0
  LOCATE FOR clientno = f_clientno
  IF FOUND()
    IF RLOCK() .OR. LockR(500)
      IF objstat = SPACE(1)
        REPLACE objstat WITH "L"
        UNLOCK
        l_action = "EDIT"
      ELSE
        UNLOCK
        ??Note("Record is being edited "+ ;
               "by another user")
      ENDIF
    ELSE
      ??Note("Record is being edited "+ ;
             "by another user")
    ENDIF
  ENDIF
CASE l_action = "SAVE"
  l_action = "READ"
  SET ORDER TO 0
  LOCATE FOR clientno = f_clientno
  IF FOUND() .AND. (RLOCK() .OR. LockR(500))
    REPLACE company WITH f_company, ;
            addr1   WITH f_addr1, ;
            addr2   WITH f_addr2, ;
            city    WITH f_city, ;
            state   WITH f_state, ;
            zip     WITH f_zip, ;
            country WITH f_country, ;
            phone   WITH f_phone , ;
            objstat WITH SPACE(1)
   ELSE
      ??Note("Cannot lock record.  Update "+;
             "of client record cancelled...")
```

```
        ENDIF
     CASE l_action = "DONE"
       * — Done working
       EXIT
     OTHERWISE      * — Safest to leave routine if
       * — we don't know what is going on...
       EXIT
   ENDCASE
ENDDO && WHILE .t.
CLOSE DATABASESRETURN
```

When the user first pulls up the record, your code stores the fields to memory variables and presents the data to the user in READ-only mode. If the user wishes to edit the record, check the `objstat` field. If objstat is blank, reserve the record for editing by dynamically locking the record, updating objstat to 'L' (locked), and immediately unlocking the record. You then display the most current memory variable copies of the fields on-screen with GETs. If the record is unavailable for editing, inform the user with Note() and display the record again using SAYs. When the user is done editing, update the data table fields for the record from the memory variables and release the object lock by clearing objstat.

Complex Objects

A common database problem is the maintenance of master/detail records across multiple tables. For example, an invoice commonly contains global invoice information that resides in a single header record in one table, as well as line items that reside in detail records in a second table.

The issue again is how to reserve an editing session on the invoice without having to use static physical locking techniques. For example, locking the header record in the parent table and the detail records in the child table would prevent either the records or tables from being locked during the user's editing session.

The solution is nearly identical to the method suggested above for reserving a simple object for editing. Add `objstat` to the invoice header table. When you begin editing the invoice, use objstat to reserve both the header and the detail items. When you are done editing, update the header and detail lines and clear the header object lock.

> **FOXPRO MAC HACK TIP**
>
> A *deadlock*, or deadly embrace, results when two users first successfully lock a different resource and then attempt to lock the resource that the other user has already locked. Unless special procedures are in place to de-escalate this situation, neither user gives any ground, and both users are prevented from continuing their work.
>
> Some database management systems automatically detect and resolve deadlocks. For example, both Oracle and Sybase contain deadlock avoidance features. FoxPro neither detects nor avoids deadlocks. As a developer, you are responsible for writing your application in such a way that deadlocks do not develop.
>
> There are at least three ways to avoid deadlocks. One approach is to lock and unlock resources only one at a time. Another method is to attempt to acquire all required locks within a loop, unlocking all resources if any lock attempt within the loop fails, and starting the process again until all locks are obtained. Finally, you can choose to lock all resources within an application in the same order, ensuring that a deadlock can never occur.

Task Locks

Many tasks must be controlled across an application or an entire database installation, even across several separate applications. When such tasks are undertaken, you may need to restrict the number of users performing the task, remove all other users from an application, or remove all other users from the entire installation. To control complex tasks requiring restricted access to an application or installation, use task locks.

Task locks control access to complex operations. Since tasks do not necessarily correspond to existing data tables, you may need to create custom data tables to handle task locking requirements. One approach is to create a system-level data table to control access to tasks.

The next listing details a custom system data table that is generic enough to be used to control task locking across several applications. Some example records have been added to demonstrate implementation details. Figure 15.10 shows a BROWSE view of this table with the sample table loaded. Use this table, or one similar to it, to support task locks in your own application. For each task and module that you wish to track or control, insert a record into the TASKLOCK table. As you perform the task, check and update the correct record in the TASKLOCK table. When you are done with the task, release the task lock.

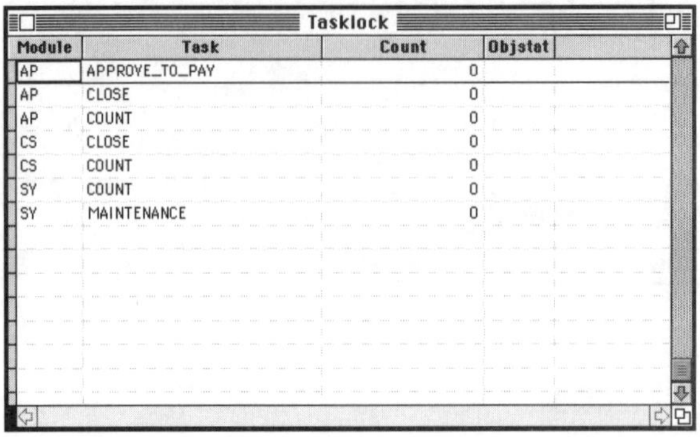

Tasklock

Module	Task	Count	Objstat
AP	APPROVE_TO_PAY	0	
AP	CLOSE	0	
AP	COUNT	0	
CS	CLOSE	0	
CS	COUNT	0	
SY	COUNT	0	
SY	MAINTENANCE	0	

Figure 15.10 *Browse View of Task Locking Data Table.*

```
* — Set up table to support
* — task locking
CREATE TABLE TASKLOCK (module     C(2), ;
                       task       C(20), ;
                       count      N(15,0), ;
                       objstat    C(1);
                       )

* — Set up indexes for the table
USE TASKLOCK EXCLUSIVEINDEX ON module     TAG module
INDEX ON task       TAG task
INDEX ON objstat    TAG objstat
SET ORDER TO 0
* — Insert some representative records
* — into the task locking table
INSERT INTO TASKLOCK (module, ;
                      task, ;
                      count, ;
                      objstat;
                      ) ;
             VALUES ('AP', ;
                      'APPROVE_TO_PAY', ;
                      0, ;
                      SPACE(0);
```

```
                  )

INSERT INTO TASKLOCK (module, ;
                  task, ;
                  count, ;
                  objstat;
                  ) ;
          VALUES ('AP', ;
                  'CLOSE', ;
                  0, ;
                  SPACE(0);
                  )

INSERT INTO TASKLOCK (module, ;
                  task, ;
                  count, ;
                  objstat;
                  ) ;
          VALUES ('AP', ;
                  'COUNT', ;
                  0, ;
                  SPACE(0);
                  )

INSERT INTO TASKLOCK (module, ;
                  task, ;
                  count, ;
                  objstat;
                  ) ;
          VALUES ('CS', ;
                  'CLOSE', ;
                  0, ;
                  SPACE(0);
                  )

INSERT INTO TASKLOCK (module, ;
                  task, ;
                  count, ;
                  objstat;
                  ) ;
          VALUES ('CS', ;
                  'COUNT', ;
```

```
                    0, ;
                    SPACE(0);
                    )

INSERT INTO TASKLOCK (module, ;
                    task, ;
                    count, ;
                    objstat;
                    ) ;
          VALUES ('SY', ;
                    'COUNT', ;
                    0, ;
                    SPACE(0);
                    )

INSERT INTO TASKLOCK (module, ;
                    task, ;
                    count, ;
                    objstat;
                    ) ;
          VALUES ('SY', ;
                    'MAINTENANCE', ;
                    0, ;
                    SPACE(0);
                    )
```

The example shown in this listing provides basic task locking support for two applications and the entire installation. Applications are identified using the `module` field. Currently defined applications are Accounts Payable ("AP") and Customer Service ("CS"). The installation itself is controlled using system-level ("SY") records. Specific tasks within applications are accessed using the `task` field. To access or change the status of any defined task, locate the corresponding record identified by <module, task> and either read or update the count or objstat fields.

Maintain current installation and application user counts with the `count` field. Increment and decrement count as users log in and out. In addition, a closing task has been defined for both AP and CS. Use the objstat flag to control the closing process just like the objstat field in the client table described above. A general maintenance task has also been defined at the system level. Access this task using the objstat field for the record. Finally, you can control access to the accounts payable approve to pay task through the objstat field for that record.

Other Locking Alternatives

Recall that in the examples presented earlier, you check to see if a resource is available, reserve the resource for update, update the resource, and finally release the resource for others to update. Because you check for problems in advance, these examples can be said to illustrate pessimistic resource locking. In *pessimistic* resource locking, you assume that there will be a conflict and deal with the situation in advance.

Programmers sometimes opt to employ an *optimistic* resource locking strategy. An optimistic strategy does not require an explicit reservation before checking out a resource. Instead, your application checks to see whether the resource has been changed by another user between the time that you began your edit and the time you wish to conduct an update. If the application detects a change made by another user, your changes are not committed to the database. This strategy is called optimistic because of the assumption that such collisions will not happen very often.

One way to implement optimistic logical locking is to capture a before-image of all affected records before editing begins. When you are ready to commit changes, physically lock the resources and compare the before image to the current image. If there have been any changes, unlock the resources and reject the user request for update. If there have been no changes, update and unlock the resources. An alternative to this approach is to use a change marker. A change marker is a logical structure that is incremented every time the object that it represents is changed.

Rushmore Multi-User Queries

FoxPro's database optimization technology is known as Rushmore. If you understand how to take advantage of this technology, you will be able to significantly reduce the time required for multi-user queries in your multi-user FoxPro Mac application.

Multi-user queries are usually returned fastest when they are retrieved using Rushmore. However, FoxPro may or may not use Rushmore on any given query. FoxPro follows a number of rules to determine whether it will use Rushmore on any given query. Rushmore's behavior in a multi-user situation doesn't vary from the general Rushmore rules you learned for queries and filter conditions earlier in this book, although following those rules becomes even more critical to your application's performance. It is in your interest to understand how to use these rules to get FoxPro to use Rushmore as often as possible in your queries.

See Also

- "Refining and Optimizing Result Set Conditions," Chapter 9

In those rare cases where you do not want to use Rushmore, you can explicitly disable it. Many FoxPro commands that make use of Rushmore have a NOOPTIMIZE option, which disables Rushmore during the execution of the command. In addition, SET OPTIMIZE OFF globally disengages Rushmore, but this is not recommended.

Chapter Wrap Up

After you have your multi-user application up and running, you may find that there are a number of opportunities to improve performance. As you continue working to optimize multi-user FoxPro, you can begin to consider additional techniques and opportunities for tuning FoxPro performance. The follow suggestions give you a place to start:

Install FoxPro Mac correctly. You may find yourself considering sophisticated techniques to help improve sluggish performance, only to find that FoxPro has not been installed properly on your network. Pay special attention to FoxPro's temporary files.

Don't forget the network. The network is part of the application. You need to ensure that the network has been selected and configured appropriately for multi-user FoxPro Mac. You may be able to make some simple, low-cost improvements to your network that will yield huge performance improvements.

Design and constantly refine appropriate table and index structures. Data structures that have been completely normalized according to academic dictum can perform exceptionally poorly. In many cases, a bit of good old-fashioned, de-normalization will help to improve performance.

Select and stick to a consistent multi-user coding strategy. In this chapter, you have learned some simple multi-user programming techniques. Whatever approach you select, be sure that you select it for the right reasons, and that you use it uniformly.

Exploit Rushmore technology. Rushmore can help you select data very quickly. You need to understand how to write queries that take full advantage of Rushmore. In addition, you may want to selectively add indexes to tables to enable Rushmore to operate most effectively.

Use temporary tables and indexes. You can open temporary tables for exclusive access. In many cases, multi-user reports will run much faster when you move data into temporary tables.

Remember the 80/20 Rule. Troublemakers usually make up a small minority of the population (fewer than 20%), yet they generally account for the vast majority of problems (greater than 80%). You can observe this phenomena in everything from automotive pollution to crime to database performance. Focus your performance-improving labor on the small number of areas that inevitably account for most of the problems, and you'll maximize the results of your effort.

16

USE EXTERNAL COMMANDS AND FUNCTIONS (XCMDS AND XFCNS): ACCESS TO MACINTOSH CAPABILITIES

by
Randy Brown

XCMDs and XFCNs are acronyms for external commands and functions. Think of XCMDs as being similar to FoxPro API libraries. They provide additional commands that do not exist in the native FoxPro language. While FoxPro does support over 600 commands and functions, much of this syntax is limited strictly to database operations. FoxPro offers only minimal access to native operating system calls. For example, FoxPro does not provide the capability to programmatically query or change your Chooser device (this controls your printer, AppleShare and other output devices). An XCMD comes in quite handy for this job, as you saw in Chapter 9.

See Also

- "Output Printed to File," Chapter 9

In addition, FoxPro for Macintosh must rely on its own custom controls, such as check boxes, dialogs, and buttons, to maintain its strong cross-platform compatibility with DOS and Windows. In this chapter I'll show you how to use true Macintosh controls within your FoxPro applications through the use of XCMDs.

First, let's back up and talk a little about the origins of XCMDs and XFCNs. Apple Computer introduced HyperCard back in 1987. It was written by Bill Atkinson (yes, the same guy who wrote MacPaint and has since moved on to new and exciting adventures in future telecommunications with General Magic). HyperCard can be thought of as a structureless kind of database (an application "erector set") in which links to data can be made to and from anywhere (HyperCard files are called "stacks" and each stack can contain many "cards"). HyperCard unfortunately only provided the **HyperTalk** (the native programming language of HyperCard) developer with about 50 commands. However, HyperCard opened up the architecture by allowing smarter developers to write and plug in their own external routines called XCMDs.

Programmers think of commands as performing some sort of action, and functions as returning some sort of value. While the intent of having both XCMDs and XFCNs was to somehow delineate this behavior, no true distinction exists between the two other than their Resource ID Types and their names.

FOXPRO MAC HACK TIP

You should not confuse Resource ID Types with File Types. Both have unique 4 letter codes that are case-sensitive. An XCMD, for example, has a Resource ID Type = 'XCMD'. Resources are contained within the resource fork of any Macintosh file. Some files such as text files (which have a File Type = 'TEXT') typically do not have resource forks. Note: if you try to open one of these in a resource editing application such as ResEdit, you will be prompted to add a new resource fork. Only one resource fork is allowed per file.

Today, you often see XCMDs, which don't perform any sort of action, and XFCNs which do. Maybe Apple should have just come out with XCMDs to avoid all the confusion. If you want guidelines for differentiating between the two forms when you write your own externals, use the following definitions:

- XCMDs: External commands perform some action and return a value, usually an error code.
- XFCNs: External functions may or may not perform action, but always return a value. If the XFCN takes an action, the value returned should reflect an error code, if a problem occurred while this action was taken.

Because of this lack of distinction, treat XCMDs and XFCNs the same when you read about them in books and articles. The one FoxPro difference is a matter of calling syntax in your programs, as you'll see shortly.

With the success of HyperCard and the XCMD standard, many applications adopted support for XCMDs, including FoxBASE+/MAC, to use two advantages. First, developers need only learn this one API standard to add external functionality to their applications. Second, the same XCMD created for HyperCard could run on another XCMD-supporting application.

> **CROSS-PLATFORM WARNING**
>
> Don't expect every XCMD ever written to run perfectly within FoxPro. You should thoroughly test a new XCMD, especially one not written specifically for FoxPro (FoxBASE+/Mac), before you use and distribute it with your application. The main reason is that XCMDs can make direct calls to native commands in the language. For example, I could use the FoxPro BROWSE command in an XCMD. If you run an XCMD created for HyperCard that uses a native HyperTalk command, FoxPro chokes when it comes to this unknown command. Another reason to be suspect to all non-FoxPro XCMDs is that the XCMD structure was expanded beyond that supported by FoxPro. Finally, XCMDs written for older Mac systems may not run properly or at all under System 7.

FoxPro for Macintosh supports only HyperCard 1.0 style XCMDs. The latest versions of HyperCard support an expanded XCMD structure. A new feature is support for external windows. In essence, you now can write an XCMD that has its own window (as a drawing program) and then have the application (or its event loop) recognize this window's existence. As I said, FoxPro does not support this. However, FoxPro has internal API support now, which goes far beyond the current XCMD standard.

The Language of XCMDs According to FoxPro

As you can imagine, there is not a plethora of commands and functions devoted to XCMDs. In fact, you may even be able to memorize all of them:

```
SET XCMDFILE TO ¦<file name>¦
LOAD <xcmd> ¦FUNCTION¦
CALL <xcmd> ¦WITH <parameters>¦ ¦TO <memvar>¦
RELEASE MODULE <xcmd>
```

If you are familiar with FoxBASE+/Mac, you will notice that the following command is not on the list:

```
SET RESOURCE TO ¦<file name>¦
```

This command served not only to register an XCMD container in FoxBASE+/Mac, but also to store any Macintosh resources needed by your application. You could store pictures (PICT resources) and have them appear in your screens and reports. Also, you could embed fonts as resources. FoxPro no longer relies on Macintosh resources primarily because the resources would be unavailable cross-platform (pictures now must be stored as separate files). The only real Mac resources of which FoxPro takes advantage are XCMDs and XFCNs, and FoxPro uses SET RESOURCE TO for another purpose, so the FoxBASE+/Mac SET RESOURCE TO command became SET XCMDFILE TO.

CROSS-PLATFORM WARNING

FoxBASE+/Mac programmers often are confused that SET RESOURCE remains in the FoxPro language but doesn't refer to a resource file in the Macintosh sense. Instead, a **FoxPro resource file** (named FOXUSER.DBF by default) is a regular database table of specified format without a resource fork. FoxPro uses resource tables to remember system window positions and attributes, store diary entries, and other housekeeping chores.

The SET XCMDFILE TO command merely establishes a pointer for FoxPro to locate XCMDs. Unlike the SET LIBRARY command, SET

XCMDFILE cannot load XCMD files in an ADDITIVE fashion. (Only one XCMDFILE can be set at a time.) You can use the SET('XCMDFILE') function to determine if another file is already in effect. Here is a sample routine that uses two XCMDs to play a sound from the Macintosh control panel.

```
* This routine uses two XCMDs to control and
* play the Mac Sound control panel.
*
* Xvolume XCMD
* Copyright © 1990 J. Randolph Brown
*
* Xvolume <Set/Get code>,<soundlevel> - this
* XCMD will set or get the sound volume
* normally adjusted using the control
* panel General cdev. Use "S" or "G" to set
* or get.
* The sound level must be between 0 - 7.
*
* Format:
*  Xvolume <GetVol/SetVol Code> <soundlevel>.
*
* Code is S or G ,
* Soundlevel is 0 - 7 for S only.
*
* Error1.
*  XCMD can only accept 1 parameters (G only)
* Error1.
*  XCMD can only accept 2 parameters (S only)
* Error2.
*  First Parameter must be S or G.
* Error3.
*  New sound level is out of range (0-7).
*
* examples: CALL Xvolume TO merr with S,6
*       CALL Xvolume TO mlevel with G
*
* Xbeep XCMD
* Copyright © 1990 J. Randolph Brown
*
```

```
* Xbeep <beepname>,<beepplays> -
* this plays a specified
* beep <beepname> which is a snd resource
* a certain # of times <beepplays>.
* It searches the resource file,
* then FoxBASE and finally the system
* for the resource.
*
* Format: XBeep <Beepname> <Beepcount>.
*    Beepname is sound,
*    Beepcount is # of times to play.
*
* Error1. Failure to load sound.
*    System Error:  error
*    (Note: see Mac manual for code)
* Error2. Beepcount must be greater then zero.
*
* examples:
*   CALL Xbeep TO merr with Clink-Klank,6
*   CALL Xbeep TO merr with Simple Beep,2
*

PRIVATE m.oldvol,m.savexfile
m.savexfile=SET('XCMDFILE')
SET XCMDFILE TO Fxuser
LOAD xvolume
LOAD xbeep
CALL xvolume WITH "G" TO m.oldvol
CALL xvolume WITH "S",4
CALL xbeep WITH "Sosumi",3
CALL xvolume WITH "S",m.oldvol
RELEASE MODULE xvolume
RELEASE MODULE xbeep
IF EMPTY(m.savexfile)
  SET XCMDFILE TO
ELSE
  SET XCMDFILE TO (m.savexfile)
ENDIF
```

You should get in the habit of error checking important XCMDs that impact other commands. In this example, if the sound failed to load, no real harm is done. On the other hand, if you are relying on the XCMD to return a proper value before continuing, you had better make sure to check the value returned by the XCMD. Be aware that XCMDs always return values as character data type. If you are checking for a numeric return value, you can check for the string equivalent of the return or you can compare the VAL() of the return to the value you want:

```
CALL myxcmd TO m.retval

IF m.retval = '1'
...
ENDIF
* or:
IF VAL(m.retval) = 1
...
ENDIF
```

Sources of XCMDs

If you are like most people, you probably don't want to write your own XCMDs. You'd just like to accumulate a neat collection of these externals in case you ever need one for a special purpose. I've put a starter set of more useful XCMDs on the source disk for this book. Many of these are from the excellent FoxBASE+/Mac public domain FoxTools 1.5 XCMD Library (I would like to thank Microsoft for making obsolete the need for many of the memo-field related XCMDs).

See Also

- Source Disk:XCMDS Folder

If you have access to CompuServe's FoxForum, the forum libraries have many public domain XCMDs you can download. CompuServe also has many Macintosh forums that contain huge selections of HyperCard XCMDs. Remember, many of these will not work with FoxPro, but you should be able to find some very useful ones. Other on-line services such as GEnie and America OnLine also have libraries of HyperCard XCMDs.

XCMDs vs. the FoxPro API

Before embarking on the task of rolling your own XCMDs, consider some of the differences between XCMDs and FoxPro API functions. If you're a person interested in writing externals for FoxPro, you should weigh the pros and cons of choosing XCMDs vs. the FoxPro API, as shown in table 16.1. Microsoft has chosen to support XCMDs primarily for backward compatibility with their FoxBASE+/Mac product, but that doesn't mean that you should neglect XCMDs as an option.

Table 16.1

Comparison of XCMDs vs APIs for Adding External Functionality to FoxPro

XCMDs	*FoxPro API*
Only one XCMDFILE allowed at a time via the SET XCMDFILE command.	Multiple libraries can be opened one at a time using the SET LIBRARY command.
Must use LOAD and CALL commands.	Can call API routines just like common UDFs and system functions.
A maximum of 16 XCMDs/XFCNs can be loaded at a time.	Unlimited API functions can be loaded.
Accesses the Mac ToolBox libraries.	Accesses both Mac ToolBox and FoxPro internal libraries.
Can be used by other applications which support XCMDs.	Used only within FoxPro, but can easily be ported to DOS and Windows versions of FoxPro.
Pre-existing wealth of XCMDs in commercial and public domain libraries.	Limited availability of API routines.

Writing XCMDs

An XCMD is what is known as a **code resource** (other types include inits and cdevs). It is a segment of code that cannot run on its own, but must be called by the currently running application (such as FoxPro or HyperCard). Because it cannot run on its own, it must exist within a file. When you build an XCMD, you actually create just the resource itself in a file specified by the development environment, as shown in figure 16.1. These segments are usually written in C, C++, or Pascal, but can also be written in BASIC or Assembler.

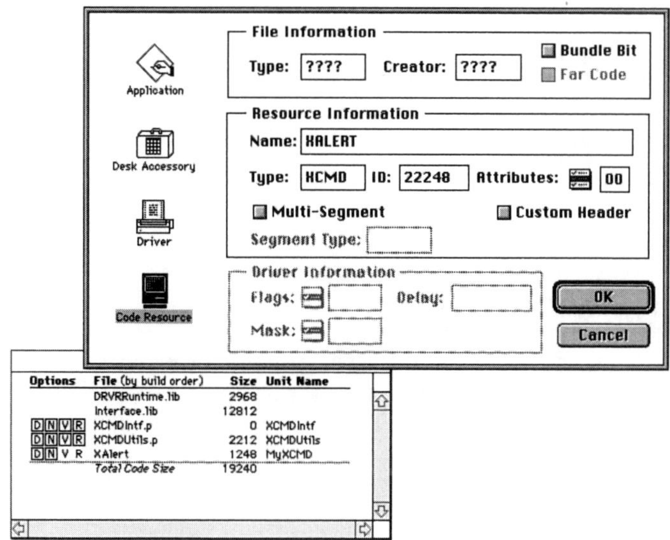

Figure 16.1 *THINK Pascal dialog to set XCMD resource information.*

This section contains the necessary elements for writing an XCMD. The programming language used for all code here is THINK Pascal (users of other languages such as C++ will need to make adjustments). Generally, all elements of the XCMD interface are contained in separate files (see table 16.2) and are linked and compiled together by the programming software. This approach is very similar to the Project Manager used in FoxPro (one fortunate difference: most of these development platforms include #INCLUDE compiler directives). The result of compilation is the XCMD code resource, which is then stored in a resource file to be later called within your FoxPro routine.

Table 16.2
Internal components of an XCMD

Internal components of an XCMD
Parameter Block
XCMD Glue Routines
XCMD Code

XCmdBlock Record

The XCmdBlock, shown here in Pascal, provides the actual interface XCMD parameter block. Through this structure, the XCMD passes its parameters back and forth to FoxPro and the Macintosh OS.

```
XCmdPtr = ^XCmdBlock;
XCmdBlock = record
   paramCount: INTEGER;
   params: array[1..16] of Handle;
   returnValue: Handle;
   passFlag: BOOLEAN;

   entryPoint: ProcPtr;
   request: INTEGER;
   result: INTEGER;
   inArgs: array[1..8] of LongInt;
   outArgs: array[1..4] of LongInt;

   {FoxBASE+/Mac Unique Fields}

   version: INTEGER;
   options: INTEGER;
   onscreen: WindowPtr;
   offscreen: Grafptr;
   printRec: THPrint;
   printPort : TPPrPort;
   foxuser: INTEGER;
   setresource: INTEGER;
   utillong1: LongInt;
   utillong2: LongInt;
```

```
utillong3: LongInt;
utillong4: LongInt;
utilhandle1: Handle;
utilhandle2: Handle;
utilhandle3: Handle;
utilhandle4: Handle;
publong: LongInt;
pubhandle: Handle;
reserved1: LongInt;
reserved2: LongInt;
END;
```

FoxPro does not include any documentation on the details of the XCmdBlock structure. FoxBASE+/Mac manuals and HyperCard XCMD books contain details of these field definitions.

XCMD Glue Routines

These routines are a set of standard routines you can use to manipulate data within your XCMD. When writing your XCMDs, you should make extensive use of these functions because they help manipulate and convert data being passed to and from FoxPro and the Macintosh OS. There are over 30 routines. Here are a few of the more common ones:

function PasToZero (paramPtr: XCmdPtr; str: Str255): Handle;

- Converts a Pascal string into a zero-terminated one.

procedure ZeroToPas (paramPtr: XCmdPtr; zeroStr: Ptr; var pasStr: Str255);

- Converts a zero-terminated string to a Pascal string.

function StrToLong (paramPtr: XCmdPtr; str: Str31): LongInt;

- Converts a Pascal string of type Str31 to an unsigned long integer.

function EvalExpr (paramPtr: XCmdPtr; expr: Str255): Handle;

- Evaluates a FoxPro expression within the XCMD. The result field in the XCmdBlock can be used to check for call success.

procedure SendCardMessage (paramPtr: XCmdPtr; msg: Str255);

- Similar to EvalExpr except it is a procedure.

function GetFieldByName (paramPtr: XCmdPtr; cardFieldFlag: BOOLEAN; fieldName: Str255): Handle;

- Returns a handle to the contents of a FoxPro database field specified by the field name. All field types can be accessed including memo and picture fields. The options field in the XCmdBlock must be set properly when working with picture fields.

procedure SetFieldByName (paramPtr: XCmdPtr; cardFieldFlag: BOOLEAN; fieldName: Str255; fieldVal: Handle);

- Similar to GetFieldByName except that it writes the contents of the handle to the field specified.

function GetGlobal (paramPtr: XCmdPtr; globName: Str255): Handle;

- Returns a handle to the contents of a memory variable.

procedure SetGlobal (paramPtr: XCmdPtr; globName: Str255; globValue: Handle);

- Sets the value of a memory variable to the contents of the handle.

Sample XCMD Code

The following Pascal code is for an XCMD that displays a standard Macintosh alert dialog. This XCMD works similarly to the FxAlert() routine in the FOXTOOLS.MLB API library. When the XCMD is called, it displays a standard alert dialog from the Macintosh Toolbox. The XCMD has certain preset dialog resources (see CONST section below), which correspond to the 12 dialogs available in FoxBASE+/Mac's ALERT NOTE command. Following the code, we will look at expanding the functionality of this XCMD by using ResEdit to create custom dialog boxes available for the XCMD to call.

```
UNIT MyXCMD;
{XCMD Template Code}
{File name:xalert.Pas    }
{History: 09/93 Original by Randy Brown. }

INTERFACE
  USES
    XCmdIntf, XCmdUtils;
```

```
  PROCEDURE Main (paramPtr: XCmdPtr);

IMPLEMENTATION

 PROCEDURE TheXCMD (paramPtr: XCmdPtr);

  VAR
   message, alrtparm, alrtdlog, retstr, mystr: str255;
   ParamStr, Parm0, Parm1, Parm2, Parm3: str255;
   atype, adlog, myerr, theItem, alertID: integer;
   tempHandle: handle;

  CONST
   LargeOK = 5877;
   SmallOK = 5878;
   LargeYes = 5879;
   SmallYes = 5880;
   LargeCon = 5881;
   SmallCon = 5882;
   LargeNo = 5883;
   SmallNo = 5884;
   LargeYesCan = 5885;
   LargeNoCan = 5886;
   SmallYesCan = 5887;
   SmallNoCan = 5888;

 PROCEDURE FAIL (errStr: Str255);
 BEGIN
   paramPtr^.returnValue := PasToZero(paramPtr, errStr);
   EXIT(TheXCMD)
 END;

  PROCEDURE WrongFormat;
   VAR
    rt, str1, str2, str3, str4, str5: str255;
  BEGIN
   rt := chr(13);
   str1 := 'XALERT Format:';
   str2 := '  CALL xalert WITH <C1>[,<C2>][,<N2>]';
   str3 := '  <C1> - alert message';
   str4 := '  <C2> - alert type (stop,caution,note)';
   str5 := '  <N2> - alert dialog id (1-12)';
```

```
  parm0 := CONCAT(str1,rt,str2,rt,str3,rt,str4,rt,str5);
  ParamText(parm0, '', '', '');
  alertID := LargeOK;
  theItem := Alert(alertID, NIL);
  Fail('Error: Incorrect XCMD format.');
 END;


BEGIN

 InitCursor;                {Make an arrow cursor}

 IF paramPtr^.paramCount = 0 THEN
  WrongFormat;

 ZeroToPas(paramPtr, paramPtr^.params[1]^, parm0);

 IF paramPtr^.paramCount = 1 THEN
  atype := 0
 ELSE
  BEGIN
   ZeroToPas(paramPtr, paramPtr^.params[2]^, alrtparm);
   IF LENGTH(alrtparm) = 1 THEN
    BEGIN
     IF StringEqual(paramPtr, 'S', alrtparm) THEN
      atype := 1
     ELSE IF StringEqual(paramPtr, 'C', alrtparm) THEN
      atype := 2
     ELSE IF StringEqual(paramPtr, 'N', alrtparm) THEN
      atype := 3
     ELSE
      atype := 4
    END
   ELSE
    BEGIN
     IF StringEqual(paramPtr, 'stop', alrtparm) THEN
      atype := 1
     ELSE IF StringEqual(paramPtr,'caution',alrtparm) THEN
      atype := 2
     ELSE IF StringEqual(paramPtr, 'note', alrtparm) THEN
      atype := 3
```

```
    ELSE
     atype := 4
   END
  END;

IF paramPtr^.paramCount < 3 THEN
 alertID := LargeOK
ELSE
 BEGIN
  ZeroToPas(paramPtr, paramPtr^.params[3]^, alrtdlog);
  adlog := StrToNum(paramPtr, alrtdlog);
  CASE adlog OF
   1:
     alertID := SmallCon;
   2:
     alertID := SmallOK;
   3:
     alertID := SmallYes;
   4:
     alertID := SmallNo;
   5:
     alertID := SmallYesCan;
   6:
     alertID := SmallNoCan;
   7:
     alertID := LargeCon;
   8:
     alertID := LargeOK;
   9:
     alertID := LargeYes;
   10:
     alertID := LargeNo;
   11:
     alertID := LargeYesCan;
   12:
     alertID := LargeNoCan;
   OTHERWISE
         alertID := adlog;
  END;
 END;
```

```
 ParamText(Parm0, '', '', '');
 CASE atype OF
  1:
    theItem := StopAlert(alertID, NIL);
  2:
    theItem := CautionAlert(alertID, NIL);
  3:
    theItem := NoteAlert(alertID, NIL);
  OTHERWISE
    theItem := Alert(alertID, NIL);
 END;

 retstr := NumToStr(paramPtr, theItem);
 paramPtr^.returnValue := PasToZero(paramPtr, retstr);

END;

PROCEDURE Main;
BEGIN
 TheXCMD(paramPtr);
END;
END.                                {End of unit}
```

The dialog you see in figure 16.2 comes up if you call the XCMD without any parameters. For those programmers new to writing XCMDs, you might want to take this approach of displaying an alert of proper parameters as part of the error handling for your XCMDs.

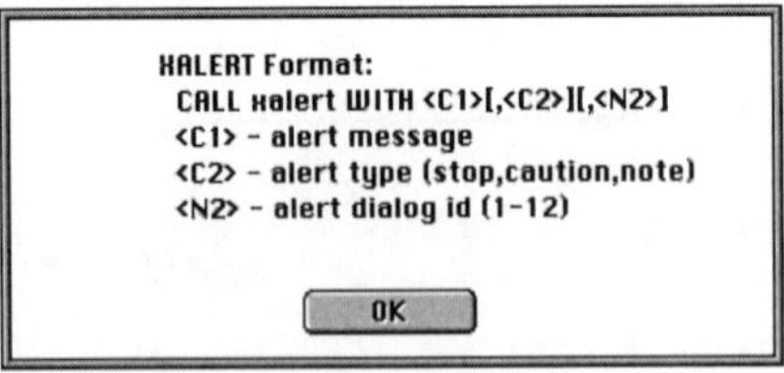

Figure 16.2 *Xalert XCMD shows required parameters if you call the XCMD without parameters.*

The Xalert XCMD actually supports more than the standard 12 alerts shown in table 16.3. You can create your own custom alerts using ResEdit. The third parameter (<N2>), if passed a number other than 1-12, can also be the Resource ID code for this custom alert.

Table 16.3
Xalert XCMD ALRT Dialog Options

Alert Size	*Button 1*	*Button 2*	*Button 3*
Small	Continue		
Small	OK		
Small	Yes *	No	
Small	Yes	No *	
Small	Yes *	No	Cancel
Small	Yes	No *	Cancel
Large	Continue		
Large	OK		
Large	Yes *	No	
Large	Yes	No *	
Large	Yes *	No	Cancel
Large	Yes	No *	Cancel

** default*

The XCMD is stored in a file called XREZ along with DITL and ALRT resources. It is these resources that can be edited to provide your own user defined alerts. Figure 16.3 shows the resources that appear when you open the XREZ file in ResEdit.

To add your own new alerts, simply copy existing DITL and ALRT resources to create new ones (see figure 16.4). The ALRT resource contains the resource describing the alert window. The DITL is a resource that houses a list of dialog controls. It is important that each of these new resources be tied together. You should probably give them the same number (make sure to renumber the DITL reference number in the ALRT resource so that it accurately refers to the correct DITL resource). Pass this new ALRT Resource ID number to the Xalert XCMD.

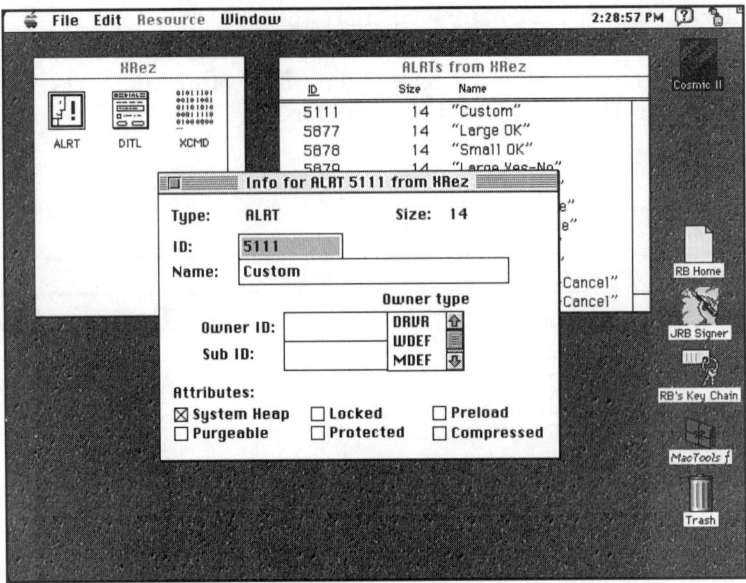

Figure 16.3 *The XREZ file opened in ResEdit shows Xalert XCMD and related resources.*

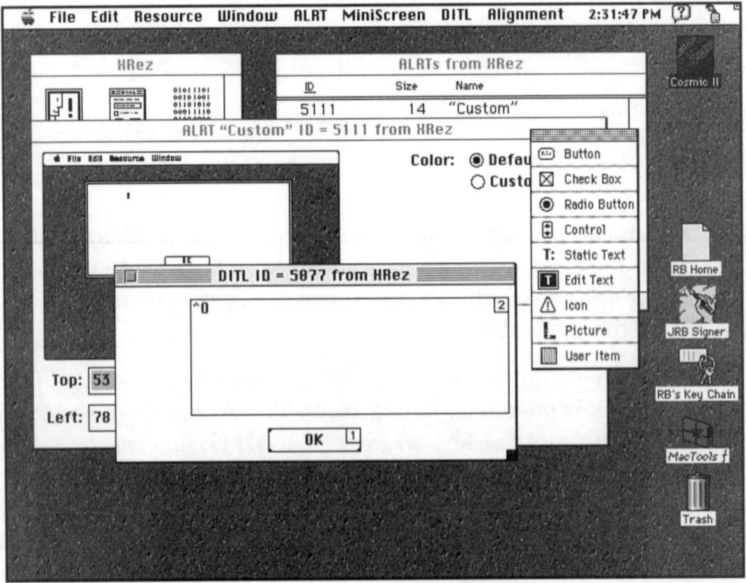

Figure 16.4 *Editing ALRT resources for Xalert XCMD in ResEdit.*

Chapter Wrap Up

XCMDs can still add great power to your applications even though their function has been partially superseded by FoxPro's API. If you have distributable applications that need external boosts and you don't have a license from Apple to bundle ASLM, you should look at XCMDs. With the abundance of XCMDs from the HyperCard libraries, you may not even need to write your own. If you do write your own XCMDs, consider sharing them with others.

17

ADD FUNCTIONALITY WITH LIBRARIES (MLBS): THE FOXPRO LIBRARY CONSTRUCTION KIT

by John R. "Doc" Livingston

FoxPro for Macintosh supplies an immense wealth of tools for your database development needs, right from the box. FoxPro's built-in power tools, rich language, and elegant user interface provide a strong base to begin developing powerful database applications. However, no application development environment can supply you with all of the facilities that you ever will require. There are times you'll want to extend the power of FoxPro Mac by creating and adding your own tools. The FoxPro Library Construction Kit (LCK) is one of the best ways to extend the power of FoxPro.

In this chapter, you'll learn how to use the FoxPro LCK to add external C routines to FoxPro for Macintosh. You'll learn the following:

- What the FoxPro LCK is.
- What the LCK does.
- How the LCK works.

- When and when not to use the LCK to write external routines.
- How to install the LCK and other required tools on your Macintosh.
- How FoxPro and FoxPro external function libraries communicate.
- How to use the LCK to write external libraries of C routines that you can integrate into your FoxPro Mac application by using the external FoxPro Application Programming Interface (API).

The FoxPro LCK

In this section, you'll explore some FoxPro Mac LCK basics. You'll learn about each of the LCK's major components, how these components work together to allow you to build shared library resources, how to access shared libraries from FoxPro, and how the LCK API differs from FoxPro Mac's HyperCard external command and external function interface.

What the LCK Is

The FoxPro LCK consists of a series of header files, library files, and tools that allow you to use the C language to write external FoxPro API functions. The FoxPro LCK for the Macintosh runs only in the Macintosh Programmer's Workshop (MPW) environment, using the MPW C compiler and the Apple Shared Library Manager (ASLM) interface and tools. The FoxPro Mac LCK works only with MPW C. It does not work with THINK C, Aztec C, or any other Macintosh C language development system.

> **FOXPRO MAC HACK TIP**
>
> The MPW environment may be a bit new to you. In the examples in this chapter, you'll learn to use only the basic MPW features required for writing, compiling, and linking FoxPro Mac API routines. If you would like a more in-depth introduction to the MPW environment and MPW C, consider *Programmer's Guide to MPW, Volume I*, by Mark Andrews (ISBN 0-201-57011-4) (Addison-Wesley Publishing Company, Inc.).

You need to understand that the FoxPro Mac LCK actually requires four separate components: MPW, MPW C, the ASLM developer's tools, and the FoxPro Mac LCK itself. In addition, if you want to do debugging, you need either MacsBug or the Apple Symbolic Application Debugging Environment (SADE).

The FoxPro Mac LCK disk contains both the LCK files and the ASLM developer's tools. MPW and MPW C are sold separately by Apple Computer through APDA. In addition, APDA supplies both MacsBug and SADE. Although all of these products are available separately from APDA, you may find it more convenient and cost-effective to license them as a bundle. E.T.O.: Essentials•Tools•Objects (ETO) is a subscription service available from APDA that will provide you with all the tools required by the FoxPro LCK to write FoxPro external API functions in the Mac environment.

FOXPRO MAC HACK TIP

ETO is available from APDA, Apple Computer, Inc., P.O. Box 319, Buffalo, NY 14207-9974, (800) 282-2732. ETO complete subscription package: part number M0895LL/C ($1295.00); Annual ETO subscription renewal: part number R0076LL/B ($400.00). Both the initial and annual subscriptions provide three issues of a CD-ROM containing all of the latest tools.

What the LCK Does

The FoxPro Mac LCK permits you to build shared library routines conforming to the Apple ASLM interface and the FoxPro API. Once built, these routines are dynamically linked into the FoxPro Mac environment through the Apple ASLM client software. After dynamic linking, these routines appear as built-in functions in FoxPro Mac.

The FoxPro LCK provides structures for communicating between your external C routines and FoxPro. In addition, it contains a rather extensive number of library routines that allow you to directly access FoxPro's internals from C. Finally, libraries written using the LCK can directly access the Macintosh user interface toolbox and operating system routines.

How the LCK Works

In the MPW environment, you begin by writing C routines conforming to the FoxPro Mac LCK API. Using the standard MPW C compiler and the FoxPro API header files, you compile these routines to object files. Finally, your object files are linked with the FoxPro API library files and the ASLM library files using the Apple BuildSharedLibrary tool, creating a shared library file with the .MLB extension. These steps are most conveniently accomplished using an MPW makefile.

The shared library file is made available to FoxPro by simply dropping it into the Extensions folder within each client computer's System folder. Shared library routines are then available to FoxPro Mac as conventional FoxPro functions.

Applicable FoxPro Commands

FoxPro Mac API library routines are not available to FoxPro Mac until they are dynamically-linked to FoxPro at run time. Use SET LIBRARY to open an external API routine and publish the functions within the routine to FoxPro. The full syntax is:

```
SET LIBRARY TO [<filename> [ADDITIVE]]
```

To activate an API library, `SET LIBRARY TO <filename>`. Include the ADDITIVE clause to keep any previously opened libraries available as additional libraries are activated. To confirm that your API libraries and functions have been registered with FoxPro, use `LIST STATUS` or `DISPLAY STATUS`. Either `LIST` or `DISPLAY STATUS` includes entries confirming all active API routines. To deactivate all API routines, use the command `SET LIBRARY TO` (without specifying a file name or `ADDITIVE`). To deactivate a single API routine, use the command `RELEASE LIBRARY <filename>`.

See Also

- FUNCTION SetLib,Source Disk:Library/Template Code:MAIN.PRG

CROSS-PLATFORM WARNING

Unlike FoxPro for DOS and Windows, the initial shipping version of FoxPro for Macintosh does not check to see if a library is already available before loading the library with the ADDITIVE keyword. If you SET LIBRARY TO a library repeatedly, you can end up with a `too many instances` error, not to mention the waste of memory this entails.

This problem is the cause of the crashes you'll get with the FXALERT conversion function the Migration Kit writes, as described by Andy in Chapter 2. Lisa's generic library-loading function in the template code for this book avoids the problem by checking SET ("LIBRARY") before loading any library. The check shouldn't be necessary, and is probably a bug, but you should follow this strategy just in case.

CROSS-PLATFORM WARNING

The SET LIBRARY command changes in FoxPro 2.6 to accommodate the addition of a single FoxPro procedure file for compatibility with dBASE IV. The FoxPro-specific ADDITIVE keywork on SET LIBRARY, however, doesn't appear to allow you to add more than one FoxPro procedure file to the library list.

You may have been working in FoxPro cross platform before upgrading to FoxPro 2.6. If so, remember to bracket any SET LIBRARY calls to a FoxPro procedure file that you write for the use of FoxPro 2.6 Windows or DOS.

See Also

- "Bracketing Code For Cross-Platform Applications," Chapter 11;
- "FoxPro for Macintosh 2.6 and Beyond," Appendix E

FoxPro assumes the extensions .PLB for MS-DOS libraries, .FLL for Windows libraries, and .MLB for Macintosh libraries. API libraries compiled for MS-DOS or Windows cannot be used with FoxPro Mac. However, in many cases source files for MS-DOS and Windows can be recompiled in the FoxPro Mac LCK environment for use with FoxPro Mac.

The LCK Versus the External Commands and Functions

XCMDs and XFCNs are routines developed to the Macintosh HyperCard API specification, also known as the XCMD API. While the FoxPro Mac LCK API interface is relatively new and is tailored to the requirements of the FoxPro developer, the XCMD API has been around for a much longer time, and is a generic standard for Macintosh applications. As a FoxPro developer, you can choose either the XCMD API or the FoxPro API to add external routines to your FoxPro Mac application.

The XCMD API is useful for taking advantage of XCMDs and XFCNs that have already been written by others for the Macintosh-only environment. The LCK API interface is the preferred approach for constructing new external routines because of its robustness, more flexible API, and compatibility with the DOS and Windows world. Consider the following issues when evaluating the best approach for your needs:

- *Availability of prebuilt tools.* Because there are a large number of XCMDs already written, you may be able to find a prebuilt, reliable XCMD to perform the task that you have in mind. FoxPro's XCMD API enables you to use the XCMD with FoxPro immediately. Here the XCMD is probably preferable to the LCK approach. You don't have to reinvent the wheel.
- *Access to the Macintosh operating system, user interface toolbox, and FoxPro internals.* Both the XCMD and the LCK interfaces provide access to the Mac OS and user interface toolbox. However, only the LCK interface provides clean access to FoxPro's internals.
- *Plug and play compatibility with DOS and Windows libraries.* XCMDs can only be used on the Macintosh. FoxPro LCK source code written for use with DOS or Windows can be recompiled for the Macintosh using the FoxPro Mac LCK.
- *API flexibility and robustness.* The LCK interface and tools are designed specifically to work with FoxPro. The data structures used to communicate between FoxPro and external libraries created with the LCK are very flexible, and the interface and tools are quite robust. On the other hand, the XCMD API is not designed especially for use with FoxPro. The XCmdBlock structure used to pass information to and from the XCMD and FoxPro can be quite limiting for FoxPro applications.

System Requirements

To create, test, and use external libraries with the FoxPro Mac LCK, you need to be able to operate both the LCK and FoxPro Mac. Minimum requirements for this complete development environment are:

- A Macintosh equipped with a Motorola 68020 CPU or higher.
- 4 MB of RAM (8 MB is recommended).
- Macintosh System 7.1 or later.
- Microsoft FoxPro for the Macintosh version 2.5 or later.
- Apple Shared Library Manager (ASLM) client software version 1.0 or later. The ASLM client software is shipped with FoxPro Mac.
- Macintosh Programmer's Workshop (MPW) version 3.2 or later (version 3.3 or later is recommended).
- MPW C version 3.2 or later (version 3.3 or later is recommended).
- ASLM Developer Tools. The ASLM Developer Tools are shipped on the FoxProLCK diskette. They are also included with ETO.
- FoxPro LCK Tools. These are also included on the FoxProLCK disk.
- (Optional) MacsBug, version 6.2 or later, is also available with the ETO package.

Installation

To get started with the FoxPro LCK, you need to install and configure a number of separate tools. I assume that you have already installed FoxPro Mac, that you have not installed MPW, and that you will be using ETO to install MPW and the related MPW tools. To install the complete LCK environment, you need to accomplish the following tasks:

- Confirm that FoxPro Mac has been properly installed, including the ASLM.
- Install MPW and MPW C.
- Install the ASLM developer's tools.
- Install the FoxPro LCK.
- (Optional) Install MacsBug.

To accomplish these tasks, complete the instructions that follow. The process described here varies slightly from the installation outlined in Microsoft's FoxPro LCK documentation. These variances allow you to isolate the ASLM tools from the rest of the MPW environment and will permit you to organize your libraries as clearly defined, stand-alone projects.

Step 1: Confirm Your FoxPro Mac Installation

You need to have a working copy of FoxPro Mac to test your FoxPro Mac LCK projects. Make sure that FoxPro Mac has been installed and configured properly. The installation procedure is outlined in Chapter 15 of this book.

Step 2: Install the ASLM Client Software

Ensure that you have the most recent version of the ASLM client software installed on your Mac.

FoxPro for Macintosh 2.5 has a separate ASLM Install disk. FoxPro 2.6's installation routine integrates the installation of the ASLM with its installation of the base product. The ASLM itself did not change between FoxPro Mac 2.5 and 2.6; only the installation did. If you use FoxPro 2.5's ASLM Install disk, or any other updated copy of the ASLM Installer you receive from Apple or other sources, insert the Apple Shared Library Manager diskette into your Mac's floppy disk drive. Double-click on the Installer icon (see figure 17.1). Select the Install button from the ASLM Installation dialog (see figure 17.2). The Apple Shared Library Manager and all required resources will be installed on your Macintosh, and any outdated files will be removed.

Figure 17.1 *The ASLM Installer.*

CROSS-PLATFORM WARNING

If you have installed an earlier version of the ASLM client software with other programs, make sure that you update your ASLM software using the version that came with FoxPro or a later version, if you have one. If you did not install FoxPro with extensions off, the update may not have occurred properly. You need to install the ASLM with extensions off, whether you're installing it separately with FoxPro 2.5 or automatically with later versions of the product.

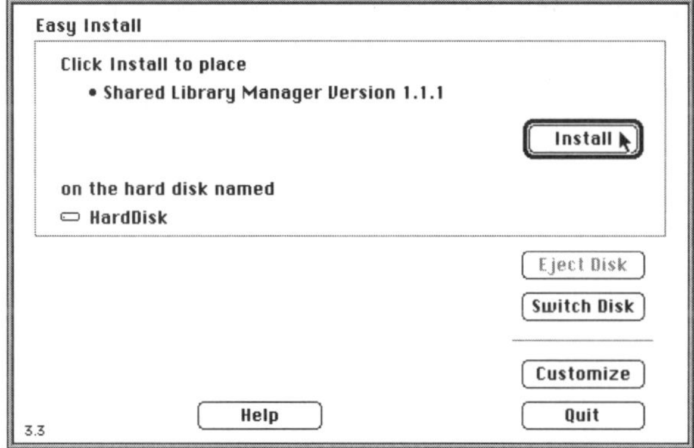

Figure 17.2 *ASLM Installer options.*

Step 3: Install MPW and MPW C

ETO contains MPW and MPW C. A complete MPW installation from your ETO CD-ROM makes both MPW and MPW C, as well as many other tools, available. To install MPW and MPW C, simply locate the "Latest MPW" on your ETO disk, create an MPW folder on your Macintosh, and copy the contents of "Latest MPW" to the MPW folder on your Mac (see figure 17.3).

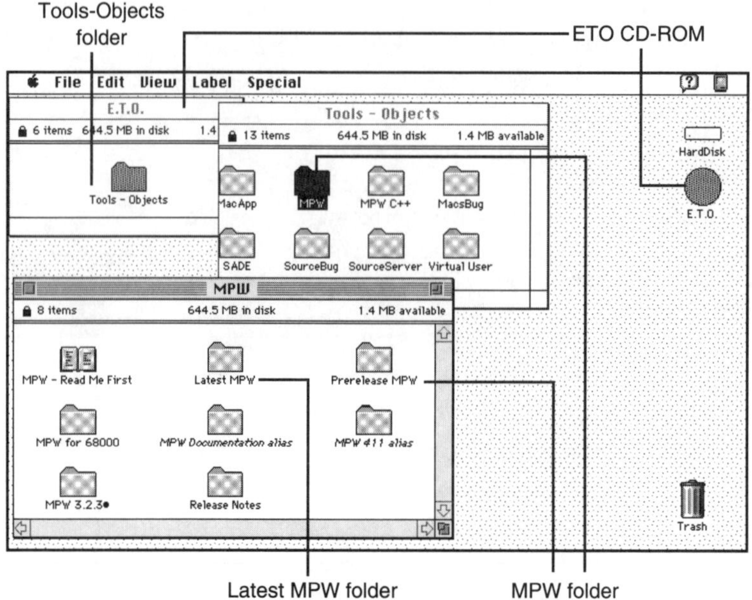

Figure 17.3 *MPW and MPW C installation.*

Step 4: Install the ASLM Developer Tools

Before you can use the FoxProLCK in the MPW environment, you need to install the ASLM developer tools in MPW. The ASLM developer tools are contained in the FoxProLCK disk. Insert the FoxProLCK disk into your Macintosh's floppy diskette drive. Open the ASLM Developer Tools folder of the FoxProLCK disk. You see 3 folders: Interfaces, Libraries, and Tools (see figure 17.4).

Copy these folders into MPW using the following procedure:

1. Create an SLMInterfaces folder within the Interfaces folder of MPW. Copy the contents of the Interfaces folder from the FoxProLCK disk into the newly-created SLMInterfaces folder (see figure 17.5).

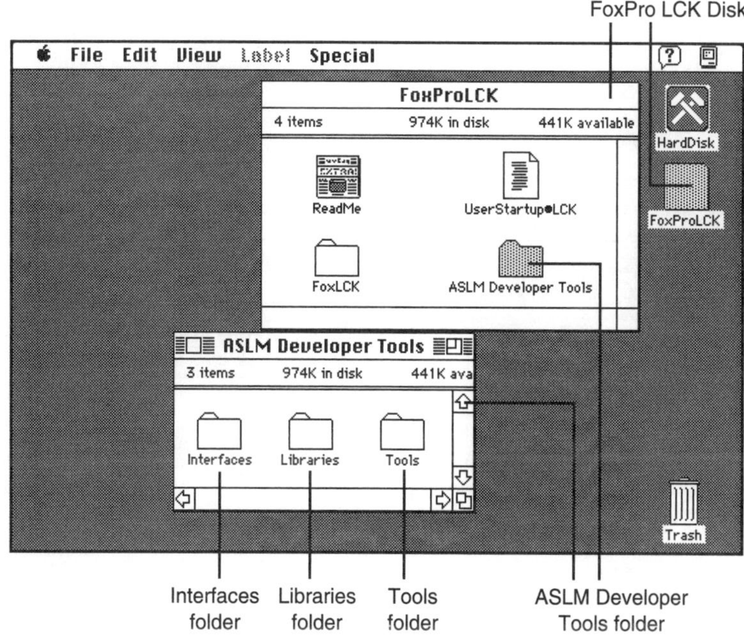

Figure 17.4 *ASLM Developer Tools.*

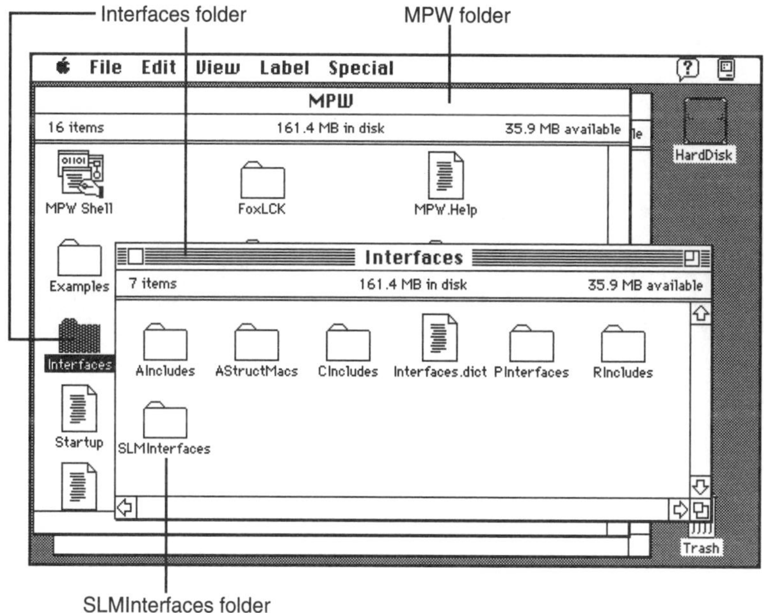

Figure 17.5 *MPW SLMInterfaces Installation.*

2. Create an SLMLibraries folder within the Libraries folder of MPW. Copy the contents of the Libraries folder from the FoxProLCK disk into the newly-created SLMLibraries folder (see figure 17.6).

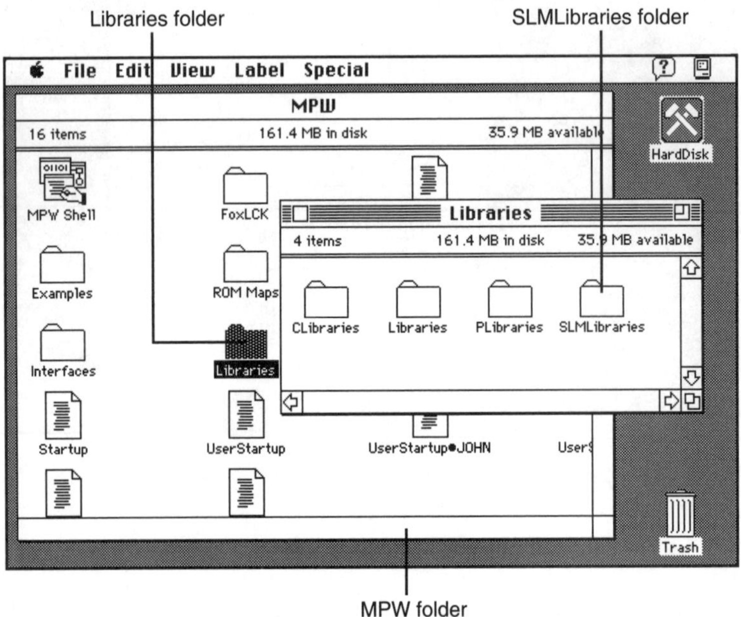

Figure 17.6 MPW SLMLibraries Installation.

3. Create an SLMTools folder within the Tools folder of MPW. Copy the contents of the Tools folder from the FoxProLCK disk into the newly-created SLMTools folder (see figure 17.7).

Note that the procedures described above vary slightly from those described in the Microsoft FoxPro Mac LCK documentation. The installation process outlined here helps you to isolate the ASLM developer tools from the generic MPW tools. This will help keep you organized when you change the configuration of MPW in the future.

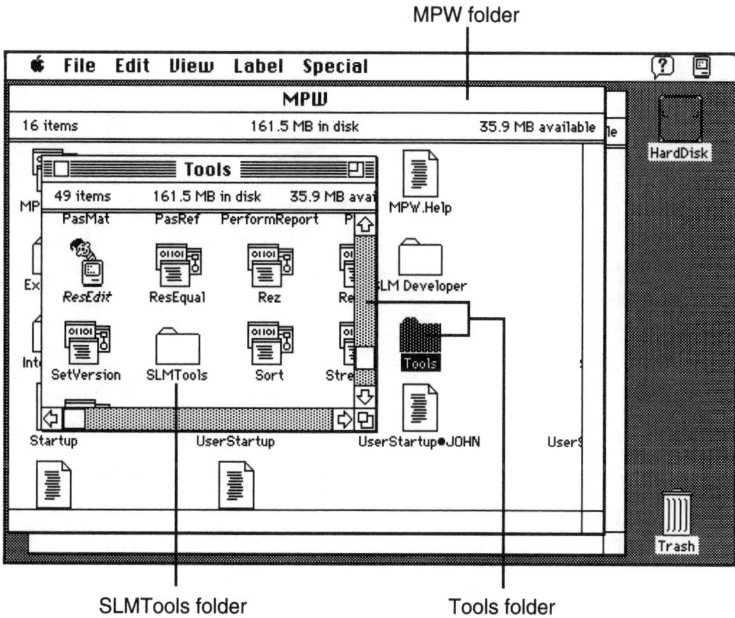

Figure 17.7 *MPW SLMTools Installation.*

Step 5: Install the FoxPro LCK

The last mandatory task is the installation of the FoxPro Mac LCK itself. The installation process suggested here also varies slightly from that presented in the Microsoft FoxPro LCK documentation. The approach outlined here allows you to set up clearly defined, stand-alone projects.

To install the FoxPro Mac LCK using the alternative, project-oriented configuration, complete the following steps:

1. Create a FoxLCK folder within your MPW folder. Create 3 folders within the FoxLCK folder: Libraries, Projects, and Samples. Finally, create two folders within the Projects folder: TestLib and Demo (see figure 17.8).

2. Insert the FoxProLCK disk into your floppy diskette drive. Open the FoxLCK folder. Note 3 folders: Source, Object, Libs. To complete the installation process, you copy items from these folders into the folders you created for the FoxLCK in MPW (see figure 17.9).

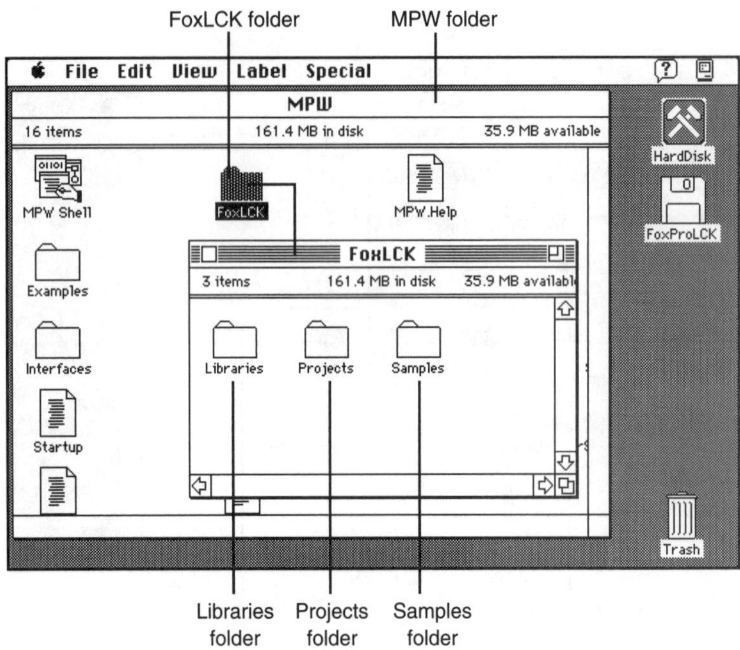

Figure 17.8 *FoxPro LCK MPW folder arrangement.*

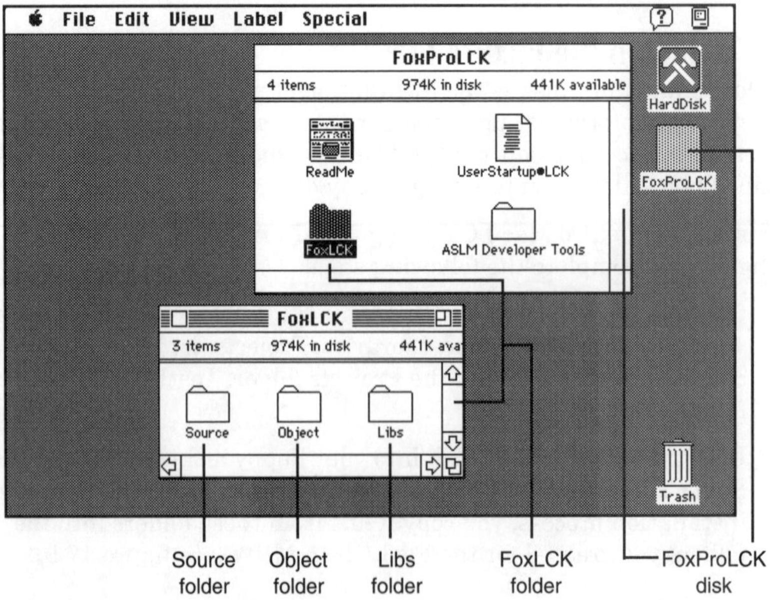

Figure 17.9 *FoxPro LCK Tools.*

3. Open the Source folder. This folder contains several sample files for creating a test library and a Samples folder containing additional material. Copy the contents of the Samples folder into the Samples folder of the FoxLCK folder in MPW. Copy MakeFile, Test.exp, and Testlib.c to the <root>:MPW:FoxLCK: Projects:Test folder that you created in the Projects folder. Copy the pro_ext.h to the following folder:<root>:MPW:Interfaces: SLMInterfaces:CIncludes (see figure 17.10).

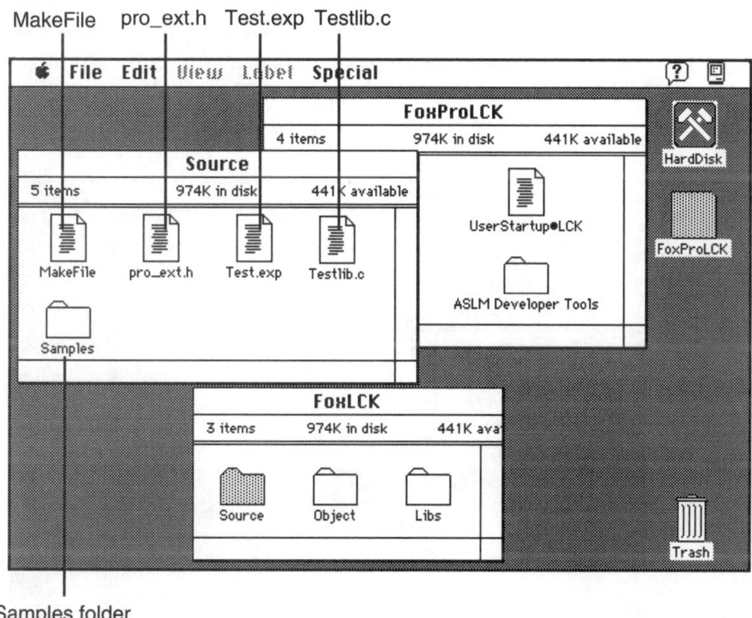

Figure 17.10 *FoxProLCK Source Folder Installation.*

FOXPRO MAC HACK TIP

You use makefiles to compile and link your FoxPro Mac API libraries in MPW. The project-oriented configuration suggested in this chapter requires makefiles that vary slightly from those supplied with the LCK. An appropriate makefile is supplied on the source disk.

See Also

- Source Disk:API/Libr Constr Kit Folder

FOXPRO MAC HACK TIP

You do not have to place the pro_ext.h file in the Interfaces folder. If you prefer, you can make a copy of it for each project, placing the copy in each project folder.

4. Open the Object folder. Copy the contents of this folder to the <root>:MPW:FoxLCK:Libraries folder (see figure 17.11). Open the Libs folder. Currently, there are no files within this folder. If there are any files here at the time of your installation, copy them to the <root>:MPW:FoxLCK:Libraries folder. The installation of all mandatory FoxPro Mac LCK components is now complete.

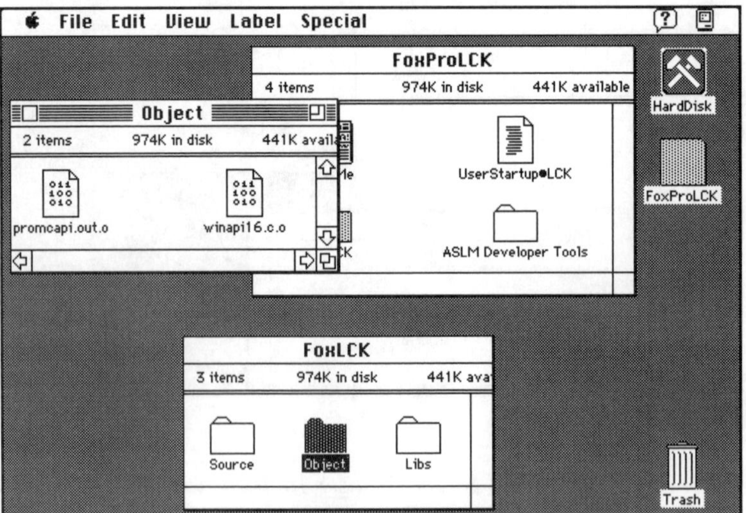

Figure 17.11 *FoxProLCK Object Folder Installation.*

5. Customize the MPW Environment. Before you can use the LCK, you need to customize the MPW environment for use with the LCK. When MPW starts up, it looks for several files in the MPW folder. Two important files are Startup and UserStartup. Startup defines and exports a number of variables used by MPW, performs some general housekeeping chores, and then calls a second command file named UserStartup. UserStartup builds several menus and can define and export additional variables and aliases.

Both Startup and UserStartup are installed at the time you install MPW. You should avoid modifying either of these files, since doing so might cause serious damage to your environment. To customize MPW, it is safer for you to create any number of custom command files named like UserStartup[B]*fileName*. MPW will execute any command file named in this manner after the basic UserStartup file has been executed. Consider using at least two custom UserStartup files: one for your LCK variable definitions and exports, and one for your own personal preferences.

To support the FoxPro Mac LCK in the installation described here, as a minimum, you need to define and export two variables: {SLMInterfaces} and {SLMLibraries}. In addition, you must add the location of the SLM tools to the {Commands} path. A UserStartup[B]CK file supporting the installation presented in this chapter is listed below:

```
# UserStartup·LCK
# A file for customizing the MPW environment
#  for the FoxPro Mac LCK

# Your UserStartup·LCK file must contain entries
#  analogous to these:

set SLMInterfaces "HardDisk:MPW:Interfaces:SLMInterfaces:"
export SLMInterfaces
set SLMLibraries "HardDisk:MPW:Libraries:SLMLibraries:"
export SLMLibraries
set Commands "{Commands},HardDisk:MPW:Tools:SLMTools:"
export Commands

# EOF UserStartup·LCK
```

FOXPRO MAC HACK TIP

This book's source disk includes two files to serve as templates for customizing MPW for the FoxPro Mac LCK installation process described here: UserStartup[B]LCK and UserStartup[B]JOHN. UserStartup[B]LCK sets up the environmental variables required for your MPW makefiles. UserStartup[B]JOHN contains a number of useful MPW command aliases.

Step 6: Install MacsBug

When you are ready to debug your FoxPro Mac API routines, Apple Computer offers several options. The simplest approach is to use MacsBug. MacsBug is also included with the ETO CD-ROM. To install MacsBug, copy the most current MacsBug file from ETO into your System Folder (see figure 17.12). After rebooting your Mac, you will see the message *Debugger installed* at the same time the *Welcome to Macintosh* message is displayed. This indicates that MacsBug is resident and ready for action.

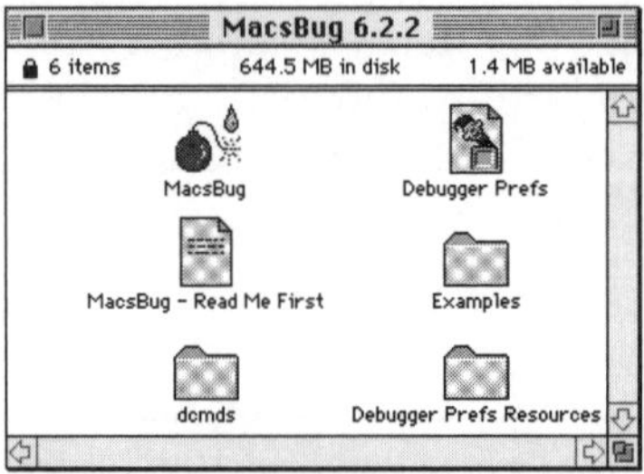

Figure 17.12 *MacsBug Installation.*

The FoxPro LCK API

To build FoxPro Mac API libraries, you need to understand how to communicate between FoxPro Mac and your API functions, and how to send data from your API routines back to FoxPro Mac. The following section describes the data structures and techniques for accomplishing this task.

Passing Parameters by Value or by Reference

You can pass parameters to FoxPro Mac functions by *value* or by *reference*. Call-by-value causes a copy of the variable to be sent to the function, leaving the value of the original variable unaffected; call-by-reference passes the address of the variable to the function, allowing the function to change the variable pointed to. Like other native FoxPro Mac functions, you can communicate with library functions that you create with the LCK by using either call-by-value or call-by-reference.

By default, FoxPro passes variables to functions by value. You can override this default by issuing the following FoxPro command:

```
SET UDFPARMS TO REFERENCE
```

To restore the default calling convention, issue the following command:

```
SET UDFPARMS TO VALUE
```

To force a variable to be passed by reference, precede the reference to the variable with @. To force a variable to be passed by value, enclose the reference to the variable with ().

To maintain an environment in which functions behave consistently, I suggest that you stick with the default of SET UDFPARMS TO VALUE and use @ to explicitly call by reference when call-by-reference is required.

The conventions used to send data from FoxPro to your API routines (as well as other FoxPro functions) are fairly straightforward. However, as you write routines with the LCK, you need to adhere to more complex rules to prepare your API functions to operate in call-by-value or call-by-reference mode.

Value and Locator Structures

The FoxPro API supports call-by-value and call-by-reference. The Value structure is used to communicate using call-by-value; the Locator structure supports the call-by-reference convention. The Value and Locator structures are listed below:

```
/* An expression's value                        */
  typedef struct {
  char            ev_type;
  char            ev_padding;
  short           ev_width;
  unsigned short  ev_length;
  long            ev_long;
  double          ev_real;
  MHANDLE         ev_handle;
} Value;

/* A reference to a database or memory variable*/
#if MAC_API       //byte for MPW byte-alignmt
typedef struct {
  char  l_type;
```

```
  char  l_extrabyte; /* Byte so struct lines up*/
  short l_where,   /* Database #; -1 for memory */
        l_NTI,     /* Variable name table offset*/
        l_offset, /* Index into database       */
        l_subs,    /* # subscripts specified    */
        l_sub1,    /* subscript integral values */
        l_sub2;
} Locator;
#else
typedef struct {
  char  l_type;
  short l_where, /* Database #; -1 for memory  */
        l_NTI,   /* Variable name table offset */
        l_offset,/* Index into database        */
        l_subs,  /* # subscripts specified     */
        l_sub1,  /* subscript integral values  */
        l_sub2;
} Locator;
#endif
```

FoxPro fills in Value and Locator structures depending upon the calling convention and data type(s) passed to the API routine. These rules are described in Chapter 2 of the *Developer's Guide to the Microsoft FoxPro Library Construction Kit*, one of the manuals included with the Professional edition of FoxPro for Macintosh.

Parameters and Parameter Blocks

The FoxPro API uses a parameter block to communicate between FoxPro and the FoxPro API routines. The name of this structure is ParamBlk. The ParamBlk structure provides the flexibility to communicate using call-by-value or call-by-reference, using any FoxPro Mac data type and any number of parameters. ParamBlk consists of an integer indicating the number of parameters being passed, followed by an array of parameters of the type Parameter. The Parameter structure is a union of a Value structure and a Locator structure: if the API structure is designed to accept call-by-value, a Value structure is used; if the API is to accept call-by-reference, a Locator structure is used. The first byte of either structure indicates the data type and calling convention expected.

```
/* A parameter to a library function.     */
typedef union {
  Value   val;
```

```
  Locator loc; /* An 'R' in l_type means  */
               /* the Locator part        */
               /* of this union is in use.*/
} Parameter;

/* A paramter list to a library function. */
typedef struct {
  short int pCount; /* Number of          */
                    /* Parameters PASSED  */
  Parameter p[1];   /* pCount Parameters  */
} ParamBlk;
```

FoxInfo and FoxTable

The FoxPro API uses the FoxInfo and FoxTable structures to publish and maintain information concerning the functions contained in API libraries at run time. Each API source file must contain instances of these structures. The FoxInfo structure makes functions within the library visible to FoxPro by telling FoxPro the name to be used for each FoxPro API function, the name of the function in the source file, the number and types of parameters passed, and the calling convention to be used. FoxTable is a linked list that tracks FoxInfo structures:

```
/* The FoxInfo structure contains descriptions */
/* of the functions contained in the library   */

typedef struct {
  char FAR * funcName;
                /* Function name (all caps)    */
  FPFI       function;
                /* Actual function address     */
  short      parmCount;
                /* # params specif or flag val */
  char FAR * parmTypes;
                /* Parameter list description  */
} FoxInfo;

/* Alternate values for parmCount in FoxInfo to*/
/* modify how FoxPro treats the function       */
#define INTERNAL      -1
                /* Not callable from FoxPro    */
#define CALLONLOAD    -2
                /* Call when lib is loaded     */
```

```
#define CALLONUNLOAD -3
               /* Call when lib is unloaded   */

typedef struct _FoxTable {
  struct _FoxTable FAR *nextLibrary;
                             /* Linked list of */
                             /* libraries      */
  short                infoCount;
                             /* # of functions */
                             /* in library     */
  FoxInfo FAR          *infoPtr;
                             /* Function list  */
} FoxTable;
```

Building, Evoking, and Debugging FoxPro Mac API Routines

To create a FoxPro Mac API library with MPW, follow these steps:

- Set up a folder for the project in the <root>:MPW:FoxLCK:Projects folder.
- Create the required source file(s), the exports file, and the makefile for the project in the project folder.
- Build the FoxPro shared library API routine using the MPW MAKE facility.
- Test the API library in FoxPro, debugging and rebuilding the API routine as required.

To illustrate this process, in this section you'll learn how to build a sample FoxPro Mac API library called DEMO.MLB. DEMO.MLB makes three functions accessible to FoxPro Mac: HELLO, XUPPERREF, and XUPPERVAL. HELLO is an API routine that throws up a window with a simple message; XUPPERREF demonstrates call-by-reference; and XUPPERVAL demonstrates call-by-value.

The Project and the Project's Required Files

As a minimum, all FoxPro Mac API library projects require three files: the source file for the library, an exports file, and an MPW makefile. The sample DEMO.MLB project folder and files are illustrated in figure 17.13:

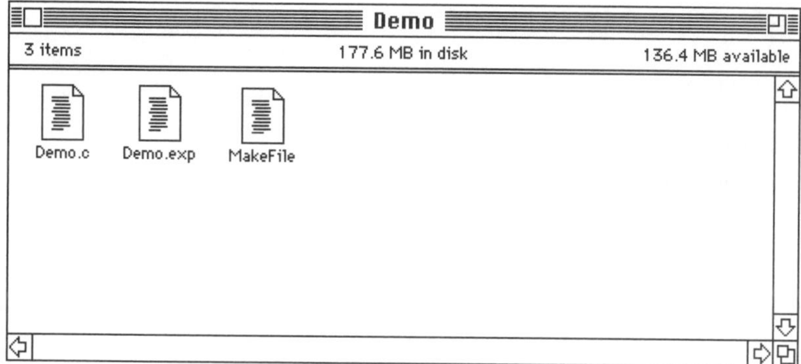

Figure 17.13 *The MPW Demo LCK Project.*

The source file contains the actual API library source code. The exports file contains entries that define the exported library and all included functions. The makefile allows the MAKE facility to generate all of the MPW commands required to compile and link the shared library resource.

- Source Disk:API/Libr Constr Kit Folder

Sample files for you to build your own version of DEMO.MLB are included on the source disk. The C language library source file is Demo.c. The supporting exports file is Demo.exp. The makefile for this project is MakeFile.

The best way to create the three required files for a project is to clone files from earlier projects. You can use the files from the DEMO.MLB project for this purpose.

The API Library Source File

Demo.c contains the C language source code for the DEMO.MLB FoxPro Mac API library. As you create projects, remember that you always need a `#include <pro_ext.h>` entry. The library's function or functions are then declared and coded. Note that more than one API function can be included in a single source code file. Include a FoxInfo entry for each function to be made available to FoxPro Mac at runtime. Finally, include a FoxTable line. The FoxTable entry from Demo.c can be inserted into your source code without modification. The source code for DEMO.MLB is listed below:

```
/* Demo.c — Demonstrates basic FoxPro Mac LCK  */
/* features                                    */
/* ©1993-1994 by John R. Livingston             */

#include <pro_ext.h>

#define DATA_TYPE_MISMATCH    302
#define INSUFFICIENT_MEMORY   182
#define NULL_STRING           '\0'


/* XToUpper converts a string to all upper case */
/* It is used internally and is not callable    */
/* from Fox                                     */
void FAR XToUpper(char FAR *cstring, unsigned short j)
{
  unsigned short i;

  for (i = 0; i < j; i++, cstring++)
  {
    if (*cstring >= 'a' && *cstring <= 'z')
      {
        *cstring = *cstring + ('A' - 'a');
      }
  }
}


/* Hello — a simple dialog                      */
void FAR Hello(ParamBlk FAR *parm)
{
  Point pt;
  WHANDLE wh;

  pt.h = 9;
  pt.v = 1;
  wh = _WOpen(10, 20, 14, 50,
```

```
         WMINIMIZE + MOVE + SHADOW + WEVENT + CLOSE,
         DIALOG_SCHEME,
         0,
         WO_DOUBLEBOX);
  if(wh != 0)
  {
    _WSetTitle(wh, "HELLO");
    _WSetFooter(wh, "WORLD");
    _WShow(wh);
    _WPosCursor(wh, pt);
    _WPutStr(wh, "Hello world");
  }
  _RetInt(0L, 1);
}


/* XUpperRef — converts a string          */
/* to all upper using call by reference   */
void FAR XUpperRef(ParamBlk FAR *parm)
{
  Value val;

  /* Place the value of the passed variable    */
  /* into val (Value structure)                */
  _Load(&parm->p[0].loc, &val);

  /* Check for errors                          */
  if (val.ev_type != 'C')
  {
    _Error(DATA_TYPE_MISMATCH);
  }

  /* Lock the handle during function call      */
  _HLock(val.ev_handle);

  /* Convert the string to upper case          */
  XToUpper(_HandToPtr(val.ev_handle),
           val.ev_length);

  /* Place string back into the calling loc    */
  /* and clean up                              */
  _HUnLock(val.ev_handle);
```

```
  _Store(&parm->p[0].loc, &val);
  _FreeHand(val.ev_handle);
}


/* XUpperVal — converts a string               */
/* to all upper using call by value            */
FAR XUpperVal(ParamBlk FAR *parm)
{

  /* Check for errors                          */
  if (! _SetHandSize(parm->p[0].val.ev_handle,
                parm->p[0].val.ev_length + 1))
  {
    _Error(INSUFFICIENT_MEMORY);
  }

  /* Null-terminate string                     */
  ((char FAR *)
   _HandToPtr(parm->p[0].val.ev_handle))
    [parm->p[0].val.ev_length] = NULL_STRING;

  /* Lock the handle during function call      */
  _HLock(parm->p[0].val.ev_handle);

  /* Convert the string to upper case          */
  XToUpper(_HandToPtr(parm->p[0].val.ev_handle),
          parm->p[0].val.ev_length);

  /* Return string to caller and clean up      */
  _HUnLock(parm->p[0].val.ev_handle);
  _RetVal(&parm->p[0].val);
}


/* FoxInfo structure — coordinates             */
/* function names and parameter descriptions   */
/* between Fox and API                         */
FoxInfo myFoxInfo[] = {
  {"XTOUPPER",  (FPFI) XToUpper, INTERNAL, "?"},
  {"HELLO",     (FPFI) Hello,           0, "?"},
```

```
  {"XUPPERREF", (FPFI) XUpperRef,       1, "R"},
  {"XUPPERVAL", (FPFI) XUpperVal,       1, "C"},
};


/* FoxTable linked list                            */
FoxTable _FoxTable = {
  (FoxTable FAR *) 0,
  sizeof(myFoxInfo)/sizeof(FoxInfo),
  myFoxInfo
};

/* EOF Demo.c                                      */
```

The Exports File

The exports file for DEMO.MLB follows. You can use this exports file as a template for other exports files by simply changing the id and version entries:

```
/* File:     Demo.exp                              */
/* Contains:
/* Exports file for the Demo function set.         */

Library
{
  id = "Fox$Demo";
  version = 1.3b6;
  flags = system7;
  heap = application,hold;
};

FunctionSet Hello
{
  id = "Fox:API$DEMO.MLB,1.3";
  version = 1.0...1.3b6;
  exports = extern pascal DispatchAPI;
};

/* EOF Demo.exp                                    */
```

The Makefile

The makefile for the DEMO.MLB project is on the source disk. To use this file as a template for new projects, you need to change the entries referring to the project's folder and file names. In addition, if your API library needs to link into libraries not included in the sample makefile, you must add entries to the makefile to include those libraries with the project. Remember that the sample makefile is tailored to the FoxPro LCK installation procedures outlined in this chapter.

Compiling, Linking, and Building the Shared Library

To compile, link, and build the DEMO.MLB FoxPro Mac API library, follow these steps:

1. Make sure that you have created the <root>:MPW:FoxLCK:Projects:Demo folder and that the DEMO.MLB, Demo.exp, and MakeFile files from the floppy disk enclosed with this book have been copied into that folder.

2. Start up MPW by opening the <root>:MPW folder and double-clicking on the MPW Shell icon (see fig. 17.14).

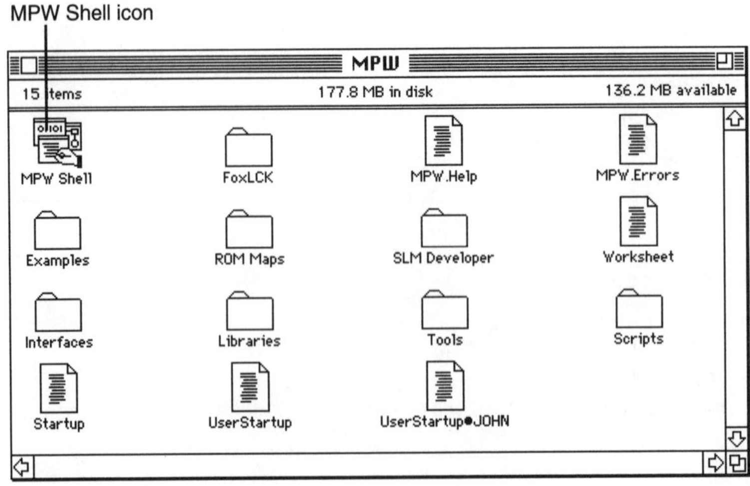

Figure 17.14 *Starting up MPW.*

3. Use the MPW Set Directory Menu and Set Directory Dialog to set the default directory to the <root>:MPW:FoxLCK:Projects:Demo folder (see figures 17.15 and 17.16).

Figure 17.15 *Using the MPW Set Directory Menu.*

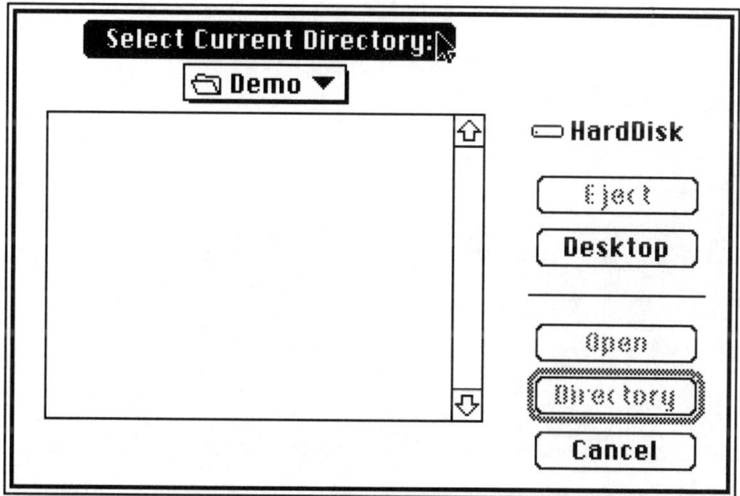

Figure 17.16 *Setting the Default Directory to the Demo Project Folder.*

4. If necessary, modify the supplied MakeFile to account for any differences in file and folder names. Demo.c and Demo.exp should not require modification.

5. Use MAKE to create the shared library resource. Type MAKE and then either the Ctrl+Return keys, or the ↵Enter key on the numeric key pad. After you type MAKE, MPW generates all of the MPW commands required to compile, link, and build the shared library resource.

   Select the generated code with your mouse and again hit the Ctrl+Return keys, or the ↵Enter key on the numeric key pad. This causes all of the MPW commands generated by MAKE to be executed, building the FoxPro DEMO.MLB file (see figure 17.17).

> **FOXPRO MAC HACK TIP**
>
> Note that when typing commands in MPW, pressing the return alone will not cause MPW to execute your commands. You must type either the combination of the Ctrl+ return keys, or the return key on the numeric keypad.

```
 File  Edit  Find  Mark  Window  Project  Directory  Build
HardDisk:MPW:Worksheet
MPW Shell
make
Echo "∂t∂tCompiling HardDisk:MPW:FoxLCK:projects:demo:demo.c"
C HardDisk:MPW:FoxLCK:projects:demo:demo.c -o HardDisk:MPW:FoxLCK:projects:demo:demo.c.o -model far -
Lib "HardDisk:MPW:FoxLCK:projects:demo:demo.c.o" "HardDisk:MPW:FoxLCK:libraries:winapi16.c.o" -o "Har
BuildSharedLibrary ∂
   HardDisk:MPW:FoxLCK:projects:demo:demo.out.o ∂
   -exp "HardDisk:MPW:FoxLCK:projects:demo:demo.exp" ∂
   -obj "HardDisk:MPW:FoxLCK:projects:demo:demo" ∂
   -lib "demo.mlb" ∂
   -resid 1 -restype cod1 ∂
   -macsbug ∂
   -sym full ∂
   -progress ∂
   -verbose ∂
   -i "HardDisk:MPW:FoxLCK:projects:demo:" -i "{SLMInterfaces}CIncludes:" -i "{CIncludes}" -p ∂
   "{SLMLibraries}LibraryManager.o" ∂
   "{CLibraries}Stdclib.o" ∂
   "HardDisk:MPW:FoxLCK:libraries:promcapi.out.o" ∂
   "{Libraries}Interface.o" ∂
   "{Libraries}Runtime.o" ∂
   -e
```

Figure 17.17 *Using MAKE to Create a Library API File.*

6. Quit MPW and open up the Demo project folder. You should see a number of new files in the project folder, including DEMO.MLB (see figure 17.18). Copy the .MLB file to the <root>:System Folder:Extensions folder. Your FoxPro Mac API library resource is now ready for testing.

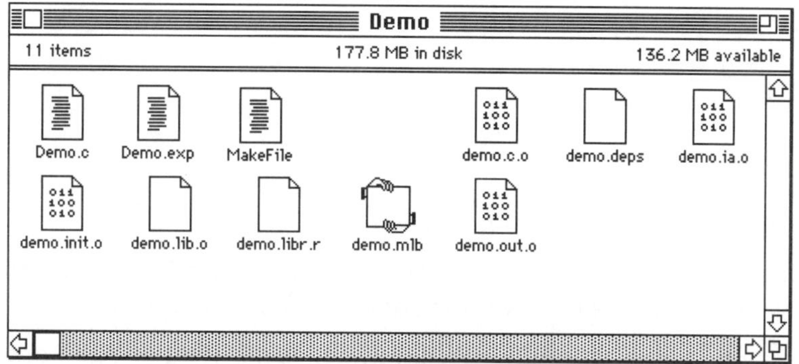

Figure 17.18 *The DEMO.MLB File.*

> **FOXPRO MAC HACK TIP**
>
> Make sure that you place the .MLB file into the Extensions folder. Simply dropping the .MLB into the system folder will not suffice. The Finder does not know where .MLB files need to be placed within the System Folder.

Evoking the API Routine

To test DEMO.MLB, start up FoxPro and enter the following commands:

```
SET TALK OFF
CLEAR
SET LIBRARY TO DEMO.MLB

m.string = 'abc'
m.retval = .f.

m.retval = HELLO()
?m.retval
?m.string

m.retval = XUPPERVAL(m.string)
?m.retval
?m.string
```

```
m.retval = XUPPERREF(@m.string)
?m.retval
?m.string

SET LIBRARY TO
```

You should note the following results:

- `m.retval = HELLO()` places a simple hello world window on your screen, updates m.retval to 0, and does not affect m.string.
- `m.retval = XUPPERVAL(m.string)` changes m.retval to 'ABC' and has no effect on m.string.
- `m.retval = XUPPERREF(@m.string)` sets m.retval to .t. and changes m.string to 'ABC'.

Debugging with MacsBug

MacsBug is Apple's low-level debugger. MacsBug functions quite differently from the source-level debugging environment that you may have encountered in THINK C. When evoked, MacsBug displays a screen allowing you to examine 680x0 assembly language, memory addresses, and the CPU's eight data and address registers. To effectively use MacsBug, you need to clearly understand Macintosh hardware.

MacsBug can be evoked in one of several ways: by a program crash, by setting a program breakpoint, or through one of several manual techniques. The FoxPro LCK provides support for program breakpoint debugging with the _BreakPoint() API library function. If you install MacsBug, when your API program reaches a call to _BreakPoint(), MacsBug is evoked, and all other activities cease. Once MacsBug is called, you can examine the hardware and toggle back and forth between the condition of the screen just before the _BreakPoint() and the debugger.

> **FOXPRO MAC HACK TIP**
>
> If you want to debug using _BreakPoint(), make sure that you have MacsBug installed. If you evoke an API routine with _BreakPoint() inserted without the debugger installed, your system will hang, and you will need to reboot. Additionally, when you are done with debugging, make sure that you remove any _BreakPoint() calls.

Chapter Wrap Up

Following the rules and instructions in this chapter, you can write simple LCK libraries. After gaining confidence at this level, you can continue to expand your skills by tackling the more advanced Macintosh user interface toolbox and operating system features that the LCK also makes available.

18

COMMUNICATE WITH OTHER MAC APPLICATIONS: APPLE EVENTS AND APPLESCRIPT

by
Randy Brown

Wouldn't it be nice if you could have FoxPro for Macintosh output a database query and have Excel automatically create a chart from the data? Wouldn't it be nice if you could insert this chart, along with an associated data table, into an executive report in your favorite word processor? Wouldn't it be nice if you could print this report for faxing or e-mailing to any destination of your choosing? All of these options can be initiated from a single FoxPro command by using AppleScript, Apple Computer's scripting language.

Microsoft first introduced interapplication communications (IAC) to the FoxPro database line with FoxPro for Windows. Both DDE (Dynamic Data Exchange) and OLE (Object Linking and Embedding) were added to conform with Microsoft Windows standards. The Mac product supports only OLE (through General fields). Unfortunately, OLE was not rapidly adopted by many Macintosh developers (with the exception of Microsoft), so OLE servers are scarce on the Mac. In addition, FoxPro for Macintosh doesn't support Apple's Publish and Subscribe. To Microsoft's credit, this decision was wise because the compound-document approach introduced with OLE proved far superior to Publish and Subscribe. Apple is fast at work with its own compound-document equivalent, called OpenDoc. Presumably, FoxPro for Macintosh will support this standard one day if and when it becomes an accepted reality.

Although OLE and OpenDoc allow applications (actually, documents in different applications) to share information, there is no true underlying language associated with them to allow applications to truly communicate with each other. For this capability, you need to resort to alternative methods. In FoxPro for Windows, DDE is the primary tool for all inter-application communications. FoxPro for Windows has a number of functions strictly devoted to DDE such as DDEAdvise, DDERequest, DDEPoke, and so on. Currently, Microsoft Excel is the only Macintosh product to support DDE. FoxPro for Macintosh doesn't support DDE. Rather, FoxPro handles IAC by using AppleScript, a far superior beast.

Before I show you how to use FoxPro with AppleScript, look at the basics. What is AppleScript (and, for that matter, DDE)? AppleScript is a system extension developed by Apple Computer that allows two or more applications to talk to each other. When people say they want to use FoxPro with AppleScript, they are only talking about one side of an equation. AppleScript is the glue in the middle that ties FoxPro to another application (not AppleScript itself). Unlike DDE, which is simply a set of protocols each application must handle in its own native language, AppleScript is a true language supported by the operating system and exposed to those applications that support it. This is a major advantage for software applications that do not have a native language. Table 18.1 shows you a few of the differences between the two IAC technologies.

Table 18.1

Differences between Interapplication Communication (IAC) standards

AppleScript	*Dynamic Data Exchange*
System supported language universal to applications.	No true language, only that which is natively supported by supporting application itself.
Primary intent is to communicate with other applications.	Primary intent is to transfer data.
Can create stand-alone AppleScript applications.	Works entirely within an application.

AppleScript	*Dynamic Data Exchange*
More comprehensive control.	Less comprehensive control.
Works only on Macintoshes.	Runs under Windows and Macintoshes (minor support).

AppleScript Resources

This chapter presents only a brief overview of the AppleScript language. Do not expect to use this chapter exclusively to learn AppleScript. Most of the concepts are only touched on at a general level. If you are at all interested in using AppleScript with your own applications, you should invest in one or more of the following references.

- *AppleScript 1.1 SDK*—This software developers' kit (with CD) put out by Apple contains everything you need to get started with AppleScript. Complete documentation is included along with many useful examples. The SDK also includes several excellent third-party goodies that assist in the process of creating AppleScript applications.
- *AppleScript Language Guide*—This is Apple Computer's definitive publication of the entire AppleScript language. The book does not have many useful examples. It should be treated only as a reference guide.
- *AppleScript Scripting Additions Guide*—This is Apple Computer's publication on the Scripting Additions it provides with AppleScript. Do not waste your money on this one! Why Apple decided not to include this material with the *AppleScript Language Guide* is anyone's guess. The next two books cover the scripting additions and offer a lot more for the money.
- *The Tao of AppleScript*—This excellent book by Derrick Schneider and put out by the Berkeley Mac Users Group (BMUG) explains AppleScript in an uncomplicated manner most non-programmers can understand. It comes with a disk of valuable scripting additions and other goodies. The book does not have a complete language reference,

so you may find certain aspects of the AppleScript language missing in this book. This book complements the *AppleScript Language Guide* quite nicely.

- *The Complete AppleScript Handbook*—Danny Goodman has taken a break from his best-selling HyperCard books to write a book on AppleScript. This book is very comprehensive, as suggested by the title. It has a wealth of examples and goes into depth on a variety of subjects not covered elsewhere. If you are new to programming, you may want to start out with *The Tao of AppleScript* because it explains things in a more simplistic manner.
- *Script Tools 1.3*—This freeware set of scripting additions by Mark Alldritt is a must for any AppleScript developer. It contains many commands for working with files and applications.
- *Jon's Commands*—This is another freeware set of scripting additions. It has many useful commands for handling files, sounds, and the clipboard. There are also some nice object classes for important system-related information.

FOXPRO MAC HACK TIP

If you have upgraded to System 7.5 or above, look for a folder named Apple Extras in your System folder. A nested folder named AppleScript contains sample scripts to automate tasks in the Finder such as turning the sound or file sharing on and off. Perhaps most important for FoxPro performance, you can change the current color depth from *within* an application! You may want to run scripts such as these from menu options on your application menus. The Apple Extras' AppleScript folder also contains text files with up-to-date information from Apple about AppleScripting.

Defining AppleScript

AppleScript is Apple Computer's common scripting language, used to control Apple Events. Understanding *Apple Events* is essential to understanding AppleScript. Apple Events are simply a set of high-level Mac system events, as opposed to low-level events such as pressing a key or clicking the mouse. These events describe communications between several applications.

What are some of the more common Apple Events? Apple has defined a registry of various suites of events, which applications support at varying levels. At the minimum level of support is the Required Suite of events. These are commands that every application should support, including the following:

- Open—Opens the specified object(s).
- Print—Prints the specified object(s).
- Quit—Quits application.
- Run—Launches application. This is equivalent to when you double-click on an application.

FoxPro for Macintosh only supports the Required Suite and one critical additional command that it includes in a *Miscellaneous* Suite.

- Do Script—Executes a script.

We can stop learning about Apple Events here because there isn't much AppleScript stuff that FoxPro supports, right? Not quite. As mentioned previously, using AppleScript is a two-sided equation, so learning about FoxPro's support of AppleScript and Apple Events is only half the work.

Examine Microsoft Excel. When I write a script (a script is the document that contains the AppleScript code—similar to a FoxPro .PRG), that script can contain any commands and objects supported by the application. A script communicating with Excel can contain many AppleScript commands because Excel supports a fairly large set. In fact, Excel supports five separate suites of Apple Events (Required, Core, Table, Charting and Excel).

How do you know which Apple Events are supported by an application? Now is as good a time as any for you to get acquainted with the *Script editor*. This is simply a text editor used for creating and compiling AppleScript scripts. When you install AppleScript, a folder is created that contains all files needed for using AppleScript including some valuable examples. This is where you can find the Script Editor. Although you will be inclined to start off using Apple's Script Editor that ships with AppleScript, you should be aware that other third-party editors exist should your scripting needs demand a more powerful tool.

The Script Editor's File menu has a special menu option called "Open Dictionary" that displays an open file dialog. The user selects any AppleScript supporting application from the open file list. A *Dictionary* is the listing of Apple Events supported by that application. In addition, the dictionary contains a definition of the commands and objects. Figure 18.1 shows the Excel events listing. Notice the italic items listed at the bottom representing Object Classes. Each object within an Object Class inherits similar characteristics.

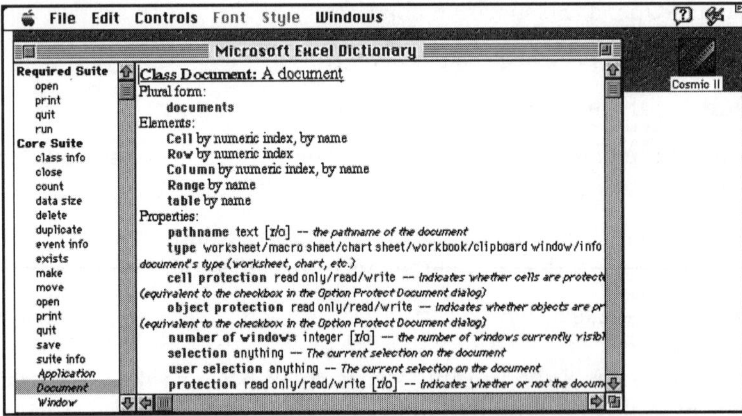

Figure 18.1 *Excel AppleScript dictionary opened in the script editor.*

Object-Oriented AppleScript

It seems that most computer languages these days are becoming object-oriented (yes, even FoxPro soon). AppleScript is no exception, although it is not fully object-oriented. In fact, if you are new to OOP (Object-Oriented Programming), AppleScript might be the place to start because it is simple to learn and has many aspects of an OO language. I'll not go into many details about using AppleScript here because there are other resources available devoted specifically to this topic.

Look at AppleScript as having two components to worry about—*Objects* and *Commands*. Each of these components has additional features that support the object-oriented nature of the language, as shown in table 18.2.

Table 18.2

AppleScripts object-oriented components

Object Class	*Commands*
Elements	Parameters
Properties	Replies

By now you are somewhat familiar with FoxPro as a language. FoxPro is known as a *procedural* language because program execution is centered around various procedures and their execution order. Object-oriented programming centers around the objects themselves. For example, as the dictionary in figure 18.1 shows, an Excel object known as a Document is selected. Excel supports other object classes such as Applications, Windows, Cells, Rows, Columns, Tables, Text, Ranges, and Charts. A Document object can contain a Cell, Table, etc. AppleScript refers to these objects contained within other objects as *Elements*. In addition, the main object (here, a Document) inherits properties of the subordinate elements (for example, Cells).

Each object has its own set of properties, which are attributes that describe the object. For example, a Cell object includes properties such as value, number format, foreground color, alignment, font, name, protection, and so on. You may be a little confused about the difference between an Object Class and an Object. Think of Objects as a fuzzy term used to describe Object Classes and their Elements. In Excel, Object Classes such as Documents can contain other Elements such as Cells (note that not all Object Classes have elements). A Cell is also considered a separate Object Class with its own set of properties.

You may be thinking, “Hey, FoxPro has objects such as Menus, Tables, Indexes, Windows, Buttons, etc., what’s the big deal.” Unfortunately, as you may well know, FoxPro suffers from a phenomenon known as “dBloat” where the language has become so large that it is virtually impossible to memorize all the syntax. It seems as though each FoxPro object has its own set of commands and functions (you can think of FoxPro functions as object properties).

In contrast, AppleScript relies on object-oriented techniques for its commands. Unlike FoxPro, which has specific commands and functions for different objects, AppleScript uses the same commands for every object; commands are transparent to the object! Look at some typical AppleScript commands for creating a new Excel Chart object:

```
— Sample Excel AppleScript commands
make Chart
set type of first Chart to three D column
set title of first Chart to Annual Sales
set has legend of first Chart to true
copy the title of first Chart to charttitle

** Sample FoxPro commands
CREATE TABLE mytable (field1 C(10), field2 m)
INDEX ON field1 TAG field1
SET FIELDS TO field1
SET ORDER TO
SET DELETED ON
m.getalias = ALIAS()
m.getorder = ORDER()
```

Notice in table 18.3 that there are no special AppleScript functions used to return specific properties of objects. Because AppleScript treats objects in a universal fashion, it has no need to use object specific functions. Both languages do use commands and variables (AppleScript refers to variables as *Identifiers*). Unlike FoxPro commands, some AppleScript commands return values (known as *Replies*). These commands are similar to FoxPro functions.

Table 18.3

Comparison of AppleScript and FoxPro object actions

Action	*FoxPro uses*	*AppleScript uses*
set property value	command	command
get property value	function	object reference

In the following example, a single command (`display dialog`) actually returns two replies, the entered text and the button selected. When there are multiple replies, they are returned in a data structure known as an AppleScript List. Note the AppleScript continuation character (¬) that is entered by typing Option-Return in the Script Editor (in other Macintosh editors you get the same character by typing Option-L.)

```
— Sample AppleScript using dialog
display dialog "Enter name for archive file:" ¬
  default answer "BACKUP.ZIP" ¬
  buttons {"One", "Two"}
copy the result to retlist
copy (text returned of retlist) to GetFileName
copy (button returned of retlist) to GetBtnName
display dialog "You selected file/button: "¬
  & GetFileName & "/" & GetBtnName ¬
  buttons {"OK"} default button "OK"
```

AppleScript commands come in four flavors, according to their origins:

- AppleScript-native
- Application
- Scripting Additions
- User-Defined

A native AppleScript command is built into the actual AppleScript extension itself. The second type is an Application command. These are the ones that belong to a specific application such as the Excel suites shown above. The third type of command is known as a Scripting Addition. The Display Dialog command is an example of this type. AppleScript searches for Scripting Additions in a folder of same name located inside the `System Folder:Extensions` folder. Any Scripting Additions located within this folder are freely available to all AppleScript supporting applications. If you are so inclined, additions can be written using your favorite development platform such as MPW. As with other applications, the complete set of commands and objects can be revealed through the Open Dictionary menu option (see figure 18.2).

The final command type is known as a User-Defined command (UDC). Think of these as being similar to FoxPro UDFs. Within a script, you can define a subroutine that can be called at various times. As with FoxPro UDFs, an AppleScript UDC can be passed parameters and can return a value to its calling command.

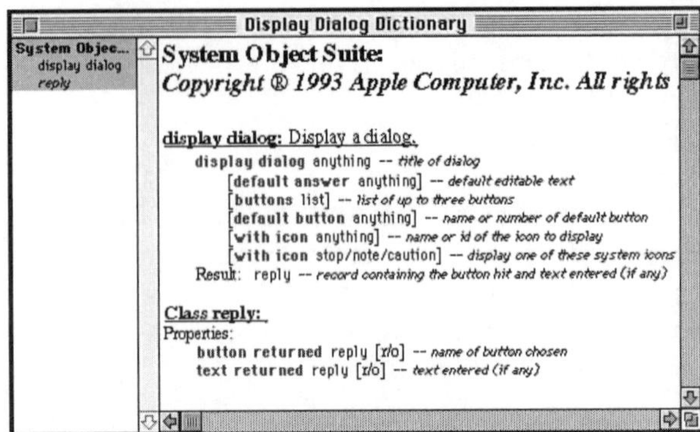

Figure 18.2 *AppleScript dictionary of Display Dialog scripting addition.*

AppleScript has its own set of data types (the correct terminology is *Values*), which in some ways correspond to those in FoxPro. The two types, Lists and Records, could be compared to FoxPro arrays and records, but AppleScript treats them as true data types. One difference between AppleScript lists and FoxPro arrays is that lists can contain other lists, as shown in table 18.4.

Table 18.4

AppleScript value class identifiers (data types)

Value class identifier	*Example*
Text	"FoxPro"
Number	12344
Boolean	true
List	{true,1,"Cosmic:",{1,2,3},4>5}
Record	{city:Yreka,state:CA,zipcode:94839}
Constant	yes
Date	date "01/15/94"
Real	1.034
Integer	-14
Reference	A reference to cell "R1C1" of document 1

AppleScript treats data types as its own unique class of *Value*. One strength of the AppleScript language is its English-like syntax. The manner in which you manipulate various objects and variables is almost equivalent to conversation. Nowhere is this syntax more evident than with object references (don't confuse this with the Value Class identifier Reference in the preceding table). For example, if you wanted to delete some words from a word processing document, you can use a command similar to the following:

```
DELETE words 10 thru 15 of the last paragraph ¬
  in Document "Jane's Essay"
```

AppleScript operators include those you are already familiar with in the FoxPro language (such as +,–,=,>,<). In addition, many Values also include English-like operators such as Equals, Is Equal To, Starts With, Ends With, Contains, Is Contained By, and Comes Before. The concatenation operator for strings in AppleScript is the "&" character. AppleScript refers to the process of converting between data types as *coercion*. For example, to change a set of numbers in a list to a string, you could use the following command:

```
COPY ({1,2,3} AS String) TO mystring
```

Even though AppleScript tends to an object-oriented approach, you still need control statements to control when and how commands are executed. When we begin to examine AppleScript code later in the chapter, you'll see many of these control statements. The following list shows some of the common control statements:

- if ... end if
- repeat ... end repeat
- tell ... end tell
- try ... on error ... end try
- considering ... end considering
- with timeout ... end timeout
- on subroutine ... end subroutine

After you become more familiar with AppleScript, you will want to exploit advanced features such as handlers and Script Objects. One of the examples later uses the `On Open` handler, which allows you to drop files onto your compiled AppleScript application.

Scripts can be compiled as applications into two formats: *Applets* and *Droplets*. Applets are compiled scripts that act like applications. You can double-click on them and they will launch just like FoxPro itself. Droplets perform an action when you drag and drop a file(s) onto them. Their scripts usually start out with something similar to the following:

```
on open (fileList)
— add commands here
end open
```

Notice the `fileList` parameter in the preceding statement. This is a list of all the files dropped onto the droplet. You can drop both files and folders. In essence, we are passing parameters to AppleScript. Theoretically, the droplet should perform some action on those items dropped onto it.

CROSS-PLATFORM WARNING

Before I jump right into more practical uses of AppleScript, you should be aware of some pitfalls associated with AppleScript. If at all possible, you should try to obtain version 1.1 or later. Prior versions (1.0 and 1.0.1) have a number of anomalies that may cause your scripts to crash. In fact, you may encounter problems with version 1.1, but Apple is making an effort to clean up AppleScript. The Script Editor sometimes has trouble compiling and recognizing applications (for example, when you use the command `Tell Application`) in older versions. Also, you will experience crashes when working with AppleScript-created droplets (you may want to make sure that the Script Editor is running to avoid this).

Editing AppleScript

Creating a script is easy. You have already seen a simple script which displays a dialog and returns the selected values. Figure 18.3 shows Apple's Script Editor creating that script. There really aren't many features in this editor— certainly not what you're accustomed to after using FoxPro for a while. The Script Editor is really bare bones, although it has nice automatic formatting and indentation. OK, I know what you're thinking here, and you're right—FoxPro's editor isn't anything to rave over.

You notice the Record and Stop buttons. These controls allow you to record sequential user actions similar to FoxPro's macro recorder. While many applications support AppleScript, very few are AppleScript-recordable. FoxPro certainly is not.

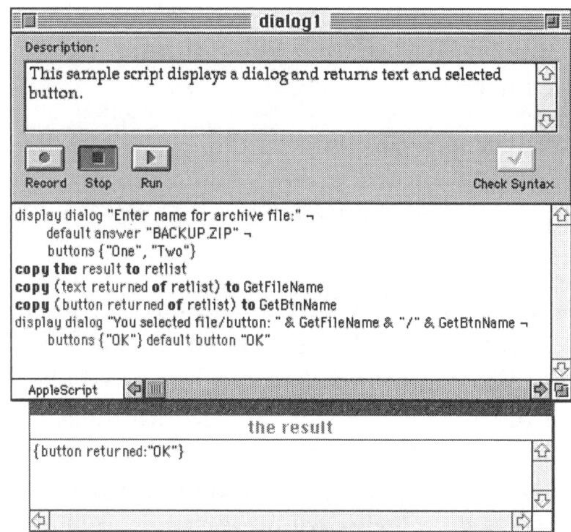

Figure 18.3 *Simple script to display a dialog.*

The Script Editor has a special window called the *Result* window. This window returns the value returned by the last AppleScript command. You can refer to its contents using the Result variable. Be careful when using this because its contents will change with every command. If you need to save the Result, use the Copy command to store it to a variable.

> **FOXPRO MAC HACK TIP**
>
> If you find that your Mac has problems running and compiling scripts, you may want to increase the application memory partition for the Script Editor. Select the Script Editor's icon and choose the Get Info menu option under the Finder.

Scripting to FoxPro

As you may know, FoxPro has a command, RUNSCRIPT, which is used to run a script from within a FoxPro program. I'll go into this later, but you may not know that other applications can talk to FoxPro. Here is a very simple script you can try. If FoxPro is not running, the script will automatically launch it for you.

```
tell application "Microsoft FoxPro"
  DO SCRIPT "WAIT WINDOW ¬
    'This is my first script' TIMEOUT 2"
end tell
```

This simple script uses the DO SCRIPT command, the only non-Required suite AppleScript command FoxPro supports. The DO SCRIPT command lets you run any FoxPro command. Although the WAIT WINDOW command is just one of many possibilities, you would most likely pass a DO command to run a program (PRG or APP) to execute a sequence of commands. You would not want to string a bunch of FoxPro commands using separate DO SCRIPT AppleScript commands because going back and forth between FoxPro and AppleScript causes a performance hit. These hits may not be all that significant, but you should try to stay within the native application if at all possible.

FOXPRO MAC HACK TIP

Notice in this script and all other scripts that text strings are delimited with double quotes. You cannot use single quotes to delimit text as you can with FoxPro. With FoxPro, it is often a good idea to use double quotes because text more often contains apostrophes (single quotes). Also, localization of strings in FoxPro for international distribution may cause conflicts if you are using single quote delimiters. Because AppleScript uses double quotes, you will have to make your FoxPro strings, those you embed in a DO SCRIPT command, single-quote-delimited.

Although not too exciting, this next script shows some of the commands that FoxPro supports from the Required Events suite (Run, Open, Print, Quit). The FoxPro INKEY() function illustrates a neat trick you can use to make FoxPro pause for a specified time.

```
— Sample AppleScript showing Required commands.
run application "Microsoft FoxPro"
tell application "Microsoft FoxPro"
  activate "Microsoft FoxPro"
  open "config.fpm"
  Do Script "=INKEY(2)"
  activate "Finder"
  Quit
end tell
```

The next and final script in this section is important in that it serves as the basis for using FoxPro as a server. The concept of using FoxPro in a client-server capacity based on AppleScript is a cool idea. Methods of requesting data can come in multiple varieties. With this script, I take the approach of requesting data by dropping a special request file on an AppleScript droplet. Here is how it works:

1. Drag a text file onto the `Fox Drop` AppleScript droplet. This file must contain a special parameter block.
2. Script starts FoxPro and runs a FoxPro program using the DO SCRIPT command.
3. FoxPro program reads the text file into a memo field where it can then process the parameter block.
4. FoxPro executes a SQL - SELECT statement based on items in the parameter block and displays the resulting set in a BROWSE.

The text file dropped must contain a parameter block with the following format. The FoxPro program checks for this and returns an error if things aren't kosher. The sample text file following the parameter block definition can be used with the Customer DBF file contained in the `:FoxPro:Tutorial:` folder.

```
*** Parameter block definition ***
* DATABASE = <table name>
* FIELDS = <field list>
* ORDER = <sort field list>
* FILTER = <filter expression>

*** Parameter block from file FOXQRY1.TXT ***
* DATABASE = CUSTOMER
* FIELDS = CNO,ONO,COMPANY,CONTACT,CITY,STATE
* ORDER = ONO
* FILTER = ONO > "3"
```

This first code listing is for the AppleScript droplet script because it runs first. Remember, if you are not using AppleScript 1.1 or higher, test it first with the script open in the Script Editor before dropping files. The application itself will not do anything if you simply double-click on it.

```
— Fox Drop AppleScript listing.
— Save as compiled application/droplet
on open (fileList)
  copy (fileList as list) to fileList
  set x to path to startup disk
  copy (x as string) & "Machete:AppleScript:" ¬
    to foxpath

  — check if empty list
  if fileList is {} then
    dodlog("You must drop a file on icon.")
    return
  end if

  — check if multiple files dropped
  if (count every item in fileList) > 1 then
    dodlog("The max # of files you can drop is 1.")
    return
  end if

  — check if folder dropped
  if last character of (fileList as string) = ":" then
    dodlog("You cannot drop folders on icon.")
    return
  end if

  — check if text type
  copy (info for file (fileList as string)) to filerec
  if file type of filerec is not contained by ¬
    {"TEXT", "F+PR", "ttro"} then
    dodlog("You can only drop text files.")
    return
  end if

  — now call FoxPro with this file
  tell application "Microsoft FoxPro"
    activate "Microsoft FoxPro"
```

```
    — ignoring application responses
    with timeout of 3600 seconds
      Do Script "DO LOCFILE('" & foxpath & ¬
        "FOXDROP.PRG','PRG',¬
        'Locate foxdrop.prg') WITH '" & ¬
          (fileList as string) & "'"
    end timeout
    — end ignoring
  end tell
end open

on dodlog(message)
  display dialog message buttons "OK" ¬
    default button "OK"
end dodlog
```

I won't review every line of these examples in depth; rather, this section highlights aspects of scripts, illustrated in the examples, that might be of use to your FoxPro scripting.

You can refer to the startup disk using the `startup disk` object. This can greatly simplify distribution of scripts as long as folder names are kept consistent.

As with FoxPro, you can create UDFs or subroutines that can be used repeatedly throughout a script. The preceding Dodlog subroutine is an example.

Applications that support AppleScript have a resource that contains definitions of the classes and commands supported. As mentioned earlier, this is known as a dictionary. File attributes, such as a file type (see check if text type statement in preceding code listing), can be obtained from the Info For File Class object, which actually is part of the File Commands scripting addition dictionary (see figure 18.4).

By default, AppleScript waits one minute when it sends a command to an application before it times out and returns an error. AppleScript will wait for that command to be executed before continuing on its own course. In our script above, most of the time you can expect the script to be completed under one minute. Using a `With Timeout` statement, we can tell AppleScript to wait a little longer. For example, this script could easily time out if the user starts the script and leaves before noticing the LOCFILE() dialog displayed. As an alternative, you could have AppleScript proceed to the next line in the script without waiting for FoxPro by using the `Ignoring Application Responses`. In our script above, this approach would probably be a better choice.

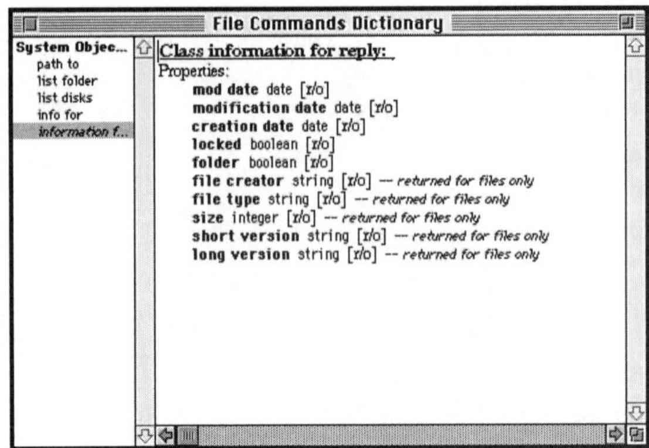

Figure 18.4 *File Commands Dictionary showing various properties.*

The code for the FoxPro program is shown in the following listing. As already mentioned, this is just the bare necessities. You probably could add far more functionality to this procedure.

```
* FoxPro FOXDROP.PRG file
#DEFINE C_TBLDATA    "* DATABASE"
#DEFINE C_FLDDATA    "* FIELDS"
#DEFINE C_ORDDATA    "* ORDER"
#DEFINE C_FILDATA    "* FILTER"
#DEFINE C_BADQUERY   "Invalid query request passed"

PARAMETER scriptfile

PRIVATE validqry
PRIVATE tblline,fldline,ordline,filline
PRIVATE tblexpr,fldexpr,ordexpr,filexpr

STORE 0 TO tblline,fldline,ordline,filline
STORE "" TO tblexpr,fldexpr,ordexpr,filexpr
m.validqry = .T.

CREATE CURSOR tmpcurs (memodata m)
APPEND BLANK
APPEND MEMO memodata FROM (m.scriptfile)
```

```
* check to make sure we have a valid fields
m.fldline = ATCLINE(C_FLDDATA,memodata)
m.tblline = ATCLINE(C_TBLDATA,memodata)
m.ordline = ATCLINE(C_ORDDATA,memodata)
m.filline = ATCLINE(C_FILDATA,memodata)

IF m.fldline = 0 OR m.tblline = 0
    m.validqry = .F.
    WAIT WINDOW C_BADQUERY TIMEOUT 2
    RETURN
ENDIF

m.tblexpr = MLINE(memodata,m.tblline)
m.tblexpr = SUBSTR(m.tblexpr,AT('=',m.tblexpr)+1)

m.fldexpr = MLINE(memodata,m.fldline)
m.fldexpr = SUBSTR(m.fldexpr,AT('=',m.fldexpr)+1)

IF m.ordline # 0
    m.ordexpr = MLINE(memodata,m.ordline)
    m.ordexpr = "ORDER BY "+;
      SUBSTR(m.ordexpr,AT('=',m.ordexpr)+1)
ENDIF

IF m.filline # 0
    m.filexpr = MLINE(memodata,m.filline)
    m.filexpr = "WHERE "+;
      SUBSTR(m.filexpr,AT('=',m.filexpr)+1)
ENDIF

USE IN tmpcurs

ON ERROR WAIT WINDOW MESSAGE()

SELECT &fldexpr FROM &tblexpr ;
  &ordexpr ;
  &filexpr ;
  INTO CURSOR Query

BROWSE NORMAL NOWAIT

ON ERROR
```

Notice the parameter statement at the top. You pass the name of the file from your script. Make sure that you review the script again because the file name passed as a parameter must be coerced into a string.

I use a FoxPro BROWSE NOWAIT command here. Remember, unless you have a `With Timeout` or `Ignoring Application Responses` statement in your script, AppleScript will time out in one minute. The NOWAIT keyword ensures that command execution continues in the script immediately.

If you want to expand this concept to an even cooler hack, consider a neat shareware utility called Folder Watcher (by Joe Zobkiw). Folder Watcher is actually a control-panel/system-extension combo that monitors the contents of any specified folder(s). Through the control panel, you can control a number of actions taken when the contents of a folder being watched change. Typically, you have the machine display a dialog and/or play a sound. The best part of the control panel is that you can have an AppleScript run when a folder changes. You can set up a folder called Requests, for example, in which you drop files that FoxPro then could automatically process through a script.

Scripting from FoxPro

Here is the only command FoxPro has devoted to AppleScript. Unlike XCMDs, values passed back from scripts are not limited to strings. Scripts, for example, can also return numeric data types.

RUNSCRIPT <script> | TO <memvar> |

Before you plan on executing this command, you'd better make sure that your Mac has AppleScript loaded, or else an error will result. You could test for this by setting up an ON ERROR routine or you could search for the AppleScript extension file(s). Apple uses the following files for running AppleScript (note: both are located in the `:System Folder: Extensions:` folder):

- AppleScript
- Apple®Event Manager

The following program checks for the existence of the AppleScript file. This program relies on a function called FxSystem() contained in the FOXTOOLS.MLB library. If you plan on including this program in a distributed application, any Macs running it will need to have the Apple Shared Library Manager (ASLM) in order to load the FOXTOOLS library.

```
* IS_ASCRIPT.PRG

#DEFINE C_ASFILE "AppleScript_"

PRIVATE hasascript,asfilename
PRIVATE saveerr,savelib,haderr

m.haderr = .F.
m.hasascript = .T.
m.asfilename = ""

m.savelib = SET('LIBRARY')
IF ATC('FOXTOOLS',m.savelib)=0
  m.saveerr = ON('ERROR')
  ON ERROR m.haderr = .T.
  SET LIBRARY TO FOXTOOLS ADDITIVE
  ON ERROR &saveerr
  IF m.haderr
    WAIT WINDOW ;
      "Could not load FoxTools library"
    RETURN .F.
  ENDIF
ENDIF

m.asfilename =fxsystem(1)+':'+C_ASFILE
m.hasascript = FILE(m.asfilename)

IF ATC('FOXTOOLS',m.savelib)=0
  RELEASE LIBRARY FOXTOOLS
ENDIF

RETURN m.hasascript
```

FoxPro scripting can be fun, but having one command can be limiting. Look closely at the preceding RUNSCRIPT command. Notice how information can be received but not passed. Part of the trick to successful scripting is finding a way to pass data from FoxPro to AppleScript. Because parameters are out of the question, you have two options: a file whose format can be used by the other application (for example, FoxPro can output tables to Excel spreadsheets), or you can use the clipboard. FoxPro has a _CLIPTEXT system variable, which contains the contents of the clipboard. If the other application can access the clipboard either through its own AppleScript application command or its own native language (or macros), you are in luck.

CROSS-PLATFORM WARNING

The following few examples require FoxPro and other large applications to run concurrently. Your Macintosh may not have enough memory to successfully run the scripts. If you want to run Excel and FoxPro together under System 7, you need a minimum of 8M—more is better. Several options exist if you are running on limited memory. First, you can set up Virtual Memory, which may be too slow for some scripts. Another alternative is to use the AppleScript Run and Quit commands to launch and terminate applications as you need more memory. The last script in the chapter, for example, uses FoxPro, Excel, and WordPerfect. After Excel finishes completing its functions, I execute a Quit command to free memory.

Excel Cross Tabs

This next example uses the first approach to pass data: FoxPro translates data to a recognizable file format. In this example, a FoxPro table is queried and the output of this query is saved to an Excel spreadsheet. FoxPro then runs a script that processes this data in Excel (see figure 18.5). Here is how it works:

1. FoxPro runs a query from a table and saves the output to a spreadsheet.
2. FoxPro next runs a script to process this new file.
3. The script opens the worksheet saved from FoxPro and runs a macro.
4. The Excel macro creates a pretty cross-tabular table from the data.

Instead of beginning with the script, I will first examine the FoxPro program because it is executed first. The Macsales table contains sales figures for various Macintosh computers by region (see figure 18.6). In our example, we want to obtain a breakdown of product by year for sales.

The MAC SALES.PRG program is extremely basic. Again, the idea is to stress the AppleScript functionality, not what we can do with FoxPro. The COPY TO TYPE XLS command is used to create the Excel spreadsheet used later in the script.

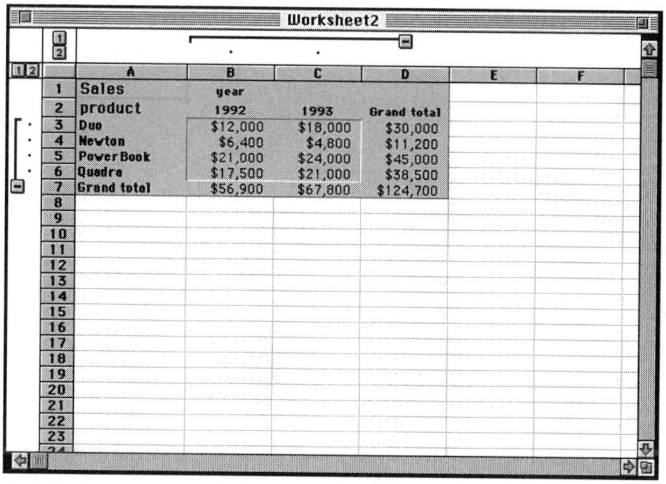

Worksheet2

	A	B	C	D
1	Sales	year		
2	product	1992	1993	Grand total
3	Duo	$12,000	$18,000	$30,000
4	Newton	$6,400	$4,800	$11,200
5	PowerBook	$21,000	$24,000	$45,000
6	Quadra	$17,500	$21,000	$38,500
7	Grand total	$56,900	$67,800	$124,700

Figure 18.5 *Results of FoxPro-Excel Cross-Tab script.*

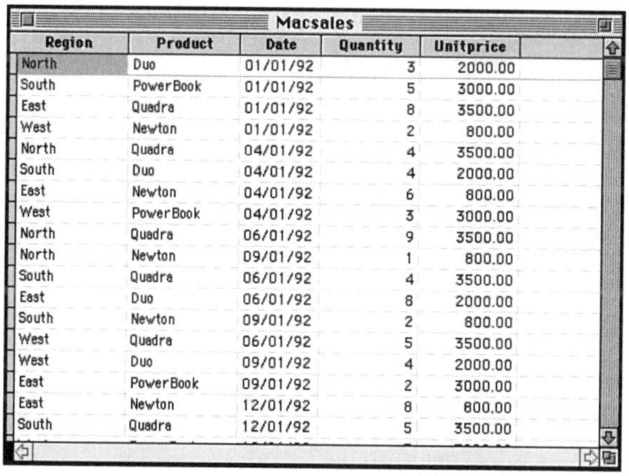

Macsales

Region	Product	Date	Quantity	Unitprice
North	Duo	01/01/92	3	2000.00
South	PowerBook	01/01/92	5	3000.00
East	Quadra	01/01/92	8	3500.00
West	Newton	01/01/92	2	800.00
North	Quadra	04/01/92	4	3500.00
South	Duo	04/01/92	4	2000.00
East	Newton	04/01/92	6	800.00
West	PowerBook	04/01/92	3	3000.00
North	Quadra	06/01/92	9	3500.00
North	Newton	09/01/92	1	800.00
South	Quadra	06/01/92	4	3500.00
East	Duo	06/01/92	8	2000.00
South	Newton	09/01/92	2	800.00
West	Quadra	06/01/92	5	3500.00
West	Duo	09/01/92	4	2000.00
East	PowerBook	09/01/92	2	3000.00
East	Newton	12/01/92	8	800.00
South	Quadra	12/01/92	5	3500.00

Figure 18.6 *FoxPro table used in Cross-Tab script.*

```
* Mac Sales program

m.filepath = SET("DEFAULT") +;
  "MACHETE:APPLESCRIPT:"
m.salesdbf = m.filepath + "MAC SALES.DBF"
m.xlsheet  = m.filepath + "XL SALES.XLS"
m.xlscript = m.filepath + "XL SCRIPT"
```

```
SET SAFETY OFF
CLOSE DATA

USE (m.salesdbf) ALIAS macsales AGAIN

SELECT product,unitprice*quantity AS sales,;
  YEAR(date) AS Year FROM macsales ;
  GROUP BY year,product ORDER BY year;
  INTO CURSOR xlcurs

COPY TO (m.xlsheet) TYPE XLS

RUNSCRIPT (m.xlscript) TO m.retval
```

There isn't anything special in this program. A variable named `m.retval` is used to obtain any values returned by the script. I haven't tested this variable in the sample procedure, but you could easily set up statements to do this. Now, look at the script that uses the results:

```
— XL Script is file name
tell application "Microsoft Excel"

  — setup AppleScript variables
  set x to path to startup disk
  copy (x as string) ¬
    & "Machete:AppleScript:" ¬
    to foxpath
  copy "XL Macros" to xlmacs
  — FoxPro query file
  copy "XL SALES.XLS" to xlsales

  — open files if not already open
  if not (Window xlmacs exists) then
    open foxpath & xlmacs
  end if
  if not (Window xlsales exists) then
    open foxpath & xlsales
  end if

  — make sure xlsales document is on top
  set the selection of Document ¬
    xlsales to "R1C1"
```

```
  — run excel macro to create cross tab
  Evaluate "run('" & xlmacs & "'!Cross_Tab)"

  — close files, see if Macro file is hidden 1st
  close Window xlsales saving no
  if visible of Window xlmacs = false then
    set visible of Window xlmacs to true
  end if
  close Window xlmacs saving no

  —bring Excel to front
  activate "Microsoft Excel"

end tell
```

Most of the meat in this script is actually part of Excel's dictionary, which I showed earlier in the chapter. The AppleScript `Evaluate` (Excel) command is similar to the `Do Script` (FoxPro) command in that it performs a native Excel command (in this case, the command is the macro you run).

In Excel, you can use the Set The Selection command to bring forward a document to the top.

Many Excel developers like to keep hidden macrosheets. You can do this by hiding the macrosheet and then quitting Excel. Excel will prompt you to save the macrosheet when terminating (select Save). The Excel AppleScript Close command has trouble closing hidden files. To do so, you first need to make them visible.

Often when you close files, the application prompts you to Save or Cancel new edits. The AppleScript Close command has an optional parameter called Saving that lets you bypass the Save dialog with a particular response.

Finally, table 18.5 shows you the Excel Cross_Tab macro contained in the `XL Macros` macrosheet file. This entire macro was created using Excel's macro recorder. Excel has a Cross Tab wizard that facilitates the creation of the CROSSTAB.CREATE command. As you begin working with scripts and spreadsheets, be aware that cell referencing in scripts is usually only by RC syntax. For instance, you can use R1C1, but may not be able to use A1.

Table 18.5

Excel Macro to create Cross Tab from XL Macro's file

```
cross tab
=ACTIVATE("XL SALES.XLS")
=SELECT("C1:C3")
=SET.DATABASE()
=CROSSTAB.CREATE({"product",0,"Auto","Auto","NNNNNNN"},{"year",0,"Auto","Auto",
  "NNNNNNN"},{"sales","SUM(sales)","YNNNN",FALSE},TRUE,TRUE,1,TRUE,TRUE)
=SELECT("crosstab_range")
=FORMAT.AUTO(13,TRUE,TRUE,TRUE,TRUE,TRUE,TRUE)
=APPLY.STYLE("Currency [0]")
=COLUMN.WIDTH(13,"C1")
=COLUMN.WIDTH(10,"C2:C10")
=FORMULA("=CROSSTAB(""Sales"",""Summary:"",values_array,TRUE,TRUE,1,TRUE)")
=SELECT("R1C1")
=RETURN("OK")
```

Notice the last line here — =RETURN(OK). If you are familiar with Excel macros, you probably are wondering why we need to return anything. For some reason, the `Evaluate` command must receive a data type with which AppleScript is familiar, and a null value is not one of them.

I already pointed out that, if possible, you are better off using the native language rather than AppleScript, and Excel is no exception. If you look at the Excel AppleScript dictionary, you see many commands and objects. Unfortunately, the command set is severely limited when compared to the command set of Excel's native macro language. Many advanced features, such as cross tabs, can be performed only within Excel.

Using ZipIt To Automate Backups

ZipIt is a wonderful archiving utility because of its cross-platform compatibility with the popular DOS products PKZIP/PKUNZIP. The following example illustrates a useful function for database developers, archiving. *Archiving* here refers to ZipIt's capability to compress user-specified files/folders into a single ZIP file. The `Zip Back` script that follows can be run without using FoxPro. In fact, there is no FoxPro program listed; you can create one with a RUNSCRIPT command to call this script if you want FoxPro to control the process.

When you first run this script, the user interface may be a little confusing. This is primarily because the script was written using native AppleScript resources.

AppleScript does not come with a scripting addition to allow for selection of a folder (similar to FoxPro's GETDIR() function). If you want a nice freeware solution (which is the recommended course of action), check out Script Tools by Mark Alldritt. This set of scripting additions includes one to select only a folder. In fact, he has included tools to allow for selection of multiple files and folders.

This script performs the following steps:

1. The user is prompted with a dialog asking for a file name to archive.
2. The user is next asked to select whether to archive the file or entire folder where that file was contained.
3. The user is prompted to specify a name used for the archive file.
4. The script processes commands with ZipIt to automate creation of a ZIP archive file.

```
— Zip Back AppleScript source
choose file with prompt "Select a file:"
copy the result as string to newfile
copy pathOf(the result) as string to getfolder

display dialog ¬
  "Do you want to backup this file only?" ¬
  buttons {"File Only", "Entire Folder"} ¬
   default button 2

copy (button returned of the result = ¬
  "Entire Folder") ¬
  to dofolder

display dialog ¬
  "Enter name for archive file:" ¬
  default answer "BACKUP.ZIP" ¬
  buttons {"OK"} ¬
  default button "OK"

copy getfolder ¬
  & (text returned of the result) ¬
  to zipFileName
```

```
tell application "ZipIt"

  New window
  activate "ZipIt"

  if dofolder then
    repeat with myitem in list folder getfolder
      Add file (getfolder & myitem)
    end repeat
  else
    Add file newfile
  end if

  with timeout of 3600 seconds
    Compress to file zipFileName
  end timeout

  quit
  return zipFileName
end tell

on pathOf(theFile) — takes an alias of fileSpec
  copy every character of (theFile as string) ¬
    to CharList
  repeat with charNum from (the number of items ¬
    in CharList) to 1 by -1
    if (item charNum of CharList) is ":" then
      return alias ((characters 1 thru charNum ¬
        of theFile) as string)
    end if
  end repeat
end pathOf
```

Okay, so I included a modified version of `Zip Back` that uses the Script Tools extensions. One nice feature of this script is that you do not need a subroutine to obtain a file's path because all the dialogs return this information for you. Before I show the script, figure 18.7 shows the dialog included with Script Tools.

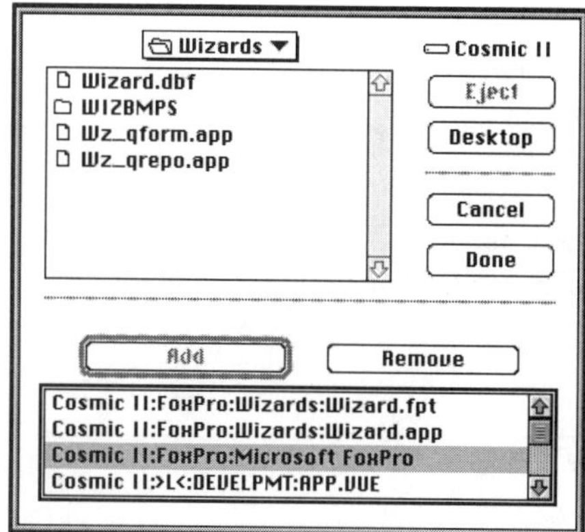

Figure 18.7 *Mark Alldritt's shareware Script Tools Choose Several Files dialog.*

```
— Zip Back script using Mark Alldritt's
— Script Tools scripting extensions.
— prompt for backup method
display dialog "What do you want to archive?" ¬
  buttons {"Files", "Folders"}

copy (button returned of the result = "Folders") ¬
  to isfolders

— get list of files/folders
if isfolders then
  copy (choose several folders) to flist
else
  copy (choose several files) to flist
end if

— get backup archive name
copy (choose new file default name "backup.zip" ¬
  with prompt "Save archive as:") to tmprec
copy ((folder returned of tmprec as string) & ¬
  filename returned of tmprec) to zipFileName

tell application "ZipIt"

  New window
  activate "ZipIt"
```

```
  repeat with myitem in flist
    Add file (myitem as string)
  end repeat

  with timeout of 3600 seconds
    Compress to file zipFileName
  end timeout

  quit
  return zipFileName
end tell
```

Document Integration

The preceding script shows off Apple's true intent with AppleScript. Apple envisioned AppleScript as the glue needed to combine the strengths of several applications. You don't want to create a nice formatted document in FoxPro. Nor do you want to use WordPerfect to produce a complex graph. This script combines the strengths of FoxPro (database querying), Excel (charting), and WordPerfect (word processing) to automate the generation of a sales report. Although this script stops here, you could add additional AppleScript commands easily that use AOCE to send this report to a number of e-mail addresses.

Again, start out with the FoxPro program. This program exploits the clipboard as the method for transferring data from FoxPro to the script. Because you are passing this data to an Excel spreadsheet, you need to format the data in a manner that Excel can handle. Excel columns are separated by Tabs and rows by Carriage Return/Line Feeds.

The table used for the query is the same used before with the Cross-Tab example (MAC SALES.DBF). This time we are querying data based on region, not product:

```
* FoxPro Regions program

#DEFINE tab CHR(9)
#DEFINE crlf CHR(13)+CHR(10)

m.filepath = SET("DEFAULT") + ;
```

```
  "MACHETE:APPLESCRIPT:"
m.salesdbf = m.filepath + "MAC SALES.DBF"
m.xlscript = m.filepath + "Create Chart"
m.tmpstr = " "

CLOSE DATA

USE (m.salesdbf) ALIAS macsales AGAIN

SELECT DISTINCT region FROM macsales ;
  INTO ARRAY rgnarr
SELECT DISTINCT YEAR(date) AS Year FROM macsales;
  ORDER BY 1;
  INTO ARRAY yeararr

* create string for clipboard
FOR i = 1 TO ALEN(yeararr)
  m.tmpstr=m.tmpstr + tab + ;
    ALLTRIM(STR(yeararr(m.i)))
ENDFOR
m.tmpstr=m.tmpstr + crlf

FOR i = 1 TO ALEN(rgnarr)
  m.tmpstr=m.tmpstr + rgnarr(m.i) +tab
  FOR j = 1 TO ALEN(yeararr)
    SUM unitprice*quantity TO m.tmpsum ;
      FOR region = rgnarr(m.i) AND ;
      YEAR(date)=yeararr(m.j)
    m.tmpstr=m.tmpstr + STR(m.tmpsum) + ;
      IIF(j=ALEN(yeararr),'',tab)
  ENDFOR
  m.tmpstr=m.tmpstr + crlf
ENDFOR

_CLIPTEXT = m.tmpstr
RUNSCRIPT (m.xlscript) TO retval
```

In this program, the FoxPro global _CLIPTEXT is used to transfer the data string created to the clipboard. This string consists of regions along the y-axis and years along the x-axis.

Now comes the fun part. The script that follows in this section is not too long, and most of it is devoted to Excel. As you read through the code, you will notice a number of tricks that may help you get around limitations with the two products. Here is what the script does:

1. FoxPro runs a query and stuffs the results into the Clipboard.
2. Excel takes the contents of the clipboard and creates a new worksheet with it.
3. The data is massaged a bit before it is used to create a 3D Column chart.
4. The script next starts WordPerfect and opens a stationery document.
5. Finally, the Excel chart is added to the WordPerfect document (see figure 18.8).

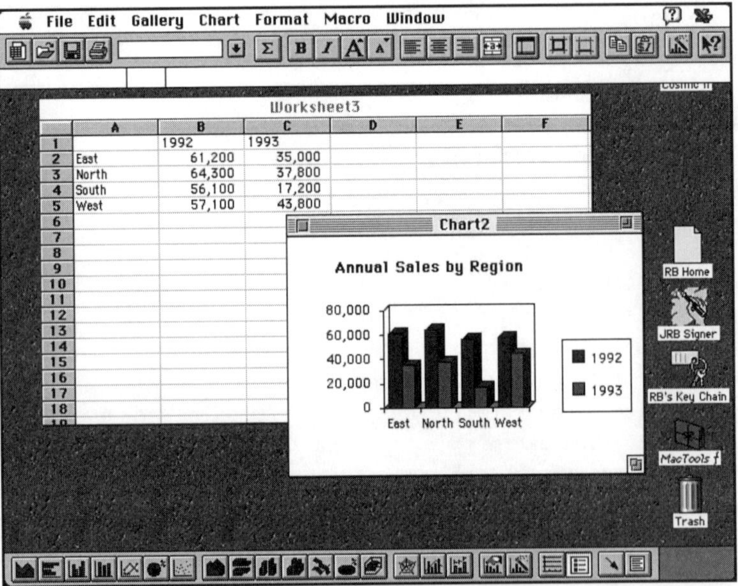

Figure 18.8 *Excel-generated chart from FoxPro query.*

```
—AppleScript script
tell application "Microsoft Excel"

  — Set up variables
  set charttitle to "Annual Sales by Region"
  set charttype to three D column
  set chartlegend to true
```

```
  — Now do the work
  activate "Microsoft Excel"
  make Document
  Evaluate "Paste()" —paste contents of clipboard
  Evaluate "APPLY.STYLE(\"Comma [0]\")"

  (* this repeat loop is used to convert Excel
  numbers into labels for the series headings *)
  repeat with snum from 2 to 99 — use large number
    copy value of Cell snum to scontents
    if scontents is equal to "" then
      exit repeat
    end if
    try
      get scontents as integer — check for number
      set the value of Cell snum to "'" & scontents
      on error — loop around
    end try
  end repeat

  make new Chart
  set type of first Chart to charttype
  set variant of first Chart to 1
  set has legend of first Chart to chartlegend
  set title of first Chart to charttitle

  copy first Chart to finalchart

  close first Document saving no
  close first Document saving no
  quit —not needed if you have enough memory
end tell

(* Need to launch WP first if not already running,
else the chart gets lost. Also, make sure you have
stationery file "Machete" loaded. *)
run application "WordPerfect"
tell application "WordPerfect"
  ignoring application responses
    activate "WordPerfect"
```

```
    — this is a stationery file
    open (a reference to file "Machete")
    make new paragraph with data finalchart
    move paragraphs 2 thru 14 to front
  end ignoring
end tell
```

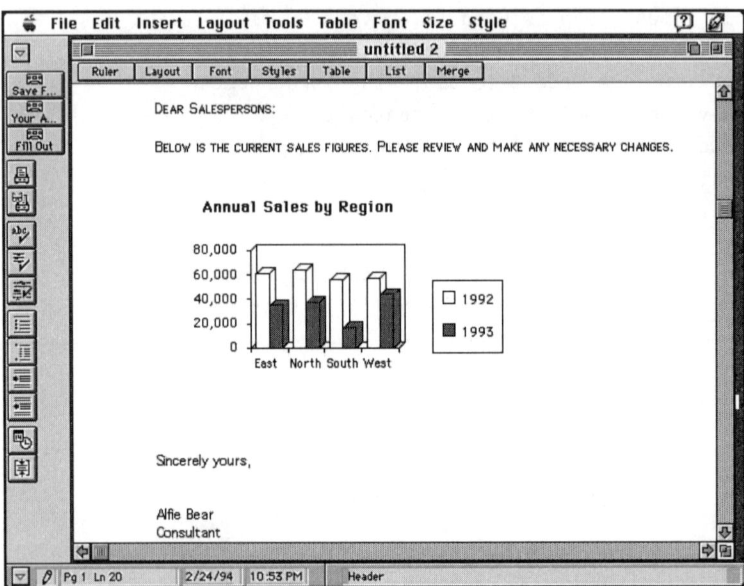

Figure 18.9 *WordPerfect final document incorporating Excel chart from FoxPro query.*

This script uses the Excel Evaluate command several times. The line `Evaluate "APPLY.STYLE(\"Comma [0]\")"` applies a number format (Comma [0]) to the selected cells. Notice the backslashes. Because AppleScript also uses double quote delimiters, the command confuses the Script Editor because there is also a set of double quotes for the Excel command. AppleScript allows you to include double quotes in your strings if you precede them with a "\" character.

The repeat loop is actually a kludge to get Excel to convert numbers (e.g., 1992, 1993) into label strings so that they will not be used as data in the chart. This happens if you try to copy and paste numeric data preceded with the single quote delimiter.

Before sending AppleScript commands to WordPerfect, you need to launch it. Usually, the Tell Application can be used. With this script, however, WordPerfect doesn't properly process the command that adds the chart (Make New Paragraph) if WordPerfect is not already running.

To accomplish this launch, a stationery file provides a stub. If you wanted to get really fancy, you could have FoxPro create a text file from a memo field and have this added as the text portion of the document. WordPerfect 3.0 supports Apple's new AOCE technology that in essence integrates e-mail into the application. One of the other reasons that you will want to consider using a stationery file is that an AOCE mailer can be attached and saved with preset e-mail addresses. Through AppleScript, you could take this script one step further by having the generated document mailed to a number of e-mail accounts.

Chapter Wrap Up

Several years after Apple Computer's first release of System 7, they've finally provided their much-hyped AppleScript extension. Even with its limitations, and although FoxPro's support for AppleScript is limited, Do Script lets you get at any FoxPro capability through this powerful System extension. FoxPro's RUNSCRIPT lets you turn around and connect with other Macintosh applications, through AppleScript, in unlimited ways. Happy scripting.

19

ENHANCE THE DEVELOPMENT PROCESS AND POLISH YOUR APPLICATION: THIRD PARTY TOOLS AND EXTENSIONS

by
Randy Brown

In this chapter, I review various utilities that can improve your productivity in FoxPro. I am not trying to put together a buyer's guide of what you *need* to work in FoxPro; each utility described here is handy for particular aspects of FoxPro application development. This chapter includes recommendations for both public domain and commercial software divided into categories by type of application. You will find a few of the shareware products on the source code disk for this book. Appendix A, "Guide to Resources," includes instructions for obtaining those items not included on the disk.

Should you use public domain and shareware software? Many people avoid noncommercial software for a number of reasons. First, some companies have corporate standards that do not allow machines to have software from sources other than a "recommended software" list. People with this policy believe that shareware is not tested as thoroughly as commercial software, although experience may argue otherwise. Commercial software companies usually offer some form of technical support. Finally, commercial companies are more apt to offer upgrades, especially when hardware and system software incompatibilities arise.

Remember that many commercial products originated as shareware. Raymond Lau's *StuffIt* is a good example. Trying out shareware on sample data before risking it on live data is always wise. Also, if you use a shareware product rather than a program placed in public domain by its author, you should register the shareware and pay the nominal usage fee the author requires. If you plan on distributing FoxPro applications that might make use of one of these goodies, do not violate its distribution policy.

Even portions of the Mac System have originated as shareware. If you have upgraded to System 7.5, you will find some of the utilities I recommend are now included with your system software! This chapter will help you understand how they're used and why they're useful with FoxPro, whether you install them with System 7.5 or integrate them into your custom Mac environment on your own.

FOXPRO MAC HACK TIP

Searching for sources of public domain software? The best places to start are the Macintosh PD libraries on CompuServe, America OnLine, and GEnie. You can also contact your local user group. User groups have sizable public domain libraries. One caveat—with the user group approach, you may not always obtain the latest version of a product as you would from an online service. Finally, you can contact a mail-order house and pay a small fee for their efforts to put together PD disks. Today, you can obtain CD-ROMs that contain hundreds of MB worth of shareware files. The Berkeley Mac Users Group (BMUG) offers their BMUG PD-ROM, which has received many accolades, at a reasonable price. BMUG is listed in the Resources appendix.

Cross-Platform Goodies

You may be new to FoxPro for Macintosh, but you probably have experience with FoxPro products on the PC. However, you may be one of the many Mac developers who never used a PC, but expect to port your FoxPro application from the Mac to the PC. Using the right tools can facilitate a successful port.

Cross-platform development on FoxPro can, for the most part, be confined to a single machine. You can create a decent-looking FoxPro for Macintosh application by using FoxPro for Windows, and vice versa. I don't recommend this approach with the DOS product because it is character-based only. At some point, however, transferring files to all platforms that will run the application is a good idea. Although this entire process really is not too complicated, even some top FoxPro PC developers had troubles accomplishing it at first. You can break the porting process into two components:

- File transfer
- File translation

File transfer refers to the physical process of moving files between platforms. There are several media to accomplish this part of the task. The easiest way is to move files back and forth over a network that supports both platforms. If you have a single Macintosh and PC, this solution may be an overkill. There are several great alternatives for very small networks (several machines) that don't require a lot of network hardware and software. In fact, a physical cable can be attached between the two.

Perhaps the easiest solution, if you have just a few machines and no network, is to transfer files by using a floppy disk. This method may be time-consuming if you have many files. In addition, large files can be quite a pain to transfer. In this chapter, I'll show you some compression utilities and evaluate their use for cross-platform work. A final alternative is to use a modem to transmit file(s) to the other platform.

File translation describes the physical manipulation of changing a file's format to another format. This process often is necessary when you move files between applications, not just between platforms. Many applications contain filters or other conversion methods for translating foreign files into a native format. You may want to work, for example, on a Lotus 1-2-3 spreadsheet (PC) with a Macintosh and all you have is Excel. After you transfer the file to the Mac, you need to translate it into Excel format.

Excel has internal translators for this, but third party products offer a more diverse array of format translators.

FoxPro is extremely flexible when it comes to translating its file formats between platforms. The binary file structure of all files—with the exception of libraries—is identical between platforms. FoxPro relies primarily on file extensions to identify file types because its roots are in the DOS environment. Although extensions simplify cross-platform development, Microsoft's approach totally ignores preservation of a Macintosh's file type and creator. You should be concerned about this for several reasons. First, there are certain commands that are enhanced to allow the use of clauses specifying creator and/or type (ADIR and GETFILE). Second, the ability to double-click an application's file (or drag and drop a file onto the application's icon) to launch the application is controlled by the file type and creator.

FOXPRO MAC HACK TIP

The ability to drag and drop files onto application icons is unique to Apple's System 7. If you drag a database file (DBF) onto the application's icon, System 7 launches FoxPro and opens the table. Unfortunately, you can drag only one file onto the icon at a time. It would be nice if FoxPro opened all files that you dragged onto it. Even if you are already running FoxPro, you can drop a database file onto the icon, and FoxPro opens it in the current work area. Be careful here: a table already opened in this work area is closed. Another trick is to have a System 7 alias of the FoxPro application icon on the desktop. You can drag and drop files on alias icons just like the real application icons.

You can start here with a few simple solutions to assist with transporting files between platforms. Remember, you need not spring for an integrated network yet. The simplest and least expensive approach is direct floppy transfer, which is a software-only solution. If you work with large files, consider using a compression utility to shrink the files to fit on floppies. If this method is still too burdensome, you can explore using a direct cable or simple network.

The following software solutions offer you different degrees of flexibility in file transfer and translation.

Macintosh PC Exchange, DOS Mounter, and Access PC

These three utilities (each is a commercial product) allow you to insert a PC-formatted floppy disk into the Mac's disk drive. Each utility is a control panel that offers a set of options including the capability to format new disks in either Mac or PC format.

These products can optionally map a specific file type and creator based on its DOS file extension. For example, you could have a FoxPro database file automatically mapped with a file type of 'F+DB' and a creator of 'FOXX'. Appendix B gives additional advice about FoxPro file types.

The PC Exchange product is marketed by Apple, included in System 7.5, and has the least impressive features. You need to know that when you insert a DOS disk into a Mac when using these programs, a new directory is created to hold any resource fork information for Mac-specific files. If you work only with PC files, you need not worry about this directory.

MacDisk for the PC

This is an equivalent PC-side utility by Insignia® Solutions (who also produce Access PC) for file transfer. MacDisk for the PC allows you to insert a Mac disk into a PC machine and works with both DOS and Windows.

MacLinkPlus

This tool, known as MLP, by DataViz, Inc., is the quintessential utility for file translation on the Macintosh. There are over 1,000 file translation paths between Mac, DOS, Windows, Apple II, NeXT, and Sun computers. Most of the translators handle word processing, spreadsheet and graphics formats, but a few useful database translators also are included.

As mentioned previously, FoxPro provides excellent cross-platform support for its files among Mac, DOS, and Windows. Also, FoxPro has internal converters for 4th Dimension, FileMaker Pro, dBASE, Paradox, and other common database formats. Make sure that what you need from MLP isn't already provided for by FoxPro.

The full version of MLP comes with a cable so that you can connect to a PC and transfer files directly. If you choose, you can purchase just the translators. You can set up default translations between the platforms so that, for example, PICT files always are translated to BMP format unless you override the default choice. This option is handy for porting images you use in FoxPro screens and reports.

Coactive Connector

This utility is a great solution by Coactive Computing Corp. for a simple MAC-PC network where sharing files and printers is your primary concern. Setup can be accomplished within a matter of minutes (no hardware cards needed), and it even runs on Windows. You are limited to 32 computers over 1,000 feet of phone line.

SoftPC, SoftWindows

These products, from Insignia® Solutions, emulate a 80×86 processor or allow you to run DOS/Windows software on a Mac. If you are a serious FoxPro PC developer, you may be disappointed with performance and speed. I suggest that you use these only with the new Apple Power Macs.

Macintosh Easy Open

This system extension by Apple Computer acts as an intermediary to assist in translating foreign file formats. For example, you can double-click on a document and Easy Open intercepts, asking you to select an appropriate beginning application. Mac Easy Open works behind-the-scenes on a Macintosh to allow you to open a document when you don't have the program that created the document. If the file's creator is known, the file is opened without going through Easy Open. Easy Open also works with the standard Mac File Open dialog to offer more choices of files.

It's important to understand that Easy Open doesn't contain translators, but instead works in conjunction with translators, such as MacLinkPlus by DataViz, Inc.

File Buddy

This highly recommended shareware utility by Laurence Harris has many wonderful file goodies worth investigating (see figure 19.1). From the point of view of cross-platform development, it is useful for changing file type and creator of PC-ported documents. You just drop a file on its icon to make changes to a variety of file attributes. In addition, File Buddy contains several options for System 7 aliases.

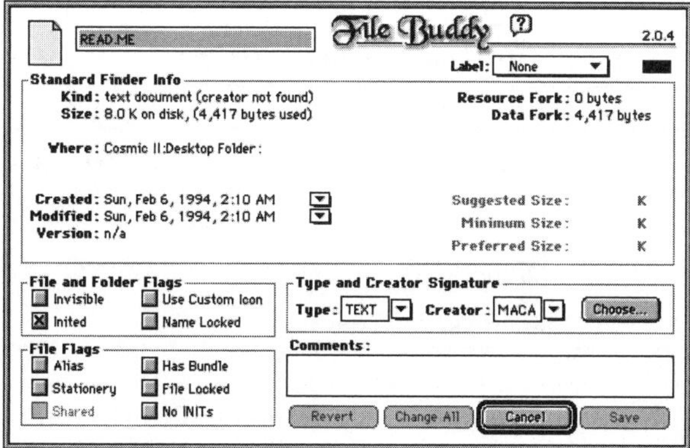

Figure 19.1 *File Buddy Shareware Utility by Laurence Harris.*

Compression Goodies

Most people are familiar with file compression utilities. These programs compress your files up to 90 percent of their original size. They also can combine multiple files together into a single compressed archive. Compressed files are popular with on-line services because they can significantly reduce the time (cost) of a download. These files are also convenient for backup, because you often can squeeze several MBs of data onto a single disk.

Table 19.1 is a guide to some of the more common extensions for files created with a compression utility. The last option (self-extracting) is offered by many vendor products including Disk Doubler (not mentioned in the table). SEA files can be decompressed without the utility itself being present. They are a little larger in size because they contain a mini-decompression engine built into the file.

Table 19.1
Comparisons of Various Compression Utilities

Extension	*Mac Utility*	*PC Utility*
ZIP	ZipIt	PKZIP, PKUNZIP
SIT	StuffIt	UnSit
CPT	Compact Pro	EXTPC
SEA	generic self-extracting	

This section reviews the popular compression tools listed in this table.

PKZIP and ZipIt

If you're a cross-platform FoxPro developer, these utilities are indispensable. Both are shareware, but you can use PKUNZIP freely if you intend to employ it only for decompression services. On the Mac side, there are several Macintosh shareware utilities that inflate ZIP files, but ZipIt seems to offer the most features and supports the latest versions of PKZIP. In addition, ZipIt is the only Mac offering that retains the directory structure of a ZIP file. ZipIt is the creation of Tommy Brown (see figure 19.2), and PKZIP is produced by PKWare, Inc.

While on the subject of PKZIP, you may need to transfer these files via CompuServe or other electronic services and bulletin boards. PKZIP is the standard for file transfer between PCs. The advent of Mac compatible PKZIP utilities such as ZipIt makes possible sending ZIP files from your Mac to a friend on CompuServe who uses a PC.

Many Mac users run the Navigator communication package to connect to CompuServe. Most Mac files have a MacBinary file header that is stripped by Navigator when you transfer a file to CompuServe. This header contains file type, creator, and resource fork information. Because ZIP files do not contain any of this information, you need to tell Navigator to bypass stripping a part of the header. Otherwise, the PC user ends up with a corrupted file. The trick is to change the file type to 'DATA'. Navigator transfers all files of this type as straight binary without any header information being lost.

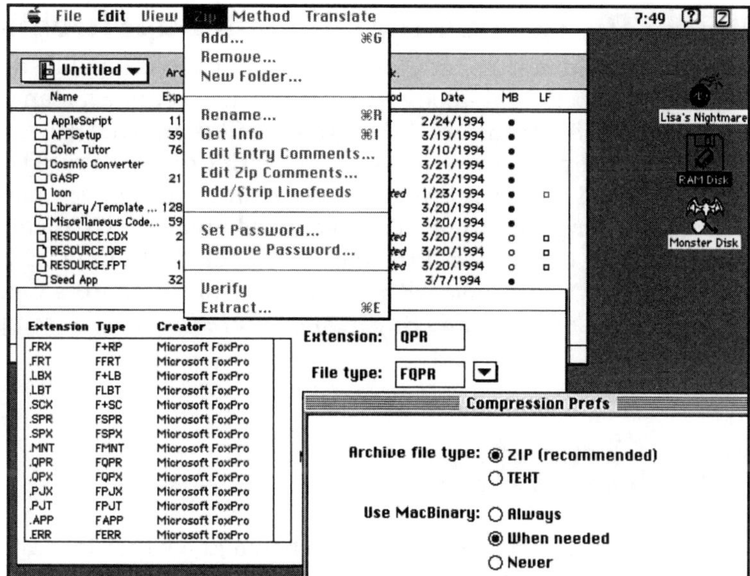

Figure 19.2 *ZipIt Shareware Utility by Tommy Brown showing its file extension-to-type and compression preference dialogs.*

PC users can download Mac files to their PCs and then transfer them successfully to a Mac. Using some of these utilities (such as MacLinkPlus PC Exchange), these files can be ported successfully with MacBinary attributes intact.

StuffIt, UnStuff

StuffIt originally was created by Raymond Lau as a public domain project. For a long time, it was the only decent compression product available for the Mac (shareware or commercial). StuffIt quickly became a standard. StuffIt now is owned and sold as commercial software by Aladdin Systems, Inc. You still can get a scaled-down shareware version called StuffIt Lite. The UnStuff PC utility makes StuffIt a practical solution for cross-platform file transfer if you choose not to go with PKZIP/ZipIt. UnStuff is written by Jody Nickel as freeware and distributed by Aladdin.

Compact Pro, Now Compress, and SuperDoubler

These are Mac-only compression utilities. Compact Pro is a public domain utility by Bill Goodman that, along with StuffIt, has become a standard for on-line services' file transfers. When you see files with a .CPT extension on-line, you know they were compressed with Compact Pro. The registered version of Compact Pro includes two utilities that you may distribute freely along with Compact Pro-created archives: Extractor, an extract-only version of Compact Pro, and "ExtractorPC" (EXTPC.EXE), a version of Extractor that people with PCs can use to decompress Compact Pro archives. Now Compress and SuperDoubler are commercial compression packages.

Virus Goodies

If you are a FoxPro user new to Macs, you should know that PCs are not the only computers prone to virus attacks. Because Macs also are susceptible, we're fortunate that some outstanding products exist to combat the nasties. Leading the way, believe it or not, is a must-have freeware utility called Disinfectant.

Disinfectant

This public domain utility by John Norstad of Northwestern University has proven to be the most up-to-date of all virus packages. The best part is that it is free. John, one of the foremost authorities on computer viruses in the Macintosh industry, is committed to rapid product updates whenever new viruses are discovered.

SAM

The Symantec Antivirus for Macintosh probably is the most popular commercial virus utility and also is a very comprehensive package. Symantec is responsive to releasing upgrade patches for new found viruses.

MacTools

This Central Point Software package may be a better alternative to SAM. For about the same price, you get not only a decent virus checker but also a full set of disk, file maintenance, and recovery utilities.

Development Goodies

Most Macintosh developers own a set of tools to help enhance productivity when working on applications. Although FoxPro comes with a wealth of native features to make life easier for the creation of that ultimate database application, you should seriously consider adopting several of these utilities if you do not already own them.

MacsBug

How often have you been working with your favorite software package when suddenly, you get the ubiquitous System La Bomba message and things go black. Usually, you have only one option at this point: click the OK button and watch your Mac reboot, taking along with it any unsaved documents you might have had opened at the time. I can't really enforce good backup habits, but I do recommend an option that will get you out of most binds. If you are serious about development, do yourself a favor and get a good debugger.

The MacsBug debugger by Apple Computer is a known standard among Mac software developers. Many on-line bulletin board services have this one. When you do encounter that System Bomb error, the debugger will intercept and allow you to return back to the Finder. Often, the problematic application is terminated (not always), and any other open applications are left intact.

> **FOXPRO MAC HACK TIP**
>
> If you are ever invited to beta test software, consider doing it only if you have a good debugger. Fortunately for Mac users, several excellent debuggers are available that won't totally bring your whole system to a halt. Windows users may not be as lucky when the General Protection Fault strikes.

ResEdit

This Apple Computer essential allows you to edit and work with any Macintosh Resource in the resource fork of any file. For example, you can

See Also

- "Visual Clues in Standard Dialogs," Chapter 11
- "Doing Windows the FoxPro Way," Chapter 12
- "Sample XCMDs," Chapter 16

change the look of dialog boxes, edit icons, create cursors, and copy XCMDs to other files. If you prefer, you even can edit FoxPro, as shown in figure 19.3. ResEdit is a powerful utility, but it also can do serious damage to files if you don't know what you are doing.

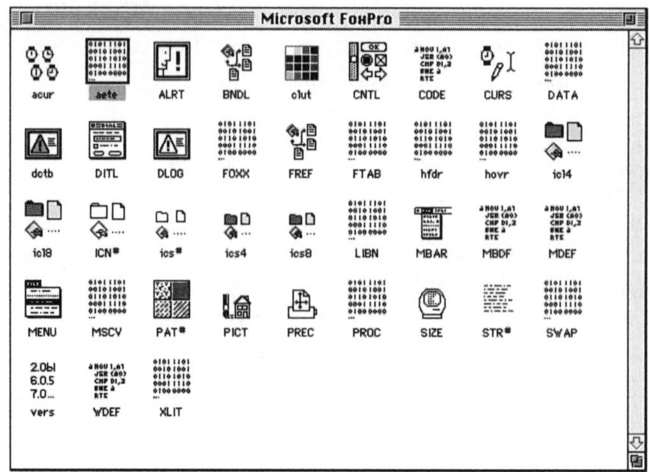

Figure 19.3 *ResEdit Utility by Apple Computer.*

PopChar

See Also

- "Keyboard Differences," Chapter 1

If you are in search of a Mac alternative to the FoxPro (DOS) ASCII Chart and Special Characters dialog, PopChar is a wonderful solution. This nifty shareware init from Günther Blaschek places a tiny icon in the top corner of your Mac and gives you instant access to the entire character set of the current font (see figure 19.4).

You even can select specific characters to copy from and paste into your applications, and PopChar gives you a handy reminder of the Mac ⌘-shifted equivalent from the character if you want to type it from the keyboard next time. It works quite well with the FoxPro editor.

Figure 19.4 *PopChar Shareware Utility by Günther Blaschek.*

MiniScreen

This control panel device by the Morgan Davis Group changes the size of the desktop on a large screen Macintosh to something smaller. It's great for software developers with full page displays who need to test their programs on smaller screen machines. Be aware that this shareware utility may have compatibility problems with certain machines and may cause them to lock up. As an alternative, the latest version of the Monitors control panel by Apple Computer offers several resolutions to choose from, including smaller 9-inch Macintosh screens.

QuicKeys

CE Software made its name in the Macintosh world with this product. QuicKeys automates everyday repetitive tasks and routines with single keystrokes. In fact, you don't even need to memorize the keyboard shortcuts because QuicKeys offers menus and palettes for storage of these. QuicKeys also interfaces nicely with AppleScript and Frontier.

> **CROSS-PLATFORM WARNING**
>
> QuicKeys enables you to create application-specific shortcuts. As mentioned previously, FoxPro is not truly compliant with many standard Macintosh interface elements because of cross-platform needs. Therefore, QuicKeys doesn't always work with FoxPro. For example, FoxPro does not use Macintosh menus in a standard way,

> so a QuicKeys shortcut that selects a series of menus may not work properly. There are ways to use QuicKeys in conjunction with FoxPro to circumvent some of these limitations. Because QuicKeys is such an asset to Mac developers, QuicKeys is discussed separately in Appendix C.

Frontier

Userland Software, Inc. beat Apple to the punch with its own scripting language. This product is compliant with Apple's Open Scripting Architecture (OSA) and has a C-like language. Consider Frontier as a more powerful alternative to Apple's AppleScript. Frontier goes to the lowest System levels and offers more features than AppleScript.

Magnet

Magnet by No Hands Software is a product that automates virtually any file-related task, using *agents*. Consider a Macintosh agent as a utility sent to perform a task for you. Magnet can synchronize, copy, move, and alias any file. In fact, it works transparently over a network. If you plan group FoxPro development efforts, look closely at this product.

SpeedyFinder7

Finally, here's an invaluable shareware utility from Victor Tan of Australia that performs many System 7 enhancements. First, you can turn off that annoying Balloon Help or, if you prefer, assign hot keys to enable it. There are a number of options to speed various Finder operations, including copying files. SpeedyFinder7 features a nice document-linking option in which you can link certain file types to specific applications, and a whole slew of additional features.

Interface Goodies

Macintoshes are meant to be fun, and adding a few interface goodies can make Mac life more interesting for the user. Along with fun, I include several utilities here because they offer functionality similar to that on another platform. For example, FoxPro for Windows and DOS allows you to minimize windows. The WindowShade control panel performs a similar function on the Mac.

Besides the plethora of commercial enhancers, an abundance of public domain software is out there for the choosing. Here are just a few of the goodies worth checking out.

Greg's Buttons

Gregory D. Landweber got bored with Apple's standard button look and feel one day, so he decided to do something about it. This public domain control panel utility changes the look of various controls including push buttons, radio buttons, and check boxes. Don't get too excited about this stuff for your FoxPro dialogs because FoxPro rolls its own controls. Greg's Buttons also has options to change dialog, window, and menu colors (see figure 19.5).

Figure 19.5 *Greg's Buttons Shareware Utility by Gregory D. Landweber.*

MenuChoice

This simple menu utility adds hierarchical menus to your Apple menu. It is a shareware product by Kerry Clendinning.

TearOFFs

This utility falls under the *way-cool* category and it even works with FoxPro's menus. Menus can be torn-off the menu bar and placed anywhere on the desktop. If you have a large monitor, this is a must-have utility by Bad Boys' Software (see figure 19.6).

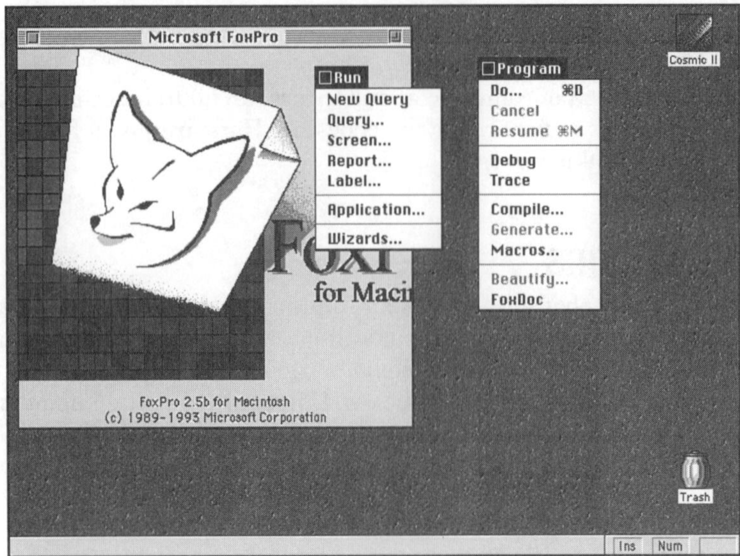

Figure 19.6 *TearOFFs Shareware Utility by Bad Boys' Software.*

WindowShade

This shareware utility by Rob Johnston rolls like windows up a window shade. You just click in the title bar of a window the number of times set in the control panel. Be forewarned that FoxPro for Macintosh does not recognize windows in a minimized state—WMIN()—so it may have limited use within a program. Interactively, WindowShade works great and cleans up your desktop working space.

CROSS-PLATFORM WARNING

In System 7.5, WindowShade is included with the system software, but FoxPro still doesn't know anything about it. To test it, DEFINE and ACTIVATE a FoxPro window with a border of SYSTEM. Click the title bar the number of times specified by the WindowShade. The FoxPro window appears minimized. Now check the WMIN() function; it still returns .F..

> In FoxPro for DOS or Windows, you can check WMIN() to decide whether you need to ZOOM WINDOW <name> NORM (to pop it back to normal size) when that window is activated during a READ. Otherwise, the user is entering data that he cannot see. Because WindowShade is now available to all Mac users, and with no WMIN() to check, we may have to add the line ZOOM WINDOW (WONTOP()) NORM in all READ ACTIVATE clauses for FoxPro for Macintosh.

SuperClock

This freeware control panel by Steve Christensen places a clock into the menu bar. The popular utility has a clock, timer, and alarm all nicely tied together. The clock has options for display format, font, color, and hourly chimes, to name only a few configurable features.

SoundMaster

This venerable control panel by Bruce Tomlin lets you assign specific sounds to various system actions such as startup, window zooming, and disk ejecting.

Performance Goodies

How can you improve the performance of FoxPro on your machine? The easiest answer is to get a fast Quadra with lots of RAM, but this option may not be prudent or possible. In this section, I explore several software solutions that may make a crucial difference to FoxPro for Macintosh's performance (and the speed of other apps) on your present hardware. Although I do not discuss software for defragmenting your hard disk here, consider a package such as MacTools, Norton Utilities, or Disk Express, because FoxPro runs much better on a clean disk with lots of free space for temporary files.

Extensions Manager and Symbionts

These two public domain utilities help manage the various system extensions, control panels, chooser devices, fonts, and other tools that get loaded into your system at startup. Both utilities allow you to turn off and on specific items through a control panel. Extensions Manager is put out by Ricardo Batista of Apple Computer, and has been included with System 7.5. Symbionts by B. Kevin Hardman offers more options and has an elegant interface (see figure 19.7). Symbionts also informs you of the amount of memory each init consumes.

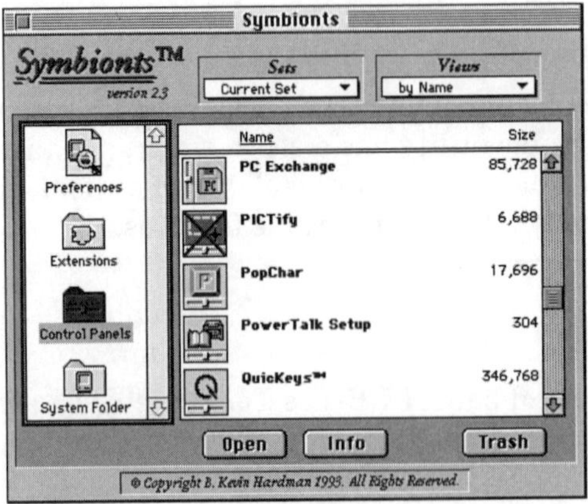

Figure 19.7 *Symbionts Shareware Utility by B. Kevin Hardman.*

RamDisk+

Ram disks have been around for years, and they allow you to set up a virtual disk drive in RAM (you, of course, must have the spare RAM). For FoxPro developers, a RAM disk can come in handy. Because there is no physical media to write to, file I/O is immensely faster. RAM disks are ideal when you work with lots of sample and temporary files. Make sure that your RAM disk is large enough to handle large temp files. Apple's System 7 comes with a RAM disk located in the Memory control panel. RamDisk+ is shareware by Roger D. Bates that is much better and offers many additional features.

RAM Doubler

Connectix just recently came out with this commercial product. It doubles the amount of RAM your Mac has without touching your hard drive. RAM Doubler works best with multiple applications open because this utility uses unallocated application memory by compressing it. Because the hard drive is left out of the equation, don't expect major performance hits. This system extension is an inexpensive solution to costly SIMM chips, even more so if you have a PowerBook or Duo. It does not consume much power, so it's equally suitable for PowerBook users. For FoxPro users with less than 16M, consider a software memory upgrade.

OptiMem

OptiMem, by Jump Development, is another commercial software memory enhancer. The difference between RAM Doubler and OptiMem is that OptiMem allows more applications to run by reducing the amount of memory needed per application. RAM Doubler allows more applications to run by effectively doubling the amount of available RAM. Both utilities accomplish the same thing. For example, you might only give FoxPro a 1,000K memory partition with OptiMem, whereas without this utility you would need a 3,000K partition.

Printing Goodies

This final section delves into a favorite subject of FoxPro developers, printing. FoxPro now provides a built-in Print Preview dialog, something not provided in FoxBASE+/Mac. The FoxPro Report Writer is already quite powerful, so you may not be able to do a lot with add-ons, but these utilities can be extremely valuable for particular jobs.

Print2Pict

Print2Pict by Baudouin Raoult is a chooser device printer driver that previews and saves printed pages to PICT files, PostCards (double-clickable applets displaying output), or the clipboard. In addition to this, FoxPro developers will love to hear that Print2Pict also outputs to a text file. I cannot recommend this utility enough. It is that good!

Adobe Type Manager

ATM is a commercial product that allows you to use PostScript fonts with non-PostScript printers/devices. While it is still sold by Adobe, ATM is bundled with many other applications, so you may already have it.

DynoPage

This wonderful print control panel by Portfolio Systems, Inc. gives you options to perform special print jobs such as multiple pages per sheet of paper, double-side output, and brochure-style printing. Over 50 page template forms, which can be modified using ResEdit, are available to use.

Toner Tuner

You can attest to the high cost of replacing toner cartridges with laser printers. This inexpensive utility by Working Software controls the amount of ink used by a printer and will pay for itself after one cartridge!

PowerPrint

This hardware/software utility by GDT Softworks lets you print from your Mac to over 1,000 PC compatible printers. GDT Softworks also sells a special version for use over LocalTalk and Novell networks.

Pierce Print Tools

QuickDraw GX is just around the corner. In fact, it may be out by the time you read this book. Why all the talk about QuickDraw GX? Apple decided to include their new system Print Manager with this extension. Pierce Print Tools (PPT) is among the first products to take advantage of these new technologies.

Although FoxPro does not currently offer support for the new print managers, PPT comes with an init that modifies the print dialog to offer these additional services to any System 7 application. You can track and manage print jobs, password protect printers, add special effects to pages (watermarks and borders), and save paper by printing multiple pages on a sheet.

Best of all, PPT will include a print extension to create Portable Digital Documents (files that allow recipients to print and preview them without having the same fonts or applications) so that you can distribute documents electronically (FoxPro users who need to print to file will love this feature—it's the *interpreter* or previewer Lisa suggests in Chapter 9).

FoxPro Goodies

One nice thing about being a FoxPro developer is the array of third-party developer tools available. Many excellent products (written in native FoxPro and/or C libraries) are already being run on FoxPro for Windows and FoxPro for DOS. You should expect many of these products to be ported to the Macintosh, if they aren't already cross-platform. I selected a few of the more popular ones to discuss here. All the products listed here are available in Macintosh-specific versions.

GENSCRNX

This wonderful public domain goodie by Ken Levy addresses limitations with GENSCRN and the best part is that you don't even need to alter GENSCRN. Ken has also written two great drivers to go with GENSCRNX—3D objects and Drag and Drop.

GENMENUX

Similar to GENSCRNX but for FoxPro menus (GENMENU), this utility also is public domain. Written by Steven Black and Andrew Ross MacNeill.

Tom Rettig's Office (TRO)

This is a full-featured FoxPro event-driven development platform. TRO now comes with a powerful accounting module.

Foxfire!

MicroMega's FoxPro reporting tool lets your users create ad-hoc queries and reports, as you learned in Chapter 9.

MUPET

The Multi-User Project Editing Tool by Flash Creative Products, Inc. This product allows for work group FoxPro development on a single project. MUPET is designed to mimic the original Project Manager but adds a number of conveniences and nice interface touches.

CAPCON

CAPCON, another multiple-user network access FoxPro Project Manager tool, by Cascade Interactive Designs, Inc., uses network and remote access, plus product life-cycle documentation, to provide a full workgroup approach to project management.

INTL Toolkit

This utility, by Steven Black, lets you localize (translate to other languages) your FoxPro screens and menus with relative ease. It works in conjunction with GENSCRNX and GENMENUX.

Chapter Wrap Up

Libraries have always been the key to successful FoxPro development. Besides having a wealth of FoxPro code libraries, you also should consider investing in a few good products and utilities that can improve on what your code already does and how the FoxPro environment functions. Just don't forget to send in those shareware payments!

A

Guide to the Source Disk and Additional Resources

by
Lisa Slater

This appendix gives a short tour of the extensive files on the source disk that accompanies this book and references to other resources we've discussed that make your work in FoxPro more enjoyable and more efficient.

Contents of the Source Disk

The source disk contains a single self-extracting archive file, which you expand on your hard disk to over 5 megabytes of material. When you fully generate the source code, as described in this section, the full space requirement is about 7 megabytes.

However, before you use the source disk with the book, you need to prepare some of the folders' contents.

Preparing To Use the Source Disk

To conserve space, and to leave as much room for additional utilities as we possibly could, we've left generated files (such as .SPRs) off the disk in most cases. We've also left off the built .APP versions of some of the included applications (Color Tutor, AD*Vantage in the developed Seed App folder, and APPSETUP). To run these applications:

1. SET your DEFAULT folder to the folder containing the project (PJX) file using SET DEFAULT TO (GETDIR()) in the Command window or use the "Working Folder" button in the View window's Folder panel.
2. Open the project. You may get a message asking if you wish to change the project's home folder. Answer "yes."
3. Use the Build button in the Project Manager to Build the Application. You may have to Locate some files that the Project Manager doesn't see on your disk immediately, especially if you move the folders out of their current relationship. If this happens, you can Locate the files for the Project Manager in one of two places:
    - A subfolder of your current folder (for example, a SCREENS folder under APPSETUP).
    - The Library/Template Code Folder.

After you point the Project Manager to one file in a given folder, it will find the rest of the files it needs in that location.

When you're in the appropriate default folder, you can also do the Build without opening the Project Manager, in the Command window, like this:

```
BUILD APP COLORS FROM COLORS
BUILD APP APPSETUP FROM APPSETUP
BUILD APP AD*VANTAGE FROM AD*VANTAGE
```

You will probably see a lot of activity as all the generated files in the Library/Template Code Folder are rebuilt on your disk for the first time.

These instructions are repeated in a ReadMe.1st text file you'll find in the home folder for the source materials.

Because of the lead-time for disk production, as well as the tremendous variety and extent of the material on this source disk, there may be small differences in the text from the source code on disk. You'll find these changes, and any other last-minute instructions we want to give you about using the disk, in a TeachText named Changes/Errata List. This file is separate from the self-extracting archive on the disk.

Exploring the Contents of the Source Disk

You're going to take a while to explore all these files! Work with the source disk by following the instructions in the book, and then continue to look through the material on your own. The following list describes the disk's folders.

The *Resource* folder contains the .DBF used to prepare the references to third-party sources you find in the second half of this chapter. Astute readers will notice that RESOURCE.DBF is a flat-file version of the COMPANY.DBF and associated contacts used in the model data structures for this book. In fact, the sample data you see in the screen shots and in the developed version of AD*Vantage, the model application, was seeded with these records of real-life people and companies.

This folder contains a special utility, BFIND.APP, which you can use to peruse the Resource records. BFIND is an enhanced version of FoxPro's BROWSE Find dialog, which I wrote to search for data across memo fields as well as across character and numeric data search, as the native Find dialog does. This extra generic utility isn't mentioned specifically in the book, but be sure to investigate BFIND.PRG to see how easily you can call the dialog with *any* BROWSE, rather than simply using it for RESOURCE.DBF.

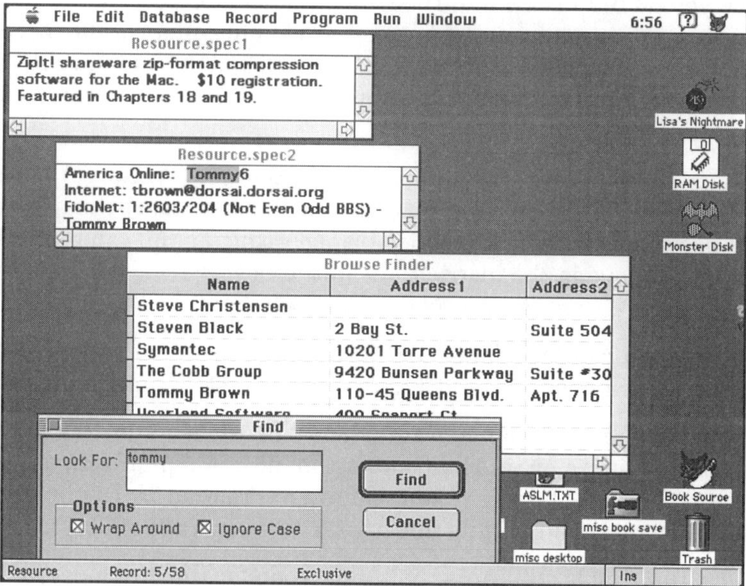

Figure A.1 *The BFIND utility at work on the Resource table.*

The *Library / Template Code* folder contains the code that's at the heart of the application-building method you use in this book. You first build a simple application using the contents of this directory in Chapter 4, and you continue using it throughout the book.

You may be a cross-platform developer who has placed the contents of this disk on a DOS machine. If so, you should be aware that *all the template code for this book is designed to work cross-platform,* containing DOS and Windows records in the screens and dialogs along with Macintosh object definitions.

The *Seed App (startup)* folder contains the data structures you use to build the model application, AD*Vantage, throughout Parts II and III of this book.

The *APPSetup* folder contains the source code for the utility you use in Chapter 6 to describe FoxPro data structures and relationships to your application. (Remember to BUILD the APPSetup.APP file on the disk before following the instructions in Chapter 6, so you can use APPSetup to generate your table-opening and maintaining programs.) You run APPSetup on the contents of the Seed App (startup) folder to begin building the AD*Vantage application.

The *Seed App (AD*Vantage developed)* folder contains the end result of the work you do in Parts II and III, starting in Chapter 6, and building the sample application from the template code plus application-specific work in the Power tools. You need to BUILD APP AD*Vantage FROM AD*Vantage before you can see the application working, as described earlier in this appendix.

Unlike the template code, the sample application (AD*Vantage) contains application-specific screens and reports that have *not* been transported. You can use the files here to practice transporting, or you can build them from scratch following the instructions in the Power Tools portions of the book.

The *GASP* folder contains Andy Griebel's utility for quick and consistent screen effects, demonstrated in Chapter 8 on the AD*Vantage files.

The *Cosmic Converter* folder contains Randy Brown's better-than-Transporter utility to handle font-management, cross-platform, described in Chapter 1 as part of the introduction to FoxPro Mac for DOS-people, and explained more thoroughly in Chapter 12's coverage of font issues.

The *Color Tutor* folder contains the source code for the developer's color utility covered in Chapter 14. Remember that you have to BUILD

COLORS.APP to use the utility, but pay close attention to the source code for this application. It's built on the template and shows you how very far from standardized the template results can be.

The *Network & Config* folder contains Doc Livingston's source code from Chapter 15, including UDFs to handle standard locking tasks in a robust manner and suggestions for configuration files and system setup.

The *XCMDS* folder contains the resources for Randy's Chapter 16, which covers using and writing these external files in FoxPro. The folder includes a *PASCAL* subfolder with the source for some of Randy's XCMDs, as featured in the chapter.

The *API/Libr Contr Kit* folder contains the source material for Chapter 17, in which Doc covers compiled libraries (.MLBs) and the FoxPro for Macintosh Library Construction Kit.

The *AppleScript* folder gives you the source code for Randy's examples of AppleScript and Apple Events in Chapter 18. (You'll find ZipIt, one of the applications with which the scripts communicate, in the Tools folder.)

The *Tools* folder includes some of the most useful public domain and shareware programs described in Randy's third party listings in Chapter 19. We couldn't fit all of his suggestions on this disk—but you'll find contact references to the authors of these files in the resource listing in this appendix and RESOURCE.DBF.

Finally, the *Miscellaneous Code Samples* folder brings together the additional source code used to illustrate various principles at scattered points in the book. You'll find:

- X_ASCII.PRG, from Chapter 1, which allows you to type ASCII code equivalents for symbols;
- SEARCH.PRG and supporting files (COMPFIND.*) from Chapter 3, providing Andy's quick and easy approach to a generic Query By Form dialog;
- AUT2.PRG and a supporting file (Entity Defs.TXT) used in Chapter 6 to demonstrate the low level file functions and importing the results of designing in a CASE design tool into FoxPro;
- DOSPRINT.PRG and a supporting DOS-only report form (QUICKDOS.FRX/FRT), used in Chapter 9 to demonstrate a cross-platform method of printing to file;
- READTEST.PRG, a simple demonstration of a way to learn about the READ command from Chapter 10;

- LGENMENU.PRG and LGENSCRN.PRG and supporting test menu and programs (AUTO_VER.* and TEST.*), from the discussion of template-writing in Chapter 11;
- CONVERT.PRG, Randy's program-only version of the Cosmic Converter approach to font conversion, discussed in Chapter 12.

Additional Notes about Your Use of the Source Disk

All four authors are very pleased to have this opportunity to share the quantity of source material with you. The material represents the fruits of hours of testing and design work.

We are frequently asked what rights the readers of our books have to use the included source materials in their own applications.

Here are some guidelines for you as you prepare to use what you've learned from us and from this book:

- By buying this book, you have the right to use the code that we've published here in your compiled applications.
- If you are a developer who distributes source code to your applications, please *attribute* the code you've drawn from this book in source code comments, just as you'd use a bibliography or footnotes to indicate others' contributions to any other work you publish.
- If you distribute the source code to a large number of VARs who go on to redistribute customized applications under their own names, please don't include large sections of our code without selling a copy of the book to the VAR as part of the sale of your product. Your implicit permission to use the code herein does not extend to others who get the code from you and haven't bought the book. Besides, the VARs are going to be a lot better informed about the code if they read the book!
- Please don't publish articles or books that include sections of our source code unless that code is clearly attributed to us and to the book.

Bottom line: You have very extensive rights to *use* the materials on the disk in your own work as a developer, as long as you don't prevent other developers from getting to know our work in its proper context.

In addition, if you use the shareware tools included on the disk, please register these tools as required by the text files provided by the shareware authors. Any additional restrictions placed by these authors on their work apply to your use of the copies you find on this disk, as they would apply to any copy of the tools from another source.

Additional Resources

The following list contains the authors' contact information for the resources used and suggested throughout *FoxPro MAChete: Hacking FoxPro for Macintosh*, Second Edition. Although we've made every effort to ensure accuracy, the prices and addresses herein may have changed by the time you read this book.

Action-Research NW

Dave Lingwood (a heck of a nice guy)
CompuServe: 70431,2101
206-244-9360

Creator of PtrType XFCN, public domain—thanks, Dave!—see Chapter 9 and the REPORTS dialogs in the Library/Template Code folder.

Adobe Systems, Inc.

1585 Charleston Road
P.O. Box 7900
Mountain View, CA 94039-7900 USA

800-833-6687

elammer@adobe.com

ATM (Adobe Type Manager) commercial software. (See Chapters 12 and 19.)

Aladdin Systems, Inc.

165 Westridge Drive
Watsonville, CA 95076 USA
408-761-6200

CompuServe: 7500,1666
AOL: ALADDIN
ALADDIN@WELL.SF.CA.US

fax: 408-761-6206

StuffIt shareware and commercial products. $25 registration fee. (See Chapter 19.)

Mark Alldritt

1571 Deep Cove Road
North Vancouver, BC V7G-1 Canada

malldrit@sfu.ca

AppleScript Script Tools freeware. (See Chapter 18.)

Robert Ameeti

Lakers Consulting
15052 Springdale St. #K
Huntington Beach, CA 92649-1151 USA

vox: 714-893-7775
fax: 714-895-7522

CompuServe: 71442,630

Robert Ameeti was the technical editor for this book. He's an expert cross-platform FoxPro developer, with a keen interest in Things Macintosh. You can thank him for a lot that's right with this book – and what's still wrong should be considered the authors' responsibility!

Apple Computer, Inc.

20525 Mariani Avenue
Cupertino, CA 95014 USA

General Apple number:
408-996-1010
TLX 171-576

APDA Tools Catalog and Orders:
800-282-2732 (U.S.)
800-637-0029 (Canada)
716-871-6555 (International)
716-871-6511 (Fax)

Apple Software Licensing questions:
408-974-4667

Developer Support:
408-974-4897

User Group Referral:
800-538-9696 ext.500

Apple Computer provides books about Macintosh programming and the Macintosh interface through Addison-Wesley Publishing Company.

Be sure to get a copy of Apple's Human Interface Guidelines, *which is updated regularly. This book contains the history behind the Desktop Interface and specifications on programming in consonance with the interface and standards.*

Apple provides developer resources and tools through APDA, an international umbrella for Apple developer associations. In particular, they publish the APDA Tools Catalog, *which lists SIGs, associations, developer contacts, along with listing books and software of interest to developers.*

Among the products and resources of which you should be aware: Mac TCP, described in Chapter 15, and PC Exchange, ASLM, System 7, ResEdit, MacsBug, QuickTime, and AppleScript software, discussed at various points in the book.

Pricing for Mac TCP:
PN# M8113Z/A: $59/single-user package
PN# M8115Z/A: $69/20-user license extension

Bad Boys' Software

P.O. Box 22248
Lincoln, NE 68542-2248 USA

America Online: BadBoys
AppleLink: EMPOWERMENT
CompuServe: >INTERNET:BadBoys@aol.com

TearOFFs shareware menu enhancer. $25 registration fee. (See Chapter 19.)

Roger D. Bates

P.O. Box 14
Beaverton, OR 97075 USA

503-591-9223

AOL: ROGERB2437

RamDisk+ shareware utility for Macintosh. $35 registration fee. (See Chapters 1 and 19.)

Baudouin Raoult

17 Home Farm Close
RG2 7TD Reading, Berkshire, England

mab@ecmwf.co.uk

Print2Pict shareware utility. $10 registration fee. (See Chapters 9 and 19.)

Steven Black

2 Bay St.
Suite 504
Kingston, ON K7K 6T7 Canada

CompuServe: 76200,2110

Contact: Micromega Systems, Inc.

Steven Black's INTL Toolkit FoxPro commercial software. Also GENX.HLP public domain. (See Chapters 13 and 19.)

Günther Blaschek

Petzoldstr. 31
A4020 Linz, Austria

gue@soft.uni-linz.ac.at

PopChar freeware utility which displays character set chart for current font. (See Chapter 1 and Chapter 19.)

BMUG (Berkeley California-based Users' Group)

1442A Walnut Street #62
Berkeley, CA 94709 USA

Bruce Linde
510-549-2684 ext. 207

bruce_linde@bmug.org

Founded in 1984, BMUG (a non-profit organization) has 12,000 members in more than 50 countries. Their slogan is, "We're in the business of giving away information."

BMUG provides books such as BMUG's Quicker QuickTime, The Tao of AppleScript, Zen and the Art of Resource Editing *(all highly recommended!). Their humongous shareware and public domain catalog is $10, and they also distribute shareware on disk and CD-ROM.*

They have various bundles of their products and services with membership, starting at a one-year contributing membership of $38.

Tommy Brown

110-45 Queens Boulevard
Apt. 716
Forest Hills, NY 11375 USA

America Online: Tommy6
Internet: tbrown@dorsai.dorsai.org
GEnie: P.L.COOPER

CompuServe: 70314,3342

ZipIt shareware ZIP-format compression software for the Mac. $10 registration fee. (Featured in Chapters 18 and 19.)

Randy Brown

CompuServe: 71141,3014
America OnLine: RandyBrwn

Cosmic Converter – shareware utility to convert FoxPro screens between GUI platforms. FoxTools XCMD Library – set of XCMDs for use with FoxPro for Macintosh Fonts, International / Localization, XCMDs, AppleScript, and Third Party specialist for this book.

Cascade Interactive Designs, Inc.

1300 Spring Street
Suite 124
Seattle, WA 98104 USA

Roy L. Gerber
CompuServe: 72311,2254

800-863-0389
vox: 206-720-1234
fax: 206-720-6211

CAPCON multi-user, multi-site FoxPro Project Editing tool, available in DOS, Windows, and Macintosh versions.

CAPCON permits multiple developers to work on projects simultaneously (only one at a time can "check out" a module, but many have access to the full code base of a Project, something impossible with the single-user FoxPro Project Manager). In addition, CAPCON is a true "workgroup product," tracking developer use of modules and user feedback about the product as it prepares incremental prototypes. Its reporting system can identify problem areas and track the progress of modules ready-to-implement.

The product offers an interface to version control software, although this option is only available when CAPCON is accessed on a DOS / Windows workstation at present.

CAPCON also prepares compressed "transfer packets" for all modules necessary for a build, for developers working at remote sites, as well as subsequent "Refresh" packets as the host module continues to be edited.

A five-user license fee for CAPCON Mac is $395. The cross-platform DOS / Win / Mac product (CAPCON is written in FoxPro, of course!) is $575. License includes single server installation and unlimited workstation installs, since users / developers may work at different locations.

CE Software, Inc.

P.O. Box 65580
West Des Moines, IA 50265 USA
515-221-1801

CompuServe: 76136,2137

800-523-7638
Phone: 515-221-1806

QuicKeys commercial product. (See Appendix C and Chapter 19.)

Central Point, Inc

15220 N.W. Greenbrier Parkway
Suite 150
Beaverton, OR 97006-5798 USA

CompuServe: GO CENTRAL
AOL: Keyword - CENTRAL

503-690-8090

MacTools commercial product. (See Chapter 19.)

Steve Christensen

USA

CompuServe: 76174,1712

America Online: stevec44

SuperClock! freeware utility. (See Chapter 19.)

Kerry Clendinning

P.O. Box 26061
Austin, TX 78755 USA

CompuServe: 76424,2214

AppleLink: KerryC

MenuChoice shareware control panel. $15 registration fee. (See Chapter 19.)

Coactive Computing

415-802-2882
fax: 415-802-1088

CompuServe: 71031,2761
AOL: COACTIVECC
BBS: 415-802-1077
coactive@netcom.com

Low-cost networking solution for Mac and PCs, using printer and parallel port connections, rather than network boards, discussed in Chapter 19.

The Cobb Group

9420 Bunsen Parkway
Suite #300
Louisville, KY 40220 USA

Back issues and subscriptions:
800-223-8720 Customer Relations

Editorial:
502-491-1900 Darren McGee

The Cobb Group publishes journals about computer programs, including The FoxPro Developer's Journal, *a monthly publication with an $89/year subscription price.*

Connectix

2600 Campus Dr. #100
San Mateo, CA 94403

415-571-5100
800-950-5880

THOM_HOGAN@CONNECTIX.COM

RAM Doubler commercial product. (See Chapter 19.)

Cornerstone Software Limited

P.O. Box 35-568
Browns Bay
Auckland, New Zealand

Judith Ansell

vox: 649-479-7433
fax: 649-479-2268

CompuServe: 100026,2244

The Kernal is a RAD system and set of developers' tools for FoxPro. Currently available in DOS and Windows versions, it demonstrates the principles of rapid development as discussed in this book. A Mac version is planned.

A beta version of Cornerstone's second product, GENHELP, a help authoring tool, created the CTUTOR.HLP used by COLORS.APP on your source disk. See Chapter 14 for COLORS.APP and for information on FoxPro's help system.

DataViz, Inc.

55 Corporate Drive
Trumbull, CT 06611 USA
203-268-0030

Applelink: DO248

800-733-0030

MacLinkPlus commercial translation software. (Discussed in Chapter 1 and Chapter 19.)

Dayna Communications, Inc.

Sorenson Research Park
849 West Levoy Drive
Salt Lake City, UT 84123 USA

801-269-7200 or
801-531-0600
800-531-0600

SUPPORT@DAYNA.COM
AppleLink:DAYNA
AOL:DAYNA.COM

DOS Mounter Plus, discussed in Chapter 15 and Chapter 19.

Pricing:
PN# DS0400: $79 / single-user package
PN# DS0410: $549 / 10-user
PN# DS0450: $2199 / 50-user
PN# DS04C0: $3999 / 100-user

Farallon Computing, Inc.

2000 Powell Street
Suite 600
Emeryville, CA 94608 USA

510-814-5100
800-949-7761

CompuServe: GO:FARAMAC
FARALLON.COM
AOL: GO:FARALLON

Makers of PhoneNet PC, described in Chapter 15.

Pricing:
PN# PT100: $199 / single-user package
Includes DOS and Windows support
Supports over 15 PC ethernet cards

NOTE: Other product bundling options available.

Flash Creative Products

1060 Main Street
Third Floor
River Edge, NJ 07661 USA

contact Avi Greengart
vox: 201-489-2500
fax: 201-489-6750

CompuServe: 71756,2444

MUPET FoxPro Project Manager Editing tool, with multi-programmer access and coordination capabilities. This product currently runs under FoxPro DOS and Windows, with a Mac port expected.

The FoxPro CodeBook, various editions, extends the EX1/EX2 Microsoft Fox example programs into a development system.

Maurice Frank

CompuServe: 72167,736

Creator of original GDMAIN() function used in APPSETUP – thanks, Maurice! (See Chapter 6.)

GDT Softworks, Inc.

4664 Lougheed Highway
Suite 188
Burnaby, BC V5C 6B7 6 Canada

800-663-6222
604-291-9121
fax: 604-291-9689

Compuserve: 72137,3246
AppleLink: GDT.MKT
AOL: GDT

PowerPrint commercial software. (See Chapters 1 and 19.)

Bill Goodman

Cyclos
P.O. Box 31417
San Francisco, CA 94131 USA

CompuServe: 71101,204
Internet: 71101.204@compuserve.com
Delet@Bill
AppleLink: CYCLOS

Compact Pro shareware compression utility. $25 registration fee. (See Chapter 19.)

Andy Griebel

Plaid Software Group
1400 West Markham, Suite 401
Little Rock, AR 72201 USA

vox: 501-375-6622
fax: 501-375-7620
CompuServe: 71441,3452

GASP – 3-D screen effects for the FoxPro Screen Builder. Migration from FoxBase and non-Xbase Mac DBMS systems specialist for this book.

B. Kevin Hardman

c/o Nivek Research
108 Kramer Court
Cary, NC 27511 USA

sybionts@hardman.pdial.interpath.net

Symbionts systems extension manager. $20 registration fee. (See Chapter 19.)

Harless Software

7373 Jefferson Highway #29
Harahan, LA 70123 USA

Wayne Harless
504-738-9172

CompuServe: 73227,2751

The Harless Color Sets, a utility written for FoxPro DOS 2.0 and its documentation, remains the standard against which all Fox color-handling and color-discussion should be measured.

Laurence Harris

1100 W. NC Highway
54 BVP #29-J
Chapel Hill, NC 27516-2826 USA

CompuServe: 76150,1027 (preferred)

AOL: LHarris
Internet: 76150.1027@compuserve.com

File Buddy shareware utility. $25 registration fee. (See Chapter 19.)

John Hosier

1936 Candlelight Drive
Chesapeake, VA 23325 USA

CompuServe: 71570,3454

Exclude phone@John H.

John's PICKER.APP, a great dual-scrollable list "mover" dialog, is part of the Library / Template Code's collection of reusable objects. The syntax for PICKER.APP is documented in PICKER.TXT in the Library / Template Code folder. The default INSTALL.DBF file in the Library / Template Code folder installs PICKER.APP as part of setup procedures for any template-based application.

Insignia Solutions Inc.

1300 Charleston Road
Mountain View, CA 94043 USA

800-848-7677
fax: 415-694-3705

AppleLink: D1437

SoftPC, Access PC, MacDisk for the PC commercial software. (See Chapter 19.)

Rob Johnston

1720 N.W. River Trail
Stuart, FL 34994-9449 USA

407-692-9199

WindowShade is a freeware utility to minimize Mac windows. (See Chapter 19.)

Gregory D. Landweber

10 Wallingford Drive
Princeton, NJ 08540 USA

Internet: gdl@maths.ox.ac.uk
CompuServe: 73131,3326

Greg's Buttons shareware interface utility. $15 registration fee. (See Chapter 19.)

Ken Levy

CompuServe: 76350,2610

GENSCRNX public domain pre- and post-processing for GENSCRN, FoxPro's screen generator program. (See Chapters 10, 11, and 19.)

John R. "Doc" Livingston

Database Online Computing
555 Bryant Street, Suite 243
Palo Alto, CA 94301 USA

vox: 415-327-8950
fax: 415-327-8990

CompuServe: 71171,567
AppleLink: LIVINGSTONJ

Network, Configuration, and LCK specialist for this book.

Andrew Ross MacNeill

Canada
CompuServe: 76100,2725

GENMENUX public domain processing for GENMENU, FoxPro's menu generator tool. (See Chapter 19.)

Micromega Systems, Inc.

832 Baker Street
San Francisco, CA 94115

contact Karyn McEwen

FoxFire! orders: 800-283-4080 ext. 885

vox: 415-346-4445
fax: 415-346-6804

CompuServe: 73354,1745

The FoxFire! Reporting and Querying Tool is a distributable, configurable application you can bundle with your applications to provide almost unlimited FoxPro "results," as we use the term in Chapter 9. (Chapter 9 also gives you a little more information about FoxFire!) Talk to MicroMega about licensing and pricing policies.

Model Systems Consultants, Inc.

721 Park Avenue
Bainbridge Island, WA 98110-2966 USA

US Contact for AUT2

Keri Anderson Healy

CompuServe: 71174,1435

vox: 206-842-1158

This listing is the United States contact for the AUT2 CASE tool and Analyst's Workbench.

Model Systems Ltd.

#1 Wendle Court
135 Wandsworth Road
Vauxhall, London, England SW8-L2Y

AUT2 Vendor Home Office

Alan Cook

vox: 71 627-5120
fax: 71 622-3139

The AUT2 CASE tool and Analyst's Workbench are used in Chapter 6. It's a real Mac application in look and feel, easy to use and supporting informal documentation of your work as you sketch out your design ideas in a natural manner. Yet underneath it is fully supported by a rigourous design methodology, SSADM (Structured Systems Analysis and Design Method).

John Norstad

Northwestern University
2129 North Campus Drive
Evanston, IL 60208 USA

j-norstad@nwu.edu

Disinfectant anti-virus freeware. (See Chapter 19.)

Now Software, Inc.

921 S.W. Washington
Suite 500
Portland, OR 97205-2823 USA

503-274-2800
800-237-3611

Applelink: NOWSOFTWARE
CompuServe: 71541,170

Now Utilities commercial software. (See Chapter 19.)

Peachpit Press, Inc.

2414 Sixth Street
Berkeley, CA 94710 USA

800-283-9444

vox: 510-548-4393
fax: 510-548-5991

AppleLink: PEACHPIT
CompuServe: 75430,1022
AOL: PEACHPRESS

The Macintosh Bible, *Naiman et al., is the best all-around book introduction to using the Macintosh. ISBN 1-56609-009-1. If you're a Mac person, you probably already have it. If you're a DOShead and reading this book, you should get a copy immediately. Peachpit offers a fine selection of Mac titles.*

Peirse & Peirse Limited Computer Consultants

P.O. Box 1
Waitakere, New Zealand 1230

Matt Peirse

CompuServe: 100033,2071

Creator of GENMENU patch—thanks, Matt! (See Chapter 11.)

Pierce Software, Inc.

719 Hibiscus Place
Suite 301
San Jose, CA 95117 USA

800-828-6554

Pierce Print Tools commercial software. (See Chapter 19.)

Pinnacle Publishing

18000 72nd Avenue South
Suite 217
Kent, WA 98032 USA

800-788-1900
vox: 206-251-1900
fax: 206-251-5057

CompuServe: GO:PINNACLE

Pinnacle publishes various Fox books and publications, including the FoxTalk Journal *and the* Pros Talk Fox *book series, along with add-on software (communications and network libraries, graphics display programs, and more) for Fox professionals.*

Portfolio Systems, Inc.

10062 Miller Avenue
Suite 201
Cupertino, CA 95014 USA

800-729-3966
fax: 802-434-7000
vox: 802-434-6400

DynoPage commercial product. (See Chapter 19.)

Rettig Micro Corporation

2532 Lincoln Blvd.
Suite 110
Marina del Rey, CA 90291-5978 USA

CompuServe: 75066,352

fax: 310-821-1162
vox: 310-301-0911

TRO order line: 800-742-7843

Tom Rettig's Office (R) is a complete VAR/Development Environment, written in cross-platform FoxPro code. TRO is arguably the most comprehensive rapid development system available for FoxPro to date.

Lisa C. Slater

SoftSpoken

CompuServe: 71333,2565

APPSETUP: data structure and relationship utility. COLOR TUTOR and PICKER: FoxPro Macintosh color system tools. BFIND: BROWSE search utility. The template code, system, and lead author for this book—blame me for whatever's missing!

St. Clair Software

2025 Mohawk Road
Upper St. Clair, PA 15241 USA

Attention: Jon Gotow

Internet: gotow@ansoft.com

CompuServe: 72330,3455

America Online: StClairSW

fax: 412-835-4402

Default Folder shareware control panel. $20 registration fee. (See Chapter 19.)

Symantec

10201 Torre Avenue
Cupertino, CA 95014 USA

800-441-7234
503-465-8440

AOL: SYMANTEC
CompuServe: GO SYMANTEC

SAM, Disk Doubler, Auto Doubler commercial software. (See Chapter 19.)

Victor Tan

42 Waratah Avenue
Randwick, NSW -2031 Australia

Internet: victort@extro.ucc.su.OZ.AU (most frequently accessed)
AppleLink: victort@extro.ucc.su.OZ.AU@INTERNET#
CompuServe: >INTERNET:victort@extro.ucc.su.OZ.AU

SpeedyFinder7 shareware utility to assist with many System 7 features. US $25 cash or registration fee. US $30 bank/personal check. Competitve site license available. (See Chapter 19.)

UserLand Software

555 Bryant St. #237
Palo Alto, CA 94301

415-366-7791

CompuServe: 72662,2132
AOL: C.FRANZI
APPLELINK: C.FRANZ

Frontier commercial software. (See Chapter 19.)

Joe Zobkiw

4000 C Knickerbocker Parkway
Raleigh, NC 27612 USA

America Online: AFL Zobkiw (checked daily)

Internet: aflzobkiw@aol.com or zobkiw@world.std.com (checked weekly)

CompuServe: >INTERNET:zobkiw@world.std.com

AppleLink: zobkiw@world.std.com@INTERNET#

Folder Watcher shareware utility. (See Chapter 18.) $20 registration fee.

FOXPRO'S USE OF FILE EXTENSIONS AND MACINTOSH FILE TYPES

by
Lisa Slater

As a Macintosh application, FoxPro assigns its various documents *file types*. As a cross-platform application, FoxPro also assigns its various documents *file extensions*, which provide information to DOS programs roughly analogous to what Macintosh file types give the Finder.

How does FoxPro reconcile these two types of systems internally? What happens when they conflict?

As a rule, you can assume that FoxPro honors the extension before the file type. Although this rule may displease Macintosh users, it was probably chosen on the theory that many files a FoxPro for Macintosh user accesses may be on a foreign platform on some other part of a network, and therefore the file may not have a file type attached.

The FoxPro commands and functions also have competing strategies for file use. If you issue the command `MODIFY COMMAND TEST.TXT` and `TEST.TXT doesn't already exist`, you'll find that FoxPro makes a laudable attempt to reconcile the extension and the file type by creating a text file instead of a program and giving the new file a text file type. If you later use the commands `MODIFY COMMAND` and `MODIFY FILE` interchangeably on this file, however, you'll find that the editing preferences FoxPro gives you by default (such as wordwrap) depend on the command you use—not on the extension *or* the file type of the file you indicate.

Using ResEdit or other utilities, as described in various sections of this book, you can easily modify a file so that its type doesn't match its file extension. *If you double-click on such a file in the Finder, Fox opens the file according to extension, not according to file type.*

For example, figure B.1 shows you a file with a .TXT extension, altered in File Buddy to have the file type of F+PR represent a program. You can see that the icon for the file changed to a program icon. However, if you double-click on this file, Fox opens it as a text file in the editor, rather than trying to compile and run it as a program. Only if a FoxPro document has no file extension, or has a file extension that FoxPro doesn't recognize, does the document open according to file type.

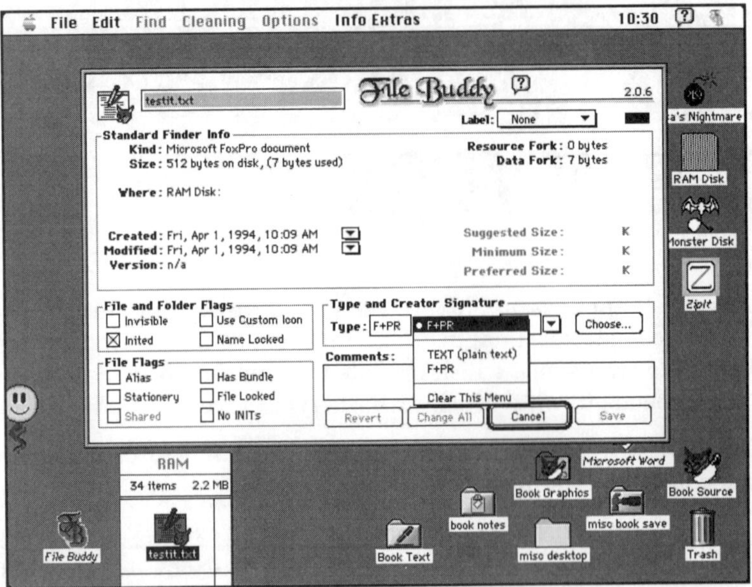

Figure B.1 *Modifying a FoxPro file type in File Buddy.*

Unfortunately, hundreds of permutations exist for the ways these systems *can* conflict, and the answer to the question of which system Fox honors isn't entirely consistent. *Even if you don't plan to do cross-platform development, try to use standard FoxPro extensions to minimize possible conflicts.*

The same advice goes for file naming conventions: *even if you don't plan to do cross-platform development, use standard DOS file names.* Otherwise, you will find yourself verifying, in each case, whether FoxPro has properly assigned a file type and extension appropriate to the file you create and its associated documents (such as its memo file, its structural index and other index files).

I can't give you a simple rule that lets you know whether FoxPro takes care of this detail if, for example, you choose to issue the command `MODIFY SCREEN "My Long Mac Name W/ No Ext"`.

Trust me. It's not worth fighting this particular battle. Use DOS conventions for file names in FoxPro and use standard extensions to match the FoxPro document type.

For this reason, I provided a chart of file types and corresponding extensions in this appendix. This chart is slightly more comprehensive and accurate than the similar chart in the *FoxPro for Macintosh Developer's Guide.*

There are still omissions on this chart. At this writing, for example, the new FoxPro 2.6 extensions (such as .CAT and .FPC) don't have corresponding Macintosh file types assigned. If you're in doubt about a particular file type, simply examine an existing file of that type in a Macintosh utility that shows you this important information.

Keep this chart handy (with your own emendations, if you discover new correspondances) when you use a utility such as DOS Mounter or ZipIt. Many such utilities allow you to keep a preference list of associated file types and extensions for cross-platform file transfers; your FoxPro work will be more seamless if you keep these preference files up-to-date (see figure B.2).

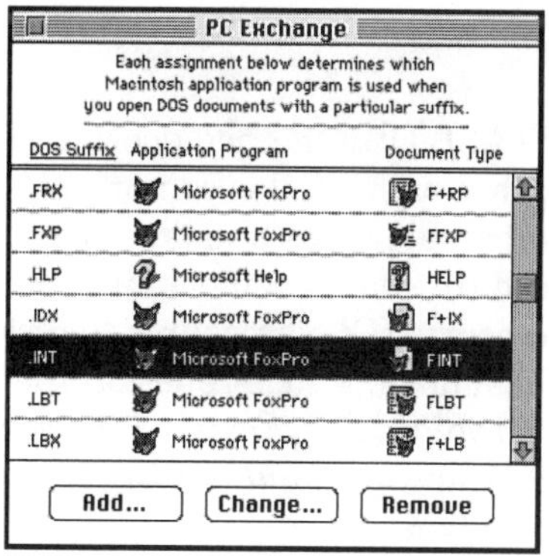

Figure B.2 *Setting extension preferences for the PC Exchange control panel.*

You also should use the information in this chart if you use the INSTALL.DBF system for adding files on disk recommended in the template code. As you may recall from Chapter 5, the setup procedures in MAIN.PRG perform a SCAN through the elements you place in INSTALL.DBF to copy application elements from the Install.Contents memo field. This SCAN contains a call to the FOXTOOLS function FxSetType() to replace the Macintosh-specific file type and creator information, which the memo field doesn't retain:

```
* get pieces that must exist on disk
* out of the app if necessary...

IF FILE("INSTALL.DBF")
   USE Install && DBF included in .APP
   m.havelib = "FOXTOOLS" $ ;
               UPPER(SET("LIBRARY",1))
   SCAN
      IF NOT FILE(ALLTRIM(Name))
        WAIT WINDOW NOWAIT ;
            "Installing "+ALLTRIM(Name)+"... "
         COPY MEMO Contents TO (ALLTRIM(Name))
         IF _MAC AND m.havelib
            = FxSetType(SYS(2027,;
                          ALLTRIM(Name)),;
                      Filetype,Creator)
         ENDIF
      ENDIF
   ENDSCAN
   WAIT CLEAR
   USE
ENDIF
```

Be aware that the INSTALL.DBF method doesn't work for libraries and other executables, and that memo fields cannot retain Macintosh resource forks along with Macintosh file types and creators. For this reason, the CHECKPRT.PRG procedure you used in Chapter 9 uses a different method to install a necessary XCMD resource to disk if the program doesn't find the file. The following code relies on the fact that *you can build any type of file into your .APP file as a File (even an .APP) and it won't be excluded. When you copy it out to disk, it retains the file type and extension and its resource fork:*

```
IF NOT FILE("Printertype.")
   * this check should exist in your
   * dialog — disable Print-to-File
   * if you don't have the right file! —
   * but repeat the check here in case
   * you mess up your dialog design
   * by adding an option to enable all
   * GETs or something

   DO Warning.SPR with ;
      "Can't check Chooser device",;
      "'PrinterType' File Missing"
  RETURN
ENDIF

PRIVATE m.xx, m.oldxcmd, m.olderror
m.success = .T.  && global
m.oldxcmd = SET("XCMDFILE",1)
m.olderror = ON("ERROR")
m.xx = ""

ON ERROR m.success = .F.

SET XCMDFILE TO PRINTERTYPE.
IF NOT m.success
   m.success = .T.
   * we've previously determined
   * that the file exists,
   * but maybe it's only built into
   * the app as a file...
   WAIT WINDOW NOWAIT ;
       "Installing PrinterType File... "
   COPY FILE "PRINTERTYPE." TO ;
        (CURDIR()+"PRINTERTYPE.")
   IF m.success
      SET XCMDFILE TO PRINTERTYPE.
   ENDIF
   WAIT CLEAR
ENDIF

IF m.success
   LOAD ptrType FUNCTION
   CALL "ptrType" TO xx
   * etc...ELSE alert dialog again...
```

Unfortunately, you can't use this trick in a standalone, executable file created with the FoxPro for Macintosh Distribution Kit; somehow, the files bound into an executable don't retain the same information as do the identical files bound into an .APP. You may want to use a small, subsidiary INSTALL.APP file your executable can call to create files on disk, if you choose to distribute using standalone executables rather than .APP files accompanied by FoxPro's runtime library (.ESL).

FOXPRO MAC HACK TIP

I like to use INSTALL.DBF for most files because it's easier to explicitly Include the one Install table than every file I need to start a new project. I also don't like to clutter a project with extraneous Included files, especially when these files are repeated in almost every application's project.

However, because INSTALL.DBF has limitations on the Macintosh, you might want a combination of INSTALL.DBF and the bound-in-file approach for your installation routines. Your SCAN can check EMPTY (Install.Contents), for example, to decide whether you want to pull a given file out of the memo field or check to see whether it's been separately bound into the .APP for copying to disk as a file. You can add an INSTALL.DBF field, indicating the new name the file should have on disk, if necessary. With a data-driven approach, you have endless possibilities.

Standalone executables have other vagaries where file types and extensions are concerned. As you note on the following chart (and contrary to what the chart in the *Developer's Guide* tells you), an executable doesn't default to a particular extension. It defaults to FOXX as its creator type, just as the executable file Microsoft FoxPro and the runtime library (FoxMac25.ESL) do. Like the development version of FoxPro and its runtime substitute, however, an executable is an APPL (application-type), not a document, and as such can be assigned any creator type. You may want to assign your executable a separate creator type, in fact, and assign certain documents associated with this application separate icons and file types from the standard Fox designations.

> **CROSS-PLATFORM WARNING**
>
> If you think that executables default to .EXE extensions, you may only have tried to create one through the Project Manager dialog. You also can create an executable by using the `BUILD EXE <name> FROM <project name> STANDALONE` syntax in the Command window. Please note that although FoxPro for Macintosh doesn't support compact executables (unlike FoxPro for Windows and DOS, you use the runtime library with .APP files only), you *must* use the STAND-ALONE keyword on this command because the cross-platform BUILD EXE command defaults to a compact executable build.

Even if you don't want to customize your applications, limited tests indicate that the Finder may be confused by multiple APPL files of the same creator type. Assigning a separate creator may make sure that your application is executed when double-clicked, as opposed to some other FOXX application-type file on disk with a later creation date.

> **FOXPRO MAC HACK TIP**
>
> If you use the Setup Wizard to create installation disks for your distributable application, be warned that this method adds the runtime library (.ESL file) to your installation disks by default. This extra two-and-a-half megabyte file is completely superfluous if you create standalone executables; it supports .APPs. Uncheck this option!
>
> In fact, be careful to decide whether you want the installation process to install the .ESL file even for .APPs because the Setup process isn't smart enough to check for other copies of the .ESL accessible to your user, even though the Finder would be smart enough to associate an .ESL in some remote folder with the .APP, because of the .APP's file type and creator. The Setup process behaves as though you need an .ESL in the same folder as your .APP—a real waste if your user has multiple FoxPro applications.

As a standalone executable, your application can have separate resources from the original Fox palette, dialogs, and so on, along with its customized icon. You learned how to use ResEdit to modify these resources in Chapter 12, starting with the standard GETFILE() dialog. An executable is a good place to put this knowledge to work.

FOXPRO MAC HACK TIP

When you assign document file types and new icons to a particular creator, such as your new FoxPro application, you may have trouble getting the Finder to recognize these assignments. After changing the BNDL resource for an application, you have to rebuild the Desktop (holding ⌘-Option when you restart) to let the Finder know about the change. If this is a completely new BNDL, you also have to set the Has BNDL check-box in ResEdit's Get File/Folder Info dialog for this file before rebuilding the Desktop.

Besides executables, relying on file types and extensions in FoxPro has a few other "gotchas." Be careful when you open a table by double-clicking in the Finder. This method works because FoxPro properly interprets the action that you want to take on a table, but FoxPro isn't smart enough to use an unoccupied work area in which to open the table. You will close any table you currently have open in the current work area when you take this action. (This behavior matches FoxPro's use of the standard Open AppleEvent on a .DBF/table document.)

You also should realize that the all-important FoxPro configuration file, CONFIG.FPM, does not have a file type of its own. CONFIG.FPM relies exclusively on the one allowable name—CONFIG.FPM—to perform its tasks. If you have separate CONFIG.FPMs for different applications or different uses, you locate them in different folders, preferably in the same folders you place your .APPs or standalone executables.

In the following table, the Mac file type and creator designations are case-sensitive, and the FoxPro file type is case-insensitive.

FoxPro File Type (and Creator— FOXX unless specified)	*Default Extension*	*Macintosh File Type*
Application	APP	FAPP
Backup Database Table, Program, or Text file	BAK	FBAK
Catalog Manager Table	FPC	F+DB
Catalog Manager Memo	FCT	F+DT
Compiled Format	PRX	FPRX
Compiled Menu	MPX	FMPX
Compiled Program	FXP	FFXP
Compiled Query	QPX	FQPX
Compiled Screen	SPX	FSPX
Compound Index	CDX	FCDX
Database Tables	DBF	F+DB
Error	ERR	FERR
Executable	none	APPL (any creator, defaults to FOXX)
Format	FMT	F+FM
FoxDoc Act. diagrams	ACT	FACT
FoxDoc Reports	DOC	FDOC
Index	IDX	F+IX
International (codepage and collation) settings	INT	FINT
Label	LBX	F+LB
Label Memo	LBT	FLBT
Library compiled for FPDOS	PLB	FPLB
Library compiled for FPMac	MLB	libr (creator OMGR)
Library compiled for FPWin	FLL	FFLL

continues

Continued

FoxPro File Type File (and Creator— FOXX unless specified)	*Default Extension*	*Macintosh File Type*
Macro File	FKY	FFKY
Mem File	MEM	F+ME
Standard .DBF's Memo	FPT	F+DT
Memo Backup	TBK	FTBK
Menu	MNX	FMNX
Menu Generated Program	MPR	FMPR
Menu Memo	MNT	FMNT
Microsoft-style Help file	HLP	HELP (creator MSHE)
Program	PRG	F+PR
Project	PJX	FPJX
Project Memo	PJT	FPJT
Query Program	QPR	FQPR
Report	FRX	F+RP
Report Memo	FRT	FFRT
Screen	SCX	F+FR
Screen-Generated Program	SPR	FSPR
Screen Memo	SCT	FSCT
Temporary file	TMP	FTMP
Text	TXT	TEXT

C

QuicKeys: Mac Developer's Tool

by
Randy Brown

QuicKeys by CE Software, Inc. is a "must have" utility, an indispensable product that Macintosh users have been parading for years. As the name suggests, QuicKeys automates virtually any action you may want to perform on the Mac with a simple keyboard shortcut. If you belong to the "rodentially challenged" minority (to borrow a phrase from Lisa Slater's vernacular—people with difficulty using a mouse), you will want to obtain this product, especially if you are new to the Macintosh.

You probably have reservations about using this kind of utility with a product that, like FoxPro, departs from some Macintosh interface standards. I was skeptical about this, too, but the more I tested and tortured it with FoxPro, the more I found QuicKeys valuable.

I will not waste valuable trees on QuicKeys basics. The manuals do an excellent job, and several good books are available, too. This appendix covers details specific to QuicKeys' use with FoxPro. Finally, many of you cross-platform developers will be interested in knowing that QuicKeys also is available on Windows.

Isn't FoxPro's Macro Editor Enough?

Why use a product like QuicKeys when you have an excellent Macro Editor already built into FoxPro? This was my first take on the product (although I have been using it for quite a while now), but I found that the Macro Editor could not do many things.

The advantage of QuicKeys is that it works with the whole Macintosh and not just with one product, such as FoxPro. Wouldn't it be great if you could have the same set of keyboard shortcuts for all the applications you use, not just FoxPro? QuicKeys allows you to do this. For example, I like having F1 activate an applications help.

Personally, I am not a big fan of the FoxPro Macro Editor. It is not that user-friendly, and it has limitations. Ask yourself, "How often do I use the Macro Editor?" If you say, "Not too often," QuicKeys may be a better solution for your needs, too.

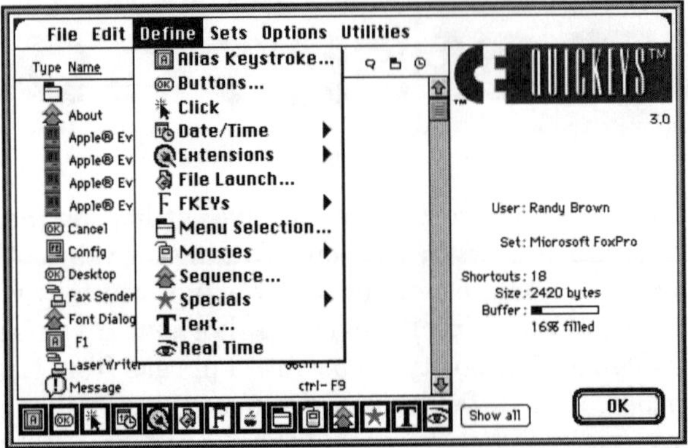

Figure C.1 *QuicKeys dialog showing typical screen set.*

QuicKeys' main dialog appears in figure C.1. The product allows you to have two types of keyboard sets. The first type is a *Universal* set that works anywhere on the Macintosh, including both Finder and any other application. The other set is an *Application* set that works only in the specific product (such as FoxPro or Excel). In addition, you can devise keyboard shortcuts to work between multiple applications, and QuicKeys supports Apple Events and AppleScript.

What Works

For all of the interface liberties Microsoft has taken with FoxPro, there is a whole lot you can do with QuicKeys in FoxPro. Here is a quick guide to get you started on those interface objects you can access through QuicKeys.

- *Menus*. FoxPro menus can be thought of as a hybrid between Macintosh and FoxPro menus. Figure C.2 shows a typical *Menu Selection* QuicKey illustrating a shortcut to select the Wizards menu item from the Run menu. QuicKeys can recognize FoxPro menu pads by name since they use true Macintosh Toolbox menus. However, the names of menu items on the menu pop-ups can only be referenced through FoxPro. Fortunately, the menu pop-ups are normal Macintosh menus, so you can reference them by position as shown in the figure.

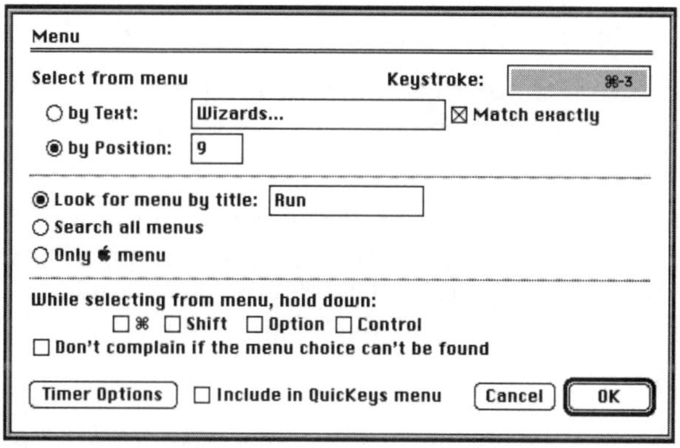

Figure C.2 *QuicKeys Menu Selection shortcut showing that you must select a menu item by position in order to work with FoxPro.*

- *Windows*. As with menus, you can access FoxPro windows with QuicKey shortcuts, but only to some degree. FoxPro uses Macintosh windows; but don't rely on the window titles, because they are internally controlled by FoxPro.

See Also

- "Window and Font Handling," Chapter 12

- *Controls*. Check boxes, pop-ups, push buttons, and other GET controls for the most part are conjured up by FoxPro's internal code. You can see this problem easily by attempting to use third party products, such as Greg's Buttons, which alter the appearance of these comparable Macintosh internal controls but have no effect on FoxPro. However, certain dialogs, such as Print, Page Setup, and GETFILE(), do use Macintosh internal controls. QuicKeys has a *Button* shortcut that clicks on a dialog button specified by name. This way you can have keyboard access to these buttons (such as OK and Cancel) for GETFILE() like dialogs. As a rule, FoxPro dialogs use a Geneva,10 font, while the Macintosh dialogs use a Chicago,12 font.
- *Keystrokes*. QuicKeys can be used to stuff the keyboard and output keystrokes to FoxPro without any problems to FoxPro.
- *Text*. Because QuicKeys can keyboard to FoxPro without conflict, you can have shortcuts which input specified text, such as the current date.
- *Apple Events / AppleScript*. QuicKeys works quite well with FoxPro when accessing FoxPro's limited Apple Event suite. FoxPro also can run scripts (using RUNSCRIPT) that make calls to QuicKeys. Because QuicKeys shortcuts each have a name, you can use an AppleScript to run them.

Because QuicKeys works primarily around key shortcuts, you can assign virtually any variable keystroke to some action. However, if you want the action tied to a menu or button, you may not be able to use the capability directly. Fortunately, QuicKeys is AppleScript savvy, which means you can run the equivalent key shortcut action through a script sent via the FoxPro RUNSCRIPT command, which in turn is attached to the button. Be sure that you define the key shortcut in the Universal key set.

Some FoxPro Examples

The following are some things I have done with QuicKeys. I have included a sample QuicKeys set on the source disk.

- *Play QuickTime movies.* FoxPro's QT OLE Server always shows the movie controls. With QuicKeys, you can also display a movie without the controls.
- *Zoom windows.* Use QuicKeys Mousies to automate window zooms. You can add this to FoxPro if you use the DOS style menus. I much prefer not having this menu item.
- *Open About This Macintosh dialog.* QuicKeys lets you swap applications to perform other actions. You might want to switch to the Finder and use the Menu Selection QuicKeys to choose this menu option under the Apple menu.
- *Show Clipboard.* Similar to the About This Macintosh dialog.
- *Change Chooser devices* (printers). QuicKeys has a special type of shortcut called a Choosy which allows you to switch printers, faxes, and other chooser devices. It also works quite nicely over a network.
- *Open Control Panels.* There are a number of ways to activate a control panel such as Monitors.
- *Change font using FoxPro's font dialog.* You can use a QuicKeys sequence to go through actions (keyboard) to change the selected font for an edit window.
- *Set up keyboard shortcuts for buttons/popups on GETFILE() dialogs.*
- *Open any FoxPro file by using the Open File Apple Event.*

Finally, if you plan to distribute your FoxPro applications with these QuicKey shortcuts, remember that QuicKeys is a commercial product. Contact CE Software about possible runtime versions or distribution licenses.

D

FOXPRO MAC, OLE, AND QUICKTIME

by Andy Griebel

With the release of FoxPro Mac comes a new capability to FoxPro tables: storing General fields or OLE objects. OLE (pronounce it *Oh Lay*, to sound like a Microsoft person) is Microsoft's method of providing Inter-Application Communication.

OLE is a standard that not many Macintosh people care about, perhaps justly so, but it's worth an appendix to let you know about yet another FoxPro feature.

The Terminology

Here is a listing of OLE terms written in an abbreviated fashion from FoxPro's perspective.

- *Objects*. An OLE object is the item—perhaps a picture image or video clip—that may be copied and pasted into another document.
- *Server*. The OLE Server is the application that created the object.
- *Container Document*. The document into which an object is Pasted. In FoxPro, the container document is a field of *General* type in a FoxPro table.
- *Client*. The OLE Client is the application that creates the container document. In this case, FoxPro is an OLE client, not an OLE server.
- *Embedding*. A normal paste is an *embed*, indicating that all the bits and bytes for this particular object are stored in the container document and nowhere else.

- *Linking*. A Paste-Link results in the container document having only "pathing" information to the actual object. This object resides "loose" on the disk and may be accessed by other applications. Updating it once on the disk means that other container documents to which it is linked see the updated version when they open this object.

OLE Objects in FoxPro Mac

I would have to say that OLE works much better in Windows than it does on Macintosh. This isn't entirely surprising because OLE is a Windows standard, not a Macintosh standard.

OLE General fields bear remarkable similarities to early Xbase memo fields in terms of usefulness. Remember when memo fields first appeared? Suddenly, it seemed like the world opened up. We could store multi-page documents, allow unlimited numbers of comments, and so on.

Then the list of things you couldn't do with memo fields started growing. You couldn't search them for data. You couldn't replace them. You couldn't have rich text formatting of individual words within one. They weren't all that reliable, either.

They've gotten a lot better, however, over the years. Lisa *loves* throwing odd types of data, and even whole files, in memo fields now, as you have seen with some of the rapid development techniques demonstrated in the book. Somewhere along the way, memo fields became totally valid and useful objects.

> **CROSS-PLATFORM WARNING**
>
> Lisa's reading this and reminds me to tell you once again that, with the advent of FoxPro Mac, there are a few things memo fields can't do properly—such as storing the file type and creator for a Macintosh file you've APPENDed in the field—and that you'll find a couple of hints about memo field problems in the "Limitations of FoxPro Mac" topic in her Color Tutor help file. She still loves memo fields and says they'll get better again!

In my opinion, General fields still are in an early phase. The list of things you can't do seems to grow as you start working with them. Just like the early memo fields, however, they're handy for what they do!

Where Does the Object Go?

When you create a general field and paste in an image, the data from that object is stored in the FPT—usually. Occasionally, the OLE server may decide to paste-link anyway. Video clips usually are done this way.

What Works, What Doesn't?

I need to be up front and say the OLE-Quicktime player has been fairly flaky on my Quadra 840AV. Nothing I can put my finger on and duplicate, just flaky. I've only got 16 megs of RAM at the time of this writing, so that may be a factor.

You can't REPLACE data in general fields directly—you have to zig-zag with a CURSOR and COPY TO techniques to manipulate them. You can't COPY TO to get the object out of the OLE field and back onto the disk—you've got to fire up the Server application and SAVE AS. Like I said, a lot like early memo fields.

What is cool is being able to use and enjoy OLE with all its limits for what it ca*n* do right. A friend of mine has a copy of TouchBase, and I wanted to duplicate this kind of functionality in FoxPro. So I wrote AndyBase, and stuck it in my Apple Menu items folder. I have the AV, and being a father, the requisite video camera. Anytime somebody comes to my office I take a video shot of them—usually just rolling tape, sometimes capturing an instant-still. I open a paint program and crop, copy, and paste the image in AndyBase. This method eats up a little disk, but it really is cool. A lot of my clients are amazed at it when they come in—so overall it pays for the extra disk space. People love pictures of themselves and others (just ask Kodak).

I absolutely love it—so this relatively "unnecessary," immature, and unsupported feature becomes one of the reasons I prefer working on the Macintosh.

Why Use OLE?

Use OLE the way I use it in AndyBase: for fun and because it's there. It comes with the product, and it makes you cross-platform ready. Going from Windows to Mac and back with OLE video images is sometimes a troublesome experience, but overall, it's the best cross-platform solution I have found.

Additional Syntax

Rather than copying and pasting, you can move data directly into a General field with a command similar to APPEND MEMO:

```
APPEND GENERAL <general field>
FROM <file>
  [LINK]
  [CLASS <ole class>]
```

In the preceding syntax, <general field> is the field in question and <file> is the object you want to bring in. If you want it to be Linked rather than Embedded, add the keyword LINK.

The OLE class is used to specify which Server document should be used to open the object, something like a combination of the file type and creator in the Macintosh environment. In Microsoft Windows, one or more classes of documents are *registered* for each OLE server in a special registration database (REGEDIT). On the Mac, the Finder's Desktop file handles the association of servers and their documents internally.

If you use the command APPEND GENERAL, realize that this is *not* one of the faster things you can do in FoxPro. In addition, don't APPEND documents repeatedly into one general field without PACKing or PACKing MEMO to eliminate file bloat.

If you design screens with general field elements, you can use the following command to duplicate the effect of double-clicking on the general field in a BROWSE:

```
@0,0 SAY the_object VERB 0
```

VERB 0 tells the OLE server to act on its document using the default action (usually EDIT or PLAY). Different servers have different available operations. To see which verbs are available for a server, rather than using VERB 0, use the command MODIFY GENERAL <fieldname> or double-click on the general field in the BROWSE, so the general field's window is active. Then check the Edit menu's Object option; it should have a hierarchical pop-up with all the available verbs for this document.

CROSS-PLATFORM WARNING

In the initial shipping version of FoxPro, be careful with this syntax (APPEND GENERAL, @.. SAY VERB, and MODIFY GENERAL). Using these commands with inappropriate types of files or an empty field can freeze FoxPro Mac solid, although error-checking is much tighter in OLE on FoxPro for Windows.

The Future

OLE continues to gain momentum in the Windows arena. With the "DOS-compatible" Power Macs (I just love the ads) becoming available, more and more barriers between the platforms will fall.

Microsoft is a *big* company. They like OLE. They want you to like it, too. I'm sure you'll see it continue to step into Macintosh-ville through subsequent enhancements.

Now, if they can just get SQL beefed up so I can select all records with general fields containing "Paisley Ties...."

FOXPRO FOR MACINTOSH 2.6 AND BEYOND

by Lisa Slater

This book was written using the designation *FoxPro for Macintosh*, without a version number, throughout. At the time we wrote the book, the current version of FoxPro for Macintosh was officially 2.5b, but this release also was the first and only FoxPro for Macintosh available.

As the first printing went to press, several important events in the Fox and Apple worlds combined to create exciting news and incipient changes for FoxPro for Macintosh users. On the Fox side, March 1994 saw the Microsoft announcement of FoxPro 2.6 for DOS and Windows. On the Apple side, the same month saw the introduction of the Power PC.

How did these events impact FoxPro for Macintosh?

A New Platform: Power Mac

Microsoft released FoxPro 2.6a in both Macintosh and PowerPC/Power Macintosh versions in late summer, 1994. Note that the standard Macintosh version 2.6 runs on the PowerPC and Power Mac in their standard-Mac-emulation modes; in fact, FoxPro for Macintosh 2.5b ran successfully in that mode.

In FoxPro 2.6, Microsoft says that the standard Macintosh and the new PowerPC-native releases have identical functionality. “Identical functionality,” however, is in the eyes of the beholder. There seem to be a few quirks in the initial shipping Power Mac version of FoxPro. For example, if you double click on a document file to launch the runtime library (ESL) version of FoxPro PowerMac, you'll crash your operating system.

Microsoft will identify these problems and fix them as they are discovered by the intrepid early-adopters of FoxPro Mac and PowerMac hardware. As always, be sure to check with Microsoft for the latest release and read any last-minute text files Microsoft adds to the home FoxPro folder.

Perhaps the only enduring difference between the two releases will be their use of shared libraries (.MLBs) because of underlying differences in the versions of System 7 that support the two environments.

Power Macs use System 7.1.2, which Apple doesn't recommend for other Macs. This version of System 7 includes a new piece of system software known as the Code Fragment Manager (CFM), which provides the capability of dynamically linked, shared libraries for native code. The CFM supersedes the ASLM. Libraries written for FoxPro for Macintosh will require re-compilation to take advantage of the CFM as a port to FoxPro for PowerPC.

The current release of CFM is said to support ASLM-type libraries and behavior, but this may change. When you run FoxPro for Macintosh *under* System 7.1.2 on a Power Mac, you can install and use the ASLM (Apple Shared Library Manager), just as you do on a regular Macintosh. If you own FoxPro for Macintosh, you have a license to the ASLM and you install it along with FoxPro to use libraries. If you distribute applications, you have to comply with Apple's licensing requirements for distributing ASLM because it's not bundled with System 7.1.2, just as it's not part of System 7.1 or System 7.5.

FOXPRO MAC HACK TIP

Although PowerPC/Power Mac users of your distributed FoxPro for Macintosh applications don't automatically have the ASLM as part of their System, the ASLM is automatically installed with the GeoPort software, which should become fairly ubiquitous on the Power Macs. Therefore it's possible that you won't need to worry about the ASLM's availability to your distributed applications on Power Macs, as a rule.

The template code for this book includes a test for the ASLM when it tries to load a shared library, which will still be valid, but we hope will become less necessary.

The distribution of System 7.5 has not changed FoxPro Mac developers' dilemma with regard to use of the ASLM. However, Apple has a history of incorporating ancillary tools previously released separately into new versions of System software. For example, AppleScript and PowerTalk became standard with System 7 Pro. If Apple bundles the ASLM, or if libraries compiled for the CFM will work directly for FoxPro for Macintosh as well as FoxPro for PowerPC, a future version of the System may end FoxPro developers' worry about the ASLM licensing requirements for distributed applications.

Meanwhile, all this speculation about shared libraries and the new Power Mac platform doesn't tell you what will be different about FoxPro for Macintosh in version 2.6.

Should you upgrade if you have version 2.5? The answer is definitely *yes*.

A New FoxPro Release: 2.6

Your first inducement to upgrade should be the ASLM if you use System 7.5. Versions of the ASLM distributed earlier than the one included with FoxPro 2.6 will cause serious system crashes in System 7.5.

You have positive incentives to upgrade as well as negative ones, however. At various points throughout the book, we mentioned some FoxPro for DOS and Windows 2.6 commands and features to which you didn't have access or which might cause an error when you ported cross-platform FoxPro applications to the Macintosh. Many new commands in 2.6 were added to allow dBASE IV users to port their applications to FoxPro without pain, and these features won't matter much to Mac users. At the least, the upgrade to 2.6 simply means that you don't have to bracket 2.6-style code that happens to use these features to avoid errors on the Macintosh platform.

A few new commands, however, can benefit users on any platform. You will want to check the help file for the topic on `What's New Since FoxPro 2.5` to familiarize yourself with the changes. We recommend that you highlight the following additions:

- *BLANK*. This new command clears the contents of a record and provides FoxPro's first attempt at null value support because it returns a record to the condition of an APPEND BLANK record. A logical field or a numeric field have *no contents* if you use BLANK on them, not just a .F. or 0 value. BLANK can be scoped and takes a FIELDS list. Its companion function, ISBLANK(), has the same capability to evaluate true-null status.

- *_SHELL*. This new system variable allows control to pass from one program to another without the use of a READ level underneath. It prevents access to the Command window in the development version of FoxPro.
- *OBJVAR()*. This new function is a superior version of VARREAD(). Its first argument is an object number, and its second argument is a READ level. If you use this function with the system variable _CUROBJ (OBJVAR(_CUROBJ), with the second argument defaulting to the current READ level), you get the same return value as VARREAD()—with an important difference: OBJVAR()'s return value is *aliased* with either the GET's table alias, if the GET is a field, or "m." if the GET is a memory variable.
- *SET LIBRARY TO*. This command, previously used only for compiled libraries, now supports a FoxPro procedure file, with the result that you can add a second open repository for global access to library procedures in your application.
- *SET FIELDS TO*. This venerable command now supports a GLOBAL keyword providing access to fields in other workareas. Although this change in SET FIELDS was made for dBASE compatibility, the current capability of SET FIELDS to support related tables and calculated values is quite significant; it creates the equivalent of a SQL View in FoxPro.
- *SET KEY*. This new command gives you the ability to limit the scope of other FoxPro commands to a value or values (using the RANGE clause) in the current index, in the same way that BROWSE's KEY clause limits the records displayed in a BROWSE. You can see that there are far-ranging implications for multi-table READs; this command can simplify navigation among records of a child table without making sure that parent-child relationship is active because the SELECTed work area is the parent. SET KEY has an IN clause to specify the work area whose records you want to limit.
- *SYS(1037)*. One small step for humankind, this function gives FoxPro for Windows and Macintosh programmatic access to the Printer Setup dialog for their respective platforms.
- *KEYBOARD <expr> CLEAR*. You can now make sure that the keyboard buffer is empty before you stuff it with characters.
- *KEYMATCH()*. You can check for duplicate index values without explicitly moving the record pointer.

- *REPLACE FROM ARRAY*. If you edit to arrays and use INSERT FROM ARRAY, you'll find this new syntax is a handy addition for editing existing records.
- *NORMALIZE()*. This function transforms expressions into a set format so that you can compare expressions at runtime. For example, you could compare an existing SET("FILTER") expression against a new set of conditions entered by a user without concern for the capitalization or operator conventions (.AND. or AND? # or NOT or <>?) with which the filter was stored.
- *SYS(2033)*. This function returns the current Mac's System, Extensions, Preferences, or Microsoft folder locations. The capability is highly significant for distributed applications because you can now figure out where you need to store FOXTOOLS.MLB (the current Extensions folder) without calling a FOXTOOLS function!

FOXPRO MAC HACK TIP

The Microsoft folder is a new method Microsoft uses to organize the extensions it distributes within the Mac Extensions folder. FoxPro 2.6 creates it if no other Microsoft application creates it first or adds files to it if it exists already.

Don't destroy Microsoft files you find in other locations, such as OLE Shared Code within the Extensions folder, even if you think they are duplicates. Some other Microsoft application you use, such as Word or Excel, may expect to find them there.

FoxPro 2.6 does not make use of any of the new features of System 7.5. In Chapter 19, we described WindowShade and mentioned that this utility is now included with the system files. As noted there, however, FoxPro programs have no way to tell that any of their windows have been "rolled up" becauseWMIN() doesn't know about WindowShade. You may want to use SYS(2033) to look for this control panel and ZOOM WINDOW (WONTOP()) NORM in your READ ACTIVATE clauses to compensate for its presence.

FoxPro's interface has problems with new System 7.5 features that go beyond your programs. If you want a good chuckle, use WindowShade to "roll up" the FoxPro Filer sometime!

Besides the new and enhanced commands and functions in FoxPro 2.6, FoxPro for Macintosh receives a greatly enhanced set of Wizards for interactive use (see figure E.1, from FoxPro for Windows 2.6).

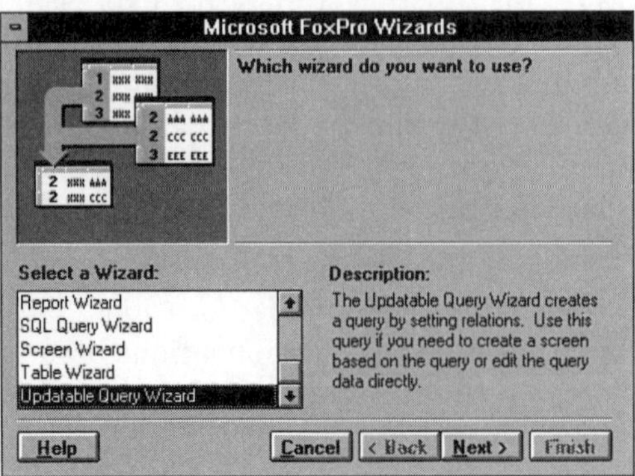

Figure E.1 *FoxPro 2.6 has new and improved Wizards on all platforms.*

Accompanying the current Report and Screen Wizards, you'll find both SQL and Updatable (table) Query facilities, a Mail-Merge Wizard, special Report Wizards targeting Labels, Group Totals, Multi-Column Reports, and (in the Professional Version) a Client-Server Wizard feature.

FoxPro 2.6 also gets a dBASE IV-style face-lift in the form of a Catalog Manager. Think of the Catalog Manager as a new way of organizing the various components of a project. A Catalog also allows you direct access to the Wizards and to generate simple applications from the tables you specify.

CROSS-PLATFORM WARNING

The Catalog Manager is only useful if you're already used to thinking in dBase IV terms (hardly a factor for most Mac developers). We think it "ghetto-izes " new users because it isolates them from the real FoxPro environment and tools. To get rid of the Catalog Manager permanently, just add the line CATMAN=OFF to your CONFIG.FPM file.

Fixes Accompany Enhancements

Throughout the book, we told you about various bugs in the current product that you need to watch for. Soon after initial release, Microsoft announced a maintenance release designed as a bug fix, and we hope that you'll find many of the items we mentioned are cured by the version of the product you receive. Among the important fixes in the maintenance upgrade are improvements in FoxPro Mac's memory handling and some serious incompatibilities with the Stylewriter and Apple LaserWriter 300 printer drivers.

Check your release date of FoxPro for Macintosh using the function VERSION(1). If you see `FoxPro 2.5b for Macintosh [Dec 4 1993 10:38:29]`, you have the original release of the product. If you see a later date, and especially if you see a later version number than 2.6a (which we used to prepare this edition of the book), test the problems we describe in this book before you worry about them!

The End is the Beginning

FoxPro 2.6 is only the beginning of the changes you should expect to see in FoxPro for Macintosh. Microsoft scheduled a 3.0 release of FoxPro for Windows for the spring of 1995. Although the Macintosh release of FoxPro 3.0 may be as much as six months later than the advent of 3.0 on PCs, you will see substantially the same syntax in all the 3.0 releases, just as you do in FoxPro 2.

Although FoxPro will still be an Xbase dialect, the new FoxPro syntax requires a significant shift in developers' approaches and techniques toward an object-oriented programming style.

That's why we've devoted space and effort to discussing object orientation as part of rapid development techniques in this book. The syntax you use will change, without a doubt—but the habits of mind you learn here will stand you in good stead as you move toward the DBMS platforms of the future.

INDEX

SYMBOLS

J-K

L

N

T

U

Y-Z